MANAGING CONFLICT IN A WORLD ADRIFT

MANAGING CONFLICT IN A WORLD ADRIFT

Chester A. Crocker
Fen Osler Hampson
Pamela Aall
editors

UNITED STATES INSTITUTE OF PEACE PRESS
Washington, D.C.

CENTRE FOR INTERNATIONAL GOVERNANCE INNOVATION
Waterloo

UNITED STATES INSTITUTE OF PEACE
2301 Constitution Avenue, NW
Washington, DC 20037
www.usip.org

To request permission to photocopy or reprint materials for course use, contact the Copyright Clearance Center at www.copyright.com. For print, electronic media, and other subsidiary rights, e-mail permissions@usip.org.

First published 2015

Printed in the United States of America

Published simultaneously in Canada by CIGI

The paper used in this publication meets the minimum requirements of American National Standards for Information Science—Permanence of Paper for Printed Library Materials, ANSI Z39.48-1984.

Library of Congress Cataloging-in-Publication Data

Managing conflict in a world adrift / edited by Chester A. Crocker, Fen Osler Hampson, and Pamela Aall.
    pages cm.
  Includes bibliographical references and index.
   ISBN 978-1-60127-222-5 (alk. paper)
  1. Conflict management—International cooperation. 2. Crisis management—International cooperation. 3. Security, International. 4. Political violence—Prevention. 5. Peace-building. 6. Peaceful change (International relations) 7. Diplomatic negotiations in international disputes. 8. World politics. I. Crocker, Chester A.
   JZ5597 .M36 2015
   303.6'9—dc23
                                                                                                2014015110

Contents

FOREWORD

Martti Ahtisaari

As this panoramic study of contemporary conflict management makes plain, ours is a messy world, and it's getting messier. Power and authority are fracturing and dispersing across the globe as US hegemony follows superpower bipolarity into the history books. Discord, dissent and outright rebellion are spreading into regions where autocratic forms of stability reigned until the recent past. National sovereignty and state legitimacy, the touchstones of the international order for more than three centuries, are increasingly diluted and contested. New actors are crowding the international stage, each demanding more of the spotlight, each reading from a different script, each rewriting its role as it goes along.

This messiness is not necessarily bad news for peace and peacemakers. Messiness can arise from anarchy and indifference, but it can also grow out of more open debates about how to move closer to a more legitimate underlying order based on a bedrock of shared principles and universal rights Messiness, however, brings many challenges and raises questions not faced by the international system for many years: If no one is in charge, who will lead the way? What are the priorities in addressing the still substantial conflict agenda, and who decides? If traditional responses and the existing institutions and leading states are no longer as willing or able as previously to shape a coherent security order, which new actors will respond to the challenge and step forward to take up some of the responsibilities for managing conflict and building peace?

The editors and authors of this volume bring widely varied perspectives to the challenges I just mentioned. Their voices are sober but not despairing. "In a world of fractured governance and diffused authority," explain Chester Crocker, Fen Osler Hampson, and Pamela Aall, "it is apparent that responding to a conflict will require a diverse portfolio of instruments and actors to deal with a wide array of different security challenges. That is because each actor (or set of actors) and institution has its own strengths and weaknesses, but no single actor or set of institutions has a decided comparative advantage (or legitimacy) over the others."

I have long believed that with pragmatic thinking, professional skill, and realistic, fact-based analysis, much can be done to build a more peaceful and decent world order. This belief, grounded in hard-won experience, is the vision that drives Crisis Management

Initiative, the organization I founded in 2000, when I left the presidency of Finland, and immersed myself in peacemaking efforts around the world. Crisis Management Initiative has been active in many parts of our messy world—from Burma to Liberia, North Africa to Indonesia—and has worked with many different actors in that world—from the African Union to the European Union, national governments to civil society organizations.

I also believe the editors are correct to point out that "there is greater order in [the world's current] 'messiness' than may first appear to be the case. Its disappointments notwithstanding, there is still value in the United Nations, including its conflict prevention abilities. Regional states and security organizations also offer an alternative, as they increasingly assert their role as legitimizers and gatekeepers of international action." Civil society leaders and organizations such as Crisis Management Initiative, too, are playing increasingly influential roles. While states may no longer dominate the international community as once they did, national leaders and the unparalleled resources they can deploy are still often decisive in determining the shape of global order and the success or failure of a specific conflict management effort. As the editors argue, in this

environment of more diffused capacity we may find that conflict management will become an improvised and situation-specific pattern of collective action.

The chapters in this timely and important volume detail the capacity of diverse actors and institutions, the variety of tools at their disposal, and the array of sources and triggers of conflict that test the ingenuity and determination of peacemakers. I hope emerging generations of students and practitioners will plunge into this volume, wrestle with the leading ideas, argue and debate the premises of the diverse authors, and keep the faith with the profession of peacemaking.

Over the course of almost twenty years— *Managing Conflict in a World Adrift* is the fourth volume in a series that dates back to 1996—the editorial team of Crocker, Hampson, and Aall have built a reputation not only for producing magisterial surveys of the conflict management field with contributions from dozens of globally influential experts and scholars but also for their own clear-sighted analyses of that field. As a policymaker and practitioner, I applaud the United States Institute of Peace and the Centre for International Governance Innovation for championing this important contribution to the field.

ACKNOWLEDGMENTS

The editors gratefully acknowledge the strong and generous support they have received from the board and leadership of the United States Institute of Peace (USIP) and the Centre for International Governance Innovation (CIGI) in producing this volume. We also wish to thank Nigel Quinney for his fine editorial guidance; Alli Phillips at USIP, who provided administrative support; Dan Snodderly at USIP who helped manage the development of the manuscript; Valerie Norville, Kay Hechler, Michelle Slavin, and other members of USIP's Publications staff who helped manage the production process; Peter Wallensteen, George Lopez, and an anonymous reviewer who read portions of the manuscript; and Carol Bonnett, Alexandra Stephenson, Anne Blayney, Lauren Amundsen, and Simon Palamar at CIGI who helped organize a highly successful authors' workshop and manage CIGI's contribution to the project.

CONTRIBUTORS

Chester A. Crocker is the James R. Schlesinger Professor of Strategic Studies at Georgetown University's Walsh School of Foreign Service and serves on the board of its Institute for the Study of Diplomacy. From 1981 to 1989, he served as assistant secretary of state for African affairs. He served on the board of the United States Institute of Peace for twenty years through 2011, including twelve years as chairman of this independent, nonpartisan institution created and funded by Congress to strengthen knowledge and practice in managing international conflict. He is a member of the World Bank's Independent Advisory Board on governance and anticorruption, and is a founding member of the Global Leadership Foundation. He consults as adviser on strategy and negotiation to a number of US and European firms, and is a member of the Council on Foreign Relations, the International Institute of Strategic Studies, and the American Academy of Diplomacy. In addition to the series of books and articles coauthored and coedited with Fen Osler Hampson and Pamela Aall, he is the author of *High Noon in Southern Africa: Making Peace in a Rough Neighborhood* (1993).

Fen Osler Hampson, Fellow of the Royal Society of Canada, is a Distinguished Fellow and director of the Global Security and Politics Program at the Centre for International Governance Innovation in Waterloo, Canada, and concurrently Chancellor's Professor at the Norman Paterson School of International Affairs, Carleton University, Ottawa, Canada. He is codirector of the Global Commission on International Governance chaired by Sweden's foreign minister, Carl Bildt. A member and former vice chair of the board of directors of the Pearson Peacekeeping Centre, a member of the Board of the Parliamentary Centre, and a former member of the Social Science Foundation Board of Trustees of the Josef Korbel School of International of International Affairs, he is the author or coauthor of ten volumes and coeditor of twenty-five others. His latest books include *The Global Power of Talk: Negotiating America's Interests* (coauthored with I. William Zartman) and *Brave New Canada: Meeting the Challenge of a Changing World* (coauthored with Derek H. Burney). He writes a weekly column for *iPOLITICS*, Canada's leading online source on Canadian politics, business and international affairs, and is a regular commentator on the CBC, CTV, Global Television, and Sun media radio and television networks.

Pamela Aall is a senior fellow at the Centre for International Governance Innovation and a senior advisor for conflict prevention and management at the United States Institute of Peace. Prior to this, she was founding provost of the Institute's Academy for International Conflict Management and Peacebuilding. Her research interests include negotiation and mediation, nonofficial organizations, civil–military relations, education and training, and the role of education in exacerbating conflict or promoting reconciliation. She is past president and current board member of Women in International Security, an organization dedicated to promoting women's professional advancement in the foreign affairs and security fields. She has also worked at the Rockefeller Foundation, the European Cultural Foundation, and the International Council for Educational Development. In 2014, she was the Sharkey Scholar at Seton Hall University. Aall has coauthored and coedited a number of books and articles, including the *Guide to IGOs, NGOs and the Military in Peace and Relief Operations* (2000). Together with Chester A. Crocker and Fen Osler Hampson, she has written and edited a series of books on international conflict management. Aall, Crocker, and Hampson are also series editors for the Routledge Studies in Security and Conflict Management.

◆ ◆ ◆

Richard K. Betts is the Arnold A. Saltzman Professor of War and Peace Studies in the Political Science Department, director of the Saltzman Institute of War and Peace Studies, and director of the International Security Policy program in the School of International and Public Affairs at Columbia University.

Sumantra Bose is professor of international and comparative politics at the London School of Economics and Political Science.

Dawn Brancati is assistant professor of political science at Washington University in St. Louis.

Graham K. Brown is associate dean (Research) in the Faculty of Humanities and Social Sciences and reader in international development in the Department of Social and Policy Sciences, University of Bath.

Martha Crenshaw is senior fellow at the Center for International Security and Cooperation (CISAC), Freeman Spogli Institute for International Studies, and a professor of political science by courtesy at Stanford University.

Michael W. Doyle is director of the Columbia Global Policy Initiative, and Harold Brown Professor of International Affairs, Law and Political Science at Columbia University.

Chantal de Jonge Oudraat is the executive and founding director of the Stockholm International Peace Research Institute (SIPRI) North America and president of Women in International Security.

Charles F. Doran is the Andrew W. Mellon Professor of International Relations at The Johns Hopkins University's School of Advanced International Studies in Washington, D.C.

Vanda Felbab-Brown is a senior fellow with the Center for 21st Century Security and Intelligence in the Foreign Policy program at the Brookings Institution.

Nils Petter Gleditsch is research professor at the Peace Research Institute Oslo (PRIO) and Professor Emeritus at the Norwegian University of Science and Technology (NTNU) in Trondheim.

Jack A. Goldstone is Hazel Professor of Public Policy at George Mason University and director of the Research Laboratory on Political Demography at the Russian Presidential Academy of National Economy and Public Administration.

David F. Gordon is Eurasia Group's chairman and head of research. He served as the director of policy planning under Secretary of State Condoleezza Rice, and held a top managerial role with the National Intelligence Council.

Sheldon Himelfarb is director of the PeaceTech Initiative at the United States institute of Peace, having previously launched its Centers of Innovation for Media/Science and Technology.

Michael J. Johnson is a MBA candidate at Carnegie Mellon and a former Eurasia Group researcher.

Bruce D. Jones is a senior fellow and the director of the Project on International Order and Strategy at the Brookings Institution, and director and senior fellow of the Center on International Cooperation at New York University.

Kathleen Kuehnast is the director of the Center for Gender and Peacebuilding at the United States Institute of Peace. She is also a member of the Council on Foreign Relations.

Ellen Laipson is president and chief executive officer of the Stimson Center, and directs its Middle East/Southwest Asia program. She serves on the International Advisory Council of the International Institute of Strategic Studies and the Secretary of State's Foreign Affairs Policy Board.

David A. Lake is the Jerri-Ann and Gary E. Jacobs Professor of Social Sciences, Distinguished Professor of Political Science, associate dean of Social Sciences, and director of the Yankelovich Center for Social Science

Research at the University of California, San Diego.

Deborah Welch Larson is professor of political science at the University of California, Los Angeles.

Tod Lindberg is a research fellow at the Hoover Institution, Stanford University. He is also a contributing editor to the *Weekly Standard* and an adjunct associate professor at Georgetown University, where he teaches in the School of Foreign Service.

Edward D. Mansfield is the Hum Rosen Professor of Political Science, chair of the Political Science Department, and director of the Christopher H. Browne Center for International Politics at the University of Pennsylvania.

Monty G. Marshall is president of Societal-Systems Research Inc., and director of the Polity IV project. He is a consultant with the United Nations, national development agencies, and international organizations.

Michael O'Hanlon is director of research and senior fellow in Foreign Policy at the Brookings Institution.

Thania Paffenholz is senior researcher at the Graduate Institute of International and Development Studies in Geneva, Switzerland. She also works as a policy advisor in support of peace processes.

Stewart Patrick is senior fellow and director of the International Institutions and Global Governance program at the Council on Foreign Relations.

Hilton Root, a policy specialist in international political economy and development, is professor of public policy at George Mason University.

Rafe Sagarin is a marine ecologist and environmental policy analyst at the Institute of the Environment, University of Arizona.

Jack Snyder is the Robert and Renée Belfer Professor of International Relations in the Political Science Department and the Saltzman Institute of War and Peace Studies at Columbia University.

Paul B. Stares is the General John W. Vessey Senior Fellow for Conflict Prevention and director of the Center for Preventive Action at the Council on Foreign Relations in Washington, D.C. He is also an adjunct professor in the Edmund A. Walsh School of Foreign Service at Georgetown University.

Frances Stewart is professor emeritus in development economics at the University of Oxford and editor of *Oxford Development Studies*.

Jane E. Stromseth is professor of law at Georgetown University, and has served in government at the State Department, the National Security Council, and the Department of Defense.

Astri Suhrke is senior researcher at the Chr. Michelsen Institute, Bergen (Norway), and a nonresident fellow at the Asia-Pacific College of Diplomacy, the Australian National University (Canberra).

Necla Tschirgi is professor of practice in human security and peacebuilding at the Kroc School of Peace Studies at the University of San Diego and co-executive editor of the *Journal of Peacebuilding and Development*.

Abiodun Williams is president of The Hague Institute for Global Justice, and a former director of strategic planning for United Nations secretaries-general Ban Ki-moon and Kofi Annan.

Paul D. Williams is associate professor of international affairs at George Washington University. He is also a nonresident senior adviser at the International Peace Institute in New York and a visiting professor at the Institute for Peace and Security Studies at Addis Ababa University in Ethiopia.

David A. Welch is a CIGI senior fellow, chair of global security at the Balsillie School of International Affairs, and professor of political science at the University of Waterloo. He is also founder of the Japan Futures Initiative.

I. William Zartman is Jacob Blaustein Distinguished Professor Emeritus of International Organization and Conflict Resolution at the Paul H. Nitze School of Advanced International Studies, Johns Hopkins University, Washington, D.C. He is a member of the steering committee of the Processes of International Negotiation (PIN) Program at Clingendael, Netherlands.

PART I

THE EVOLVING GLOBAL SECURITY ENVIRONMENT

1

The Center Cannot Hold
Conflict Management in an Era of Diffusion

Chester A. Crocker, Fen Osler Hampson,
and Pamela Aall

The state of the world has been called many names—the post–Cold War era, the post-9/11 era, a G-Zero world (in which no country dominates the global agenda), the end of the unipolar moment, the era of failed states, a postmodernist world, the age of terrorism, the rise of the rest, and the Pacific century. None of these labels adequately describes today's world. Yet, they point to a common denominator—the global order is breaking apart, national sovereignty is changing, boundary lines are becoming more fluid, new norms are forming, old norms are withering away. There is, in short, a systemic transformation occurring in which some regions are on the rise, some in decline, and some in open revolt. There are new actors that operate under new authorities, using new approaches and methodologies. In this diffusion of agency, authority, and action, it seems that the world has slipped its moorings and is drifting.

What impact will these changes have for practitioners, scholars, and institutions of conflict management? This chapter looks at the characteristics of the evolving international environment, reviews how the different international relations schools view this evolution, identifies four conflict types that can be anticipated over the next decade, and examines how the conflict management field is adjusting to the changing challenges to peace and security.

Not long ago, the situation looked very different. Writing in 2005, Zbigniew Brzezinski foresaw that "the central challenge of our time is posed not by global terrorism, but rather by the intensifying turbulence caused by the phenomenon of *global political awakening*. That awakening is socially massive and politically radicalizing."[1] This scenario, which foresaw that the world's somnolent would rise into political awareness and demand change in the relationship between rulers and the ruled, became reality a few years later, as popular uprisings brought down autocratic leaders in Egypt, Libya, and Tunisia. The "global" aspect of these uprisings was not just that popular movements overthrew these autocratic regimes, but that these revolts were part of a shift in regional power dynamics, giving regional political leadership—which had long rested in the hands of Iranians, Turks, Israelis, and Americans—to the Arabs themselves.[2]

The patterns of turmoil unleashed by the self-immolation of a Tunisian fruit vendor had numerous, deep-seated origins.[3] But three factors seem to have been central: the impact of demographic pressures, including a youth bulge that constituted a ready pile of political tinder; an increasing societal awareness that there were alternatives to a sterile and humiliating status quo; and the technological drivers of that awareness in the form of regional—if not global—communications media, powerfully supplemented by social media. While Middle East experts expressed doubts that the transitions would lead to more democratic societies, many analysts and journalists were swept away by visions of political empowerment in the Middle East.[4]

Troubled transitions in Egypt and Libya and a vicious civil war in Syria have sobered this optimistic view. While mobilized publics did awake from the shackles of authoritarian rule and repressive regimes themselves awoke to the power of the street and mass protest movements, there were also more disturbing stirrings. Among the most threatening were extremist elements and criminal networks that exploited conditions of extreme poverty and weak and ineffective governance for their own purposes, using the tools of terrorism, intimidation, and organized violence.

Beyond the Middle East and North Africa, other awakenings are still works in progress, still capable of generating hope, uncertainty, apprehension, and dismay, whether sequentially or simultaneously. There is the continued mobilization of publics in a variety of weak or so-called transitional democracies. These situations highlight the gap between good governance and state institutions, and the inability of governments in these transitional democracies to accommodate the interests of a newly mobilized public and emerging civil society. There is also an economic dimension as several large developing nations, who are flexing their muscles in noneconomic arenas. Many people across the world sense a power shift toward the emerging Asian states and away from the West. Whether this is indeed the case is yet to be seen, but even the perception of a shift will have an impact on international security and conflict management structures and governance.

If the concept of "awakening" has so many diverse meanings, can take so many directions, and can elicit such divergent reactions, can it usefully guide the analysis of where the international system is heading? Diverse actors appear to awaken for their own reasons and their resulting actions will reflect this diversity of motivations. The net systemic impact of these interactions is far from clear. The contributors to the current volume reflect the reality that the international system's future trajectory has not yet been determined. For this reason, the editors of this volume recognize the importance of the new forces and new dynamics identified above. But the best metaphor to capture the current conflict management challenge is the one introduced at the start of this chapter: the world as a ship that has broken away from its moorings in stormy seas. No one can tell where it will end up or whether its crew can regain control and pilot it to safer, more predictable waters. Today's conflict managers in international organizations, regional groupings, individual governments, and nonofficial organizations are in a situation like that of the crew in a ship adrift. Hence, the title of this volume.

Obvious challenges exist to exploring the geographic and cultural limits of the global ferment seen in all of its various manifestations. First, there is the challenge of trying to determine how widespread will be the potential "demonstration effect" (a phenomenon where events in one place act as an example for people elsewhere) of this turmoil in places as diverse as the post-Soviet states, China, Cuba, Zimbabwe, and other autocracies. The behavior of leaders in these places suggests that—whatever one may think of the likely scenarios—they consider themselves to be vulnerable to spontaneous pressures from "below."

A second challenge is identifying the nature of the relationship between political change and violent conflict. On the regional or global scale, when political regimes define themselves by reference to clashing norms of legitimacy, the more powerful among them may desire to export their systems and principles. Examples include the wars triggered by the Reformation in Europe and the systemic upheavals occasioned by the Wilsonian urge to make the world safe for democracy. On a national or societal level, when the very essence of regime legitimacy becomes an issue, instability tends to follow, as seen in the contemporary cleavage between Sunni- and Shia-dominated political systems, and within specific states such as Syria, Iraq, Bahrain, and Afghanistan.

The process of establishing normative clarity within a society can itself trigger civil war. Moreover, lured by perceived security threats or opportunities for expansion, political elites may look outside their borders and seek to shape the environment in which their system can thrive, a process that can lead to regional, interstate conflict.[5] Ethnonational principles as well as ideological or confessional ones can set such dynamics in motion. Old-fashioned nationalistic impulses can also be whipped up in an instant in this media-enabled age, in response to perceived slights or a unilateral fait accompli. Nationalistic behavior is not a surprising outcome when major states experience severe development, governance, and environmental strains.

In those cases of street-power uprisings, the link to conflict will vary from society to society. In some places, nonviolent action may simply reflect the urge to remove a discredited autocrat and force a genuine political opening—as happened in the Philippines, Serbia, and more recently, Burma. In other places—Georgia, for example—people-power movements may be a response to, or an effort to preempt, stolen or suspect elections. In Lebanon, the mass movement was a response to the Syrian-inspired assassination of a leader. The Libya, Yemen, and Syria cases point to the extreme danger that nonviolence will meet violent state brutality and descend into outright warfare with the potential for regional spillover into neighboring states. As the Egyptian case illustrates, removing the dictator is only the first chapter in what may be a protracted political evolution.

A third, broader challenge concerns conflict management. Will the practice of conflict management be able to keep up with the emerging systemic and societal transformations that are under way, with the new actors, new actions, and new authorities? Will international organizations, states, or private groups have the motivation, capability, and the means to manage the messy, transborder, ethnically complex conflicts spreading across regional terrain? Will the conflict management crew in a world adrift have the necessary resources, the right charts and compass, and the capacity to work together? Will they be capable of divining the primary dangers and organizing to deal with them?

The commonplace observation that today's conflicts are overwhelmingly local and internal needs to be held up to the mirror of historical experience as well as to be judged by current events. Can the conflicts in Cyprus, Afghanistan, Syria, Sudan, Kashmir, and the Democratic Republic of the

Congo be termed "internal" in any meaningful sense? Even when a conflict appears to be purely internal—such as in the Basque region of Spain, Mindanao in the Philippines, or Northern Ireland—powerful neighbors have played roles as partisans or third parties.[6] Neighbors and regional lead states are likely to be the "first responders" when turbulence turns into violent conflict. The actions of Qatar, Iran, and Turkey in recent Arab cases illustrate this point.

These three challenges can be expressed as questions: (1) Are we in the midst of a global political shift where power moves from central institutions (i.e., governments, the United Nations, or the G8) to smaller, more distributed units? (2) What is the nature of the relationship between political (or social or economic) change and the outbreak and spread of conflict? and (3) What are the consequences of these factors for conflict management? Together, this trio of questions creates a framework for understanding the demands of conflict management in the near future and forms the basis of a large exploration of this topic.[7]

This chapter argues that we are entering an era characterized by contests—contests over legitimacy, governance, and geopolitical spaces. At the same time, there is an ongoing diffusion of expertise, power, initiative, and agency in international relations, leading to an autonomous, ambiguous, and asymmetrical world order where there are, in effect, no first responders to conflicts when they break out—or to those that continue to burn. But this view may be too pessimistic. While governments/states (and intergovernmental organizations) remain centrally important in conflict and conflict management, they increasingly are sharing their roles with a growing list of others, both within their own societies and within the so-called international community. Conflict has become more distributed, but conflict management has become distributed, too.

In order to make distributed conflict management work, however, the conflict management players need to recognize that they need to work through teams and coalitions, throwing diplomatic energy into developing coordinated and layered responses, and working closely with regional and local actors that have the knowledge, legitimacy, and capacity to act in constructive ways. Providing security and conflict management in this environment is a team effort, but it is not an organized, highly structured game like football. Nor is it a relay race, in which one player does his or her best, and then hands off to another. This is perhaps a new game, where the central challenge is to devise new rules of engagement and cooperation among a diverse group of participants whose fields of action and core objectives differ. There may not be a controlling central "captain" of the ship in a world adrift, but if crew members cannot devise some basis for joint and parallel action, the implications for conflict management are troubling.

DIFFERENT SCHOOLS, DIFFERENT TEAMS

It is not only practitioners who are challenged by the new environment. Scholars disagree on many aspects, as well. That international relations scholars are divided about the direction in which the world is moving should not surprise. The traditional major paradigms in international relations—realism, liberalism, and constructivism—have long pointed to different causes of peace and conflict in the international system, as have more recent schools of thought, including feminism and environmentalist approaches that also have a strong impact on policy.[8] The intensity of those debates, with their deep and lasting implications for foreign policy and the management of international relations, is now even more acute as international relations scholars ponder an uncertain future.[9]

Realist School

To many realists, the world appears to be entering a period of heightened instability with growing potential for interstate conflict as the tectonic plates of the international system shift with the rise of China and other emerging economies of the developing world, such as India and Brazil.[10] In a recent intelligence forecast, for example, the US National Intelligence Council argues that the era of US global primacy—the so-called unipolar moment of the post–Cold War era—is finally over with the rise of the world's emerging economies.[11] Realists believe that since the time of ancient Greece great power transitions in world politics have had deeply unsettling consequences. When Thucydides wrote about the origins of the Peloponnesian wars, he identified the culprits as the rise in the power of Athens and the fear this created in Sparta.

Some realists believe that this drama is now being reenacted in the United States' relations with China. Like Athens, which bullied its smaller neighbors in the Aegean Sea, China is now doing the same as it asserts its territorial claims in the South and East China Seas. As Graham Allison notes, "For six decades after the second world war, an American 'Pax Pacifica' has provided the security and economic framework within which Asian countries have produced the most rapid economic growth in history. However, having emerged as a great power that will overtake the US in the next decade to become the largest economy in the world, it is not surprising that China will demand revisions to the rules established by others."[12] Whether China and the United States can avoid what Allison calls the "Thucydides Trap" remains an open question. Other realists argue that the analogy is misplaced on both theoretical and empirical grounds.[13] In their view, China may be "rising" but the United States is not a "declining" power, and there are still major gaps in the two countries' respective economic and military capabilities.

Liberal School

For liberal international relations scholars, there is much more stability in the international system and less anarchy than meets the eye. In terms of great power relations, for example, liberal international relations scholars argue that both the United States and China have simply too much at stake to reenact Thucydides' account of the origins of the Peloponnesian wars between Athens and Sparta. In their view, when the British economist and Nobel laureate, Sir Norman Angell, forecast in his book *The Great Illusion* (1910) that the forces of globalization would inevitably create a more peaceful world, he was not wrong, just perhaps fifty or sixty years too early with his forecast. "Commercial development," he wrote, "is broadly illustrating one profound truth: that the real basis of social morality is self-interest. If the subject of rivalry between nations is business, the code which has come to dominate business must necessarily come to dominate the conduct of governments."[14] For liberal scholars, this is the story of US-China relations in recent years. China and the United States are two of the most highly economically interdependent economies in the world.[15] More generally, economics and the changing forces of production through global "value chains," in which the production of goods and services is no longer contained within the boundaries of a single nation, are also drivers of tightly woven global economic interdependence.[16]

Liberals are also at pains to point out that none of the current major powers of the international system—or any of the so-called rising powers—seeks to challenge it through a revolutionary foreign policy. Although the former Soviet Union and, perhaps to a lesser extent, China once viewed themselves as revolutionary powers, this is no longer the case. Russia's leaders harbor great power ambitions, but those ambitions are confined largely to its periphery and its economy is too weak for it to play any kind of serious imperial, expansionist role. China, with its embrace of free markets and capitalism, is very much a status quo power in terms of the global political economy. So, too, is India. Russia and China have key positions in the world's leading international institutions, the United Nations in particular, through their seats on the Security Council. For liberal scholars, international institutions exert a powerful stabilizing effect on the international system and the behavior of its component actors.

According to the liberal tradition, another pillar of the current order is the embrace of democracy in many parts of the globe. Since the overthrow of Portugal's dictatorial regime in April 1974, the number of democracies in the world has multiplied dramatically. Before the start of this global trend toward democracy, there were roughly forty countries that could be classified as more or less democratic. Today there are eighty-seven countries designated as free and democratic, representing 43 percent of the global population, and another sixty that are "partly free."[17] The flourishing of democracy is seen by liberal scholars as a positive force for world peace and global order, a view that is supported by a wealth of empirical research on this matter.[18]

Constructivist School

In contrast to realists, constructivists believe that changes in the distribution of material power are socially indeterminate.[19] For them, the implications of the rise of the BRICs (a neologism referring collectively to rising powers such as Brazil, Russia, India, and China) are unclear. Constructivists also ascribe greater powers to institutions than do neoliberal institutionalist scholars: in addition

to reducing transaction costs, altering payoffs, and increasing the quantity and quality of available information, institutions also configure actor interests, values, and even identities.[20] Scholars are thus confronted by multiple possible futures, though not all are equally likely, and all involve the exercise of social power.[21]

These views lead to concrete (if probabilistic) conclusions about the implications of the rise of China, for example. One view is that China is likely to continue along a path leading to greater integration into the international system.[22] Despite a revolutionary period in the early history of the People's Republic, China is now reconciled to modern diplomacy and international law; indeed, it is rapidly becoming more skillful in employing these practices. Another view emphasizes the influence of realist thought on Chinese grand strategy, suggesting the possibility that China will increasingly turn to balancing behavior (though, notably, these scholars decline to categorize China as a revisionist power).[23]

The prospects for maintaining and strengthening international order thus depend on the orientation of emerging powers toward critical institutions of the modern international system. Like scholars of the English school, constructivists place emphasis on the importance of rules and practices of diplomacy and international law;[24] they do not maintain that the world is necessarily becoming a more peaceful place. Indeed, it clearly sometimes operates in what might be called a realist manner. The key is that, to the extent it does so in particular regions at particular times, this is due not to the immutable character of anarchy but rather because such practices have been socially constructed among a set of actors. Anarchy is, in Alexander Wendt's terms, what states make of it.[25] Such a conclusion is natural, given that constructivism is first and foremost a social theory rather than a theory of international relations; while many constructivists working in international relations are essentially liberal in their philosophical views and normative beliefs, it is equally possible to imagine what Samuel Barkin and others have called "realist constructivism."[26]

The key to maintaining and strengthening social order is to maintain the robustness, and especially the legitimacy, of key norms, rules, practices, and institutions. Diplomacy, international law, and peaceful dispute resolution are essential at the system level, as are the laws of armed conflict. Fragile and failed states must be addressed with transitional justice and reconciliation efforts, peace education, and the strengthening of human rights cultures. All such efforts will take time, however, and all must be tailored to fit local cultures.[27]

Environmentalists

This school is controversial, especially when it focuses on causality issues. This school can be referred to as the environmentalist school of conflict because it focuses on the role of resource scarcity and broader environmental factors, such as the onset of climate change, as conflict drivers. According to this school, environmental degradation, population growth, and climate change are increasingly key contributing factors, if not triggers, to the outbreak-of-conflict equation.[28] Some studies, for example, have shown that the onset of drought and growing desertification in sub-Saharan Africa have exacerbated interethnic and tribal tensions, as displaced groups are forced to move into neighboring areas where demand outstrips resources to secure their livelihood.[29] Even the Arab Spring apparently had roots in the hidden stresses of climate change, which has adversely affected agricultural production and raised food prices, thereby helping to fuel the upheavals that toppled or challenged authoritarian regimes in Egypt and Syria,

according to a recent study.[30] However, in regions that traditionally have not been arenas of conflict, such as the Arctic, there is also the potential for new conflicts, with the scramble to exploit mineral resources and develop new transportation corridors as global warming opens up the North and the Arctic ice pack recedes.

Competition for resources, both renewable and nonrenewable, is a key source of conflict in the environmentalists' understanding of conflict processes, although intergroup rivalries and historical patterns of enmity also enter into the scarcity-as-a-driver-of-conflict equation.[31] According to environmentalists, climate change and the onset of severe weather patterns—especially in vulnerable coastal areas, where much of the world's population is concentrated—will create new stresses and social and political tensions in the future. So, too, will growing climate stresses create greater demands on the world's food supplies and the availability of fresh water.[32] These factors do not signify the emergence of a theory of resource-driven determinism; rather, they encourage reflection on the impact of accelerating natural resource development and burgeoning demographic growth in regions and countries with weak or poor governance. The pressures caused by such changes can lead to social conflict, which, in certain circumstances, can descend into violence.[33]

These strains of thought on the dynamics of international relations speak to the kinds of contests that are emerging over legitimacy, governance, and the control of geopolitical spaces. Among realist, liberal international, and constructivist scholars, there is widespread recognition that the international system is fracturing and that power is becoming more widely diffused, not only in terms of the distribution of power between states but also in the relationship between states and their citizens, with the rise and engagement of civil society in many corners of the globe. Like many realists, liberals, and constructivists, environmentalists see a fracturing of regional and global systems, especially when it comes to the management of scarce resources and the environment. They believe that unless more effective preventive and mitigation measures can be found to deal with resource scarcity and environmental stresses, bringing peace to war-torn nations and regions will remain an elusive goal. As useful as these paradigms are in organizing analytical and practical approaches to conflict, they have yet to contend fully with the increasing dispersion and fragmentation of political will and authority in the international system.

AGREEING ON THE PLAYING FIELD: AN EMERGING TYPOLOGY OF CONFLICTS

The diffusion of agency, authority, and action may be characteristic of the new global environment, but it does not describe the kinds of conflicts that can be anticipated in the near future. Are there patterns that can be discerned about the nature and dynamics of conflict over the next decade? While prediction, especially in international relations, is a risky business, this chapter will go so far as to describe four kinds of conflicts that are likely to occur in the near future. In offering our own typology of extant and emerging conflict patterns, the authors of this chapter recognize that there are many different ways to parse the world of international conflict. Some studies focus on the intrastate-versus-interstate dimensions to such conflicts,[34] although we believe that this dichotomy is somewhat artificial, because today's conflicts have a tendency to "spill into" as well as "spill over" porous national boundaries.[35] Other studies stress the role of variables such as ethnicity,[36] "greed, creed and need,"[37] horizontal inequalities,[38] social marginalization and injustice,[39] relative deprivation, "the financial viability of rebel organizations,"[40] and "acute poverty combined with critical

failures of governance."[41] The goal here is not to rehearse the extensive list of sources that are offered in the conflict literature, but to demarcate a few simple patterns that are especially salient to policymakers and that need to be considered in different strategies and tools of conflict management.

Conflicts over Legitimacy

This is an emergent—or more accurately, reemergent—type of conflict, and its future shape and scope are only dimly visible today. This first type, discussed at length previously, will grab the attention of both regional and global actors. The risk of spillover and regional spread is clear. Unless handled skillfully by major powers, this type of conflict risks drawing in those powers on behalf of contending sides, creating a fresh layer of polarization.

Conflicts Arising from Weak States

A second, more familiar category of conflict results from state fragility or failure leading to political collapse, a vacuum of authority, and humanitarian crisis. Such scenarios emerged with a vengeance after the Cold War ended and bipolarity came to a sudden end. Numerous factors contribute to the weak-state phenomenon, including the spread of criminal networks that undermine legitimate state authority, trade in arms and looted commodities, economic stagnation, the politics of greed and corruption that hollow out state institutions, and the manipulation of sectarian and ethnic diversity by political entrepreneurs. As a result, state weakness takes many forms and can descend into conflict along several pathways, some of which are more threatening to international order and the interests of major powers than others.[42] A major share of such conflicts are recurrent cases, in which peace agreements break down (such as in the Democratic Republic of Congo and Sudan), and intractable cases, in which peace efforts fail to get at the underlying sources of violent strife (such as the Naxalite conflict in India, the Muslim insurgency in southern Thailand, or the Tuareg rebellions affecting Mali and Niger).

There is little reason to expect a decline in the number of conflicts flowing from fragile states with weak institutions. Many of the affected polities are still relatively "new," and a period of time may be needed to build durable political institutions and to reduce the impact of personalized rule through patronage networks. External actors will be drawn into these largely internal conflicts selectively when there are overwhelming humanitarian arguments for applying some version of the responsibility to protect principle, or when there is a risk of a weak state falling into the hands of criminals, pirates, or terrorist groups. Cases such as northern Nigeria, the southern Thailand insurgency, and the Mindanao conflict in the Philippines illustrate the risk that strictly "local" conflict dynamics can be hijacked by outside extremists. Increasingly, regional bodies will be the default responders in this category of conflicts. No major powers want to "own" them, which helps to explain why the United Nations is often drawn in to dampen down things and manage or mitigate the turbulence. In reality, however, major powers will not stand aloof when the stakes appear high enough: they will act selectively, inconsistently, and within a UN mandate when possible.

Existential Conflicts

A third category of conflicts revolves around the perception of existential threats; in other words, threats to the existence or viability of one group due to the actions or attitudes of another group or groups. Because of the zero-sum nature of the dispute, these conflicts often become intractable. These existential conflicts are often found in turbulent zones that result from the collapse of empires and other complex multiethnic structures during or after major wars. A substantial portion of the most intractable cases derive from the circumstances and decisions made when things fell apart. Kashmir, Cyprus, the Balkan wars, the Korean Peninsula, the Armenian-Azerbaijan dispute over Nagorno-Karabakh, and even the Israeli-Palestinian case all contain a variant of this group of what could be called "imperial legacy conflicts." Such cases are impacted by the political rivalries of successor or neighboring states, captive to forces larger than the immediate territorial confines of the contested land.[43] Due to their escalatory risks and the problem of the proliferation of weapons of mass destruction, these cases will continue to form a major challenge for conflict management. External powers will be drawn in as patrons, mediators, and peacekeepers, but they will seldom enjoy the experience. Regional bodies are more likely to mirror the divisions that fuel these conflicts than to make effective contributions to managing them.

Major Interstate Conflict

A fourth type of case is the possibility of a return to armed confrontation and outright conflict between great powers and/or rival regional powers. As discussed above, various schools of thought come to distinctly different conclusions about the emerging international system and the relationships among its most powerful states. However much war has been devalued and delegitimized as an instrument of national policy over the decades, it may be unwise to discount the chance that major state rivalry, structural tests of strength, or sheer miscalculation could trigger outbreaks of interstate war. A careful examination of scenarios that could draw the United States and China (or China and various combinations of neighbors) into armed hostilities leads to the recognition that peaceful coexistence is not inevitable, and to a heightened appreciation of the importance of managing and deflecting these risks.[44] Interstate war risks in South Asia and the Middle East/Persian Gulf must also be considered as ongoing challenges for conflict management. It may also be the case that, absent direct armed confrontation and violence (where the costs of direct armed conflict are deemed to be too high), advanced and emerging economic powers may resort to other, less direct (and stealthier) confrontational means such as cyber warfare to pursue their broader economic and strategic goals. As has been seen, such attacks have the potential to cripple critical infrastructure and wreak wider economic havoc, which in turn might cause a major loss of life.[45]

In considering this category of potential conflict in the emerging global order, the bad news is that only major, powerful actors can hope to manage the conflicts between and among each other. This places a premium on diplomacy and sustained engagement in conflict prevention and strengthened bilateral communication, especially in politically fragmented regions that lack shared security institutions. The UN Security Council cannot be expected to be an effective conflict manager in such scenarios unless the permanent five members (Great Britain, China, France, Russia, and the United States) and other major states (such as Japan, India, Germany, and Brazil) enable it to do so through their own policies and by developing habits of responsible behavior and cooperation.

The good news is that the world's most powerful states are increasingly caught up in networks and webs of interdependency that severely constrain their freedom of action. Those networks—financial, communications and information technology, energy and commodity trade, among others—may be understood as an elaborate conflict-prevention mechanism (akin, perhaps, to mutually as-

sured destruction in the US-Soviet balance of power). If elites are fully aware of their import, they will recognize their growing vulnerability to a transformed and more "fragile" strategic environment that includes risks of economic and infrastructural collapse. Such a world may not be less conflictual, but it could evolve into complex patterns of "entangled rivalry" in which military competition gradually gives way to nonviolent interactions and where states work together with a wide range of other actors to manage the conflict agenda.[46]

Conflict Trends

While these four types of clashes may describe the future conflict environment, it is possible that the total amount of conflict in that environment is decreasing. In fact, recent research into conflict trends seems to indicate that there is no reason to worry too much about escalating rates of violence around the world. A range of empirical research using statistical analysis indicates that armed conflict has been on a long-term secular decline since the final years of the Cold War and that an increasing share of today's wars are either being brought under control by successful conflict management or are recurrences of earlier fights that continue to burn underground before once again igniting into open violence.[47] The significance of such trends depends on the baselines established and the methodologies and definitions chosen, but it is clear that a positive trend was in place through the middle of the last decade.

Trends are reversible, however, and there is some limited quantitative evidence that war's decline has stopped and fresh outbreaks of intrastate conflict are continuing to occur. This should hardly be surprising in an age of global financial crisis, the political "awakening" discussed above, the relative rise of powerful states in Asia, and the continuation of intractable conflict zones in South Asia, the Horn of Africa, and parts of the Middle East. According to one recent analysis, the potential for continued outbreaks of *intrastate* conflict appears to be highest in parts of Africa, the Middle East, and South Asia, while there are also reasons for concern that interstate conflict—quiescent for a decade—could reemerge as a result both of broader global political and economic trends and of the impact of unresolved regional conflict dynamics.[48]

CHALLENGES FOR CONFLICT MANAGEMENT

How will the field and institutions of conflict management adjust in order to remain effective? Just as the actors, authorities, and actions affecting conflict have expanded beyond a more centralized system—epitomized by the Cold War—to more diffuse, decentralized structures, there have been changes in conflict management to address these new challenges. Sometimes these changes come about in reaction to events or policies in the preceding period. Their experiences in World War II led a number of formerly neutral countries, such as Norway, to enter into a robust alliance with the United States and other European allies. At the end of the Cold War, however, those alliances were allowed to wither as countries celebrated the "end of history"[49] and, at least in North America and Europe, focused energies on developing informal collaboration within a community of like-minded nations.[50] After the terrorist attacks on the United States and western European countries in the first decade of the new century, formal alliances were back in fashion. NATO rebounded and undertook its biggest campaign to date, in Afghanistan. After wearying conflicts in Iraq and Afghanistan, key Western actors again underwent a transformation, this time away from the practice of war; not toward neutrality, but toward conflict prevention.

Diffusion of Strategy: The Case of Conflict Prevention

Looking forward at a turbulent future and backward at a turbulent past, it is not surprising that a number of international actors have begun to stress the importance of conflict prevention.[51] The United Nations, the European Union, the Organization for Security and Cooperation in Europe (OSCE), the World Bank, the United Kingdom's Department for International Development, and the US military have all embraced a commitment to preventing conflict. At this stage, it is worth pausing to consider whether prevention is an appropriate response to all four types of conflict discussed above.

In some ways, the global commitment to conflict prevention has seen remarkable growth since the early 1990s. When the Carnegie Corporation launched its Commission on Preventing Deadly Conflict in 1994, it was after five years of dramatic geopolitical changes that sometimes erupted into violence. Building on the defining work of the UN secretary-general Boutros Boutros-Ghali, the Carnegie Commission approached conflict in much the same way as physicians approached the development of preventive medicine: (1) it is important to encourage healthy practices (e.g., transparency in political and economic decision making) to avoid conditions that might lead to conflict; (2) if conflict seems likely, it is important to address the factors that will trigger conflict; and (3) if conflict has already erupted, a critical response is to limit the influence of factors that exacerbate conflict.[52] The commission recommended that early warning should lead to early action in all three of these scenarios. The recommendations were directed at the United Nations and at states capable of affecting the situation.[53]

After a brief heyday of conflict management optimism in the early 1990s, troubling events in the Balkans, Africa, and Haiti produced skepticism that the attempts to bolster political will among the five permanent members of the UN Security Council would lead to any change in global responses to impending or deteriorating conflict. However, public opinion, at least in democratic nations, was in fact changing around this issue. In 2001, a group of experts led by former Australian prime minister Gareth Evans and Algerian diplomat Mohammed Sahnoun issued the report of the International Commission on Intervention and State Sovereignty, examining the conditions and limitations of outside intervention on humanitarian grounds.[54] The commission recommended that in cases in which states are unable to protect their citizens, or are themselves the agents of serious abuse, the international community had a duty to intercede. Three years later, UN Secretary-General Kofi Annan established the High Level Panel on Threats, Challenges and Change, which took the step of officially recommending collective international action in the face of violence, whether as threats to national and international security or as gross human rights violations to individuals and groups. This was followed in 2005 by the UN General Assembly World Summit, which brought together 191 heads of state to endorse the responsibility to protect, or R2P, principle.[55] In endorsing this principle, most of the world's nations recognized that protecting individuals from gross human rights abuses trumped state sovereignty. Preventive intervention—collective action to ward off abuses before they happened—seemed a short step away.

However, prevention—whether for humanitarian purposes or simply to stop conflict—has been applied both sparingly and sporadically.[56] In 2011, the R2P principle was invoked by the UN Security Council and a number of powerful states to justify action in support of Libyan rebels

and against Muammar Gaddafi. Unusual as it was, that action exposed the fundamental weakness of collective preventive action by sovereign states: the difficulty of reaching and maintaining agreement among independent entities that have different interests and different capabilities. Russia and China agreed reluctantly to approve international intervention in the Libyan case, but reacted negatively to the operation, led by Western states with some Arab support, and refused to make a precedent out of that collective action. When the conflict in Syria broke out, they repeatedly vetoed UN resolutions to impose sanctions on the Syrian government and rejected General Assembly calls for more concerted action. Without their support, the UN Security Council could not authorize measures to protect individuals from extreme violence in Syria. At this point, it was clear that the UN resolution–based commitment to stop state-sponsored violence and to prevent bloodshed was hostage—like most collective action—to the least-enthusiastic permanent member's willingness to support the engagement.

This example also illustrates some of the contradictions involved in preventing conflict, whether it is preventing conflict from breaking out, or preventing human rights abuses and mass violence in the midst of a conflict. Critics contend that conflict prevention prizes stability over change, stopping the violence over settling the issues for once and all. They point to a number of autocratic regimes in the Middle East—such as Egypt, Libya, and Saudi Arabia—where the suppression of dissent may have prevented conflict, but it also repressed democratic development. Preventing conflict, in their eyes, may be fighting against the tide of history by silencing voices that need to be heard. Proponents of conflict prevention, however, contend that averting or stopping violence allows parties to consider the costs of conflict and return to politics as a means of resolving issues. They believe that returning the conflict to political negotiation promotes a democratic solution and provides legitimacy among all sides for the ultimate settlement.

Returning to the schools of thought discussion, much of the earlier and contemporary discussion on conflict prevention is rooted in the liberal internationalist paradigm insofar as it stresses the importance of strengthening governance and the development of democracy at the national level, and international and regional institutions at the systemic and subsystemic levels. Realists would contend that such faith is misplaced insofar as security dilemmas at the national level and the power disequilibria at the systemic level are drivers of conflict and not susceptible to confidence-building measures. Fundamentally, these political dynamics raise barriers to preventive measures unless they are backed by coercive power. Constructivists would argue that old habits and patterns of conflict die hard and require extended normative change and the institutionalization of norms and values that would inhibit conflict, such as the promotion of transitional justice and war crimes accountability (other examples include the Responsibility to Protect and the anti-personnel landmines convention). Environmentalists argue that more attention should be paid to the "globalization of hazard" and, when it comes to global stressors such as climate change, to how to mitigate its sources and better manage the consequences of social and economic disruption.[57] These schools overlap to some extent in their sources of skepticism and the particular emphasis they place on different kinds of policy remedies.

What this disagreement makes clear is that prevention is not and should not be an automatic response to the outbreak of conflict. In the typology of conflicts discussed above—(1) conflicts over legitimacy, (2) failed states, (3) existential conflicts, and (4) interstate wars—conflict prevention by outsiders is most likely to be effective in those situations in which no one is really in charge (failed or failing states), and in those situations in which strong political elites are engaged in a kind of escalatory cycle, trying to scare their opponents into concessions (interstate conflict). A conflict-prevention role in interstate conflict might be to avert circumstances in which regional powers decide to fight with one another; for instance, Israel and Iran, China and Japan, or India and Pakistan. For the other types of conflict—over legitimacy and existential conflicts—conflict prevention consists not so much in stopping the violence as in preventing its spread to surrounding countries and promoting governance capacity and legitimacy as pathways to peace and security.

That said, in situations of transition, the international community's response to political awakenings will help to shape the context in which they occur—taking decisive military action as NATO members did in Libya, will produce an entirely different normative context than pushing for negotiated transitions, as happened in Yemen. If major powers and the international community quickly recognize rebels as legitimate future governments and back them in various ways, they are potentially encouraging more would-be rebels to take to the street. Whether such recognition will prevent conflict or lead to more violent confrontations, however, is dependent entirely on the case at hand.

These examples show that while the idea and embrace of conflict prevention has spread over the past ten years, its implementation remains a situation-dependent response. Attractive as it is as an overall strategic approach, it is only a partial response to the rapid changes in the international conflict environment. And if recent history is a guide, the embrace of conflict prevention may be temporary, lasting only as long as circumstances permit. Another international flare-up or catastrophe could send the community of nations back to a more martial approach to managing conflict, or discredit the idea of prevention entirely. The challenge for conflict managers, both inside and outside government, is to smooth out the cycles, to develop a holistic view of responding to conflict and building peace that incorporates prevention, diplomacy, peacekeeping, humanitarian intervention, social and political reform, and economic development—not as distinct entities, but as policies that refer to and build on each other, and support a larger conflict-management vision.

Diffusion of Responsibility: From Orchestration to Improvisation

The goal of developing a holistic conflict management strategy would be difficult at any time, but is even more challenging at a moment when the leadership and infrastructure for coordinated action are in flux. The changes in the nature of international and intrastate conflict have presented the principal institutions of conflict response with serious challenges to their roles and operations, and have changed the competencies needed to promote peace. The time-honored division of labor between the military and civilian agencies has dissolved into a swirl of overlap and duplication, but has also created gaps where neither soldiers nor diplomats are taking the lead. The United Nations has had a mixed record in filling these gaps, partly because the powerful nations find it increasingly hard to agree after a brief post–Cold War honeymoon and partly because the United States and Russia left it little room to maneuver in the complex environments of Iraq, Afghanistan, Syria, and Ukraine. UN Security Council resolutions, once seen as the necessary go-ahead for collective international action, are sometimes sought before an engagement (Libya) and

sometimes after an intervention in order to provide ex post facto justification (Kosovo); and sometimes an intervention occurs after its sponsors—recognizing the likelihood of vetoes—opt not to seek explicit authorization by the Security Council (for instance, as happened with the 2003 invasion of Iraq). Nongovernmental organizations (NGOs) have stepped into the breach in some instances, but are usually too small, diverse, and underresourced in their operations and goals to substitute for coordinated international action by governments or intergovernmental organizations. While institutions try to find their place in this new world, they at times join together in temporary, relatively unstructured collective ventures to address specific problems.

In a world adrift, the international system is one of fractured governance and diffused authority, and it is apparent that responding to conflict will require a diverse portfolio of instruments and actors to deal with a wide array of different security challenges. That is because each actor (or set of actors) and institution has its own strengths and weaknesses, but no single actor or set of institutions has a decided comparative advantage (or legitimacy) over the others. The real world is one of a plenitude of issues from regional rivalries to the spread of nuclear materials and weapons, from transnational organized crime and terrorism to cyber security, and conflicts of the more traditional variety that occur within and between states. Many of these challenges, by their very nature, are best met—in fact, can only be—met by collective effort. In the descriptive phrase of Richard Haass of the Council on Foreign Relations, it is a world of "messy multilateralism."[58]

However, there is greater order in that "messiness" than may first appear to be the case. Its disappointments notwithstanding, there is still value in the United Nations, including its conflict prevention abilities.

Regional states and security organizations also offer an alternative, as they increasingly assert their role as legitimizers and gatekeepers of international action. As a consequence, conflict management may well take on a distinctly regionalized hue. Regions, however, are seldom unanimous or coherent in their political alignments, and few regions have their own coercive toolkits. Their capacity constraints suggest the possibility of continued experimentation with hybrid models of global and regional coordination, typically on a case-by-case basis, as exemplified in a number of African conflicts.

Beyond the United Nations, there is a wide variety of evolving multilateral approaches to deal with the collective-action problems of a complex and globalized world that escape the United Nations. They include the "new" and not so new minilateralism (typically understood as getting together "the smallest possible number of countries needed to have the largest possible impact on solving a particular problem") of coalitions of the willing.[59] And there is resurgent regionalism and improvised forms of security management—what are sometimes termed collective conflict management—to deal with new security challenges.[60] Leaders of powerful states, international organizations, and civil society increasingly have to deal with conflict in a world where rules, hierarchies, objectives, and even outcomes are not clear.

In other words, there will be growing pressure for adaptable and flexible conflict management mechanisms. That reflects the reality that power and authority are diffusing in several different ways. One model is where diffusion is a conscious "outsourcing" action taken by powerful states and global bodies such as the World Bank and the United Nations, which seek to empower security partners and launch capacity-building initiatives at the regional level. Diffusion can also be the result of demands by local or regional actors to be the primary gatekeepers and legitimizers of conflict management activity. A third approach is where power diffusion is the result of laissez-faire attitudes ("let nature take its course") in global power centers, leading to situations in which local and regional actors follow their survival instincts and "do what they must" in their own interests. A fourth model features market-based power diffusion where willing buyers interact with willing sellers of security and conflict management services (e.g., mediation, training, security contracting, arms sales) in a marketplace constrained by hardly anything except national and regional norms and regulations.

In this environment of contested spaces and diffused capacity, collective conflict management will become the norm as institutions struggle to resolve problems rather than establish new modi operandi. This will mean that they will not only have to reach out to other third-party institutions and to understand local or regional conflict management cultures but they will also have to be prepared to operate in situations where leadership may change on a regular basis, where the lines of authority are unstated and fluid, and where their best judgment (rather than instructions from the home office) will make the critical difference between moving a step forward and moving a step back. The conflict management "crew" in a world adrift will need to be flexible, informed and intuitive, creative and careful, entrepreneurial and even-handed. Building this capacity into the world's conflict management leadership and institutions will be a critical task.

NOTES

1. Zbigniew Brzezinski, "The Dilemma of the Last Sovereign," *American Interest*, Autumn 2005. Brzezinski summed up the potential this way:

[T]he ongoing political awakening is now global in its geographic scope, with no continent or even region still largely politically passive; it is comprehensive in its social scale, with only very remote peasant communities still immune to political stimuli; it is strikingly youthful in its demographic profile and thus more receptive to rapid political mobilization; and much of its inspiration is transnational in origin because of the cumulative impact of literacy and mass communications.

2. Bassma Kodmani, "The Imported, Supported, and Homegrown Security of the Arab World," in *Rewiring Regional Security in a Fragmented World,* ed. Chester A. Crocker, Fen Osler Hampson, and Pamela Aall (Washington, DC: United States Institute of Peace Press, 2011).

3. In December 2010, a Tunisian fruit vendor, Mohamed Bouazizi, set himself alight in protest of the harassment he received from local government officials. His death is widely cited as the spark for popular antigovernment movements in Tunisia, Libya, Egypt, Yemen, Bahrain, and Syria.

4. Jon B. Alterman, "The Revolution Will Not Be Tweeted," *Washington Quarterly* 34, no. 4 (Fall 2011): 103–16.

5. John Owen, *The Clash of Ideas in World Politics: Transnational Networks, States, and Regime Change 1510–2010* (Princeton, NJ: Princeton University Press, 2010).

6. See the discussion of a wide range of contemporary cases in, "Cross Border Peacebuilding: Accord 22," *Conciliation Resources,* 2011, http://www.c-r.org/accord/cross-border.

7. Others are also grappling with these questions. The 2014 book edited by Mark Lagon and Clark Arend (*Human Dignity and the Future of International Relations* [forthcoming, 2014]) revisits Hedley Bull's arguments from the 1970s that the world was entering a neomedieval period. See Hedley Bull, *The Anarchical Society: A Study of Order in World Politics* (New York: Columbia University Press, 1977). Although their focus is on the preservation and protection of human dignity, their analysis is relevant to conflict management as well:

If we accept the proposition that the international system is becoming something akin to

what Bull called neo-medieval, what does this mean for human dignity? At some level, it would mean that the traditional system of accountability is being loosed from its moorings. In a system where states have legal and moral legitimacy because they are to be accountable to their citizens, intergovernmental organizations have legitimacy because they are creations of states. . . . But when we suddenly fast forward to a world where states are losing some of their monopoly of legitimacy through the presence of powerful non-state, non-state-created, actors, it becomes a challenge to find such accountability. Perhaps it lies somehow in the concept of 'human rights'?" (Lagon and Arend, p. 5)

8. On the traditional perspectives, see Christian Reus-Smit and Duncan Snidal, eds., *Oxford Handbook on International Relations* (Oxford: Oxford University Press, 2010).

9. It is beyond the bounds of this chapter to consider all of these different schools here. Instead, we have focused our discussion on the major, traditional international relations paradigms and some of the key debates about the world's geopolitical future that are anchored in these different paradigms. However, it is important to recognize that other approaches—especially the feminist school—have had a major impact on thinking about peace and conflict. The feminist school looks at how men and women intersect with and are affected by conflict. It examines how unrecognized assumptions about the gendered nature of conflict determine the analysis of violent conflict, and lead to conclusions relevant only to armed actors while ignoring women and girls who often play significant roles in conflict. Feminists consider conflict as a masculinized activity, much as some consider international relations as a masculinized field of study. The feminist perspective believes that long-term peace is not achievable until the academic and practitioner communities expand their views of the impact war has on individuals as perpetrators, victims, and conflict managers, especially in terms of the gendered roles. On feminist theories see, for example, J. Ann Tickner, *Gendering World Politics* (New York: Columbia University Press, 2001); Lorraine Code, *Encyclopedia of Feminist*

Theories (London: Routledge, 2002): Cynthia Enloe, *The Curious Feminist: Searching for Women in a New Age of Empire* (Berkeley: University of California Press, 2004): Carol Cohn, "Sex and Death in the Rational World of Defense Intellectuals" *Signs* 12, no. 4 (Summer 1987): 687–718; and Spike V. Peterson, "Transgressing Boundaries: Theories of Knowledge, Gender and International Relations," *Millennium:Journal of International Studies* 21, no. 2 (1992): 183–206. For faith-based theories of international relations, see, for example, J. Fox, "Religion as an Overlooked Element of International Relations," *International Studies Review* 3 (2002): 53–73; and Daniel Philpott, "Has the Study of Global Politics Found Religion?" *Annual Review of Political Science* 12 (June 2009): 183–202.

10. For an important discussion and assessment of these trends from a realist perspective, see Charles L. Glaser, *Rational Theory of International Politics: The Logic of Competition and Cooperation* (Princeton, NJ: Princeton University Press, 2010), and his review and critique of the realist debate about China's rise, "Will China's Rise Lead to War?" *Foreign Affairs* 90, no. 2 (March/April 2011): 80.

11. National Intelligence Council, *Global Trends 2030: Alternative Worlds* (Washington, DC: National Intelligence Council, 2012), http://www.dni .gov/files/documents/GlobalTrends_2030.pdf.

12. Graham Allison, "Thucydides's Trap Has Been Sprung in the Pacific," *Financial Times*, August 21, 2012, http://www.ft.com/cms/s/0/5d695b5a -ead3-11e1-984b-00144feab49a.html#axzz2Fo DyxgiK.

13. See Charles F. Doran, "Power Cycle Theory and the Ascendance of China: Peaceful or Stormy?" *SAIS Review* 32, no. 1 (Winter–Spring 2012): 73–87, http://muse.jhu.edu/login?auth=0& type=summary&url=/journals/sais_review/v032/32 .1.doran.html; and Charles F. Doran, *Systems in Crisis: New Imperatives of High Politics at Century's End* (Cambridge: Cambridge University Press, 1991).

14. Norman Angell, *The Great Illusion* (New York: Cosimo, 2010), 73.

15. See, for example, Jerald D. Finn, ed., *China-U.S. Economic and Geopolitical Relations* (New York: Nova Science, 2007); and Marcus Noland, "US-China Economic Relations," Working Paper no. 96-6 (Peterson Institute for International Economics, Washington, DC, 2012), http://www .iie.com/publications/wp/wp.cfm?ResearchID=162.

16. See, for example, World Trade Organization, *Trade Patterns and Global Value Chains in East Asia: From Trade in Goods to Trade in Tasks* (Geneva: World Trade Organization, 2011), http:// www.wto.org/english/res_e/booksp_e/stat_trade pat_globvalchains_e.pdf.

17. Freedom House, *Freedom in the World* (Washington, DC: Freedom House, 2012), 3.

18. See, for example, Bruce Russett, *Grasping the Democratic Peace: Principles for a Post–Cold War World* (Princeton, NJ: Princeton University Press, 1993).

19. We are grateful for the assistance of Mark Raymond in drafting this section.

20. Emmanuel Adler, "Seizing the Middle Ground: Constructivism in International Relations," *European Journal of International Relations* 3, no. 3 (1997); Ted Hopf, "The Promise of Constructivism in International Relations Theory," *International Security* 23, no. 1 (1998): 171–200; and Martha Finnemore and Kathryn Sikkink, "Taking Stock: The Constructivist Research Program in International Relations and Comparative Politics," *Annual Review of Political Science* 4, no. 3 (2002).

21. For a constructivist view on how to think in a rigorous way about "prediction" in international relations, see Michael N. Barnett and Robert Duvall, "Power in International Politics," *International Organization* 59, no. 1 (2005): 39–75; and S. Bernstein et al., "God Gave Physics the Easy Problems: Adapting Social Science to an Unpredictable World," *European Journal of International Relations* 6, no. 1 (2002): 43–76.

22. Shogo Suzuki, *Civilization and Empire: China and Japan's Encounter with European International Society* (London: Routledge, 2009).

23. A. I. Johnston, *Cultural Realism: Strategic Culture and Grand Strategy in Chinese History* (Princeton, NJ: Princeton University Press, 1995); and A. I. Johnston, "Is China a Status Quo Power?" *International Security* 27, no. 4 (1995): 5–56.

24. Bull, *Anarchical Society.*

25. Alexander Wendt, "Anarchy Is What States Make of It: The Social Construction of Power Politics," *International Organization* 46, no. 2 (1992): 391–425.

26. J. S. Barkin, *Realist Constructivism: Rethinking International Relations Theory* (Cambridge: Cambridge University Press, 2010).

27. Amitav Acharya, "How Ideas Spread: Whose Norms Matter? Norm Localization and Institutional Change in Asian Regionalism," *International Organization* 58, no. 2 (2004): 239–75.

28. Thomas F. Homer-Dixon, "Environmental Scarcities and Violent Conflict: Evidence from Cases," *International Security* 19, no. 1 (Summer, 1994): 5–40; and Thomas F. Homer-Dixon, *Environment Scarcity and Violence* (Princeton, NJ: Princeton University Press, 1990). For critiques of causal arguments that purport to show that there is a clear link between environmental scarcity and conflict, see Ragnhild Nordås and Nils Petter Gleditsch, "Climate Change and Conflict," *Political Geography* 26, no. 6 (August 2007): 627–38; and Nils Petter Gleditsch, "Armed Conflict and the Environment: A Critique of the Literature," *Journal of Peace Research* 35, no. 3 (May 1998): 381–400; Solomon M. Hsiang, Marshall Burke, and Edward Miguel, "Quantifying the Influence of Climate on Human Conflict," *Science* 341, no. 6151 (2013).

29. See, for example, Robert H. Bates, *When Things Fall Apart: State Failure in Late-Century Africa* (Cambridge: Cambridge University Press, 2008).

30. Caitlin E. Werrell and Francesco Femia, *The Arab Spring and Climate Change: A Climate and Security Correlations Series* (Washington, DC: Century for American Progress, February 2013), http://www.americanprogress.org/wp-content/uploads/2013/02/ClimateChangeArabSpring.pdf.

31. Nils Petter Gleditsch and Ole Magnus Theisen, "Resources, the Environment and Conflict," in *The Routledge Handbook of Security Studies*, ed. Thierry Balzacq and Myriam Dunn Cavelty (London: Routledge, 2010): 221–32; and Nils Petter Gleditsch and Ole Magnus Theisen, "Implications of Climate Change for Armed Conflict," in *The Social Dimensions of Climate Change: Equity and Vulnerability in a Warming World*, ed. Robin Mearns and Andrew Norton (Washington, DC: World Bank, 2010): 75–101.

32. See Clionadh Raleigh and Henrik Urdal, "Climate Change, Environmental Degradation and Armed Conflict," *Political Geography* 26 (2007): 674–94; and Charles J. Vörösmarty et al.,

"Global Water Resources: Vulnerability from Climate Change and Population Growth," *Science* 289 (2000): 284–88. However, as with much scholarship in the environmentalist world, there is much disagreement on this issue. Nils Petter Gleditsch argues the opposite—that water has seldom produced conflict except in the sense that neighbors fight and neighbors share rivers—in a number of works, including in chapter 9 of this volume.

33. Jack A. Goldstone, "The New Population Bomb: The Four Megatrends That Will Change the World," *Foreign Affairs* 89, no. 1 (2010): 31.

34. M. R. Sarkees, F. W. Wayman, and J. D. Singer, "Inter-State, Intra-State, and Extra-State Wars: A Comprehensive Look at Their Distribution over Time, 1816–1997," *International Studies Quarterly* 47 (2003): 49–70; and Muzaffer Ercan Yilmaz, "Intra-state Conflicts in the Post–Cold War Era," *International Journal on World Peace* 24, no. 4 (2007): 11–33.

35. See, for example, Monica Duffy Toft, *The Geography of Ethnic Violence: Identity, Interests, and the Indivisibility of Territory* (Princeton, NJ: Princeton University Press, 2004).

36. Ted Robert Gurr, "Peoples against States: Ethnopolitical Conflict and the Changing World System," *International Studies Quarterly* 38, no. 3 (1994): 347–77; and Ted Robert Gurr, *Minorities at Risk. A Global View of Ethnopolitical Conflict* (Washington, DC: United States Institute of Peace Press, 1993).

37. Mats Berdal, "Beyond Greed and Grievance: And Not Too Soon," *Review of International Studies* 31 (2005): 687–98.

38. Frances Stewart and Valpy Fitzgerald, *War and Underdevelopment*, 2 vols. (Oxford: Oxford University Press, 2001).

39. Roger Petersen, *Understanding Ethnic Violence: Fear, Hatred, and Resentment in Twentieth-Century Eastern Europe* (Cambridge: Cambridge University Press, 2002).

40. Paul Collier, "Economic Causes of Civil War and Their Implications for Policy" (research working paper, World Bank, Washington, DC, 2000); and Paul Collier et al., *Breaking the Conflict Trap: Civil War and Development Policy* (Washington, DC: World Bank; New York: Oxford University Press, 2003).

41. James D. Fearon and David D. Laitin, "Ethnicity, Insurgency, and Civil War," *American Political Science Review* 97 (2003): 75–90.

42. Stewart Patrick, *Weak Links: Fragile States, Global Threats and International Security* (New York: Oxford University Press, 2011).

43. Sumantra Bose, *Contested Lands: Israel-Palestine, Kashmir, Bosnia, Cyprus and Sri Lanka* (Cambridge, MA: Harvard University Press, 2007).

44. James Dobbins, "War with China," *Survival* 54, no. 4 (August–September 2012): 7–24.

45. See, for example, Ron Diebert, *Black Code: Inside the Battle for Cyberspace* (Toronto: Random House Canada, 2013).

46. Michael J. Mazarr, "Rivalry's New Face," *Survival* 54, no. 4 (August–September 2012): 83–106.

47. Monty G. Marshall and Benjamin R. Cole, *Global Report 2011: Conflict, Governance, and State Fragility* (Vienna, VA; Center for Systematic Peace, 2011); Human Security Centre, *Human Security Report 2005: War and Peace in the 21st Century* (New York: Oxford University Press, 2005); and J. Joseph Hewitt, Jonathan Wilkenfeld, and Ted Robert Gurr, with Birger Heldt, eds., *Peace and Conflict 2012* (College Park, MD: Center for International Development and Conflict Management, University of Maryland, 2012).

48. National Intelligence Council, *Global Trends 2030*, 53–65. Lotta Themnér and Peter Wallensteen, "Armed Conflict, 1946–2012," *Journal of Peace Research* 50, no. 4 (2013): 509–21; and Håvard Hegre et al., "Predicting Armed Conflict, 2011–2050," *International Studies Quarterly* 57, no. 2 (2013): 250–70.

49. Francis Fukuyama, *The End of History and the Last Man* (New York: Simon and Schuster, 2006).

50. See Tod Lindberg's chapter on the international community, chapter 30 in this volume.

51. For a full discussion of conflict prevention, see chapter 27 in this volume, by Paul Stares. See also Michael S. Lund, *Preventing Violent Conflicts: A Strategy for Preventive Diplomacy Conflict Prevention* (Washington, DC: United States Institute of Peace Press, 1995); and David Malone and Fen Osler Hampson, eds., *From Reaction to Conflict Prevention: Opportunities for the UN System* (Boulder, CO: Lynne Rienner, 2002). One of the few studies comparing disputes with and without preventive action is Magnus Öberg, Frida Möller, and Peter Wallensteen, "Early Conflict Prevention in Ethnic Crises, 1990–98: A New Dataset," *Conflict Management and Peace Science* 26, no. 1 (2009): 67–91.

52. Boutros Boutros-Ghali, in his *Agenda for Peace* (1992), used a very broad three-part definition of preventive diplomacy: (1) steps to "prevent disputes from arising between parties'; (2) steps to prevent existing disputes "from escalating into conflicts"; and (3) steps "to limit the spread of the latter when they occur" (Boutros Boutros-Ghali, *An Agenda for Peace,* June 17, 1992, A/47/277 S/24111, p. 5). Some have called the first "structural prevention" (and criticized it as stretching the concept too far); and the second, "operational prevention" in which the third party checks the slide to violence.

53. Paraphrasing Carnegie Commission on Preventing Deadly Conflict, *Preventing Deadly Conflict: Final Report* (Washington, DC: Carnegie Commission on Preventing Deadly Conflict, 1997), xiii.

54. International Commission on Intervention and State Sovereignty, *Responsibility to Protect* (Ottawa, ON: International Development Research Centre, 2001).

55. "The international community, through the United Nations, also has the responsibility to use appropriate diplomatic, humanitarian, and other peaceful means, in accordance with Chapters VI and VIII of the Charter, to help protect populations from genocide, war crimes, ethnic cleansing and crimes against humanity. In this context, we are prepared to take collective action, in a timely and decisive manner, through the Security Council, in accordance with the Charter, including Chapter VII, on a case-by-case basis and in cooperation with relevant regional organizations as appropriate, should peaceful means be inadequate and national authorities are manifestly failing to protect their populations from genocide, war crimes, ethnic cleansing and crimes against humanity." United Nations General Assembly, "2005 World Summit Outcome," October 24, 2005, A/RES/60/1, para.139.

56. The best-known and rarely duplicated case of preventive deployment was in Macedonia under UNPROFOR (the United Nations Protection Force) and then UNPREDEP (the United Nations Preventive Deployment Force).

57. In the words of Thomas Friedman, "Scientists like to say that, when it comes to climate change, we need to manage what is unavoidable and avoid what is unmanageable. That requires collective action globally to mitigate as much climate change as we can and the building of resilient states locally to adapt to what we can't mitigate." Thomas L. Friedman, "The Scary Hidden Stressor," *New York Times*, March 2, 2013.

58. Richard N. Haass, "The Case for Messy Multilateralism," *Financial Times,* January 5, 2010, http://www.ft.com/intl/cms/s/18d8f8b6-fa2f -11de-beed-00144feab49a,Authorised=false.html ?_i_location=http%3A%2F%2Fwww.ft.com %2Fcms%2Fs%2F0%2F18d8f8b6-fa2f-11de-beed -00144feab49a.html&_i_referer=#axzz289 og598s.

59. Moses Naim, "Minilateralism: The Magic Number to Get Real International Action," *Foreign Policy* 173 (July/August 2009): 135.

60. Chester A. Crocker, Fen Osler Hampson, and Pamela Aall, eds., *Rewiring Regional Security in a Fragmented World* (Washington, DC: United States Institute of Peace Press, 2011); and Chester A. Crocker, Fen Osler Hampson, and Pamela Aall, "Collective Conflict Management: A New Formula for Global Peace and Security." *International Affairs* 87, no.1 (January 2011): 39–59.

2

THE SHIFTING LANDSCAPE OF CONFLICT MANAGEMENT

David A. Welch

Conflict is a broad term that can be used to describe any interaction in which the parties have incompatible preferences. These interactions can range from the banal (two people disagreeing over who should take out the trash) to the catastrophic (World Wars I and II). In a perfect world, there would be no conflict; everyone would live in harmony. But in the real world, conflict is common and represents a daily management challenge. A conflict managed well will be prevented from getting out of hand until a resolution can be found or the underlying issue goes away. Poor conflict management may not merely fail to prevent escalation, but hasten it.

The kinds of conflicts that students of world politics are most interested in are those that arise between groups of people who are well enough organized and well enough armed to cause significant levels of death and destruction. Nonlethal conflicts are important as well, of course; trade disputes and competitive currency devaluations, for example, can be very costly. But this chapter concentrates on (those fortunately rare) conflicts that have the poten-

tial to turn violent. What are various ways of managing these? Which of those ways are most useful, and when? Does history teach us any lessons about how best to manage conflict so as to give genuine resolution the best possible chance? How have conflict management challenges changed over time? These are questions that I explore here.

PATTERNS OF VIOLENT CONFLICT

Before one can explore the best ways of managing conflict, one must have a general understanding of what is to be avoided. It is important to recognize that no two wars are exactly alike. They all vary in respect to one or more of the "five Ws":

- Identity of the parties (who?)
- Intensity (what?)
- Frequency and duration (when?)
- Geographical location (where?)
- Underlying issues (why?)[1]

The enormous variability in the historical record poses a significant challenge to scholars who seek to understand the causes of wars.[2] Nevertheless, in recent decades several interesting and important patterns and trends have become evident.[3]

With respect to the identity of the parties, wars are increasingly being fought over issues internal to (rather than between) states (see Figure 1).[4] Not surprisingly, because militias and paramilitary forces operate on smaller scales and deploy less firepower than the armed forces of well-functioning states, this tends to reduce the intensity of war (Figure 2). The difficulty of monitoring these kinds of wars makes it difficult to know exactly how deadly they are; as Figure 3 illustrates, there is quite a gap between the lowest and highest estimates of annual battle-related deaths.[5]

The frequency of war varies by type and era. As Figure 1 shows, postwar decoloniza-tion effectively brought extrasystemic wars to an end; but although war in general increased in frequency during the Cold War, it has been in decline since.[6] Intrastate wars tend to last the longest—14.4 years on average, compared to 11.3 years for internationalized intrastate wars, 4.8 years for interstate wars, and 5.1 years for extrasystemic wars. Except for interstate wars, the trend has been for the duration of wars to increase (Figure 4).[7]

Some parts of the world are more war prone than others. Asia and Africa are home to most of the wars in the world, followed by the Middle East, the Americas, and Europe (Figure 5). But of particular note is the existence of specific zones of peace that no longer experience either interstate or intrastate war. Such zones can be found today in Eu-

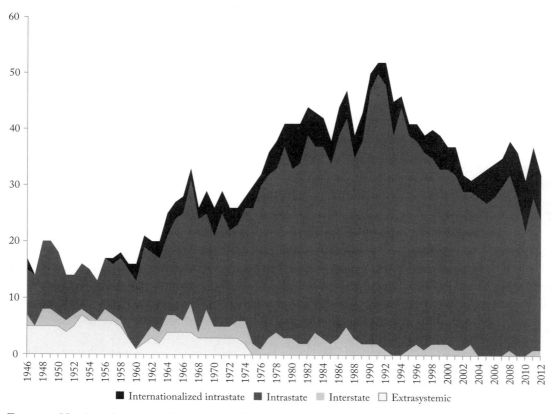

Figure 1. Number of armed conflicts by type, 1946–2012

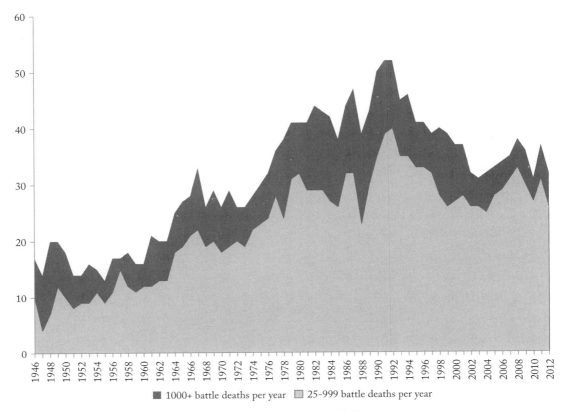

Figure 2. Number of armed conflicts by level of intensity, 1946–2012

rope, North America, and Australasia. In these so-called pluralistic security communities, in which the threat or use of force plays no role in the relations between states, all countries have dependable expectations of peaceful conflict management.[8] Some have argued that the members of the Association of Southeast Asian Nations (ASEAN) are a nascent pluralistic security community, but although "the ASEAN way" has reduced the risks of interstate war in the region, there remains a great deal of violent substate conflict in Southeast Asia.[9]

Arguably, the most important question to answer when attempting to improve conflict management is the "why?" question—but determining underlying issues is also often a very difficult task. Parties to a conflict always provide some account of their motives,

and no doubt some of the time their self-reports are accurate. But ulterior motives can also be at work, and in some cases, the parties may not even be fully aware of the reasons why they have one set of preferences rather than another. Take, for example, Japan's ongoing island disputes with South Korea (over Dokdo/Takeshima) and China (over the Senkaku/Diaoyu Islands), both of which have become tense in recent years. All three countries insist that the islands in question are theirs by historical right. Occasionally, officials in one country or another will refer to the disputed islands' economic or strategic value as well. So justice and instrumental utility are among the motives the parties express. But whether or not Japanese, Korean, or Chinese leaders actually believe that the islands are theirs by right (the working assumption

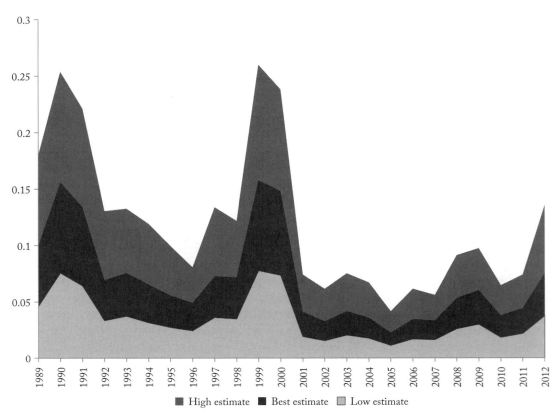

Figure 3. Estimates of total battle-related deaths in millions, 1989–2012

is that most do), and whether or not they value the islands for economic or strategic reasons (the working assumption is that most do not—at least not much), most analysts insist that what these conflicts are primarily about is national pride. The islands have become symbols of and lightning rods for national antipathy and unresolved historical grievances. Yet no leader admits it openly. The situation brings to mind the outbreak of the Peloponnesian War in 432 BCE, about which Thucydides wrote: "The Spartans voted that the treaty had been broken, and that war must be declared, not so much because they were persuaded by the arguments of the allies, as because they feared the growth of the power of the Athenians, seeing most of Hellas [Greece] already subject to them."[10] In fact, no Spartan made this argument, and yet many people—Thucydides

included—confidently assert that this was what was on their minds.[11]

Diagnosing a conflict properly is vital to ending it. If simple disagreement over historical title is driving a territorial dispute, then impartial adjudication or arbitration would seem to be the obvious solution. If economic or strategic motives predominate, then seeking a negotiated settlement involving a quid pro quo may be the best way forward. But taking someone to court or offering to pay them off is not going to satisfy them if what they really want is to humiliate you.

Second-guessing stated motives is a tricky business for which standard social-scientific methods of inquiry are not especially well designed. One cannot always determine through measurement and observation what is really driving a conflict. But careful con-

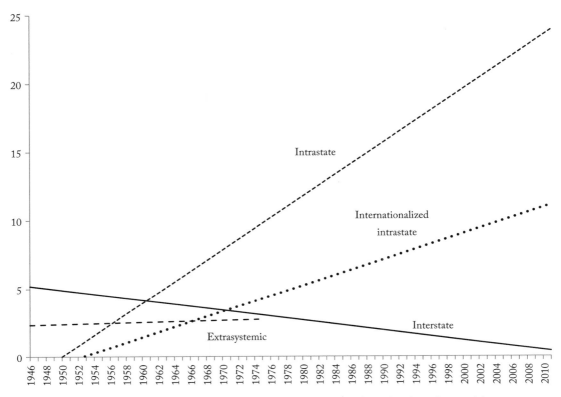

Figure 4. Linear duration trends by conflict type in years, 1946–2011 (completed conflicts only)

textual analysis can often supply what is needed when documentary or testimonial evidence is lacking. Consider, for example, the dispute between the United States and Canada over Machias Seal Island in the Gulf of Maine or between Canada and Denmark over Hans Island in the high Arctic. The overwhelming majority of Americans and Canadians have never even heard of the former, and few of those who have heard about it actually care. And although the latter has made it into the news in recent years, it has been treated primarily as a source of mirth. This nonchalance is a function of the fact that Canada's relations with both the United States and Denmark are congenial. There is no serious nationalist antipathy, no sense of historical grievance, no suspicion, and no fear. If Japan enjoyed similar relations with its neighbors, its island disputes would not be so dangerous.

Not only is understanding the nature of a conflict important for identifying possible routes to ultimate resolution, it is vital for finding ways of preventing it from exploding in the meantime. Here it is useful to distinguish among three types of causes: "deep causes," "intermediate causes," and "proximate causes." Think of a conflict as analogous to a bomb. There would be no danger of a bomb going off if no one had figured out how design a bomb in the first place (a deep cause). Even with a design, there would be no danger of an explosion until someone took the trouble to assemble a bomb (an intermediate cause). Even with a fully assembled bomb, there would be no danger of an explosion until and unless something triggered it (a proximate cause). Conflict prevention is about preventing bombs from being assembled. Conflict resolution is about dismantling them. Conflict management—the subject of this

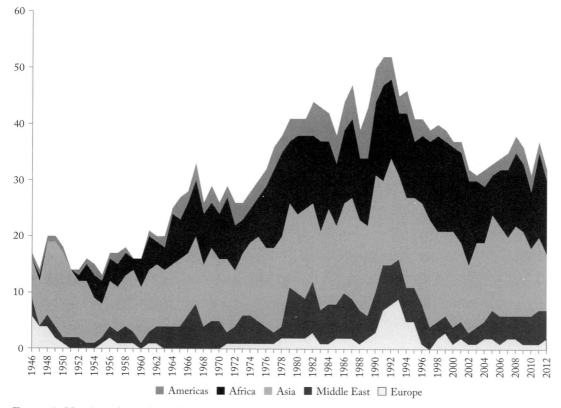

Figure 5. Number of armed conflicts by region, 1946–2012

chapter—is about making sure that they never go off. What are various ways of accomplishing this?

AGENTS AND STRUCTURES, LEVELS OF ANALYSIS

A useful place to begin is to recognize that all conflicts take place in a larger context. This raises the question of whether the best way to manage conflict is to target the context or the actors. Sociologists have long distinguished between "structures" and "agents." Take, for example, the increasing problem of head injuries in certain competitive team sports. One way of trying to reduce head injuries is to alter the rules so that players do not collide with each other so frequently or so violently.[12] This is alter-

ing the structure of the game. Other ways of trying to reduce head injuries are to educate players about the dangers of concussions, purge violent players from the rosters, or require that players wear more effective head gear. These kinds of changes target the agents.

North American International Relations (IR) scholars have become increasingly familiar with the concepts of structure and agency as European "constructivism" has moved into mainstream IR theory, thanks in large part to the efforts of Ohio State political scientist Alexander Wendt.[13] Constructivism is the view that agents and structures are "co-constitutive" and evolve over time through interaction.

Even prior to the embrace of constructivism on North American shores in the 1990s,

North American scholars were comfortable thinking in terms of levels of analysis, typically distinguishing among three or four. The highest level of analysis is the Westphalian system of sovereign states (the system level); the next highest is the sovereign states themselves (the unit level); and the lowest level encompasses leaders of states—the men and women who make foreign policy decisions (the individual level).[14] Some scholars have found it helpful to delineate a level in between the latter two, the bureaucratic level, which explains the behavior of states in terms of the interactions of subunits of government.[15]

It is an interesting question how well the structure/agent distinction maps onto levels of analysis.[16] One way of thinking about it is to say, for example, that states are agents in the Westphalian system, which is a political system with a particular structure very different from other kinds of historical political systems (e.g., imperial, tributary, or feudal systems). Systemic IR theorists such as "structural realists" or "neo-realists" are comfortable explaining the behavior of units (sovereign states) in terms of systemic structural features, the most important of which they generally consider to be anarchy, or the absence of a higher authority above states. The incentives and constraints that the structural features of the Westphalian system impose on actors, such theorists believe, result in predictable patterns of behavior, such as the balance of power. They believe also that the configuration of the units within the system has an important effect on the system's properties.

For example, according to Kenneth Waltz, bipolar systems (those with two great powers) are less war prone than multipolar systems (those with three or more great powers), and the war proneness of a system increases as the number of great powers rises. The reason for this is that when there

are only two great powers, they have no doubt who their potential enemy is, can readily monitor each other's capabilities, and can rationally make internal adjustments to prevent a dangerous imbalance of power from developing. With three or more great powers in the system, however, external balancing by means of alliances is the dominant way of preserving an overall balance of power, and problems with monitoring and trust reduce certainty.[17]

Unit-level scholars tend to point the causal arrow in the other direction. An important characteristic of the system as a whole (such as its war proneness) may crucially depend, in their view, on the characteristics of states. The most famous unit-level proposition—the "liberal peace" thesis, which has an intellectual pedigree that dates to Immanuel Kant—is that a world full of liberal democracies would be much more peaceful than a world full of authoritarian states.[18] There is debate about the reasons for this, but the absence of examples of liberal democracies going to war with one another is certainly striking. Of course, "states" are themselves, in a sense, "systems," the units of which are political institutions configured in various ways, as well as citizens, corporations, and civil society groups. One can explore agent-structure interactions within states just as readily as one can explore them between states and the international system as a whole.

At the lowest level of analysis are individual human beings. Scholars may ask questions (for example) about the personality traits of individual leaders, the impact of cognition and emotion on decision making, the relevance of sex or gender, or the particular lessons leaders draw from history or experience. The focus here is on what happens within the individual human brain, and the goal is to determine the extent to which (and why) people with different personalities or life experiences behave differently when they make foreign policy choices. One can make a strong case, for example, that all leaders are susceptible to certain kinds of biases and errors, because psychological research shows that these are part of being human. But one can make an equally strong case that World War II would not have happened if Adolf Hitler had not been chancellor of Germany.[19]

The key difference between constructivists who focus on understanding the interaction between agents and structures and IR theorists who employ the levels of analysis device is that the latter tend to look at only one direction of causality. From a constructivist perspective, this is a mistake: agents and structures always interact and always co-evolve. But it may be a forgivable mistake. Depending on the questions one asks or the problems one wants to solve, there may be an advantage to treating either structure or agents as fixed and seeing how one affects the other. Over a short time scale, for example, many structures do not and cannot change enough to make a practical difference, in which case, one might as well focus on the behavior of the actors operating within it. In times of great upheaval, in contrast (for example, during a major revolution), the actors may not change but the context in which they operate may change dramatically.

In my view, both the agent/structure distinction and levels of analysis can be helpful when attempting to determine the best way of managing conflicts in general, but managing a particular conflict may require focusing on one thing rather than another. To some extent, how one tackles the basic question of how much effort to put into altering context and how much into changing actors is a matter of expedience. History is full of examples of both successful and unsuccessful conflict management, and a consideration of theory and history can help develop the skill for identifying fruitful approaches.

MANAGING INTERSTATE CONFLICT: LESSONS FROM BISMARCK'S EUROPE AND THE COLD WAR

The period 1871–1914 was a time of relative peace for much of Europe, at least as far as the great powers were concerned. Britain, France, and Russia had clashed in the Crimean War (1853–56); Prussia and Austria had fought in the Seven Weeks War (1866); and France and Prussia had fought in the Franco-Prussian War (1870–71), which resulted in the unification of Germany under Prussian rule, leaving Europe with six acknowledged great powers: Britain, France, Germany, Italy, Austria-Hungary, and Russia. Although many of these countries engaged in overseas colonial rivalry during this period, occasionally resulting in brief intense crises that threatened to escalate to war,[20] in fact there was no direct combat between any two European great powers between the Franco-Prussian War and World War I. Was this luck or successful conflict management?

There can be no question that there was a great deal of conflict in Europe during this period, if one understands conflict as the existence of incompatible preferences. In addition to colonial rivalries, the great powers jockeyed for strategic advantage, modernized and industrialized competitively, engaged in arms races, and had various ongoing territorial disputes. But the fact that there was no great power war is remarkable and can largely be attributed to successful diplomacy.

The chief architect of European peace during this time was German chancellor Otto von Bismarck, who had deliberately engineered both the Seven Weeks War and the Franco-Prussian War with an eye toward using these conflicts to unite much of German-speaking Europe under Prussian rule.[21] Once he had achieved German unification, he turned his energies toward preventing further conflict on the continent to provide space for the consolidation and growth of the new

Germany. His chosen mechanism for this was alliance politics, and in particular he sought to ensure that Germany would never be surrounded by a hostile coalition or left without adequate support from allies of its own. In other words, he sought to maintain a favorable balance of power.

In this task, Bismarck was highly successful. The nightmare scenario, from a German perspective, was an alliance between Russia and France, which in a time of war would threaten Germany from both sides. If Britain were to join in a Franco-Russian coalition, Germany would be both surrounded and overmatched—the only other two great powers in Europe with which Germany could ally would be Austria-Hungary, a sickly and divided empire in evident decline owing both to its failure to industrialize and to worsening ethnic-nationalist tensions (particularly in the Balkans); and Italy, which in every dimension (population, territory, economy, military capability) was the weakest of the European great powers and had no realistic prospects of ascent. Bismarck successfully prevented a Franco-Russian alliance and deftly managed relations with Britain so as to encourage London in its general aversion to European entanglements. But Bismarck resigned in 1890 after falling out of favor with Kaiser Wilhelm II, who replaced him with Count Leo von Caprivi, a far less skilled diplomatist. Just two years after Bismarck's departure, France and Russia concluded an alliance. In 1904, Britain and France formed an entente, which led in 1907 to an informal tripartite bloc that included Russia. Germany was now surrounded. Seven years later, Europe exploded into war.

Although Bismarck's conflict management strategy succeeded in keeping Europe peaceful for a long time, ultimately this policy was not enough to maintain peace. For one thing, it depended too heavily on Bismarck—and this, of course, is an individual-level factor, not a systemic structural one. In addition, Germany had earned France's enduring hostility at the close of the Franco-Prussian War by annexing two of its eastern provinces, Alsace and Lorraine. The Prussian military considered these provinces valuable strategically, but failed to appreciate the cost in France's enduring enmity. France steadfastly maintained that the sine qua non of improved relations with Germany was the return of these lost provinces.[22] For this reason, as much as anything else, France was keen on seeking allies against Germany. This powerful irredentist sentiment was a unit-level (sociological) factor that could be traced to widely shared moral outrage (an inflamed sense of justice, an individual factor).[23] Other unit-level factors were at work as well, including intensifying ethnic nationalism in the Balkans, which threatened to tear apart one of Germany's only great power allies. All these factors combined to make Europe highly combustible in 1914. The assassination of Austrian Archduke Franz Ferdinand in the streets of Sarajevo on June 28 proved to be the spark that set the fuse alight.

Whereas the nineteenth-century European system was multipolar, the Cold War system (1945–91) was bipolar: the United States and the Soviet Union were by far the most powerful countries in the world. Not only was the configuration of units different, but so too was its scope, for the Cold War took place on a global scale. The early Cold War was marked by a series of acute crises that threatened to explode, of which the most notable were two crises over Berlin (1948–49 and 1961) and the Cuban missile crisis (1962). Thereafter, the superpowers did a better job of avoiding direct confrontations that might escalate to war even though tensions remained—waxing and waning, but always present—and even though the two countries fought many wars by proxy (e.g., in Vietnam, Angola, Afghanistan, and Nicaragua). The fact that the superpowers avoided direct military conflict during this period is cold comfort to the people who suffered in these proxy wars, but is nonetheless remarkable. Why were they able to do this?

Recall Waltz's argument that bipolar systems are more stable than multipolar systems because of the relative ease of balancing.[24] This argument provides one possible explanation for the absence of "hot" war between the superpowers, but it is not the only one, and this consideration alone does not help us understand why nineteenth-century European great powers managed to avoid war for almost the same length of time. In fact, because internal adjustment is the primary mechanism available to maintain a balance of power in a bipolar world, the fact that the Soviet Union was ultimately unable to adjust—and collapsed in the course of attempting to reform so as to be able to adjust—suggests that the Cold War balance of power failed. But neorealists such as Waltz point to an unprecedented feature of the Cold War system that they believe explains its peacefulness: the existence of nuclear weapons. The fact that even an ailing and declining Soviet Union possessed more than enough nuclear weaponry to destroy the United States many times over, they suggest, can be credited with maintaining peace. Waltz goes even further to argue that the pacifying effects of nuclear weaponry can be generalized—that the measured spread of nuclear weapons is, in fact, "more to be welcomed rather than feared."[25]

It is fair to say that relatively few people think favorably of nuclear proliferation in general. In fact, there is a near-consensus globally that the nuclear nonproliferation regime is among the most important pillars of global security today.[26] The backbone of the regime is the 1970 Nuclear Non-Proliferation Treaty, to which 188 states are currently party, leaving only five outside (India, Israel, North Korea, Pakistan, and South Sudan).

Either neorealists know something that most of the world does not, or there is a basic flaw in the neorealist argument.[27] In my view, it is the latter. The basic flaw is captured succinctly by the classic episode of the 1970s sitcom *All in the Family* in which Archie Bunker proposes ending the problem of airliner hijacking by arming all the passengers.[28] Leaders of states are not perfectly rational actors uninhibited by emotion, lack of information, or misperception;[29] some do not even value survival above all else; and even if this were otherwise, they do not fully control the actions of their militaries. It is no great catastrophe if things go badly in the confusion and heat of a crisis, provided that no one wields lethal force; but if they do yield lethal force, people die. We know for certain that things will sometimes go badly in a crisis, and if lethal force comes in the form of nuclear weaponry, hundreds of thousands or millions of people could die.

In fact, the Cold War illustrates the importance of not relying on nuclear stalemate to preserve the peace. The closest the world came to nuclear war during that period was the 1962 Cuban missile crisis—a nuclear crisis precipitated by the Soviet deployment of nuclear weapons of the kind that Waltz would have applauded as redressing an imbalance of power. In this case, nuclear weapons were all problem and no solution.[30] At least in part, the fact that the superpowers avoided nuclear Armageddon in October 1962 was, as Dean Acheson would later remark, "sheer dumb luck."[31] But a crucial factor was the ability of US president John F. Kennedy and Soviet chairman Nikita Khrushchev to cultivate empathy—the mutual understanding of each other's perspective and predicament—which enabled them both to see that ultimately they each had the same fundamental fear: that mistakes, misperceptions, inadvertence, or breakdowns in command and control would result in runaway escalation.[32]

The Cuban missile crisis illustrates the importance of considering certain individual-level attributes when managing conflict in a time of immediate great peril: namely, empathy, circumspection, a willingness to find mutually face-saving paths to de-escalation, and skill at diplomacy and negotiation.[33] In October 1962, there was simply no time to try to alter context; but, fortunately for the world, both superpowers were led by men who had the capacity to learn quickly on the fly. This international-political equivalent of a near-death experience had a salutary effect on subsequent context, for it led directly and deliberately to collaborative efforts to enhance the clarity of the superpowers' "rules of the road" and to strengthen norms against strategic surprise.[34] Kennedy's assassination and Khrushchev's ouster limited the "stickiness" of the lessons these two leaders learned during the heat of crisis— neither of their immediate successors, nor many of their later ones, felt or internalized the same lessons—but ultimately the two leaders who did the most to turn around US–Soviet relations did. Ronald Reagan and Mikhail Gorbachev came to appreciate that they shared the same main problem: preventing accidents, misperceptions, or breakdowns in chains of command from leading to inadvertent nuclear war.[35] They also understood the value of open channels of communication, greater military transparency, and various other confidence and security building measures, such as military-to-military contacts.

A final crucial difference between Bismarck's Europe and the Cold War was the development of robust mechanisms of security governance. In the late nineteenth century, there were no analogues to the United Nations (UN) or to various regional security organs such as the Organization of American States (OAS), ASEAN, the Organization of African Unity (OAU), the Conference on Security and Co-operation in Europe (CSCE),

or the European Community (EC).[36] Bilateral summits were rare, and there were no regular institutionalized multilateral summits such as the G7 or G8. As time passed, non-state actors became more numerous and more important, taking on an increasing variety of roles in managing disputes. One particularly important Cold War innovation was the invention of peacekeeping, or the insertion between warring parties of armed but neutral third-country soldiers generally operating under the UN banner for the purpose of reducing the danger and incidence of direct conflict and buying time for negotiated settlements of disputes. Most of these developments took place with an eye toward reducing the frequency and severity of interstate war, but they have proven their value in managing intrastate conflict as well. The OSCE and the EU, for example, played vital roles in helping to bring peace to the Balkans after the violent breakup of the former Yugoslavia in the 1990s. It is difficult to say how much credit should be given to these various organs, actors, and practices for preventing great power war, but whether their contributions were vital or marginal, they were clearly positive.

MANAGING INTRASTATE CONFLICT: IN SEARCH OF POST–COLD WAR LESSONS

As Figure 1 shows, intrastate conflict is not a recent phenomenon, but it has only recently begun to attract the kind of attention from scholars and policymakers that interstate conflict attracted. As a result, the international community's response to intrastate conflict is in flux. To a very large extent, we are learning by doing.

Why has it taken so long for intrastate conflict to attract the attention that it deserves? To some extent, "intrastate conflict" was not a recognizable category in places that were not yet constituted as "states." The modern state as we know it is not quite 400 years old, and for most of its history, it existed only in Europe. During that time, no systematic academic discipline was devoted to the study of international relations, let alone the causes, dynamics, and resolution of large-scale organized violence as such.[37] The Westphalian state became genuinely global only as a result of postwar decolonization, which took place at the same time as the Cold War, when the imperative of avoiding a third world war dominated academic and policy agendas. (In any case, far from seeking ways of ending intrastate conflict, the superpowers often fueled it for strategic or ideological reasons.)[38] In addition, the many former European colonies tended to be jealous of their newly acquired sovereignty; norms against intervention were stronger; the international community had fewer legal tools and quasi-legal instruments (such as the doctrine of the responsibility to protect, or R2P) with which to justify it;[39] and fewer nonstate actors and civil society groups were active on the ground.[40] A slew of relevant concepts that are familiar today had not yet been invented, let alone operationalized or institutionalized. These include peacebuilding;[41] peace support operations;[42] demobilization, disarmament, and reintegration (DDR);[43] security sector reform;[44] constitution building;[45] truth and reconciliation commissions;[46] international criminal tribunals;[47] and the International Criminal Court.[48]

In the past twenty years or so, intrastate conflict has attracted an astonishing degree of attention. Scholars and policymakers are doing their best to make up for lost time. Both the rapid evolution of the field and the relatively short period during which new practices and techniques have been attempted make it difficult to assess the effectiveness of strategies for managing intrastate conflict. Indicators of failure are clear enough: a conflict management strategy has failed if violence breaks out, intensifies, or spreads; a conflict management strategy is working if violence does not break out or declines. But what does one call an uneasy peace with no clear road to resolution? Is this a "success" or "not-yet failure"? And what does one say of a case where violence is episodic but there is secular progress toward peace?

The common wisdom holds that, with enough patience, political will, money, expertise, and manpower, and if the international actors work hard enough on fixing everything that is broken in a conflict zone—lack of basic goods and services, inadequate infrastructure, dysfunctional and/or corrupt state institutions, non-inclusive political processes—violence is more likely to be kept at bay. The order in which one does things, and the precise way in which one does them, must be tailored to context, and success must be gauged in a context-sensitive way.[49] But this all sounds somewhat platitudinous: if this is the template, how does one know what to blame if conflict management fails? How does one know what to credit when it succeeds?[50] In times of limited patience, political will, and resources, how does one know what to prioritize? Only experience with a large number of cases that vary in approach can provide reliable answers to questions such as these, and arguably we have neither as of yet.

Put another way, unlike managing interstate conflict—something with which the international community has a great deal of experience that provides lessons—intrastate conflict management is an experiment in progress, and so lessons learned are hard to discern. But one can separate out potential therapeutic pathways conceptually. As with interstate conflict, one can imagine attempting to manage intrastate conflict by working on either structures or agents.[51] Potentially relevant structures may be found at both the international system level and the unit level.

Not all the international system levers that might be helpful for managing interstate conflict are available for managing intrastate conflict. There is no obvious Bismarckian or Waltzian solution, for example, to the ongoing civil war in Syria. Nevertheless, what is feasible depends in part on what is permissible, so the normative and legal context does affect available conflict management approaches. The normative and legal structure of the international system changes over time both in response to prior experience (path dependence) and as a result of the efforts of norm entrepreneurs (conscious agency). From the perspective of intrastate conflict management, the most significant change in the normative structure of the international system in recent years has been the rise of R2P, which has fundamentally altered the nature of sovereignty itself.

In the past, sovereignty—the right to rule—was understood as something very nearly absolute. Such were the terms and conditions of membership in the club of sovereign states that each member's primary obligation was to respect the other members' sovereign autonomy. The norm against interfering in others' domestic affairs was strong, and exceptions were rare.[52] Within any given state's national territory, its government had virtually unfettered right to act as it saw fit. This is no longer true. Sovereign autonomy is increasingly conditional. States now must meet certain minimum standards for the treatment of their own people. In particular, they must neither commit nor permit mass atrocities within their boundaries. The doctrine of R2P obliges the international community both to help states meet this standard and to enforce it if necessary, including (as a last resort) by means of military action.[53] To paraphrase the old American Express slogan: membership in the club has its privileges, but increasingly it comes with obligations.[54]

Because international system structure levers are limited in modern intrastate conflict management, a great deal of effort targets the states themselves. This is hardly surprising, as intrastate conflict is by definition conflict within the borders of a particular state. Recall that states are themselves "systems" when seen from the perspective of the unit level of analysis. What structural features of states predict susceptibility to violent internal conflict?

As Ernie Regehr argues, probably the single most important risk factor for civil conflict is poverty: "The wars of the recent past were overwhelmingly fought on the territories of states at the low end of the human development scale."[55] Additional risk factors include political and social grievances, identity conflict, the existence of groups that have the ability and will to wield violence on a large scale, and "the perceived absence of effective pathways for nonviolent conflict resolution."[56] The last of these drivers is clearly structural: the availability of pathways for nonviolent conflict resolution is a function of both institutions and norms. Not surprisingly, much of the literature on intrastate conflict stresses the importance of development (to raise people out of poverty), state building, and constitutionally mandated representative or inclusive government.

Sometimes, however, the best way of managing (or perhaps even resolving) intrastate conflict is to work on the actors. Occasionally, the single most effective way of dealing with intrastate conflict is to take out one of the parties. This is easiest when a particularly charismatic leader without an obvious successor is keeping the conflict alive. Peru became a much more peaceful place, for instance, when Abimael Guzmán, leader of the Maoist *Sendero Luminoso* (Shining Path) guerrilla movement, was arrested in 1992—although the way in which Peru did battle with Guzmán's group left wounds and a legacy of distrust that were major obstacles to peacebuilding in their own right.[57]

Most leaders can be substituted, however, in which case, if leaders are key actors, the only viable approach is to work on their interests. In the wake of the Taliban's ouster in 2001, for example, most Afghan warlords simply wanted to consolidate their power bases and rule locally—a recipe for continued low-level civil war and a fractured political landscape. But the goal of a united, representative, ultimately democratic Afghanistan required persuading the warlords to relinquish old ways and commit to building a federal Afghan state. This was the objective of the Bonn Agreement, which bought the warlords' cooperation in the coin of national offices and rents from corruption. There was, of course, an element of paradox in this. As Dipali Mukhopadhyay puts it:

> In Afghanistan, this pattern of bargaining and compromise, reinforced by parallel counterterrorism and counterinsurgency campaigns, can be framed as a kind of racketeering arrangement: warlord governors and their subordinates pose a danger to the state but, when approached with certain carrots and sticks, they shield the state from the very threat they create.[58]

In cases where leaders are not necessarily key actors—for example, when successful conflict management and progress toward ultimate conflict resolution requires buy-in at a grassroots level—engineering identity or interest change is a genuinely daunting task. The preferred mechanism in recent decades has been the truth and reconciliation commission (TRC), which is designed to help both victims and perpetrators of conflict clear the psychological obstacles to thinking of themselves as stakeholders in a future common enterprise. It does so by providing opportunities not so much to establish "truth," which is always contested (at least on the margin), but to give voice to and rehumanize former enemies. Experience with TRCs is limited, but increasing, and the international community should soon be in a position to assess how and when a TRC is most effective.[59]

CONFLICT MANAGEMENT IN A GLOBALIZING WORLD

Conflict management involves many choices. In both interstate and intrastate conflicts, conflict managers can spend time, energy, and resources attempting to manipulate the context of the conflict (structure), the parties to the conflict (agents), or both. This choice can arise at the level of the international system or within the boundaries of an affected state. Depending on the choice, there may be additional questions. Who takes the lead? Who shares the burdens? Which of the available instruments should be tried first? How does one gauge success? What do we do in case of failure?

It would be helpful to have a road map or an algorithm to navigate these decisions, but we do not.[60] For the most part we must rely upon a combination of theory and history. Some of the time this will be enough; much of the time it will not. Novel situations arise from time to time. Even when there is enough knowledge and experience on which to make sound judgments, we will occasionally misdiagnose the problem or look in the wrong places for insight on how to deal with it.[61] Such mistakes can be extremely costly. What might work well in one case might not work at all in another, or might even make a difficult situation worse.

At present we seem to have a fairly good handle on interstate conflict management. There is a long historical record upon which to draw, and context is becoming somewhat more conflict-management friendly. Norms of peaceful conflict resolution are now quite strong at the international level, and ample mechanisms are available. It is small wonder that interstate war is in decline. It is too soon to declare the problem solved, and no doubt interstate war will occur from time to time (one hopes not in places or in situations that threaten to escalate to nuclear or great power war), but the trend is clearly positive. This is not, of course, an argument for complacence, merely for optimism.

Intrastate conflict is quite another matter. Although both the incidence and the deadliness of intrastate conflict have declined from their Cold War highs, the international community has far less experience dealing with it in a concerted way and is still largely learning by doing. And yet, the very ground beneath the classroom is shifting rapidly. New forces, new processes, new players, new trends, new developments—some welcome, some unwelcome, most simply disorienting—complicate both the learning and the doing. What are some of the most important changes?

The simplest and most abstract is *globalization*, a term that first gained currency in the early 1980s[62] but that quickly became a fixed feature of our analytical toolkit. Unfortunately, no two people seem to agree exactly what it means, but at its core is the idea that things increasingly happen on a global scale. Not only do people and systems operate over greater and greater distances, they do so more quickly and more intensely, thanks to the development of communications and transportation technologies and the spread of English as a lingua franca. From my perspective, globalization has two main implications. First, it has almost entirely eliminated strangeness. In most cases, this is a positive development, for what is strange is difficult to understand, and what is difficult to understand is easy to fear and to hate. Second, it has fundamentally altered the nature of power.

Power is another term that people use readily enough but whose meaning is sometimes unclear. At its simplest level, it is the ability to achieve one's goals.[63] There are two main ways of doing this: by wielding carrots and/or sticks (hard power), which alters cost-benefit calculations; or by persuading other people by argument or by example to want what you want (soft power).[64] Globalization has complicated both. At the transnational and interpersonal level, the information revolution has eroded states' capacities to manage the message. Today, it is possible to communicate directly with almost anyone on the planet almost instantaneously. Fifty years ago, this was possible only by telephone, a device still unknown in many parts of the world; according to Source Digit, global cell phone penetration reached 91 percent in the third quarter of 2012, with 6.4 billion subscribers.[65] Email, Facebook, Twitter, LinkedIn, and various social networks provide additional channels. If we once lived in a world with six degrees of separation, there are almost certainly fewer now.[66]

New communications technologies do not immunize people from the prying eyes of the state, and some countries exert considerable effort to censor; but as the Arab Spring revolts demonstrated, today's communication tools make it easier for people to see how others live and when their own governments are performing poorly. These tools also make it easier to mobilize and coordinate popular pressure.[67] Not only is it easier to communicate globally, it is easier to move money (legitimately or illegitimately), smuggle drugs, smuggle humans, spread disease, hack or disrupt computers and networks, and disseminate hatred and falsehood. At the transnational level, the world is a fascinating mess.[68]

Economically, the world is increasingly multipolar. Whereas in 1944 the United States' share of global economic output was 35 percent, by 2012 it had dropped to 22 percent. Meanwhile, China's share rose rapidly, to 11 percent; Japan's stands at 8 percent, and the Euro zone (collectively) is at 17 percent.[69]

The world is still very much unipolar militarily, however.[70] The United States accounts today for 40 percent of global military spending—as much as the next ten countries combined, and four times as much as the next-highest spending country, China.[71] Moreover, the US military enjoys qualitative advantages in every major category (weaponry, training, battlefield management). In many parts of the world, if the United States cannot solve a problem militarily, no one can. Of course, it is the rare problem in the modern world that has a solely military solution. The tight interconnectedness of a globalized world means problems are likely to have social, cultural, economic, political, and even environmental causes. In most cases, this means that they must also have corresponding social, cultural, economic, political, and environmental solutions. Accordingly, conflict management in the modern world—be it interstate conflict management or intrastate conflict management—is, and must be, multifaceted, multidimensional, and multistakeholder. The bad news is that this makes conflict management significantly more complex than in days of yore. The good news is that it opens up new possibilities for creativity and cooperation, and increases the value of success—as the chapters that follow so clearly reveal.

NOTES

For helpful comments and suggestions, I would like to thank Aisha Ahmad, Joseph S. Nye Jr., Mark Raymond, Peter Wallensteen, and the participants in the "Conflict Management and Global Governance in an Age of Awakening" workshop at the Balsillie School of International Affairs, Waterloo, Ontario, January 26, 2013.

1. These five questions are central to the United States Institute of Peace Narrative Analysis

Framework; see Matthew Levinger, *Conflict Analysis: Understanding Causes, Unlocking Solutions* (Washington, DC: United States Institute of Peace Press, 2013), 225–26.

2. Meredith Reid Sarkees and Frank Whelon Wayman, *Resort to War: A Data Guide to Inter-State, Extra-State, Intra-State, and Non-State Wars, 1816–2007* (Washington, DC: CQ Press, 2010); and Jody B. Lear, Diane Macaulay, and Meredith Reid Sarkees, eds., *Advancing Peace Research: Leaving Traces, Selected Articles by J. David Singer* (Abingdon, UK: Routledge, 2012).

3. See, for example, Levinger, *Conflict Analysis,* 29–59. Unless otherwise noted, the following discussion and figures use data from the UCDP/PRIO Armed Conflict Dataset v.4-2013 (1946–2012), http://www.pcr.uu.se/research/ucdp/datasets/ucdp_prio_armed_conflict_dataset (accessed January 6, 2014), for the most recent presentation of which, see Lotta Themnér and Peter Wallensteen, "Armed Conflict, 1946–2012," *Journal of Peace Research* 50, no. 4 (2013): 509–21.

4. Among other things, this undermines Samuel Huntington's original formulation of the "clash of civilizations" hypothesis, which would lead us to expect that wars should increasingly be fought between states on opposite sides of grand cultural divides. Samuel P. Huntington, "The Clash of Civilizations?" *Foreign Affairs* 72, no. 3 (1993): 22–49; Samuel P. Huntington, *The Clash of Civilizations and the Remaking of World Order* (New York: Simon and Schuster, 1996); and David A. Welch, "The 'Clash of Civilizations' Thesis as an Argument and as a Phenomenon," *Security Studies* 6, no. 4 (1997): 185–204.

5. Data for Figure 3 are from the UCDP Battle-Related Deaths Dataset v.5-2013, 1989–2012, http://www.pcr.uu.se/research/ucdp/datasets/ucdp_battle-related_deaths_dataset (accessed February 3, 2014). Note that battle deaths are usually a minority of deaths in modern war.

6. On the general decline in violence, see Steven Pinker, *The Better Angels of Our Nature: Why Violence Has Declined* (New York: Viking, 2011).

7. See chapter 10 in this volume, Sumantra Bose, "National Self-Determination Conflicts: Explaining Endurance and Intractability."

8. Emanuel Adler and Michael Barnett, *Security Communities* (Cambridge: Cambridge University Press, 1998); Veronica M. Kitchen, "Argument and Identity Change in the Atlantic Security Community," *Security Dialogue* 40, no. 1 (2009): 95–114.

9. Amitav Acharya, *Constructing a Security Community in Southeast Asia: ASEAN and the Problem of Regional Order* (London: Routledge, 2001); Donald K. Emmerson, "Security, Community, and Democracy in Southeast Asia: Analyzing ASEAN," *Japanese Journal of Political Science* 6, no. 2 (2005): 165–85.

10. Robert B. Strassler and Richard Crawley, eds., *The Landmark Thucydides: A Comprehensive Guide to the Peloponnesian War* (New York: Free Press, 1996), section 1.88.

11. David A. Welch, "Why International Relations Theorists Should Stop Reading Thucydides," *Review of International Studies* 29, no. 3 (2003): 304–5.

12. One could imagine accomplishing this with two different kinds of rules change: increasing penalties for hits; and/or adjusting the actual rules of play such that players do not find themselves encountering each other at high velocity quite so often.

13. Alexander Wendt, "The Agent-Structure Problem in International Relations Theory," *International Organization* 41, no. 3 (1987): 335–70; Alexander Wendt, "Anarchy Is What States Make of It: The Social Construction of Power Politics," *International Organization* 46, no. 2 (1992): 391–425; and Alexander Wendt, *Social Theory of International Politics* (Cambridge: Cambridge University Press, 1999).

14. Seminal works include Kenneth N. Waltz, *Man, the State and War* (New York: Columbia University Press, 1959); and J. David Singer, "The Levels of Analysis Problem in International Relations," in *International Politics and Foreign Policy*, ed. James N. Rosenau (New York: Free Press, 1969). For recent applications of levels of analysis to interstate and intrastate conflict, see Jack S. Levy, "International Sources of Interstate and Intrastate War," in *Leashing the Dogs of War: Conflict Management in a Divided World*, ed. Chester A. Crocker, Fen Osler Hampson, and Pamela R. Aall (Washington, DC: United States Institute of Peace Press, 2006); and Jack S. Levy, "Theories of Interstate and Intrastate War: A Levels-of-Analysis Approach," in *Turbulent Peace: The Chal-*

lenges of Managing International Conflict, ed. Chester A. Crocker, Fen Osler Hampson, and Pamela R. Aall (Washington, DC: United States Institute of Peace Press, 2001).

15. Most scholars treat bureaucratic politics as a unit-level phenomenon. See, for example, Morton H. Halperin, Priscilla Clapp, and Arnold Kanter, *Bureaucratic Politics and Foreign Policy*, 2nd ed. (Washington, DC: Brookings Institution Press, 2006). Cf. David A. Welch, "A Positive Science of Bureaucratic Politics?" *Mershon International Studies Review* 42, no. 2 (1998): 210–16.

16. For a lively debate on this subject, see Alexander Wendt, "Bridging the Theory/Meta-Theory Gap in International Relations," *Review of International Studies* 17, no. 4 (1991): 383–92; and Martin Hollis and Steve Smith, "Beware of Gurus: Structure and Action in International Relations," *Review of International Studies* 17, no. 4 (1991): 393–410; Alexander Wendt, "Levels of Analysis vs. Agents and Structures: Part III," *Review of International Studies* 18, no. 2 (1992): 181–85; Martin Hollis and Steve Smith, "Structure and Action: Further Comment," *Review of International Studies* 18, no. 2 (1992): 187–88.

17. Kenneth N. Waltz, *Theory of International Politics* (New York: Random House, 1979), 134–36.

18. There are many variations on the "liberal peace" or "democratic peace" thesis, but this is the one that strikes me as the most defensible given ongoing debates. For seminal treatments, see Michael Doyle, "Liberalism and World Politics," *American Political Science Review* 80, no. 4 (1986): 1151–69; John M. Owen, "How Liberalism Produces Democratic Peace," *International Security* 19, no. 2 (1994): 87–125; and Bruce M. Russett, *Grasping the Democratic Peace: Principles for a Post-Cold War World*, 2nd ed. (Princeton, NJ: Princeton University Press, 1995).

19. Alan Bullock, *Hitler: A Study in Tyranny* (New York: Harper and Row, 1971); Fritz Redlick, *Hitler: Diagnosis of a Destructive Prophet* (New York: Oxford University Press, 1999).

20. Prominent examples include the Fashoda crisis between Britain and France in the Sudan (1989) and the Agadir crisis between Germany and France/Britain in Morocco (1911).

21. Bismarck openly boasted of this later in life; Robert Howard Lord, *The Origins of the War of*

1870: New Documents from the German Archives (New York: Russell and Russell, 1966), 71, 95; and Otto Fürst von Bismarck, *Bismarck, the Man and the Statesman: Being the Reflections and Reminiscences of Otto, Prince Von Bismarck*, trans., Arthur John Butler, vol. II (New York: Harper and Brothers, 1898), 98–100.

22. Michael Howard, *The Franco-Prussian War: The German Invasion of France, 1870–1871* (New York: Macmillan, 1962), 447–48; and Bernadotte Everly Schmitt, *The Coming of the War, 1914*, vol. 1 (New York: Charles Scribner's Sons, 1930), 67–68.

23. David A. Welch, *Justice and the Genesis of War* (Cambridge: Cambridge University Press, 1993), 76–94.

24. See note 17.

25. Kenneth N. Waltz, *The Spread of Nuclear Weapons: More May Be Better,* Adelphi Paper no. 171 (London: International Institute for Strategic Studies, 1981), 21.

26. See chapter 26 in this volume, Michael O'Hanlon, "Dealing with Proliferation: The Nuclear Abolitionist Vision versus Practical Tools for Today's Extremist States."

27. See, generally, Scott D. Sagan and Kenneth N. Waltz, *The Spread of Nuclear Weapons: A Debate* (New York: W. W. Norton, 1995).

28. Http://www.youtube.com/watch?v=68xSoecsoq0. In the wake of the 2012 mass shooting at the Sandy Hook Elementary School in Newton, CT, the National Rifle Association similarly proposed stationing armed guards in every school. Eric Lightblau and Motoko Rich, "N.R.A. Envisions 'a Good Guy with a Gun' in Every School," *New York Times*, December 22, 2012.

29. See chapter 15 in this volume, Deborah Welch Larson, "Misperception, Overconfidence, and Communication Failure between Rising and Status-Quo States."

30. James G. Blight and David A. Welch, "Risking 'the Destruction of Nations': Lessons of the Cuban Missile Crisis for New and Aspiring Nuclear States," *Security Studies* 4, no. 4 (1995): 811–50.

31. Dean Acheson, "Dean Acheson's Version of Robert Kennedy's Version of the Cuban Missile Affair," *Esquire*, February 1969.

32. James G. Blight and Janet M. Lang, *The Armageddon Letters: Kennedy, Khrushchev, Castro in the Cuban Missile Crisis* (Lanham, MD: Rowman and Littlefield, 2012); and Don Munton and David A. Welch, *The Cuban Missile Crisis: A Concise History*, 2nd ed. (New York: Oxford University Press, 2011).

33. David A. Welch, "The Cuban Missile Crisis," in *The Oxford Handbook of Modern Diplomacy*, ed. Andrew F. Cooper, Jorge Heine, and Ramesh Thakur (New York: Oxford University Press, 2013).

34. Joseph S. Nye Jr., "Nuclear Learning and US-Soviet Security Regimes," *International Organization* 41, no. 3 (1987): 371–402.

35. Beth A. Fischer, *The Reagan Reversal: Foreign Policy and the End of the Cold War* (Columbia: University of Missouri Press, 1997); Richard Ned Lebow and Janice Gross Stein, *We All Lost the Cold War* (Princeton, NJ: Princeton University Press, 1994); and George Bush and Brent Scowcroft, *A World Transformed* (New York: Knopf, 1998).

36. After the Cold War, the latter three further formalized and institutionalized. The EC became the European Union (EU) in 1993; the CSCE became the Organization for Security and Cooperation in Europe (OSCE) in 1994; and the OAU became the African Union (AU) in 2000.

37. David A. Welch, "Tolstoy the International Relations Theorist," in *War and Peace across Disciplines*, ed. Donna Tussing Orwin and Rick McPeak (Ithaca, NY: Cornell University Press, 2012), 175.

38. Mary Kaldor, *New and Old Wars: Organized Violence in a Global Era,* 3rd ed. (Cambridge: Polity Press, 2012). Stathis Kalyvas cautions us, however, not to draw too dramatic a distinction between Cold War and post–Cold War civil wars; Stathis N. Kalyvas, "'New' and 'Old' Civil Wars: A Valid Distinction?" *World Politics* 54 (2001): 99–118. See also Stathis N. Kalyvas, *The Logic of Violence in Civil War* (Cambridge: Cambridge University Press, 2006).

39. Gareth J. Evans, *The Responsibility to Protect: Ending Mass Atrocity Crimes Once and for All* (Washington, DC: Brookings Institution Press,

2008); Cristina G. Badescu, *Humanitarian Intervention and the Responsibility to Protect: Security and Human Rights* (London: Routledge, 2011); and Theresa Reinold, *Sovereignty and the Responsibility to Protect: The Power of Norms and the Norms of the Powerful* (London: Routledge, 2013).

40. See chapters 5 and 16 in this volume, Abiodun Williams, "The Changing Normative Environment for Conflict Management"; and Chester A. Crocker, Fen Osler Hampson, and Pamela Aall, "The Piccolo, Trumpet, and Bass Fiddle: The Orchestration of Collective Conflict Management."

41. Fernando Cavalcante, "Contemporary Debates on Peacebuilding," *Journal of Intervention and Statebuilding* 5, no. 4 (2011): 419–29. Peacebuilding and peace support operations both evolved from peacekeeping, which was a Cold War invention intended primarily to address the problem of interstate war, but which later also demonstrated its utility in intrastate conflicts. See Michael W. Doyle and Nicholas Sambanis, "International Peacebuilding: A Theoretical and Quantitative Analysis," *American Political Science Review* 94, no. 4 (2000): 779–801; and Virginia Page Fortna and Lise Morje Howard, "Pitfalls and Prospects in the Peacekeeping Literature," in *Annual Review of Political Science* (2008). See also chapters 31 and 33 in this volume, Michael W. Doyle, "Postbellum Peacebuilding: Law, Justice, and Democratic Peacebuilding"; and Jane E. Stromseth, "Peacebuilding and Transitional Justice: The Road Ahead."

42. Kobi Michael and Eyal Ben-Ari, "Contemporary Peace Support Operations: The Primacy of the Military and Internal Contradictions," *Armed Forces & Society* 37, no. 4 (2011): 657–79.

43. Johanna Söderström, "The Political Consequences of Reintegration Programmes in Current Peace-Building: A Framework for Analysis," *Conflict, Security & Development* 13, no. 1 (2013): 87–116.

44. Monica Duffy Toft, *Securing the Peace: The Durable Settlement of Civil Wars* (Princeton, NJ: Princeton University Press, 2010).

45. Wayne J. Norman, *Negotiating Nationalism: Nation-Building, Federalism, and Secession in the Multinational State* (Oxford: Oxford University Press, 2006).

46. Beth Rushton, "Truth and Reconciliation? The Experience of Truth Commissions," *Australian Journal of International Affairs* 60, no. 1 (2006): 125–41; Etienne Mullet, Félix Neto, and María da Conceição Pinto, "What Can Reasonably Be Expected from a Truth Commission: A Preliminary Examination of East Timorese Views," *Peace and Conflict: Journal of Peace Psychology* 14, no. 4 (2008): 369–93; and Michal Hirsch, Megan MacKenzie, and Mohamed Sesay, "Measuring the Impacts of Truth and Reconciliation Commissions: Placing the Global 'Success' of TRCs in Local Perspective," *Cooperation and Conflict* 47, no. 3 (2012): 386–403.

47. Karen J. Alter, "The Evolving International Judiciary," *Annual Review of Law and Social Science* 7 (2011): 387–415.

48. William Schabas, *An Introduction to the International Criminal Court*, 2nd ed. (Cambridge: Cambridge University Press, 2004); Sibylle Scheipers, *Negotiating Sovereignty and Human Rights: International Society and the International Criminal Court* (Manchester, England: Manchester University Press, 2009).

49. See, for example, "Key to Successful Peacebuilding Efforts Is Political Will, Ban Tells Security Council," *UN News Centre* (2010), http://www.un.org/apps/news/story.asp?Cr=peacebuilding&NewsID=34393#.UdWDCPnVB8E (accessed July 4, 2013); Charles T. Call, "Knowing Peace When You See It: Setting Standards for Peacebuilding Success," *Civil Wars* 10, no. 2 (2008): 173–94.

50. The difficulty is apparent in the "not yet fully failed" case of Afghanistan, where critiques of peacebuilding efforts generally have the air of plausibility but are vulnerable to the criticism that they are arbitrarily selective. A good example is Isaac Kfir, "'Peacebuilding' in Afghanistan: A Bridge Too Far?" *Defence Studies* 12, no. 2 (2012): 149–78.

51. That the international community typically works on both simultaneously is understandable, but complicates inference.

52. Rare, but less rare than many people believe. See Jack Donnelly, "Sovereign Inequalities and Hierarchy in Anarchy: American Power and International Society," *European Journal of International Relations* 12, no. 2 (2006): 139–70.

53. See note 39.

54. It is important to note, however, that people interpret R2P "obligations" differently in different conflicts. R2P was cited as the basis for intervention in Libya in 2011, for example, but as of the time of writing it has not resulted in a similar international response to the civil war in Syria.

55. Ernie Regehr, "Armed Conflict: Trends and Drivers," The Simons Foundation, http://www.thesimonsfoundation.ca/sites/all/files/Armed%20Conflict%20-%20Trends%20and%20Drivers%20by%20Ernie%20Regehr_0.pdf (accessed July 4, 2013). See also chapter 12 in this volume, Graham K. Brown and Frances Stewart, "Economic and Political Causes of Conflict: An Overview and Some Policy Implications." It is tempting to say that "failed" or "failing" states are particularly susceptible to violent internal conflict, although there is some risk of circularity here—for it is not always clear whether low state capacity is more cause or consequence of violent conflict. In any case, there is some reason to believe that the terms "failed state" or "failing state" convey as much information about the labelers as about the labeled; Daniel Halvorson, *States of Disorder: Understanding State Failure and Intervention in the Periphery* (Burlington, VT: Ashgate, 2013).

56. Regehr, "Armed Conflict." See also Paul Collier and Anke Heoeffler, "Greed and Grievance in Civil War," *Oxford Economic Papers* 56, no. 4 (2004): 563–95; and Paul Collier and Anke Heoeffler, "On Economic Causes of Civil Wars," *Oxford Economic Papers* 50, no. 4 (1998): 563–73.

57. Caroline Yezer, "Who Wants to Know? Rumors, Suspicions, and Opposition to Truth-Telling in Ayacucho," *Latin American and Caribbean Ethnic Studies* 3, no. 3 (2008): 271–89; Pablo Dreyfus, "When All the Evils Come Together," *Journal of Contemporary Criminal Justice* 15, no. 4 (1999): 370–96.

58. Dipali Mukhopadhyay, *Warriors as Bureaucrats: The Afghan Experience* (Washington, DC: Carnegie Endowment for the Humanities Middle Eastern Program, 2009), 21. See also Thomas H. Johnson, "Afghanistan's Post-Taliban Transition: The State of State-Building after War," *Central Asian Survey* 25, nos. 1–2 (2006): 1–26.

59. See note 46.

60. A number of helpful conflict assessment frameworks and conflict mapping tools are available, however; see Levinger, *Conflict Analysis,* 223–29.

61. See, for example, David A. Welch, "Culture and Emotion as Obstacles to Good Judgment: The Case of Argentina's Invasion of the Falklands/Malvinas," in *Good Judgment in Foreign Policy: Theory and Application*, ed. Stanley A. Renshon and Deborah W. Larson (Lanham, MD: Rowman and Littlefield, 2003).

62. Its use has leveled off since 2004; see http://bit.ly/14vvKPn.

63. Joseph S. Nye Jr. and David A. Welch, *Understanding Global Conflict and Cooperation*, 9th ed. (New York: Pearson/Longman, 2012), 43.

64. Joseph S. Nye Jr., *Soft Power: The Means to Success in World Politics* (New York: PublicAffairs, 2004).

65. Http://sourcedigit.com/1264-global-mobile-penetration-q3-2012.

66. "Facebook Users Average 3.74 Degrees of Separation," *BBC News Technology* (2011), http://www.bbc.co.uk/news/technology-15844230 (accessed July 5, 2013).

67. Sarah Anne Rennick, "Personal Grievance Sharing, Frame Alignment, and Hybrid Organisational Structures: The Role of Social Media in North Africa's 2011 Uprisings," *Journal of Contemporary African Studies* 31, no. 2 (2013): 156–74.

68. Joseph S. Nye Jr., *The Future of Power* (New York: PublicAffairs, 2011), xv.

69. Christopher Chase-Dunn, Andrew K. Jorgenson, and Shoon Lio, "The Trajectory of the United States in the World-System: A Quantitative Reflection," *Sociological Perspectives* 48, no. 2 (2005): 241; and World Bank, "GDP Ranking," in the the World Bank data catalog, http://data.worldbank.org/data-catalog/GDP-ranking-table (accessed July 5, 2013).

70. Put another way, power in the world today is distributed differently than at any time in history—diffuse at the transnational level, multipolar economically, and unipolar militarily. Moreover, it is shifting between countries (most noticeably toward the Indo-Pacific) and toward nonstate actors. Nye, *The Future of Power*, xv.

71. In constant 2011 US dollars; SIPRI Military Expenditures Database, in the Stockholm International Peace Research Institute, http://www .sipri.org/research/armaments/milex/milex_data

base. US military superiority, coupled with the dollar's role as the world's premier currency, somewhat compensates for America's relative economic decline; see Carla Norrlöf, *America's Global Advantage: US Hegemony and International Cooperation* (Cambridge: Cambridge University Press, 2010).

3

US POWER IN A G-0 WORLD
IMPLICATIONS FOR CONFLICT AND STABILITY

David F. Gordon and Michael J. Johnson

INTRODUCTION: THE G-0 WORLD AFTER THE GLOBAL WAR ON TERROR

While the United States was preoccupied with the Global War on Terror (GWOT), a world of more diffuse power, diverse actors, and complex interests emerged. A new G-0 (G-Zero) world has been created by the erosion of two key elements of late-twentieth-century stability: a decade of war and a financial crisis has reduced US willingness to exercise leadership, while the rise of state capitalism has undermined the post–World War II consensus on global economic and financial rules. Technological surprises in energy and weaponry have also reordered the global landscape, but to cross-cutting purposes. New weaponry has empowered weaker states and nonstates vis-à-vis their stronger foes, but a revolution in energy technology has ensured that the United States will remain the world's most powerful nation even as its role changes. While the United States remains the only truly global power, US policymakers will be challenged to develop new methods of leadership in a more crowded and diverse international environment.

For the first decade of the twenty-first century, US foreign and security policy was rightly dominated by the GWOT. From the 9/11 attacks to the killing of Osama bin Laden, the United States focused on counterterrorism, while its other security and economic priorities were somewhat relegated. Whereas the United States had played the lead role in ushering in the globalization era in the 1990s, the globalization agenda became less significant after 9/11 as Washington viewed both trans-Atlantic and trans-Pacific relations through the prism of counterterrorism. Relations with many European friends eroded because of the war in Iraq, and relations with Southeast Asian nations such as the Philippines and Indonesia became dominated by counterterror cooperation.

However, the killing of bin Laden in May 2011 marked the beginning of the end of the GWOT as the preeminent driver of US foreign and security policy. It is not that global terrorism has gone away as a threat, but that US foreign and security policies are returning to what is, in some sense, the post–Cold War "normal" of a fluctuating range of priorities. At the end of 2011, the remaining US troops withdrew from Iraq, and the Obama administration began expediting the US withdrawal from Afghanistan. Although counterterror operations remain a tactical priority for military and intelligence operators, they are no longer the primary driver of foreign policy.

While the United States was in the midst of the GWOT era, a fundamentally different global environment took shape. With the rise of state capitalism and rapid growth of developing countries, economics became increasingly important in geopolitics. And more players and interests entered the world stage. While geopolitics was becoming more crowded, the US appetite for it diminished. Through the middle of the first decade of the twenty-first century, interstate relations and international institutions took a back seat to counterterror and counterinsurgency efforts in the Middle East and South Asia. As the decade came to an end, the United States retreated inward. After a decade of war, the US populace had become wary of large-scale military involvements overseas. And the financial crisis consumed US policymakers while also imposing reputational costs on the country internationally. So, the United States became less willing to lead, while others were less willing to follow. But no other country or group emerged to assume the United States' place. Europe and Japan have been consumed by internal challenges, and the "emerging" powers have neither the capability nor desire to take on global leadership.

These developments undoubtedly weakened the post–World War II international system, but they also led to premature declarations of US decline. The United States has indeed become more selective in its international leadership. It now focuses mainly on countries or regions that are economically critical or that pose global security risks. But even as it narrows its priorities, it remains the only great power with global reach diplomatically and militarily. Just as critically, the US economy has shown resilience and dynamism after being devastated by the financial crisis. Aggressive measures taken by US policymakers prevented another Great Depression, and the emergence of hydraulic fracturing has ushered in a new US energy boom. This energy boom has helped drive the US recovery and has made the United States an attractive partner for energy importers such as Japan. Countries that just a few years ago saw it as a declining power are realizing that the United States is again on the rise as an economic and international force.

All these developments have led to at least a temporary G-0 world of every country for itself and of economics largely driving geopolitics. The United States remains the most active and powerful country, but it is exercising leadership more selectively. At the same time, the rise of state capitalism has broken the consensus on international economic norms, weakening multilateral institutions, and technological diffusion has empowered weaker state and nonstate actors. While US officials do not use the term "G-0," the December 2012 National Intelligence Council Global Trends study largely adopted this framework for thinking about the future, and the major conceptual foreign policy contribution of the first Obama administration was to explicate a strategy of economic statecraft consistent with the G-0 construct.[1] In 2011, the US ratified free trade agreements with South Korea, Colombia, and Panama, all of which had been awaiting congressional approval since the Bush administration. And the United States is also looking to complete sweeping trade deals in the Asia-Pacific and with Europe.

Going forward, the Obama administration apparently wishes to build its larger geopolitical relationships on these economic foundations.

The G-0 world is and will continue to be rocky. Neither WTO-type "megalateralism" nor a stable multipolarity with clear roles and relationships will define it. Conflict management will suffer as the United States will be hesitant to organize cooperative responses to conflict. We will see fewer interventions like those in Kuwait and Kosovo, and more crises that simmer and potentially spiral outward like the current civil war in Syria. During the 2012 election, a common refrain from both President Obama and Governor Romney was that China will fill the void should the United States pull back from its global leadership role. That is not going to happen. China and all potential successors are even more consumed with internal issues than is the United States. The Eurozone crisis has thrown Germany and other European powers into a prolonged period of crisis management, and rising powers such as China, Brazil, and India are constrained by low per capita GDP, risk of social instability, and immature militaries. The result is a US-constructed world order replaced by a more anarchic, less predictable one.

COMPETITIVE INTERDEPENDENCE: THE CHALLENGE OF STATE CAPITALISM

One major driver of the G-0 world is the rise of state capitalism—an economic system that is distinct from, yet integrated with, free-market capitalism. As opposed to the firm-centric, profit-maximizing basis of free-market capitalism, state capitalism is about ensuring that market activity and wealth serve the interests of the state and those who run it. Further, the political control required by state capitalism goes hand in hand with authoritarian political institutions. Thus, state capitalism engenders different economic and political values than those of free-market capitalism.

Nevertheless, the rivalry between free-market and state capitalisms is fundamentally distinct from the rivalry between capitalism and communism during the Cold War. Then, the economies of the United States and the capitalist bloc were largely independent of the economies of the Soviet Union, China, and the communist bloc. As a result, the United States was able to construct a world order centered on a group of like-minded nations that generally shared liberal, free-market values. In contrast, today, state and free-market capitalist economies are very much intertwined, and state capitalism represents a broad spectrum. State capitalist countries, led by China, have largely embraced international trade and investment. The Chinese and US economies are highly integrated, with over $500 billion in trade in goods and services in 2011.[2] In contrast to the isolated economic decision making of Soviet leaders, leaders in state capitalist countries make investment and regulatory decisions that affect global markets. When many emerging markets began to liberalize in the 1990s, they nevertheless maintained control of strategic sectors, limiting Western investment opportunities. In the 2000s, many emerging markets, such as China and the United Arab Emirates, set up state-run sovereign wealth funds which they used to invest internationally and become major players in global capital flows.

These competing, yet interdependent, economic approaches prevent a consensus on global economic rules from emerging. Two major areas of contention between state and free-market capitalist countries are state-owned enterprises (SOEs) and national champions, such as Russia's oil and gas giant, Rosneft, and China's oil giant, CNOOC (China National Offshore Oil Corporation). These firms are heavily subsidized by the government and are allowed to dominate a sector, putting foreign competitors at a severe disadvantage in trade and investment. Governments provide SOEs and national champions the inside track to many contracts, and government subsidies reduce SOEs' financing costs and give them unfair pricing advantages. State control of the economy and these entities is also a major source of wealth for government leaders and bureaucrats. In just one example, the family of former Chinese prime minister Wen Jiabao is reportedly worth $2.7 billion due to government connections and deals with SOEs.[3] State control of firms, therefore, not only threatens competition, transparency, and accountability, but also secures the livelihood of government officials.

State capitalist countries view SOEs and national champions as instruments to advance their foreign policy objectives. State capitalist governments can use domestic firms to secure access to strategic resources or as carrots to influence a foreign government's behavior. China, in particular, has been notable for its use of nonconditional development assistance to secure access to strategic resources for its SOEs.[4] Thus, SOEs and national champions move beyond the realm of profit-seeking entities and function as tools of geopolitical competition for resources and influence. This underscores the difficulty in developing rules of the road for the G-0 world. Regulatory rules that weaken or limit state-controlled firms would reduce state control of the economy and take away sources of income for bureaucrats. But just as importantly, such rules would also take away an important geopolitical tool for state capitalist states. Because such entities are at the core of state capitalism while much less critical to free-market capitalism, key countries cannot agree on rules and restrictions for them. With state capitalism here to stay for the foreseeable future, developing a global consensus, like that which existed after World War II, will remain elusive.

UNITED STATES RESURGENT: THE COMING DECLINE OF THE ENERGY OLIGOPOLY

Even as state capitalism has undermined the Washington-led multilateralism of the post–World War II era, technological changes are allowing the United States to secure its position atop the new G-0 order. Surprising technological developments in energy and weaponry have upset the global balance of power—reducing or frustrating the power of established players and empowering new ones. By far the most influential recent technological surprise has been in energy. As the end of the first decade of the twenty-first century approached, the conventional wisdom was that technological shifts would facilitate non-carbon energy. With climate change receiving ever-growing attention and sizeable government investments in alternative energies such as solar and biofuel, the next big thing in energy appeared to be coming from the "green energy" sector. However, technological breakthroughs in horizontal drilling and hydraulic fracturing turned these expectations on their head. Oil and gas resources that are locked in tight shale formations were once too difficult and expensive to access. But the new drilling technology has made extracting these resources much easier, more efficient, and more economical.

This technological advance has challenged the energy oligopoly of national oil companies that was increasingly dominating the world of conventional carbon extraction. Conventional oil and gas reserves are largely concentrated in a small number of countries such as Saudi Arabia, Russia, and Qatar, which has allowed them to dictate the terms of supplying critical energy resources. As a result, they have an outsized influence in geopolitics. Russia can use this leverage to pressure governments it disagrees with, while Saudi Arabia's cooperation is needed when restricting Iranian oil exports. Conventional reserves undoubtedly remain important to global energy markets, but unconventional drilling has opened up many more avenues of supply and is poised to reduce the leverage of the traditional energy titans. Given that unconventional oil and gas supplies are more widely distributed, a key factor in determining the global distribution of power has become which countries have the expertise and the technology to exploit their reserves.

The United States is, unsurprisingly, a major source of this expertise and technology. US companies have been at the forefront of perfecting the new drilling techniques, which have unlocked vast domestic oil and gas reserves. The International Energy Agency estimates that, because of unconventional drilling, the United States will surpass Saudi Arabia as the world's leading producer of crude oil in 2020.[5] A similar story can be told for US production of liquefied natural gas (LNG). The US Energy Information Administration (EIA) estimates that annual shale gas production in key formations grew 350 percent between 2007 and 2011. In its *Annual Energy Outlook 2013,* the EIA projects that, as a result of this rapid growth, the United States will produce more natural gas than it consumes by 2020.

Thus, while unconventional drilling has fragmented the global energy landscape and reinforced the G-0, it has also created the conditions for a US resurgence. The new energy boom has the potential to turn the global narrative of power trends on its head over the next decade. The mantra of US decline could disappear to be replaced with the narrative of US resurgence. The United States should see its soft power grow as countries throughout the world view US power as more resilient than it has appeared since the 2008 financial crisis. Should the United States continue to develop its domestic resources, and open up the export

spigots, countries in Asia and Europe will see it as a more reliable source than Iran or Russia. While the United States will not return to a position of unmatched hegemony, it now appears that the 2008 financial crisis did not portend the country's secular decline, as doomsayers predicted. The United States will continue to be the world's premier economic and military power, even as the rise of state capitalism and developing economies has reduced its relative power. Many people have assumed the United States would be a loser in the G-0 world, but the rest of the world, rather than the American people, is more likely to endure the brunt of the consequences.

THE COUNTERREVOLUTION IN MILITARY AFFAIRS

While the advances in energy technology are boosting the outlook for US power, other developments across the technological spectrum have made the exertion of US power more challenging. In the late 1990s and the early years of this century, US military planners were optimistic that high-end technology—the so-called Revolution in Military Affairs (RMA)—would provide an increasing military edge to the United States and its allies. But, in the last decade, the United States had its main objectives in Iraq and Afghanistan frustrated because of the rapid development of asymmetric technologies, especially improvised explosive devices (IEDs). These low-tech devices have been the main cause of US deaths in both countries, and the United States has been at pains to keep ahead of their technological evolution. It invested billions of dollars into technology to counteract IEDs and yet found that dogs remain the most effective detection devices.

Mid-range technological developments have also empowered nonstate actors and frustrated their more powerful state adversaries. Except for an occasional suicide bomber,

Hamas and Hezbollah were previously unable to reach deep across the Israeli border. Rocketry advances in the Middle East, however, have multiplied their power projection capabilities. Such advances were on display with thousands of Hezbollah rocket attacks during the 2006 Lebanon war and thousands of Hamas rocket attacks during the 2012 Gaza conflict. Mid-range technology developments have also helped strengthen states vis-à-vis much stronger foes. Iran has developed small and swift boats that it uses to harass US naval assets in the Persian Gulf and could use to disrupt, at least temporarily, global trade in the Strait of Hormuz.

Perhaps of greatest concern to the United States is the development of Anti-Access/Area-Denial (A2AD) weaponry by China. The purpose of this technology is to deny an adversary access to a certain territory or make access prohibitively costly. Examples include anti-ship ballistic missiles (ASBMs), which could be used to target US aircraft carriers at standoff ranges, and directed energy weapons, which could be used to neutralize US command and control assets.[6] While China remains far behind the US military in overall technology and operational capabilities, A2AD technology could help mitigate their weaknesses and embolden them to push the limits of a confrontation with the United States.

All these new technological developments reinforce G-0 dynamics. From IEDs to rocketry to A2AD weaponry, these technologies allow weaker actors to block or frustrate the policies of stronger states. They enhance the ability of insurgent groups to undermine conflict-management efforts and help narrow the perceived gap between the US military and its rivals. It is not that US military dominance is going away. Rather, it is getting ever-harder to translate that dominance into compellence of adversaries.

Sustaining Stability: Trading Institutions for Interdependence

Absent a global hegemon, and given the empowerment of an unprecedented number of actors, some thought that we were on the verge of a flowering of multilateralism in order to ensure stability. But the relative waning of US power has not engendered more international cooperation and stronger multilateralism; if anything, the opposite has occurred. Effective cooperation demands leadership, and, as discussed, that is in short supply.

In this context, stability and cooperation must be produced more organically, rather than imposed from above. The cornerstones of this organically produced stability are most likely to be found in economic growth and interdependence. Despite disagreement from some realists,[7] a sizeable body of scholarly research supports the hypothesis that economic interdependence reduces the likelihood of violent conflict.[8] It does so by increasing the perception of the costs of conflict or by creating channels for credible signaling. Recent studies from Erik Gartzke and others reinforce the economic interdependence hypothesis.[9] Using a more robust and precise measure of interdependence than previously employed, these studies find that open and developed capital markets, monetary coordination, direct investment flows, and economic development (measured by per capita GDP) reduce the likelihood of conflict. These measures of interdependence go beyond trade flows and more accurately capture the dynamics at play in the G-0 world. It is not simply the exchange of goods and services that will incentivize peace and cooperation, but a growing middle class and the thick web of international economic and financial relationships.

With growth fostered by economic interdependence, countries perceive a stake in the international order and are less likely to take actions to threaten that order. Regional stability and peace have been major components of the rapid development of emerging markets such as China and Brazil. This stable environment has allowed them to devote significant resources and attention to their domestic economy, and has facilitated growth in trade and investment with foreign countries. Critically, economic development has also created expectations of continued growth. Many governments in developing countries, China being the most notable example, have staked their legitimacy largely on the ability to deliver consistent growth and rising standards of living. Any disruptions to growth threaten that legitimacy and put popular support at risk. With their legitimacy on the line, leaders in the rising great powers have strong incentives to adopt foreign policies conducive to such growth.

Developed countries similarly have strong economic incentives to avoid violent conflict. The rise of developing countries injects new dynamism into the world economy, allowing developed countries to export high-value products and capital, and to import cheap consumer products. International stability also allows them to expend relatively little on military budgets—even US military spending as a percentage of GDP remains historically low—freeing up resources for more popular spending on domestic priorities. Finally, ever-growing trade and investment flows create constituencies in both developed and developing countries that serve as a check on military conflict. Powerful interests that profit from international trade and investment help reduce the likelihood of conflicts should tensions rise. Those interests also create more channels of communication between countries, fostering dialogue and helping to minimize misunderstanding during crises.

There is, however, a converse to the positive webs woven by economic interdepen-

dence and growth. Economic stagnation or contraction weakens and destroys those webs, reducing a country's stake in the international order. Those who fail to reap the benefits of the international economic order and concomitant peace and stability lack the incentives to preserve it. Economic failure also reduces the number of stakeholders that can positively constrain governments. Whereas powerful actors with stakes in foreign trade and investment multiply as the economy grows and interdependence deepens, powerful economic interests contract and international ties weaken in failing economies.

Rather than preserving peace and stability, the leaders of states on the margins of the international economy have incentives to undermine peace and stability for political gain. Without economic growth, leaders, especially those who lack democratic legitimacy, must look for other sources of legitimacy. As a result, they may stake their claim to rule on being defenders of the nation and seek external scapegoats for internal problems. Many historical cases also suggest that external scapegoating can be a motivating factor for leaders to pursue conflict.[10] Elites challenged by economic turmoil and/or elite competition can seek diversionary wars with the hope of unifying the regime and increasing popular legitimacy. Jack Levy and Lily Vakili argue that economic crises, domestic illegitimacy, and elite disunity can produce diversionary behavior in authoritarian regimes. North Korea exemplifies this dynamic. Overseeing an economy with few ties to the outside world and desperate to hold onto power, its leaders have persistently engaged in provocations and flouted international censure. The lack of economic growth produces perverted incentives—it minimizes conflict's downside while increasing its upside.

Herein lies perhaps the greatest weakness of the G-0 world: peace and stability are produced much more organically and, thus, are much more beyond the control of governments. In past eras of strong international institutions and global hegemons, coalitions could be organized and credible sticks and carrots employed to deter bad behavior internationally. The period following the fall of the Berlin Wall was particularly tumultuous, as internal conflicts kept in check by the Cold War suddenly erupted. But because the United States emerged from the Cold War riding a wave of confidence and with an appetite for international activism, it organized robust international responses to various crises as they broke out throughout the world. With Russia recovering from the collapse of the Soviet Union and China only beginning its economic ascent, the international political environment was also more conducive to US leadership. Managing their own internal development, potential veto players were unwilling to mount staunch opposition against the sole global superpower. Working through the United Nations, the United States led protection forces and peacekeeping missions throughout the world, most notably in Africa, Haiti, and Bosnia. Even if these missions did not achieve all their aims, UN intervention prevented worst-case humanitarian crises and/or regional instability.

The G-0 world has made the conflict management that defined the 1990s much more difficult to conduct. A decade of war and a focus on domestic growth has reduced US willingness and ability to organize coalitions to address crises, and the rise of large developing states makes agreeing upon responses even more difficult. Eyeing US and Western geopolitical interests with suspicion, China and Russia are often intransigent in responding to US-led initiatives. Furthermore, as conflict is more likely to break out in regions with less economic growth and interdependence, the international community has less material incentive

to actively intervene. Conflicts in countries and regions on the margins of the global economy simply cost less to those in other regions. As conflicts break out on the margins, from Mali to Syria, the United States and other global powers have a reduced appetite for spearheading responses. This is exacerbated by a more complicated international political environment. The United States and its allies often have different interests than Russia and China in any given conflict, preventing a unified response through the United Nations. With the international community often unable or unwilling to undertake conflict management, stability has now become more dependent on variables such as economic growth and interdependence. This leaves policymakers with fewer and much less direct tools to prevent instability. In the G-0 world, beyond promoting trade and open markets, US policymakers and others can do little to foster domestic economic policies and conditions in foreign countries conducive to growth and interdependence.

ASIA'S BOOM AND THE CAPITALIST PEACE

Asia is the region in which economic growth and interdependence has the greatest opportunity to prevent conflict and foster conflict management. More than any other region, Asia benefited from the economic booms of the 1990s and 2000s. Asia's share of the global economy has grown dramatically in the past two decades, rising from 25 percent of global GDP in 1990 to 36 percent of global GDP in 2012. Excluding Japan, its share has grown from 14 percent in 1990 to 30 percent in 2012. The per capita GDP of developing Asia[11] has grown by almost five times in the same period, while that of the newly industrialized countries (NICs) of South Korea, Taiwan, Hong Kong, and Singapore has grown by almost four times.[12]

This had led to a dramatic growth in the Asian middle class. Asia has also seen rapid growth in two key elements of economic interdependence: foreign direct investment and trade. Asia's developing economies saw net direct investment rise from $46 billion in 2000 to $224 billion in 2010.[13] Exports and imports also grew by double digits each year from 2002 until 2008, and trade growth quickly recovered after the global financial crisis, jumping by double digits in 2010. Meanwhile, Asia's developed economies have increasingly become a source of capital. Japan's net lending grew from 2.9 percent of GDP between 1998 and 2005 to 3.5 percent of GDP from 2006 to 2011. Net lending by the NICs grew even more, from 5.7 percent of GDP between 1998 and 2005 to 6.6 percent of GDP from 2006 to 2011.[14] Between the NICs and Japan, exports and imports have grown faster than GDP in nine of thirteen years since 2000. And, as in developing Asia, after exports and imports fell in 2009, they quickly recovered and grew by double digits in 2010.[15]

In Asia, therefore, we see all the economic variables that reduce the likelihood of violent conflict: economic growth, growing per capita GDP, robust trade flows, and robust capital flows. With the benefits of economic growth disbursed among the developed and developing economies, the countries of the region have strong incentives to avoid escalating conflicts and to participate in crisis management should intraregional conflict break out. Asia's importance to the world economy also incentivizes active involvement by major powers such as the United States and European Union in Asian geopolitical affairs. Economies both within and outside the region would experience significant economic shocks from instability. Thus, should tensions rise, countries around the globe are sure to actively play a role in conflict prevention or crisis management.

The attraction and value of Asia's economy was the major driver of President Obama's "pivot to Asia," the administration's most significant foreign policy initiative during its first term. Most of the discussion around the pivot has focused on its security dimension. Indeed, it was the credibility of the security side that responded to what was worrying the United States' Asian allies and partners in the context of a rising and more assertive China.

But critical to the pivot is its economic dimension, the Trans-Pacific Partnership (TPP), a sweeping free trade agreement that would include countries from North and South America and East Asia. With Japan announcing its intention to join talks in March 2013, TPP member states constitute nearly 40 percent of global GDP. The economic dimension of TPP would be impossible without the security pivot. Asian countries see the United States as a check on growing Chinese power, a belief that will be reinforced by the US energy boom. Japan, in particular, is seeking access to US exports of LNG as part of a potential TPP. At its core, the TPP embodies the G-0 order in which security relationships are intermingled with economic ones. The United States will use the appeal of its large market, abundant capital, and newfound energy resources to forge closer ties across Asia. These closer ties will then ultimately serve as a platform for closer security relations, both with traditional US allies such as Japan and South Korea, and with new partners such as Vietnam and the Philippines.

Given rising Chinese assertiveness and growing nationalism across the region, Asia's economic interdependence and the US pivot are more important than ever to regional stability. These two elements will serve as critical brakes on conflict escalation. In 2012, China-Japan tensions reached levels unseen in recent history. Island disputes in the East China Sea led to attacks on Japanese businesses in China and hurt the investment climate between the two nations. Similar tensions have arisen recently in the South China Sea between China and members of the Association of Southeast Asian Nations (ASEAN). Although tensions moderated somewhat in 2013 from their 2012 peak, events such as Prime Minister Shinzo Abe's visit to the Yasukuni Shrine and the announcement of the Chinese Air Defense Identification Zone indicate that issues between the two nations will not be resolved anytime soon. With a new Chinese leadership, this nationalism will not quickly abate as Chinese leaders push territorial claims in order to establish their credibility. Nevertheless, economic interdependence will play an important role in keeping a lid on Chinese nationalism and other nationalisms throughout the region. Chinese leaders, so dependent on export-led economic growth for legitimacy, are unlikely to push their brinkmanship to a point that would seriously damage trade relations. The same can be said for China's East Asian neighbors, whose explosive growth has largely been fueled by Chinese trade and investment. In returning its focus to the region and finding so many willing partners, the United States will also play an important role in reducing conflict in the region. The US relationship with multiple interested parties can restrain any escalation as well as assure allies of their security from Chinese aggression. Just as importantly, the US presence will make China extra prudent in limiting provocative actions.

Nevertheless, even as the United States serves as a check on China's territorial ambitions, the economic interdependence between the two limits the force of what are otherwise strong downward pressures on their bilateral relationship. Unlike the United States and the Soviet Union, the United States and China benefit from each other's success. Both are large and growing markets for one another. China is the United States' second-largest trading partner and the largest foreign holder of US Treasury bonds, while the United States is China's largest trading partner and a major supplier of direct investment, investing $60.5 billion in China in 2010.[16] While the two countries are potential strategic rivals, they have strong economic incentives to develop a cooperative relationship. The loss of one another as trade and investment partners would be economically devastating.

Importantly, both China and the United States remain optimistic about their interdependence, but in ways that are not easy to reconcile. For the United States, interdependence is seen as fostering China as a more responsible regional and global stakeholder. For China, interdependence is seen as minimizing the possibility that the United States will actively seek to limit China's rise. The good news is that both countries perceive a shared interest in a flourishing and stable Asia. A more forthright and regular dialogue between both countries would go a long way to smoothing tensions that arise from these two different perspectives. The United States, in particular, could more clearly convey its interest in Chinese economic growth and explain its relationship with China's neighbors in terms of regional stability.

But risks remain that could threaten regional peace and stability, especially if US-China relations continue to be defined by fickleness and lack of transparency. Most prominent among these risks is a sustained Chinese economic crisis. To be sure, such a crisis appears unlikely in the near term. Even in a historically adverse situation such as the 2008 financial crisis, the Chinese government showed competence in managing the decline in external demand and stimulating growth. Nevertheless, such a scenario remains possible in the medium term, especially if China does not rebalance its economy away from growth almost entirely dependent on investment and exports. The Chinese economy is the heart of the Asian economy, and any significant slowdown would produce tremors across regional economies and weaken the ties that bind the countries together. Most ominously, this slowdown would incentivize China's leaders to seek external scapegoats. The Chinese Communist Party (CCP) has built its legitimacy on delivering economic growth and representing the aspirations of the nation. If the pillar of economic growth crumbles, Chinese leaders would be forced to rely even more on nationalism. They might stake their rule on being protectors of the nation, and, thus, be more likely to engage provocatively around territorial claims. A desperate CCP could see a short and contained militarized conflict with the United States or Japan as a small price to pay for continued rule. But even a limited conflict could quickly spiral out of control.

US actions could also inadvertently trigger such instability. China is weary of the US pivot, seeing it as an effort by the United States to encircle a rising China. To reassure China, the United States must maintain transparency in its efforts and continue to engage with it. Neglecting either of these reassurance mechanisms could cause Chinese leaders to confront the United States somewhere in the region. Alternatively, if allies begin to doubt US commitments, this could also lead to a conflict. Should the United States fail to maintain its traditional security arrangements or grow its budding ones, or should the United States fail to make the necessary compromises to reach an agreement on the TPP, the sense of security among China's neighbors would erode. Without these security or economic commitments, allies and partners would have reason to doubt US commitment in much more costly scenarios. They would be more likely to take preventive measures or react

more aggressively to China's territorial provocations, significantly increasing the prospect of conflict.

Conflict could also arise from US allies feeling too comfortable with their security. A hand-in-glove relationship with the US military could cause US allies to feel enabled to engage in brinkmanship with China. After all, should they get in over their heads, the United States would come riding to the rescue. Old allies such as Japan and South Korea are unlikely to engage in brinkmanship, but there is some risk that allies new to US partnerships, such as the Philippines or Vietnam, might feel enabled to engage in provocative actions. The United States, therefore, should set clear terms of engagement so partners know the circumstances in which it will intervene. Further, while the United States should worry little about Japanese or South Korean brinkmanship, continued strong ties between both allies is critical. The Japan–South Korea friendship is a cornerstone of regional security, keeping a check on China's territorial claims and deterring North Korean aggression. Rising nationalism in Japan and South Korea could create a dangerous regional dynamic.

All the risks above are further heightened by Anti-Access Area-Denial (A2AD) technology, designed to prevent American air and naval forces from operating near the Chinese mainland. China would not intentionally seek a long, drawn-out conflict with the United States. Only if it saw the opportunity for a quick victory over the United States or Japan, for example, would it provoke a militarized conflict. A2AD technology such as the DF-21A "carrier killer" missile might give China confidence that it could quickly destroy a US aircraft carrier and take out critical US command and control assets. China could calculate that, with some initial embarrassments, the United States would rather sue for peace than risk further losses merely to defend small islands in the South China Sea. This certainly would be a dangerous game. Most wars begin with one or both sides expecting quick resolution. Nevertheless, if China feels cornered by one of the scenarios above, it may feel that its new military assets are suited to bring about such a resolution.

These risks are real, and the United States should plan for any of these contingencies. But they are also unlikely. Even a short downturn in China would not necessarily lead to conflict. Chinese leaders are just as likely to double down on interdependence, looking for new markets to pull them out of the downturn. So long as Asian countries continue to see the enormous upside of economic growth, and the damage that would result from war, regional tensions will remain in check. The enormous upside will also help mitigate the friction between state and free-market capitalist countries in the region. Interdependence and growth will not produce clear guidelines for the treatment of SOEs or intellectual property, but they will remind regional players that the fruits of economic openness and interdependence outweigh regulatory disagreements.

THE "SPOILER" REGION: AN ECONOMICALLY STAGNANT MIDDLE EAST

In contrast to Asia, the Middle East and North Africa region is a spoiler for global security, rather than an opportunity; it stands as the poster child of the dangers that arise from economic stagnation and contraction. The Middle East was largely left out of the boom of the 2000s. Its per capita GDP grew by only 120 percent between 1990 and 2012, and its share of global GDP was nearly flat.[17] Its trade performance has been similarly disappointing, with exports growing by double digits in only two years between 1990 and 2012, and imports grow-

ing by double digits in only four years during the same period, despite the low base.[18] And while net direct investment grew from $5 billion in 2000 to a peak of $64 billion in 2009, it has since fallen dramatically, coming in below $30 billion in both 2011 and 2012.[19] These data mask the severe economic difficulties facing many countries in the region, especially the populous oil-importing countries. The GDP of oil importers in the Middle East grew at a mere 1.4 percent in 2011, and final 2012 growth is projected to come in at 1.2 percent. This is compared with growth of 3.9 percent and 6.6 percent, respectively, for oil exporters.[20] But, even the oil exporters of the region have fundamentally weak economies almost entirely dependent upon the price of oil for growth. Further, their relatively stronger growth has not fostered the interdependence conducive to cooperative relations. Instead, the growth is largely fueled by exporting oil outside the region rather than intraregional trade. The web of interdependence, thus, remains weak, even during periods of regional growth.

Egypt is emblematic of these dire conditions, which is particularly dangerous given its importance to the Middle East. It is, in many ways, the bellwether of stability in the region. Egypt's peace treaty with Israel ended an era of frequent Arab-Israeli wars, and the fall of Mubarak transformed the Arab Spring into a regional uprising. But the economic malaise that triggered the 2011 uprising has only worsened since then. After GDP grew at 5.1 percent in 2010, it has since stalled, growing at 1.8 percent in 2011 and 2.2 percent in 2012. Trade has also been contracting. Year-on-year, exports fell by 5.4 percent in 2011 and 7.8 percent in 2012. And while imports grew by 3.4 percent in 2012, they contracted by 5.2 percent in 2010 and 2.8 percent in 2011.[21] The high hopes of 2011 faded under the short-lived administration of President Morsi. The economy has continued to deteriorate, political polarization has worsened, and General Sisi is highly unlikely to reverse any of these negative trends. These developments bode ill for the region. Without growth and political stability, Egypt cannot serve as the hub for regional trade and investment that its geographic location and population size would seem to endow, nor is it in a position to play a sustained leadership role in regional affairs.

Due to these weak economic underpinnings throughout the region, there is less ability for economic interdependence to foster peace in the Middle East. Because the international environment has not been a source of abundance for many Middle Eastern countries, they have less of a stake in the international system and have not developed a strong association between external stability and growth. On the contrary, Middle East leaders, whose legitimacy and popularity are seriously threatened by weak growth and lack of accountability, are much more prone to see potential upsides to international conflict. Creating external enemies and casting themselves as "defenders of the nation" provide leaders an attractive source of legitimacy in economically weak, autocratic countries. Even in democratizing countries, weak economic growth and domestic instability could push leaders to scapegoat external enemies like, in Egypt's case, Israel.

The post–Arab Spring Middle East, in fact, presents a particularly dangerous confluence of events. While regional growth continues to stagnate, the toppling of the Egyptian and Tunisian autocracies creates dangers on both the political and economic fronts. As the Arab Spring has evolved into an unstable Arab Summer, sectarian conflicts and the resurgence of extremism are creating a vicious downward political cycle. At the center of both resurgent sectarianism and extremism is Syria, where an initially peaceful democracy struggle has become a violent confrontation between domestic and regional sectarian forces and threatens to spill over, increasing risks in Iraq, Jordan, and Lebanon. The conflict in Syria is made particularly dangerous with Saudi Arabia and Iran taking the lead in covertly aiding their sectarian allies. Iran, in particular, would appear particularly prone to escalation, though aggressive moves on its part are constrained for the time being due to the ongoing nuclear negotiations. More than ever, leaders in the Middle East are engaging in sectarian brinkmanship, and unlike their counterparts in an economically growing and internationally integrated Asia, they have much less incentive to tread carefully.

In addition to the regional forces heightening the risk of conflict, the broader global dynamics of G-0 add to that risk. The Obama administration had hoped (and expected) that the Assad regime in Syria would fall, one way or another. But that didn't happen, and the president severely diminished US regional credibility when he promised and then backtracked on a military intervention in early September 2013. The United States is now caught between its opposition to reprising its role as Middle East military "enforcer" and the lack of a credible alternative option for resolving the conflict. Rising powers neither have the operational capabilities nor the resources to take over this role, while the European powers are consumed with the Eurozone crisis. Among global powers, parochial interests, especially Russia's relationship with the Syrian regime, have ruled the day over concerns of broader regional instability. But even as the conflict continues to spiral outward, there is little likelihood of military intervention. At this point, only if global energy markets are threatened or if Al Qaeda can claim and hold territory for an extended period of time will the major powers see a compelling reason to act.

While the case of Syria offers an example of the downside risks of G-0, Iran offers an example of not only downside risks but also creative responses to manage risks. In a sense, the response to Iranian nuclear development is a perfect storm of conflict management in the G-0 world. While serving as a harbinger for the decline of traditional institutions, it has produced a quintessential G-0 institution that is strengthened by technological surprises. Despite being a signatory of the Nuclear Non-Proliferation Treaty (NPT), Iran flaunted its treaty obligations even after it was discovered developing nuclear technology in the early 2000s. In particular, it took advantage of a United States that was consumed with Iraq, Afghanistan, and the broader GWOT. The deteriorating situation in Iraq after 2003 was particularly favorable for Iran in that it required the United States to pour more resources into Iraq, and gave the Iranians a field on which to combat the United States. Obviously as well, critical players such as Russia and China often chose to prioritize their bilateral relationships with Iran over the enforcement of the NPT.

While weakened global institutions and receding US leadership allowed the Iranian nuclear crisis to grow, recent geopolitical and technological developments give us a glimpse into a new form of conflict management. As the United States has reduced its counterinsurgency operations in the Middle East and South Asia, it has committed more resources to Iran and built a very diverse coalition to enforce ever-tightening financial sanctions. This coalition is indicative of G-0—it has no formal membership, but is ad hoc and composed of like-minded and not-so-like-minded nations. As Iranian nuclear development has progressed, and US and EU pressure has increased, China and Russia have been brought along reluctantly and, at a minimum, tolerated stronger sanc-

tions. These are not uniform sanctions emanating from a single institution, but rather a patchwork of complementary sanctions from the United States, United Nations, and European Union. Further, different nations play different roles. UN Security Council resolutions have played a crucial legitimating role, the United States and European Union are active in ensuring compliance, while other nations play a more passive role. India and South Korea, for example, have reduced oil purchases from Iran, but play no role in ensuring that other nations comply.

Bolstering the US-led coalition have been two critical technological developments. First, the US energy boom has strengthened the hand of US policymakers, as it has with other foreign policy challenges. Iran previously believed that its oil reserves served as a bulwark against the harshest of sanctions. Neither the United States nor the United Nations, it thought, would want to turn the screws too tightly for fear of seriously disrupting global energy markets. But with hydraulic fracturing boosting US oil production, the loss of Iranian oil has not had the negative effects that Iranian leaders once counted on. US oil production and a boost in production from Saudi Arabia has also allowed the United States to get other nations on board with oil sanctions.

Second, while the US energy boom has created the conditions for harsh sanctions, a technological breakthrough in financial intelligence has given the United States the ability to effectively enforce those sanctions. In the past, economic tools to influence geopolitical outcomes have been either too blunt or too weak. Conditional aid, for instance, has not been coercive enough. It is generally dispersed without strict oversight of compliance. Further, aid recipients often have multiple sources of aid, limiting the leverage of any single donor. This is increasingly the case. Should an African country find US conditions too burdensome, China often provides unconditional aid in exchange for some type of political or market access. Trade sanctions, on the other hand, were easily violated as enforcing nations couldn't prevent leakages. Sanctioned nations used alternative supplier networks to evade detection and keep the flow of goods going.

Over the last decade, however, the United States built a solid capability to uncover the identity of terrorist financial networks and found that disrupting finances could be a critical element of fighting terrorism. Underscoring the priority of this mission, the US Treasury created the Office of Terrorism and Financial Intelligence. This agency spurred a revolution in economic sanctions. It learned how to follow the money. It developed an unprecedented ability to map and disrupt financial networks, while preventing leakages. Critical in a G-0 world, these capabilities have enhanced the US ability to enforce financial sanctions and create incentives for participating in them.

The United States has leveraged this technical expertise and infrastructure to craft the harshest economic sanctions to date against Iran. Up until mid-2012, Iranian leaders bragged of their resilience to international sanctions. But then sanctions began to bite, and Iranian rhetoric underwent a dramatic shift. Instead of being mocked as ineffectual, sanctions became another part of the US conspiracy to undermine the Islamic Revolution. As 2013 began, they had devastated Iranian oil exports and led to a major currency crisis. Critically, the breakthrough in financial intelligence has given the United States the ability to deny others access to US financial markets. Losing access to US financial markets, the deepest and most liquid in the world, is a much more economically damaging consequence for most nations than just losing US trade. Even nations who

trade relatively little with the United States do not want to risk losing access to its financial markets. This serves as a powerful deterrent for other nations who may consider violating sanctions and doing business with Iran. While it remains to be seen whether the sanctions will ultimately achieve their strategic objective, they have triggered severe hardship in Iran, leading to the election of moderate president Hassan Rouhani and the opening of ongoing negotiations for a final status settlement on the nuclear issue. In a crisis that began because of weakened international institutions and US neglect, an ad hoc coalition—borne out of arm twisting and US revolutions in energy and economic sanctions—has emerged as a model for conflict management in the G-0 world.

From the G-20 to the G-2: The Future of International Institutions

The challenges and opportunities outlined above provide policymakers a glimpse into the emerging, but limited, levers of power in the G-0 world. This world will require the United States and others to reimagine international institutions. We will no longer have an international system dominated by broad universalist institutions or competing blocs, such as those that defined the post–World War II era. Power is now more widely distributed, and interests more varied. Thus, the outlook is bleak for challenges that require dozens of actors, with initiatives such as a global climate-change regime doomed to failure. Aligning economic and regulatory policies across economies of vastly different sizes, levels of growth, and stages of development has proven impossible. The General Agreement on Tariffs and Trade was effective in bringing down nonagricultural tariff barriers between advanced liberal democracies, but the World Trade Organization has been ineffective at coordinating regulatory, investment, and agricultural policies among developed and developing countries.

To meet the challenges of G-0, the United States will instead have to focus on two main models: creating coalitions of the like-minded and coalitions of the non-like-minded. Some of these arrangements will involve formal membership, while some will be situational and ad hoc. Some will address a specific issue or challenge, while others will be more expansive and address sets of issues. Regional trade deals that the United States is pursuing with Asia-Pacific nations and the European Union are archetypes of coalitions of the like-minded. The TPP is composed of a group of nations excited about the market access that an eventual free trade agreement will produce. Rather than joining reluctantly because of international pressure, the TPP has seen nations join enthusiastically, with each new member stirring greater interest among nonmembers.

Not every coalition will be composed of enthusiastic members willingly coming together. Some, like the G-20, will remain groupings of the non-likeminded, reflecting the make-up of the G-0 world, with members reluctantly working to manage conflicts and crises not of their choosing. The G-20 initially emerged in 1999 as a forum for dialogue between finance ministers of developed and developing countries. This ad hoc coalition emerged out of a realization that developed countries needed a forum for dialogue with an increasingly powerful developing world. When the global financial crisis hit in 2008, the Bush administration proposed raising the status of the G-20 to the head-of-state level, to allow a broad grouping of the world's financial powers to be the focal point for crisis management.

The most important future coalition of the non-likeminded, however, will be the G-2—the United States and China. Buzz around this grouping peaked during the financial crisis, but it remains critical to global stability. Even though the United States is being drawn into Asia to, at least substantially, balance *against* China, working *with* China will be key to the global geopolitical and economic trajectory. The US-China relationship is currently ad hoc, sporadic, and tumultuous. The two countries must develop a regularized framework to ensure that their relationship is more stable and, thus, better able to address global challenges. The US-China Strategic and Economic Dialogue is a good start, but should be expanded to entail more regular meetings between officials below the ministerial level. Such a framework is especially critical for military affairs. The United States and China should work to develop a general understanding of acceptable military behavior so that a routine patrol by a US surveillance ship doesn't escalate into a crisis. A regularized framework should also ensure that communication channels remain open during periods of heightened tension to reduce the risk of escalation. With a protocol to help ease the major friction points in the US-China relationship, the two countries can then more constructively engage on broader geopolitical challenges. However, even a more regularized relationship will not produce a G-2 entirely on US terms. China will remain a state capitalist country for the foreseeable future, and US leaders must work with Chinese leaders despite their different worldviews.

Right now, the G-2 remains unattainable, with China unwilling to be drawn in and the United States still believing in a Washington-led model. But we are no longer in a bipolar world in which a balance of fear between the two most powerful nations can create stability. The G-0 world is one with more varied and widespread risks than seen during the Cold War. However, it is also a world in which economic interdepen-

dence has the opportunity to nearly eliminate the catastrophic risks that defined the
Cold War era. To push catastrophic risks beyond the pale and limit the lesser ones, the
world's two largest economies must realize
that their mutual interests trump their mutual suspicions.

NOTES

1. National Intelligence Council, "Global
Trends 2030," December 2012, http://www.dni.gov
/files/documents/GlobalTrends_2030.pdf.

2. US Census Bureau, "Trade in Goods with
China," http://www.census.gov/foreign-trade/bal
ance/c5700.html.

3. David Barboza, "Billions in Hidden Riches
for Family of Chinese Leader," *New York Times*,
October 25, 2012, http://www.nytimes.com/2012
/10/26/business/global/family-of-wen-jiabao-holds
-a-hidden-fortune-in-china.html?pagewanted
=all.

4. Shanthi Kalathil, "Influence for Sale? China's Trade, Investment and Assistance Policies in
Southeast Asia," *East and South China Seas Bulletin*
4 (Center for a New American Security, September
2012), http://www.cnas.org/files/documents/publi
cations/CNAS_ESCA_bulletin4.pdf.

5. Lananh Nguyen, "U.S. Oil Output to
Overtake Saudi Arabia's by 2020," Bloomberg
News, November 12, 2012, http://www.bloom
berg.com/news/2012-11-12/u-s-to-overtake-saudi
-arabia-s-oil-production-by-2020-iea-says.html.

6. Jan van Tol, Mark Gunzinger, Andrew
Krepinevich, and Jim Thomas, *AirSea Battle: A
Point-of-Departure Operational Concept* (Washington, DC: Center for Strategic and Budgetary Assessments, 2010), 1, 20–21.

7. Kenneth Waltz, "Globalization and Gov-
ernance," *PS: Political Science and Politics* 32, no. 4
(December 1999): 693–700; and David Rowe,
"The Tragedy of Liberalism: How Globalization
Caused the First World War," *Security Studies* 14,
no. 3 (2005): 407–47.

8. Erik Gartzke, "The Capitalist Peace,"
American Journal of Political Science 51, no. 1 (Janu-
ary 2007): 166–91; Erik Gartzke, Quan Li, and
Charles Boehmer, "Investing in the Peace: Eco-

nomic Interdependence and International Conflict," *International Organization* 55, no. 2 (Spring
2001): 391–438; Solomon William Polachek,
"Conflict and Trade," *Journal of Conflict Resolution*
24, no. 1 (March 1980): 55–78; Bruce M. Russett
and John R. Oneal, *Triangulating Peace: Democracy, Interdependence, and International Organizations* (New York: W. W. Norton, 2001); Edward D.
Mansfield and Jack Snyder, "Incomplete Democratization and the Outbreak of Military Disputes," *International Studies Quarterly* 46, no. 4
(December 2002): 529–49; and Susan McMil-
lan, "Interdependence and Conflict," *Mershon
International Studies Review* 41, no. 1 (May 1997):
33–58.

9. Gartzke, "The Capitalist Peace"; and
Gartzke, Li, and Boehmer, "Investing in the Peace."

10. Jack S. Levy, "The Diversionary Theory of
War," in *Handbook of War Studies*, ed. Manus I.
Midlarsky (Boston, MA: Unwin Hyman, 1989),
259–88; Jack S. Levy and Lily I. Vakili, "Diver-
sionary Action by Authoritarian Regimes: Ar-
gentina in the Falklands/Malvinas Case," in *The
Internationalization of Communal Strife*, ed. Manus
I. Midlarsky (London: Routledge, 1992), 118–46;
and T. Clifton Morgan and Kenneth N. Bickers,
"Domestic Discontent and the External Use of
Force," *Journal of Conflict Resolution* 36, no. 1 (1992):
25–52.

11. Afghanistan, Bangladesh, Bhutan, Brunei
Darussalam, Burma/Myanmar, Cambodia, China,
Fiji, India, Indonesia, Kiribati, Laos, Malaysia,
Maldives, Nepal, Pakistan, Papua New Guinea,
Philippines, Samoa, Solomon Islands, Sri Lanka,
Thailand, Timor-Leste, Tonga, Tuvalu, Vanuatu,
and Vietnam.

12. International Monetary Fund (IMF),
"World Economic Outlook Database," October
2012.

13. Ibid.

14. IMF, "World Economic Outlook October
2012: Coping with High Debt and Sluggish
Growth," 214.

15. IMF, "World Economic Outlook Database."

16. Office of the United States Trade Representative, "The People's Republic of China," http://
www.ustr.gov/countries-regions/china-mongolia
-taiwan/peoples-republic-china.

17. IMF, "World Economic Outlook Database."

18. Ibid.

19. Ibid.

20. IMF, "Coping with High Debt and Sluggish Growth," 82.

21. Egypt Country Office, "Egypt Economic Quarterly Review," 3 (April 2013), African Development Bank Group, http://www.afdb.org/filead min/uploads/afdb/Documents/Publications/Egypt %20Economic%20Quarterly%20Review%20 -%20Volume%203%20-%20April%202013.pdf.

4

THE POWER CYCLE, TERRITORIAL SECURITY, AND PEACE IN THE TWENTY-FIRST CENTURY

Charles F. Doran

What causes systems transformation and the massive warfare historically associated with it? What is it about the rise and decline of great powers that has repeatedly proved so traumatic? The overriding concern of statecraft today is that quintessential problem of world order which, a century ago, preoccupied both the founders of the field of international relations and world statesmen negotiating international regimes as they witnessed history's plunge into World War I. At issue now, as then, is how to integrate an increasingly powerful great state into the existing global balance of power and community of nations collectively experiencing the challenges of structural change, something that has proven to be extraordinarily difficult. But we now have much greater understanding of the dynamic that drives this structural change, and of the stakes and surprises embedded within it. Today, as it has throughout history, a "single dynamic" of structural

change is contouring the power cycles of all the great powers and, thereby, the expectations that each state has regarding its future security and foreign policy role.[1] Therein the analyst will find both cause and solution regarding history's so-called dilemma of peaceful change.

The assessments offered in this chapter derive from this foundational claim at the heart of power cycle theory. "Power cycle theory" is a dynamic understanding of history that is anchored in, and speaks to, the particulars of state power and foreign policy behavior as they evolve, moment by moment, across long periods of history. In this historical dynamic, nothing is deterministic; everything is emergent. These patterns of structural change, and the historical behavioral responses to them, offer important lessons for emergent statecraft.

Today, two states, China and India, accounting for nearly 40 percent of the world's population, have embarked on the ascent to the rank of great power, with attendant international political consequences that are perilous for them and for world order in the twenty-first century. China has been accelerating up its power cycle for several decades now, and like rising great powers throughout history, it has begun an incessant push for a greater foreign policy role. But the single dynamic imposes ineluctable structural constraints on the trajectory of ascendancy that China will have to confront. The very same principles of relative power change that have always mapped the structural trends of history are shaping China's power cycle, and that cycle will contain the same critical points of suddenly shifted trends that have challenged every other rising power historically and that, all too frequently, have ended in major war.

After establishing the stakes and challenges confronting the existing world order by the rise of China, this chapter goes on to spotlight the errors and the dangers inherent in "hegemon-challenger" notions that have come to dominate the thinking of many academics and policymakers. Those ideas egregiously mislead. This chapter presents a conception of world politics that is pluralist rather than hegemonic, that is based on balance rather than hierarchy, and that differentiates the "leadership" characterizing the present open and accommodating international system from the imagined "hegemony" (political domination and control) of the largest state purportedly dictating the rules and benefits at will. The power cycle conception of statecraft, detailed in the third part of the chapter, undergirds the "dynamic equilibrium" proposed in the final part as a guide to world order properly attuned to the dynamic of changing power and role.

THE IMPORTANCE OF AMERICAN LEADERSHIP IN A DANGEROUS WORLD

The American Foreign Policy Objective: To Perpetuate a System That Is Open and Accommodating

At the climax of World War II, although the United States had the capacity to squelch opponents that lay in economic and political ruins, and to establish a self-serving economic system that exploited small competitors, the United States did not do so. Even though it possessed one-half of the world's GDP and most of the active military capability, the United States chose not to emulate the practice at the end of the Franco-Prussian War (1871) and at the end of World War I (1919) that extracted reparations from the defeated states. Instead, despite awareness that the system it helped establish would eventually leave it in relative decline as other states grew larger and more powerful because of the strategy, the United States sought to create a liberal trading and commercial order through the General Agreement on Tariffs and Trade (GATT), in which weaker and smaller states also could prosper, thus increasing the prospect for territorial stability and world peace. This liberal trade and political order, based on the principles of openness and equal economic opportunity, endures today. World war has not returned. More personal and national wealth has been generated in these intervening years—in this open and accommodating system—than in all prior intervals of world history combined.

But as the twenty-first century unfolds, rising states such as China, India, and Brazil have similar decisions to make. Will they help build a world order that perpetuates openness and economic fairness? Or will they choose to dominate their neighbors politically and perhaps militarily? Will they defend this liberal trade and commercial order? Or will they try to replace it with a kind of neo-mercantilism that exploits smaller and weaker states? This is the paramount question of strategy that faces contemporary world politics.

Nowhere else today is this question etched more sharply than in the South China Sea. Based on three decades of phenomenal growth and extraordinarily hard work, China has lifted 300 million citizens out of poverty. It has built an economy that soon will exceed the size of that of each of its rivals. It plans a one-thousand-ship navy. How will China deal with its near neighbors such as South Korea, the Philippines, Vietnam, Indonesia, and Malaysia, many of which claim sovereignty over the very same islands and seabed as does China? While claiming Taiwan as a province, will China continue to respect the democratic norms that govern Taiwan's 23 million citizens? Will China avoid a major war with other great powers such as Japan, Russia, and India as these states, like China, traverse their cycles of relative power and make judgments about their future security and foreign policy role vis-à-vis use of these waters?

How China answers these questions regarding the South China Sea will, positively or negatively, affect the rules and norms of world order for the remainder of the twenty-first century. Much of the world's trade passes through these waters. The high seas everywhere must remain unobstructed. Among the great powers themselves, the South China Sea is symbolic of the larger struggle within Asian politics more generally and ultimately within global international politics. It will provide signals as to, among other things, whether the liberal trade and commercial order can perpetuate itself.

China's Twenty-first-Century Imperative: To Forge Its Role within the Pluralistic, Decentralized International System of Interdependent Nation-States

The huge dilemma that China faces today—and the crux of the problem for order maintenance in the twenty-first century—is anchored in the fact that China's international political role in the modern world of interdependent nation-states is too different from its ancient past regarding contemporary structural circumstance, and yet is too similar culturally and politically to that past and to its incarnation within nineteenth- and twentieth-century world politics.

Perhaps the most profound difference between ancient China and its role, and modern China and its role, apart from the degrees of industrialization, is that modern China is totally interdependent with the rest of the world. The Middle Kingdom isolated itself. It was a world withdrawn, a world unto itself. Modern China in an economic and commercial sense is totally interactive with North America, Europe, Africa, the Middle East, South America, and of course the rest of Asia. Modern China is a fully conjoint and interdependent member of the international system in a way that ancient China did not want to be and therefore conspicuously was not. In the twenty-first century, rising China possesses aspirations to become the largest member of the international system, a position from which it hopes to express predominance.

Yet, in another sense, ancient China and contemporary China are culturally and politically similar. They are both inextricably and preferentially autocratic. Indeed, modern China is attempting to pioneer, in stark contrast with democratic capitalism, a new concept of capitalism where the private sector plays a negligible decision-making role. China is attempting to become an economic model in which the government-controlled corporation replaces the private multinational corporation, and government intervention shapes and drives the economy. In that conception of capitalism and of commercial enterprise, ancient China and modern China hold much in common. Hierarchy within the Communist Party is very similar to hierarchy within the Imperial Court. The emperor's modern equivalent is the head of the Communist Party. The ancient Chinese court is today the politburo.

But because the modern international system is pluralistic, a rift emerges between the imperatives for world order and China's continuing penchant for autocracy. Established at the Peace of Westphalia (1648) and enshrined in the UN Charter, the decentralized nation-state system is composed of multiple, independent actors with their own sovereignties. It is anarchic and balance oriented. No state kowtows to a single government. This conception clashes with the hierarchic vision of foreign relations manifested by an autocratic China, for instance, in its contact with its near neighbors in the South China Sea.

The very nature of the international system is at stake. The principle characteristic of the negotiated framework of open commercial interaction established when the United States assumed a leadership position in world affairs in 1947 (via the GATT) was that the smallest members of this trading system would benefit through their capacity to specialize externally within an open exchange of goods and services. All states would prosper, and the largest member of this system accepted that other governments would eventually eclipse its financial, commercial, and trade superiority in relative terms through the operation of the marketplace. A convergence of wealth would take place, and that was good. The trading system was expressly not zero-sum.

In contrast, China, a beneficiary of that system, prefers to deal with each state bilaterally in a way that enables it to dominate commercially because of its huge, growing size. China's preference for hierarchy extends to a notion of global economics that is unabashedly neo-mercantilist, as evidenced by its manipulation of its exchange rate, its cyber theft, and its disregard of intellectual property rights wherein it benefits at the expense of other nations. China prefers to import raw materials and export manufactured goods in an export-oriented economy that, because of its size and trading pattern, places a strain on the liberal international trading order. In a trading order in which countries expect to exchange goods and services broadly, in a reciprocal and balanced fashion, neo-mercantilism disrupts and distorts as it exploits.

A disjuncture exists between China's desire for harmony in Asia and its expanding claims for ownership of deep-sea resources and for control of transit through the high-seas areas. The problem is that China believes, because of its historical self-image and its size and potential for future growth, that it has a right *to dominate* its neighbors, *to own* and *to extract* a disproportionate amount of seabed resources, *to control* the sea lanes, to *exclude* foreign navies from its offshore waters even on the high seas, and *unilaterally to determine* the nature of world order in Asia. From the Chinese perspective, the United States just gets in the way. China is rapidly convincing itself (i.e., its populace) that the United States is the source of trouble, not its own heavy-handed behavior toward its neighbors. I italicized the actions, or verbs, but focus equally on the objects of those actions—the stakes vis-à-vis China's neighbors. Nationalism historically has arisen precisely from such a mixture of assertiveness, on the one hand, and delusions about conspiracy on the part of governments that will not yield to such blandishments, on the other.

The Challenge in the Asia-Pacific: Military Confrontation

Demonstrations and violence occurred all over China, triggered by a crisis in September 2012 involving the purchase by Japan of several uninhabited islands in the Senkaku (Diaoyu) chain. Two of Japan's largest retailing networks, Fast Retailing and Aeon, shuttered a majority of their Chinese stores. Stock for each company fell on the Nikkei 225 index. Nissan Motor Company, the largest Japanese automaker operating in China, stopped production at two of its factories. Honda, Nissan, and Toyota all experienced damage to their Chinese retail outlets. They also suffered steep drops there in the sale of Japanese-branded cars.

All this turmoil resulted from the decision of the prime minister of Japan, Yoshihiko Noda, to purchase several small islands so as to preempt the nationalist governor of Tokyo, Shintaro Ishihara, from buying these islands himself. During the crisis, eight Chinese warships shadowed the islands. Frigates from the Japanese navy and fighter jets from the Japanese air force, in turn, patrolled the area in a show of force.

Yet war did not break out, much less major war on the scale of World War I or II; war was scarcely even a background concern. Since 1995, many similar crises have occurred between China and its neighbors in the South China Sea. Yet no massive military confrontations have resulted. Have we just been lucky? Concern about escalation of the dispute was not lacking. A high-level US diplomatic delegation echoed Secretary of State Hillary Clinton's warning that war could break out over miscommunication, misperception, or accidental miscalculation. Although nothing was settled in terms of dispute resolution, peace once again prevailed.

Historically, as policy analysts and journalists have increasingly emphasized, the rise and fall of great powers is implicated in the origin of the most massive wars of history—usually interpreted today as a contest for supremacy between a declining hegemon and a rising challenger. But for which great powers, under what circumstances, and in which intervals of history is the collapse into major warfare most likely? Are all intervals of history equally vulnerable to this collapse? Does the mere fact of rise and decline make war inevitable? Or is there something specific about structural change that nations find so traumatic and threatening that they believe war is the appropriate or inevitable choice? Surely, great powers have ascended and descended their power cycle in certain intervals of history without impinging on the security of their neighbors. What does history tell us about the dynamic of rise and decline that could be more informative and more analytically helpful in policy terms as we move further into the twenty-first century?

Regarding the September 2012 crisis over the Senkaku/Diaoyu Islands, scholars and journalists have identified a number of purported explanations for the events and the subsequent escalation of discord: a transition of power in China to the "Fifth Generation" leadership; elite conflict at a very high level, including the Bo Xilai affair; and slipping economic growth because of world recession. Under the circumstances, Japan could appear from the Chinese perspective to be exploiting Chinese weaknesses. Behind all these short-term considerations lies the Chinese sense of historical injury, highlighted perhaps by the allegedly purposeful Japanese timing of Prime Minister Noda's announcement. The announcement of the decision to buy the islands fell on the July anniversary of the 1937 Marco Polo Bridge incident, which marked the start of Japan's effort to conquer China. For those in China believing in conspiracy, the sale of the islands occurred just a few days in advance of the anniversary of the Japanese invasion of Manchuria in 1931. Each of these "irritants" could be used separately or together to explain the timing of the purchases, the sensitivity involved, and the resulting escalation of tension, as though the possible loss of oil and natural gas in the vicinity were not sufficient grounds for Chinese protest.

The problem is that these supposed irritants only explain why the crisis occurred, not why the interval remained peaceful. While these irritants are catalytic of crisis, they cannot explain why the crisis, serious as it was, did *not* lead to war.

From the perspective of power cycle theory, the explanation for why this crisis did not lead to war, and for why future crises—perhaps similar in nature—are more likely to precipitate major war, lies in the deeper structural undercurrents of change that affect the rise and decline of states abruptly and counterintuitively. Since the origin of the modern state system in the late fifteenth century, "systems transformation"—a monumental transformation of structure and expectations that is experienced in statecraft as "shifting tides of history"—has upset world order on six occasions, stoking the fire of systems-wide war in five of the six: the Thirty Years' War (1618–48), the wars of Louis XIV (1667–97) and of the Spanish Succession (1701–14), and the Napoleonic Wars (1795–1815)—each of which engulfed all of Europe; and the two twentieth-century world wars (1914–19 and 1939–45) that enmeshed the globe.[2] Systems transformation *preceded* each of the wars. Unlike the surface irritants that come and go, these systems transformations are massive, unpredictable, and intractable. Understanding how structural undercurrents cause the shifting tides of systems transformation can help us understand why the rise and decline of states can trigger major war in some structural intervals but not in others, a relation-

ship confirmed empirically with strong statistical evidence. Power cycle analysis will undergird our assessment of whether China's rise is likely to be peaceful or stormy, and why.

NAVIGATING STATECRAFT IN A DANGEROUS WORLD: POWER CYCLE THEORY VS. HEGEMONIC STRUCTURAL INTERPRETATIONS

The power cycle perspective stands in stark contrast to some assumptions and competing structural theories[3] that, in recent decades, have begun to influence strategic thinking both in the United States and around the world, particularly in Asia. These conceptual differences are fundamental to assessment, as the following warrants regarding power cycle analysis attest.

Warrants of Power Cycle Theory

1. The structure of the international system is *competitive and plural, not hegemonic*. In particular, no actor (hegemon) is capable of imposing its will on matters internal to the central system of principal powers. This warrant captures the essence of the nation-state system.

   1a. *Leadership is not hegemony (domination and unilateralism).* Hegemony is incompatible with pluralism and balance. This distinction lies at the heart of world order.[4]

   1b. The purported "hegemonic leadership" notion of world order—the view that peaceful systems are characterized by the "hegemony" of a single state that creates its rules and benefits—is a distortion of the structural and strategic reality and dangerously misleads.

   1c. The thesis that structural change is a contest for this hegemonic position between a rising and a declining state at the top of the hierarchy distorts the reality of structural change, and yet has become so widely accepted that its fallacious reasoning must be unmasked.

2. World politics is *dynamic*; power and statecraft are dynamic, and that dynamic must be understood. Systems are not static entities. Power cycle theory unites the structural (state and system) and the behavioral (power and statecraft) aspects of world politics in its single dynamic of power and role. It explains the evolution of systems structure, and the associated concerns of statecraft, via the emergent cyclical dynamic of states' *relative* rise and decline (see Figure 1).

    2a. The principles of the power cycle reveal the *unique perspective of statecraft* in the expectations and unexpected nonlinearities of relative power (structural) change in contrast to the perspective of absolute trends.

    2b. Beware the expectations induced by absolute power trends. Do not underestimate the power of the undercurrents of structural change, and the bounds of the system, to abruptly surprise and to so fracture expectations that major war becomes, as it has so frequently in history, not merely an option but an inevitability too late to manage peacefully.

3. *Foreign policy role* is the behavioral component of statecraft over which states fight and may find compromise. It is a medium of exchange (bargaining currency) whereby structural change can be assimilated and world order legitimized. Territorial security is non-negotiable.

3a. Therein lies the clue to resolving the dilemma of peaceful change.

Why Not Hegemony and Why Not the Single Challenger Model?

Perhaps the most damaging impact of the "hegemonic" thesis is that China is likely to adopt it with alacrity, justifying Chinese actions on grounds that even democratic governments have claimed (China will assert) that such unilateral domination is a legitimate form of world order. As history suggests, the great powers are likely to reject such a claim to authority wholeheartedly if China tries to assume this foreign policy role. The crucial problem with the hegemon-challenger model is that it is wrong in terms of both conception and policy implication.

Instead of the hierarchy implied in the hierarchic notion, world politics has always been composed of a balance among members of the central system. Currently that system is composed of the United States, Japan, the principal EU countries or a surrogate thereof, China, and Russia, with India waiting in the wings. Only one of these countries has global reach, the United States. But this does not mean that the United States can act alone, nor that it does act alone or only on its own terms. Nor when China becomes the largest actor in the system will its size justify the attribution "hegemonic." Leadership, not hegemony, is what helps get things done and helps protect the functioning of the international system to the security and benefit of all states.

The hegemon-challenger model tries to explain history's world wars by arguing that war occurs at a "transition" when, as the challenger's power exceeds (transitions) that of the existing hegemon, they go to war to determine who will predominate and determine the future system's rules and benefits.[5] When this "dueling dyad" model of

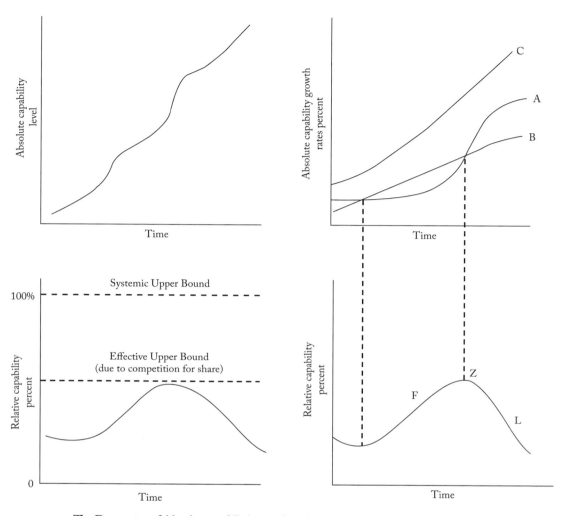

The Dynamics of Absolute and Relative Capability: Principles of the Power Cycle

*Curves of absolute growth rate (depicted is an accelerating system):
       A: major power system   B: state B   C: entire system

*Critical points:
       F: first inflection point   Z: zenith   L: second inflection point

Figure 1. The "single dynamic" of changing systems structure: bounds on elative growth

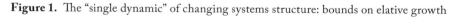

Source: Charles F. Doran, *The Politics of Assimilation: Hegemony and Its Aftermath* (Baltimore, MD: Johns Hopkins University Press, 1971), 193.

structural change was tested empirically against the pluralistic, balance-oriented model of the power cycle regarding the outbreak of major war, the results were definitive. In the power cycle model, major war is more likely than in normal diplomatic inter-

vals when a great power passes through "a critical point" on its power cycle (where the tides of history shift). In these empirical tests, a transition does not explain the war outcome unless it coincides with a critical point; but when a great power traverses a critical point of nonlinearity on its power cycle, the war outcome is highly probable.[6]

In the future, the less said about hegemony in academic and policy circles, and the more done reflecting political leadership as far as the United States is concerned, the better. Perhaps it is not too late to discourage China from trying to adopt the false and dangerously misleading hegemonic model as a guide to its own strategic thought. Unfortunately, for reasons of history, culture, and authoritarian institutional structures, China may well choose to apply the notion of international political domination to the conduct of its own foreign policy according to what it erroneously may believe are historically valid and scientifically sound political principles. If so, world politics will be much the worse for such misbegotten beliefs.

Let us specify the issue more precisely vis-à-vis contemporary concern regarding order maintenance in the Asia-Pacific. In particular, let us specify why the assimilation of China into the global balance of power cannot be cast as a "dueling dyad" between China and the United States.

1. This oversimplification of hegemon versus challenger misconstrues the global balance of power for an exclusive contest between the United States and China. It completely ignores the stakes (and capabilities) that Japan, Russia, India, South Korea, Australia, Indonesia, Vietnam, and others have in the competition with China, for example, in the South China Sea. Worse yet, some analysts in China would like to believe that the United States is the sole arbiter of power in the South China Sea and that, by ousting the United States from the region, China will inherit this mantle. But such a perversion of the dynamics of trade and naval movement in the South China Sea, a passage that witnesses the transit of half the world's shipping (by weight), is far too reductionist. The current naval capacities of Japan and Russia, including their strategic and submarine capacity, are scarcely to be ignored. India also is a country that in the future China dare not slight.

2. This oversimplification ignores not only the stakes in the region but also the structural reality underlying those stakes. China faces competition for power share from other governments climbing their own power cycles. India, the huge rising country at the bottom of the central system, will increasingly take power share away from China, impinging on China's rate of increase in relative power, forcing China into slower relative growth at China's first inflection point and ultimately to a Chinese peak. The stakes and problems in assimilating China peacefully are encapsulated in the structural dynamic vis-à-vis all members of the central system.

3. On the view that China's assimilation into the global balance is a bilateral contest for supremacy between the United States and China, China's relationship with its neighbors takes on the quality of an old-fashioned battle for territory. But China's rise has little if anything to do with territory. It involves a struggle for foreign policy role, with naval role being central. China is trying to redefine and amplify its foreign policy role. The United States and other members of the central system are trying to assure that this new Chinese foreign policy role is compatible with the interests of other states and legitimate in the eyes of the world community—including, in particular, the other great powers

that have the capacity to dispute outcomes.

"International political legitimacy" involves two components of order maintenance: (a) no great power will use force to challenge the existing configuration of foreign policy roles, and (b) at least one great power will come to the defense of the existing configuration of world order if that order is challenged by aggression. The political legitimacy of transit and resource development in the South China Sea is currently being tested.

4. Never has a government achieved hegemony over the central system of states. Such a situation lacks international political legitimacy and invites defensive force to roll it back. Repeatedly, states have attempted military hegemony, and repeatedly they have been rolled back. The international system is a decentralized (anarchic) nation-state system. Governments have jealously guarded their own security and the decentralized nation-state character of that system since its origins in the late fifteenth century. This is what is at stake in the Asia-Pacific today.

In sum, leadership is not hegemony, and the hegemonic view of foreign policy conduct is false. If the maintenance of world order is perceived as one-sided and decisively self-serving, impinging grossly and negatively on other great powers, the equilibrium of power and role is likely to be upset. Five "world wars" resulted when other governments rolled back an effort to establish hegemony, itself triggered by the trauma of a sudden shift in future expectations. As history shows and power cycle theory argues, the central system is pluralistic and composed of states that seek a rough equilibrium

regarding role and power amid structural change.

POWER CYCLE THEORY AND STATECRAFT

History and the State Power Cycle

Structural change takes place incrementally across long periods of history.[7] The United States' rise on the state power cycle took more than 175 years. Decline in US relative power could involve similarly long intervals.[8] China's rise is taking many decades. Why do we care?

Change on a state's power cycle is always "of the moment" in foreign policy terms, reflecting the state's well-founded expectations for its future security and foreign policy–role attainment. We should care because there are ineluctable shocks and surprises within the "single dynamic" structuring these power cycles and role expectations, and, as history records, states do not easily adjust to these "shifting tides of history." As explained in opening this chapter, power cycle theory is anchored in and speaks to the particulars of state power and foreign policy behavior as they evolve, moment by moment, across long periods of history. Everything is emergent; nothing is deterministic.

From the power cycle perspective, *power* is what government officials and diplomats perceive it to be. Perceptions of power have been shown to be highly correlated with a bundle of indicators of national capability—variables such as GDP, per capita wealth, size of armed forces, military spending, population size, and the capacity for technological innovation—that together facilitate a state's ability to carry out a foreign policy role and, hence, compose the state power cycle. Most importantly, the power cycle is a cycle of "relative" power in a very specific sense. Each state in the central system (or a regional system) possesses a percentage share of overall power in that system at any given time. States in the system "compete" for relative power share, where the "competition for share" depends on the differing levels and rates of absolute growth among the states comprising the system at each moment of time. But there are undercurrents within this structural dynamic that create the "critical shifts" at issue in power cycle theory. To discern history's dynamic, we must understand how historical trends and suddenly shifted trends on the state power cycles impact the expectations and behaviors of statecraft.

Power cycle theory discloses meanings and perceptions embedded in the power cycle trajectory, meanings that capture at once the structures, concerns, and behaviors of international politics experienced at a particular moment of statecraft. As schematically depicted in Figure 1, it establishes the fundamental principles of the "single dynamic" whereby *differences in absolute growth rate* across states in the system *set the power cycles in motion* (via alterations of the systemic average absolute growth rate), creating a particular nonlinear pattern of change on each state's relative power trajectory, which is interpreted as reflecting the "perspective of statecraft"—thereby giving a very specific meaning to the concern that the "tides of history" have changed, a meaning absent from balance-of-power assessment. Competition for power share creates powerful undercurrents that contour structural change via "critical shifts in the trend" of the component state power cycles, so-called critical points.

Each of these critical points matter in an existential sense as the state traverses its cycle as a major power (see Figure 2), creating a crisis of foreign policy expectations:

- A *lower turning point* beginning a state cycle, when the state suddenly

takes off on a trajectory of incremental but ever-accelerating rise in relative power: the state experiences the "birth throes of a major power" as it envisions and strategizes about the possibilities and challenges of its new political future.

- An *inflection point* on the state's rising trajectory, when the state's vigorous accelerating rise in relative power suddenly shifts into a decelerating rise (the curvature changes from concave up to concave down): the state experiences the "trauma of constrained ascendency," realizing for the first time ineluctable limits on its capacity for future power and role enhancement.

- An *upper turning point* ending the state's rise (at its maximum in relative power), when the state suddenly shifts onto a trajectory of incremental but accelerating relative decline: the state experiences the "trauma of expectations foregone" as it is forced to confront not only an abrupt end to its rising expectations but, as well, its future as a declining state.

- An *inflection point* on its declining trajectory, where the state's accelerating decline in relative power suddenly shifts into decelerating decline (the curvature changes from concave down to concave up): the state experiences the "hopes and illusions of the second wind" which encourage an unwarranted strategic exuberance.

- A *lower turning point* at the end of the cycle: the state experiences its "demise as a major power" inducing it to grasp at this last chance to assert its claims before it drops out of the central system.

Each critical point thus corresponds in the state's experience to a time when the tides of history have shifted in the international system.

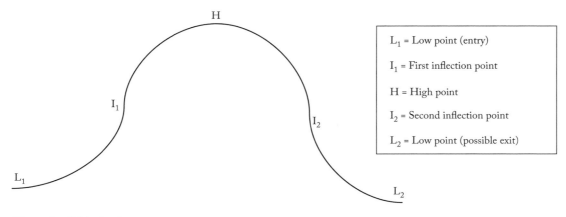

Figure 2. Critical points matter

Legend: Depicts a state's relative power share in the central system across time. Note the lack of symmetry on the rising and declining segments. The amplitude and period varies with state and historical system, as contoured by the single dynamic relating the differential levels and rates of absolute growth at each point in time.

Why is this nonlinear change unanticipated and abrupt? There are conflicting messages and surprises in *relative versus absolute* change; changes in absolute power can egregiously mislead. As the principles of the power cycle explain, and as empirical studies of both individual and aggregate power indicators have shown, even at the moment of a state's greatest achievement in terms of *absolute* power growth, the state can be driven into *relative* decline by the "bounds of the system"—that is, by *competition for power share* from even a much smaller state. The undiminished dynamism of Germany's *absolute* power ascendancy prior to World War I, for example, made some historians believe that the rise of German *relative* power would continue at such elevated rates that Germany was destined to become the "master of Europe." But while contemporaneous statesmen saw ever-greater increases in *absolute* growth for Germany, they also saw an abrupt halt in its prior rapid gain in *relative share.* The German leadership on the eve of the war confronted the trauma of foregone expectations, and subsequent empirical analysis on German coal, steel, and oil production reveals the striking contradiction

between absolute and relative growth that made this abrupt halt in Germany's rise in relative power so shocking.[9]

At least as abrupt and surprising are the contradictions between the state's absolute and relative power growth at the first inflection point, where the rising state first feels the impact of the bounds of the system. According to the principles of the power cycle, a state gains in relative share to the extent that its absolute growth rate is greater than the systemic average. Initially, this growth rate advantage yields accelerating growth. But, as the state continues its accelerating rise, it also increasingly weights the systemic average, so that the state ultimately attains a level of relative power at which its previously increasing growth-rate advantage ends; thereafter, the state increasingly competes against itself for increased share. At that time and level, the state goes through its first inflection point. Even when the absolute-growth-rate differentials throughout the system remain unaltered, the state's rising trajectory abruptly shifts from acceleration to deceleration.

The bounds of the system thus contour a nonlinear rise in relative power wherein the state's future expectations, long improving at an accelerating rate, are abruptly inverted into a decelerating rate. For a major power, this sudden shift creates the trauma of constrained ascendancy, a change that is especially challenging for statecraft in that it is so perversely unexpected and unyielding.[10]

The occurrence of major war may appear random, but when it is examined against this type of structural change, an astonishing regularity emerges—a relationship that persists for a variety of types of structural change (military and economic) and for various measures of major war (intensity, duration, and magnitude). The relationship is particularly strong regarding the critical structural change postulated in power cycle theory.[11] In an atmosphere of high political uncertainty and invitation to belligerence, the probability of war increases sharply following each interval of abrupt, unanticipated, massive structural change known as systems transformation.

The singularity of major war becomes clear. At critical points on the power cycle, a sudden shift in structural trend is sharply identifiable, and the probability of major war surges.[12] At these points, the state will confront a discontinuity in its foreign policy expectations regarding future role and security. Gaps between power and role come to the surface and ricochet through the system, demanding resolution.[13] A discontinuity of expectations is a traumatic challenge to foreign policy conduct. Japan experienced such a shock at its first inflection point in 1935–39, highlighting its perceived problem of access to commodities and natural resources. Unable to accept its suddenly declining rate of power increase, and its commodity restrictions, Japan used force at Pearl Harbor to try to revert to an accelerating trend and to gain access to resources.

In normal periods of history, when change in relative power is essentially linear, statecraft is very much like chess. The number of principal actors in the central system is readily perceived. The relative power of each actor is known or can easily be estimated. Rules of the game of diplomacy are understood and largely adhered to. A concept of balance emerges whose limits are respected. Political stability prevails amid structural change.

But when a principal power passes through a critical point on its power cycle, and especially when several states do so at about the same time (systems transformation), everything changes. The flat chessboard is now twisted and distorted—none of the prior assumptions about statecraft are sustainable. The number of principal actors is not known; the impact of the new relative power trajectories on long-standing foreign policy expectations is impossible to estimate; no one knows whether the prior rules of the game of diplomacy will be observed. Balance arrangements are turned upside down. As Paul Nitze said in the midst of the 1989 systems transformation, "All is uncertainty."[14]

Of the six systems transformations that have occurred since the origins of the modern state system, only the most recent, that occurring in 1989 with the collapse of the Soviet Union, ended peacefully and without loss of security for any of the major states in the system. Rather, the members of the system allowed Germany to become unified, and Russia voluntarily dissociated itself from its most diverse, costly, and troublesome "republics."

In the power cycle conception of world order, major war is a singular event, and it is passage through critical points of radical structural change on state power cycles that creates conditions for major war. More deterrent challenges also occur at these critical points, and more deterrence failures result.[15] Both alliances and deterrence attempt to mitigate the enormous uncertainty that arises as several states pass through critical points on their power cycles in the same interval of history, the circumstance that we call systems transformation. The focused interpretability of the theory, and its underlying plausibility in terms of the practice of statecraft, make the theory easy to assess empirically and lend credence to the highly significant statistical results that reinforce its validity as tested in the past two centuries of historical experience.

Historical Analogy: Wrong Responses to Systems in Crisis

Will the world this century repeat the mistakes of the early twentieth century? This is the coded question implicit in expressions such as "peaceful rise" or "peaceful development." Will a rising China succumb to tactics that lead to major war, as did rising Germany in 1907–14, and declining Germany in 1935–39? Each great power went through a critical point on its power cycle between 1880 and 1914, some more than once. Never had world politics seen so much radical structural change for so many states. This was not just movement up and down the international power hierarchy (so-called power shifts), which is always happening. Rather, for each of these states, this transformation involved a unique, abrupt inversion of its prior trend of relative power change, and hence an inversion of its prior expectations. The tides of history had shifted, taking states along new uncharted trajectories. The system could not absorb the political uncertainty, the gargantuan unpredictable change, and the belligerence. It ruptured in 1914.

World War I was not a contest between a purported hegemon (Britain) and a challenger (Germany); Britain had many challengers, Germany many opponents. Nor was this a preemptive war by Russia, much less by Germany. If, for Germany, Russia was the exclusive target, then how could the

alliance between France and Britain, automatically bringing them into the confrontation, be ignored? A preemptive war that would precipitate crisis with every other major state made no strategic sense. Rather, as Rousseau said of war in general, Europe on the heels of radical systems transformation fell into war because there was nothing to stop it.

War happened because of failures of policy in the long period of Germany's astonishing rise. For decades, the system of older great powers had done nothing to accommodate the rise of Germany with appropriate and legitimate role and status before it was too late, and before Germany's relative power abruptly peaked and turned into decline. The international system had become severely disequilibrated in terms of power and role. Upholders of systemic order—Britain, France, and Austria-Hungary—were frightened by Germany's astonishing growth in power and attempted to halt Germany's ambitions by encircling it. But Germany was an ascendant state whose power could not be constrained, and who would not be denied a place in the sun. From 1880 to 1914, the declining older states—each of whom experienced the "hopes and illusions of the second wind" of the second inflection point that invite strategic overconfidence—refused to adjust and to yield any diplomatic perquisites or foreign policy role to Germany, either among the colonies or within the central system. In 1914, shocked to discover that it had peaked in relative power (notwithstanding its greatest absolute increases ever), Germany experienced the "trauma of expectations foregone" and moved the system into war as the only "solution" to its sense of severe role deprivation.

Prior to World War II, radical structural change again occurred on a monumental scale. Germany went through the second inflection point, where its accelerating decline abruptly began to decelerate, fueling

Hitler's overconfidence. Passing through a first inflection point, where their accelerating rise shifted into deceleration, both Japan and Italy confronted the "trauma of constrained ascendancy" that accentuates perceptions of role deprivation. All this occurred in two short decades, amid the struggle to recover from the ruins of World War I and amid the worst economic depression in modern history. Systems transformation again precipitated world war in 1939.

Unfortunately, the architects of world order in the interwar period once again made huge mistakes. Although Germany had actualized its military power to a very high degree, it was now in abject decline in terms of its latent base of relative power. The Soviet Union and the United States towered over Germany in relative power terms, as Hitler knew and said in his speeches. As a declining state, Germany could make no further claims on the system for a larger systemic role; and Hitler's aggressive intentions were illegitimate and unacceptable. The proper strategic response to an expansionist Germany was opposition and balance. But for reasons of wartime exhaustion, the misapplication of the lessons of Versailles, and isolationism, Britain, France, the Soviet Union, and the United States succeeded only in appeasing Germany. The Nazis, along with Imperial Japan, exploited this global state of malaise.

Lessons and Warnings

China today is not likely to try to roll over its neighbors in a campaign of territorial expansionism, as did Louis XIV's and Napoleon's France; Bismarckian and Wilhelmine and Nazi Germany; and Imperial Japan. But China has not yet had to confront the bounds of the system. Events in the South China Sea and the East China Sea have not led to war because the structural preconditions for war involving China and its neighbors do not yet exist. However, when China passes through its first inflection point, the attitudinal and behavioral preconditions will be established for conflict, both to diffuse across actors and to escalate in terms of magnitude. When systems transformation returns in the twenty-first century, every spark of regional tension could lead to a fire of global proportion. Structural change precipitates a higher probability of war.

DYNAMIC EQUILIBRIUM IN THE CONTEMPORARY CENTRAL SYSTEM

Hegemony (unilateral domination) at the global level is impossible in the twenty-first century (and historically has never occurred in the central system), and thus perhaps world politics will tend toward multipolarity, as a number of analysts have concluded. But because true multipolarity means that a single power is predominant and exclusive in every region, the international system cannot be a genuine multipolar system either.

While a single regional power may prevail in North America (United States) and South America (Brazil), one does not prevail in Europe, where neither Germany nor France nor Britain can dominate alone, and where Russia is both a European and an Asian power. Nor is a single dominant regional power evident in Africa. Asia is the most fragmented region of all, with India and China vying for a role of predominance while Japan and Russia also claim a legitimate role in the Asian system. China will figure strongly in Asian affairs but not as a powerhouse capable of excluding other Asian contenders for leadership roles. The multipolarity characterization fails because most regions cannot claim the existence of a single regional hegemon.

Moreover, for multipolarity to prevail, a single regional power must not only predominate over other regional polities; it must also exclude nonregional states from exercising power within the region. Most governments at the regional level will be unable to do this or will not want to adopt such a role. Finally, true multipolarity fails because some polities (the United States, perhaps China) will exercise a global role. Their reach will extend worldwide, albeit in contention with the reach of predominant actors inside each region. Such a mix of power, with at least two players extending globally, will not conform to the rules of true multipolarity, which associates the power of a single predominant state with each region and with that region alone.

Alternatively, the central system of states might constitute a "classical balance of power" such as characterized the nineteenth century, in which Britain, Russia, France, Austria-Hungary, and Prussia (Germany) were the leading players. In the twenty-first century, the leading actors will be the United States, China, Europe (depending on the success of the European Union), Japan, Russia, and India. The central system will contain an Asia-Pacific focus, with the United States, China, Japan, Russia, and India all more or less competing for foreign policy role within that sphere.

Yet while the balance of power is a valid depiction of interaction in normal intervals of statecraft, when everything is rather predictable and stable, it is not a reliable understanding of strategic demands and responses during intervals of extreme structural change. The balance of power historically was able to preserve the territorial security of most of the leading states, but it failed spectacularly to prevent major war during the Thirty Years' War or the Napoleonic Wars, for example. In such intervals of massive systems transformation, the balance of power proved to be too rigid; its "rules of balance" broke down, and major war resulted.

According to power cycle theory, "political equilibrium" (world order) is mutually and reciprocally constructed by all the members of the central system, albeit disproportionately. The largest members weigh more heavily in decisions. Adjustment is "of the moment," continuous, and incremental. World order is composed of a synchronicity of changing power and foreign policy role. An equilibrium of power and of legitimate foreign policy role within the central system preserves the integrity of the system and the territorial security of each of the members. The largest members—based on key capability indicators such as GDP, per capita wealth, and military spending—can carry out more functions, assume more responsibilities, and influence a larger number of, and more significant, political outcomes.

A concept of "dynamic equilibrium" is thus necessary to guide order maintenance during structural transformation, when violent up-and-down movements on the state power cycles twist and wrench the horizontal chessboard of strategic calculation. What are the characteristics of dynamic equilibrium? The principal characteristic is that the movements of states' rise and decline on their power cycles must fully be taken into account when attempting to deter aggression by governments willing to use force to alter their strategic fate.

Recall that the declining states France and Britain failed to allow Germany a "place in the sun" during the long Wilhelmine period, which would have acknowledged Germany's quest as a rising state for a larger international political role, albeit a role that had to be deemed legitimate by the other great powers. Germany feared encirclement by a tight balance of power. It protested its perceived lack of recognition. When in 1914 the "bounds of the system" abruptly halted Germany's rise (despite its accelerating absolute growth) and pulled it onto a declining trajectory, Germany experienced the "trauma of expectations foregone." World War I resulted.

Exactly the opposite set of strategic responses was necessary for a dynamic equilibrium to work in the face of aggression by Hitler. Germany by then was in abject relative decline, a completely different structural situation. Also, actualizing its power to a very high degree, Nazi Germany threatened other states. The principles of dynamic equilibrium require opposition and balance as the strategy for dealing with Nazi Germany. But by trying to "erase" the mistakes made prior to World War I, the great powers failed to apply the correct strategy of opposition and balance to a declining state that was a potential challenger to world stability in the 1930s.

Dynamic equilibrium requires that the defenders of world order employ the correct strategy, determined by the nature of structural change, to uphold the integrity of that system. The rule-guiding strategy in order maintenance is that rising states cannot be constrained (and declining states cannot be artificially bolstered) *vis-à-vis legitimate role acquisition*. While foreign policy role *cannot be lacking in malleability* in the face of structural change, all foreign policy role *must be determined as legitimate* by each member of the central system.

In the twenty-first century, force is not warranted against a rising China's effort to obtain, without force, a larger foreign policy role that is declared legitimate by its neighbors. A tight balance of power around China will cause it to scream "encirclement," just as did Germany in the interval 1905–14. A larger political role for a rising China is only natural and expected, although that larger role cannot come at the cost of the territorial sovereignty and integrity of its neighbors.

Events in the South China Seas highlight these principles of dynamic equilibrium. In normal intervals of statecraft, the pushing and shoving in the South China Sea for valid claims of sovereignty can be absorbed by the system without violence. Diplomacy and sound sense will prevail. The prudent involvement of the United States can help preserve dynamic equilibrium.

Yet systems transformation will return: the tides of history will abruptly shift, altering expectations throughout the system, and casting all the events in the South China Sea and the East China Sea—involving as well Taiwan, India, Japan, and multiple other actors—in a harsher light. Japan has already peaked on its power cycle. When China passes its first inflection point on its rising cycle, the conditions will be set for highly stressful interaction in which dynamic equilibrium will be severely tested. A passage by the United States through its second inflection point will only exacerbate these tensions.

While China should not be confronted with a tight balance of power, and while its quest for a larger foreign policy role ought to be channeled into constructive pathways, such as upholding World Trade Organization rules and peacekeeping, China must observe the law of the high seas and managed development of seabed resources. China cannot grab all the South China Sea at the cost of its smaller neighbors. Engagement of China must not be confused with appeasement.

The United States will continue to maintain its alliances with Australia, Japan, and South Korea, for example. These are structural anchors of world order in Asia. China may attempt to induce governments such as Cambodia and Laos to bandwagon. But as developmental projects in both countries reveal (projects paid for by local governments and destructive of the physical environments), bandwagoning with China may become a highly unequal and damaging enterprise for a smaller neighbor.

Yet dynamic equilibrium can absorb bandwagoning as well as alliance. Dynamic equilibrium is a constructive response to the inevitable surges and challenges associated with systems transformation. Properly applied, the principles of dynamic equilibrium can assimilate China and India into the larger community of nations without default or major war. Balance alone will not work. Engagement as well as resistance to illegitimate demands for foreign policy role can guide restless governments passing through critical points, whether on the rising or the declining side of their respective power cycles.

Dynamic equilibrium corrects the mistakes of the classical balance of power in a structural environment of massive, abrupt alterations of trajectory at critical points on state power cycles. Dynamic equilibrium is necessary in an era of irremediable and otherwise catastrophic structural change. This chapter rejects the hegemonic, multipolar, and classical balance-of-power models for world order in the twenty-first century in favor of a model of dynamic equilibrium that will enable governments to better manage the tremors of systems transformation.

NOTES

1. Power cycle theory was first articulated in published form in Charles F. Doran, *The Politics of Assimilation: Hegemony and Its Aftermath* (Baltimore, MD: Johns Hopkins University Press, 1971). For a full elaboration, see Charles F. Doran, *Systems in Crisis: New Imperatives of High Politics at Century's End* (Cambridge: Cambridge University Press, 1991); and the special issue "Power Cycle Theory and Global Politics" of the *International Political Science Review* 24, no. 1 (January 2003).

2. Doran, *The Politics of Assimilation*, assesses the three European systems transformations and ensuing wars from the power cycle perspective. Doran, *Systems in Crisis*, examines the two twentieth-century failures of systems transformation as well as the impending systems transformation involving the Soviet Union.

3. Kenneth Organski and Jacek Kugler, *The War Ledger* (Chicago: University of Chicago Press, 1980), expands and applies power transition theory; Robert Gilpin, *War and Change in World Politics*

(Cambridge: Cambridge University Press, 1980), explicates hegemonic stability theory; George Modelski and William Thompson, *Seapower in Global Politics* (Seattle: University of Washington Press, 1988), develops long cycle theory; and Stephen Brooks and William Wohlforth, *World Out of Balance: International Relations and the Challenge of American Primacy* (Princeton, NJ: Princeton University Press, 2008) elaborates a notion of unipolarity.

4. Joseph S. Nye Jr., *Bound to Lead: The Changing Nature of American Power* (New York: Basic Books, 1990), emphasizes the importance of distinguishing between hegemony based on domination and control, and a state carrying out a leadership role. The United States, being more powerful than other nation-states, was more capable of carrying out leadership functions in the system. Zbigniew Brzezinski, *The Choice: Global Domination or Global Leadership* (New York: Basic Books, 2004), explaining that these choices are far different in concept and in their possibility, argues that a failure to understand this reality underscores the policy missteps of the move to "unilateralism" of the early 2000s. The range of responses by actors "balancing" against such unilateralism is excellently represented in the essays in Davis B. Bobrow, ed., *Hegemony Constrained: Evasion, Modification, and Resistance to American Foreign Policy* (Pittsburgh, PA: University of Pittsburgh Press, 2008); see also the review of this volume, Charles F. Doran, "Fooling Oneself: The Mythology of Hegemony," *International Studies Review* 11 (2009): 177–81.

5. An enormous number of empirical studies have been made of these hegemon-challenger theories with varying degrees of support. But as Robert Jervis observed regarding the fundamental claim that hegemony (concentration of power) is necessary for maintaining world order, these theories have been "battered by encounters with evidence." Robert Jervis, "Unipolarity: A Structural Perspective," *World Politics* 61, no. 1 (2009): 188–213, at 193.

6. Charles F. Doran, "Systemic Disequilibrium, Foreign Policy Role, and the Power Cycle: Challenges for Research Design," *Journal of Conflict Resolution* 33, no. 3 (1989): 371–401.

7. This section of the chapter is drawn, with some alteration, from the presentation in Charles

F. Doran, "Power Cycle Theory and the Ascendance of China: Peaceful or Stormy?" *SAIS Review* 32, no. 1 (2012): 73–87.

8. Joseph S. Nye Jr., *The Future of Power* (New York: PublicAffairs, 2011), 187–204.

9. Charles F. Doran, "World War I from the Perspective of Power Cycle Theory: Recognition, 'Adjustment Delusions,' and the 'Trauma of Expectations Foregone," in *The International Politics of Recognition*, ed. Thomas Lindemann and Erik Ringmar (Boulder, CO: Paradigm, 2010).

10. For more on these principles and how they shape the power cycle and affect state behavior, see Doran, *Politics of Assimilation*, 191–94, 210; Doran, *Systems in Crisis*, 4–14, 59–68 (which includes helpful "seeing is believing" computer simulations), 82–89, 260–67 (the mathematical appendix), and the entries marked with an asterisk in the index; and Charles F. Doran, "Economics, Philosophy of History, and the 'Single Dynamic' of Power Cycle Theory: Expectations, Competition, and Statecraft," *International Political Science Review* 24, no. 1 (2003): 13–49, in particular 17–27 and 39–43.

11. Charles F. Doran and Wes Parsons, "War and the Cycle of Relative Power," *American Political Science Review* 74 (1980): 947–65; Lui Hebron and Patrick James, "Great Powers, Cycles of Relative Capability, and Crises in World Politics," *International Interactions* 23 (1997): 145–73; and Jacob Heim, "Tapping the Power of Structural Change: Power Cycle Theory as an Instrument in the Toolbox of National Security Decision-Making," *SAIS Review* 30, no. 2 (2009): 113–27.

12. For a full explication of these concepts see Doran, *Systems in Crisis*.

13. For an examination of the origins of different types of foreign policy roles and their interaction with the power cycle dynamic, see William J. Lahneman, "Changing Power Cycles and Foreign Policy Role–Power Realignments: Asia, Europe, and North America," *International Political Science Review* 24, no. 1 (2003): 97–111.

14. Paul Nitze, in an address at Johns Hopkins University, School of Advanced International Studies, upon his return from a European conference in the fall of 1989. Following detailed commentary on the impact of the Soviet economic reforms, the debt situation, the attitudes of the European allies, and the future course of US foreign policy in the aftermath of containment, he encapsulated the structural situation and its challenges: "All is uncertainty." See Doran, *Systems in Crisis*, 247.

15. Daniel Y. Chiu, "International Alliances in the Power Cycle Theory of State Behavior," *International Political Science Review* 24, no. 1 (2003): 123–36; Brock F. Tessman and Steve Chan, "Power Cycles, Risk Propensity, and Great-Power Deterrence," *Journal of Conflict Resolution* 48, no. 2 (2004): 131–53; and Trita Parsi, *Treacherous Alliance: The Secret Dealings of Israel, Iran and the United States* (New Haven, CT: Yale University Press, 1987).

5

THE CHANGING NORMATIVE ENVIRONMENT FOR CONFLICT MANAGEMENT

Abiodun Williams

There is a striking omission in the indexes to *Managing Global Chaos*, *Turbulent Peace*, and *Leashing the Dogs of War*, the three magisterial predecessors to this volume: none of them include an entry for "norms" or "normative development." The effort to build the norms of collective conflict management is not new and has become increasingly central to strategies to prevent, manage, and resolve violent conflict. These norms continue to evolve in light of new challenges and changes in the strategic global environment—even as theorists and practitioners of conflict management frequently use the terms "norm" and "normative" as though they were self-evident and unproblematic.

Today, the conflict management environment is far more daunting than anyone could have envisaged in the heady days following the end of the Cold War over two decades ago. There is a great range of complex and often interrelated threats to international peace and security, including classic interstate conflicts, civil wars, and intrastate conflicts that continue to erupt with troubling regularity, with an increasing ratio of civilian to military casualties. Complex regional conflicts are intertwined with emerging threats such as terrorism, transnational organized crime, and piracy. The types of warring parties in violent conflicts are more diverse, with non-state actors and criminal networks playing more prominent roles. Governments and the general publics of different countries vary widely in their perceptions of the nature of these threats, their relative importance, and their causes and solutions. In addition, the threats appear against a backdrop of other new challenges, such as climate change and the illegal exploitation of natural resources.

Armed conflicts, and intrastate conflicts in particular, are not a new challenge. However, our understanding of civil wars and similar conflicts has changed in recent years, with a greater appreciation of the interrelationships between the domestic and international, local and regional factors that cause and fuel such conflicts. There is also more awareness of the ways in which global structures and processes, including the proliferation of small arms, the illegal trade and exploitation of natural resources, and the spread of HIV/AIDS, can obstruct transitions to peace.

At the same time, the gradual alignment of interests and ideas among major powers in the post–Cold War era has facilitated the expansion of multilateral conflict management resources and the involvement of peacebuilders in violent conflict.[1] The number and diversity of institutions dedicated to conflict management has increased rapidly, as local and international nongovernmental organizations (NGOs), regional bodies, and international organizations have become increasingly proactive in preventing and resolving deadly conflict. New conflict management instruments are being developed and refined, including international criminal tribunals, satellite-based conflict-mapping tools, and "conflict commodity" certification schemes.

THE VARIOUS MEANINGS OF "NORM"

A norm can be understood in a sociological sense as a reflection of an established or common pattern of behavior, or in an ethical sense as the ideal standard of appropriate behavior. Martha Finnemore defines the term as "observable patterns of behavior for actors which can prescribe future actions."[2] Norms can be seen as either aspirational or effective, attributes that exist at either end of a continuum. Aspirational norms set a goal to which the international community should aspire. They are, as Alex Bellamy puts it, "the guide to institutional reform and behavioral change."[3] Effective norms are established practices of acceptable behavior or standards to which states are widely expected to adhere.

Norms are commonly introduced by so-called norm entrepreneurs, who are invariably well-placed individuals whose prominence enhances their ability to promote norms and prompt change in the international system. These actors also possess strong notions about appropriate standards of behavior. The role they play as catalysts is of paramount importance to understanding how a norm is crafted and how future buy-in from state and non-state actors is bolstered. To facilitate this process, norm entrepreneurs employ "language that names, interprets and dramatizes" new issues.[4] The framing of norms is done in a way that persuades states that any such normative change ultimately serves their interests. Martha Finnemore and Kathryn Sikkink posit that the mission of these agents is to "change the utility functions of other players to reflect some new normative commitment."[5] As their acceptance grows, norms are said to be emerging. Once the international community acknowledges the reality of a norm through debate or action, it moves along the aforementioned continuum from aspirational to effective. Norms become embedded as they approach effectiveness, strengthening through broad rhetorical support and appropriate behavior. Others erode as they slide back toward aspiration—perhaps following the adoption of contrary ideas, abnormal behavior, or normative competition—or sink into irrelevance. Embedded norms may be codified into international law, such as the Geneva Conventions or the United Nations Charter. At this codification stage, norm entrepreneurs have established a critical mass of support and pushed the norm beyond the tipping point.[6]

There is, however, a myriad of factors that engender this proliferation, whereby a strongly desired pattern of behavior evolves into a more universally accepted norm. First, the number of states that endorse the new practices is evidently important, but exactly *which* states choose to affirm those norms will prove to be indispensable. As Finnemore and Sikkink explain, the first stage is led almost entirely by norm entrepreneurs endeavoring to convince international actors to embrace new standards of behavior, while the second phase of a norm cycle is characterized by leading states trying to foster greater support from others. This "norm cascade" is largely a function of

> an active process of international socialization intended to induce norm breakers to become norm followers. . . . In the context of international politics, socialization involves diplomatic praise and censure, either bilateral or multilateral, which is reinforced by material sanctions and incentives.[7]

As such, states that endorse and seek to diffuse new standards rely greatly on resources, leverage, and an organizational platform.[8] These determined and influential actors use their platforms to "launch their crusades" and emphasize the import of a norm.[9]

Norms can constrain conflict managers as they consider both the effectiveness and appropriateness of their options. In setting standards for appropriate or ideal behavior, norms may complicate a decision maker's choice between the normative optimal and more politically expedient or effective alternatives. The decision to conduct an air campaign over Kosovo without Security Council authorization in 1999 reflects the complexity of conflict management issues. The international community may, at times, disregard normal procedures, driven by political considerations or competing norms. Repeated abnormal behavior eventually leads to a corrective response or norm erosion.

The normative environment for conflict management thus is dynamic and can be understood as a constantly evolving balance of related norms.[10] The body of existing norms, and their placement along the continuum between aspirational and effective, form the normative context against which conflict management practices occur. Change in the normative context can be the result of numerous factors. New aspirations articulated by a norm entrepreneur can spur the international community to action, as when former UN secretary-general Kofi Annan in the late 1990s urged UN member states to resolve the tension between the principles of state sovereignty and the international community's responsibility to respond to massive human rights violations, such as genocide and ethnic cleansing.

The normative context for conflict management may also evolve organically, as the nature of a conflict changes. Warring parties may find new avenues for violence, or peacebuilding actors may develop new instruments to manage conflict. In both cases, the group of norms will steer peacebuilders' expected behavior. World events may prompt the international community to question existing norms or lament their absence in aspects of conflict management in dire need of standards or structure. The transnational nature of emerging threats and the role of non-state actors in violent conflicts have spurred the quest for innovative normative responses. The actions of regional institutions or norm entrepreneurs can realign the distribution of norms along the continuum, changing the normative context. The African Union's transition from upholding a norm of nonintervention to embracing a norm of non-indifference, five years after the Rwandan genocide, illustrates how conscience-shocking events can trigger normative and institutional change at the regional level and generate new ideas about the international community's role in conflict management more broadly.

Since the end of World War II, multilateralism has evolved from an experimental practice into an important and multifaceted tool that states use to find solutions to common problems. It has also become a firmly embedded norm in international affairs. In contrast, changes in the conduct of warfare have eroded the inviolability of noncombatants as a long-standing norm. The 1949 Geneva Conventions traditionally protected humanitarian aid workers, including UN officials and NGO representatives, operating in conflict zones. This codified norm effectively shielded civilian noncombatants from attacks by warring parties. However, the killing of Red Cross nurses in Chechnya in 1996 and the 2003 killing of the UN secretary-general's special representative in Iraq, Sergio Vieira de Mello, illustrate the erosion of this norm. The violation of established norms usually causes anxiety within the international system as it undermines expectations and patterns of conduct. If the violators are states, it can result in their punishment or isolation, restraining and limiting conflict.

Dealing with non-state armed actors who violate norms constitutes an even greater challenge given their inherently subversive nature, political aims, and tactics. Yet despite these complexities, the international community has evinced a commitment to upholding principles that govern intra- and interstate warfare. A report published by the United States Institute of Peace highlights the contribution of NGOs, such as the International Committee of the Red Cross and Geneva Call, as norm entrepreneurs in this regard. According to the study,

> [these organizations] use different approaches in dealing with armed actors, but they have the same goal: to persuade rebel groups, militias, tribal chiefs, and other armed actors to accept international norms and change their behavior as well as their internal rules and doctrines accordingly. The international norms involve, for example, the protection of civilians, the ban of certain means of warfare

(such as landmines and child soldiers), and the appropriate treatment of prisoners.[11]

These are not the only cases where the international community has recognized the importance of safeguarding appropriate behavior in conflict settings. While state and non-state actors may contravene the normative frameworks previously discussed, international bodies have been established to rectify and mitigate those egregious practices. The Rome Statute, which established the International Criminal Court, is an example of the international community making a concerted effort to demonstrate accountability and strengthen norm enforcement for state and non-state actors alike through criminal justice.

THE CHANGING NATURE OF STATE SOVEREIGNTY

National sovereignty is one of the most influential norms in the conduct of international relations and the management of violent conflict in particular. For centuries, sovereignty has structured the internal relationship between the ruling regime and its citizens, as well as the external interaction between a sovereign power and other states. In today's evolving peace and security environment, sovereignty plays a dual role: While the legal codification of this effective norm has helped reduce the occurrence of interstate conflict, the principle also constrains the ability of international peacebuilders to counter the potentially destructive role of abusive regimes in civil conflicts.

Hans Morgenthau defined sovereignty as "the supreme legal authority of the nation to give and enforce the law within a certain territory and, in consequence, independence from the authority of any other nation and equality with it under international law."[12] In a similar vein, Hedley Bull noted that sovereignty includes "internal sovereignty, which means supremacy over all other authorities within that territory and population," and "external sovereignty, by which is meant not supremacy but independence of outside authorities. The sovereignty of states, both internal and external, may be said to exist both at a normative level and at a factual level."[13] Thus, in principle, states have equal legal status regardless of differences in their attributes. Sovereignty is both intrinsic to states and a status other rulers recognize.

The Peace of Westphalia in 1648, which ended the Thirty Years' War in Europe, established a system of sovereign entities whose potentates were no longer subservient to an external political authority, be it the Holy Roman Emperor or the pope and the Roman Catholic Church. It also established the basic principles of the modern state system: the territorial inviolability of the state, its authority to rule its own citizens, its monopoly over the control of the means of force within its borders, its right to negotiate treaties and conduct foreign relations with other states, and its freedom from interference. The sovereignty norm encapsulated these legal rights and responsibilities while asserting the primacy of states and independence from outside authority. Over time, the principles underlying national sovereignty became codified in international law, making sovereignty the most embedded of the conflict management norms discussed in this chapter.

National sovereignty as an international norm remains a powerful deterrent to interstate conflict. It is a protective shield against the domination of weaker states by more powerful states. The first principle of the United Nations is the sovereign equality of all its members.[14] However, this refers to juridical equality; in practice, some states are more equal than others, as reflected in the Security Council, in which the great powers at the time of the United Nations' creation have permanent membership. Another fun-

damental principle enshrined in the UN Charter is the requirement that all members "shall refrain in their international relations from the threat or use of force against the territorial integrity or political independence of any state."[15] A third principle is nonintervention; the charter forbids the United Nations from "interven[ing] in matters which are essentially within the domestic jurisdiction of any state."[16] Breach of sovereignty remains one of the gravest violations of the international order. As Michael Walzer pointed out, the defense of Kuwait's sovereignty, its "political survival," was the cardinal moral argument justifying the 1991 Gulf War.[17] But the prohibition against intervention can be set aside if the Security Council determines that a matter threatens international peace and security and decides to apply enforcement measures under Chapter VII.

Sovereignty also allows a regime to manage internal conflict, including through the legitimate use of force. Conversely, sovereignty restricts the menu of options for international peacebuilders keen to mitigate the effects of intrastate conflict and protect civilians threatened by repressive regimes. The external application of both coercive instruments and humanitarian assistance in intrastate wars requires the consent of the host regime, a likely primary actor in any civil conflict. Would-be interveners usually encounter the roadblock of national sovereignty, allowing grave human rights abuses to occur without effective action to prevent or stop them.

Nevertheless, growing concern about human rights atrocities such as genocide, mass killing, ethnic cleansing, rape, and torture is redefining the meaning of sovereignty. Two decades ago, in an address at the University of Bordeaux, then–UN secretary-general Javier Pérez de Cuéllar urged reflection on the relation between the principle of sovereignty and concern for human rights. He said,

"Has not a balance been established between the rights of states, as confirmed by the Charter, and the rights of the individual, as confirmed by the Universal Declaration? We are clearly witnessing what is probably an irresistible shift in public attitudes towards the belief that the defense of the oppressed in the name of morality should prevail over frontiers and legal documents."[18] And, as Alex Bellamy points out, "sovereignty has almost always entailed responsibilities in one form or another. What changes is not the connection between sovereignty and responsibility, but the scope of the relevant responsibilities."[19] The understanding that sovereign regimes have an obligation to protect their people from grave human rights abuses, whether committed by insiders or outsiders, is taking hold, challenging the principles of nonintervention, territorial integrity, and a state's monopoly on the legitimate use of force.

Since the mid-1990s, the meaning of sovereignty has also been redefined by the United Nations' role as a transitional administrator in Kosovo, Eastern Slavonia, and Timor-Leste, all places where it explicitly assumed many of the duties and responsibilities of a sovereign authority. In the Eastern Slavonia region of Croatia, the mandate of the United Nations Transitional Authority in Eastern Slavonia (UNTAES) was reintegration of the breakaway province in a short time frame. Although the mission sought to promote an atmosphere of confidence among all ethnic groups of the local population, it was not obliged to seek full public consent in pursuit of its goal of reintegration. Not surprisingly, as the United Nations is an intergovernmental organization of sovereign states, it has carried out this role with a certain ambivalence. Indeed, the appellation of "transitional administrator" underlines the temporary and limited nature of the UN role and reflects member states' reluctance; many of them are not eager to see the Security Council involved in sensitive issues of internal governance.

The meaning of sovereignty continues to evolve and be shaped by new principles, but the norm is by no means disappearing. The age of nations is not yet over, and the forces of the new millennium have not toppled the norm. States both large and small have a vested interest in the continuation of unconditional national sovereignty. However, the demands of peoples and the imperatives of a globalized world will continue to catalyze debates about more visionary and humane conceptions of sovereignty.

CIVILIAN PROTECTION NORMS

The advent of total war in the early twentieth century forced the international political elite to reevaluate their ability to respond to crises and their understanding of international conflict dynamics. The immense suffering of innocent civilians as a recent trend in violent conflict reinvigorates doubts over the international system's ability to reach its goal of "sav[ing] succeeding generations from the scourge of war . . . [and] reaffirm[ing] faith in fundamental human rights."[20] Actors in armed conflict do not invariably protect civilians from harm; in some cases, civilians are targeted specifically for tactical purposes.

Whereas norms of protection have featured in UN peacebuilding doctrine only recently, multiple humanitarian organizations, most notably the International Committee of the Red Cross, have long been mandated to ensure civilian protection in the field. That is not to say that the United Nations and other organizations have remained idle in response to the human security concerns of their constituents. The earliest documents directed toward the human toll of war include the first two Geneva Conventions, agreed in 1864 and 1906. The conventions and their additional protocols reflect the evolving humanitarian concern for civilian protection in war. However, while the community of states largely agreed to abide by the proper standards of interstate engagement, the international legal framework remains inadequate to address new forms of conflict, in which civilians are increasingly targeted within state borders, resulting in fierce discussions concerning the relation between state responsibility and national sovereignty. The remainder of this section will introduce two norms—the responsibility to protect and the protection of civilians—that jointly constitute the normative foundation for civilian protection.

The Normative Development of the Responsibility to Protect

The growing global constituency to prevent mass killing is a defining normative development in today's conflict management environment. Neighboring countries, regional hegemons, and intergovernmental organizations have traditionally lacked the legal framework and political will to formulate an adequate response to large-scale atrocities, from the Armenian massacres by the Ottomans to the killing fields in Cambodia. Throughout the twentieth century, an international community under construction often ignored man-made human suffering in desolate countries of little strategic interest. Humanitarian considerations did not appear prominently in states' decision-making calculations until the 1990s, as the human security paradigm took hold and the world witnessed the slaughter of millions of civilians in Rwanda and the western Balkans. The end of the Cold War superpower rivalry did not bring about the end of history,[21] but the proliferation of genocide, ethnic cleansing, and other types of mass violence committed within the borders of sovereign states. These heinous acts raised the question of whether the international community had a right to intervene militarily in cases of mass suffering. Today, the ability of political elites to ignore mass slaughter is no longer an option, as the combination of instant-access media and established preventive practices has cast indifference in a very pale light. The capstone achievement of these confluent forces is the emerging norm of the responsibility to protect, or R2P.

The normative emergence of R2P illustrates the general direction the world aspires to take toward preventing mass atrocities. In his Millennium Report in 2000, former UN secretary-general Kofi Annan questioned the perceived incompatibility between national sovereignty as enshrined in the UN Charter and the protection of civilians from gross human rights abuses through humanitarian intervention.[22] The International Commission on Intervention and State Sovereignty (ICISS) laid the groundwork to overcome this conundrum by shifting the debate from a "right to intervene" to a "responsibility" of both sovereign states and the international community "to protect" civilians through prevention, reaction, and rebuilding efforts.[23] Following arduous political deliberations, heads of state and government adopted the responsibility to protect at the 2005 World Summit. The outcome document established the three pillars of R2P:

1. Each individual State has the responsibility to protect its populations from genocide, war crimes, ethnic cleansing and crimes against humanity.
2. The international community should . . . encourage and help States to exercise this responsibility.
3. The international community, through the United Nations, also has the responsibility . . . to take collective action should peaceful means be inadequate and national authorities manifestly fail to protect their populations.[24]

More than a decade after the ICISS report, R2P serves as a political alarm bell, bolstering the will of the international community to urgently consider all available means in cases of imminent or ongoing mass atrocities. It remains unclear whether R2P is a new normative framework or a reincarnation of past norms that never fully embedded themselves. Clarifying this matter may reveal whether the norm can be strengthened further, or whether atrocity prevention efforts have fallen into the trap of eternal aspiration. R2P does not create new law; rather, it reminds all sovereign nations to abide by existing principles concerning the protection of civilians under international humanitarian law. Case-specific references to R2P by senior UN officials, regional organizations, national governments, and civil society organizations have become more frequent in recent years. Since 2005, the principle has been invoked about ten times in response to crisis situations. Yet the norm remains in its aspirational stages, as its invocation to prevent atrocities is disturbingly inconsistent. R2P was instrumental in driving Security Council initiatives in Côte d'Ivoire and Libya, but remains absent in discussions about Somalia and the Democratic Republic of the Congo (DRC).

As an aspirational political practice, R2P faces conceptual, operational, and political challenges. On the conceptual level, the underlying principles of the responsibility to protect remain in flux. While the broad parameters are firmly set, disagreements persist on the legal significance of the term "ethnic cleansing," one of the four R2P crimes; the comprehensiveness of the responsibility to prevent; and the thresholds for the use of force. Brazilian president Dilma Rousseff contributed to the conceptual debate at the UN General Assembly in September 2011, when she emphasized the international community's responsibility while protecting (RwP). Brazil's norm entrepreneurship with the RwP initiative "was aimed at promoting or clarifying, but not at detracting from, changing or substituting R2P."[25] To shape the debate on the use of humanitarian force and the R2P principle after Libya, Brazil repackaged the do-no-harm principle, urging for strict limitations on the use of military coercion and mechanisms to avoid the misuse of R2P. The concept note sent to the United Nations outlining this new standard insisted that R2P and RwP ought to "evolve together, based on an agreed set of fundamental principles, parameters and procedures."[26] Yet critics argue that the norms reveal competing imperatives: R2P, they argue, is largely predicated on a determination to use whatever means are available to thwart the commission of heinous crimes, whereas RwP demands that military force be used as a last resort and enumerates far more requirements for the international community to appropriately engage in humanitarian interventions. "While R2P emphasizes the limits of state sovereignty, RwP reimposes limits on the international community's ability to override sovereignty in order to protect populations."[27] But the gap between R2P and RwP is not insurmountable, and they both have the same fundamental objective: the prevention of genocide and mass atrocities. Although raising numerous concerns, the RwP initiative is, all things considered, a constructive proposal that largely complements existing agreements and could help bridge the deep divide between advocates and opponents that obstructs a normative convergence on R2P. Apart from the consideration of RwP, operational debates have gradually replaced conceptual discussions at the United Nations. The question is no longer what the new acronym entails, but how it can be implemented. The responsibility to prevent serves as "the single most important dimension of the responsibility to protect"[28] and enjoys the broadest support among member states.

Translating the growing normative support for atrocity prevention into functioning institutions and effective policy presents a second daunting challenge. Many operational questions—who needs to act, when, how, and under what circumstances—have yet to find concrete answers. The practice of R2P still proceeds in an ad hoc fashion, as different atrocities require customized responses. The analytical search for the structural drivers or early warning signs of mass atrocities remains inconclusive, while many questions linger about the appropriate measures to effectively prevent atrocities in a given context. Experience with conflict management activities and previous R2P operations provide general lessons about the utility of traditional peacebuilding tools in atrocity situations. Effective R2P action requires accurate analysis and early warning, long-term structural engagement, and direct or operational measures for crisis prevention, response, and mitigation. Two traditional conflict management tools have proven to be particularly apt in certain contexts for enhancing operational efforts vis-à-vis prevention and response: political missions and preventive deployments. Both types of undertakings have been carried out in areas threatened by actual and imminent atrocity, and arguably have mitigated the risk or effects of such violent crimes. Through persuasion and deterrence, these two approaches could contribute to the prevention of mass atrocities by dissuading "potential perpetrators to refrain from atrocity planning and embrace nonviolent options to achieve strategic objectives."[29] In some cases, particularly when a government is targeting its own people under the cover of power patrons, the missing ingredient may not be political will, but rather our ability to respond effectively with the tools at our disposal and within the limits of the international legal framework. These two models constitute only a few of the many instruments in the toolbox available to buttress those national capacities. Yet a note of caution: the central operational challenge remains the lack of training, doctrine, and planning to prevent atrocities through civilian or military means, at both the national and international level.

The uneven political support for R2P's application in concrete cases presents a third persisting challenge. R2P remains the focus of heated deliberation between rejectionists and advocates[30] at the UN General Assembly and Security Council, revealing the fragility of this emerging norm. While there is widespread agreement on the need to prevent atrocities through peaceful means, a handful of member states continue to oppose the norm's invocation and implementation. Opponents are particularly wary of the potential threat R2P may pose to national sovereignty and question the utility of military force to protect civilians. The differing levels of normative support for R2P have caused inconsistencies in its practical application. A notable contrast in this regard is the decision to robustly intervene in Libya while remaining idle in the face of ongoing atrocities in Sri Lanka or Syria.

Despite the challenges, R2P plays a significant role in today's conflict management environment. The proliferation of early warning systems, the creation of a network of senior R2P focal points at the national level, and, most recently, the establishment of an interagency Atrocity Prevention Board within the US government illustrate the momentum of the global atrocity prevention agenda. State sovereignty no longer serves as a license to kill. Comparing the attitudes of the international community toward the conflicts in Kosovo and Syria illustrates a larger node of progress. In reacting to Kosovo, the pro-intervention side was on the defensive, struggling to make its case to the larger opposition. With Syria, the dynamics have reversed: even though the perceived options for effective action are limited and the world continues to stand by, those advocating for intervention on the grounds of R2P have put the nonintervention side on the defense.

Amid attempts to alter the conflict management context and transform R2P into an effective norm, opponents fear that the principle may increasingly cause competition with the norm of sovereignty. However, as the previous section indicates, this assumption applies an outdated interpretation of the sovereignty norm. R2P stipulates that if a state does not exercise its sovereign responsibilities and manifestly fails to protect its citizens, the responsibility is transferred to the international community.[31] States referred to as "manifestly failing" under this provision fall into two categories. States unable to fulfill their duties in protecting their civilians almost always request help when needed. Unwilling states—often those authorities directly or indirectly involved in the violations occurring—represent the true obstacle to R2P effectiveness. R2P poses a visible threat only to this core group of states, which upholds an absolutist interpretation of national sovereignty.

The Normative Development of the Protection of Civilians

Recent trends in armed conflict—namely the persistent lack of respect for international humanitarian law, and the increased targeting and suffering of innocent bystanders— triggered the normative emergence of the protection of civilians in the late 1990s. In little over a decade, the principle became deeply embedded in UN operations, aiming to "obtain full respect for the rights of all individuals in accordance with international law . . . regardless of their age, gender, social ethnic, national, religious, or other background."[32] In 1999, the UN Security Council first expressed its "willingness to

respond to situations of armed conflict where civilians are being targeted" by taking "appropriate measures."[33] Shortly after, the United Nations Mission in Sierra Leone (UNAMSIL) became the first peacekeeping operation explicitly mandated to protect civilians following a number of protection failures in post–Cold War interventions. Protecting civilians has since become an integral part of most UN peacekeeping operations, mitigating human suffering in South Sudan, Côte d'Ivoire, and other volatile conflict zones. Despite the efforts by the UN Department of Peacekeeping Operations (DPKO) to develop a conceptual framework for civilian protection, a comprehensive doctrine or toolkit for implementing UN protection activities remains an important lacuna.

The protection of civilians refers to any measure taken by states, non-state actors, and intergovernmental organizations in times of armed conflict to protect civilians from immediate physical threats and guarantee human rights. Operationally, this practice encompasses both coercive and peaceful measures taken during the resolution phase of the conflict cycle: the provision of medical assistance, food, and housing; human rights training for security forces; the enforcement of rules of engagement; and the resort to transitional justice mechanisms. International protection efforts may reduce the risk to civilians by targeting potential perpetrators or empowering local communities. Yet external actors' abilities to provide protection remain constrained in the direst humanitarian situations, when they are unable to access the civilians most in need. Because the access of humanitarian actors depends on their perceived impartiality and the host state's consent, their effectiveness remains limited when the host regime itself is primarily responsible for the insecurity. The bilateral or multilateral use of military tools to protect civilians may further complicate the ability of humanitarian NGOs to operate in conflict zones, as recently illustrated in Libya, where the UN Security Council unanimously authorized "all necessary measures . . . to protect civilians and civilian populated areas under threat."[34] Several humanitarian NGOs, including Doctors Without Borders, lamented the references to the protection of civilians and the responsibility to protect to justify the NATO air campaign, as it hampered the perceived impartiality of the NGOs' activities based on the same stated humanitarian principles.

The protection of civilians strongly overlaps with R2P; both are grounded in the same humanitarian objectives and legal principles. Like R2P, the protection of civilians stresses the primary role of the state and warring parties to ensure civilian protection, and recognizes the necessity of military force in exceptional cases. Despite these similarities, there are important conceptual and procedural distinctions between the two norms. The focus of the protection of civilians is broader than R2P in that it adopts a much lower threshold, extending the protection of civilians beyond the four R2P crimes (genocide, war crimes, ethnic cleansing, and crimes against humanity). R2P develops responsibilities for states and the international community in times of both peace and ongoing conflict, whereas the protection of civilians is restricted to the latter category. While R2P has been discussed thematically within the General Assembly only since 2009, the protection of civilians has featured on the Security Council agenda since 1999. It appears the protection of civilians is more firmly embedded as an international norm. One could only question the significance of this comparison given the continued large-scale suffering of civilians worldwide.

MAKING CONFLICT PREVENTION A NORM

It is widely acknowledged that preventing violent conflicts is preferable to taking action to resolve them after they have erupted. Prevention saves lives and is cheaper than reaction and rebuilding. In 1945, the victors of World War II established the United Nations in an effort to find a better way to prevent deadly conflict. In marked contrast to peacekeeping, the founders explicitly embedded conflict prevention in the UN Charter. According to Article 1(1), the first purpose of the United Nations is "to maintain international peace and security, and to that end: to take effective collective measures for the prevention and removal of threats to the peace." Chapter VI of the charter contains an array of options to settle disputes by peaceful means.[35] During the Cold War, the United Nations' use of preventive diplomacy, peacekeeping operations, and peaceful methods to settle disputes were aimed at preventing disputes from escalating into armed conflicts and local wars from sparking a global war between the United States and the Soviet Union.[36]

In the aftermath of the Cold War, the Security Council invited UN secretary-general Boutros Boutros-Ghali to prepare a report on "the capacity of the United Nations for preventive diplomacy, for peacemaking and for peace-keeping."[37] In his 1992 report "An Agenda for Peace," Boutros-Ghali declared that "the most desirable and efficient employment of diplomacy is to ease tensions before they result in conflict—or, if conflict breaks out, to act swiftly to contain it and resolve its underlying causes."[38] He suggested that "preventive diplomacy requires measures to create confidence; it needs early warning based on information gathering and informal or formal fact-finding; it may also involve preventive deployment and, in some situations, demilitarized zones."[39]

Five years later, in 1997, an influential report by the Carnegie Commission on Preventing Deadly Conflict gave new impetus to the idea of prevention. The report, *Preventing Deadly Conflict*, distinguished two broad categories of strategies for prevention: operational prevention, meaning measures applicable in the face of immediate crisis, such as preventive diplomacy, economic sanctions, and preventive deployment; and structural prevention, meaning measures to address the root causes of conflict and to build the long-term conditions for sustainable peace. Structural prevention comprises two general types of strategies: the development by governments of international regimes to promote cooperation among states, and the efforts of governments to ensure security, justice, and well-being for their citizens.[40]

In his role as a norm entrepreneur, Kofi Annan emphasized the normative importance of conflict prevention during his tenure as UN secretary-general and was widely identified with the prevention agenda. In his 1999 report "Facing the Humanitarian Challenge: Towards a Culture of Prevention," Annan asserted that "for the United Nations, there is no higher goal, no deeper commitment and no greater ambition than preventing armed conflict."[41] In his 2001 report "Prevention of Armed Conflict," the secretary-general stressed that "the imperative for effective conflict prevention goes beyond creating a culture, establishing mechanisms or summoning political will. The United Nations also has a moral responsibility to ensure that genocides such as that perpetrated in Rwanda are prevented from ever happening again."[42] Annan's allusion to genocide was a reminder that genocide and mass atrocities invariably occur in the context of war, and, consequently, preventing armed conflict must be a part of

genocide prevention strategies. The report argued that the primary responsibility for conflict prevention rests with national governments, with civil society playing an important role. The United Nations and the international community should support national efforts for conflict prevention and assist in building national capacity in this field.

The moral imperative to reduce the risk and prevalence of war was also a central theme in Annan's 2005 report "In Larger Freedom," whose title, taken from the UN Charter, encapsulates the report's vision of development, security, and human rights as equal and mutually interdependent parts of a seamless whole. The outgoing secretary-general emphasized that

> no task is more fundamental to the United Nations than the prevention and resolution of deadly conflict. Prevention, in particular, must be central to all our efforts, from combating poverty and promoting sustainable development; through strengthening national capacities to manage conflict, promoting democracy and the rule of law, and curbing the flow of small arms and light weapons; to directing preventive operational activities, such as the use of good offices, Security Council missions and preventive deployments.[43]

Annan's successor, Secretary-General Ban Ki-moon, has called conflict prevention "the best guarantee of global security."[44] He has urged reinvigorating preventive diplomacy, and in 2011 issued the first UN report on using preventive diplomacy to resolve tensions and crises before they escalate.[45]

In recent years, the Security Council and General Assembly also have given increasing importance to the prevention of conflict, especially civil war, and the need to give serious attention to its root causes. In August 2001, the Security Council adopted a resolution on Annan's conflict prevention report—the first of its kind on the subject—

without dissent.[46] In July 2010, under Nigeria's presidency, the council held a thematic debate on preventive diplomacy and issued a presidential statement.[47] Another presidential statement on prevention followed in September 2010 during Turkey's presidency.[48] In 2003, the General Assembly called to strengthen the United Nations' capacity to carry out more effectively its responsibilities for preventing armed conflict.[49] And in the 2005 World Summit Outcome, all heads of state and government unanimously declared:

> We stress the importance of prevention of armed conflict in accordance with the purposes and principles of the Charter and solemnly renew our commitment to promote a culture of prevention of armed conflict as a means of effectively addressing the interconnected security and development challenges faced by peoples throughout the world, as well as to strengthen the capacity of the United Nations for the prevention of armed conflict.[50]

The normative justification for conflict prevention has not been restricted to the United Nations. Several regional organizations, powerful and not-so-powerful governments, and civil society organizations have made official policy statements about their commitment to conflict prevention.[51]

In the two decades since Boutros-Ghali authored "An Agenda for Peace," increasingly more experience has been gained in preventing conflict in regional flashpoints and vulnerable areas, such as Macedonia, and Kenya. The UN Preventive Deployment Force (UNPREDEP) deployed in Macedonia from 1992 to 1999 was an unprecedented and successful mission, helping to deter the external and internal threats to the country and to preserve its stability.[52] Following the outbreak of post-electoral violence in Kenya in 2007, the African Union and its Panel of Eminent African Personalities, headed by

former secretary-general Kofi Annan, with UN support, played a vital role in restoring peace.

Key challenges impede the further embedding of prevention as an international norm. The most important is that where conflict prevention works, the result—absence of conflict—is often invisible. In addition, national decision makers often operate in two- to four-year cycles, while comprehensive prevention strategies require long-term commitments. Leaders of countries in need of preventive action are often hesitant to admit a problem is present. Despite these challenges, which are daunting but hardly insurmountable, a global norm of prevention is slowly but surely edging its way toward acceptance and effectiveness. There is a growing consensus that if deadly conflict is not inevitable and successful prevention is possible, international actors have a moral obligation to do whatever they can to resolve disputes before they become violent, to reverse the spread or escalation of deadly conflict, and to prevent the recurrence of violence in postconflict societies.

A NEW ERA OF ACCOUNTABILITY

The post–Cold War period offered a nurturing climate for the role of accountability as a norm in conflict management. Increased attention to the rule of law as a prerequisite for sustainable peace and postconflict reconciliation enhanced the application of transitional justice mechanisms in societies awakening from conflict. Ad hoc criminal tribunals were established in the former Yugoslavia and Rwanda in an effort to hold perpetrators accountable for the war crimes committed against civilians. Since the entry into force of the Rome Statute of the International Criminal Court (ICC) in 2002, a standing legal body can prosecute individuals accused of war crimes, crimes against humanity, genocide, and crimes of aggression for the first time in history. The creation of the ICC demonstrates the international community's determination to "put an end to impunity for the perpetrators of these crimes and thus to contribute to the prevention of such crimes."[53] Together with the International Court of Justice (ICJ), the primary judicial organ of the United Nations, adjudicating disputes between states since its creation in 1945, the ICC provides a solid permanent institutional framework for international justice. As UN secretary-general Ban Ki-moon stated at the General Assembly in January 2012, "We have entered a new age of accountability."[54]

Though commonly applied in the peace and security domain, the term "accountability" allows for various interpretations. *Political accountability* refers to the responsibility that heads of state and politicians carry toward their constituencies. *Financial accountability* includes the responsibility of aid recipients toward their donors for transparency and auditing purposes. This section focuses on *criminal accountability* as reflected in domestic and international rules, procedures, and institutions that reckon with war crimes and other abuses committed during violent conflict. Transitional justice mechanisms are key vehicles to criminal accountability, as they may introduce a sense of closure and justice while addressing grievances in countries emerging from conflict.[55]

Despite the widespread acknowledgement of legal principles concerning lawful engagement in warfare (*jus ad bellum*) and acceptable conduct in wartime (*jus in bello*), the consideration of punishment for perpetrators of war crimes is a historically recent phenomenon. International criminal accountability was first introduced during the Nuremburg and Tokyo tribunals following World War II. Norm entrepreneurs since have continued to institutionalize and codify criminal accountability, embedding the

norm much further than prevention or protection norms. Numerous attempts to pursue criminal accountability have triggered a cascading effect for the norm; regional courts, the Special Court for Sierra Leone, and other hybrid international-national tribunals in Cambodia and Bosnia have emerged as conflict management tools just in the past twenty years. At Nuremberg, war crimes and crimes against humanity were generally understood in international law as engendering liability only when perpetrated during battles between states. Today's transitional justice mechanisms, including the international criminal tribunals and the ICC, uphold jurisdiction over mass atrocities even when committed in conflicts "not of an international character."[56]

While the application of international justice mechanisms expands, justice and accountability is still preferably achieved at the national level through an independent judiciary, providing legitimacy to formal state institutions or even tribal, religious, or other customary systems of justice. Indeed, one of the key challenges for the ICC is determining how best to apply the principle of complementarity, deferring to local justice processes where they are legitimate and fair. As Gareth Evans states, "in some contexts traditional justice may be a viable complement, or alternative, to conventional state-administered justice systems, given that establishing conventional forms of governance in post-conflict settings, or in countries where states are fragile, is complex and time consuming."[57] Often domestic justice systems lack the capacity or the perceived impartiality to provide accountability in a postconflict society, particularly if the crimes are beyond atrocious in scale and intensity, and particularly where those crimes were perpetrated by members of one ethnic or religious group against another and the postconflict courts and government are dominated by one of those groups. In those instances, regional or international justice mechanisms may be indispensable complements.

Despite the rapid codification of accountability as a norm, huge gaps persist. Most notable is an absence of supranational authority, particularly to bring great-power victors to justice. An indicted Omar al-Bashir has not been handed over by Sudan, and jurisprudence is shaken as the United States refuses to accept ICC authority. A common consideration in the search for criminal accountability includes the scope of guilt attributed. Prosecutors can either target those leaders "who bear the greatest responsibility for serious violations of international humanitarian law,"[58] as in the case of the Special Court for Sierra Leone, or target the far broader range of perpetrators involved in the actual conduct of genocide, as in Rwanda. A minority claim is that a public review of wartime atrocities is not even desirable, as it enflames passions rather than calming them down.[59] In this view, forgiveness of all actors through silent or formal amnesty is the preferred road to a peaceful postconflict society.

Despite setbacks, however, international efforts to create a functioning international justice system have recently passed a number of historic milestones. Thomas Lubanga, founder of the Union of Congolese Patriots in the DRC, became the first person convicted by the ICC in March of 2012. One month later, Charles Taylor, former president of Liberia, was found guilty of war crimes by the Special Court for Sierra Leone. Even with these significant advances, the road toward an effective international justice system remains long. Though the principle of sovereign impunity is definitely no longer in effect, the work toward criminal accountability for actors in conflict persists.

CONCLUSION

Norms guide conflict management, reflecting aspirations for behavior and also constraining conflict managers as they consider their options. Conflict management norms remain in flux given the evolving nature of violent conflict, the rise of humanitarian concerns, and the continued search for effective and appropriate ways to manage violent conflict. As a result of this dynamism, norms may compete, overlap, strengthen, or even evaporate. But shaped by the path its constitutive norms have set forth, conflict management is advancing steadily in the international environment toward acceptance as practice.[60]

While conflict management practice is increasingly guided by nascent norms, several aspects remain in dire need of standards and structure. A significant lacuna for the peacebuilding community is determining the appropriate intervening actor, particularly when coercive measures are required. Despite its primary responsibility for maintaining international peace and security, the Security Council at times fails to perform its core task, given its outdated and inefficient decision-making structure. The modern era birthed by the Cold War's end proved fertile ground for the creation of alternative peacebuilding actors, both inside and outside the state apparatus. While regional organizations and humanitarian NGOs increasingly complement the work of the United Nations, a disconnect between the firmly established necessity for action and the less-congealed cast of actors has prevented strong, unified action, from Rwanda through Syria. The growing pool of conflict management actors requires task division and a systematized response mechanism guiding international mandates and field operations. The existing peacebuilding norms also struggle to counter the destabilizing role that non-state actors play in violent conflict. Insurgents, guerilla movements, and paramilitary organizations often fall outside the remit of international normative regulations given the state-centric international law paradigm.[61]

Since the Cold War, international involvement in violent conflict has expanded, and the most embedded of all conflict management norms—national sovereignty—has been perceived to give ground to the nascent norms of protection, prevention, and accountability. States at the receiving end of international interventions may welcome external support in managing conflicts they were unable to resolve internally. Governments applying repressive tactics to maintain stability or control, however, fear national sovereignty is no longer a shield of impunity. Although the underlying principles may compete to some extent, the norms that constitute the framework for conflict management interact and jointly evolve while protecting the interests of all stakeholders involved. Kofi Annan recognized this transformation: "State sovereignty," he argued, "in its most basic sense, is being redefined—not least by the forces of globalisation and international co-operation. States are now widely understood to be instruments at the service of their peoples, and not vice versa."[62]

The normative context for conflict management reflects a new understanding of the role international organizations, non-state actors, peacebuilders, and humanitarians play in mitigating the negative effects of war. Peacebuilders should derive encouragement from recent UN action emphasizing partnerships "in the area of conflict prevention, resolution and management"[63] as they strive toward making war a thing of the past. The dominance of intrastate conflict, the increased accusations of moral indifference for inaction, and the acknowledged self-interest of states to resolve conflict multilaterally will continue to shape the contemporary normative framework for peacebuilding. International efforts to protect civilians, act early to prevent violent conflict, and hold perpetrators accountable will lead to new institutions, laws, and practice, allowing our aspirations to become reality over time.

NOTES

1. Gilles Andréani, "Global Conflict Management and the Pursuit of Peace," in *Rewiring Regional Security in a Fragmented World*, ed. Chester A. Crocker, Fen Osler Hampson, and Pamela Aall (Washington, DC: United States Institute of Peace Press, 2011), 26.

2. Martha Finnemore, "Constructing Norms of Humanitarian Intervention," in *Conflict after the Cold War: Arguments on Causes of War and Peace*, 4th ed., ed. Richard K. Betts (Boston: Pearson, 2012), 263–64.

3. Alex J. Bellamy, *Responsibility to Protect: The Global Effort to End Mass Atrocities* (Cambridge, England: Polity Press, 2009), 6.

4. Martha Finnemore and Kathryn Sikkink, "International Norm Dynamics and Political Change," *International Organization* 52, no. 4 (1998): 897.

5. Ibid., 914.

6. Finnemore and Sikkink, "International Norm Dynamics."

7. Ibid., 102.

8. Ibid.

9. Ramesh Thakur, *The United Nations, Peace and Security: From Collective Security to the Responsibility to Protect* (New York: Cambridge University Press, 2006), 13.

10. Quoted in Thakur, *United Nations, Peace and Security*, 15.

11. Claudia Hofmann and Ulrich Schneckener, "NGOs and Nonstate Armed Actors: Improving Compliance with International Norms," Special Report no. 284 (United States Institute of Peace, Washington, DC, July 2011), 2.

12. Hans J. Morgenthau, *Politics among Nations: The Struggle for Power and Peace*, 5th ed. (New York: Knopf, 1978), 321.

13. Hedley Bull, *The Anarchical Society: A Study of Order in World Politics* (London: Macmillan, 1977), 8.

14. See Charter of the United Nations, Article 2(1).

15. Ibid., Article 2(4).

16. Ibid., Article 2(7).

17. Michael Walzer, "A Just War?" in *The Gulf War Reader*, ed. Micah L. Sifry and Christopher Cerf (New York: Times Books, 1991), 302–6

18. UN Secretary-General Javier Pérez de Cuéllar, address delivered at the University of Bordeaux (UN press release SG/SM/4560), April 24, 1991.

19. Bellamy, *Responsibility to Protect*, 33.

20. See the Charter of the United Nations, preamble.

21. Francis Fukuyama, *The End of History and the Last Man* (New York: Free Press, 1992).

22. Kofi A. Annan, "'We the People': The Role of the United Nations in the 21st Century," Millennium Report of the Secretary-General (UN document A/54/2000), March 27, 2000.

23. International Commission on Intervention and State Sovereignty (ICISS), *The Responsibility to Protect: Report of the International Commission on Intervention and State Sovereignty* (Ottawa, ON: International Development Research Centre, 2001).

24. See the 2005 World Summit Outcome Document (UN document A/60/L.1), October 24, 2005, paras. 138–39.

25. Andreas S. Kolb, "The Responsibility to Protect (R2P) and the Responsibility while Protecting (RwP): Friends or Foes?" Global Governance Institute Analysis Paper 6/2012 (Global Governance Institute, Brussels, September 2012), 9.

26. UN Permanent Representative Maria Luiza Ribiero Viotti, "Responsibility while Protecting: Elements for the Development and Promotion of a Concept" (UN document A/66/551–S/2011/701), November 11, 2011, clause 11.

27. Xenia Avezov, "'Responsibility while Protecting': Are We Asking the Wrong Questions?" (Stockholm International Peace Research Institute, January 2013), http://www.sipri.org/media/newsletter/essay/Avezov_Jan13.

28. ICISS, *Responsibility to Protect*, xi.

29. Jonas Claes, "Atrocity Prevention through Persuasion and Deterrence: Political Missions and Preventive Deployments," Peace Brief no. 128 (United States Institute of Peace, Washington, DC, June 2012), 2.

30. See Jonas Claes, "Protecting Civilians from Mass Atrocities: Meeting the Challenge of R2P Rejectionism," *Global Responsibility to Protect* 4, no. 1 (2012), 67–97, for elaboration on R2P opposition, including a study of the basis states use for rejecting it.

31. 2005 World Summit Outcome Document, paragraph 139.

32. UN Office for the Coordination of Humanitarian Affairs (OCHA), "Thematic Areas: Protection," http://www.unocha.org/what-we-do/policy/thematic-areas/protection.

33. United Nations Security Council (UNSC) Resolution 1265 (UN document S/RES/1265), September 17, 1999, clause 10.

34. UNSC Resolution 1973 (UN document S/RES/1973), March 17, 2011, clause 4.

35. Those options include negotiation, inquiry, mediation, conciliation, arbitration, judicial settlement, resort to regional agencies or arrangements, or other peaceful means of the choice of the disputing parties.

36. See, for example, Bertrand G. Ramcharan, *Preventive Diplomacy at the UN* (Bloomington: Indiana University Press, 2008).

37. Boutros Boutros-Ghali, "An Agenda for Peace," Report of the Secretary-General (UN document A/47/277–S/24111), June 17, 1992, para. 1.

38. Ibid., para. 23.

39. Ibid.

40. Carnegie Commission on Preventing Deadly Conflict, *Preventing Deadly Conflict: Final Report* (Washington, DC: Carnegie Corporation of New York, 1997), 39–102

41. Kofi A. Annan, "Facing the Humanitarian Challenge: Towards a Culture of Prevention" (New York: United Nations, 1999), para. 36. This report was also published as the introduction to the annual Report of the Secretary-General on the Work of the Organization (UN document A/54/1), August 31, 1999.

42. Kofi A. Annan, "Prevention of Armed Conflict," Report of the Secretary-General (UN document A/55/985–S/2001/574), June 7, 2001, executive summary.

43. Kofi A. Annan, "In Larger Freedom: Towards Development, Security and Human Rights for All," Report of the Secretary-General (UN document A/59/2005), March 21, 2005, para. 106.

44. Secretary-General Ban Ki-moon, "Remarks at the Opening of the 67th Session of the General Assembly," September 18, 2012.

45. Ban Ki-moon, "Preventive Diplomacy: Delivering Results," Report of the Secretary-General (UN document S/2011/552), August 26, 2011.

46. UNSC Resolution 1366 (UN document S/RES/1366), August 30, 2001.

47. UNSC, "Statement by the President of the Security Council" (UN document S/PRST/2010/14), July 16, 2010.

48. UNSC, "Statement by the President of the Security Council" (UN document S/PRST/2010/18), September 23, 2010.

49. General Assembly Resolution 57/337 (UN document A/RES/57/337), July 18, 2003.

50. 2005 World Summit Outcome, para. 74.

51. For an overview of these various official pronouncements, see Lawrence Woocher, "Preventing Violent Conflict: Assessing Progress, Meeting Challenges," Special Report no. 231 (United States Institute of Peace, Washington, DC, September 2009).

52. Abiodun Williams, *Preventing War: The United Nations and Macedonia* (Lanham, MD: Rowman and Littlefield, 2000).

53. Rome Statute of the International Criminal Court (UN document A/CONF.183/9), July 17, 1998, preamble.

54. Secretary-General Ban Ki-moon, "Remarks to the General Assembly on His Five-Year Action Agenda: "The Future We Want," January 25, 2012.

55. Transitional justice mechanisms, of course, include criminal prosecution as well as a range of noncriminal options, such as Truth and Reconciliation Commissions, compensation measures, and noncriminal vetting processes that are beyond the scope of this chapter.

56. Rome Statute, articles 6–8.

57. Gareth Evans, *The Responsibility to Protect: Ending Mass Atrocity Crimes Once and For All* (Washington, DC: Brookings Institution Press, 2008), 167.

58. Agreement between the United Nations and the Government of Sierra Leone on the Establishment of a Special Court for Sierra Leone, January 16, 2002, article 1.

59. Neil J. Kritz, "The Rule of Law in Conflict Management," in *Leashing the Dogs of War*, ed. Crocker, Hampson, and Aall (Washington, DC: US Institute of Peace, 2007), 410–11.

60. Finnemore and Sikkink, "International Norm Dynamics," 905–7.

61. Noelle Higgins, "The Regulation of Armed Non-State Actors: Promoting the Application of the Laws of War to Conflicts Involving National Liberation Movements," *Human Rights Brief* 17, no. 1 (2009): 12–18, available at American University, Washington College of Law, http://www.wcl.american.edu/hrbrief/17/1higgins.pdf.

62. Kofi Annan, "Two Concepts of Sovereignty," *The Economist*, September 16, 1999.

63. UNSC Resolution 2033 (UN document S/RES/2033), January 12, 2012.

6

CONFLICT AND COOPERATION IN THE GLOBAL COMMONS

Stewart Patrick

Strategic competition in the twenty-first century will focus on access to and control over the "global commons." This phrase denotes those physical or virtual spaces that no nation controls but on which all rely for security and prosperity. The most important global commons are the oceans, outer space, and cyberspace. Collectively, they "constitute the vital connective tissue of the international system," facilitating the global flow of goods, capital, people, and ideas.[1] Ensuring free and unencumbered access to each domain is a core US national interest.

Since World War II, the ability of the United States, largely alone, to guarantee the global commons has been a critical foundation of world order.[2] Supremacy at sea and more recently in outer- and cyberspace has also conferred geopolitical advantages, permitting the United States to project its power globally and facilitating a distinctive "American way of war."[3] This hegemonic role is waning, however, as the global commons become more crowded, cutthroat, and conflictual. In each domain, emerging powers and private actors are staking new claims, scrambling for advantage, and challenging existing rules. This "democratization of the global commons" elevates risks of confrontation, as potential US adversaries adopt asymmetric strategies to counter traditional US advantages, and as nonstate actors seek to exploit governance gaps for illicit activities.[4] But it also introduces new opportunities for creative partnerships between established and emerging powers, and between public- and private-sector actors.[5]

Preserving the openness, stability, and resilience of the global commons will require updating existing multilateral norms and institutions regulating the maritime, outer-space, and cyber domains to new threats and actors. Preserving an open global commons, as the Pentagon's 2012 Defense Strategic Guidance points out, will require the United States to forge agreement with like-minded nations, rising powers, and private stakeholders not only on rules of the road but also on sustainable divisions of labor.[6]

This will not be easy. Because access to the global commons is a public good[7]—the benefits of which are, in principle, universally shared—rational actors are often tempted to "free ride" on the efforts of others. Accordingly, public goods tend to be undersupplied.[8] Historically, overcoming global collective action problems has required either a hegemonic power able and willing to shoulder disproportionate burdens to provide public goods or, alternatively, a negotiated multilateral agreement in which nations decide what goods to provide and how to apportion costs of their provision, what rules should govern their sustainable use, and how to enforce standards and sanction violators.[9] The United States' waning hegemony makes the latter approach the only realistic option.

Success will require the United States and other established nations to persuade emerging powers that they have a strong stake in the integrity of—and an interest in helping to sustain—an open global commons. Many of today's rising countries perceive prevailing norms, rules, and privileges stacked against them and—preoccupied with internal development—are reluctant to accept global burdens. Enlisting their support may require reopening fundamental debates over rules and granting them greater voice in reformed global institutions.

Policymakers will also need to think more creatively about the design of global institutions. Given the complexity of the global commons, they cannot be governed simply by formal organizations like the United Nations and its agencies. In the future, more flexible coalitions of the willing and relevant, akin to the Group of Twenty (G20) or the parties to the Nuclear Security Summit, will be at least as important as treaty-based bodies. Effective governance may also be provided by transgovernmental networks of regulators who possess relevant technical expertise, or by regional bodies. Finally, new global governance mechanisms will increasingly rely on innovative public-

private partnerships that marry public authority with private initiative. The challenge will be to ensure the complementarity between such "minilateral" mechanisms and nimble networks, and the standing, treaty-based entities that bring universality, legitimacy, and enforcement capacity to global problems.[10]

OUTER SPACE

International rules governing the uses of outer space have become outdated, as that domain becomes more "congested, contested, and competitive."[11] The number of actors operating in space has skyrocketed, as nations and private corporations vie for scarce orbital slots for their satellites and slices of a finite radio-frequency spectrum. More worrisome, geopolitical competition among "spacefaring" nations, both established and emerging, raises the specter of a space arms race. Unfortunately, there is little global consensus on the regulatory regime needed to ensure the stability and sustainable use of Earth's final frontier.

Guaranteed access to outer space is a cornerstone of global security and prosperity. Space-based satellites and systems facilitate communications, commerce, and finance; enable navigation, transportation, and meteorological and scientific observations; and support intelligence gathering and military operations. No country has a greater stake in these benefits than the United States, which relies on space-based systems to track storms, measure Arctic sea ice, assess damage from natural disasters, monitor illicit drug trafficking, conduct remote sensing of terrorist havens, and verify compliance with arms control agreements, among other functions.[12] American corporations and citizens, meanwhile, use telecommunications satellites and global positioning systems to transfer money, ship goods, enjoy smartphone service, and map current locations and travel destinations.

For decades, the United States enjoyed unquestioned dominance in space. Even today, it accounts for three-quarters of official space funding worldwide, and US public and private corporations own more than 40 percent of orbiting satellites. This era is fading, however, as new nations and private companies with distinct interests, capacities, and intentions exploit the heavens for military, commercial, and scientific purposes. Already, nine countries and the European Space Agency (ESA) have proven orbital launch capabilities (with several waiting in the wings),[13] and nearly sixty nations or government consortia regulate civil, commercial, and military satellites.[14] Assured access to outer space is endangered by three disturbing trends: the rapid accumulation of space debris, the growing risk of collision between space vehicles, and the looming weaponization of space.

As of 2012, more than twenty-two thousand pieces of space junk larger than a softball, and another three hundred thousand fragments between one and ten centimeters in diameter, were orbiting Earth at a speed of twenty thousand miles an hour. The impact of any one item with a satellite or spacecraft could be catastrophic. On consecutive days in September 2012, the International Space Station narrowly escaped being struck by part of a defunct Russian satellite and a piece of an old Indian rocket.[15] The danger of collisions between space vehicles is also growing. In February 2009, a nonfunctioning Russian satellite collided with an active Iridium communications satellite, destroying the latter and creating an enormous debris field.[16] Unless the accumulation of debris can be slowed and space traffic management improved, the risks of operating in orbit will become prohibitive.

Most worrisome is the possibility that space will become a setting for offensive military competition. Current military uses of satellites are largely passive—they assist intelligence gathering, reconnaissance, monitoring, and surveillance, and they facilitate land-based systems. No weapons, as such, are deployed in space. And yet the overlap between benign and military technologies creates potential dual-use dilemmas. Already, major space powers have the means to interfere with, disable, or destroy other nations' satellites. Many analysts predict a space arms race, including the deployment of kinetic energy weapons, directed energy weapons (lasers and particle beams), and conventional munitions delivered to (or from) orbit. Such a "Wild West" scenario would make miscalculation more likely and create opportunities for showdowns.[17]

China provided a glimpse of the possible future in January 2007, when it destroyed a defunct polar-orbiting Chinese weather satellite with a ground-based antisatellite (ASAT) missile—generating a debris field of 2,500 items larger than ten centimeters.[18] A year later, in February 2008, the US Navy eliminated an obsolete reconnaissance satellite with a modified missile defense interceptor.[19]

Because no nation can hope to control outer space in perpetuity, a prudent course for the United States would be to support new norms and rules to mitigate congestion, share information, and establish confidence-building mechanisms to manage competition, as well as create dispute resolution procedures to keep competition within peaceful bounds. Unfortunately, none of the pressing issues mentioned above—debris, collisions, or militarization—are adequately addressed by the current international legal regime, which has failed to keep pace with technological developments and geopolitical trends.

The foundational convention governing national conduct in outer space remains the Outer Space Treaty[20] (OST), which came into force in 1967. It establishes several important principles. It declares space to be "the province of all mankind," not subject to sovereignty claims but open to exploration by all, consistent with peaceful purposes and international law. States are responsible for all space activities (governmental or private) under their national jurisdiction and can be held liable for damages. They must avoid contaminating space and "celestial bodies," and consult prior to activities hindering others' peaceful uses. Finally, the OST prohibits the establishment of military bases, installations, and fortifications; the testing of weapons or conducting of military maneuvers; the placement into orbit or on celestial bodies of nuclear or other weapons of mass destruction; and interference with technical means of verifying compliance with arms control agreements. At the same time—and potentially incongruously—states retain the right to use space assets in pursuing their inherent right to individual and collective self-defense.

The OST has notable gaps, however. It lacks a dispute resolution mechanism, says nothing about space debris and collision avoidance, and inadequately addresses interference with space assets of other countries. To ensure secure access, promote responsible conduct, and diminish the risk of arms races, established and emerging spacefaring nations need to agree on new rules of the road.

To date, multilateral efforts to regulate space relations have been conducted primarily within the UN Committee on the Peaceful Uses of Outer Space (COPUOS). Created in 1958 as an ad hoc body of the General Assembly, COPUOS comprises seventy-one member states and includes a Legal Subcommittee and a Scientific and Technical Subcommittee. Given its unwieldy size and consensus-based decision making, COPUOS has struggled to address emerging space challenges.

Nevertheless, the United Nations remains a preferred venue for negotiations by many new spacefaring nations, as well as developing countries. In 2011, at the request of the UN General Assembly, Secretary-General Ban Ki-moon established a Group of Governmental Experts (GGE) on Transparency and Confidence-Building Measures (TCBMs) in Outer Space Activities, a fifteen-member panel including representatives from all five permanent members of the Security Council. The group's objective is to create a consensus report on TCBMs to which states can voluntarily adhere. The United States hosted the second of three planned meetings in April 2013, though the outcome of the process remained uncertain.

Any reform of global space governance will require leadership from the United States, a repository of the most advanced space technologies and scientific expertise. It has already taken the lead in promoting space situational awareness globally, through its US Strategic Command's Joint Space Operations Center (JSpOC). Using an earth-based system of monitors and sensors, JSpOC collects data on space debris and provides this free of charge to foreign government and commercial space operators, including in China, India, Brazil, and Russia.[21] At the same time, the United States has grown reliant on the capabilities of partners. NASA, for instance, cooperates with the ESA to gather meteorological data critical for responding to natural disasters and (in the case of hostilities) military planning. Such burden-sharing arrangements are likely to spread as nations pool capabilities to create "virtual constellations" of satellites.

Whether the United States should defend its long-standing outer-space primacy or adopt a more multilateral course remains a topic of debate. For its part, the administration of George W. Bush resisted new international arrangements it believed might compromise US freedom of action.[22] The succeeding administration of Barack Obama reinvigorated US space diplomacy as part of its broader effort to integrate emerging powers as responsible pillars of a renewed multilateral order.[23] Its National Space Policy (2010), premised on the "shared interest of all nations . . . to help prevent mishaps, misperceptions, and mistrust," sought to foster an accessible and sustainable outer-space domain open to all "without interference."[24]

The obstacles to improved multilateral governance of outer space are formidable. First, some rising powers suspect that new regulations are intended to consolidate advantages enjoyed by established powers and restrain newcomers' space ambitions and capabilities. Second, not all spacefaring nations—notably China—are committed to transparency in their space activities, a sine qua non for an effective governance regime. Third, even if spacefaring nations commit to a common set of norms, no regime exists to monitor compliance or sanction proscribed behavior.

Suggestions for reforming outer-space governance range from a binding multilateral treaty banning space weapons to an informal agreement on rules of conduct.[25] The most prominent treaty proposal is a joint Chinese-Russian draft titled "Treaty on the Prevention of the Placement of Weapons in Outer Space, the Threat or Use of Force Against Outer Space Objects" (PPWT), submitted in February 2008 to the international Conference on Disarmament (CD). It would fill an important gap in international space law by prohibiting nations from placing any weapons in outer space or threatening force against space objects.[26]

The United States has deemed the draft treaty "fundamentally flawed" on several grounds. Most fundamentally, the PPWT focuses on space-based weapons that have yet to materialize, while omitting mention of kinetic, ground-based ASAT systems that have already wrought havoc in space. It is also vague about the "executive organization" anticipated to implement and ensure compliance with the treaty; fails to define critical concepts such as "weapons in space" and "the threat or use of force"; blurs offensive and defensive weapons systems; lacks verification measures providing for the inspection of launch payloads; and fails to solve the dual-use dilemma (specifically, that many space technologies can have both peaceful and military purposes, making blanket efforts to ban them unrealistic). Finally, any such treaty would need to be negotiated within the consensus-based CD, notorious for its paralysis.[27]

Given problems with the treaty-based approach, the Obama administration has focused on a more promising near-term objective: a nonbinding "International Code of Conduct for Outer Space Activities."[28] Building on an existing European draft, the code would establish broad principles and parameters of state behavior, including the adoption of new policies and procedures for mitigating space debris, minimizing the possibility of collisions, and avoiding intentional interference against space objects. It would also address ASAT tests, with adherents pledging (in the words of the EU draft) to "refrain from intentional destruction of any on-orbit space object or other harmful activities which may generate long-lived space debris."

A truly effective international code, however, would need additional provisions. These include a commitment to provide advance notice of space launches and maneuvers, as well as the placement of satellites in orbit. Most important, the code must ban offensive weapons in space—something upon which China and Russia will insist and to which the United States should readily consent.[29]

Admittedly, a voluntary code implies a lesser obligation than a legally binding multilateral treaty. But it offers the best chance in the short term to establish new norms of behavior and could make outer space a less dangerous place, particularly if it multilateralized some of the situational awareness functions currently performed by JSpOC. By increasing the transparency of space operations, the code promises to help reduce debris-generating events, lower the risk of collisions, and diminish misunderstandings and misperceptions that might otherwise lead to conflict.[30]

A code of conduct would also avoid a lengthy treaty ratification debate in the United States, because it could be adopted by White House executive order. To be sure, such an approach would raise partisan hackles. In February 2011, thirty-seven Republican senators declared themselves "deeply concerned" about potential US endorsement of the EU code of conduct.[31] "Taken literally," conservatives John Bolton and John Yoo complained the following year, such a code "could limit [US] freedom of action in space," including development of space-based antiballistic missiles, testing of antisatellite weapons, and gathering of intelligence.[32]

These concerns are overwrought. According to the Pentagon, nothing in the planned code would hinder US intelligence collection or missile defense. Moreover, a ban on space-based and antisatellite weapons is a reasonable concession to prevent an unpredictable arms race in outer space. For its part, the Obama administration says it will not sign any agreement that "in any way constrains our national security-related activities in space or our ability to protect the United States and our allies."[33]

As it pursues a code, the United States should consider sponsoring a standing, "minilateral" consultative forum of space-faring nations. In principle, the G20, which already includes most spacefaring nations, could play this role.[34] Given G20 members' misgivings of mission creep, however, a more plausible approach might be to create a dedicated consultative body analogous to the Major Economies Forum on Energy and Climate (MEF).[35]

THE MARITIME COMMONS

Covering 71 percent of Earth's surface, the oceans are the global commons with the longest history of interstate competition. The first major effort to establish rules governing access to, exploitation of, and conduct on the high seas dates from the early seventeenth century. In 1609, the Dutch jurist Hugo Grotius published *Mare Liberum* (The Free Sea), establishing that the open ocean, being outside sovereign state control, must be open to free passage and commercial use by all nations. Today, freedom of the seas is more essential than ever to global commerce, transportation, and security. Like outer space, however, the oceans are growing more congested, contested, and competitive.

The legal bedrock of contemporary ocean governance is the UN Convention on the Law of the Sea (UNCLOS), which opened for signature in 1982 and entered into force in 1994. The most complex multilateral treaty every negotiated, UNCLOS defines state rights and responsibilities in their use and management of the world's oceans. It confers on each coastal state national jurisdiction over "territorial seas" extending 12 nautical miles from shore; establishes additional "exclusive economic zones" (EEZs) extending two hundred miles from shore (and up to 550 miles for "natural" extensions of the continental shelf); and clarifies rules for transit through "international straits." It also addresses issues of maritime traffic, pollution, and division of natural resources on the high seas. Finally, it serves as the main forum for dispute resolution on ocean-related issues. To date, 162 countries and the European Union have ratified UNCLOS. The United States is not a party.[36]

The US failure to accede to UNCLOS is ironic, given US history. Winning independence in a world of mercantilist empires, the young republic launched its initial foreign military actions to defend freedom of navigation and commerce—first against the Barbary corsairs and, in 1812, against Great Britain.[37] The nation's subsequent rise to world power deepened these convictions. In 1890, Alfred Thayer Mahan, president of the US Naval War College, published his famous treatise on the geopolitical significance of the oceans, describing them as "a wide commons."[38] Nearly three decades later, the United States entered World War I following Germany's resumption of unrestricted submarine warfare. Ensuring "absolute freedom of the seas" became a core US war aim, incorporated in Woodrow Wilson's Fourteen Points of January 1918.

By 1945, the United States had become not just a proponent but the ultimate guarantor of the ocean commons. It emerged from World War II with the world's most powerful navy—some twelve hundred ships, including dozens of aircraft carriers. During the Cold War and after, the US Navy both bolstered regional power balances in Asia, Europe, and the Middle East, and defended the rights of all nations to unencumbered access to the high seas. US naval mastery was the handmaiden of globalization. But this was less altruism than enlightened self-interest, because an open ocean helped the United States project power from maritime platforms and pursue defense in depth.[39]

Global prosperity is more tightly linked than ever to freedom of the seas. Since 1970, the value of global exports has expanded by 5,000 percent—just over fifteen times faster than global GDP.[40] Ninety percent of this trade—some 8 billion tons, worth over $18 trillion annually in 2012[41]—is carried on the world's container ships, a merchant fleet of more than 100,000 vessels registered in more than 150 nations and crewed by 1.5 million sailors.[42] Today's global supply chains and "just in time" inventory systems depend on reliable maritime traffic. But these flows are vulnerable to disruptions, notably in narrow "choke points" (such as the straits of Hormuz and Malacca), through which some three-quarters of global shipping passes.[43]

Beyond serving as a highway for trade, the oceans advance global prosperity in other ways. The EEZs contain a vast majority of the world's offshore deposits of oil and gas, as well as stocks of fish, the main source of protein for one-sixth of humanity. The fact that 40 percent of humanity lives within one hundred kilometers of a coast only adds to the oceans' strategic and commercial importance.[44]

However, the historically open maritime domain is at risk. First, new maritime powers are seeking blue-water capabilities or employing asymmetric strategies to deny others access to regional waters. Second, nations are embroiled in competing maritime sovereignty claims, particularly in East Asia. Third, geopolitical and economic competition is heating up in the warming Arctic, as nations dispute extended continental shelves, control of new sea routes, and rights to exploit undersea mineral and fossil fuel deposits. Fourth, malignant nonstate actors threaten merchant shipping. Addressing these problems will require bolstering existing governance regimes, both global (e.g., UNCLOS) and regional (e.g., the Arctic Council).

To begin with, the ongoing diffusion of global power jeopardizes the historic US ability to guarantee freedom of the seas. True, the US Navy remains in a class by itself, with a battle fleet tonnage greater than the next thirteen largest navies combined.[45] But new maritime powers, including China and India, are emerging.[46] Aiming to constrain US naval operations and influence in its region, China has adopted a strategy of "far sea defense" and launched its first aircraft carrier. It has also expanded its Anti-Access/Area-Denial capabilities—including mines, antiship ballistic and cruise missiles, mini-submarines, and wake-homing torpedoes—to force the US Navy to operate from a greater distance. In the Persian Gulf, Iran is developing similar capabilities, including "swarm formations" of small but fast ships.[47]

When it comes to maritime conflict, the biggest potential flashpoints are in East Asia.[48] In the South China Sea—through which more than $5 trillion of commerce (including more than 90 percent of Chinese trade) passes each year—China is locked in a dispute with Brunei, Malaysia, the Philippines, Taiwan, and Vietnam over some 2.2 million square miles of ocean, the contested islets therein, and the exploitation of undersea oil and gas reserves.[49] Beijing has advanced a historically dubious "nine-dash" formula implying Chinese sovereignty over more than 80 percent of the South China Sea, insisted (contrary to UNCLOS) that foreign warships must obtain permission to transit its EEZ, sent security vessels to confront its rivals on the ocean, and intimidated corporations assisting ASEAN nations in oil and gas exploration.[50] China has taken similarly unsettling actions in the East China Sea, where it disputes long-standing Japanese claims of jurisdiction over the Senkaku/Diaoyu Islands. In November 2013, Beijing unilaterally declared an "air defense identification zone" encompassing much of these waters, heightening regional tensions.[51]

Beijing's expansive claims reflect a drive for regional hegemony, reminiscent of US moves to control the Caribbean basin a century ago. Chinese assertiveness poses serious risks for East Asian stability, however. The most dangerous contingency would be a direct US-Chinese naval clash, perhaps in response to US freedom-of-navigation operations in China's littoral waters.[52] A Sino-American confrontation could also occur from the reckless actions of a formal treaty ally (e.g., Japan or the Philippines) or an emerging US partner (e.g., Vietnam). In providing strategic reassurance to partners, the United States must avoid offering them a blank check that sets disaster in motion.[53] Ultimately, peaceful resolution of competing claims in the South China Sea will require China to drop its resistance to a binding code of conduct consistent with international law. In the East China Sea, it will necessitate Sino-Japanese rapprochement. In both cases, a major impediment to conflict resolution is China's resistance to any solution that would facilitate a continued, robust US naval presence in its offshore waters.

Maritime competition has also increased in the Arctic. Bounded by the Arctic Circle (66°33′ north latitude), the Arctic includes 6 percent of the Earth's surface, divided in roughly equal thirds among dry land, continental shelf (to five hundred meters), and deep water. Historically, inhospitable climate and geography have stymied attempts to exploit this region's vast resources. As climate change continues unabated, these constraints are fast disappearing. In summer 2012, Arctic sea ice contracted to its smallest size since record keeping began, reducing the ice cap to well below half its size fifty years ago, and scientists suggest the Arctic may be ice-free in summer by 2035.[54] These dramatic changes have lured governments as well as private corporations north, in the hopes of exploiting undersea oil and gas deposits, as well as the fabled Northwest Passage and Northern Sea Route.[55]

This geopolitical and economic competition has led some breathless commentators to speak of a new "scramble," even a "Cold War."[56] Others worry such predictions could be self-fulfilling.[57] Such fears seem overblown given the history of resolving Arctic disputes peacefully, the presence of institutions such as the Arctic Council, and incentives favoring cooperation among the five Arctic nations: Russia, the United States, Canada, Norway, and (by virtue of its control over Greenland) Denmark.

There are at least three plausible triggers for Arctic conflict: competition over energy and mineral resources, boundary disputes over territorial seas and "extended" EEZs, and jurisdictional disagreements over new trade routes. According to US Geological Survey estimates, the Arctic may hold between a fifth and a quarter of the world's undiscovered oil and gas deposits.[58] Whether these become commercially viable, however, depends on numerous factors—including future global demand and prices, the cost of extractive equipment that can function in frigid conditions, the political climate regarding offshore drilling, and new opportunities in other regions. Several Arctic nations are also embroiled in disputes over the boundaries of territorial seas and the fisheries and fossil fuels therein.[59] In none of these cases, however, is any party likely to threaten, much less resort to, violence.

Potentially more difficult to resolve are disputes over "extended" continental shelves, particularly Russia's insistence to exclusive rights over 460,000 square miles of resource-rich Arctic waters.[60] To reinforce its claim, Russia in 2007 dispatched two submarines to place and photograph Russian flags on the seabed beneath the North Pole, subsequently ordering the first post–Cold War strategic bomber flights over the pole. Still, confrontation has since cooled, with the five Arctic nations in 2008 signing the Ilulissat Declaration, affirming their commitment to address any overlapping claims in a peaceful and orderly manner. They have since done so, including a 2010 agreement between Norway and Russia settling a long-standing dispute near the Svalbard archipelago.

Finally, disagreements over trans-Arctic sea routes could exacerbate political frictions, as countries dispute what waters are internal, territorial, contiguous, part of EEZs, or international (five categories of decreasing national jurisdiction). The United States and European Union, for example, regard the Northwest Passage as an international strait, whereas Canada insists that portions adjacent to the Canadian Arctic Archipelago are "historic internal waters" in which it can restrict transit of other nations' vessels. This dispute is likely to be resolved diplomatically, however, particularly given the 1988 bilateral US-Canada Arctic Cooperation Agreement. Going forward, one might expect joint US-Canadian cooperation in policing the thousands of miles of Arctic coastline.[61]

Some experts believe that the Arctic needs a comprehensive multilateral treaty to reconcile competing sovereignty claims, handle navigation issues, facilitate collective energy development, manage fisheries, and address pollution and environmental concerns.[62] It may make more sense to strengthen and adapt existing multilateral institutions, beginning with UNCLOS.[63] Geologists estimate that 85 to 90 percent of the Arctic Ocean's undiscovered oil and gas deposits are contained in nondisputed EEZs, suggesting that Arctic nations can exploit them unilaterally. The UN Commission on the Limits of the Continental Shelf (UNCLCS), meanwhile, offers a mechanism (albeit advisory) to determine the validity of "extended EEZ" claims. Finally, UNCLOS includes a framework for determining which straits are international and, via Article 234, provides for coastal states to enforce more stringent environmental regulations in ice-covered waters.[64]

A second worthy step would be to bolster the Arctic Council, comprising the five Arctic nations plus Finland and Sweden (as well as three northern indigenous peoples' organizations). Although this forum has historically avoided contentious boundary and legal disputes, it has a role to play in codifying guidelines on oil and gas development, sponsoring collaborative mapping of the continental shelf, creating a regional monitoring network, and modernizing systems for navigation, traffic management, and environmental protection.

Security of the ocean commons is also threatened by violent nonstate actors, notably pirates, terrorists, and other criminals. Maritime terrorism, though limited to date, remains a risk, as evinced by the 2000 attack by Al Qaeda on the US destroyer *Cole* in the port of Aden, followed two years later by an attack on a French supertanker. More significant has been piracy, which has enjoyed a disturbing renaissance in the twenty-first century. The epicenter has been the Horn of Africa, where Somali pirates, taking advantage of the collapse of the Somali state, launched increasingly brazen attacks in one of the world's busiest shipping corridors.[65] The most spectacular was the 2008 hijacking of the Saudi oil tanker MV *Sirius Star*, more than five hundred miles off Kenya's coast.[66]

After peaking in 2011 in 235 separate incidents, piracy off Somalia has declined precipitously, thanks to escalating multilateral responses.[67] These included increasingly assertive UN Security Council resolutions authorizing "all necessary means" to fight Somali piracy at sea and on land.[68] At sea, an unprecedented, loosely coordinated multinational armada emerged. This included a US Navy–led coalition (Combined Task Force 151), the European Union's first naval mission (Operation Atalanta), and ships under national command from ten other countries (China, Indonesia, Iran, India, Japan, Malaysia, South Korea, Russia, Saudi Arabia, and Yemen).[69] Besides the involvement of intergovernmental organizations and state governments, this exercise in "collective conflict management"[70] also relied on cooperation with the private sector, notably major shipping companies.

The single most important step the United States could take to strengthen ocean governance is to finally accede to UNCLOS, as recommended by the last four US presidents, as well as US military leaders, the business community, and environmental groups. Remaining apart not only reduces the treaty's effectiveness but also undermines US national interests and global leadership.[71] Absent from the UNCLOS, the United States cannot take part in the last great partitioning of sovereign space on Earth—forfeiting an opportunity to extend its own jurisdiction over vast areas along its Arctic, Atlantic, Gulf, and Pacific coasts. Nor can it serve on the International Seabed Authority, where (thanks to assertive US diplomacy during treaty negotiations) it would enjoy an effective veto. The US stance also undermines the credibility of US commitments to a rule-based international order, while emboldening revisionist powers seeking to throw their regional weight around.[72]

Washington should subsequently lead negotiations to update the treaty, now more than three decades old.[73] Priorities should include enhanced provisions for surveillance, capacity building, and enforcement—so that parties can improve maritime domain awareness, implement treaty obligations, and hold violators to account—as well as provisions for the challenges of maritime pollution, overfishing, unregulated offshore drilling, and maritime crimes, from piracy to drug smuggling. To better manage tensions in the Arctic, the revised convention should also expand Article 234 provisions on ice-covered areas. Finally, the treaty should include a framework to assess progress toward these goals.

Ensuring an open, secure, and resilient maritime commons will ultimately require multilevel governance efforts, with cooperation among international, regional, national, and local partners, both public and private. One of the most promising regional initiatives is the Regional Cooperation Agreement on Combating Piracy and Armed Robbery against Ships in Asia (ReCAAP), involving nineteen nations.[74] Securing the oceans will also necessitate new maritime consortia linking government authorities to commercial shipping operators—the largest three of which collectively possess a fleet three times as large as the twelve hundred vessels in the world's navies.[75] An early step should be to improve maritime domain awareness, perhaps by including commercial operators in the US Navy's Maritime Safety and Security Information System (MSSIS), particularly in high-risk waters.[76]

THE CYBER COMMONS

Unlike the maritime and outer-space domains, cyberspace is a purely human construction, a digital world composed of interlocking information technology networks and infrastructures that permit the transmission of massive data through the Internet, telecommunications systems, and computers. Because it operates across national jurisdictions and is (in principle) accessible to all, cyberspace may be considered part of the global commons.[77] It is an increasingly indispensable one, economically, socially, and politically. Although calculations of its economic value are necessarily approximations, a 2012 report by Boston Consulting Group suggests that the Internet economy already amounts to 4.1 percent of GDP across all G20 countries. A report by the McKinsey Global Institute that same year predicted that social media could add $1.3 trillion to the $14 trillion US economy.[78] Meanwhile, cyberspace has connected individuals and groups in new and sometimes revolutionary ways, transforming politics, societies, and lifestyles around the world.

Besides being a human invention, the cyber commons differs from its maritime and outer-space analogues in at least two major respects. First, its physical infrastructure is located primarily in sovereign states and owned by governments, corporations, or individuals, leaving the domain susceptible to interference and fragmentation. Second, most of this infrastructure, including exchanges, servers, and routers, remains in private hands.[79] In the United States, where that figure is 85 percent, the US military and Department of Homeland Security both rely heavily on the private sector to ensure both access to and security of cyber infrastructure.

The United States, where the digital age began, has been the premier national champion of an open, decentralized, and secure cyber domain that remains largely in private hands. This posture reflects the United States' long-standing belief that the free flow of information and ideas is a core component of a just and open world and an essential bulwark against fascist, totalitarian, and authoritarian alternatives to political liberty.[80]

This US vision is in jeopardy thanks to threats from three sources. The first is international disagreement over *cyber governance*—specifically, which entity should regulate cyberspace. To the degree that today's Internet is "governed," the primary regulatory institution remains the Internet Corporation for Assigned Names and Numbers (ICANN), an independent, nonprofit corporation based in Los Angeles. Licensed and loosely supervised by the US Department of Commerce, ICANN and the National Telecommunications and Information Administration (NTIA) manage protocol identifiers and domain names, including operation of root name servers that permit communication among Internet hosts. The outsized role of ICANN—and widespread perception of US (and broader Western) control over the Internet—remains a sore point for authoritarian and developing states, including the BRICS (Brazil, Russia, India, China, and South Africa), who would prefer the International Telecommunication Union (ITU) to perform this regulatory function and bring the Internet under intergovernmental control. International criticism of the US role in Internet governance has grown in the wake of revelations by former US government contractor Edward Snowden during 2013 of the massive scope of the US National Security Agency's PRISM program, which allows the United States to eavesdrop on the private communications of foreign leaders and citizens.

Founded in 1865 as the International Telegraphic Union, the ITU is the leading international standard-setting agency for a variety of telecommunications issues, including the allocation of orbital slots for satellites, the division of the radio spectrum, and the harmonization of mobile phone networks. The yawning gap in its portfolio remains the Internet, which was just emerging in 1988, the last time the ITU endorsed a significant overhaul of telecommunications regulations.[81]

At the December 2012 World Conference on International Telecommunications (WCIT), the Russian government sought to close this gap, submitting a proposal supported by China calling for ITU member states to enjoy "equal rights to manage the Internet," including assigning Internet numbers and addresses and developing Internet infrastructure. Senior ITU officials also endorsed a new treaty to ensure "the free flow of information," promote "affordable and equitable access for all," and encourage "ongoing innovation and market growth."[82] Behind this rhetorical concern with equity and multilateral management, a cohort of authoritarian governments (including Russia, China, Iran, and Cuba) pursued a narrower agenda: placing the Internet firmly in government hands to better control citizen access to information and restrict privacy.

The United States, the European Union, and the private sector mobilized to block this gambit. The misguided plan, complained the US ambassador to the WCIT, would allow governments to "manage the content of what goes via the Internet, what people are looking at, what they're saying." Such "invasive" proposals "fundamentally violate everything that we believe in[,] in terms of democracy and opportunities for individuals."[83] The ITU conference adjourned without consensus, although 89 of 144 countries accepted the revised regulations.

The second major challenge is the growing epidemic of *cyber crime*. Today, most cyber attacks occur against the private sector, and the overwhelming motive is economic—financial gain from stealing proprietary information. Beyond such intrusions, cyber criminals also threaten to compromise the global supply chain, by inserting malicious code in application software, computer microprocessors, or even the world's 4.5 billion cell phones.[84]

The global scale of cyber crime is unclear and perhaps unknowable. But US officials have offered some mind-boggling figures. In 2012, General Keith Alexander, director of the US National Security Agency, estimated its global cost at $1 trillion—of which $250 billion was borne by US businesses. It constituted, he claimed, "the greatest transfer of wealth in history." Many experts have dismissed these estimates as vastly inflated,[85] but there is no doubt that cyber crime is both lucrative and increasing. In President Obama's words, "This cyber threat is one of the most serious economic and national security challenges we face as a nation. . . . We're not as prepared as we should be, as a government or as a country."[86]

Unfortunately, the odds are stacked heavily in favor of attackers. Would-be defenders must patrol an almost limitless perimeter; and while an attack can occur in seconds, it can take weeks to track down its origin. Moreover, fewer than 2 percent of cyber criminals are successfully prosecuted.[87] Given such odds, many firms simply accept vulnerability and associated losses as a cost of doing business. The CIA estimates that businesses could stymie 80 to 90 percent of cyber attacks "by consistently applying standard practices and technologies."[88] But firms, having many priorities (such as maximizing shareholder value, advancing market position, and reducing regulatory burdens), often tolerate a greater cyber insecurity than national authorities consider prudent.

The growing sophistication of computer viruses, worms, and botnets has brought about a dramatic deterioration in what an epidemiologist might term "cyber public health."[89] Unfortunately, multilateral efforts to detect, prevent, and respond lag behind analogous strides in global health governance. There is no equivalent to the World Health Organization's International Health Regulations, which mandate immediate national access for WHO scientists investigating a pandemic event. Nor is there any parallel to the WHO's Global Outbreak Alert and Response Network, which might allow nations to respond collectively to "cyber outbreaks" and quarantine infected networks and devices.[90]

Another promising multilateral response would be to create a body similar to the intergovernmental Financial Action Task Force, created in 1989 to combat money laundering (and now terrorist financing). Beginning with like-minded foreign partners, US officials would seek to negotiate common national standards, regulations, and enforcement procedures regarding cyber crime; agree on a system of multilateral peer review; and institute a process to name and shame noncooperating jurisdictions failing to meet baseline commitments. Such a body could facilitate law enforcement cooperation in deterring and prosecuting

cross-border cyber crime.[91] Alongside these efforts, the United States might explore ways to globalize the Council of Europe's useful Cybercrime Convention.

Finally, reducing cyber crime will require public authorities to persuade industries to harden their cybersecurity systems. To alter private incentives, governments may need to provide tax breaks for investments, limit corporate legal liability, and harmonize standards and rules globally to discourage regulatory arbitrage.[92] Governments will also need robust public-private partnerships to manage vulnerable supply chains, including software, microchips, and cell phones.

A major difficulty in combating cyber crime is the problem of attribution, including distinguishing between attacks launched by private criminals versus those launched (or sponsored) by states themselves. Thieves, activists, and terrorists typically employ many of the same methods as states.

This brings us to the third major flashpoint: the growing specter of *cyber conflict*— even *cyber war*—among sovereign states. Dozens of nations have begun to develop doctrines and capabilities to conduct "information operations," not only to infiltrate but, if necessary, to disrupt and destroy the critical digital infrastructure—both military and civilian—of hostile states. In some cases, governments have already launched or tacitly endorsed proxy attacks on their nation's adversaries. In response, the United States established a new Cyber Command within the Department of Defense in 2010, and announced a planned fivefold increase in its personnel in January 2013.[93]

At the multilateral level, little tangible progress has been made in mitigating the risk of cyber conflict. Part of the problem is conceptual. There is no broadly accepted definition of what constitutes a "cyber attack," nor any global consensus on the permissible range of responses. The frequent difficulty of identifying perpetrators also complicates traditional forms of deterrence and retaliation.[94]

Consider attacks emanating from Russian territory on the cyber infrastructure of neighboring countries.[95] In 2007, a concerted attack on Estonia, following the removal of a Soviet-era statue from Tallinn's main square, disabled the websites of the prime minister, president, and justice and foreign ministries, as well as parliamentary email. The next year, Georgia suffered similar attacks during Russia's military intervention in two breakaway provinces. In both cases, evidence suggested the attacks were conducted by civilians against civilian targets, though with at least tacit endorsement from Moscow. Beyond the attribution question, were these incidents acts of "war," and, if so, should the military have a role in countering them? In the former case, Estonia explicitly invoked NATO collective defense provisions, requesting assistance. The alliance agreed merely to "study" the issue, though it subsequently established a Cooperative Cyber Defense Center of Excellence in Tallinn.

Nor, conversely, are there any commonly accepted norms or principles regarding government cyber attacks on private entities in foreign jurisdictions. In 2012, a malware attack, possibly designed by a state actor, was discovered to be reading and exporting data from Lebanese banks. This "Gauss virus" appeared designed for cyber espionage, namely tracking financial transactions potentially destined for terrorists or "rogue" states. But the operation also showed how porous the line between "private" and "public" targets could become.[96]

Some experts dismiss the threat of a cyber "war" as overblown, noting that not a single person is known to have died as a result of a state-sponsored cyber attack— suggesting that such activity is akin to less violent, if still problematic, state practices such as "subversion, espionage, and sabotage."[97] Still, one could imagine a cyber conflict causing significant loss of life if it disabled, say, an air traffic control system, a set of nuclear reactors, or a hospital network. Moreover, cyber weapons can cause physical damage, if not (yet) human casualties. The Stuxnet virus, an alleged US-Israeli operation against Iran's uranium enrichment program, succeeded (according to the International Atomic Energy Agency) in disabling 984 centrifuges at the Natanz nuclear facility. The militarization of cyberspace, in other words, has begun.[98] At a minimum, all future interstate military conflicts will involve a cyber component.

Unfortunately, the normative and legal framework governing cyber war has lagged behind these developments. There is no international consensus on what constitutes an act of cyber warfare, on what legal rules should govern state cyber weapons,[99] or on permissible and proportional responses to any attack. The novel nature of cyber weapons and the fuzzy line between military and civilian targets further complicates accord on rules of cyber engagement. The resulting uncertainty raises the risk of escalation in the wake of any future perceived state-sponsored cyber attack.

Efforts to fill this legal vacuum have been rudimentary. In 1998, the ITU adopted a nonbinding commitment to avoid "disrupting the operation of telecommunications installations within the jurisdiction of other Member States." Additionally, the UN World Summit on the Information Society (2003–5) was silent on cyber conflict. More recently, in 2011, the United Kingdom held a worldwide Cybersecurity Summit. Intended to develop international "rules of the road" to clarify "norms of acceptable behavior" in cyberspace, the meeting achieved nothing concrete.[100]

A major point of contention is whether existing laws of war can be extended to cyber warfare, or whether an entirely new body of international law is needed.[101] Advocates of the former position cite the applicability of the Geneva Conventions (1949), especially Additional Protocol I, which (under Article 36) obliges any state developing or acquiring "a new weapon, means of warfare or methods of warfare . . . to determine whether its employment would, in some or all circumstances, be prohibited by this Protocol or by any other rule of international law applicable."[102] Historically, nations have extended existing laws of war to new technologies, from submarines to bombers and weapons of mass destruction. Others insist that novel cyber weapons require a new, treaty-based legal regime and associated arms control processes.

The main stumbling block to a new treaty is disagreement between the United States and Europe, on the one hand, and Russia and China, on the other hand, on the definition of cybersecurity and the best way to achieve it. Whereas Western governments tend to define it as maintaining the Internet's physical integrity, authoritarian governments conceive of it as "information security," implying the right to restrict transmission of, control access to, and censor ideas or data that could undermine internal stability, or threaten regime survival.[103]

In September 2011, China, Russia, Tajikistan, and Uzbekistan proposed a new International Code of Conduct for Information Security with two main provisions.[104] The first would have obliged all states not to use communications networks to "carry out hostile activities or acts of aggression" or to "proliferate information weapons and related technologies." Western countries rejected this on the grounds that it could prevent the development of cyber technology to defend against offensive cyber attacks.[105] The second would have committed

all states to "curb dissemination of information which incites terrorism, secessionism, extremism, or undermines other countries' political, economic, and social stability, as well as their spiritual and cultural environment." Western governments rejected this as a blatant defense of censorship. The proposal has subsequently gone nowhere.

Russia and China have also advocated including cyber weapons in disarmament, arms control, and nonproliferation negotiations, and US officials have explored this option.[106] There are, however, major differences between cyber and nuclear weapons. Cyber deterrence, for example, is much more complicated. The doctrine of mutually assured destruction "worked" because the target of a nuclear attack would know immediately that it had been attacked and could identify the attacker. In contrast, an attack in cyberspace may not be immediately apparent, and the attacker can remain anonymous, disguise itself as another actor, or conceal its location. Moreover, whereas a nuclear attack is essentially binary (it either occurs or does not), cyber attacks include multiple gradations between limited cyber espionage and all-out cyber war. Finally, cyber weapons pose enormous challenges for nonproliferation and verification. Unlike nuclear weapons, they require no special controlled material or restricted expertise to construct. Their digital nature also creates monitoring hurdles, implying a deeply intrusive inspection regime requiring countries and the private sector to open their digital infrastructure to external investigation and scrutiny—risking the exposure not only of critical national defense assets but also of proprietary technology, software, and business secrets.

Given these political disagreements and practical obstacles, it is unrealistic to believe a single UN treaty could simultaneously address the challenges of regulating cyber warfare, countering cyber crime, and protecting the civil liberties of Internet users.[107] More realistic is a piecemeal approach to negotiating new rules of engagement, particularly on issues of state responsibility for offensive cyber operations and cyber crime attacks launched from sovereign territory, as well as criteria for retaliation. In July 2010, the United States and eighteen other nations (including China and Russia) agreed on the need to work cooperatively to reduce the threat of cyber attacks. They also endorsed a UN role in establishing norms of responsible behavior in cyberspace.[108] Moving forward, US diplomats must reach out to emerging powers, particularly dynamic democracies such as India and Brazil, to bolster their support for Internet openness, as well as security.

High on the international agenda should be developing transparency and confidence-building measures, such as a new global information-sharing network on cyber attacks, and "hot lines" to defuse tension during crises. States should also negotiate commitments to preserve humanitarian fundamentals in the event of a cyber conflict.[109] Two other important steps to reducing tensions in cyberspace would be multilateral agreements not to attack the Internet's "root" servers and to outlaw, through codification and international and domestic prosecution, all denial-of-service (DOS) attacks. Root servers are fundamental to connecting readable URLs (web addresses) to their actual, machine-specific, numeric IP addresses, and preserving their integrity is fundamental to an open cyber commons.[110] Nations should also agree to ban DOS attacks, which serve only purposes of sabotage and which could affect all Internet users within a given geographic area.

Even as it advances a constructive governance agenda for cyberspace, the United States must deal with continued diplomatic fallout from the "Snowden affair." The episode has raised profound questions about expectations of privacy in Internet communications. In an effort to forge new global rules on this topic, Brazilian president Dilma Rousseff invited nations to attend a meeting on the future of Internet governance in São Paulo in April 2014.

CONCLUSION

Deepening integration, accelerating technological change, and the diffusion of power have made the global commons more important to global prosperity, more critical to international security, and more accessible to state and nonstate actors. Managing rising competition while preserving the openness of the maritime, outer-space, and cyber domains will be a fundamental challenge for global peace and security in the twenty-first century. As US hegemony declines, maintaining the stability of the global commons will require innovative forms of multilateral cooperation. Long-standing institutions such as the United Nations and treaty regimes such as the OST and UNCLOS will share space with more pragmatic forms of collective action, including coalitions of the willing, nonbinding codes of conduct, and public-private partnerships.

For the United States and other established powers, a precondition for success will be integrating today's emerging powers into a reformed set of institutions, both global and informal, in the face of these new challenges and opportunities.[111] This will be no easy task, given political differences between the world's status quo powers and its up-and-comers over the content of international rules, the division of authority within multilateral bodies, and the costs of sustaining an open global commons. Emerging powers must be persuaded that benefits will be broadly shared, while established nations will insist that existing norms be strengthened rather than diluted.

NOTES

The author is deeply grateful to Isabella Bennett for her research and editorial assistance with this chapter.

1. Scott Jasper and Scott Moreland, "Introduction: A Comprehensive Approach," in *Conflict and Cooperation in the Global Commons: A Comprehensive Approach for International Security*, ed. Scott Jasper (Washington, DC: Georgetown University Press, 2012), 1–2. This chapter does not address airspace, a fourth global commons.

2. Barry R. Posen, "Command of the Commons: The Military Foundation of U.S. Hegemony," *International Security* 28, no. 1 (Summer 2003): 5–46.

3. This refers to "the doctrine of joint operational access—getting forward, staying forward, and operating along secure lines of communication." Paul S. Giarra, "Assuring Joint Operational Access," in Jasper, *Conflict and Cooperation*, 141.

4. Schuyler Foerster, "Strategies of Deterrence," in Jasper, *Conflict and Cooperation*, 60.

5. Abraham M. Denmark and James Mulvenon, *Contested Commons: The Future of American Power in a Multipolar World* (Washington, DC: Center for a New American Security, January 2010), http://www.cnas.org/files/documents/publications/CNAS%20Contested%20Commons_1.pdf.

6. US Department of Defense, "Sustaining U.S. Global Leadership: Priorities for 21st Century Defense," January 2012, http://www.defense.gov/news/defense_strategic_guidance.pdf.

7. Unlike private goods, public goods cannot be denied to other parties; moreover, use by one actor does not (at least initially) detract from use by others. In technical terms, public goods are "nonexcludable" and "non-rival."

8. Public goods can also suffer from the "tragedy of the commons," as self-interested actors overexploit resources they consider inexhaustible or race to compete for shares in situations of perceived scarcity.

9. This paragraph draws on Sandra R. Leavitt, "Problems in Collective Action," in Jasper, *Conflict and Cooperation*, 23–25.

10. Stewart Patrick, "Prix Fixe *and* à la Carte: Avoiding False Multilateral Choices," *Washington Quarterly* 32, no. 4 (2009): 77–95.

11. Deputy Secretary of Defense William Lynn, "Remarks on Space Policy at U.S. Strategic Command Space Symposium" (Omaha, Nebraska, November 3, 2010), http://www.defense.gov/speeches/speech.aspx?speechid=1515.

12. Micah Zenko, "A Code of Conduct for Outer Space," Policy Innovation Memorandum no. 10 (Council on Foreign Relations, Washington, DC, November 2011), http://www.cfr.org/space/code-conduct-outer-space/p26556.

13. *Wikipedia*, "Timeline of First Orbital Launches by Country," http://en.wikipedia.org/wiki/Timeline_of_first_orbital_launches_by_country.

14. Isabella Bennett, "U.S. Space Policy and the Challenge of Integrating Emerging Powers" (meeting notes for a workshop, Council on Foreign Relations, Washington, DC, June 30, 2011), http://www.cfr.org/projects/world/workshop-on-us-space-policy-the-challenge-of-integrating-emerging-powers/pr1551.

15. CBSNews.com, "Back-to-Back Near Misses on Space Station," September 28, 2012, http://www.cbsnews.com/8301-205_162-57522636/back-to-back-near-misses-on-space-station/.

16. CBSNews.com, "U.S. and Russian Satellites Collide," February 12, 2009, http://www.cbsnews.com/2100-205_162-4792976.html.

17. Bruce W. MacDonald, "China, Space Weapons, and U.S. Security," Council Special Report no. 38 (Council on Foreign Relations, Washington, DC, September 2008), http://www.cfr.org/china/china-space-weapons-us-security/p16707.

18. Leonard David, "China's Anti-Satellite Test: Worrisome Debris Cloud Circles Earth," February 2, 2007, *Space.com*, http://www.space.com/3415-china-anti-satellite-test-worrisome-debris-cloud-circles-earth.html.

19. Michael Krepon, "Setting Norms for Activities in Space," in Jasper, *Conflict and Cooperation*, 203.

20. Formally, the Treaty on Principles Governing the Activities of States in the Exploration and Use of Outer Space, including the Moon and

Other Celestial Bodies. See United Nations Treaty Collection, http://treaties.un.org/Pages/showDetails.aspx?objid=0800000280128cbd.

21. Bennett, "U.S. Space Policy."

22. The US national space policy of August 2006 explicitly stated, "The United States will oppose the development of new legal regimes or other restrictions that seek to prohibit or limit U.S. access to or uses of space." See the unclassified document posted by the Federation of American Scientists, http://www.fas.org/irp/offdocs/nspd/space.pdf.

23. Conversations with Pentagon and State Department officials, 2011. See also "National Security Strategy of the United States," May 2010, The White House, http://www.whitehouse.gov/sites/default/files/rss_viewer/national_security_strategy.pdf.

24. "National Space Policy of the United States of America," June 28, 2010, p. 3, The White House, http://www.whitehouse.gov/sites/default/files/national_space_policy_6-28-10.pdf. See also "Fact Sheet: The National Space Policy," The White House, June 28, 2010, http://www.whitehouse.gov/the-press-office/fact-sheet-national-space-policy. Michael Krepon has advocated for a US-led "space assurance regime"; see Krepon, *Space Assurance or Space Dominance: The Case Against Weaponizing Space* (Washington, DC: Stimson Center, 2003).

25. Krepon, "Setting Norms," 207.

26. "China and Russia Jointly Submitted the Draft Treaty on PPWT to the Conference on Disarmament," PRC Ministry of Foreign Affairs, http://www.fmprc.gov.cn/eng/wjb/zzjg/jks/jkxw/t408634.htm; and Jinyuan Su, "The 'Peaceful Purposes' Principle in Outer Space and the Russia-China PPWT Proposal," *Space Policy* 26 (2010): 81–90.

27. This paragraph draws on Gilead Sher, "Setting Rules for Outer Space" (panelist paper, Council of Councils annual meeting, March 10–12, 2013).

28. Secretary of State Hillary Rodham Clinton, "International Code of Conduct for Outer Space Activities" (press statement, US Department of State), January 17, 2012, http://www.state.gov/secretary/rm/2012/01/180969.htm.

29. Zenko, "Code of Conduct for Outer Space."

30. Rose Gottemoeller, "A Code of Conduct for Outer Space, as Seen from the State Department," letter to the editor, *New York Times*, March 16, 2012, http://www.nytimes.com/2012/03/16/opinion/a-code-for-outer-space-as-seen-from-the-state-dept.html?_r=0.

31. Eli Lake, "Republicans Wary of EU Code for Space Activity," *Washington Times*, February 3, 2011, http://www.washingtontimes.com/news/2011/feb/3/republicans-wary-of-eu-code-for-space-activity/?page=all.

32. John Bolton and John Yoo, "Hands off the Heavens," *New York Times*, March 8, 2012, http://www.nytimes.com/2012/03/09/opinion/hands-off-the-heavens.html?_r=1&.

33. Clinton, "International Code of Conduct." See also "An International Code of Conduct for Outer Space Activities," Fact Sheet, US Department of State, http://www.state.gov/r/pa/pl/2012/180998.htm; and Frank A. Rose, "Pursuing an International Code of Conduct for the Security and Sustainability of the Space Environment" (remarks at the National Space Symposium, Colorado Springs, April 18, 2012), http://www.state.gov/t/avc/rls/188088.htm.

34. Of course, the G20 does not include emerging spacefaring nations North Korea or Iran, neither of which should be invited into such a forum.

35. The MEF consists of the world's seventeen largest greenhouse gas emitters.

36. Council on Foreign Relations, "The Global Oceans Regime" (issue brief, Washington, DC, June 2013), http://www.cfr.org/oceans/global-oceans-regime/p21035.

37. Mlada Bukovansky, "American Identity and Neutral Rights from Independence to the War of 1812," *International Organization* 51, no. 2 (1997): 209–43.

38. Alfred Thayer Mahan, *The Influence of Sea Power on History, 1660–1783*.

39. Sam J. Tangredi, "The Maritime Commons and Military Power," in Jasper, *Conflict and Cooperation*, 72–73.

40. *International Trade Statistics 2009*, World Trade Organization, http://www.wto.org/english/res_e/statis_e/its2009_e/its2009_e.pdf, p. 173.

41. "International Trade and Market Access Data," 2012, World Trade Organization, http://www.wto.org/english/res_e/statis_e/statis_bis_e.htm?solution=WTO&path=/Dashboards/MAPS&file=Map.wcdf&bookmarkState={%22impl%22:%22client%22,%22params%22:{%22langParam%22:%22en%22}}.

42. "International Shipping Facts and Figures" (Maritime Knowledge Center, International Maritime Organization, March 6, 2012), http://www.imo.org/KnowledgeCentre/ShipsAndShippingFactsAndFigures/TheRoleandImportanceofInternationalShipping/Documents/International%20Shipping%20-%20Facts%20and%20Figures.pdf, 9.

43. Stewart Patrick, *Weak Links: Fragile States, Global Threats, and International Security* (New York: Oxford University Press, 2011), 182–83; and US Energy Information Administration, "World Oil Transit Chokepoints," August 22, 2012, http://www.eia.gov/countries/regions-topics.cfm?fips=wotc&trk=p3.

44. Center for International Earth Science Information Network (CIESIN), "Percentage of Total Population Living in Coastal Areas," http://sedac.ciesin.columbia.edu/es/papers/Coastal_Zone_Pop_Method.pdf.

45. US Navy, "Status of the Navy," http://www.navy.mil/navydata/nav_legacy.asp?id=146.

46. Nitin Gokhale, "The Indian Navy's Big Ambitions," *The Diplomat*, May 10, 2012, http://thediplomat.com/2012/05/10/the-indian-navy%E2%80%99s-big-ambitions/.

47. Tara Murphy, "Security Challenges in the 21st Century Global Commons," *Yale Journal of International Affairs* 5 (Spring/Summer 2010): 32–33.

48. "China's Aggressive New Diplomacy," *Wall Street Journal*, October 1, 2010, http://online.wsj.com/article/SB10001424052748704483004575523710432896610.html.

49. Robert Beckman, "Islands or Rocks? Evolving Dispute in the South China Sea" (S. Rajaratnam School of International Studies, May 10, 2011), http://www.rsis.edu.sg/publications/Perspective/RSIS0752011.pdf.

50. Sam Bateman, "UNCLOS and Its Limitations as the Foundation for a Regional Maritime Security Regime," *Korean Journal of Defense Analysis* 19, no. 3 (2007): 27–56.

51. "China Declares Air Defense Zone in East China Sea amid Row," Reuters, November 23, 2013, http://www.bloomberg.com/news/2013-11-23/china-declares-air-defense-zone-in-east-china-sea-amid-japan-row.html.

52. Bonnie S. Glaser, "Armed Clash in the South China Sea," Contingency Planning Memo no. 14 (Council on Foreign Relations, Washington, DC, April 2012), http://www.cfr.org/world/armed-clash-south-china-sea/p27883.

53. Stewart Patrick, "Turbulent Waters: The United States, China, and the South China Sea," *The Internationalist* (blog), November 2, 2012, Council on Foreign Relations, http://blogs.cfr.org/patrick/2012/11/02/turbulent-waters-the-united-states-china-and-the-south-china-sea/.

54. Scott G. Borgerson, "The Coming Arctic Boom: As the Ice Melts, the Region Heats Up," *Foreign Affairs* 92, no. 4 (July/August 2013): 76–89.

55. The former corridor could reduce the distance from Rotterdam to Seattle by 2,000 miles, or 25 percent; the latter could reduce the distance between Rotterdam and Yokohama more than 40 percent, from 11,200 to 6,500 miles.

56. Scott G. Borgerson, "Arctic Meltdown: The Economic and Security Implications of Global Warming," *Foreign Affairs* 87, no. 2 (March/April 2008): 63–77; and Oran R. Young, "The Future of the Arctic: Cauldron of Conflict or Zone of Peace?" *International Affairs* 87, no. 1 (January 2011): 185–93.

57. Zdeněk Kříž and Filip Chrášťanský, "Existing Conflicts in the Arctic and the Risk of Escalation: Rhetoric and Reality," *Perspectives: Central European Review of International Affairs* 20, no. 1 (2012): 111–39.

58. Borgerson, "Coming Arctic Boom." The Arctic region also contains huge stores of minerals, from zinc to palladium to rare earths—though these are conveniently located almost entirely in the sovereign territories of states.

59. These include disagreements between the United States and Russia in the Bering Sea; the United States and Canada in the Beaufort Sea; Canada and Denmark (Greenland) in the Davis Strait; and Norway and Russia in the Barents Sea.

60. This claim is based on Russia's insistence that the underwater Lomonosov Ridge is a natural continuation of the Siberian continental shelf.

61. While skirting the sovereignty issue, the 1988 agreement requires the United States always to request—and Canada always to grant—free passage of US naval vessels.

62. Borgerson, "Arctic Meltdown."

63. Kříž and Chráštanský, "Existing Conflicts in the Arctic," 111; and Ian G. Brosnan, Thomas M. Leschine, and Edward L. Miles, "Cooperation or Conflict in a Changing Arctic?" *Ocean Development and International Law* 42 (2011): 173–210.

64. Brosnan et al., "Cooperation or Conflict."

65. Lauren Ploch, Christopher M. Blanchard, Ronald O'Rourke, R. Chuck Mason, and Rawle O. King, "Piracy off the Horn of Africa," Congressional Research Service Report for Congress, R40528, April 27, 2011.

66. Patrick, *Weak Links*, 160–62.

67. International Chamber of Commerce, "IMB Reports Drop in Somali Piracy, But Warns against Complacency," October 22, 2012, http://www.iccwbo.org/News/Articles/2012/IMB-reports-drop-in-Somali-piracy,-but-warns-against-complacency/.

68. Relevant resolutions include UNSCR 1816, UNSCR 1846, and UNSCR 1851. A subsequent resolution (UNSCR 1910), endorsing the creation of an international tribunal to prosecute pirates, went nowhere after objections raised in the US Senate.

69. Bruce Jones, "Beyond Blocs: The West, Rising Powers, and Interest-Based International Cooperation," Stanley Foundation Policy Analysis Brief, October 2011, http://www.stanleyfoundation.org/publications/pab/JonesPAB1011B.pdf.

70. Chester A. Crocker, Fen Osler Hampson, and Pamela Aall, eds., *Rewiring Regional Security in a Fragmented World* (Washington, DC: United States Institute of Peace Press, 2011), 547.

71. Scott G. Borgerson, "The National Interest and the Law of the Sea," Council Special Report no. 46 (Council on Foreign Relations, Washington, DC, May 2009), http://www.cfr.org/global-governance/national-interest-law-sea/p19156.

72. Thomas Wright, "Outlaw of the Sea: The Senate Republicans' UNCLOS Blunder," August 7, 2012, *Foreign Affairs*, http://www.foreignaffairs.com/articles/137815/thomas-wright/outlaw-of-the-sea.

73. Bateman, "UNCLOS and Its Limitations."

74. Susan Page Hocevar, "Building Collaborative Capacity for Maritime Security," in Jasper, *Conflict and Cooperation*, 124–31.

75. Jasper and Moreland, "Introduction," 11.

76. Gordan E. Van Hook, "Maritime Security Consortiums," in Jasper, *Conflict and Cooperation*, 174–77.

77. Larry Clinton, "Cyber Security Social Contract," in Jasper, *Conflict and Cooperation*, 185–86.

78. Boston Consulting Group, "The Internet Economy in the G20," March 19, 2012, https://www.bcgperspectives.com/content/articles/media_entertainment_strategic_planning_4_2_trillion_opportunity_internet_economy_g20/; and Quentin Hardy, "McKinsey Says Social Media Could Add $1.3 Trillion to the Economy," *Bits* (blog), July 25, 2012, *New York Times*, http://bits.blogs.nytimes.com/2012/07/25/mckinsey-says-social-media-adds-1-3-trillion-to-the-economy/.

79. Jasper and Moreland, "Introduction," 9.

80. Frank A. Ninkovich, *The Diplomacy of Ideas: U.S. Foreign Policy and Cultural Relations 1938–1950* (Cambridge: Cambridge University Press, 1981).

81. Krishna Jayakar, "Globalization and the Legitimacy of International Telecommunications Standard-Setting Organizations," *Indiana Journal of Global Legal Studies* 5 (1998): 711–38.

82. International Telecommunication Union, "WCIT-12: Conference Overview," http://www.itu.int/en/wcit-12/Pages/overview.aspx.

83. Ambassador Terry Kramer, cited in Stewart Patrick, "UN Control of the Internet? An Idea Whose Time Will Never Come," *The Internationalist* (blog), December 4, 2012, Council on Foreign Relations, http://blogs.cfr.org/patrick/2012/12/04/un-control-of-the-internet-an-idea-whose-time-will-never-come/.

84. Kevin G. Coleman, "Aggression in Cyberspace," in Jasper, *Conflict and Cooperation*, 105–22.

85. Peter Maass and Megha Rajagopalan, "Does Cybercrime Really Cost $1 Trillion?" August 1, 2012, *ProPublica*, http://www.propublica.org/article/does-cybercrime-really-cost-1-trillion.

86. The White House, "Remarks from the President on Securing Our Nation's Cyber-Infrastructure" (East Room, May 29, 2009), http://www.whitehouse.gov/the_press_office/Remarks-by-the-President-on-Securing-Our-Nations-Cyber-Infrastructure.

87. Clinton, "Cyber Security Social Contract," 187.

88. Clinton, "Cyber Security Social Contract," 187–88.

89. "'Botnets' Run Wild," *Washington Post*, January 24, 2013.

90. The closest analogue is the Forum of Incident Response and Security Teams (FIRST), a network of top computer security experts founded in 1989 to share information about viruses, which has minimal powers. See the forum's website at http://www.first.org.

91. Robert K. Knake, "Internet Governance in an Age of Cyber Insecurity," Council Special Report no. 56 (Council on Foreign Relations, Washington, DC, September 2010), 18.

92. Clinton, "Cyber Security Social Contract," 189–90.

93. Ellen Nakashima, "Pentagon to Boost Cybersecurity Force," *Washington Post*, January 27, 2013, http://articles.washingtonpost.com/2013-01-27/world/36583575_1_cyber-protection-forces-cyber-command-cybersecurity.

94. Denmark and Mulvenon, *Contested Commons*, 150; and Duncan Hollis, "Why States Need an International Law for Information Operations," *Lewis & Clark Law Review* 11 (2007): 1023–61.

95. Knake, "Internet Governance in an Age of Cyber Insecurity," 24.

96. Katherine Maher, "Did the Bounds of Cyber War Just Expand to Banks and Neutral States?" *The Atlantic*, August 27, 2012.

97. Thomas Rid, "Cyber War Will Not Take Place," *Journal of Strategic Studies* 35, no. 1 (2012): 5–32.

98. A more recent example is the Flame virus; see "'Flame' Virus Explained: How It Works and Who's Behind It" (interview with Vitaly Kamlyuk), May 30, 2012, *RT* (previously Russia Today), http://rt.com/news/flame-virus-cyber-war-536/.

99. Duncan Hollis, "An e-SOS for Cyberspace," *Opinio Juris* (blog), July 13, 2011, http://opiniojuris.org/2011/07/13/an-e-sos-for-cyberspace-2/.

100. Anthony Rutkowski, "Public International Law of the International Telecommunication Instruments: Cyber Security Treaty Provisions since 1850," *INFO* 13, no. 1 (2011): 15; "World Summit on the Information Society: First Phase, Geneva," International Telecommunication Union, http://www.itu.int/wsis/geneva/index.html; EastWest Institute, "Second Worldwide Cybersecurity Summit: London, June 1–2, 2011," http://www.cybersummit2011.com/; BBC News, "London Hosts Cyberspace Security Conference," November 1, 2011, http://www.bbc.co.uk/news/technology-15533786; and Bryan Glick, "London Cybersecurity Conference: A Missed Opportunity?" *Computer Weekly Editor's Blog*, November 4, 2011, http://www.computerweekly.com/blogs/editors-blog/2011/11/london-cybersecurity-conference.html.

101. Hollis, "Why States Need an International Law."

102. The Additional Protocol further establishes that in the absence of a formal legal standard, "civilians and combatants remain under the protection and authority of the principles of international law derived from established custom, from the principles of humanity and from the dictates of public conscience. Additional Protocol (I) to the Geneva Conventions, https://treaties.un.org/doc/Publication/UNTS/Volume%201125/volume-1125-I-17512-English.pdf." Cited in Hollis, "Why States Need an International Law," 1037.

103. Adam Segal and Matthew Waxman, "Why a Cybersecurity Treaty Is a Pipe Dream," *Global Public Square* (blog), October 27, 2011, CNN, http://globalpublicsquare.blogs.cnn.com/2011/10/27/why-a-cybersecurity-treaty-is-a-pipe-dream/.

104. "China, Russia and Other Countries Submit the Document of International Code of Conduct for Information Security to the United Nations," PRC Ministry of Foreign Affairs, http://www.fmprc.gov.cn/eng/wjdt/wshd/t858978.htm.

105. Knake, "Internet Governance in an Age of Cyber Insecurity," 22–23.

106. In 2011, a *Christian Science Monitor* writer reported that the United States was "actively engaged in informal discussions" to model cyber weapons treaties on nuclear arms talks.

107. Segal and Waxman, "Why a Cybersecurity Treaty Is a Pipe Dream."

108. Coleman, "Aggression in Cyber Space," 114–16.

109. Duncan Hollis, "E-war Rules of Engagement," *Los Angeles Times*, October 8, 2007, http://www.latimes.com/news/la-oe-hollis8oct08,0,5514026.story; and Hollis, "An e-SOS for Cyberspace."

110. Knake, "Internet Governance in an Age of Cyber Insecurity," 24.

111. Stewart Patrick, "Irresponsible Stakeholders? The Difficulty of Integrating Rising Powers," *Foreign Affairs* 89, no. 6 (November/December 2010): 44–53.

7

FROM SOMNOLENCE TO TURBULENCE
THE GLOBAL AWAKENING

Ellen Laipson

This chapter (written in the turbulent spring of 2013) addresses the security implications of two key phenomena of recent world history: the political mobilization of peoples around the globe, including significant cases of nonviolent mobilization since the end of the Cold War; and the role that modern communications technologies have played in this era of individual and collective empowerment. The analysis explores whether or how these dimensions of international political behavior are unique or distinct as compared with those of earlier periods, and whether they change significantly the way in which states or other governance institutions function.

The Arab Awakening that began in late 2010 has given rise to the notion that the arc of history is complete; citizens' empowerment and demand for representation in seats of power are now universal norms, even if the trend toward self-determination has not been consolidated or sustained in all locales, and occasionally suffers from setbacks in states on the path to democracy. The notion of a "global awakening" is, in the abstract, a powerful and uplifting view of the human condition and the shift in power from institutions to individuals. In the gritty reality of nation-states, however, the struggle continues. Political leaders in places where the awakening has recently occurred embrace it only reluctantly and insist that sovereign territories still face threats from enemies within and without. In fact, the awakening and its technological enablers have empowered not only the good guys—the earnest would-be democrats in the last regions of the world to surf the democratization wave—but also the bad guys, who have benefitted from weakening controls by states and by transnational tools of communication and commerce. The security agenda for states and societies has evolved, to be sure, but a democratizing world is not necessarily a safer or more peaceful world.

The notion of individual empowerment as an enduring and significant part of the global landscape is gaining traction. The latest quadrennial study by the National Intelligence Council, "Global Trends 2030: Alternative Worlds," released in December 2012, names individual empowerment as the first and, by implication, most important of four megatrends of the next two decades. It states that "it is both a cause and an effect of most other trends, including the expanding global economy, rapid growth of the developing countries, and widespread exploitation of new communications and manufacturing technologies."[1] The study begins to tease out the long-term ramifications of reducing extreme poverty, expanding the middle class, closing the education and gender gaps, and using the power of technology to further all these trends. As for the political and security ramifications, "Global Trends 2030" sees a world with considerable ideological conflict, not over the big ideas that animated the twentieth century—democracy, fascism, and communism—but over the role of religion in global politics. Coupled with a concern about rising or reemerging forms of nationalism, particularly in East Asia, one can imagine a twenty-first-century agenda that lurches between very nineteenth-century issues of borders and religious wars, and a global culture of highly networked and wired young, middle-class people who eschew traditional politics and national identities. This suggests a conceptually confusing picture for governments, but it draws together in a compelling way the two animating themes of this chapter.

THE ARAB SPRING: EMPIRICAL PROOF OF THE AWAKENING?

The dramatic upheaval in several key Arab states beginning in late 2010 is the most recent manifestation of the themes of this chapter: the awakening of citizens demanding rights in nondemocratic societies; the conduct of the awakening, at least in its early

stages, without resort to violence; and the power of modern communications technology to diffuse information and ideas, which contributed to, if not determined, the political outcomes in key cases. One recalls the surge of optimism and hope that accompanied the dramatic events of Tunisia in late 2010 and Egypt in early 2011 that quickly toppled two longtime autocrats, President Zine el Abidine Ben Ali of Tunisia (in office 1987–2011) and President Hosni Mubarak of Egypt (in office 1981–2011). The spontaneous outpouring of frustration at political and economic inequality, and the peaceful demand for dignity and political change, captured the imagination of the world and prompted comparisons to earlier nonviolent uprisings that led to revolutionary change in disparate parts of the world. The marches and sit-ins in Tunis and Cairo were also notable for their demographic diversity. It was not just blue-jeans-clad youth who took to the streets, but middle-class families, organized labor, professionals, and, over time, more traditional elements from Islamist social and political forces.

The early phases of the Arab Awakening were notable for the absence of violence by protestors and by the regimes themselves. Much will be written about the remarkable restraint of the Tunisian and Egyptian militaries, and the drama of those soldiers' refusal to use force against their citizens, even when the threat to regime stability was acute. There is considerable evidence that protestors were quite purposeful and well trained in their decision to eschew violence, and were influenced, directly or indirectly, by historic precedents in eastern Europe and by the conceptual thinkers who espoused nonviolence as the most effective way to achieve political change. The eighty-five-year-old Gene Sharp, a retired political science professor and founder of the Albert Einstein Institute, had his moment of fame when young Arab activists identified his writings on nonviolent action as influential.

In the decade before the events of 2010, US-funded programs to spread democratic values, to train young activists in using information technology, and to develop political parties and nongovernmental organizations also contributed to the outcomes in the Arab Spring, even if those "soft power" inputs were not recognized at the time. Academic institutions and more activist and training-focused groups such as the International Center on Nonviolent Conflict, the National Endowment for Democracy, and the United States Institute of Peace spent years engaging young people in developing some of the technical and functional skills needed for conflict prevention, and for more open communications and political environments.

Arab scholars in the first decade of the new century were looking back at the rise of Islamism and its more radical expressions as the main source of opposition to authoritarianism. Shadi Hamid compared Islamist social movements with violent extremists to assess their relative degree of success in effecting political change. He argued that violent extremists were not very "consequential" in the history of systemic political change in the region, as compared to "mass-based Islamist groups and parties with grassroots support and religious legitimacy." Writing in 2009, he conceded that nonviolent action and civil resistance have not been particularly effective, but that it was remarkable that political opposition in the Middle East has historically *not* moved to violence.[2]

The extraordinarily rapid fall of the autocrats was determined in part by the roles of the military in both states: their refusal to fire on unarmed demonstrators and their ability to see their institutional interests as independent of the regimes they had long served was unanticipated by many regional experts, who expected regimes to maintain their hold on power through coercion if need be. In a study that addressed what regional experts had said about prospects for

change in the Middle East before it happened, it was clear that many think-tank scholars had begun to ponder the emerging tensions between the Egyptian military and the regime of Hosni Mubarak. But they were not able to confidently connect the dots between professional soldiers subtly distancing themselves from their political leaders, and the mass participation of citizens who were fed up with those leaders, perhaps for different reasons.[3]

In rapid succession in 2011, revolts emerged in Libya, Yemen, Bahrain, and Syria. While Libya was initially also nonviolent, these other cases included considerable violence by regime forces, and in all cases but Bahrain led to armed militia and political-military environments that looked increasingly like civil war. (Bahrain's level of violence has remained low; Shia opposition conducts daily acts of disobedience, but against regime property, not persons.)

By early 2013, Libya joined Tunisia and Egypt in a post-authoritarian moment that is politically dynamic and full of security uncertainties. Yemen is a unique situation where citizens' empowerment had emerged over many years, and where the current political transition may be little more than an intra-elite arrangement, not a fundamental realignment of power. Syria is the national and regional tragedy that plays to general perceptions of Arab world intrigue, violence, and perfidy, and profoundly alters the notion that the Arab world uprisings were largely peaceful. They were peaceful where regimes fell quickly, but prone to violence where regimes chose to resist change.

Yet a few years after it began, the Arab Awakening is a political scientist's nightmare. It does not prove or disprove any theory about political change, does not conform with past democratization waves, and may be too raw and recent to allow us to draw any conclusions that will stand the test of time. Arab intellectuals debate the Arab

Spring: Has it become a travesty of its original purpose? Will the would-be democrats find themselves living under new types of nondemocratic rule, or under reconstituted authoritarian regimes? Egypt and Syria appear to be lurching between forces that work to preserve the state's coercive power at all costs. In Egypt in early 2014, it manifests as a return to authoritarianism, and in Syria as a form of chaos that could lead to state collapse. Tunisia and Libya are weak states with profound security vacuums, but still on a path to building more representative systems, albeit in conditions where societal cohesion and consensus appear lacking. Tunisia alone deserves credit for staying on course, and the completion of a new constitution in February 2014 is a critical milestone for the country and the region. Yemen confounds the citizens who revolted because powerful elements of the old system and the old culture remain in place. The current snapshot of the region would suggest that the empowerment perceived in the first year has devolved to a disempowerment of the would-be democrats, as far as political sway is concerned.

Nonetheless, with respect to the broad theme of individual empowerment, evidence abounds that people from all walks of life in the Arab world are enjoying a new freedom of expression and are participating in the public space in ways that are unprecedented. There is a proliferation of media outlets, nongovernmental organizations, and enterprises that suggests a passionate commitment to public participation. The growth of NGOs, however, is not transformative without a partnership or balancing force in transparent and accessible government structures. Citizens' access to decision makers and to political processes is still limited, and the new social pact between government and the governed that was the promise of the Arab Spring appears illusory now.

The Islamization of politics in Tunisia and Libya in the immediate aftermath of change at the top, the short-lived ascendance of the Muslim Brotherhood into the halls of power in Egypt, and the sectarian overlay to the struggle in Syria further complicate the picture. These deep cultural dimensions of this period of transition could well converge with the broad trajectory toward more representative government, but in the short run, they appear to work at cross purposes with the core values and principles of citizens' empowerment. Some of the religious underpinnings of ascendant political power actually emphasize collective rights and interests and obedience to power, above the more secular focus on the individual as the unit of political action. Rather than a linear progression of empowerment of the previously powerless, the region is replete with complex cases of power redistributed, and of nonviolent strategies giving way to more traditional struggles between doctrinaire political organizations or between weakened regimes and armed ragtag bands of rebels and loosely formed militia.

It is also worth noting that the awakening has touched only part of the Arab world. According to the United Nations Development Programme's data, of the 360 million Arabs included in their count of Arab states, less than half live in countries of the Arab Spring (144 million is the total population of Egypt, Libya, Syria, Tunisia, and Yemen). According to Freedom House's slightly different formula, only 2 percent of the 395 million Arabs they count live in countries rated as "free," six Arab states are considered partly free, and ten are characterized as not free.[4]

The Arab Spring's early peaceful demand for change in 2010 and 2011 was not precedent setting; rather, it was the culmination of the twentieth-century saga so ably documented by Peter Ackerman and Jack Duvall in *A Force More Powerful: A Century of Nonviolent Conflict*.[5] Their stories of successful nonviolent political change include Russia in 1905, Gandhi's work in India from the 1920s to independence in the 1940s, and Poland in the 1980s. Yet a valid comparison of those cases to the protests of the early twenty-first century requires longer reflection; in the examples given by Ackerman and Duvall, the point at which the opposition forces knew they were successful varied from weeks to decades, reminding us that it is too early to judge whether the Arab Spring cases will make the threshold for an updated volume on the subject.

SOCIAL MEDIA AND ITS TRANSFORMATIVE POWER *PLUS ÇA CHANGE?*

The second theme of this chapter is the role of social media as a transformative aspect of a changing global security environment. As with the notion of citizens' empowerment, the conventional view is that the development and spread of mass communications devices and services, including Facebook, Twitter, and cell-phone texting, have profoundly changed societal relations and are well along the way to changing state-society relations. Many believe that the near universality of access to information technology has been a powerful driver for greater egalitarian and democratic distribution of power and influence, and that the quantity and quality of this phenomenon in the early twenty-first century has far exceeded the role of technology in earlier generations, such as the use of cassette recordings to spread the revolution in Iran in the late 1970s, or the use of cell phones to mobilize voters in the Philippines in the 1980s. Some believe too much attention has been paid to social media as a driver of the Arab Spring; seasoned Arab observer Jon Alterman believes that satellite television was the real game changer in exposing Arab publics to a wider world, and to galvanizing society in Egypt and beyond

with the riveting scenes of Tahrir Square in late 2010.[6]

The commercial world is ahead of the political world in its efforts to exploit these communications for the purposes of commerce and profit, but intelligence analysts are learning new data-mining techniques to try to derive political content from social media. Politicians ignore tweeting at their own peril. The use of social media appears to be de rigueur for public figures, from the president of the United States to the pope. But do we understand its actual power and its limits?

To use the Arab Spring again as the empirical case, cyber activism was hailed as both a cause and an outcome of the revolts that spread across North Africa after late 2010. According to Courtney Radsch, Internet access in Egypt expanded from 13 percent in 2005 to 40 percent in 2011.[7] Twitter and Facebook became "an integral part of any political protest," but she explains that despite the embrace of Facebook by over 16 million users in the Arab region, access did not correlate with political upheaval; many users were expatriates, and in some of the countries where political expression was suppressed, user communities were simply too small to matter. Global Voices Online is a blog aggregator cofounded by Tunisian journalist and activist Sami Ben Gharbeia. As Radsch notes, many of the posts were critical of incumbent power, but only Egyptian posts spoke openly of the desire for wholesale political change.[8] While the messages overall did not predict revolution, the spread of the technology was a powerful tool for mobilizing street protests and advertising state-sponsored abuses, and only those who cared to monitor the youth culture came to conclude that a bottom-up political shift was under way.[9] Nonetheless, Egypt stands out as a powerful example of social media's potential impact; it was the only place where blogs and Facebook explicitly talked about revolutionary change.

Social media was spreading long before the outbreak of fearlessness, and one notable feature was its rapid movement across borders, allowing a new version of pan-Arab awareness and identity for young people that had long faded as a political idea for their parents. Ironically, just as each Arab state has come to see its history as distinct from that of other states, and as political models across the region vary from traditional monarchy to liberal democracy, the social media phenomenon may generate unintended political significance by creating deeper links and solidarity across national boundaries for younger citizens.

There are many cases beyond the Middle East that have also provided strong evidence of social media's power in mobilizing and aggregating societal discontent into political messages, but these cases are inconclusive about its ultimate effectiveness as a driver of democratization. Clay Shirky has outlined how, in the last decade, social media usage caused a specific outcome—the defeat of an incumbent leader—in the Philippines, Spain, and Moldova, but failed to achieve the same outcome in Belarus, Iran, and Thailand.[10] He explains that social media is a precursor to political activism; it can be useful in strengthening the public space, but political change usually comes after, not at the same time as, that process. In hindsight, even some who celebrated the power of social media in the early months of the Arab Spring later made the distinction between social mobilization and political action. Once change occurred in several Arab capitals, in fact, the relative importance of mass communication shifted to the government side, and Arab activists realized that generating crowds was not sufficient to effect institutional change or the slow process of political reform.

Analysts continue to refine and shade their understanding of the relevance of social media in other transitions in the post-Cold War period, in many cases revising their initial views about the centrality and causality of social media in determining political outcomes. Overall, experts believe that cell-phone use has had less impact than what was originally understood in the color revolutions.[11] Some of the limits relate to what portion of the public has access and can afford these new technologies. In other cases, the social media was useful in sharing information, but was not sufficient to sustain protests or to ensure that the initial agents of change were still players once the transition took place. Many associate Ukraine's Orange Revolution with one of the first uses of the Internet as a tool for nonviolent protests. In late 2004–early 2005, the Internet was still relatively young and not controlled by the state. It was effective in spreading information and in monitoring election results, but the outcome of the revolution was mixed: corruption went down, but no former government officials were ever charged. In April 2009, tiny Moldova had its "Twitter Revolution" when young activists, to their great surprise, produced twenty thousand people on the steps of the parliament and forced a recount of the general election results. And in the Russian Duma elections in 2011 and presidential elections in 2012, Facebook and smart phones were used to monitor election fraud and to mobilize voters.

Social media's rise has also, paradoxically, created new opportunities for states to enhance control over their citizenry in various ways. First, just allowing citizens access to the Internet and other global media has been a way to placate populations and compensate for the lack of other, more political forms of freedom and self-expression. Arab intellectuals such as Ghassan Salamé have pointed out the self-interested way in which Egypt, for example, opened its media space out of recognition that tourists and foreign investors expected such services. The government also was willing, reluctantly perhaps, to allow ordinary citizens access to entertainment and media outlets without fully understanding the longer-term implications of such access. In the states of the former Soviet Union and in China, state manipulation of the new media, and the new media's utility for monitoring citizens' activities and reading preferences, constitute yet another a chapter in the tools of authoritarianism and do not correlate well with more individual freedom and democratization.[12] Even in more open societies, new debates have emerged about the downsides and risks of cyber tools for privacy and even for social and psychological well-being.

IMPLICATIONS FOR NATIONAL SECURITY AND CONFLICT MANAGEMENT

The security implications of these trends are indirect and diffuse. Other chapters in this volume address how states and international institutions need to develop more agile responses for a complex and evolving threat environment. For this chapter, the issue is how do the recent trends in citizen empowerment and in mass communications affect security processes and outcomes? At a fundamental level, where intuition counts for more than empirical data, citizens' empowerment and more participatory politics mean that the security agenda is exposed to a greater diversity of views, and more open media means that governments must share information about threats and could find the process of decision making about security issues compromised by the public demand for transparency. In theory, the trend could mean a dramatic erosion in the monopoly states have enjoyed on information that has security consequences. Whether better-informed citizens develop more coherent and consensual views of matters of national security remains to be seen; one can see an upside to more involvement by citizens in

security decision making that could result, perhaps, in less willingness to send young men and women into battle, but one could also imagine mass mobilization around a perceived enemy or threat that could push a government to be more aggressive than a more deliberative process would choose. In addition, a more open process and a larger set of actors could also constrain states from responding to specific threats in a timely and effective way.

One cannot generalize about how the evolving threat environment that combines traditional geopolitical threats, such as maritime disputes in the East or South China Sea, with nontraditional threats, such as climate change, terrorism, and cyber attacks, will affect publics that are more aware and more informed than earlier generations. The Egypt case, in the immediate post-Mubarak period, suggests that some post-authoritarian societies will want to focus on domestic issues of poverty and justice more than external issues used by old regimes to create solidarity and loyalty to power, and to distract publics from their domestic failings. The formal aspects of Egypt's foreign policy did not change right after the revolution, but the revolution was decidedly not about national security or foreign policy. A conclusion one could draw in the case of Egypt is that newly empowered citizens may look at security problems in a practical way, and prefer that a nation's resources be spent on its citizens, not on external adventures.

To the extent that governments in many regions have used external threats to rally popular support for a regime that may not be delivering services or fulfilling a state-society compact, informed citizens, journalists, and parliaments with more clout may find the formal protocols of national security decision making to be lacking. They could well call for reviews of past policies, assistance relationships, and alliances, and the resulting exposure could create uncertainties about a country's position on various international problems. Libya's democratic transitions have brought to the fore inexperienced political forces in key positions, and could easily create uncertainty about national positions on regional and international issues. The recent turmoil in Mali, for example, could pose serious challenges to the countries of North Africa that have not yet rebuilt their security institutions after the revolutions and are unskilled in building consensus over political divisions.

At the same time, empowered and informed citizens could build cross-border coalitions that could become useful, even effective tools in conflict management. Citizens able to communicate across a conflict zone could shame governments and attract international support in ways that could reduce violence and promote negotiated solutions. This might not produce strong, optimal agreements, but would reflect a constantly evolving, ad hoc approach to conflict management in an era of weak government.

On balance, however, the uncertainties about the true intentions and capabilities of newly empowered citizens outweigh the possible paradigms of ideals-driven behavior in a more open world. Information and political freedom draw on all the impulses of human nature, and create endless opportunities for conflict and strife within societies and between states. For today's Middle East, for example, where less than half its citizens live in countries that have shed authoritarianism, the prospects for political tension have risen, and the gaps in outlook and capacity between the Gulf oil-rich states and the Mediterranean Rim countries have grown. This may not lead directly to armed conflict or war, but it raises significant issues about the ability of governments and institutions to respond to demands for jobs and justice, and to maintain control of borders

and security in a region fraught with threats and competing ideas about governance.

Notes

1. National Intelligence Council (Office of the Director of National Intelligence), "Global Trends 2030: Alternative Worlds," December 2012, iii.

2. Shadi Hamid, "Islamists and Nonviolent Action," in *Civilian Jihad: Nonviolent Struggle, Democratization, and Governance in the Middle East*, ed. Maria Stephan (New York: Palgrave-Macmillan, 2009), 65–67.

3. Ellen Laipson, ed., *Seismic Shift: Understanding Change in the Middle East* (Washington, DC: Stimson Center, 2011), 103.

4. Freedom House, "Middle East and North Africa," http://www.freedomhouse.org/regions/middle-east-and-north-africa.

5. Peter Ackerman and Jack Duvall, *A Force More Powerful: A Century of Nonviolent Conflict* (New York: Palgrave-Macmillan, 2000), in particular the chapters "Russia, 1905: The People Strike," "India: Movement for Self-Rule," and "Poland: Power from Solidarity," 13–174.

6. Jon Alterman, "The Revolution Will Not Be Tweeted," *Washington Quarterly* 34, no. 3 (2011): 203–16.

7. Courtney Radsch, "Blogosphere and Social Media," in Laipson, *Seismic Shift*, 67–81.

8. Ibid., 72.

9. Robin Wright, *Dreams and Shadows: The Future of the Middle East* (New York: Penguin, 2008).

10. Clay Shirky, "The Political Power of Social Media: Technology, the Public Sphere, and Political Change," *Foreign Affairs* 90, no. 1 (2011): 28–41.

11. The Yellow Revolution in the Philippines (1986), Rose in Georgia (2003), Orange in Ukraine (2004–5), Green in Iran (2009), and their botanical variants, Cedar in Lebanon (2005), Saffron in Myanmar (2007), and Jasmine in Tunisia (2010).

12. See Evgeny Morozov, *The Net Delusion: The Dark Side of Internet Freedom* (New York: Public Affairs, 2011).

8

PROMISE AND PERIL
THE ROLE OF TECHNOLOGY-ENABLED NETWORKS IN CONFLICT MITIGATION

Sheldon Himelfarb

An insurgency remotely detonates a bomb beneath a hotel used as the administrative headquarters of an occupying army.[1] A citizen group broadcasts peace messages over community radio to encourage rebel soldiers to give up their arms and return home.[2] Dissidents use underground printing presses to produce banned publications calling for civil disobedience.[3]

Competition between technology-enabled networks has always been a facet of conflicts involving organized groups of non-state actors, each trying to leverage the best tools available to its advantage. However, what is fundamentally different in today's competition between these networks is a new capability, powered by the march of information technology, which enables large portions of the world's population to become media-makers for a global audience. For the first time in human history, people across the planet—including those in the most impoverished countries, where international conflict finds fertile ground—have the ability to send photographs, text, voice, and data around the globe with the push of a button.

Even in relatively undeveloped places such as Afghanistan—ranked 175th out of 182 countries in the United Nations' 2013 Human Development Index[4]—mobile phone and Internet penetrations have boomed over the past few years. A 2012 survey conducted by the US Agency for International Development (USAID) and Internews showed that the number of people with access to mobile phones in Afghanistan went up from 1.7 million in 2006 to over 17 million in 2012,[5] a penetration of around 63 percent, despite illiteracy being about 70 percent.[6] Between 2000 and 2012, percentage increases in Internet penetration skyrocketed in the world's poorest regions: Africa saw an increase of 3,607 percent; the Middle East, 2,640 percent; and Asia, 842

People are more aware of conflict in other countries

percent. At the time of this writing (early 2014), these regions together accounted for over 55 percent of the world's Internet users.[7]

This chapter explores the implications of this unprecedented technological capability for governance and conflict management around the world—the new networks that these technologies have given rise to, the immediate impacts they are having, and the long-term changes they are likely to create. Specifically, it argues that technology enables these networks to strengthen and expand what some call the "public sphere," inflecting many of the most pervasive causes of conflict in positive ways. Most importantly, this expanded public sphere enhances the potential of governments and local communities to detect and respond to emerging conflicts.

Progress in technology-enabled conflict management, however, is not necessarily unidirectional. Just as competition between technology-enabled networks is nothing new, nor is the uncertainty surrounding the evolution and impact of information technologies on society. As the World Economic Forum noted in its *Global Risks 2013* report: "The global risk of *massive digital misinformation* sits at the centre of a constellation of technological and geopolitical risks ranging from *terrorism* to *cyber attacks* and *the failure of global governance*. . . . [H]yperconnectivity could enable 'digital wildfires' to wreak havoc in the real world."[8] Thus, this chapter also discusses a range of networks—authoritarian, illicit, commercial, and others—threatening to undermine emerging new conflict management capabilities. Specifically, it looks at the risk of massive digital misinformation and other factors at work in the still-nascent debate over Internet freedom, and how the results of that debate could either nurture or impede progress in peacemaking.

THREE TYPES OF NETWORKS

Until recently, both media attention and academic research have focused on two kinds of activist networks: those that have leveraged social media to mobilize people for political or social change, and those that have effectively used the Internet to further their terror and cyber-war goals through recruitment, fundraising, or cyber attacks. Both types of networks obviously have major implications for world politics and conflict, but there is a third form—community-based and more squarely aimed at conflict prevention—that is steadily gaining significance.

Activist Networks for Political or Social Change

This first category of networks has been closely associated, at least in the public consciousness, with the power of social media to share ideas, raise awareness, coordinate activists, and ultimately catalyze a number of large-scale movements for political or social change. The 2013 Euromaidan protests in Ukraine were sparked in part by a YouTube video made by a woman named Yoka Marusherska; it was only the latest in a series of Ukrainian protest movements seeded through social media since the early 2000s. In Colombia, the "Million Voices against the FARC" Facebook group instigated a wave of protest rallies across two hundred cities worldwide, including in forty-five cities and towns in Colombia itself. Following the protests, the FARC came to the table to engage in meaningful, if fragile, peace talks with the Colombian government. Egypt's 2011 protests against the Mubarak regime's human rights violations were fueled in part by Wael Ghonim's "We Are All Khaled Said" Facebook group. The YouTube video produced by the nongovernmental organization (NGO) Invisible Children led to a "Kony 2012 Campaign" to bring Lord's Resistance Army (LRA) leader Joseph Kony to trial in the International Criminal Court.

These phenomena have sparked a number of vigorous debates among academics, researchers, and public intellectuals over the role of new technologies in large-scale social and political change. Some of these analysts and observers—who have been dubbed "cyber utopians" and "cyber optimists"—argue that new technologies have played a critical role in fomenting and sustaining the Arab Spring and other political watersheds. Others—the so-called cyber skeptics—have argued that technology does not create the necessary conditions for large-scale social change and may in fact foster more effective authoritarian repression, surveillance, and control.[9] At various points between these two extremes are many commentators weighing in with large, social-media data sets in hopes of creating an evidence-based understanding of the causal mechanisms that tie new technologies to political transformation.[10] The dust is unlikely to settle on these issues at any time in the near future, as the tools and methods of analysis continue to evolve and improve.

Networks for Terror and Cybercrime

The second category of technology-enabled networks that has gained considerable attention in global affairs consists of networks intent on fostering terror, crime, or cyber "anarchy." In February 2013, James Clapper, the director of National Intelligence, told a US congressional committee that cyber attacks and cyber espionage had supplanted terrorism as the top security threat facing the United States.[11] Governments, companies, and international organizations, increasingly concerned about the vulnerabilities created when critical infrastructure—water, transportation, energy, and the like—are tied into the Internet, have struggled to develop

better defensive capabilities. (The options under consideration for tackling the threat—and their implications for conflict management capabilities—are discussed later in this chapter.) Just a handful of examples illustrate the complexity of the cyber landscape:

- In 2013, there were reports that major US media companies, including the *Wall Street Journal* and the *New York Times*, had been infiltrated by Chinese hackers, allegedly backed by the Chinese military.
- In 2010, the Stuxnet virus, believed to have been created by Israel and US government–backed hackers, was used to attack Iran's nuclear facilities.
- Since 2008, a collective of "activist" hackers known as Anonymous have claimed responsibility for a number of cyber attacks on governments and companies.

What these attacks have in common is that they pose the same challenges: namely, determining with confidence the source of the action, and then responding to it. To date, responses have been mostly defensive, such as hardened firewalls, improved encryption, and increased security training. However, terror networks such as Al Qaeda, and individual cyberterrorists such as Irhaby 007, have prompted a different, more-offensive response to their use of the Internet to raise funds, recruit members, and advise followers on where and when to take action. Government intelligence agencies and citizen groups alike have actively monitored their websites, attempted to infiltrate their chat rooms, and taken action that have ranged from crippling denial-of-service (DOS) attacks, to legal action against the Internet service providers (ISPs) on whose servers the terrorist sites reside, to outright arrest.[12]

Experts agree that the international regulatory environment has not kept pace with either the diversity of these threats or the magnitude of their destructive power. And, as this chapter discusses later, the changes proposed to deal with these inadequacies have enormous implications, especially for the newest category of networks using new technologies for conflict prevention and peacebuilding.

Networks for Local and Regional Conflict Management

Much less well known than the two preceding groupings is a category that encompasses the growing number of networks that use technology to try to reduce the specific triggers of violent conflict. In fact, it is becoming difficult to think of a single issue in the conflict management field—election violence, refugee resettlement, corruption, disarmament and demobilization, interethnic hatred, land disputes, gender violence, and so on—that has not been the target of technology-enabled networks, especially social media networks, working actively and creatively to prevent or reduce conflict. Even if these networks have not always been successful, their efforts have been strikingly numerous and diverse, as the following examples demonstrate.

Examples

- Kenya's March 2013 elections sparked numerous technology-based initiatives aimed at preventing a repeat of the violence that followed elections in 2008, and had noteworthy success.[13] Mobile phone provider Safaricom donated 50 million SMS text messages to a local peacebuilding organization, Sisi Ni Amani ("We Are Peace"), to send to its more than fifty thousand subscribers in an effort to prevent violence and quell rumors.[14] Google's Kenya Elections Hub provided voters with a number of online tools, including online registration confirmation and polling station locators.[15] The Umati project used online crowd-sourcing tools to monitor media (both conventional and social) for instances of hate speech and incitement to violence in the run-up to the election.[16] This information also fed into the Uchaguzi project, an election-monitoring map, that crowd-sourced from "wananchi (citizens), election observers, humanitarian response agencies, civil society, community-based organizations, law enforcement agencies, digital humanitarians etc. to monitor elections in near-real time."[17]

- The Intergovernmental Authority on Development (IGAD), a regional organization comprising Djibouti, Eritrea, Ethiopia, Kenya, Somalia, Sudan, and Uganda, have developed the Conflict Early Warning (CEWARN) program, using cell phones, high-frequency radios, and high-gain antenna phones to collect reports on conflict incidents and vulnerabilities from a network of partners on the ground. Among the partners are local government leaders, civil society organizations, research entities, and trained field monitors. Although its data-analysis tools are in an early stage of development, CEWARN uses the collected information to forecast, over both the short term and the long term, where violence is likely to occur. Technology operates at two levels in this program: it allows the networks of partners to become sources of data; and it builds communication paths between communities (usually local tribes) at risk of violent conflict with one another. Admittedly, converting this information into policies and/or actions by IGAD members remains a challenge. Due to the sensitivity of this information, member countries are often reluctant to let incidents come to light. Consequently, the CEWARN program is building capacity within a regional network of governmental and NGOs to bypass country-level responders and to address conflict flashpoints at the local level. Although CEWARN still "lacks an effective response component," these efforts will be key to ensuring that reports lead to timely action.[18]

- In Haiti, the women's organization Kofaviv has successfully used technology not only to respond to instances of sexual violence (e.g., creating the only twenty-four-hour hotline for sexual violence in Haiti) but also to create a network of local women at risk of attack. Sexual violence against women in Haiti has a history as both a widespread criminal act, caused by chronic insecurity and a politically motivated act of violence.[19] Kofaviv uses FrontlineSMS software to send urgent security alerts to Haitians, manage its network of agents working in local communities, and connect victims to healthcare and legal representation.[20]

- In the Chiapas region of Mexico, where land disputes are brewing over resource-rich tracts of land currently occupied by indigenous populations at risk of being evicted by the government, the organization Digital Democracy has trained indigenous populations to use digital maps to demarcate their land for the first time, allowing them to see the implications of their land sales and agreements for their livelihoods and to capture data on "land use, sustainability, government actions and potential threats to their way of life."[21]

- In Iraq, the Center for Negotiation and Conflict Management (CNCM), a network of trained local conflict mediators, is using digital mapping tools such as Ushahidi along with messaging tool FrontlineSMS to identify and act on signs of conflict in the areas where CNCM mediates disputes. According to one of those who helped design the project, "The CNCM Dispute Mapping and Early Warning System will collect data on trends in the disputes handled by the Centre, data related to the conflict context in Iraq, and data on changing perceptions of people on key triggers of conflict. The collection and visualization of these sources of data will allow the . . . team to better monitor past activities and better respond to new developments."[22]

- The "Blue Bucket Brigade" series of YouTube videos designed to name-and-shame high-profile traffic violators was but one of many efforts in Russia to fight the endemic culture of corruption. Blogging and microblogging sites have also been on the frontlines of these battles to improve governance.[23]

Thus, the combination of cell phones, the Internet, and social media is rapidly becoming ubiquitous in conflict zones, and people are using these tools with mixed success—but success nonetheless—to prevent violence. As scholar Joseph Bock wrote in his recent book, *The Technology of Nonviolence*, "Once peacekeeping was the purview of international forces, but today local citizens often take violence prevention into their own hands, thanks in part to social media."[24] Underlying this new role for communities in peacebuilding are changes in the public sphere ushered in by the new enabling technologies.

EXPANDING AND STRENGTHENING THE PUBLIC SPHERE

The concept of the public sphere, most closely associated with Jürgen Habermas, denotes the "realm of our social life in which something approaching public opinion can be formed. A portion of the public sphere comes into being in every conversation in which private individuals assemble to form a public body."[25] According to Emory University professor Noelle McAfee, the public sphere is the result of people "coming together to figure out what to do on matters of common concern."[26] It is the wider sociopolitical foundation on which civil society is built, and is therefore a key part of the way people articulate their preferences to the state and, in turn, hold the state accountable for realizing those preferences.

The last decade has seen a vigorous conversation among leading Internet thinkers on the relationship between the public sphere and online discourse. According to one of the earliest voices in this discussion, Clay Shirky, social media is a tool that strengthens the public sphere; and a robust and active public sphere is necessary to increase political freedoms around the world.[27] Larry Diamond, another leading commentator, echoes this sentiment and points toward a highly controlled society—China—to best understand this phenomenon. Even in such a political environment, he writes, citizens use new technology to "report the news, expose wrongdoing, express opinions, mobilize protest, monitor elections, scrutinize government, deepen participation, and expand the horizons of freedom." The Chinese blogosphere plays host to a number of dissident and critical voices, especially those raised against government censorship and surveillance.[28] Chinese citizens have used microblogging site *Weibo* to identify corrupt officials; in Nanjing in 2008, for example, an online photo of a public official wearing a

luxury watch led to a public outcry, an official investigation, and, finally, the official's incarceration for bribery. In 2012, Yang Dacai, the head of the Safety Supervision Bureau in Shaanxi Province, was jailed for bribery after online activists shared photos of Yang wearing similarly extravagant accessories, far beyond the economic reach of the average civil servant.[29]

For researchers such as Diamond and Shirky, the Internet's decentralized architecture, the spread of cell phones, and the sheer popularity of social-network applications have combined to produce a revolution in social activism, making it easier than ever for civil society in countries such as China to mobilize. But some commentators take issue with this assertion, again in the context of the long-running debate between cyber skeptics and cyber optimists. According to writer Malcolm Gladwell, for example, a crucial distinction exists between traditional activism and its online variant. Social media, on the one hand, is effective at building loosely affiliated networks, which are the opposite in structure and character of effective social-change movements of the past. These past movements had hierarchies, rules, procedures, and centralized control. Online structure, on the other hand, "makes networks enormously resilient and adaptable in low-risk situations," which a conflict setting, of course, is not. Gladwell, like many others, finds digital activism to be a weak substitute for the kind of activism that requires close relationships and close collaboration, and that produced the Civil Rights movement of the 1960s and 1970s.[30]

Zeynep Tufekci, a fellow at Princeton University's Center for Information Technology Policy, takes issue with Gladwell's assertion, writing that it is a "widespread conceptual error and rests upon an inadequate understanding of these concepts. Large pools of weaker ties are crucial to being able to build robust networks of stronger ties—and Internet use is a key to this process."[31] Or, as Mathew Ingram, a senior writer and blogger for *GigaOM*, puts it: "What [social networking sites] are very good at doing . . . is connecting people in very simple ways, and making those connections in a very fast and widely-distributed manner. This is the power of a networked society and of cheap, real-time communication networks."[32]

It is fitting that the last word on these debates go to the activists themselves, whose voices are quite clear. Activists from Syria, Egypt, Colombia, and elsewhere speak of concrete gains thanks to social media. Says Ahed al Hendi, head of CyberDissidents. org, a Syrian activist organization: "Facebook taught us and the social media how to be more rational, how to build campaigns about human rights, and raise awareness in the country."[33] Rafif Joujeti from the Free Syria Foundation declares: "I think the role of social media has played a huge part not just in making sure the world knows the truth but also in organizing and maturing things like concepts of civil society in Syria, organizing different types of groups, encouraging debate and more thought."[34] Wael Ghonim, who launched the "We Are All Khaled Said" Egyptian Facebook group, asserts: "Platforms like YouTube, Twitter, Facebook were helping us a lot because it basically gave us the impression that, 'Wow, I'm not alone. There are a lot of people who are frustrated.'"[35] And according to Oscar Morales, who launched the "Million Voices against the FARC" Facebook group: "The campaign convinced people to say: 'We don't tolerate the kidnappings and we want their freedom.' On the day of the protest, February 4, 2008, the whole country was surprised by how many people marched. More than 500,000 people joined our Facebook group. Months later many freed hostages said they'd heard our protest in captivity on a radio and it gave them hope they'd survive."[36]

Clearly, activists for social change find the new technologies, and their interaction with conventional technologies such as radio, television, and print, to be valuable tools in expanding the public sphere, with profound implications for governance and political movements worldwide. On the other side of the debate, although there is acceptance that the public sphere is expanding, it is seen to be expanding in the form of more networks, "loosely affiliated" with "weaker ties," that are more likely to perpetuate the political or social status quo than to be change agents.[37]

Nonetheless, there *is* common ground—namely, the shared recognition that there is an expanding, more-networked public sphere in a world where 3 billion people are expected to enter the global middle class over the next two decades and therefore have greater access to technology in their daily lives. This expansion holds new promise for progress on one of the central challenges in conflict management: connecting early warning to early action.

EARLY ACTION

For decades, the twin challenges of sensing emerging violence early and taking early action to save lives has preoccupied peace-building practitioners, many of whom watched in horror as more than two thousand people died every day in the 1994 Rwandan genocide. The need for speed is clear. Researchers have also established that the probability of reaching nonviolent solutions, instead of using military ones, is highest in what is called the "early gestation phase" of a conflict.[38]

There have been promising developments in both regards, thanks to the technological enablement of networks. Localized shifts in sentiment and incitement—bellwethers of oncoming violence—are increasingly revealed in publicly accessible communications over social media. Moreover, networks of monitors use cell phone calls and text messages to communicate quickly as dangerous situations emerge, improving the probability of early action.

Two cases in point are Brazil and Kenya. Brazil has one of the highest rates of social media participation in the developing world, a factor that researchers say has contributed to a wide array of innovative and relatively effective programs, spawned by civic organizations and governments alike, designed to alert citizens and police of imminent violence in the country's impoverished favelas.[39] In Kenya, as discussed earlier, the elections in 2013 were relatively peaceful for many reasons, one of which seems to have been the extensive networks deploying innovative technology projects such as PeaceTXT, which the New York Times described, as a "text messaging service that sends out blasts of pro-peace messages to specific areas when trouble is brewing."[40]

Much has been written over the years about the shortcomings of systems designed to provide early warning and early response to conflict management, but technology may be tackling some of these shortcomings.[41] In 2009, for example, the OECD report on "The Future of Conflict Early Warning and Response" noted that "an external, interventionist and state-centric approach in early warning systems fuels disjointed, top-down responses in situations that require integrated, multi-level action."[42] The report went on to describe the state-of-the-art at that moment as "the use of email and websites for dissemination, and communication technology for data collection. Governmental and some intergovernmental systems do benefit from access to and resources for satellites and GIS in their analysis and reporting. However, access to technology remains very unequal among systems and the field of conflict early warning lags far behind in

the use of innovative technologies and Web 2.0 applications."[43]

Just four years later, the systems have changed significantly, due in great measure to the ubiquity of technology-enabled networks. As Patrick Meier, an expert on this subject, has written, whereas early warning and response systems were once "state-centric, institutional and top-down," today they are more "people-centered," using free, readily available software run "by the community, for the community."[44] He goes on to explain that the thrust of conflict early warning systems was once to extract data from conflict zones to satisfy Western interests; in contrast, current systems favor democratization of information collection and access. He concludes: "This distributed, bottom-up approach stands in stark contrast to the model followed by first- and second-generation conflict early warning systems."[45]

There is good reason to think that these systems will continue to improve, thanks to the expanding public sphere and its ability to generate massive amounts of new and valuable information, commonly referred to as "Big Data." Not only are unprecedented volumes of information about human dynamics and sentiment—the "DNA" of conflict—being shared on social networking sites such as Facebook, Twitter, Flicker, Tumblr, Google Plus, and YouTube, but the technological capabilities to analyze this vast treasure trove of information are also becoming cheaper and more effective.[46] In Haiti, for instance, cell phone data was a reliable predictor of post-disaster mass population movements, and such awareness can be valuable in assisting and even saving the lives of war refugees.[47]

Experts point out that they are still unable to use these kinds of tools and data sets to predict violence before it erupts. As political scientist Jay Ulfeder, part of a team at the Holocaust Museum in Washington, D.C., working on developing a forecasting model for atrocity prevention, writes: "when it comes to predicting major political crises like wars, coups, and popular uprisings, there are many plausible predictors for which we don't have any data at all, and much of what we do have is too sparse or too noisy to incorporate into carefully designed forecasting models."[48] Moreover, as many others have noted, history teaches that early response does not necessarily follow early warning. But even with those caveats in mind, it is clear that by strengthening and expanding the public sphere, technology helps create an environment in which both early warning and early action *can* occur.

GOING GLOBAL

The discussion up to this point has focused largely on local, national, and some regional conflict situations. But humanity's most pressing problems, such as climate change, financial stability, and resource management, each of which has profound implications for future conflicts, are global in scale.

Yet here, too, can be seen the emergence of international networks that aspire to address different facets of these problems. The Transparency International coalition, for instance, is working to reduce corruption worldwide, while the Yala-Young Leaders Movement uses social media to counter ethnic, religious, and sectarian hatred in the Middle East. In some cases, the results achieved by these international networks have been impressive. The media attention that the Kony 2012 social media movement drummed up prompted both the African Union and the US Congress to take action. In March 2012, the African Union formed a five-thousand-strong force to "stop Kony with military hardware," and in August 2012, the US Congress passed a resolution "calling for the US to continue to enhance its mobility, intelligence and logistical support of regional forces protecting civilians

and pursuing the LRA."[49] The International Red Cross crowdsourced tens of millions of dollars in disaster relief for Haiti in record time, using a cell phone–based texting campaign: "Text Haiti 90999." The "Half the Sky" multimedia campaign (including television, Twitter, and a Facebook game) has helped to propel international awareness of gender violence.[50]

There is reason to believe these technologically enabled international networks will continue to improve their effectiveness in pressuring governments and large institutions to act. Today's information and communication platforms lower the barriers for vast numbers of ordinary people to coordinate, motivate, and engage in consequential action, thereby steering conflict management and peacebuilding in positive directions. But continued progress is by no means a certainty.

THE OTHER TRENDLINE: CYBER VIOLENCE

In the Indian city of Bangalore in August 2012, a series of false rumors spread via text messaging and social media led to the exodus of five thousand Assamese students from the city. The students feared that they would be attacked in retaliation for communal violence in their home state, thousands of miles northeast of Bangalore.[51]

In July 2012, persons on Twitter pretending to be the Russian interior minister Vladimir Kolokoltsev caused global crude oil prices to spike by tweeting that Syria's president Bashar al-Assad "has been killed or injured."[52] In Mexico, drug cartels target those who post comments against them on blogs and social media. In September 2011, they decapitated a female blogger as retribution for her online activities.[53]

The same loose architecture that enables activists to leverage the Internet and other communication technologies for positive social change also makes these tools the weapons of choice for illicit networks. Terrorist networks have long tried to exploit this vulnerability, and continue to do so today, according to law enforcement officials who have testified about cyber attacks planned by Al Qaeda and its affiliates against critical US infrastructure. Now organized crime and state-sponsored actors have joined their ranks, leading one recent task force on cyber security to conclude that it is "becoming more difficult to disaggregate the interrelationship among cybercriminals, states, terrorists, traditional organized crime syndications, drug traffickers and others."[54]

This coalescence among violent actors may pose the greatest threat to the gains made by today's technology-enabled peace-building networks. Cyber warfare is undoubtedly on the rise, as the 2013 *Worldwide Threat Assessment* by the US Intelligence Community attests, listing cyber threats as the number one threat to US national security. "State and non-state actors increasingly exploit the Internet to achieve strategic objectives," the report explains,

> while many governments—shaken by the role the Internet has played in political instability and regime change—seek to increase their control over content in cyberspace. The growing use of cyber capabilities to achieve strategic goals is also outpacing the development of a shared understanding of norms of behavior, increasing the chances for miscalculations and misunderstandings that could lead to unintended escalation.[55]

In this environment of both escalating danger and deteriorating norms, "Internet freedom has come to mean different things to different constituencies," writes cyber commentator, Evgeny Morozov. "To some it is an Internet free from government censorship or surveillance, a question of an individual's freedom to information. To others, it is the freedom to challenge authority and to organize in order to bring down governments—authoritarian and democratic alike."[56] These competing interpretations were on the table in December 2012, when the international community came together to negotiate a global telecommunications treaty in Dubai. Russia, China, and Iran were joined by other countries in an alliance favoring more state and UN control of Internet governance; the United States and its allies sought to preserve the multistakeholder governance model that currently "provides a forum for governments, the commercial sector, academia, and civil society to deliberate and reach consensus on Internet organization and technical standards."[57] According to US officials, this model is vital in order "to protect freedom of expression and the free flow of online information."[58]

At final count, 89 of 144 countries signed on to the treaty in Dubai, but the United States and most European countries were not among them. While disagreements on various issues—including spam and roaming charges for mobile phones—combined to cause this rift, government control over the Internet was the most significant cause of contention between Western and non-Western powers.[59] After days of contentious debate, the treaty negotiations ended without an agreement among the major powers, leaving the sides to continue their attempts to take advantage of the weak international regulatory environment.

With ever-increasing frequency, US and Canadian companies report that their commercial systems and intellectual property have been breached by the Chinese military. Iran has offered credible evidence that the Stuxnet virus targeting its nuclear centrifuges probably had its origins in the US and Israeli military establishments.[60] And revelations by former US National Security Agency (NSA) analyst Edward Snowden have spotlighted a massive program of covert surveillance of users' Internet activities through the use of programs such as XKeyscore that permit "ongoing 'real-time' interception" of activities.[61] Domestically, the program was met with widespread accusations of government overreach and violations of individual privacy. Internationally, allies of the United States such as the European Union described the news as "a serious matter which will have a severe impact on EU-U.S. relations."[62] Much like the governments it found itself at loggerheads with on the Dubai treaty, the United States argued that these kinds of surveillance programs enabled it "to defend the nation and to protect US and allied troops abroad."[63]

Rogue activity on all sides adds tinder to an already volatile online environment where, in 2012, a YouTube video titled *Innocence of Muslims* sparked riots across the planet, causing more than fifty deaths because of its disrespect of the Muslim faith. The case prompted widespread debate over what constitutes reasonable limits to freedom of speech online, including the right to online anonymity that is so vital to agents of change working under repressive regimes. And if the international community were to agree that there were some limits to free speech online—just as there are protections against shouting "fire" in a crowded theater—then who would be the appropriate arbiter and enforcer of such limits?

As a report issued by the World Economic Forum notes, the issues are complex and difficult, partly "because social media is a recent phenomenon, and digital social norms are not yet well established."[64] Other observers attribute some of the complexity to the very architecture of the Internet itself, that is, the degree of anonymity that it accords to all users, whether affiliated with illicit, criminal or terror networks or with networks of democracy activists.[65] Regardless of the explanation, it is clear that the stakes are growing and the urgency increasing, due to the pres-

sures for greater control and regulation in the face of increased cyber warfare. Some estimates place the number of global hacking attempts during one quarter of 2012 alone at close to 1 billion.[66]

So, in addition to their destructive nature, these trends threaten a free Internet. Currently, users take their freedom to navigate through cyberspace for granted, but that could change. Three of every five new Internet users now come from the global South and East, shifting the center of gravity on regulatory and other issues away from Washington and Brussels, making it increasingly likely that significant governance changes will occur. If countries such as Russia and China prevail in their arguments and tactics for governing their citizens' online access, the prospects will grow of a more balkanized Internet, one defined and limited by national telecommunications providers.[67]

CONCLUSION: THE GREAT UNKNOWNS

Even in a more tightly controlled, somewhat balkanized Internet, it is likely that local activists will continue to expose injustices, organize against violence, and pressure governments to be more transparent and responsive, much as Chinese netizens have. Were more countries to adopt "the Great Firewall of China," however, the potential to create the global collaboration needed to solve the biggest issues facing humanity could be undermined. Problem solving on a global scale will require tapping into "networks [that] span the globe in a tightly-knit, broad web of activity, interaction, personalization."[68]

Problem solving may also require something else that technology-enabled networks have struggled mightily with: leadership. Over the past decade, as technology has empowered civil society, hierarchies have dissipated and power has been pushed down from governments and large institutions to networks of technology-enabled citizens.

One of the defining characteristics of these new networks has been their relatively leaderless qualities, with activists functioning as nodes within these networks.

In some instances, this leaderless quality has been a great advantage. As Alec Ross, the US Department of State's innovation advisor from 2009 to 2013, observed, the nodal, leaderless quality of the revolutionary movement in Tunisia made it impossible for President Zine el Abidine Ben Ali to quash it. However, a quite different outcome was seen in Egypt. There, too, networks of leaderless local activists helped bring down the regime—but once Hosni Mubarak government's had been toppled, they struggled to get a seat at the table at which new policies were made. This was in stark contrast to other popular uprisings in modern history, where a charismatic figure such as Nelson Mandela or Lech Walesa galvanized a movement and then went on to lead a successful government. Lacking strong leadership, the youth and liberal groups that had started the uprisings in Tahrir Square soon fell victim to dissension and in-fighting.[69] The better-organized Muslim Brotherhood then filled the leadership vacuum, took office, and subsequently ushered in a wave of restrictions on free speech—restrictions that led, at least in part, to the 2013 political crisis in Egypt in which President Mohamed Morsi was removed from office by the Egyptian military, further destabilizing the country.

At the time of this writing (early 2014), it is far from clear whose Internet governance proposals, whose architecture, and, therefore, whose networks of activists and netizens will be more prevalent in a decade's time. If, however, one assumes that the current architecture will be accepted and that the past decade is a prelude to the next one, there is reason to be sanguine about the future of conflict management and peacebuilding in the hands of technology-enabled networks. As Thomas Goetz of *Wired* magazine ar-gues, in order to "spot the future" of technology innovation, we must "bank on openness." The world of business innovation has always rewarded openness and transparency over structure and hierarchy.[70]

This seems to be a good bet when it comes to the Internet profile that has been so vital to the success of the technology-enabled networks—local, national, and international—that have been innovators in conflict prevention and peacebuilding. Not only were the reforms proposed in Dubai resoundingly defeated but also, in January 2012, when the US government proposed the Stop Online Piracy Act (SOPA) and the Protect Intellectual Property Act (PIPA), the largest online protest movement in history fought back. Clay Shirky declared that SOPA and PIPA were "an attempt to create a privatized form of international censorship, and . . . they would have a profound and chilling effect on any form of public conversation among ordinary citizens."[71] Internet pioneers Vint Cerf and Tim Berners-Lee agreed with Shirky, and an estimated 10 million voting citizens expressed their opposition to the acts, largely through online petitions.[72] This, too, was a virtual, leaderless movement that raised money through crowd-funding, and that determinedly—and successfully—campaigned against the proposed legislation to ensure what it regarded as essential: a free and open Internet.

NOTES

The author wishes to acknowledge the valuable assistance of Anand Varghese in the preparation of this chapter.

1. Harvey W. Kushner, *Encyclopedia of Terrorism* (Thousand Oaks, CA: Sage, 2003), 181.

2. Andrew Green, "Uganda: Using Community Radio to Heal after Kony's War," *Inter Press Service*, January 31, 2012, 2013, www.ipsnews.net /2012/01/uganda-using-community-radio-to-heal -after-konyrsquos-war/.

3. Keith Henderson, "Poland's Vigorous Underground Press," *Christian Science Monitor*, January 21, 1986, http://www.csmonitor.com/1986/0121/dpole.html.

4. United Nations Development Programme, *Human Development Report 2013*, last modified 2013, http://hdr.undp.org/en/media/HDR2013_EN_Summary.pdf. The *Human Development Reports* are based on the Human Development Index, a tool developed by the United Nations to measure and rank countries' levels of social and economic development based on four criteria: life expectancy at birth, mean years of schooling, expected years of schooling, and gross national income per capita. See *Investopedia*, http://www.investopedia.com/terms/h/human-development-index-hdi.asp.

5. Javid Hamdard, "The State of Telecommunications and Internet in Afghanistan: Six Years Later" (assessment report prepared for USAID and Internews, March, 2012), 9, http://www.internews.org/sites/default/files/resources/Internews_TelecomInternet_Afghanistan_2012-04.pdf.

6. *CIA World Fact Book*, s.v. "Afghanistan," last modified June 2013, accessed June 18, 2013, https://www.cia.gov/library/publications/the-world-factbook/geos/af.html.

7. *Internet World Statistics*, http://www.internetworldstats.com/stats.htm.

8. "Digital Wildfires in a Hyperconnected World," *World Economic Forum*, http://reports.weforum.org/global-risks-2013/risk-case-1/digital-wildfires-in-a-hyperconnected-world/.

9. Malcolm Gladwell, "Small Change: Why the Revolution Will Not Be Tweeted," *New Yorker*, October 4, 2010, http://www.newyorker.com/reporting/2010/10/04/101004fa_fact_gladwell; Evgeny Morozov, *The Net Delusion: The Dark Side of Internet Freedom* (New York: PublicAffairs, 2012).

10. Sean Aday et al., "Blogs and Bullets: New Media in Contentious Politics," Peaceworks no. 65 (United States Institute of Peace, Washington, DC, September 2010), http://www.usip.org/publications/blogs-and-bullets-new-media-in-contentious-politics; and Sean Aday et al., "Blogs and Bullets II: New Media and Conflict after the Arab Spring," Peaceworks no. 80 (United States Institute of Peace, Washington, DC, July 2012), http://www.usip.org/publications/blogs-and-bullets-ii-new-media-and-conflict-after-the-arab-spring.

11. Luis Martinez, "Intel Heads Now Fear Cyber Attack More Than Terror," *ABC News*, March 13, 2013, abcnews.go.com/Blotter/intel-heads-now-fear-cyber-attack-terror/story?id=18719593.

12. Faye Bowers, "Terrorists Spread Their Messages Online," *Christian Science Monitor*, July 28, 2004, http://www.csmonitor.com/2004/0728/p03s01-usgn.html.

13. Kelly Gilblom, "Why Were Kenya's Elections Peaceful? Technology Provides Only a Partial Explanation," *TechPresident*, April 4, 2013, http://techpresident.com/news/wegov/23691/kenya-technology-proved-useful-tool-not-reason-peaceful-elections.

14. "Kenya Votes: Peaceniks Use Mobiles to Cool Election Tempers," *New Internationalist*, http://newint.org/blog/2013/02/14/kenya-election-peace-initiatives/.

15. Curt Hopkins, "How Technology Is Shaping the Decisive Kenyan Elections," *Daily Dot*, February 13, 2013, http://www.dailydot.com/politics/kenyan-election-2013-technology-umati/.

16. "Monitoring Dangerous Speech: Umati Update," *Ushahidi* (blog), January 18, 2013, http://blog.ushahidi.com/2013/01/18/monitoring-dangerous-speech-umati-update/.

17. *Uchaguzi*, https://uchaguzi.co.ke/info/index/5.

18. Joseph G. Bock, *The Technology of Nonviolence: Social Media and Violence Prevention* (Boston: MIT Press, 2012), 127–34.

19. "War on Women: Time for Action to End Sexual Violence in Conflict," *Nobel Women's Initative*, May 2011, http://www.nobelwomensinitiative.org/wp-content/archive/stories/Conference_Ottawa_Women_Forging_a_New_Security/war-on-women-web.pdf.

20. "FrontlineSMSat7: KOFAVIV Supporting Haitian Women," blog entry by Sean Martin McDonald, October 26, 2012, http://www.frontlinesms.com/2012/10/26/frontlinesmsat7-kofaviv-supporting-haitian-women/.

21. "Equal Footing: Fighting Forced Evictions in Chiapas," *Digital Democracy*, http://digital-democracy.org/what-we-do/programs/chiapas-program/.

22. Helena Puig Larrauri, "What the Red Dots Are For, or Why We Map (Part1: Iraq)," *Let Them Talk* (blog), February 18, 2013, http://letthemtalk

.org/2013/02/18/what-the-red-dots-are-for-or-why
-we-map-part-1-iraq/.

23. Bruce Etling, Robert Faris, and John Pal-
frey, "Political Change in the Digital Age: The Fragility and Promise of Online Organizing" (Berkman
Center for Internet and Society, Harvard University, 2010), http://cyber.law.harvard.edu/publica
tions/2010/political_change_in_the_digital_age;
Larry Diamond, "Liberation Technology," *Journal
of Democracy* 21, no. 3 (July 2010): 69–83, http://
muse.jhu.edu/journals/jod/summary/v021/21.3
.diamond.html.

24. Bock, *Technology of Nonviolence.*

25. Jürgen Habermas, "The Public Sphere: An
Encyclopedia Article (1964)," http://www.socpol
.unimi.it/docenti/barisione/documenti/File/2008
-09/Habermas%20(1964)%20-%20The%20Public
%20Sphere.pdf.

26. Noelle McAfee, "Civil Society, or the Public
Sphere?" *GonePublic: Philosophy, Politics, & Public
Life* (blog), July 24, 2009, http://gonepublic.net
/2009/07/24/civil-society-or-the-public-sphere/.

27. Clay Shirky, "The Political Power of Social
Media: Technology, the Public Sphere, and Political Change," *Foreign Affairs* 90, no. 1 (January/Feb-
ruary 2011), http://www.foreignaffairs.com/articles
/67038/clay-shirky/the-political-power-of-social
-media.

28. Diamond, "Liberation Technology."

29. Peter Ford, "Corrupt Officials Beware: China's Twitter Empowers Citizen-Vigilantes," *Christian Science Monitor*, September 4, 2012, http://www
.csmonitor.com/World/Global-News/2012/0904
/Corrupt-officials-beware-China-s-Twitter-empow
ers-citizen-vigilantes.

30. Gladwell, "Small Change."

31. Zeynep Tufekci, "What Gladwell Gets
Wrong: The Real Problem Is Scale Mismatch (Plus,
Weak and Strong Ties Are Complementary and
Supportive)," *Technosociology* (blog), 2010 http://
technosociology.org/?p=178.

32. Mathew Ingram, "Gladwell Still Missing
the Point about Social Media and Activism,"
GigaOM, February 3, 2011, http://gigaom.com
/2011/02/03/gladwell-still-missing-the-point-about
-social-media-and-activism/.

33. Ahed al Hendi, remarks at "Groundtruth:
New Media, Technology, and the Syria Crisis," a

seminar held at the United States Institute of
Peace, Washington, DC, October 2, 2012, http://
www.usip.org/events/groundtruth-new-media
-technology-and-the-syria-crisis.

34. Rafif Joujeti, remarks at "Groundtruth:
New Media, Technology, and the Syria Crisis," a
seminar held at the United States Institute of Peace,
Washington, DC, October 2, 2012, http://www
.usip.org/events/groundtruth-new-media-technol
ogy-and-the-syria-crisis.

35. "Wael Ghonim: Inside the Egyptian Revolution," *TED Talk* (video recording of speech
presented at a TED [Technology, Entertainment,
Design] conference, March 2011), http://www.ted
.com/talks/wael_ghonim_inside_the_egyptian_
revolution.html.

36. "Oscar Morales: 'How I Used Facebook to
Protest against FARC,'" *Metro News*, http://metro
.co.uk/2010/02/08/oscar-morales-how-i-used-face
book-to-protest-against-farc-85760/.

37. Gladwell, "Small Change."

38. Malcom Chalmers, "Spending to Save? An
Analysis of the Cost Effectiveness of Conflict Prevention" (report prepared for the Department for
International Development, United Kingdom, June
12, 2004), http://www.csae.ox.ac.uk/conferences
/2004-BB/papers/Chalmers-CSAE-BB2004.pdf.

39. Robert Muggah and Gustavo Diniz, "Using
Information and Communication Technologies for
Violence Prevention in Latin America," in *New
Technology and the Prevention of Violence and Conflict*,
ed. Francesco Mancini (New York: International
Peace Institute, April 2013), 28–41, http://www
.ipinst.org/media/pdf/publications/ipi_epub_new
_technology_final.pdf.

40. Jeffrey Gettleman, "On Eve of Vote, Fragile
Valley in Kenya Faces New Divisions," *New York
Times*, last modified March 2, 2013, http://www
.nytimes.com/2013/03/03/world/africa/on-eve-of
-vote-fragile-valley-in-kenya-faces-new-divisions
.html?pagewanted=all&_r=0.

41. Herbert Wulf and Tobias Debiel, "Systemic
Disconnects: Why Regional Organisations Fail to
Use Early Warning and Response Mechanisms,"
Global Governance 16, no. 4 (2010): 525–47, http://
www.wulf-herbert.de/GG.pdf; David Nyheim,
"Preventing Violence, War and State Collapse: The
Future of Conflict Early Warning and Response"

(report prepared for the Organisation for Economic Co-operation and Development [OECD], 2009), http://reliefweb.int/sites/reliefweb.int/files/resources /318BF9C6C8868F4EC12576DF0048FE82 -OECD-jun2009.pdf.

42. Ibid., 31.

43. Ibid., 17.

44. Patrick Meier, "Early Warning Systems and the Prevention of Violent Conflict," in *Peacebuilding in the Information Age: Sifting Hype from Reality*, ed. Daniel Staiffacher et al. (ICT for Peace Foundation, January 2011), 12, http://ict4peace.org/wp -content/uploads/2011/01/Peacebuilding-in-the -Information-Age-Sifting-Hype-from-Reality .pdf.

45. Ibid., 13.

46. Emmanuel Letouzé, Patrick Meier, and Patrick Vinck, "Big Data for Conflict Prevention: New Oil and Old Fires," in "New Technology and the Prevention of Violence and Conflict," ed. Francesco Mancini (International Peace Institute, New York, April 2013), 4–27, http://www.ipinst.org/media /pdf/publications/ipi_epub_new_technology_final .pdf.

47. Liat Clark, "Mobile Data Could Predict How Populations Will Move after Disasters," *Wired*, June 19, 2012, http://www.wired.co.uk/news /archive/2012-06-19/disaster-population-predic tions.

48. Michael D. Ward and Nils Metternich, "Predicting the Future Is Easier than It Looks," *Foreign Policy* website, November 16, 2012, http:// www.foreignpolicy.com/articles/2012/11/16/pre dicting_the_future_is_easier_than_it_looks.

49. Conal Urquhart, "Joseph Kony: African Union Brigade to Hunt Down LRA Leader," *Guardian*, March 24, 2012, http://www.guardian .co.uk/world/2012/mar/24/joseph-kony-african -union-brigade; Office of US Senator Christopher Coons of Delaware, "Senate Condemns Crimes of Joseph Kony and Lord's Resistance Army" (news release, August 3, 2012), http://www.coons.senate .gov/newsroom/releases/release/senate-condemns -crimes-of-joseph-kony-and-lords-resistance -army.

50. Maura O'Neill, "Half the Sky: Building a Movement through Media and Technology," *Half the Sky Movement* (blog), April 29, 2013,

http://www.halftheskymovement.org/blog/entry /half-the-sky-building-a-movement-through-me dia-technology.

51. Associated Press in Bangalore, "Indians from Assam Flee 'Muslim threats' in Bangalore," *Guardian*, August 16, 2012, http://www.guardian .co.uk/world/2012/aug/16/indians-assam-muslim -threats-bangalore.

52. Amanda Willis, "Twitter Death Rumor Leads to Spike in Oil Prices," *Mashable*, August 7, 2012, http://mashable.com/2012/08/07/twitter-ru mor-oil-price/.

53. Neal Ungerleider, "Mexican Narcogangs' War on Digital Media," *Fast Company*, October 5, 2011, http://www.fastcompany.com/1785413/mex ican-narcogangs-war-digital-media.

54. Kristin Lord and Travis Sharp, eds., "America's Cyber Future: Security and Prosperity in the Information Age" (Center for New American Security, Washington, DC, June 2011), http://www .cnas.org/files/documents/publications/CNAS _Cyber_Volume%20I_0.pdf.

55. James Clapper, Senate Select Committee on Intelligence, "Worldwide Threat Assessment of the US Intelligence Community," March 12, 2013, http://www.intelligence.senate.gov/130312/clap per.pdf.

56. Evgeny Morozov, "Whither Internet Control," *Journal of Democracy* 22, no. 2 (April 2011), http://www.journalofdemocracy.org/sites/default /files/Morozov-22-2.pdf

57. Clapper, "Worldwide Threat Assessment."

58. Ibid.

59. Matt Smith, "Global Telecom Treaty without Net Controls Signed by 89 Nations," Reuters, December 14, 2012, http://www.reuters.com/article /2012/12/14/us-telecom-treaty-idUSBRE8BD 18820121214.

60. Ken Dilanian, "Chinese Army Hackers Blamed for Stealing U.S., Canadian Trade Secrets," *Twin Cities*, February 19, 2013, http://www .twincities.com/national/ci_22624663/chinese -army-hackers-blamed-stealing-u-s-canadian.

61. Glenn Greenwald, "XKeyscore: NSA Tool Collects 'Nearly Everything a User Does on the Internet,'" *Guardian*, July 31, 2013, http://www. theguardian.com/world/2013/jul/31/nsa-top-secret -program-online-data.

62. Mark Memmot, "'Furious' EU Demands Answers after New Report of NSA Spying," *The Two-Way* (blog), June 30, 2013, http://www.npr.org/blogs/thetwo-way/2013/06/30/197284754/furious-eu-demands-answers-after-new-report-of-nsa-spying.

63. Greenwald, "XKeyscore."

64. "Digital Wildfires in a Hyperconnected World," *World Economic Forum*, http://reports.weforum.org/global-risks-2013/risk-case-1/digital-wildfires-in-a-hyperconnected-world/.

65. "Computer Says No," *Economist*, June 22, 2013, http://www.economist.com/news/international/21579816-denial-service-attacks-over-internet-are-growing-easier-and-more-powerful-their.

66. Nick Summers, "Hacking Attempts Will Pass One Billion in Q4 2012, Claims Information Assurance Firm," *The Next Web*, November 11, 2012, http://thenextweb.com/insider/2012/11/12/hacking-attempts-to-pass-one-billion-in-final-quarter-of-2012-claims-information-assurance-firm/.

67. Rafal Rohozinski, presentation at a workshop, "Sensing and Shaping Emerging Conflicts," National Academy of Sciences, Washington, DC, October 11, 2012.

68. Zeynep Tufekci, "What Gladwell Gets Wrong."

69. Lourdes Garcia-Navarro, "Egypt's Youth Groups Struggle to Find One Voice," National Public Radio website, February 16, 2011, http://www.npr.org/2011/02/16/133785818/egypts-youth-groups-struggle-to-find-one-voice.

70. Thomas Goetz, "How to Spot the Future," *Wired*, April 24, 2012, http://www.wired.com/business/2012/04/ff_spotfuture/all/1.

71. Clay Shirky, "SOPA and PIPA Would Create a Consumption-Only Internet," *Guardian*, January 18, 2012, http://www.guardian.co.uk/commentisfree/cifamerica/2012/jan/18/sopa-pipa-consumption-only-internet.

72. Jonathan Weisman, "After an Online Firestorm, Congress Shelves Antipiracy Bills," *New York Times*, January 20, 2012, http://www.nytimes.com/2012/01/21/technology/senate-postpones-piracy-vote.html?_r=0; Declan McCullagh, "Vint Cerf: SOPA Means 'Unprecedented Censorship' of the Web," CNet, December 15, 2011, http://news.cnet.com/8301-31921_3-57344028-281/vint-cerf-sopa-means-unprecedented-censorship-of-the-web/; Dan Worth, "Web Inventor Tim Berners-Lee Slams SOPA and PIPA Legislation," *V3*, January 18, 2012, http://www.v3.co.uk/v3-uk/news/2139758/web-inventor-tim-berners-lee-slams-sopa-pipa-legislation.

9

CLIMATE CHANGE, ENVIRONMENTAL STRESS, AND CONFLICT

Nils Petter Gleditsch

"Darfur is the first of many climate wars," UN secretary-general Ban Ki-moon has said on several occasions.[1] President Obama, in his Nobel Peace Prize lecture in 2009, claimed that there is little scientific dispute that if humans do nothing, climate change will generate "more drought, more famine, more mass displacement—all of which will fuel more conflict for decades."[2] He would have been more to the point had he said that there is very little scientific agreement on any of this.

Until recently, the most important documents defining the agenda for the debate on climate change, the assessment reports from the Intergovernmental Panel on Climate Change, have dealt only in a cursory way with the prospects of armed conflict.[3] However, the views of these two leading statesmen have added weight to a point of view increasingly accepted among NGOs and in policy circles that climate change is emerging as a threat to national security. A study prepared for the US Department of Defense envisions rapid climate change leading to famine, disease, weather-related disasters, floods of refugees, offensive military aggression, and nuclear proliferation.[4] The neo-Malthusian view of conflict resulting from increased resource scarcity has been given greater attention with the rising concern over human-made climate change.

ALTERNATIVE CONCEPTS OF SECURITY

After the emergence of two totalitarian movements in Europe in the 1920s and the repeated defeats of liberal internationalism, the realist school of thought dominated in international relations. Realism emphasizes the struggle for territory and resources. In this perspective, patterns of conflict and cooperation are based mainly on the struggle for power—military, economic, and political. A country can strengthen its position through conquest or alliance building and will tend to do so unless checked by countervailing power. In the realist view, the international system is anarchic, with unclear norms and weak institutions that cannot prevent aggression from states that challenge the established order. Security is mainly a zero-sum game in which a gain for one state is a loss for another.

Yet, the field of international relations has never universally accepted a purely realist notion of security. The main challenge comes from the liberal (or idealist) view, which anchors peace in economic development, democracy, interdependence, and international law and organization.[5] The liberal worldview has gained strength in the recent observations on the waning of violence as a tool in human affairs. Steven Pinker and others have argued that there is a long-term decline not just in war and civil war but also in violence more generally and that this trend has continued in the post–Cold War period and after 9/11.[6] The recent "awakening" of public protest in autocratic states, notably in the Middle East, has taken a violent turn after a largely nonviolent start. A sharp increase of battle deaths in armed conflict was reported for 2012 relative to the previous year, particularly because of the armed conflict in Syria, but the level was still much lower than at the end of the Cold War.[7]

In the past few decades, and particularly after the end of the Cold War, traditional notions of security have been subject to intense scrutiny. In a major challenge to Cold War realism, the Palme Commission launched the concept of common security, a positive-sum notion in which the greater security of one state is seen to mutually reinforce that of another.[8] A more radical challenge was put forward with the notion of comprehensive security, which widened the scope of the traditional concerns,[9] followed by human security, which focuses on the security of the individual rather than the state. Human security is broadly defined by the UN Development Programme as "safety from such chronic threats as hunger, disease

and repression" and also "protection from sudden and hurtful disruptions in the patterns of daily life."[10] On another side of the debate, the *Human Security Report* focuses on "violent threats to individuals."[11] Its survey includes interstate war and international crises, civil war, genocide, politicide and serious human rights abuses, and military coups.

In addition to freedom from violence, a wider notion of security might include:

- Political security, defined as the freedom from dictatorship and other arbitrary government (tracking political security involves looking at patterns of democratic governance and respect for human rights)[12]
- Economic and social security, defined as the freedom from poverty and want[13]
- Cultural security, defined as the freedom from ethnic or religious domination[14]
- Environmental security, defined as the freedom from environmental destruction and resource scarcity, which is the topic of this chapter

The idea of a wider conception of security was originally promoted by scholars and activists who wanted to undermine the influence of traditional power-political thinking of international relations. After the end of the Cold War, national security establishments in the West embraced the idea of a broad concept of security. In part, this may have been a way to define a new role for themselves in a world that had robbed them of their main enemy. As early as 1991, the North Atlantic Treaty Organization (NATO) acknowledged that "security and stability have political, economic, social, and environmental elements as well as the indispensable defense dimension."[15] Expanding the concept of security was also seen as an appropriate response to a set of new challenges in the international relations of the post–Cold War period. The UN Secretary-General's High-Level Panel on Threats, Challenges, and Change also embraced a wide notion of collective security.[16] The panel identified poverty, infectious disease, and environmental degradation as three major threats to security, along with armed conflict, terrorism, organized crime, and weapons of mass destruction.

A comprehensive notion of security is not without problems. There is a danger of labeling any problem or strain as "insecurity." Observers might take heed from the discussion about an extended concept of violence in the late 1960s and early 1970s. The concept of structural violence, originally a precise notion applied to deaths caused by the unequal distribution of resources, became so diluted that almost any perceived injustice could be defined as violence.[17] Structural violence became a political slogan and eventually self-destructed in peace research. The term "insecurity" should be reserved for major threats to human life. With this caveat in mind, I turn to the environmental component of comprehensive security.

ENVIRONMENTAL SECURITY

The concern for how environmental degradation or environmental stress may lead to insecurity is at the core a question of the scarcity of resources. Thomas Malthus suggested that hunger is inevitable because the human population grows exponentially while food production can increase only in linear fashion.[18] Thus, at some point, the available food per capita will fall below the minimum needed to sustain the population, and a crisis will be inevitable. Neo-Malthusian thinking follows the same general logic but applies it to a wide range of resources.[19] Thus, numerous writers have commented on anticipated "water stress,"

based on the idea that finite amounts of available freshwater will have to be shared by an increasing number of people.[20] In the mid-1970s, following the oil embargo organized by Arab oil-producing countries, concern arose that the supply of minerals and energy sources might soon become deficient. More recently, the "peak oil" movement has predicted the end of the oil age, leading to fundamental changes in the modern economy and increased international tension.[21]

Global scarcity is a sufficient but not necessary condition for local scarcities. Thomas Homer-Dixon, a prominent proponent of the view that environmental factors play an important role in generating and exacerbating armed conflict, distinguishes among three forms of resource scarcity:

- Demand-induced scarcity, which results from population growth
- Supply-induced scarcity, which results from the depletion or degradation of a resource
- Structural scarcity, which refers to the distribution of the resource[22]

The classical Malthusian model lies at the intersection of supply and demand, when the quantity of the resource can no longer keep pace with the growth of the population. Many neo-Malthusians, particularly those on the political left, put at least equal emphasis on distributional issues.

Resource scarcity can occur without environmental stress, simply because a nonrenewable source runs dry or demand exceeds what a renewable source can supply. In the event of environmental stress—usually understood to mean a human-made disturbance of the ecosystem—the supply of the resource will dwindle more rapidly. Any form of environmental stress can be translated into a problem of resource supply. Pollution of freshwater resources reduces the supply of water that can be used for drinking or food production. Air pollution reduces the supply of fresh air. Thus, all environmental problems can be interpreted as resource scarcity problems, but not vice versa. I follow standard terminology in talking about "environmental security," but it might have been preferable to talk about "resource security."

An extensive literature has emerged on the conceptual problem of how to define security so that it includes environmental concerns.[23] From this literature, one may distill three important goals:

- To prevent war and armed conflict as a result of resource scarcity and environmental stress.
- To prevent disasters other than war resulting from scarcity and degradation.
- To prevent the erosion of the carrying capacity of the Earth, resulting in the loss of environmental sustainability in the future.

All three are deliberately phrased in anthropocentric terms. Even more radical notions of environmental security can be found in the literature. Proponents of "deep ecology" advocate a biocentric view that gives equal weight to the rights of animals, trees, and even inanimate objects of nature, such as mountains.[24] Because none of these can speak for themselves, such rights must nevertheless be formulated and advocated by humans.

The first goal of environmental security is discussed in the next section. This is followed by a shorter discussion of the other two goals.

ENVIRONMENTAL INSECURITY AS ARMED CONFLICT

Despite the recent flurry of interest, the idea that resource constraints may lead to con-

flict is not a new one. In fact, it is one of the oldest ideas in research on conflict and peace. In one of the classics in the field, *A Study of War,* Quincy Wright devotes a long chapter to the relationship between war and resource use.[25] Similarly, in *Statistics of Deadly Quarrels,* Lewis Richardson discusses economic causes of war, including the desire to acquire territory and the control of "sources of essential commodities."[26]

Above all, the struggle over territory is generally recognized to be the most pervasive form of armed conflict. Wright notes that "practically all primitive people will fight to defend their territory, if necessary."[27] Kalevi Holsti concludes that among interstate wars between 1648 and 1989, territory was by far the most important issue category.[28] John Vasquez found that 80 to 90 percent of all the wars listed by Holsti involved territory-related issues, with only a slight decline after World II.[29] Paul Huth, in a study of the period 1950–90, characterizes territorial disputes as "one of the enduring features of international politics."[30] The territorial explanation for war is also consistent with the finding that wars occur most frequently between neighbors[31] and between proximate countries.[32]

Many territorial conflicts concern the exclusive economic zones on the continental shelf. Although the symbolism of underwater territory is not as potent as that of "the soil of our fathers," the value in economic and strategic terms may be enormous. In the 1960s, the unilateral declaration of 200-nautical-mile fishery zones by several Latin American coastal states provoked conflict with states with ocean-going fishing vessels. At about the same time, deep-sea drilling for oil and natural gas and the prospects of harvesting minerals on the ocean floor led to increased interest in exploiting the extended coastal zones beyond the fisheries. This further increased the conflict of interest between coastal states and states with a regional or global reach in their commercial activities. After a long, drawn-out process, a compromise was reached in the form of the United Nations Convention on the Law of the Sea (UNCLOS) in 1982. UNCLOS did not enter into force until 1994 and still has not been ratified by the United States, but its provisions are generally respected. One of its results was that an area comprising one-third of the total world ocean surface, almost as much as the world's total land area, was added to the territory of individual nations.[33]

In addition to territory itself, several other resources are commonly seen as worth fighting for. One such resource is strategic raw materials. When President Dwight D. Eisenhower, in a 1954 radio address, justified the strategic importance of defending "exposed areas of the world" from Soviet subversion, he cited, among other things, "necessary materials we get from them" such as tin, tungsten, rubber, and manganese."[34] Another resource that is commonly fought for is energy sources, the most obvious example being oil supplies from the Persian Gulf, often mentioned as a factor in the 1990–91 Persian Gulf War and the more recent Iraq War. A third is shared water resources, which potentially gives rise to conflicts over water use or navigation rights. More than 250 major river systems are shared by two or more countries, and many of them are subject to unresolved disputes.[35] A fourth resource arguably worth fighting for is food. Disagreements about shared fishery resources have occasioned confrontations between fishing vessels and armed vessels of coastal states,[36] even in the North Atlantic area, where most conflicts are solved peacefully. Increasing food prices have given rise to violent domestic riots,[37] and in Indonesia in 1998, food prices may have contributed to the downfall of the Suharto regime. The widespread concern that environmental change might lead to armed conflict was re-

flected in the awarding of the 2004 Nobel Peace Prize to Wangari Maathai and in 2007 to the Intergovernmental Panel on Climate Change (IPCC) and Al Gore, the first such prizes to be awarded to environmentalists.[38]

Despite the growing concern about the consequences of environmental disruption, there is limited systematic empirical evidence for its potential effect on armed conflict. A number of case studies have linked environmental factors to individual armed conflicts, some of them built on elaborate theoretical models.[39] It is difficult, however, to generalize from them because of uncertainty about how representative the cases are. Homer-Dixon in particular has been criticized for studying only cases where there is armed conflict as well as environmental destruction.[40] No systematic comparison is provided with cases where armed conflict does not erupt—even though these cases may also suffer from environmental stress. Thus, it is difficult to draw any conclusions about causes of violence from Homer-Dixon's work. Such case studies may supply persuasive post facto explanations for why things went wrong in Chiapas or Rwanda, but their value in terms of predicting future armed conflict is limited.[41] Other case studies cast doubt on the importance of resource scarcity and climate change in generating conflict in Kenya, Mali, and Darfur. Several case studies of Kenya, for example, have concluded that there is more conflict in years following wet years, which may imply that cattle-raiding and similar communal conflicts are driven more by opportunism than by scarcity.[42] Studies of Darfur have questioned the "climate war" interpretation propagated by the UN secretary-general.[43]

Wenche Hauge and Tanja Ellingsen integrated soil erosion, deforestation, and lack of clean freshwater into a more general model of civil war data from the 1990s.[44] They concluded that environmental degradation to some extent does stimulate the incidence of armed conflict, particularly small conflicts, although less so than economic and political factors. The State Failure Task Force, on the other hand, found little evidence for a direct influence of environmental degradation, and neither did Ole Magnus Theisen.[45] Indra de Soysa criticized the use of scarcity variables that conflate levels and rates of change. Using World Bank data on total per capita stock of natural capital as his measure of natural resource availability, he concluded that resource scarcity has little if any relationship to armed conflict.[46] Helga Malmin Binningsbø, de Soysa, and Gleditsch found the ecological footprint—a general and frequently cited indicator of the overall human load on the environment—to be associated with internal peace rather than with armed conflict.[47]

When the third IPCC assessment report was published in 2007, little research had yet been conducted on the relationship between climate change and conflict, so there was little evidence to synthesize and assess.[48] There is now more research, including disaggregated studies at the subnational level[49] (because climate change impacts do not follow national boundaries), but recent summaries of the literature tend to conclude that climate change so far has not been an important factor in armed conflict and that, for the degree of climate change foreseen in the IPCC scenarios, this trend is unlikely to change in the near to intermediate future.[50]

Environmental stress may be seen as contributing to the outbreak of conflict. But it can also be interpreted as a symptom of various forms of societal failure, such as authoritarian rule, lack of international cooperation, poverty, excessive consumption in rich countries, and globalization of the economy. These same phenomena may be linked to armed conflict, and thus the link between environmental deterioration and conflict may be spurious, at least in part.

Possible interaction effects must also be considered. Both Homer-Dixon and Günther Bächler conclude that whether or not an environmental conflict passes over the threshold to violence is dependent on sociopolitical factors.[51]

Some case studies suggest that environmental conflicts arise primarily between different ethnic or national groups. Examples are conflicts between the Hema and the Lendu in the Ituri region of the Democratic Republic of Congo (DRC), the Hutus and the Tutsis in Rwanda and Burundi, and farmers and cattle herders in the Darfur region of Sudan. In particular, states where the government is too weak to maintain a monopoly on violence may be prone to civil war, but also to communal conflict if the authorities are unable or unwilling to intervene and settle the issue.[52] Michael Ross suggests that resource-rich states may suffer from a lack of governmental control because the easy availability of resource rents makes it unnecessary for the government to develop and enforce a tax-collecting infrastructure.[53]

There is a plausible argument that climate change may be more likely to stimulate intercommunal violence than civil war, that is, violence directed against other groups rather than against the government, but so far there have been few cross-national studies. One recent study using a new data set from the Uppsala Conflict Data Program suggests that in Sub-Saharan Africa between 1990 and 2008, large negative deviations from normal rainfall are associated with a higher risk of communal conflict. The study also finds some evidence that the effect is amplified in regions inhabited by politically excluded ethno-political groups.[54] Another recent study using the Social Conflict in Africa Database finds that such rainfall deviations are associated with all types of political conflict, although wetter years are more likely to suffer from violent events.[55] However, a review of several studies finds the evidence so far to be inconclusive. Moreover, it has also been observed that authoritarian governments in countries such as Sudan and Kenya have used divide-and-rule tactics against communal groups in order to prop up the status of their own regimes, while blaming climate change and environmental stress.[56]

There are few studies of environmental stress and conflict between states. One such study at the national level found that population density, soil degradation, and an overall measure of environmental scarcity were associated with participation in militarized interstate disputes, but that there was no such effect for water scarcity, fish catch, or land burden.[57] Several statistical studies have found that shared freshwater resources are associated with interstate disputes. But because almost all neighboring states share at least one river, the effect of shared freshwater resources is difficult to distinguish from a contiguity effect.[58] Another study found that water scarcity increases the risk of militarized conflict, but that institutionalized agreements can offset the risk.[59] These studies do not identify the issues involved in conflicts between countries sharing a river basin.

Aaron Wolf contends that water scarcity can hardly ever be identified as a direct cause of international crises.[60] Many scholars have pointed to the Middle East as an area where water is a source of considerable tension.[61] But the conflicts between Israel and its neighbors as well as conflicts between Arab states are motivated by a host of ideological and political issues and by the issue of disputed land territory. Water can, at best, be viewed as one of several conflict issues in the region. In fact, Wolf concludes categorically that "water was neither a cause nor a goal of any Arab-Israeli warfare."[62] Peter Gleick argues that increasing scarcity may make water "an increasingly salient element of interstate politics, including violent conflict."

He identifies 225 historical and ongoing instances where water is related to conflict.[63] In most of these disputes, however, water is an instrument of war or a strategic target, rather than a resource at the root of the dispute. Because there is little evidence linking environmental stress to international conflict, one would not expect climate change to play a major role either. Erik Gartzke argues that economic development, which drives climate change, also lowers the risk of interstate conflict. Therefore, even if climate change drives conflict, the effect may not be visible if it is overshadowed by the peacebuilding effect of economic development.[64] The same argument can be made for other types of armed conflict.

Terrorism has been linked to environmental stress. Terrorist activity, such as the events on 9/11, has been interpreted as resulting from deprivation and frustration, among Muslims, among Arabs, and among Third World immigrants in Western countries. However, the kind of frustration that might lead a person to join a terrorist movement is mainly economic (poverty) or religious (discrimination) rather than environmental. Most cases of "environmental terrorism" are acts of war, such as the deliberate oil spills in Kuwait in the aftermath of the Iraqi invasion in 1990–91.[65] Some radical environmental groups have engaged in violence, sabotage, and other forms of "ecoterror" in pursuit of their goals.[66] But such activities have not led to major losses of life, and they are ideologically inspired rather than a result of scarcity.

ENVIRONMENTAL INSECURITY AS DISASTERS OTHER THAN WAR

Armed conflict is direct violence between two or more organized parties. But environmental stresses and strains can kill in very different ways. Scarcity of freshwater, while not robustly associated with large-scale armed conflict, is certainly a major source of disease in poor countries. Wolf asserts that more than a billion people lack access to safe freshwater, that almost three billion people do not have access to fresh sanitation, and that more than five million people die every year from water-related diseases or inadequate sanitation.[67] Although these numbers are rough estimates, they indicate that the loss of life from such slow environmental disasters is far greater than those from war. Only very major wars, like the two world wars, can rival such figures. In addition to its direct effects on human health, water shortage is a major threat to food security in dry areas that are too poor to compensate for crop failures by food imports.

Although the scarcity of clear freshwater and the lack of proper sanitation facilities may be the biggest environmental problem of our time, many other environmental problems also pose a threat to human security. The use of lead as an additive in gasoline led to extensive pollution and health hazards until a ban was implemented in most countries starting in the 1990s. Some studies claim that lead poisoning may have played a role in the rise and fall of crime in industrialized countries in the last half of the twentieth century.[68]

The chemical spill from an accident at a factory in Bhopal, India, in 1984 is reported to have caused more than two thousand immediate deaths and over half-a-million injuries.[69] The reduction of the Aral Sea to some 10 to 25 percent of its former area and volume, one of the most dramatic human-made environmental disasters in the twentieth century, continues to degrade the lives of thousands of people.[70] This is just one in a series of environmental catastrophes resulting from Soviet policies that gave priority to rapid industrial development at the expense of the environment and with little regard to human life;[71] similar problems have arisen in

China.[72] Clearly, environmental stress can expose humans to very serious risks, even in cases where the stresses do not (and are unlikely ever to) result in armed conflict within or between nations. Of course, actions of war also have long-term environmental effects, which are incidental to the war effort but can claim a large number of lives.[73] The nuclear bombings of Hiroshima and Nagasaki in 1945 provide clear examples.

Various infectious diseases such as HIV/AIDS, Ebola, and the avian influenza have raised the specter of major human disasters that are as destructive as major wars. A pandemic—a global outbreak of a new type or subtype of disease—differs from seasonal outbreaks or epidemics of diseases that have been circulating previously. The Spanish flu in 1918–19 may have killed as many as fifty million people worldwide. The Asian flu (1957–58) and the Hong Kong flu (1968–69) were also major killers but at a smaller order of magnitude. Although progress has been made in slowing the spread and the effects of the HIV virus, AIDS continues to be a major source of death—estimated at 1.7 million worldwide in 2011.[74] Climate change is expected to increase the spread of some tropical diseases such as malaria, a substantial but declining cause of death (655,000 casualties worldwide in 2011, down by 25 percent since 2000).[75] Globalization of the economy and increased human mobility are factors that probably increase the rapid spread of pandemics, but the accompanying economic progress and the globalization of health services make for more effective responses to them. War also has a deleterious effect on health.[76] In this way, traditional security concerns such as armed conflict interact with the broader human security agenda.

Natural disasters can also be as forceful at killing as war. The Indian Ocean tsunami in December 2004 and the Haiti earthquake in January 2010 each killed well over

200,000 people. In the period 2002–11, natural disasters claimed more than 1.2 million lives.[77] This number exceeds by a wide margin the number of battle-related deaths in all wars during the same period, although it is probably less than the total of conflict-related deaths.[78] Although extremely serious, natural disasters are rare events. Large volcanic eruptions or meteor strikes could potentially kill millions. These infrequent but very large disasters, such as pandemics, are part of the hazardous physical environment. The issue for environmental policy is whether human activities, such as human-induced climate change, exacerbate the disaster rate. The UN High-Level Panel interprets the "dramatic increase in major disasters witnessed in the last 50 years" as evidence of how environmental stress exacerbates the destructive potential of natural catastrophes, but this remains a contested issue.[79] Around 60 percent of disaster-related loss of human life in the most recent decade was due to geological disasters, which are unlikely to be influenced by climatic change. The rest is due to climate-related disasters, whose frequency and severity are expected to increase with global warming.[80] The rapid increase in the number of recorded natural disasters (some of which is probably due to improved reporting) is not matched by statistics on human casualties.

ENVIRONMENTAL INSECURITY AS THE EROSION OF THE CARRYING CAPACITY

Environmental stress is not a new phenomenon, as is well known to anyone who has read descriptions of streets with running sewers in ancient Rome or conditions in industrial cities in Britain in the nineteenth century. But environmental concern is greater today, and there is also a feeling that at the present very high level of general consumption, humans are straining the global limits in an unprecedented way.

Examples can be found where environmental damage to nature has long-term—or even more or less permanent—effects. The Central Plateau of Spain and the Highlands of Scotland are unlikely to regain the forests that were destroyed by shipbuilding and overgrazing. If the more pessimistic views of the annual loss of species are anywhere near correct,[81] humankind stands to lose not only the aesthetic value of a variety of exotic species but also the genetic variability that is valuable in medical research.

Global warming poses the most serious potential challenge to the future sustainability of human civilization. If the sea level rises by several feet, life will become very difficult in low-lying areas of Bangladesh and the Maldives. Cornucopians point to the failure of many past predictions of gloom, such as the periodic warnings of global hunger issued by biologists such as Paul Ehrlich and environmentalists such as Lester Brown.[82] Negative news, even of future events that may never happen, often get more publicity than the slow but steady improvements in agricultural productivity or the worldwide reduction in population growth.[83] Predictions of future disasters cannot be ignored, but neither can the possibilities of countermeasures to avert the most disastrous consequences.

CONDITIONS OF ENVIRONMENTAL INSECURITY

Resource and environmental factors undoubtedly play some role in human insecurity, although the strength of the relationship is debated. However, the environmental effect is tempered by other factors associated with insecurity. The resource and environmental factors in conflict must be considered in the context of a multifaceted view of armed conflict. In this section, I examine some of the factors that must be part of such a broader view.[84]

POLITICS

Democratic politics may influence the relationship between the environment and conflict through its effect on environmental policy and practice, but also through its effect on the way environmental conflicts are handled.

Everything else being equal, well-established political democracies are likely to demonstrate enlightened environmental policies.[85] Democracies tend to be open to trial and error, they are responsive to the victims of environmental stress, they participate in international organizations, and they conclude agreements to alleviate environmental problems. Environmental activists in democratic countries frequently have considerable disagreements with the environmental policies of their own countries. These very complaints form an essential part of the self-adjusting political processes in democracies. This point was brought home with particular force following the exposure of the vast environmental disasters caused by the governments of the Soviet Union and Communist China, in complete disregard for the welfare of their citizens and not held in check by any organized opposition. Democracies are much less likely to let environmental problems deteriorate enough for armed conflict to be a real risk.

The relationship between environmental stress and conflict is also influenced by the phenomenon known as democratic peace.[86] Democracies rarely if ever fight one another, even at low levels of violence. Even fairly minor resource conflicts such as the "cod wars," the "turbot wars," and other fishery clashes in the North Atlantic are regarded with embarrassment by the democracies involved. Thus, democracies make great efforts to settle such conflicts before anyone gets killed. If democracies rarely fight one another for any reason, it is not likely that they will start fighting each other over re-source or environmental matters. Stable democracies rarely if ever experience serious levels of violent challenges to their governments; this is unlikely to be different for environmental conflicts.[87] Unstable democracies or intermediate regimes, on the other hand, are likely to experience more conflict than stable autocracies, as evidenced most recently in states in political transition in the Middle East.[88] The social and political awakening in autocratic states could lead to more conflict until the new regimes stabilize and could weaken state capacity, with negative results for environmental policy.

ECONOMICS

Economic development may influence environmental behavior in two ways. First, wealth has a strong effect on environmental sustainability. Early economic progress in general, and industrialization in particular, is intimately associated with unhealthy working conditions, smog, acid rain, and pollution of freshwater resources. This has led many environmentalists to conclude that economic development, and capitalism in particular, are intrinsically harmful to the environment, following the IPAT formula, in which the environmental impact by definition is equal to the product of population, affluence, and technology.[89]

But at an advanced stage of industrialization, and even more so in postindustrial societies, the trend may be reversed. An affluent society can afford to invest in new technologies to clean up pollution in industry, agriculture, and waste disposal. In addition, such a society places a high value on human resources and takes care to avoid death and incapacitation of its highly educated labor force. In an economically advanced economy, traditional indicators of environmental stress—such as the lack of clean water, unhealthy sanitation, deforestation, and air pollution in the cities—start to decline because economic development has gone beyond a certain level. Many forms of environmental stress are primarily poverty problems, although the Brundtland Commission report's general identification of environmental unsustainability with poverty elimination is probably more politically than empirically based.[90] The three environmental problems studied by Hauge and Ellingsen—deforestation, soil erosion, and lack of freshwater—are all closely related to economic development; that is, the higher the economic development, the lower the degree of environmental deterioration.[91] Early industrialization reinforces some of these problems and creates additional forms of environmental stress, such as urban and industrial pollution, during a period when economic growth takes precedence over all other concerns. This gives rise to an inverted U-shaped relationship between economic development and environmental stress, sometimes called an environmental Kuznets curve (EKC).[92] Other environmental problems, such as the emission of carbon dioxide (CO_2) and other greenhouse gases, keep increasing with economic development. Despite the mounting scientific evidence, these problems have not been fully recognized as true environmental concerns. But if the development of alternative sources of energy or CO_2 capture and storage succeed, a solution is likely to be promoted by highly developed countries with the application of initially very expensive new technology.

Environmental disasters that at first glance may seem to derive from poor economic conditions are frequently the result of poor economic policy decisions. As Amartya Sen has pointed out, India has not suffered any major famine since independence, in spite of frequent crop failures and endemic starvation.[93] He attributes this to the policies of the Indian government operating under the constraints of political democracy and a free press. These constraints were much weaker

under colonial rule, when India experienced several large-scale famines. Similarly, the Chinese government was unable or unwilling to prevent the disaster in the agricultural sector resulting from the Great Leap Forward policy in 1958–60 and, as a result, tens of millions of people died.[94] Recent North Korean famines have resulted more from economic mismanagement rather than from environmental misfortune. Yet, economic policy cannot provide a short-term cure for poverty that is irrevocably intertwined with large-scale undernourishment and poor health. To root out these problems, long-term economic growth and technological progress are called for.

Economic development can have a restraining influence on violent behavior in environmental conflict, because wealth is negatively associated with interstate as well as intrastate armed conflict.[95] Wealthy individuals and groups stand to lose more if war breaks out. If wealth is widespread, it is likely to act as a general deterrent to participation in major violence. Rich countries trade more, and trade promotes peaceful relations, a phenomenon called "liberal peace."[96]

CULTURAL FACTORS

Many countries are seriously divided between ethnic and religious groups fighting for dominance of the state (or for secession from it). Several studies have found ethnic dominance or polarization to be related to internal conflict.[97] Most of the cases studied by Homer-Dixon and his colleagues concern highly divided or segregated societies (Chiapas, South Africa, Rwanda, and Gaza). Although environmental factors may have contributed to conflict in South Africa, Valery Percival and Homer-Dixon recognize that it is impossible to overlook the ethnic basis of the conflict, given that white colonialists treated black Africans and "colored" people as creatures of a lower order.[98]

Where ethnic groups cooperate, the prospects of negotiated and cooperative solutions to environmental problems are good. Where they do not, environmental factors add to the problems created by the cultural conflict.

CONFLICT HISTORY

One of the strongest factors in accounting for current armed conflict, internal as well as external, is a history of armed conflict.[99] Armed conflict can have destructive effects on the environment, as shown by the wars in Vietnam, Afghanistan, and elsewhere.[100] Human and material destruction of the environment at a vast scale in turn increases the scarcity of resources, possibly to the point where violent conflict over scarce resources is a real possibility. In Vietnam, for example, intensive bombing and defoliation caused substantial damage to forests and agricultural land. Hard-hit countries may move into a vicious cycle of poverty, authoritarian rule, environmental stress, and violence. War leads to environmental destruction, which in turn—mixed with poor government and poverty—may fuel new conflict.

ENVIRONMENTAL CHANGE AND RESOURCE SCARCITY

Environmental change is continuously occurring as a result of processes that are beyond the control of humans. Periods of global warming and cooling occurred long before human activity became so pervasive and widespread that it could influence such basic global processes.

In the environmental debate, neo-Malthusian doomsayers regularly clash with cornucopian prophets of environmental optimism.[101] "The Earth is rich. If there is poverty, it is because of human betrayal," wrote the Norwegian poet Nordahl Grieg in 1936,[102] at a time when socialists still held to

technological optimism. Today, radical environmentalists tend to prefer the image of "Spaceship Earth," a repository of limited resources that capitalism is rapidly squandering. The international best-seller *The Limits to Growth* is a prime example, predicting scarcities in a number of strategic minerals and other raw materials.[103] A similar line was taken by Georg Borgström and others who predicted worldwide food shortages.[104] Lester Brown points to the impending crises that will occur if and when China joins the company of the affluent and its citizens adopt Western-style nutritional habits.[105] However, writers such as John Maddox, Julian Simon, and Bjørn Lomborg have argued that improved technology and human ingenuity will continue to enable humans to overcome material scarcity, particularly if we use market mechanisms to set appropriate prices for scarce resources.[106] Despite widespread malnutrition, most international experts in agriculture have a relatively optimistic view of the long-term capacity of global agriculture to feed the future world population.[107] In the mid-1970s, the oil crisis was seen as the precursor of a series of similar crises in strategic minerals, such as copper, but the subsequent decline in raw material prices put an end to this view. More recently, raw material prices have risen, mostly as a result of rapid economic development in large countries such as China, India, and Brazil. It remains to be seen whether the long-term trend toward lower prices for raw materials will be broken.

This debate has implications for conflict scenarios. If the optimists are correct, resources are not generally scarce and predictions of increased global strife over resources are unlikely to come true. If the environmental pessimists are correct, humans are constantly eroding the carrying capacity of the global environment and resource use is already beyond sustainable levels. Then one would expect the competition for resources to get ever fiercer, eventually to the point where it may break the norms of nonviolent behavior, perhaps even within and between democracies.

In the debate about the total volume of global resources, the environmental optimists have responded effectively to the neo-Malthusians. But for the purpose of analyzing conflict behavior, the question of the availability of the resources is more important. Although global resources may be abundant, local resources may not be sufficient. In other words, the key to avoiding serious and increasing resource scarcities lies in the question of distribution, within and between nations. This takes one back to the issues of economic and political structure. If people cannot afford to buy food or other basic necessities, or if authoritarian political structures prevent them from making use of available resources, overall abundance will not help. In such cases, starvation amid plenty will result. Thousands will continue to die from unclean freshwater, while others drink bottled mineral water at $1,000 per cubic meter.[108]

SCARCITY OR A RESOURCE CURSE?

A perspective on civil war adopted by many economists is that civil war is occasioned more by economic and geographical opportunity than by real or perceived grievances.[109] This perspective sees resources as relevant to the conflict, but turns the neo-Malthusian perspective on its head: abundant natural resources are likely to hinder rather than stimulate growth and to stimulate authoritarian government. Accumulation through economic development is usually associated with the development of democratic institutions. But countries whose wealth has been built quickly on oil and other raw materials, notably many countries in North Africa and the Middle East, tend to lag behind other

countries at the same level of wealth in the development of their political institutions. Resource abundance may also lead to conflict, partly because politically obsolete structures refuse to give way, but also because control over some or all of the resources can be captured by opposition groups that use them to fund their rebel movements, as illustrated by diamond-smuggling rebels in Angola and rebels in Colombia and Peru funded by drug sales.

The typical measure of natural resource dependence adopted in the study of economic opportunity in civil war is exports of primary product as a share of gross domestic product (GDP), but this measure has been criticized because it lumps lootable and non-lootable natural resources.[110] Other studies look at specific lootable resources, such as oil, timber, or diamonds, with more mixed results.[111] These studies have shown that being a major oil exporter seems to be related to the onset of civil war, and the same is true for lootable diamonds after the end of the Cold War.

THE ROLE OF POPULATION PRESSURE

High resource consumption and rapid population growth are the twin pillars of neo-Malthusian scenarios of future resource scarcities. But global population growth is leveling off. The 2012 United Nations Medium Projection estimates a global population of 10.9 billion by 2100. Many developing countries have followed industrialized countries in fertility reduction: by the 2005–10 period, global fertility stood at 2.53 children per woman (down from 4.95 in 1950–55), and it was expected to decrease to 2.24 by 2045–50 and to 1.99 a half-century later.[112] Although many of the least-developed countries, particularly in Africa (and despite AIDS), will continue to have high population growth for some time, the threat of global overpopulation is largely gone. The main concern today is with Third World countries that combine rapid population growth with poor development prospects. In the developed world, the greater worry is the "graying" of the population.

Although population pressure is a popular explanation for armed conflict, extant research provides limited support. Henrik Urdal finds little validation for neo-Malthusian hypotheses relating population density and land scarcity to internal conflict but does find some limited effect of a high rate of population growth combined with land scarcity.[113] Ester Boserup concludes in an influential book that population growth stimulates innovation and reform in agriculture,[114] which has important implications for economic development and potentially for peace. Jaroslav Tir and Paul Diehl found no significant relationship between population density and interstate conflict, but a modest effect of population growth on interstate conflict.[115] There is little or no evidence that population growth increased the probability of states initiating a conflict or escalating it all the way to war. Population pressure is unlikely to reverse the prevailing trend toward a reduction in violence, although it may be an important local factor in certain areas.[116] Urdal finds "youth bulges," that is, a high share of the adult population in the 15–24 age bracket, to be associated with internal conflict, but this is more of a distributional problem than one of available resources overall.[117]

Some researchers have extrapolated from studies of rats and other animals in very crowded conditions and have foreseen additional friction and conflict in human beings living under similar conditions. However, in order for such studies to be relevant, population densities would have to be a great deal higher, and the freedom of movement a great deal lower, than what obtains in most human settlements. Indeed, the most crowded states in the world, city-states like Singapore

and Hong Kong, are rather peaceful internally and externally, as far as group conflicts are concerned. Although much of the environmental security literature expects the urbanization resulting from climate change to lead to more violence, cities generally offer improved economic opportunities. The level of urbanization is associated with a lower level of civil war,[118] and there is no systematic connection between the growth of cities and urban social disorder.[119] Crime tends to be higher in urban areas, but this can probably be better accounted for by improved opportunities and greater anonymity than by resource scarcity.[120]

ENVIRONMENTAL COOPERATION

Environmental insecurity does not necessarily involve dramatic events such as armed struggle, mass starvation, or extensive and serious degradation. Resource and environmental problems can be handled by piecemeal reform and peaceful conflict resolution. Conflict of interest is endemic among human groups and individuals and may well increase in a world of increasing population and further globalization. But most scarcity conflicts are handled by nonviolent means. Indeed, a conflict of interest may stimulate increased collaboration, in order to regulate the use of the contested resource. The enormous "privatization" of sea territory that was completed with the Law of the Sea Treaty proceeded remarkably peacefully.[121] Wolf argues that although "water wars" are extremely rare, cooperation over shared water resources is quite common. He records 3,600 water treaties since the year 805, mainly over navigation rights.[122] Several major international rivers, such as the Rhine, the Danube, and the Mekong, have interstate river commissions that provide for discussion and resolution of conflicts of interest among the riparian states. Even in the Middle East, countries that were at hot war several times during the Cold War have been able to work out agreements relating to the use of water.[123] In the early 1960s, in the middle of the Cold War, Norway and the Soviet Union were able to agree on a large scheme for the joint exploitation of the Pasvik River for hydroelectric power, across the East-West divide. The consequences of climate change are not just cross-national but global, and new agreements and international institutions will have to be established in order to tackle them.

ENVIRONMENTAL INSECURITY?

Few, if any, conflicts justify single-issue labels such as "environmental conflict" or "climate conflict." One can always relate a specific conflict to several issue dimensions, and the issues mutually influence one another. Resource and environmental issues do indeed play a role in conflict, but the relationship is modified by the political, economic, and cultural factors at work in armed conflict generally. In many cases, environmental stress may more appropriately be seen as an intervening variable between poverty and poor governance on the one hand and armed conflict on the other. In this sense, environmental stress may be more appropriately viewed as a symptom that something has gone wrong than as a cause of the world's ills. Although climate change has bolstered the scarcity model of conflict, research to date has failed to change this assessment in a major way. Some scholars have also warned against the potential negative consequences of militarizing the climate change issue[124] or possible conflict-inducing effects of well-intentioned but ill-conceived policies for climate change mitigation or adaptation.[125]

For policymakers, as well NGOs and grassroots activists, a crucial question is at what point in the causal chain one can intervene to change things for the better. Political institutions may present the most effective short-term intervention points because they can be changed relatively abruptly. However, the dispersion of agency in international relations, noted in the introduction to this volume, may imply that the most effective means to improve human security in the long term, such as increasing economic development, do not necessarily result from political decisions. In any case, the most important function of the environmental indicators is that they can serve effectively as warning lights, particularly in a world of growing environmental consciousness. Climate change is a serious global problem for a variety of reasons. The World Values Survey found widespread international concern about global warming, and a recent survey of experts placed rising greenhouse gas emissions as one of the most likely five current risks (but not top five in terms of the consequences).[126] The breadth of consequences of global climate change makes it not unreasonable to characterize it as a threat to human security, even though the consequences for armed conflict do not appear to be among the major challenges.[127]

NOTES

My work on these issues has been supported by the Research Council of Norway and the United States Institute of Peace. I am grateful for help and comments from a number of colleagues, notably Henrik Urdal and Halvard Buhaug, and from the editors of this volume, none of whom are responsible for errors in the final version.

1. Ban Ki-moon, "A Climate Culprit in Darfur," *Washington Post,* June 16, 2007, http://www.washingtonpost.com/wp-dyn/content/article/2007/06/15/AR2007061501857.html.

2. President Barack H. Obama, Acceptance Speech for the Nobel Peace Prize, Oslo, December 10, 2009, http://www.nobelprize.org/nobel_prizes/peace/laureates/2009/obama-lecture.html (accessed March 1, 2013).

3. *IPCC Third Assessment Report: Climate Change 2001* (Geneva: Intergovernmental Panel on Climate Change, 2001); *IPCC Fourth Assessment Report: Climate Change 2007* (Geneva: IPCC, 2007), http://www.ipcc.ch. Ragnhild Nordås and Nils Petter Gleditsch, "The IPCC, Human Security, and the Climate-Conflict Nexus," in *Climate Change and Human Security*, Michael Redclift and Marco Grasso, ed. (London: Elgar, 2013), 67–88. See also note 127.

4. Peter Schwartz and Doug Randall, *An Abrupt Climate Change Scenario and Its Implications for United States National Security* (Washington, DC: Environmental Media Services, 2003), http://www.gbn.com/articles/pdfs/Abrupt%20Climate%20Change%20February%202004.pdf (accessed January 8, 2013).

5. Bruce Russett and John R. Oneal, *Triangulating Peace: Democracy, Interdependence, and International Organizations* (New York: W. W. Norton, 2001); and Nils Petter Gleditsch, "The Liberal Moment Fifteen Years On: Presidential Address, International Studies Association," *International Studies Quarterly* 52, no. 4 (2008): 691–712.

6. Joshua S. Goldstein, *Winning the War on War* (New York: Dutton, 2011); Steven Pinker, *The Better Angels of Our Nature* (New York: Viking, 2011). For discussion, see Azar Gat, "Is War Declining—and Why?" *Journal of Peace Research* 50, no. 2 (2013): 149–57; Nils Petter Gleditsch, Steven Pinker, Bradley A. Thayer, Jack S. Levy, and William R. Thompson, "The Decline of War," *International Studies Review* 15, no. 3 (2013): 396–419.

7. Lotta Themnér and Peter Wallensteen, "Armed Conflicts, 1946–2012," *Journal of Peace Research* 50, no. 4 (2013): 509–21 and, for the time series data, http://www.pcr.uu.se/research/ucdp/datasets/ucdp_battle-related_deaths_dataset/(accessed August 6, 2013).

8. Olof Palme et al., *Common Security: A Blueprint for Survival* (New York: Simon and Schuster for Independent Commission on Disarmament and Security Issues, 1982).

9. Arthur Westing, "Environmental Component of Comprehensive Security," *Bulletin of Peace Proposals* 20, no. 2 (1989): 129–34.

10. United Nations Development Programme, *Human Development Report 1994* (Oxford: Oxford University Press, 1994), 23.

11. Human Security Centre, *Human Security Report 2005: War and Peace in the 21st Century* (Oxford: Oxford University Press, 2005), viii; and Human Security Report Project, *Human Security Report 2012: Sexual Violence, Education, and War: Beyond the Mainstream Narrative* (Vancouver: Human Security Press, 2012), both available at http://www.humansecurityreport.org/ (accessed January 7, 2013).

12. Standard sources for measuring democratic governance can be found in Keith Jaggers and Ted Robert Gurr, "Tracking Democracy's Third Wave with the Polity III Data," *Journal of Peace Research* 32, no. 4 (1995): 469–82; Tatu Vanhanen, "A New Dataset for Measuring Democracy, 1810–1998," *Journal of Peace Research* 37, no. 2 (2000): 251–65; and Freedom House, *Freedom in the World: The Annual Survey of Political Rights and Civil Liberties* (annual since 1972), most recent (2014) edition at http://www.freedomhouse.org (accessed January 28, 2014).

13. Economic and social security is commonly measured by national product per capita, http://pwt.econ.upenn.edu/ (accessed January 10, 2013). A useful alternative measure is life expectancy.

14. For a prominent example of work in this area, see Ted Robert Gurr, *Peoples versus States: Minorities at Risk in the New Century* (Washington, DC: United States Institute of Peace Press, 2000).

15. See point 24 in "The Alliance's New Strategic Concept," agreed on at the North Atlantic Council, Rome, November 7–8, 1991, http://www.nato.int/cps/en/natolive/official_texts_23847.htm (accessed January 10, 2013).

16. United Nations High-Level Panel on Threats, Challenges, and Change, *A More Secure World: Our Shared Responsibility* (New York: United Nations, 2004).

17. Johan Galtung, "Violence, Peace, and Peace Research," *Journal of Peace Research* 6, no. 3 (1969): 167–91. See also Nils Petter Gleditsch, Håvard Strand, and Jonas Nordkvelle, "Peace Research—Just the Study of War?" *Journal of Peace Research* 51, no. 2 (2014).

18. Thomas Robert Malthus, *An Essay on the Principle of Population: Or a View of Its Past and Present Effects on Human Happiness: With an Inquiry into Our Prospects Respecting the Future Removal or Mitigation of the Evils which It Occasions*

(1798, 1803; reprinted: Cambridge: Cambridge University Press, 1992).

19. Nils Petter Gleditsch, "Environmental Conflict: Neomalthusians vs. Cornucopians," in *Security and the Environment in the Mediterranean: Conceptualising Security and Environmental Conflicts,* Hans Günter Brauch, P. H. Liotta, Antonio Marquina, Paul F. Rogers, and Mohammad El-Sayed Selim, ed. (Berlin: Springer, 2003), 477–85.

20. Malin Falkenmark, "Global Water Issues Confronting Humanity," *Journal of Peace Research* 27, no. 2 (1990): 177–90.

21. Colin J. Campbell, "Understanding Peak Oil," http://www.peakoil.net/about-peak-oil (accessed January 7, 2013).

22. Homer-Dixon specifically refers to scarcity of renewable resources, which he calls "environmental scarcity." But the general argument applies equally to nonrenewable resources. For a critique of Homer-Dixon, see Nils Petter Gleditsch and Henrik Urdal, "Ecoviolence? Links between Population Growth, Environmental Scarcity, and Violent Conflict in Thomas Homer-Dixon's Work," *Journal of International Affairs* 56, no. 1 (2002): 283–302.

23. Barry Buzan, Ole Wæver, and Jaap de Wilde, *Security: A New Framework for Analysis* (Boulder, CO: Lynne Rienner, 1998); and Westing, "Environmental Component."

24. Arne Næss, "A Defense of the Deep Ecology Movement," *Environmental Ethics* 6, no. 3 (1984): 265–70.

25. Quincy Wright, *A Study of War,* 2nd ed. (Chicago: University of Chicago Press, 1965), 1146–97. This edition has a commentary on war since 1942.

26. Lewis F. Richardson, *Statistics of Deadly Quarrels,* ed. Quincy Wright and C. C. Lienau (Pittsburgh, PA: Quadrangle, 1960), 205–10.

27. Wright, *Study of War,* 76.

28. Kalevi Holsti, *Peace and War: Armed Conflicts and International Order 1648–1989* (Cambridge: Cambridge University Press, 1991), 307.

29. John Vasquez, *The War Puzzle* (Cambridge: Cambridge University Press, 1993), 130.

30. Paul K. Huth, *Standing Your Ground: Territorial Disputes and International Conflict* (Ann Arbor, MI: University of Michigan Press, 1996), 5.

31. Stuart Bremer, "Dangerous Dyads: Conditions Affecting the Likelihood of Interstate War, 1816–1965," *Journal of Conflict Resolution* 36, no. 2 (1992): 309–41.

32. Nils Petter Gleditsch, "Geography, Democracy, and Peace," *International Interactions* 20, no. 4 (1995): 297–323.

33. Jennifer Bailey, "States, Stocks, and Sovereignty: High Seas Fishing and the Expansion of State Sovereignty," in *Conflict and the Environment,* Nils Petter Gleditsch, ed. (Dordrecht, the Netherlands: Kluwer Academic, 1997), 215–34.

34. Dwight D. Eisenhower: "Radio and Television Address to the American People on the State of the Nation," April 5, 1954 (The American Presidency Project, University of California Santa Barbara), http://www.presidency.ucsb.edu/ws/index.php?pid=10201 (accessed January 9, 2013).

35. Aaron T. Wolf, Jeffrey A. Natharius, Jeffrey J. Danielson, Brian S. Ward, and Jan K. Pender, "International River Basins of the World," *Water Resources Development* 15, no. 4 (1999): 387–427.

36. Marvin S. Soroos, "The Turbot War: Resolution of an International Fishery Dispute," in *Conflict and the Environment,* Nils Petter Gleditsch, ed. (Dordrecht, the Netherlands: Kluwer Academic, 1997), 235–52.

37. Indra de Soysa and Nils Petter Gleditsch, with Michael Gibson, Margareta Sollenberg, and Arthur Westing, *To Cultivate Peace: Agriculture in a World of Conflict,* PRIO Report no. 1 (International Peace Research Institute, Oslo, and Future Harvest, Washington, DC, 1999), http://www.future-harvest.org.

38. See http://nobelpeaceprize.org/en_GB/laureates/. For a critical view of the Nobel Committee's justification for the 2004 award, see Nils Petter Gleditsch and Henrik Urdal, "Roots of Conflict: Don't Blame Environmental Decay for the Next War," *International Herald Tribune,* November 22, 2004, 10, www.nytimes.com/2004/11/22/opinion/22iht-ednils_ed3_.html (accessed March 4, 2013).

39. Thomas Homer-Dixon and Jessica Blitt, eds., *Ecoviolence: Links among Environment, Population, and Security* (Lanham, MD: Rowman and Littlefield, 1998); and Günther Bächler, *Violence* *through Environmental Discrimination* (Dordrecht, the Netherlands: Kluwer Academic, 1999).

40. Thomas Homer-Dixon, *Environment, Scarcity, and Violence* (Princeton, NJ: Princeton University Press, 1999).

41. For a more detailed critique along these lines, see Nils Petter Gleditsch, "Armed Conflict and the Environment: A Critique of the Literature," *Journal of Peace Research* 35, no. 3 (1998): 381–400. For a response, see Daniel Schwartz, Tom Deligiannis, and Thomas Homer-Dixon, "The Environment and Violent Conflict," in *Environmental Conflict*, Paul F. Diehl and Nils Petter Gleditsch, ed. (Boulder, CO: Westview, 2001), 273–94. For a brief rejoinder, see Nils Petter Gleditsch, "Armed Conflict and the Environment," in *Environmental Conflict*, 264.

42. Wario R. Adano, Ton Dietz, Karen Witsenburg, and Fred Zaal, "Climate Change, Violent Conflict and Local Institutions in Kenya's Drylands," *Journal of Peace Research* 49, no. 1 (2012): 65–80; Ole Magnus Theisen, "Climate Clashes? Weather Variability, Land Pressure, and Organized Violence in Kenya, 1989–2004," *Journal of Peace Research* 49, no. 1 (2012): 81–96.

43. Ian A. Brown, "Assessing Eco-scarcity as a Cause of the Outbreak of Conflict in Darfur: A Remote Sensing Approach," *International Journal of Remote Sensing* 31, no. 10 (2010): 2513–20; Michael Kevane and Leslie Gray, "Darfur: Rainfall and Conflict," *Environmental Research Letters* 3, no. 3 (2008): 1–10.

44. Wenche Hauge and Tanja Ellingsen, "Beyond Environmental Security: Causal Pathways to Conflict," *Journal of Peace Research* 35, no. 3 (1998): 299–317.

45. Daniel Esty et al., *State Failure Task Force Report: Phase II* (Washington, DC: State Failure Task Force, 1998); and Ole Magnus Theisen, "Blood and Soil? Resource Scarcity and Internal Armed Conflict Revisited," *Journal of Peace Research* 45, no. 6 (2012): 801–18.

46. Indra de Soysa, "Paradise Is a Bazaar? Greed, Creed, and Governance in Civil War, 1989–99," *Journal of Peace Research* 39, no. 4 (2002): 395–416; Indra de Soysa, "Ecoviolence: Shrinking Pie or Honey Pot?" *Global Environmental Politics* 2, no. 4 (2000): 1–27.

47. Helga Malmin Binningsbø, Indra de Soysa, and Nils Petter Gleditsch, "Green Giant, or Straw Man? Environmental Pressure and Civil Conflict, 1961–99," *Population and Environment* 28, no. 6 (2007): 337–53.

48. The fifth assessment report from the IPCC will contain a separate chapter on human security. IPCC, "Agreed Reference Material for the IPCC Fifth Assessment Report, http://www.ipcc.ch/pdf/ar5/ar5-outline-compilation.pdf (accessed August 6, 2013). See also note 127.

49. Ole Magnus Theisen, Helge Holtermann, and Halvard Buhaug, "Climate Wars? Assessing the Claim that Drought Breeds Conflict," *International Security* 36, no. 3 (2011/12): 79–106; John O'Loughlin, Frank D. W. Witmer, Andrew M. Linke, Arlene Laing, Andrew Gettelman, and Jimy Dudhia, "Climate Variability and Conflict Risk in East Africa, 1990–2009," *PNAS* 109, no. 45 (2012): 18344–49.

50. Ragnhild Nordås and Nils Petter Gleditsch, "Climate Change and Conflict," *Political Geography* 26, no. 6 (2007): 627–38; Thomas Bernauer, Tobias Böhmelt, and Vally Koubi, "Environmental Changes and Violent Conflict," *Environmental Research Letters* 7, no. 1 (2012), doi:10.1088/1748-9326/7/1/015601; Nils Petter Gleditsch, "Whither the Weather? Climate Change and Conflict," *Journal of Peace Research* 49, no. 1 (2012): 4–9; Jürgen Scheffran, Michael Brzoska, Jasmin Kominek, P. Michael Link, and Janpeter Schilling, "Climate Change and Violent Conflict," *Science* 336, no. 6083 (2012): 869–71; and Ole Magnus Theisen, Nils Petter Gleditsch, and Halvard Buhaug, "Is Climate Change a Driver of Armed Conflict?" *Climatic Change* 117, no. 3 (2013): 613–25. For a debate on the implications of increased temperature for conflict in Africa, see Marshall B. Burke, Edward Miguel, Shanker Satyanath, John A. Dykema, and David B. Lobell, "Warming Increases the Risk of Civil War in Africa," *PNAS* 106, no. 49 (2009): 20670–74; and Halvard Buhaug, "Climate Not to Blame for African Civil Wars," *PNAS* 107, no. 38 (2010): 16477–82. A study that labels itself a meta-study of the literature, Solomon M. Hsiang, Marshall Burke, and Edward Miguel, "Quantifying the Influence of Climate on Human Conflict," *Science* 341 (August 1, 2012), doi:10.1126/science.1235367, finds evidence for a strong causal link between climatic events and human conflict "across a range of spatial and temporal scales and across all major regions of the world," but the accuracy of this assessment was immediately questioned by other scholars (see, e.g., John Bohannon, "Study Links Climate Change and Violence, Battle Ensues," *Science* 341 [August 2, 2013]: 444–45, doi:10.1126/science.341.6145.444), and Halvard Buhang et al., "One Effect to Rule Them All? A Comment on Climate and Conflict," *Climate Change* (2014).

51. Bächler, *Violence through Environmental Discrimination.*

52. James D. Fearon and David Laitin, "Ethnicity, Insurgency, and Civil War," *American Political Science Review* 97, no. 1 (2003): 75–90.

53. Michael Ross, "What Do We Know about Natural Resources and Civil War," *Journal of Peace Research* 41, no. 3 (2004): 337–56.

54. Hanne Fjelde and Nina von Uexkull, "Climate Triggers: Rainfall Anomalies, Vulnerability and Communal Conflict in Sub-Saharan Africa," *Political Geography* 31, no. 7 (2012): 444–53.

55. Cullen Hendrix and Idean Salehyan, "Climate Change, Rainfall, and Social Conflict in Africa," *Journal of Peace Research* 49, no. 1 (2012): 35–50.

56. Idean Salehyan, "From Climate Change to Conflict? No Consensus Yet," *Journal of Peace Research* 45, no. 3 (2008): 315–26.

57. Phillip Stalley, "Environmental Scarcity and International Conflict," *Conflict Management and Peace Science* 20, no. 2 (2003): 33–58.

58. Kathryn Furlong, Nils Petter Gleditsch, and Håvard Hegre, "Geographic Opportunity and Neomalthusian Willingness: Boundaries, Shared Rivers, and Conflict," *International Interactions* 32, no. 1 (2006): 79–108; Marit Brochmann and Nils Petter Gleditsch, "Shared Rivers and Conflict—A Reconsideration," *Political Geography* 31, no. 8 (2012): 519–27.

59. Theodora-Ismene Gizelis and Amanda E. Wooden, "Water Resources, Institutions, and Intrastate Conflict," *Political Geography* 29, no. 8 (2010): 444–53.

60. Aaron T. Wolf, "'Water Wars' and Water Reality: Conflict and Cooperation along International Waterways," in *Environmental Change, Ad-* *aptation, and Human Security,* Steve Lonergan, ed. (Dordrecht, the Netherlands: Kluwer Academic, 1999), 254. Wolf uses data from Michael Brecher and Jonathan Wilkenfeld, *A Study of Crisis* (Ann Arbor: University of Michigan Press, 1997).

61. Miriam R. Lowi, "Bridging the Divide—Transboundary Disputes and the Case of the West-Bank Water," *International Security* 18, no. 1 (1993): 113–38.

62. Wolf, "'Water Wars' and Water Reality."

63. Peter H. Gleick, "Water and Conflict: Fresh Water Resources and International Security," *International Security* 18, no. 1 (1993): 79–112; and Peter H. Gleick, "Water Conflict Chronology" (Oakland, CA: Pacific Institute, 2010), www.worldwater.org/conflict/list/ (accessed January 8, 2011).

64. Erik Gartzke, "Could Climate Change Cause Peace?" *Journal of Peace Research* 49, no. 1 (2012): 177–91.

65. Daniel M. Schwarz, "Environmental Terrorism: Analyzing the Concept," *Journal of Peace Research* 35, no. 4 (1998): 483–96.

66. Edward V. Badolato, "Environmental Terrorism—A Case Study," *Terrorism* 14, no. 4 (1991): 237–39, http://en.wikipedia.org/wiki/Animal_Liberation_Front (accessed January 8, 2013).

67. Aaron T. Wolf, "Water and Human Security," *AVISO: An Information Bulletin on Global Environmental Change and Human Security* 3 (1999): 1.

68. *Wikipedia,* s.v. "tetraethyllead," http://en.wikipedia.org/wiki/Tetraethyllead; and Kevin Drum, "Crime Is at Its Lowest Level in 50 Years. A Simple Molecule May Be the Reason Why," *Mother Jones,* January 3, 2013, http://www.motherjones.com/kevin-drum/2013/01/lead-crime-connection (accessed January 9, 2013).

69. *Wikipedia,* s.v. "Bhopal disaster," http://en.wikipedia.org/wiki/Bhopal_disaster (accessed January 9, 2013). For a discussion of how industrial accidents are likely to be exacerbated in wartime, see Arthur Westing, *Environmental Hazards of War: Releasing Dangerous Forces in an Industrialized World* (London: Sage, for PRIO and UNEP, 1990).

70. *Wikipedia,* s.v. "Aral Sea," http://en.wikipedia.org/wiki/Aral_Sea (accessed January 9, 2013).

Following the building of a dam in 2008, the Aral Sea has been slowly expanding again.

71. Murray Feshbach and Albert Friendly Jr., *Ecocide in the USSR: Health and Nature under Siege* (New York: Basic Books, 1992).

72. Vaclav Smil, *China's Environmental Crisis: An Inquiry into the Limits of National Development* (Armonk, NY: M. E. Sharpe, 1993).

73. Arthur H. Westing, *Pioneer on the Environmental Impact of War* (Heidelberg: Springer, 2012).

74. Joint United Nations Programme on HIV/AIDS (UNAIDS), http://www.unaids.org/en/dataanalysis/ (Geneva: UNAIDS, 2013) (accessed January 9, 2013).

75. *IPCC Fourth Assessment Report;* "Climate Change and Malaria, Scenario for 2050" (Arendal: GRID, 2005), http://www.grida.no/graphicslib/detail/climate-change-and-malaria-scenario-for-2050_bffe; "Malaria Deaths are Down but Progress Remains Fragile" (news release, World Health Organization, Geneva, 2011), http://www.who.int/mediacentre/news/releases/2011/malaria_report_20111213/en/index.html (accessed January 9, 2013).

76. Zaryab Iqbal, *War and the Health of Nations* (Stanford, CA: Stanford University Press, 2010). *Human Security Report 2009* (Vancouver: Human Security Report Project, 2009) provides some evidence that the health effect of recent armed conflicts are more difficult to discern because the conflicts are generally smaller, the secular trends in health improvement are greater, and the international response to human disasters is more effective.

77. *World Disasters Report 2012* (Geneva: International Federation of Red Cross and Red Crescent Societies, 2012), http://www.ifrcmedia.org/assets/pages/wdr2012/.

78. For a discussion about war deaths versus battle deaths, see Bethany Lacina and Nils Petter Gleditsch, "Monitoring Trends in Global Combat: A New Dataset of Battle Deaths," *European Journal of Population* 21, no. 2 (2005): 145–66, http://www.prio.no/cscw/cross/battledeaths (accessed March 4, 2013).

79. UN High-Level Panel on Threats, Challenges, and Change, *A More Secure World.*

80. *IPCC Fourth Assessment Report.*

81. Norman Myers argues that the loss of animal species runs into the thousands every year. Julian Simon and Bjørn Lomborg argue that very few cases of species extinction are documented. See Norman Myers and Julian Simon, *Scarcity or Abundance? A Debate on the Environment* (New York: W. W. Norton, 1994); and Bjørn Lomborg, *The Skeptical Environmentalist: Measuring the Real State of the World* (Cambridge: Cambridge University Press, 2001).

82. Paul Ehrlich, *The Population Bomb* (New York: Ballantine, 1968); and Lester Brown, *Who Will Feed China? Wake-up Call for a Small Planet*, Environmental Alert Series (Washington, DC: WorldWatch Institute, 1995).

83. *The State of Food and Agriculture* (Rome: Food and Agriculture Organization, 2012), http://www.fao.org/publications/sofa/en/ (accessed January 9, 2013).

84. Nils Petter Gleditsch, "Environmental Conflict and the Democratic Peace," in *Conflict and the Environment*, Nils Petter Gleditsch, ed. (Dordrecht, the Netherlands: Kluwer Academic, 1997), 91–106.

85. See Nils Petter Gleditsch and Bjørn Otto Sverdrup, "Democracy and the Environment," in *Human Security and the Environment: International Comparisons*, Edward A. Page and Michael Redclift, ed. (Cheltenham, UK: Edward Elgar, 2002), 45–79; and Rodger A. Payne, "Freedom and the Environment," *Journal of Democracy* 6, no. 3 (1995): 41–55. For a different view, see Manus Midlarsky, "Democracy and the Environment: An Empirical Assessment," *Journal of Peace Research* 35, no. 3 (1998): 341–61. Eric Neumayer argues that democracies are primarily stronger in their environmental commitment, not in environmental results. Eric Neumayer, "Do Democracies Exhibit Stronger International Environmental Commitment? A Cross-Country Analysis," *Journal of Peace Research* 39, no. 2 (2002): 101–12.

86. Nils Petter Gleditsch and Håvard Hegre, "Peace and Democracy: Three Levels of Analysis," *Journal of Conflict Resolution* 41, no. 2 (1997): 283–310.

87. Håvard Hegre, Tanja Ellingsen, Nils Petter Gleditsch, and Scott Gates, "Towards a Democratic Civil Peace? Democracy, Political Change, and Civil War, 1816–1992," *American Political Science Review* 95, no. 1 (2001): 17–33.

88. Ibid; see also Edward D. Mansfield and Jack Snyder, *Electing to Fight: Why Emerging Democracies Go to War* (Cambridge, MA: MIT Press, 2007).

89. However, if A is operationalized as GDP/cap and T as I/GDP, the IPAT formula is simply a tautology. Jordi Roca, "The IPAT Formula and Its Limitations," *Ecological Economics* 42, nos. 1–2 (2002): 1–2.

90. Gro Harlem Brundtland et al., *Our Common Future* (New York: Oxford University Press, 1988).

91. Hauge and Ellingsen, "Beyond Environmental Security." For empirical illustrations relating to air pollution, see Lomborg, *The Skeptical Environmentalist*, chap. 15.

92. Matthew A. Cole, "Development, Trade, and the Environment: How Robust Is the Environmental Kuznets Curve?" *Environment and Development Economics* 8, no. 4 (2003): 557–80.

93. Amartya Sen, "Liberty and Poverty: Political Rights and Economics," *New Republic*, January 10, 1994, 31–37.

94. Frank Dikötter, *Mao's Great Famine: The History of China's Most Devastating Catastrophe, 1958–62* (London: Bloomsbury, 2010).

95. Håvard Hegre, "Development and the Liberal Peace: What Does It Take to Be a Trading State?" *Journal of Peace Research* 27, no. 1 (2000): 5–30; and Hegre et al., "Towards a Democratic Peace?"

96. Russett and Oneal, *Triangulating Peace*.

97. Tanja Ellingsen, "Colorful Community or Ethnic Witches' Brew? Multiethnicity and Domestic Conflict during and after the Cold War," *Journal of Conflict Resolution* 44, no. 2 (2000): 228–49; and Marta Reynal-Querol, "Ethnicity, Political Systems, and Civil Wars," *Journal of Conflict Resolution* 46, no. 1 (2002): 29–54.

98. Valery Percival and Thomas Homer-Dixon, "Environmental Scarcity and Violent Conflict: The Case of South Africa," *Journal of Peace Research* 35, no. 3 (1998): 279–98.

99. Arvid Raknerud and Håvard Hegre, "The Hazard of War: Reassessing the Evidence for the

Democratic Peace," *Journal of Peace Research* 34, no. 4 (1997): 385–404; and Hegre et al., "Towards a Democratic Civil Peace?"

100. Arthur Westing, *Explosive Remnants of War: Mitigating the Environmental Effects* (London: Taylor and Francis, for Stockholm International Peace Research Institute, 1985); and Westing, *Environmental Hazards of War*.

101. For a pointed confrontation, see Myers and Simon, *Scarcity or Abundance?*

102. *Wikipedia*, s.v. "Til Ungdommen," http://en.wikipedia.org/wiki/Til_Ungdommen (accessed January 9, 2013).

103. Donella H. Meadows, Dennis L. Meadows, Jørgen Randers, and William W. Behrens III, *The Limits to Growth: A Report for the Club of Rome's Project on the Predicament of Mankind* (New York: Universe, 1972).

104. Georg Borgström, *The Hungry Planet: The Modern World at the Edge of Famine*, 2nd. ed. (New York: Macmillan, 1972).

105. Brown, *Who Will Feed China?*

106. John Maddox, *The Doomsday Syndrome* (New York: McGraw-Hill, 1972); Julian L. Simon, *The Ultimate Resource 2* (Princeton, NJ: Princeton University Press, 1996); and Lomborg, *The Skeptical Environmentalist*.

107. Vaclav Smil, "How Many People Can the Earth Feed?" *Population and Development Review* 20, no. 2 (1994): 255–92.

108. Peter Beaumont, "Water and Armed Conflict in the Middle East—Fantasy or Reality?" in *Conflict and the Environment*, Nils Petter Gleditsch, ed. (Dordrecht, the Netherlands: Kluwer Academic, 1997).

109. Paul Collier and Anke Hoeffler, "Greed and Grievance in Civil War?" *Oxford Economic Papers* 56, no. 4 (2004): 563–95; and Michael Ross, "What Do We Know about Natural Resources and Civil War," *Journal of Peace Research* 41, no. 3 (2004): 483–96.

110. James D. Fearon, "Primary Commodity Exports and Civil War," *Journal of Conflict Resolution* 49, no. 4 (2005): 483–507.

111. Päivi Lujala, Nils Petter Gleditsch, and Elisabeth Gilmore, "A Diamond Curse? Civil War and a Lootable Resource," *Journal of Conflict Resolution* 49, no. 4 (2005): 538–63.

112. *World Population Prospects, the 2012 Revision.* (New York: United Nations, Population Division, 2013), http://esa.un.org/unpd/wpp/Documentation /pdf/WPP2012_%20KEY%20FINDINGS.pdf (accessed August 6, 2013).

113. Henrik Urdal, "People vs. Malthus: Population Pressure, Environmental Degradation, and Armed Conflict Revisited," *Journal of Peace Research* 42, no. 4 (2005): 417–34.

114. Ester Boserup, *The Conditions of Agricultural Growth: The Economics of Agrarian Change under Population Pressure* (London: Allan and Unwin, 1965).

115. Jaroslav Tir and Paul F. Diehl, "Demographic Pressure and Interstate Conflict: Linking Population Growth and Density to Militarized Disputes and Wars, 1930–89," *Journal of Peace Research* 35, no. 3 (1998): 319–39.

116. Marijke Verpoorten, "Leave None to Claim the Land: A Malthusian Catastrophe in Rwanda?" *Journal of Peace Research* 49, no. 4 (2012): 547–63.

117. Henrik Urdal, "The Devil in the Demographics: The Effect of Youth Bulges on Domestic Armed Conflict, 1950–2000," *International Studies Quarterly* 50, no. 3 (2006): 607–29.

118. Collier and Hoeffler, "Greed and Grievance in Civil War," 563–95.

119. Halvard Buhaug and Henrik Urdal, "An Urbanization Bomb? Population Growth and Social Disorder in Cities," *Global Environmental Change* 23, no. 1 (2013): 1–10.

120. Eric Neumayer, "Inequality and Violent Crime: Evidence from Data on Robbery and Violent Theft," *Journal of Peace Research* 42, no. 1 (2005): 101–12.

121. Bailey, "States, Stocks, and Sovereignty," 222.

122. Wolf, "'Water Wars' and Water Reality"; and Aaron T. Wolf, "The Transboundary Freshwater Dispute Database Project," *Water International* 24, no. 2 (1999): 160–63. Data from http://terra.geo .orst.edu/users.tfdd/.

123. Steve C. Lonergan, "Water Resources and Conflict: Examples from the Middle East," in *Conflict and the Environment,* Nils Petter Gleditsch, ed. (Dordrecht, the Netherlands: Kluwer Academic, 1997).

124. Salehyan, "From Climate Change to Conflict?" 323.

125. Geoffrey D. Dabelko, Lauren Herzer, Schuyler Null, Meaghan Parker, and Russell Sticklo, eds., "Backdraft: The Conflict Potential of Climate Change Adaptation and Mitigation," *Environmental Change and Security Program Report* 14, no. 2 (2013), http://wilsoncenter.org/sites/default/files /ECSP_REPORT_14_2_BACKDRAFT.pdf (accessed August 6, 2013).

126. Berit Kvaløy, Henning Finseraas, and Ola Listhaug, "The Publics' Concern for Global Warming: A Cross-National Study of 47 Countries," *Journal of Peace Research* 49, no. 1 (2012): 11–22; and Lee Howell, ed., *Global Risks 2013* (Geneva: World Economic Forum, 2013), http://www3.weforum .org/docs/WEF_GlobalRisks_Report_2013.pdf (accessed January 9, 2013).

127. The Fifth Assessment Report of the IPCC in its report from Working Group II, released on March 31, 2014, provides a more comprehensive review of the possible consequences of climate change from conflict. However, different chapters are somewhat inconsistent, ranging from complete dismissal in one to warnings of serious future climate-related conflicts in another. For a brief critical comment on the report, see Nils Petler Gleditsch, "Climate Change and War," http://blogs.prio.org/2014/04 /climate-change-and-war/, posted April 17, 2014.

10

NATIONAL SELF-DETERMINATION CONFLICTS
EXPLAINING ENDURANCE AND INTRACTABILITY

Sumantra Bose

In an era of change and upheaval, one genre of dispute continues to prove immutable more often than not. It is defined by clashing perspectives and agendas of "national self-determination" (NSD), the late modern political doctrine that asserts the right of a community of people proclaimed as a "nation" by its community leaders to govern itself in its own sovereign state. A distinct territory is the sine qua non of any sovereign state. When two (or more) "national" communities make the same territory the focus of their respective claims to NSD, conflicts that are *enduring* (of protracted duration, measured in decades) and *intractable* (very difficult to resolve peaceably through negotiation and compromise) are born. The metaphor of a "zero-sum game" often accurately describes such conflicts.

Why is this so? What is it about conflicts between "national" peoples over a land that makes this genre of dispute so resistant to resolution? This chapter dissects the major reasons for the endurance and intractability of NSD conflicts, and shows how a broadly common set of factors account for their stubborn resilience across the diverse contexts of the Middle East (Israel and the Palestinians), South Asia (Kashmir), the Balkans (Bosnia and Herzegovina), and the eastern Mediterranean (Cyprus). The chapter emphasizes the ideological nature of these disputes, and the existential fears of the communities engaged in them, as the key factors. It then goes on to survey the efforts to make peace in the above cases of protracted conflict and highlight the lessons that emerge for the practice of peacemaking in NSD disputes. It concludes, through a broad-brush comparison of these cases, by reflecting on the challenge posed by NSD conflicts to international peace and security in the early twenty-first century.

IDEOLOGICAL UNDERPINNINGS

The endurance and intractability of NSD conflicts are rooted in the (often intensely) ideological nature of these disputes. When claims to NSD are articulated and justified in ideological terms, it becomes difficult to step back and recognize that rival claims may have some validity too, the first enabling condition for negotiation and compromise. The degree to which (clashing) ideological beliefs permeate NSD claims and conflicts—the strength of the claimants' conviction of moral "rightness"—is somewhat variable across cases, but this bedrock feature is rarely, if ever, absent in NSD struggles. Generally, the greater the ideological fervor underlying an NSD conflict, the more likely it is to be enduring and intractable.

The Israeli-Palestinian conflict is a case in point. The conflict in its current incarnation originated about one hundred years ago, in the second decade of the last century, as the pioneer leaders of the Zionist movement—which first appeared in the second half of the 1890s among a small fraction of the Jews then living in East-Central Europe and the Russian Empire—stepped up their political and diplomatic campaign. The objective of Zionism since the inception of the ideology was the establishment of a Jewish "national home" in the land of Palestine, regarded as the ancient homeland of the Jewish people despite its being located several thousand miles distant from the heart of Europe and populated by an overwhelming majority of Arabs, mostly Muslim and the rest Christian. This seemed a rather far-fetched agenda at the time, including to most Jews in East-Central Europe and the territories of the Russian Empire, among whom a variety of socialist and communist movements considerably outweighed Zionism in appeal through the 1930s.

Yet the Zionist movement's deficit in realist terms was compensated by its strength of ideological conviction, and resolute purpose flowing from that conviction. The movement for the return of the Jewish people—whom the Zionists defined as a nation rather than a scattering of minorities across various states and societies in Europe and the Middle East—to the "land of Israel" became a serious project in the 1920s and 1930s, as skilled and persuasive Zionist leaders gained sympathy and sanction for their nation-state–building program from the British government in London and its colonial officials governing Palestine. Between the end of World War I and the beginning of World War II, at least 365,000 Jews, the overwhelming majority from East-Central Europe and the former Russian Empire, arrived to settle in Palestine, and the "national home" idea—thinly veiled code for a Jewish nation-state in Palestine—acquired its critical mass of would-be citizens. In late 1946, a quasi census conducted by the British authorities counted 608,227 Jews living in Palestine, along with 1,364,332 Arabs.

During the three decades before the establishment in 1948 of the State of Israel on nearly 77 percent of Palestine, Zionism was characterized by an intense ideological spirit. In its framework of belief, the right of Jews from anywhere in the world to not just live in but to set up a Jewish national state in Palestine was simply unquestionable, the fulfillment of historical destiny.[1] The Zionist movement presented its vision of a Jewish nation-state in Palestine as *the* solution to the predicament of Jewish communities, principally those in the eastern half of Europe, who faced problems ranging from discrimination to pogroms. The movement was permeated by belief in the moral rightness of its case and cause. By the late 1930s, this very modern NSD movement with millenarian overtones and a message of collective salvation and rebirth was firmly entrenched in Palestine.

After World War II and the Holocaust, the moral legitimacy of this claim to NSD grew dramatically; thus, in November 1947, amid the deepening chill of the Cold War, both the United States and the Soviet Union voted in the United Nations in favor of the proposal to establish a Jewish state on about 56 percent of Palestine, disregarding the objections of Arab countries. The right of Jews to live in and govern themselves in the land of Palestine was affirmed. This was a triumph for the once implausible ideology of Zionism. The prophecy of Theodor Herzl after the first Zionist congress in Basel, Switzerland, in 1897 was vindicated: "At Basel, I founded the Jewish State. If I said this out loud today, I would be greeted with universal laughter. Perhaps in five years, and certainly in fifty, everyone will know it."[2]

More than six decades after the emergence of Israel, the unswerving ideological faith that powered Zionism has proved to be a tiger difficult to dismount, and the operational strategy of the movement since its inception—acquisition of (more and more) land in Palestine for Jewish people and the Jewish state—has proved difficult, perhaps impossible, to draw back from. That there is another people with a reasonable claim to self-determination in the land of Palestine/Israel is difficult to accommodate in most versions of the discourse and practice of Zionism. Until twenty-five years ago, even the term "Palestinians" was a rarity in public discourse in Israel.

The conflict over Kashmir has proved similarly enduring and intractable fundamentally because of the territory's status as a core element of hegemonic ideological narratives prevalent in India and Pakistan. Since the inception of the *idea* of Pakistan as a Muslim homeland in the subcontinent in the early 1930s, nearly a decade and a half before the formation of Pakistan as a sovereign state in 1947, Kashmir has been an integral part of the Pakistan concept. (In the original formulation, the letter *k* in Pakistan stood for Kashmir, alongside Punjab, the Frontier or "Afghan" province, Sind, and Baluchistan.) The leaders who founded Pakistan as the purported realization of the right to self-determination of the subcontinent's Muslims believed that Kashmir belonged to Pakistan because of its population's 77 percent Muslim majority, its greater territorial contiguity with Pakistan than with India, and its ethnic ties to elements of the Muslim population of Punjab.

Since the end of the first India-Pakistan war over Kashmir in early 1949, however, the greater part of the disputed territory and the bulk (about three-fourths) of the population—currently over 13 million of 17 to 18 million people—have been on India's side of the cease-fire line (known since 1972 as the Line of Control, or LOC). This has made Kashmir Pakistan's sacred national cause since the late 1940s, and motivated attempts to challenge the de facto border using force (notably in 1965 and 1999). In the dominant national narrative, Pakistan is incomplete without Kashmir, which is rhetorically referred to as Pakistan's missing *shah rug* (jugular vein).

The Pakistani narrative has a mirror-image counterpart in India, that India would be incomplete without Kashmir. The hegemonic Indian narrative of Kashmir as an *atut ang* (integral part) of India emerged in the 1950s with official sponsorship, and asserts that the presence of Kashmir in the Indian Union of (currently) twenty-nine states is essential to the validation of India's secular and inclusive credentials, because the Indian state of Jammu and Kashmir is the only state of India with a Muslim majority (about two-thirds). The centrality accorded to Kashmir in this narrative is questionable because

India has about 170 million Muslim citizens outside of Jammu and Kashmir, and their status could serve to validate India's secular and inclusive credentials. Likewise, the myth of a unitary Muslim "nation" in the subcontinent that underpinned the creation of Pakistan imploded spectacularly in 1971, when the eastern wing of Pakistan broke away to become the sovereign state of Bangladesh.

Nevertheless, the fact remains that both India and Pakistan have chosen to make Kashmir absolutely central to their identities as states, and that the respective ideological stances have wide resonance with the elites and publics in both countries. This narrows the space for meaningful negotiation on the dispute, because any substantive concessions by either side are prone to be viewed as compromising not just national interest but the national *identity* of the state. The logjam of ideological narratives is the essential starting point of explaining why the Kashmir conflict has proved so enduring and intractable.

The frozen conflict on Cyprus also has its roots in an ideological construct of national self-determination. This was crisply expressed in 1971 by Archbishop Makarios, the preeminent Greek Cypriot leader: "Cyprus is a Greek island. It was Greek from the dawn of history and it shall remain Greek forever. We have taken it over as a wholly Greek island and we shall preserve it as an undivided Greek island until we hand it over to mother Greece."[3]

This was simply the Cypriot version of the Megali Idea, or Great Idea, which harked back to the glory of the Macedonian and Byzantine empires and envisaged the unity of all "Hellenic" territories in a single Greek state. Until four decades ago, it had massive resonance among Greek Cypriots, who considered enosis (union) with Greece logical and inevitable given Cyprus's Hellenic character since antiquity and the large Greek

majority on Cyprus, 77 percent of the population when Cyprus became independent in 1960. The Megali Idea's solution for Cyprus was the doomsday scenario of Turkish Cypriots. As early as 1930, a Turkish Cypriot leader explained why: "We vehemently protest [the enosis demand] as we have always done. We believe that if Cyprus were annexed to Greece there would be no chance of life for the Moslems in Cyprus."[4] Turkish Cypriots who feared extinction often cited the example of Crete, another Mediterranean island, whose longstanding Turkish community had dwindled to nearly zero after its absorption into Greece in 1913.

The power of the Megali Idea and its pan-Hellenic vision explains why most Greek Cypriots regarded the constitution of independent Cyprus as an abomination. This constitution, negotiated in Zurich in 1959 by the foreign ministers of Turkey and Greece and presented as a fait accompli to Cypriot leaders, prescribed a government based on principles of equality and power-sharing between the Greek Cypriots and the Turkish Cypriot minority of 18 percent. The composition and procedures of the legislative, executive, and judicial branches were to reflect these principles. In addition, Turkish Cypriots were guaranteed a 30 percent share of the police and the civil service; a 40 percent share of the army; municipal autonomy for the Turkish Cypriot parts of the island's major towns; and equal status of Turkish and Greek as official languages. This was possibly the first example of full-blown "consociational" government in practice, mandated by a formal constitution (Lebanon's national pact of 1943 was an unwritten "gentlemen's agreement" between Maronite and Sunni notables), long before this form of government was prescribed by political scientists for divided societies starting in the 1970s.[5] The constitution also forbade the enosis of Cyprus with Greece.

To most Greek Cypriots, this form of government violated both the ancient Hellenic essence of Cyprus and the modern principle of democratic government: majority rule. In late 1963, President Makarios presented a list of thirteen constitutional amendments to his Turkish Cypriot vice president; collectively, they amounted to the replacement of the 1959–60 constitution with a majoritarian form of government. Violence approximating civil war erupted on Cyprus almost immediately, and a chain of events led eventually to Turkey's military invasion of the island and its de facto partition in 1974, with the self-declared "Turkish Republic of Northern Cyprus" across 37 percent of the island, recognized only by Turkey and protected by a 35,000-strong Turkish military force.

Since 1974, the idea of enosis with Greece has faded away among Greek Cypriots, but two beliefs have remained prevalent among them: that Cyprus is historically a Greek island and that its form of government should reflect the fact that Greek Cypriots are a large majority of the population. Three out of four Greek Cypriots (76 percent) rejected a UN proposal for Cyprus's reunification as a confederated union of Greek Cypriot and Turkish Cypriot "constituent states" when it was put to referendum in both parts of the island in 2004. Two out of three Turkish Cypriots (65 percent) voted in favor, but the proposal required concurrent majorities in the two communities to come into effect and therefore failed.

EXISTENTIAL ANXIETIES

The Turkish Cypriots saw the Greek Cypriot understanding of national self-determination as a mortal threat to their survival as a people in their shared homeland. Soon after the end of World War I, Arab Palestinians had also sensed the existential threat posed by the takeoff of the Zionist program of building a Jewish national home in Palestine. In 1920, fighting erupted around a Jewish settlement in the Galilee (post-1948 northern Israel), followed by deadly clashes between Jews and Arabs in the old city of Jerusalem. In 1921, protests against Jewish immigration from Europe in Jaffa, the ancient port town just south of Tel Aviv (founded in 1909), led to widespread violence. On the orders of the British high commissioner of Palestine, who was Jewish and a Zionist supporter, Arab rioters were strafed from the air. In 1929, a march by a militant wing of Zionism (the Revisionist Zionists) on the Western (Wailing) Wall in Jerusalem sparked violence across Palestine. (Seven decades later, a similar visit by Ariel Sharon to the Temple Mount site triggered the second Palestinian intifada in autumn 2000.) Amid this violence, 133 Jews died—including 67 members of Hebron's pre-Zionist Jewish community—and 116 Arabs were killed, mostly by the British police and military.

As Jewish immigration to Palestine from Europe, particularly Poland and its adjacent regions, picked up again from 1932 after a relative decline from 1927 to 1931, large Arab protest demonstrations in Jerusalem and Jaffa were violently suppressed by the British authorities in 1933. In 1935, immigration peaked as 66,472 Jewish persons arrived to settle in Palestine. In November 1935, Sheikh Izz al-Din al-Qassam, a fiery preacher from Haifa who had been calling for armed rebellion, was killed in a skirmish with British police near the town of Jenin, which is today in the northern West Bank. (Hamas's armed wing, formed after the start of the first Palestinian intifada in the Gaza Strip and the West Bank in December 1987, was named the Qassam Brigades in his honor.) In 1936, a large-scale Arab Palestinian insurgency erupted and lasted until 1939. About five thousand insurgents were killed in that three-year period, including

112 captured men hanged by the British authorities, who were assisted in their counterinsurgency operations by specially formed groups of Jewish auxiliaries.

The Arab population of Palestine was quite right to discern a dire existential threat in the British-abetted Zionist program. It was also perfectly understandable that their leaders angrily rejected a British proposal in 1937 to divide Palestine into Arab and Jewish states. This proposal envisaged the creation of a Jewish state across one-third of Palestine's territory and an Arab state in most of the remainder, while a swath extending inland from Jaffa on the coast to Jerusalem and Bethlehem would be retained under British control. The Palestinians were outraged at the prospect of a land-grabbing movement overwhelmingly comprising recent settlers from Europe being given a state covering one-third of their homeland. Moreover, that state would take in the whole of the Galilee as well as the entire coastal plain stretching from Haifa to Tel Aviv (the heartland of Israel from 1948 till today), an area inhabited by a quarter-million Arabs. A decade later, the UN proposal for the partition of Palestine, passed by majority vote in the General Assembly, gave nearly 56 percent of Palestine to the Jewish state, an area inhabited by over four hundred thousand Arabs. At the time, even after three decades of Jewish immigration under Zionist auspices, Arabs represented 68 percent of the 2 million people living in Palestine (down from about 92 percent in 1920).

Since 1948, the notion of a people facing an existential threat has been associated above all with Israel. The identity of the principal purveyors of that peril has shifted over time—from Nasser's pan-Arabist Egypt of the 1950s and 1960s; to Yasser Arafat's Palestine Liberation Organization in the 1970s and 1980s; to Iran, Hamas, and Hezbollah today. Yet the perception among (most) Israelis of being a people whose

nation-state is in mortal peril has remained constant over time, even as Israel has emerged since 1967 as an unassailable military power in the Middle East, fortified by a strategic superpower alliance. But perception does matter, often acutely, and the perception of an existential threat from a hostile "other" (or "others") helps explain why NSD conflicts are so often viewed in zero-sum terms by protagonists, and therefore prove enduring and intractable.

During the Bosnian war of April 1992 to November 1995, many Bosnian Serbs seemed to be influenced by such a sense of existential threat. In the cold light of reality, this sense of collective peril was clearly dubious. The Bosnian Serbs composed a large proportion of Bosnia and Herzegovina's population, about 1.5 million out of 4.4 million people in 1991, alongside about 2 million Bosnian Muslims and eight hundred thousand Bosnian Croats. Extensive areas in the north, west, and east of Bosnia and Herzegovina had Bosnian Serb majorities or pluralities. Moreover, Serbia was literally next door on the eastern border (as was Montenegro).

In the thickening fog of imminent war in late 1991 and early 1992, however, reason and rationality took a distinct back seat to fear and anger. Most Bosnian Serbs had a strong attachment to the federal, multinational state of Yugoslavia created at the end of World War II by the victorious Yugoslav communist movement led by Josip Broz "Tito." (Both Bosnian Serbs and Croatian Serbs were very numerous in Yugoslavia's antifascist resistance struggle, Nazi-occupied Europe's largest, between 1941 and 1945.) Serb nationalist ideologues had from time to time raised the slogan of "all Serbs in one state." The framework of Titoist Yugoslavia did put all Serbs in one state, but an avowedly multinational and federal state shared on the basis of constitutional equality with the other major southern Slav peoples (Croats,

Slovenes, Macedonians, Montenegrins, and—from the 1960s, when they were fully recognized as a "constituent nation" of Yugoslavia—Bosnian Muslims), a very different model of state from the centralized and Serbia-dominated Yugoslavia that existed from the end of World War I until the spring of 1941. When this framework of coexistence—encapsulated by the slogan *bratstvo i jedinstvo*, or "brotherhood and unity"—crumbled rapidly in 1990–91 and Slovenia and Croatia seceded from Yugoslavia, many Bosnian Serbs still hoped that a reduced Yugoslav federation consisting of Serbia, Bosnia and Herzegovina, Montenegro, and Macedonia would be preserved.

That hope faded in late 1991 when the emerging dominant leadership of the Bosnian Muslim community decided to push for Bosnia and Herzegovina to become a sovereign state, with tactical support from Bosnian Croat nationalists. In a February 1992 referendum on Bosnia's independence, 98 percent of the citizens who participated voted "yes." The turnout was 63 percent, and the missing 37 percent consisted overwhelmingly of Bosnian Serbs, who boycotted the referendum en masse. By this time, Bosnia and Herzegovina was in the grip of bitter polarization between Bosnian Muslims supportive of an independent state and Bosnian Serbs viscerally opposed to it. In early April 1992, the United States announced recognition of Bosnia and Herzegovina's sovereignty, primarily on the basis of the referendum that had produced a majority in favor; this was an illusion, because many and perhaps most Bosnian Croats had voted "yes" tactically to end any chance of a residual Yugoslav federation, not because of their enthusiasm for a united, sovereign Bosnia and Herzegovina.

The Bosnian war, Europe's worst armed conflict since 1945, began almost immediately. About 110,000 Bosnians were killed in the conflict, of whom about 60 percent were combatants and 40 percent were civilians. Bosnian Muslims constituted about two-thirds of the dead, and five-sixths of the civilian dead. (The Bosnian Serbs suffered significantly too, especially in combatant casualties: 20,649 Bosnian Serbs were killed in action during the war.) Over half of Bosnia and Herzegovina's population—2.3 million people belonging to all three ethnonational communities—were internally displaced or became refugees abroad as a result of "ethnic cleansing," the driving logic of the war.

The existential crisis perceived by most Bosnian Serbs can be explained by two mutually reinforcing factors: the context of state (and social) breakdown in the early 1990s, and the dark shadow of memories of past conflicts and atrocities. In the second half of 1991, several areas of Croatia bordering Bosnia and Herzegovina experienced severe fighting between the forces of the self-declared sovereign Croatian state and members of the Croatian Serb minority (this minority, about one in eight of Croatia's population, was much smaller and more vulnerable than Bosnia's Serb community). In early 1992, the fighting in Croatia stalemated, and UN peacekeeping forces deployed to police a fragile suspension of hostilities, but the full-fledged war in Croatia and international recognition of Croatia's independence in early 1992 (primarily at Germany's initiative) aggravated Bosnian Serb anxieties. The collapse of Yugoslavia's communist regime had led to state failure and generated an acute version of what international relations scholars call a "security dilemma" among Bosnia's ethnonational groups. Most Bosnian Serbs were dead set against becoming citizens of an independent Bosnia and Herzegovina, where they were outnumbered by Bosnian Muslims and where (in their view) an anti-Yugoslav, anti-Serb alliance of Bosnian Muslims and Bosnian Croats had taken shape. In the former

Yugoslavia, "minority" status was regarded not as reassuring, but as portending subordination or worse.

The crisis of the early 1990s also reawakened memories among Bosnian Serbs of the violence that ravaged Axis-occupied Yugoslavia between 1941 and 1945. During that period, the large Serb populations of Croatia and of Bosnia and Herzegovina were subjected to mass killings and other atrocities by a fascist Croatian movement allied with Nazi Germany. It is not possible to reliably quantify the toll, but the killing happened on a large scale, and it is likely that several hundred thousand Croatian and Bosnian Serbs were massacred in towns and villages or died in concentration camps. In Bosnia and Herzegovina, the mass murder of Serbs, which peaked between 1941 and 1943, was abetted by some Bosnian Muslims (while other Bosnian Muslims fought alongside Bosnian Serbs in the resistance). In the late 1980s and early 1990s, demagogic Serb politicians and media in Serbia, Croatia, and Bosnia played up what had happened to Serbs less than fifty years earlier, and the fearmongering had a significant effect on Bosnian Serbs.

For most of the Bosnian war, Bosnian Serb forces controlled two-thirds of the territory of Bosnia and Herzegovina, from where hundreds of thousands of Bosnian Muslims and tens of thousands of Bosnian Croats were expelled, often amid great violence. During the endgame of the war in the late summer and early autumn of 1995, the Bosnian Serbs lost substantial chunks of this territory to Bosnian Muslim and Croatian/Bosnian Croat offensives, but were able to hold on to about half of Bosnia and Herzegovina. This was the territory, in the northwestern and eastern part of the country, on which Republika Srpska (the Serb Republic) was recognized as a radically autonomous "entity" of a nominally united state of Bosnia and Herzegovina as part of the agreement to end the war negotiated on the Wright-Patterson Air Force Base in Dayton, Ohio, in November 1995.

Almost two decades after the war's end, the divisions that tore Bosnia and Herzegovina apart between 1992 and 1995 have not healed, despite a protracted and wide-ranging international effort to build a functioning state in which all three ethnonational communities have a shared stake.[6] The Serb Republic zealously guards its "state within a state" status, and its leaders make noises about full independence—a very popular position among Bosnian Serbs. Most Bosnian Muslims are deeply disillusioned with the "Dayton state," which they (rightly) regard as hardly a state except on paper. There is widespread grievance among Bosnian Croats that they do not have a unitary, autonomous territory on the Serb Republic model and have to make do with a lesser degree of autonomy in a dysfunctional "Federation of Bosnia and Herzegovina," the second "entity" or state within a state, which they share with far more numerous Bosnian Muslims. Carl von Clausewitz, the early-nineteenth-century Prussian general and military thinker, famously called war the continuation of politics by other means. Inverting Clausewitz, post-1995 Bosnia and Herzegovina has been a study in politics as the continuation of war by other means. That reveals the intractable and enduring nature of NSD disputes, which even landmark peace agreements and purposive third-party interventions struggle to resolve.

ELUSIVE PEACE

Efforts to find a solution to the sixty-six-year-old Kashmir dispute have never moved beyond expressions of good intent. In July 1972, after summit-level talks in India, Prime Ministers Indira Gandhi of India and Zulfiqar Ali Bhutto of Pakistan signed the Simla Agreement, named after the town in north India where the talks were held. The immediate context of the agreement was the 1971 crisis in the subcontinent centered on East Pakistan (Bangladesh) that culminated in December 1971 in the defeat and breakup of Pakistan in the third India-Pakistan war. The agreement "resolved that the two countries put an end to the conflict and confrontation that have hitherto marred their relationship and work for . . . a friendly and harmonious relationship and . . . durable peace on the subcontinent . . . reconciliation and good neighborliness." In an implicit but obvious reference to Kashmir, the agreement stipulated that "the basic issues and causes of conflicts which have bedeviled relations . . . for the last twenty-five years shall be resolved by peaceful means . . . through bilateral negotiations or other peaceful means mutually agreed." The agreement explicitly stated that "in Jammu and Kashmir, the Line of Control resulting from the ceasefire of 17 December 1971 shall be respected by both sides without prejudice to the recognized positions of either side [on the Kashmir dispute]. Neither side shall seek to alter it unilaterally, irrespective of mutual differences and legal interpretations. Both sides . . . undertake to refrain from the threat or use of force in violation of this Line." The agreement's concluding clause stated that "both Governments agree that their Heads will meet again at a mutually convenient time in the future and that, in the meanwhile, the representatives of the two sides will meet to discuss the modalities and arrangements for the establishment of durable peace and normalization of relations."[7]

The substantive peace process visualized by this declaration did not materialize, and four decades later the Kashmir dispute is still in limbo. In the meanwhile, the international dispute over Kashmir has been complicated by the messy legacy of a large-scale insurgency that broke out in 1990 in large parts of Indian-administered Kashmir,

and ebbed only after a decade and a half of brutal fighting between insurgents seeking either independence or merger with Pakistan and the Indian security forces.

A ray of hope briefly appeared in February 1999 after summit-level talks in Pakistan, when Prime Ministers Atal Behari Vajpayee of India and Nawaz Sharif of Pakistan issued a promising "Lahore Declaration" (named after the city in Pakistan). The declaration asserted that "an environment of peace and security is in the supreme national interest of both countries and the resolution of all outstanding issues, including Jammu and Kashmir, is essential for this purpose." The leaders agreed to "intensify efforts to resolve all issues, including Jammu and Kashmir . . . , recognizing that the nuclear dimension of the security environment of the two countries adds to their responsibility for avoidance of conflict [after the Indian and Pakistani nuclear test explosions of May 1998]." The Lahore Declaration spoke of "the determination of both countries to implement the Simla Agreement in letter and spirit."[8] At the time of the declaration, Pakistani military units had already infiltrated the Indian side of the Line of Control in a remote and sparsely populated high-altitude area, in a secret, high-level operation directed by the then Pakistani army chief, Pervez Musharraf. The Indians discovered the intrusion in early May 1999, and a border war raged in the zone of infiltration until mid-July. In 2002, after a terrorist raid on India's Parliament in New Delhi, India mobilized hundreds of thousands of troops on the international border with Pakistan and the LOC, and Pakistan responded similarly, further raising tensions on the subcontinent.

The reasons for the stillborn nature of peace diplomacy on Kashmir are complex, but the root cause lies in competing ideological claims connected to the identities of India and Pakistan as states. Since a relative thaw in India-Pakistan relations began in late 2003, a cease-fire on the Line of Control has generally held, albeit with numerous localized violations. In "confidence-building" measures undertaken since 2005, limited travel and trade across the LOC are permitted. But a settlement to the Kashmir conflict remains a remote prospect.

The Kashmir case raises two questions that apply to peace processes worldwide. First, are deliberately slow, gradualist approaches to NSD disputes that emphasize "confidence building" and piecemeal, incremental progress likely to produce results, that is, a conducive context for substantive agreement and settlement? The answer is "not likely" in the case of the Kashmir conflict. (The terror attack on Mumbai in late 2008 by Lashkar-e-Taiba, a Pakistani jihadi organization that has close ties to the Pakistani military and has been active in Kashmir since the mid-1990s, set the clock back further on a halting bilateral dialogue that appeared to be going nowhere slowly.) Second, can a framework to settle the Kashmir dispute emerge through bilateral diplomacy alone, that is, without support and facilitation by a third party or parties? The answer is "probably not."

Yet even where a comprehensive peace agreement has been reached, and thanks to decisive intervention by a third party (the United States)—in the case of Bosnia's Dayton agreement—the NSD dispute has not been laid to rest and simmers on, despite massive international support and engagement in the postwar "implementation" phase. Between November 1999 and April 2004, the United Nations attempted to engineer a comprehensive, "big bang" settlement to the Cyprus dispute (the Annan Plan), which won backing from the governments in both Ankara and Athens but failed because it was rejected in referendum by the vast majority (76 percent) of the island's Greek Cypriot ethnonational majority (who represent about

80 percent of the population of Cyprus). The experiences of Bosnia and Cyprus reveal the limits to the efficacy of third-party engagement in polarized NSD disputes, as well as of the "comprehensive solution" approach to such conflicts. Yet even the deliberately incremental model of peacemaking has its pitfalls, as revealed in the failure of the 1993–2000 "Oslo process" between Israel and the Palestinians, which also showed that the role of the de facto third party—here the United States—can be not just ineffective but perhaps even inimical to the prospects of settlement because of the third party's special relationship with one of the parties to the dispute.

The reasons for the failure of the Oslo process are complex and contested. Some commentators such as the Palestinian American intellectual Edward Said argued that the process was doomed from the outset because it was structured entirely on Israel's terms.[9] Others such as Ron Pundak, who was an Israeli representative to the 1993 Norway "back channel" that gave rise to the process, say that the process was not structurally flawed but failed because of numerous breaches and violations by both sides, particularly Israel.[10] This chapter has argued that the underlying causes of the debacle were the Jewish state's ideological roots and the "existential threat" mentality that permeates most of the Israeli establishment and much of the Israeli public. Of course, there were proximate causes as well. The role of "spoilers" was especially damaging, on both sides. The hostility of the mainstream right wing in Israeli politics played a major role in the downfall of the Oslo process, as did the violence—particularly suicide attacks perpetrated within Israel—of the rising Islamist stream of Palestinian politics represented by the Hamas movement.

Two vital points, both of broader relevance to the challenge of making peace in NSD disputes, should be made about the

Oslo process and its tragic fate. First, the process was based on an explicitly incremental strategy of crafting peace. Thus, the three core issues of the Israeli-Palestinian conflict—the borders of the putative Palestinian state, the issue of Jerusalem, and the Palestinian refugee question—were put in abeyance, "kicked down the road," so to speak. According to the 1993 timetable, negotiations on these issues were meant to start by 1998 and conclude by 2000. By 1998, the peace process was in free fall. In autumn 2000, by a cruel twist of fate exactly when the process was supposed to culminate in a comprehensive Israeli-Palestinian peace, the process died amid a massive outbreak of violence. The expectation that piecemeal agreements, such as the interim accord on limited Palestinian self-rule on the West Bank (Oslo II) signed in Washington in September 1995, would improve the Israeli-Palestinian relationship and pave the way to a final settlement proved misplaced. Instead, the relationship turned more and more poisonous between 1993 and 2000. In my own detailed account of the rise and fall of Oslo, I have noted that the way the process actually unfolded turned the logic of incremental progress on its head and that seven years of "confidence building" turned into a confidence-destroying morass.[11]

Second, as the Oslo process unraveled, the role of the United States—effectively the third party in the Israeli-Palestinian dispute—was not effective. American scholars and practitioners have noted that the US administration during the second term of the Clinton presidency was sympathetic to the Palestinians' burning aspiration to a viable state.[12] Even Dennis Ross, the openly pro-Israel US special envoy to the Middle East from 1989 to 2001, recalls in his memoirs that "both Madeleine [Albright, secretary of state] and Sandy [Berger, national security adviser] . . . feared that Bibi [Netanyahu, Israel's Likud prime minister from

May 1996 to May 1999] was trying to deliberately destroy the Oslo process [and felt that] . . . we needed to resist him now and confront him." Ross also recalls that after the Labor Party's Ehud Barak succeeded Netanyahu as prime minister in May 1999, Albright was "mystified by Barak's behavior" in putting the dying process with the Palestinians on a back burner while he focused, without success, on reaching a deal with the Hafez al-Assad regime in Syria. Yet the administration's sympathy for the Palestinians and its deep concern about the behavior of the Israeli government did not translate into timely and effective pressure on the latter. Ross writes that "our involvement was desired strongly by both sides but especially by the Palestinians," and that "Arafat saw us as his equalizer with the Israelis."[13] But in practice, the United States did not act to mitigate, and effectively deepened, the very asymmetrical power relationship between Israel and the Palestinians. The reluctance to pressure the key strategic ally in the region may have been reinforced by the influence of the so-called "Israel lobby" in the United States.[14]

Yet it is important to remember that comprehensive peace blueprints that tried to strike an evenhanded balance between the protagonists have also not fully resolved NSD conflicts. The Dayton agreement aimed to simultaneously accommodate the Bosnian Serbs (by conceding the radically autonomous Republika Srpska on nearly one-half of Bosnia and Herzegovina's territory) and the Bosnian Muslims (by preserving a nominally united state of Bosnia and Herzegovina, and strengthening common institutions through the activism of a postwar international supervisory presence). In the words of the country's first international supervisor after the war, Dayton "balance[d] the reality of division with structures of cooperation and integration, and is based on the hope that over time the imperative of integration in the country and the region will be the dominant factor."[15] Almost two decades on, however, that hope has not yet been realized. Bosnia and Herzegovina is still deeply divided on ethnonational fault lines, and the contradiction between the NSD preferences of its ethnonational communities is still sharp and polarized.

In Cyprus, the attempt by the United Nations' comprehensive blueprint (the Annan Plan) to simultaneously accommodate the Greek Cypriot quest for the island's re-unification and the Turkish Cypriot quest for security and territorialized autonomy had many features—general and specific—similar to the Dayton agreement. The proposal for a confederated "United Cyprus Republic," consisting of a self-governing Greek Cypriot "constituent state" on 72 percent of Cyprus and a Turkish Cypriot constituent state over the remaining territory in the north of the island, foundered in 2004 as the Greek Cypriots resoundingly rejected it in referendum.[16] For most Greek Cypriots, the Annan Plan amounted to a modified version of the partition of the island that resulted from the 1974 Turkish invasion, and it did not recognize either the Hellenic essence of the island or the fact of the large Greek Cypriot majority in Cyprus's population. If the Dayton agreement had been put to identical parallel referenda among Bosnia's three ethnonational groups, it is likely that all three communities would have rejected it, albeit for very different reasons explained earlier in this essay.

CONCLUSION

So are NSD conflicts fated to fester? On the basis of the empirical evidence to date, the answer is generally "yes." Does that matter for international—regional and global—security? The answer to this question is widely variable and depends on the degree of instability and the broader implications of an unresolved NSD dispute.

Through the 1960s and the first half of the 1970s, the conflict on Cyprus was regarded as a potential flashpoint for a wider armed conflict that would draw in Turkey and Greece. That would have jeopardized peace and security in an arc much beyond the eastern Mediterranean island. The risk of a face-off between Turkey and Greece was particularly unwelcome to the United States because both countries were member states of the North Atlantic Treaty Organization and US allies against the Soviet Union–led bloc.

Since the decisive Turkish military intervention that sealed the island's *taksim* ("division" in Turkish) in 1974, the risk of Cyprus becoming the focal point of regional hostilities has ceased, and the island's dispute has been gradually consigned to the ranks of "frozen conflicts." The end of the Cold War and the Soviet Union in the early 1990s sharply downgraded the island's strategic significance to the United States and its allies. Although the Cyprus dispute is unresolved, there is no risk of armed hostilities on the island, let alone regional spillover. In 2004, the governments in both Athens and Ankara supported the United Nations' Annan Plan as a long-term settlement. After the plan's failure, the post-1974 status quo—de facto partition—looks increasingly permanent. Renewed negotiations between the two sides in the last few years, facilitated by the United Nations (which has been stuck in a peacekeeping role on Cyprus since 1964), have not progressed well, though there is some hope of progress as of early 2014. The economic meltdown of 2013 in the part of Cyprus under the authority of the Greek Cypriot government has made reunification unattractive, and indeed irrational, from the Turkish Cypriots' perspective. It is far more attractive, and rational, for the Turkish

Cypriot state in northern Cyprus to instead continue and deepen its status as a political and economic appendage of Turkey—one of the world's fastest growing economies in the early twenty-first century. The "Green Line" that runs horizontally across Cyprus for about 220 kilometers and divides north from south has become a long-term reality, but it carries no risk of armed conflict, internal or international. In short, unlike the 1960s and 1970s, Cyprus's ethnonational conflict poses no threat to international peace and security. In that sense, the failure of the Annan Plan is relatively inconsequential.

The meltdown in the western Balkans due to the disintegration of the Yugoslav federation triggered a series of wars: first in Croatia (1991–95), then in Bosnia and Herzegovina (1992–95), and a few years later in Kosovo (1998–99). In 2001, another former Yugoslav federal unit and successor-state, Macedonia, also came perilously close to descending into armed conflict between its Slav Macedonian majority and the ethnic Albanian minority that makes up about one-quarter of the population. The Bosnian war resulted directly from the wider regional crisis and was its single worst episode. Bosnia and Herzegovina, with the most multinational population of the former Yugoslavia's constituent units—about 45 percent Bosnian Muslim, 35 percent Bosnian Serb, and 18 percent Bosnian Croat—also had a complex and troubled twentieth-century history of relations between these communities. Prior to the establishment of Titoist Yugoslavia after World War II, radical nationalists in both Serbia and Croatia harbored annexationist ideas about Bosnia and Herzegovina (whose landlocked territory is wedged between Croatia to the west and north, and Serbia and Montenegro to the east). Following the implosion of Titoist Yugoslavia, Bosnia and Herzegovina became the site of a violent three-way collision between the national-

isms of its communities, a brutal conflict significantly exacerbated by the material support given by the then governments of Croatia and Serbia to their Bosnian kinpeoples. The Bosnia mayhem had to prompt Western intervention. It was an armed conflict in a region of Europe at the end of the twentieth century that lasted three and a half years, killed more than one hundred thousand people, and produced over 2 million refugees. After several failed European attempts, the United States decisively intervened in the second half of 1995, and its coercive diplomacy ended the war.

Almost two decades later, Bosnia and Herzegovina remains divided and polarized, but there is practically no risk of renewed armed conflict. The extraordinary violence that set it aflame in 1992 and kept it in the world headlines for the next four years was due to the lethal conjuncture of a wider regional breakdown of state and society with Bosnia's own dormant tinderbox characteristics. Today, Bosnia and Herzegovina is a small country of 4 million people in southeastern Europe that is economically weak and politically disunited. But it is peaceful, and very likely to remain so. The three ethnonationalist armies of the Bosnian war that fielded a quarter-million combatants between them have long demobilized and disappeared. The Inter-Entity Boundary Line (IEBL), which snakes across the country for 1,100 kilometers from the northwest to the southeast and separates Republika Srpska from the Federation of Bosnia and Herzegovina, appears on maps and is an important political border, but on the ground it is barely apparent. It is, of course, a contentious line that most Bosnian Muslims would like erased and most Bosnian Serbs are anxious to preserve. But like Cyprus's Green Line, it is extremely unlikely to be a flashpoint for armed hostilities at any time in the foreseeable future. Bosnia's NSD conundrum continues, but that does not pose a threat to regional peace and security (nor does Kosovo's disputed independence, despite the strong rhetoric over that dispute in the region and across the world, and the conflict between Serbia and Kosovo over the Serb-populated area of northern Kosovo). The Dayton settlement has clearly not fostered integration and cooperation over time. If that is the benchmark of success, Dayton is a failure. But if the criteria are more modest—ending a war, enabling limited returns of refugees to the places from where they were expelled, and finding a way to put a lid on the region's most incendiary problem following the breakup of Yugoslavia—Dayton and the American intervention that produced it can be regarded as a qualified success.

It is not possible to be as sanguine about the Kashmir and Israeli-Palestinian conflicts. In these two cases, the status quo is volatile and rife with potential for escalation leading to major crises. This is not to say that regional war is imminent or inevitable in either the Middle East or South Asia. But to the extent that even a low degree of risk exists, that is sufficient argument against the default option of leaving these NSD disputes to fester cancerously.

In the subcontinent, incidents of mass terrorism (on the lines of the late 2008 Mumbai attack, or worse) and localized hostilities on the 742-kilometer Line of Control in Kashmir have the potential to trigger a major regional crisis. It is not possible to say with confidence that the India-Pakistan crises of 1999 and 2002 will not recur. Popular protests in the Kashmir Valley against Indian authority in 2008 and 2010 show that the problem is volatile at the intrastate level as well. The rise of fundamentalist forces in Pakistan that do not recognize borders or norms of interstate behavior adds a dangerous dimension to the conflict. For India, a rising power in the early twenty-first century, the problem of Kashmir is burdensome

baggage it would be wise to try and ameliorate.

The Israeli-Palestinian impasse since the collapse of the Oslo process is a core element of regional instability in the Middle East in the early twenty-first century, and breaking that impasse is crucial to building stability in the region. The recurrent mini-crises since 2008 centered on Gaza, and the 2006 international conflict between Israel and Lebanon's Hezbollah, are reminders of just how volatile the region is in the absence of an Israeli-Palestinian modus vivendi. The anti-authoritarian Arab revolutions since 2011 are remaking the political landscape of the Middle East, in at least some cases in a generally democratic direction, and the dubious props for the region's status quo provided for several decades by such regimes as Mubarak's Egypt (and even the Assads' Syria) are giving way to a new and much more uncertain regional order. Amid such ferment and change, the deadlock between Israel and the Palestinians sticks out like a sore thumb.

The irony of these festering disputes is that the basic contours of plausible settlements have been clear in the Israeli-Palestinian case for two decades and in the case of Kashmir for a decade. In the former case, the sine qua non is a Palestinian state whose border with Israel would approximate the pre-June 1967 "Green Line," with its capital in East Jerusalem and the right of return for Palestinian refugees and their descendants to the Palestinian state. In the latter case, it is democratization and political autonomy on both sides of the Line of Control and particularly on the Indian side, with the LOC converted over time into a "soft border" between the Indian and Pakistani Kashmirs.[17]

Untangling the Israeli-Palestinian and Kashmir disputes would require most felicitous conjunctures of circumstances and forces. Such conjunctures, which would provide openings for constructive and effective support roles by third parties, may emerge only in the sobering context, or aftermath, of major international crises triggered by these disputes. International peace and security in the early twenty-first century requires that these two intractable disputes in the Middle East and South Asia become amenable to negotiation and compromise, sooner rather than later, and ideally without the perverse catalyst of an escalation of regional conflict.

NOTES

1. Walter Laqueur, *A History of Zionism* (London: Tauris Parke Paperbacks, 2003).

2. Sumantra Bose, *Contested Lands: Israel-Palestine, Kashmir, Bosnia, Cyprus, and Sri Lanka* (Cambridge, MA: Harvard University Press, 2007), 212.

3. Ibid., 84–85.

4. Ibid., 64.

5. Arend Lijphart, *Democracies: Patterns of Majoritarian and Consensus Government in Twenty-One Countries* (New Haven, CT: Yale University Press, 1984).

6. See Sumantra Bose, *Bosnia after Dayton: Nationalist Partition and International Intervention* (New York: Oxford University Press, 2002); and Bose, *Contested Lands*, 105–53.

7. Bose, *Contested Lands*, 185–86.

8. Ibid., 188.

9. Edward Said, *The End of the Peace Process: Oslo and After* (London: Granta Books, 2002).

10. Ron Pundak, "From Oslo to Taba: What Went Wrong?" *Survival* 43, no. 3 (Autumn 2001): 31–45.

11. Bose, *Contested Lands*, 239–89.

12. See William Quandt, "Clinton and the Arab-Israeli Conflict: The Limits of Incrementalism," *Journal of Palestine Studies* 30, no. 2 (Winter 2001): 26–40; and Hussein Agha and Robert Malley, "Camp David: The Tragedy of Errors," *New York Review of Books*, August 9, 2001.

13. Dennis Ross, *The Missing Peace: The Inside Story of the Fight for Middle East Peace* (New York: Farrar, Straus and Giroux, 2004), 339, 502, 768–71.

14. John Mearsheimer and Stephen Walt, "The Israel Lobby," *London Review of Books*, March 23, 2006.

15. Carl Bildt, *Peace Journey: The Struggle for Peace in Bosnia* (London: Weidenfeld and Nicholson, 1998), 392.

16. On the Annan Plan and its failure, see Bose, *Contested Lands*, 90–104.

17. Sumantra Bose, *Kashmir: Roots of Conflict, Paths to Peace* (Cambridge, MA: Harvard University Press, 2003), 201–65.

PART II

THE TRIGGERS OF VIOLENT CONFLICT IN THE EMERGING SECURITY ENVIRONMENT

11

A Not So Great Awakening?
Early Elections, Weak Institutions, and the Risk of Violence

Jack Snyder, Dawn Brancati, and Edward D. Mansfield

Presidents Bill Clinton and George W. Bush, as well as human rights advocates and neo-conservative publicists, have argued that promoting democracy abroad promotes peace. Indeed, it is true that mature, stable democracies have not fought wars against each other, and they rarely suffer from civil wars. But the path to the democratic peace is not always smooth. Democratic transitions in Lebanon, Iraq, Afghanistan, and the Palestinian Authority that turned violent were the bane of the Bush administration's "war on terror" and its plans for a new Middle East. The "Arab Awakening," or "Arab Spring," of 2011 raised hopes of democratization throughout the Middle East, but more often led to violence, repression, and tense stalemate. Likewise, during the 1990s, competitive elections held in the early stages of political transition led to major civil wars in Algeria, Burundi, and Yugoslavia.

These examples are hardly unique. Throughout the nineteenth and twentieth centuries, states that became stalled in the initial stages of a democratizing transition faced a heightened risk of civil war.[1] When authoritarian regimes break down, a panoply of elite factions and popular groups jockey for power in a setting where repressive state authority has been weakened, yet democratic institutions are insufficiently developed to take their place. The lack of institutional means to regulate or repress factional strife can lead to civil war.[2]

In some cases, war results from a gap between rising demands for political participation and the lagging development of the political institutions needed to accommodate those demands. In these circumstances, old elites as well as newly rising elites are likely to turn to ideological appeals to win mass support. Populist ideology serves as a substitute for institutions that are too weak to legitimize political power.

These ideological appeals can be based on almost any social cleavage—ethnicity, religious sect, tribe, class, economic sector, or urban/rural. Elites, however, tend to prefer nationalism, ethnicity, and sectarianism, because these ideologies play down the economic conflict of interest between elites and masses, emphasizing instead the purportedly more fundamental commonalities of blood and culture. Threatened authoritarian elites may gamble for resurrection by playing the nationalist, ethnic, or religious card in the hope of gaining a mass following by invoking threats from outsiders. Rising elites may find that ethnic or religious groups are easier to mobilize than class or secular constituencies when institutions that cut across traditional cultural groupings are poorly developed.

The potential for danger in the early phase of a transition can be heightened when the international community mounts pressure for early elections. Over the past two decades, states emerging from civil war have been holding elections sooner than was the case in previous eras. The earlier such elections are held, the greater is the likelihood of the country slipping back into war. A recurrence of conflict is especially likely if elections precede military demobilization and the strengthening of state institutions, although power-sharing agreements and robust international peacekeeping can sometimes reduce the risk posed by early elections. One implication of these research findings, discussed below, is that international democracy promotion efforts should focus less on pushing for elections and more on fostering circumstances that facilitate success when elections are held.

SUCCESSFUL TRANSITIONS

Not all countries experience significant violence during democratic transitions. Brazil, Chile, Hungary, Poland, South Korea, and Taiwan offer recent examples of peaceful transitions. But liberal democratic appeals based on full electoral and legal accountability are likely to succeed only when favorable conditions, such as effective political and legal institutions, accompany the early stages of a democratic transition.[3] This is a

story as old as democracy itself: Great Britain's nineteenth-century path toward mass electoral politics was smoothed by the preexisting strength of its legal system, representative institutions, and free press. Building effective state institutions before holding fully competitive mass elections is a key to reducing the risk of violence during a democratic transition. In addition to robust institutions, other conditions facilitating peaceful democratic consolidation include a fairly high level of economic development, the absence of extreme income inequality, a diversified economy that is not based largely on oil production (which tempts factions to use force to seize this prize), the absence of deep identity-based divisions within society, prior experience with democracy, and democratic neighbors.[4]

As Robert Dahl and Samuel Huntington observed more than four decades ago, the British-style sequence of forging effective state institutions prior to starting a democratic transition has become increasingly rare, though it does still occur.[5] Postapartheid South Africa followed such a sequence with some success in the 1990s, adapting apartheid-era institutions to the needs of postapartheid democracy despite shortcomings with respect to some other facilitators of democratic consolidation such as ethnic homogeneity and income equality. That this favorable sequence is unlikely to unfold in future transitions is precisely why democratization may often go awry, as recently occurred in parts of the Middle East.

THE MIDDLE EAST AND THE ARAB SPRING

During the past decade, various Middle Eastern countries have held elections, causing some observers to hope that a wave of democracy and peace might spread through the region. Frequently, however, these elections have produced outcomes that have frustrated and disappointed democracy advocates. Lebanon, Iraq, the Palestinian territories, and other Middle Eastern states have elected ethnic militants, sectarian extremists, terrorists, Holocaust deniers, and nuclear proliferation advocates, contributing to both civil and international conflict.[6]

Huntington argued that instability and violence are "in large part the product of rapid social change and the rapid mobilization of new groups into politics coupled with the slow development of political institutions."[7] At the heart of the Arab Spring lie disaffected groups that have been mobilized and are demanding a greater role in politics. In those Arab countries with somewhat greater institutional capacity, such as Tunisia and (marginally) Egypt, violence has been limited despite sometimes-divisive elections. In countries with weaker political institutions, such as Libya, Syria, and Yemen, the Arab Awakening has precipitated substantial violence and instability.

A measure of government effectiveness included in the Worldwide Governance Indicators permits a comparison across states that have experienced popular uprisings during the Arab Spring. This measure is based on the perceptions of individuals working in the private sector, the public sector, and nongovernmental organizations throughout the world. It captures "perceptions of the quality of public services, the quality of the civil service and the degree of its independence from political pressures, the quality of policy formation and implementation, and the credibility of the government's commitment to such policies."[8]

In 2010, before the masses took to the streets to demand political and economic reform, the governmental effectiveness of Libya was among the bottom 10 percent of countries worldwide. Yemen was among the worst 14 percent. Syria was among the worst 35 percent. None of the Middle Eastern countries that have avoided large-scale civil vio-

lence during popular mobilization in the Arab Spring score as poorly, including Bahrain (70th percentile), Jordan (57th percentile), Morocco (49th percentile), Egypt (40th percentile), and Tunisia (63rd percentile).

These estimates should be treated cautiously because they reflect individuals' perceptions of government effectiveness and because the factors being assessed do not exhaust the institutions needed to manage social change and political mobilization, such as professionalized media and constructive civil society organizations. Nonetheless, there has been a striking tendency for the Middle Eastern countries that are perceived to have the least effective governments to experience the most serious domestic violence when popular movements arise. Algeria (33rd percentile) is an exception that proves the rule: despite the limitations of its capacity for constructive governance, the regime weathered the Arab Spring without violence because it distributed oil revenue widely among the population and militarily deterred any popular push for democratization. It endured an election-fueled civil war in the 1990s, and the Algerian people were loath to risk a rerun.

In some respects, Syria's domestic institutions were considerably stronger than those of Libya and Yemen. Syria had been vested with highly centralized coercive and administrative institutions, which tempted the regime to use this capacity to repress the opposition at the cost of a bloody civil war. But Syria's participatory and legal institutions are very weak, and its bureaucracy has long been marked by massive corruption. Successful democratization requires all these types of institutions, and transitions in countries whose participatory and legal institutions are as weak as Syria's rarely sustain movement in a liberal direction.[9]

Libya, Syria, and Yemen were not only institutionally weak but also ethnically and geographically splintered. Libya, for example, is deeply divided along territorial and tribal lines. Muammar Gaddafi actively used these divisions to ward off potential opposition and maintain power. In the aftermath of his regime, they will severely complicate efforts to promote democracy in Libya.[10] The situation in Yemen is not much better. In 1962, Yemen split into two countries. North Yemen and South Yemen reunified in 1990, but fought a bloody civil war in 1994. Deep divisions remain between these regions. Yemen is also beset by cleavages among parties, tribes, and warlords. Like Gaddafi, Ali Abdullah Saleh's ruling strategy centered on manipulating these divisions.[11] Syria is marked by splits among numerous religious and ethnic groups. Sunnis outnumber other religious groups—including the Alawites, which is the Assad family's religious community—by roughly fourfold, but have faced oppression and exclusion from political influence for decades. Such internal divisions and grievances would place exceptional demands on the political institutions of any postconflict regime, not least one facing demands for increased popular participation in politics.

DANGERS OF EARLY POSTCONFLICT ELECTIONS

Democracy advocates have long favored early elections in countries emerging from authoritarianism and violent conflict. In light of the fact that democracies do not fight each other and tend to settle internal disagreements peacefully, these advocates have reasoned that democratic transitions yield peace, and that the sooner such transitions occur, the better. In their view, pushing autocratic war-prone regimes along the fast track toward democracy should break the power of violent authoritarian elites, accustom people to the habits of democratic participation, provide legitimacy for new leaders, and, in cases, of international peacekeeping

or military occupation, hasten the withdrawal of foreign forces. "It is the practice of democracy that makes a nation ready for democracy," opined President George W. Bush, "and every nation can start on this path."[12]

However, recent troubled transitions to democracy have raised doubts, even among some staunch democracy advocates, about whether early elections actually are beneficial for peace and democracy. As in Bosnia after the 1995 Dayton Accords, early elections may cement the power of former combatants, who remain the best organized groups in the immediate aftermath of conflict, whereas progressive, programmatic political parties typically do not have time to organize to overcome communal barriers. Moreover, early elections typically take place when the rule of law is weak, making it more likely that elections will suffer from irregularities and that losers will refuse to accept the results peacefully. For these reasons, the short-term chance of peace and the long-term prospect for democratic consolidation might both be improved by postponing fully competitive elections until some progress has been made in strengthening the institutions needed to make democracy work, including competent state bureaucracies, independent courts, professional media, integrative political parties, and functioning market economies.

Today, this issue takes on greater urgency because postconflict elections are being held much sooner than in the past. The average time between the end of a civil war and the first postconflict election has been cut in half since the end of the Cold War. Prior to 1989, an average of 5.6 years passed before countries held their first postconflict election. Since 1989, this figure has fallen to 2.7 years.[13]

Much of this trend is due to international urging. In Bosnia, for example, the early timing of elections was to justify the exit of

US occupation troops. Since the end of the Cold War, foreign countries have increasingly pressured civil war–ridden countries to end their conflicts with negotiated agreements and to hold elections in the expectation that democracy will promote peace and stability.[14] As Séverine Autesserre shows in her research on eastern Congo, prioritizing electoral politics—instead of directly addressing local security problems and building the institutional capacity of the state—often fails to achieve these goals.[15]

Based on an original dataset of all post–civil war elections that occurred between 1945 and 2008, Brancati and Snyder find that holding elections too soon after a civil war raises the risk of war occurring again.[16] On average, waiting five years to hold the first election reduces the chance of war recurring by one-third. However, the study finds that early elections do not necessarily increase the risk of war under all circumstances. Decisive victories, demobilization of rebel armies, and international peacekeeping diminish the fighting capacity of former combatants who might otherwise be tempted to return to war when faced with unfavorable election results. Effective institutional reforms can help new pro-reform actors come to power. But if elections are held before adequate administrative and legal institutions are put in place or before former rebels are demobilized, the risk of going back through the revolving door into civil war increases.

Liberia's elections in 1997 illustrate the danger of holding elections when institutions are weak, whereas its 2005 elections illustrate the stabilizing role elections can play in an improved institutional setting. Liberia held presidential and legislative elections, supervised by a West African peacekeeping force, two years after signing the 1995 Abuja Accords. Former warlord Charles Taylor wielded enormous advantages over his opponents due to his pervasive organizational network, his monopoly over the media, and

his extensive military and financial resources. Bloody resistance from bands of local warlords marred pre-election disarmament efforts. Many voters supported Taylor because they expected him to devastate the country in renewed fighting if he lost. Nonetheless, Taylor's exploitative, arbitrary rule after his election provoked resistance and a renewed civil war in 1999.[17]

In contrast, Liberia's 2005 elections took place in a more highly institutionalized setting, overseen by a substantial contingent of fifteen thousand UN peacekeepers. These elections achieved much better results, although they too were held only two years after signing a peace treaty. Because Taylor had fled the country, a single candidate or party did not dominate the 2005 elections. Demobilization occurred prior to the elections, which ran more smoothly than before. Political institutions needed for democratic elections were better developed as well. Prior to the elections, Liberia's media was liberalized, and some media outlets, such as Star Radio, offered reasonably balanced coverage of the elections. An independent electoral commission, despite shortcomings, maintained neutrality, and, unlike in previous elections, political groupings were genuine parties, not just unreformed rebel groups. Ultimately, disputes about the electoral process were settled in court, not on the battlefield.

Power-sharing agreements between rival factions in postconflict settings offer another method for reducing the risk of early elections. An agreement to share power regardless of the outcome of the election can reassure both sides that they will have a place in government, reducing the chances of them rejecting the election results and returning to war.[18] Examples include the power-sharing deals in South Africa following violence at the end of the apartheid regime, in Mozambique after the long civil war between Frelimo and Renamo, and in Sudan at the end of the civil war between North and

South. Power sharing, however, can some-times cause instability in the short run or in the long run if it is not combined with other favorable conditions, such as peacekeeping or strong governmental institutions.

In the short term, powerful groups that are accustomed to ruling outright may resist the implementation of agreements that re-quire them to share power.[19] In Burundi in 1993, for example, international aid donors insisted that the military dictatorship led by the Tutsi minority hold elections. The elec-tions were won by the majority ethnic Hutu candidate, Melchior Ndadaye. When the new president moved to institute power-sharing arrangements that would have inte-grated Hutus into the formerly all-Tutsi officer corps, the military assassinated him, plunging Burundi into another, even more intense civil war. Power sharing imposed by international donors also contributed to the onset of the Rwanda genocide by excluding from power the militant Hutu government faction that controlled armed security forces and machete-wielding militias.

Power sharing can increase the odds of a return to war in the long term by allowing leaders to govern in an arbitrary and exploit-ative manner with little risk of losing office. By locking former combatants into positions of authority, power-sharing institutions pro-vide group leaders with little incentive to broaden their support bases beyond old cleavage lines and tend to reduce demo-cratic accountability to a process of appeal-ing to narrow constituencies. Power-sharing arrangements tended to freeze and deepen lines of conflict for this reason in Lebanon and Yugoslavia.[20]

International actors have been part of the problem of premature elections, but they have sometimes also been part of the solu-tion. Internationals have often pushed for early elections in risky conditions, when re-cently warring factions remain well armed and able to use violence to contend for power.

Indeed, international actors have helped cre-ate these conditions in the first place by press-ing warring factions to reach settlements before one side has defeated the other.[21] How-ever, international actors can sometimes cre-ate conditions that mitigate the risk posed by early elections when they provide robust peacekeeping, facilitate the demobilization of armed forces, back power-sharing agree-ments, and help build robust political insti-tutions. Thus, international pressure in favor of early elections strengthens peace when it provides these stabilizing instruments, but it undermines peace when it is not backed by effective means to achieve stable democracy.

ELECTIONS TIMING IN THE MIDDLE EAST

These conclusions about the dangers of early elections after civil wars are relevant to a few recent cases in the Middle East, and broader arguments about the consequences of pre-mature elections illuminate the Egyptian experience. Early elections have been nei-ther a magic cure-all in these societies nor the main cause of their problems. On bal-ance, some of these countries would argu-ably have been better off delaying elections.

Libya held elections for its General Na-tional Assembly in July 2012, less than a year after the ouster of dictator Muammar Gaddafi in a bloody civil war. The elections proceeded with little violence despite the presence of many local militias still well armed following the war. The party of act-ing premier Mahmoud Jibril, a moderate secularist political science PhD educated at the University of Pittsburgh, prevailed in the voting, outpolling the Muslim Brotherhood slate. This was a surprisingly good outcome, considering that Libya manifested many of the risk factors for danger with early elec-tions: rebel groups still under arms, weak state institutions, a poor legal system, no peace-keepers, and the absence of a strong power-sharing framework. Indeed, all was not entirely well despite the lack of major turmoil around the elections. Subsequently, the US ambassador and diplomatic outpost in Benghazi was attacked and Libya witnessed the collapse of two governments in quick succession, squabbles with the International Criminal Court stemming from its inability to ensure due process in the case of Gaddafi's son, slow progress in drafting a permanent constitution, and an inability to disarm local militias. Early elections do not seem to have made the situation worse, but they did not prevent instability.

Iraq held parliamentary elections in January 2005, less than two years after the toppling of Saddam Hussein in the context of ongoing insurgency and sectarian violence. The United States, still militarily occupying the country, had hoped to delay elections, but the Shiite religious majority bloc insisted on holding elections that it knew it would win in a loose coalition with Kurdish ethnic parties. The United States had hoped that a delay would improve the chances of parties that were trying to appeal to voters across ethnic and sectarian lines, particularly the Iraqi List party of Ayad Allawi, the US-appointed interim prime minister. Iraqi List won only 14 percent of the vote. Narrowly sectarian or ethnic parties won the other 86 percent. Parties representing the formerly ruling Sunni minority gained few seats due to the combined effects of a Sunni boycott of the election, fear of violence at polling places, and an electoral system that grouped votes into a single national pool rather than by local districts.

As in the case of the Bosnian elections shortly after the Dayton Accords, political mobilization and voting in Iraq followed the cleavage lines of previous struggles and of cultural networks in traditional society. There was a need for culturally cross-cutting organizations based on trade unions or civic networks to be created anew, a daunting pro-

cess in a setting polarized by violence. Early elections did not cause the civil violence, which was already under way, but early elections arguably unnecessarily exacerbated the polarization of Iraqi politics along identity lines.

Lebanon held elections in 2005, shortly after Syria withdrew its military forces, ending a three-decade occupation triggered by the Lebanese civil war.[22] These elections were structured in accordance with a 1989 adjustment of the country's traditional power-sharing system, the breakdown of which had led to civil war in 1975. These elections produced a governing coalition of various religious factions, including the well-armed Hezbollah Shia group that acted as a state within the state in its southern Lebanon enclave, facing its sworn enemy Israel. Although this arrangement sustained an uneasy peace in Lebanon, it did not check Hezbollah's ability to provoke war with Israel, which retaliated not only in southern Lebanon but also in air attacks against Hezbollah targets in Beirut. Lebanon's early elections following Syria's withdrawal did nothing to reduce this unstable polity's risk of violence, and they may have exacerbated it.

Egypt held parliamentary elections in November 2011, less than a year after the ouster of President Hosni Mubarak, and it held presidential elections in May and June 2012. Although these were in no way post-conflict elections, they nonetheless raised the question of whether premature elections might play into the hands of antidemocratic or narrowly sectarian political groups that reflect the divisions of the old authoritarian regime. The Muslim Brotherhood, realizing that it was the best organized mass-based political group in the country, pushed energetically for quick elections. Urban secular progressives who had spearheaded the Tahrir Square demonstrations leading to Mubarak's resignation realized that they were poorly organized in many tiny parties, and so preferred a slower pace. Some progressives worried that too slow a pace would allow the Supreme Council of the Armed Forces to entrench the sovereign role it had assumed in the wake of Mubarak's departure.

Early elections did help Brotherhood candidates dominate the parliamentary election. The candidates of the two well-organized remnants of the old regime, the military and the Brotherhood, prevailed in the first round of the presidential election. A secular socialist trade union candidate, Hamdi Sabahi, came out of nowhere in the last two weeks of the campaign to win nearly 21 percent of the vote, just behind the Brotherhood candidate Mohammad Morsi and the military candidate Ahmed Shafik. Given more time to organize and strike bargains with two other centrist candidates, Abdel Foutouh and Amr Moussa, who gained a total of nearly 29 percent in the first round, Sabahi could have created a dominant coalition far more committed to democracy and civil rights than either candidate in the runoff. Hurried, unsuccessful discussions of such a coalition, motivated by the desire to block Shafik's candidacy, came too late, after the first round of the presidential election, when the coalition would have had to coalesce around Morsi and the Brotherhood. Arguably, the civil violence, sectarian tension, and political instability in Egypt following Morsi's victory could have been minimized if a more deliberate electoral pace had allowed time for a new centrist alliance to coalesce around the moderate Islamist Foutouh, who might have reassured the Brotherhood's constituency, and the Mubarak-era diplomat Moussa, who might have reassured the secularists of the old regime.

Election timing had less dramatic effects elsewhere in the Arab Awakening. Tunisia's early elections went well enough, because various facilitating conditions were in place. Yemen's one-candidate "election" is not rel-evant to the theory. Overall, the track record of the Arab Awakening provides no support for a policy of rushing to the polls.

SEQUENCING TRANSITIONS: DILEMMAS AND SOLUTIONS

Our point is not only that democratization is often violent[23] but also that premature, out-of-sequence attempts to democratize may make subsequent efforts to democratize more difficult and more violent than they would otherwise be. When elections are held in an institutional wasteland like Iraq, for example, political competition typically coalesces around and reinforces the ethnic and sectarian divisions in traditional society. To forge liberal, secular coalitions that cut across cultural divisions, it is usually necessary to have impartial state institutions that provide a framework for civic action and a focal point for civic loyalty.[24] Without reasonably effective civic institutions, the outcome in culturally diverse societies is likely to resemble that of Iraq and Lebanon. Once a country starts on an illiberal trajectory, ideas are unleashed and institutions are established that tend to continue propelling it along that trajectory. A key danger is that premature democratization will push a country down this path.

When will gradual or partial steps be helpful, and when will claims to be sequencing the transition simply serve as excuses for authoritarians who seek to subvert progress toward democracy? Dictators in countries like Tunisia have used reforms tactically to co-opt, divide, and weaken resistance to autocracy.[25] However, dictators in Chile, South Korea, Taiwan, and Malaysia have presided over economic and administrative reforms that have had the unintended consequence of improving the country's subsequent chances for a successful democratic transition. At least some authoritarian leaders seek to increase the efficiency of their state and its economy, in part to strengthen their regime against potential external and internal foes. Toward this end, they may work to professionalize the bureaucracy, reduce corruption by lower-level officials, collect taxes in a more orderly way, rationalize business regulations, and enhance the competitiveness of exports. They may aim for an outcome like Singapore, modern but run by one party, yet inadvertently wind up like Taiwan, with a thriving middle class, a law-governed capitalist economy, and a highly skilled and educated populace that is ready for and demands multiparty democracy.[26]

That said, dictators are not the most likely initiators of well-sequenced reforms leading to democracy. This role is more commonly played by moderate groups that seek to curtail the power of the old authoritarian elite, but that also fear a rapid descent into the chaos of mass politics. Historically, a constructive role has sometimes been played by partial reforms that are designed to protect a liberalizing coalition, like the British Whigs and liberals; from a backlash by threatened traditional elites, like the Tories; and from radical mass groups, like the working-class Chartists. Similarly, in more recent times, reformers like South Africa's Nelson Mandela may bargain with repressive old elites like the apartheid regime in order to contain the demands of militant advocates of racial or tribal confrontation. Controlled reforms create a breathing space in which the reformers can put in place rule of law guarantees that reassure all constituencies while they negotiate golden parachutes with old elites to induce them to relinquish power—for example, the amnesties gained by cooperation with South Africa's Truth and Reconciliation Commission. As for the precise mechanisms of sequencing or gradualism, a variety of tactics might be useful in the right hands: pacts regularizing the protection of elites' property rights and personal security, rule of law reform that starts with

the bureaucracy and the economy, professionalized but regulated news media, and the internal democratization of ruling elite institutions such as the ruling party. Such expedients have effectively facilitated peaceful democratic transitions in Brazil, Chile, El Salvador, Mozambique, Poland, South Africa, South Korea, Taiwan, and elsewhere.

Thinking about the impact that outsiders can have on the trajectory and sequence of the political development of a transitional country commonly gravitates to insistent, active measures: military interventions to topple dictators, humanitarian interventions to stop atrocities and remake institutions, democracy assistance packages to export "color revolutions," donor ultimatums to hold elections and institute power sharing, and NGO naming and shaming to demand rights and accountability. Such efforts can sometimes yield improvements if the country is small, the commitment is long term, and a comprehensive package of reforms is thoughtfully put in place.[27] Often, however, such dramatic, coercive efforts have no lasting effect, or a negative one. The more dramatic the intervention, the more likely it is to destabilize local equilibria of power, touching off struggles among local forces to protect or improve their position in the altered environment.[28] Likewise, the export of popular awakenings through standard methods of protest ("color revolution in a box") can sometimes succeed in toppling dictators already weakened by their own incompetence, but the follow-up with NGOs' "anticorruption and rule of law reform in a box" turns out to be more difficult. Street-led color revolutions in places like Georgia, Kyrgyzstan, and the Middle East often put in place regimes that end up a couple of years later having the same Freedom House democracy rating the previous regime had.[29] Even worse, the populist politics sprouted in a false democratic spring may grow illiberal political movements and entrench militant ideologies, such as the Salafism, in post-awakening Egypt, making future democratization that much harder.

A better approach to fostering democratic change may be to create a political ecology that facilitates liberalization when it occurs naturally and provides incentives to choose a liberal path voluntarily. Research shows that peaceful democratic consolidation is far more likely when the international setting creates a friendly environment for the transitional state. Peaceful consolidation is also much more likely when democratic transition occurs in an already democratic neighborhood. On a larger scale, new democracies thrived better in the well-institutionalized post–1945 international environment of the Bretton Woods system and NATO than they did in the rickety interwar era of the League of Nations and the Dawes Plan. Statistical studies show that in the nineteenth century, the best predictors of democratization were domestic factors, whereas in more recent decades, international factors have become increasingly important.[30] It seems likely that one of the most important contributions that developed democracies can make to promoting peaceful consolidation of new democracies is to invest in the overall stability of international financial, trade, and security systems—operating systems that are always running in the background, which reforming states can plug into as needed. Etel Solingen has written persuasively on the importance of anchoring regional political orders in a liberal international trading system to encourage the prospective emergence of liberalizing ruling coalitions in regions such as the Middle East.[31]

In a somewhat more active mode, providing conditional access to special "club goods" of liberal democracy has also proved an effective tool for promoting democracy. The European Union's conditional terms for membership are a powerful example. The European Union's astute tactics in conditioning Romanian and Slovak accession on the adoption of policies to guarantee the rights of minorities, backed by strengthened rule of law, helped support the efforts of democratic coalitions to create favorable conditions for transition. Another example is the European Union's Cotonou trade agreement with many of its former colonies, conditioning benefits on verified compliance with human rights norms.[32]

Such "open door" policies send the signal that the benefits of membership in the liberal club are available to states that are ready to liberalize. This tactic strengthens the hand of progressive elements in the country, who can argue that liberalization will work if it is tried and who will gain resources by following this path. At the same time, the opened door, unlike the banged-on door, relieves progressives in developing countries of the burden of seeming like the stalking horse of the insistent neo-liberal imperialists.

Most important, open door strategies do not depend on the heroic assumption that outsiders can foresee the political consequences of coercing locals to hold elections, introduce power sharing, or undertake reforms. International donors thought they knew how to encourage reform in Burundi and Rwanda in the early 1990s, but instead they inadvertently heightened incentives for ethnic mayhem. If the assumptions behind open door strategies are wrong, the incentives will not work, but no additional harm is done, and the incentives can stay in place for later, whenever the moment is ripe. Good timing is everything in reform.

NOTES

1. Håvard Hegre, Tanja Ellingsen, Scott Gates, and Nils Petter Gleditsch, "Toward a Civil Democratic Peace? Democracy, Political Change, and Civil War, 1816–1992," *American Political Science Review* 95 (March 2001): 33–48; Jack A. Goldstone, Robert H. Bates, Ted Robert Gurr, Michael Lustik, Monty G. Marshall, Jay Ulfelder, and Mark

Woodward, "A Global Forecasting Model of Political Instability," (paper presented at the annual meeting of the American Political Science Association, Washington, DC, September 1–4, 2005).

2. Edward D. Mansfield and Jack Snyder, *Electing to Fight: Why Emerging Democracies Go to War* (Cambridge, MA: MIT Press, 2005); Hegre et al., "Toward a Civil Democratic Peace?" 34.

3. Mansfield and Snyder, *Electing to Fight*, 61–62; and Edward D. Mansfield and Jack Snyder, "Democratization and Civil War," chap. 8 in *Power and Progress: International Politics in Transition,* ed. Jack Snyder (London: Routledge, 2012).

4. Thomas Carothers, "How Democracies Emerge: The 'Sequencing' Fallacy," *Journal of Democracy* 18 (January 2007): 12–27; Daniel Byman, "Constructing a Democratic Iraq: Challenges and Opportunities," *International Security* 28, no. 1 (Summer 2003), 47–78; and Bruce Moon, "Long Time Coming: Prospects for Democracy in Iraq," *International Security* 33, no. 4 (Spring 2009): 115–48.

5. Samuel P. Huntington, *Political Order in Changing Societies* (New Haven, CT: Yale University Press, 1968); and Robert A. Dahl, *Polyarchy: Participation and Opposition* (New Haven, CT: Yale University Press, 1971).

6. This section draws on Edward D. Mansfield and Jack Snyder, "Democratization and the Arab Spring," *International Interactions* 38, no. 5 (2012): 722–33; and Edward D. Mansfield and Jack Snyder, "Prone to Violence: The Paradox of the Democratic Peace," *The National Interest* 82 (Winter 2005/06): 39–45.

7. Huntington, *Political Order*, 4.

8. Daniel Kaufmann, Art Kraay, and Massimo Mastruzzi, *The Worldwide Governance Indicators: Methodology and Analytical Issues,* World Bank Policy Research Working Paper no. 5430 (World Bank, Washington, DC, 2010), available at http://siteresources.worldbank.org/INTMACRO/Resources/WPS5430.pdf, and their 2011 update, available at www.govindicators.org.

9. Jack L. Snyder, *From Voting to Violence: Democratization and Nationalist Conflict.* (New York: W. W. Norton, 2000), 74–81.

10. Lisa Anderson, "Demystifying the Arab Spring," *Foreign Affairs* 90, no. 3 (2011): 6.

11. Ibrahim Sharqieh, "Yemen: The Search for Stability and Development," in *The Arab Awakening: America and the Transformation of the Middle East*, by Kenneth M. Pollack et al. (Washington, DC: Brookings Institution Press, 2011).

12. George W. Bush, "Remarks by the President at the 20th Anniversary of the National Endowment for Democracy" (speech, Washington, DC, November 6, 2003).

13. Dawn Brancati and Jack Snyder, "Time to Kill: The Impact of Election Timing on Post-Conflict Stability," *Journal of Conflict Resolution* 57, no. 5 (October 2013).

14. Virginia Page Fortna, "Where Have All the Victories Gone? War Outcomes in Historical Perspective" (paper presented at the annual meeting of the International Studies Association, Honolulu, HI, March 5, 2005); and Page Fortna, "Has Violence Declined in World Politics?" *Perspectives on Politics* 11, no. 2 (June 2013): 566–70.

15. Séverine Autesserre, *The Trouble with the Congo: Local Violence and the Failure of International Peacebuilding* (New York: Cambridge University Press, 2010).

16. Dawn Brancati and Jack Snyder, "Rushing to the Polls: The Causes of Premature Post-Conflict Elections," *Journal of Conflict Resolution* 55, no. 3 (2011), 469–92; Brancati and Snyder, "Time to Kill."

17. Roland Paris, *At War's End: Building Peace after Civil Conflict* (New York: Cambridge University Press, 2004); and Adekeye Adebajo, *Building Peace in West Africa: Liberia, Sierra Leone, and Guinea-Bissau* (Boulder, CO: Lynne Rienner, 2002).

18. Madhav Joshi and T. David Mason, "Civil War Settlements, Size of Governing Coalition and Durability of Peace in the Post–Civil War States," *International Interactions* 37, no. 4 (2011): 388–413.

19. Karl Derouen, Jenna Lea, and Peter Wallensteen, "The Duration of Civil Peace Agreements," *Conflict Management and Peace Science* 26 (September 2009): 367–87.

20. Philip G. Roeder and Donald Rothchild, *Sustainable Peace: Power and Democracy after Civil Wars* (Ithaca, NY: Cornell University Press, 2005). Roeder and Rothchild recommend "power dividing" arrangements that separate powers in different branches of government in a way that encourages alliances that cut across rival factions. Although Brancati and Snyder did not test this hypothesis, this arrangement may have long-term advantages that could serve as a corrective to power sharing's tendency to reify groups.

21. Suzanne Werner and Amy Yuen, "Making and Keeping Peace," *International Organization* 59, no. 2 (Spring 2005): 261–92.

22. Because Syrian-influenced elections were held during the occupation, the freer 2005 election technically does not fit the criteria used by Brancati and Snyder for a first post–civil war election.

23. Sheri Berman, "The Vain Hope for 'Correct' Timing," *Journal of Democracy* 18, no. 3 (2007): 14–17.

24. Note, however, the argument of Dominica Koter that strong local leaders forge cross-ethnic coalitions in most regions of Senegal, preventing the divisive ethnic polarization that prevails in the otherwise comparable case of Benin. See Dominica Koter, "King Makers: Local Leaders and Ethnic Politics in Africa," *World Politics* 65, no. 2 (April 2013): 187–233.

25. Eva Bellin, *Stalled Democracy: Capital, Labor and the Paradox of State-Sponsored Development* (Ithaca, NY: Cornell University Press, 2002).

26. On the role of financially independent business groups in shoring up democratic opposition parties in Africa, see Leonardo R. Arriola, "Capital and Opposition in Africa: Coalition Building in Multiethnic Societies," *World Politics* 6, no. 2 (April 2013): 233–72.

27. Michael W. Doyle and Nicholas Sambanis, *Making War and Building Peace* (Princeton, NJ: Princeton University Press, 2006).

28. Simon Collard-Wexler, "Understanding Resistance to Foreign Occupation" (PhD diss., Columbia University, 2013).

29. Mark R. Beissinger, "Structure and Example in Modular Political Phenomena: The Diffusion of Bulldozer/Rose/Orange/Tulip Revolutions," *Perspectives on Politics* 5, no. 2 (June 2007): 259–76.

30. Carles Boix, "Democracy, Development, and the International System," *American Political Science Review* 105, no. 4 (November 2011): 809–28.

31. Etel Solingen, *Regional Orders at Century's Dawn: Global and Domestic Influences on Grand Strategy* (Princeton, NJ: Princeton University Press, 1998), 165–214.

32. Emilie M. Hafner-Burton, *Forced to Be Good: Why Trade Agreements Boost Human Rights* (Ithaca, NY: Cornell University Press, 2009).

12

Economic and Political Causes of Conflict
An Overview and Some Policy Implications

Graham K. Brown and Frances Stewart

Violent conflict is undoubtedly a major cause of underdevelopment. Both country studies and cross-country regressions have demonstrated the heavy economic costs of civil wars. Indeed, twenty-two out of the thirty-one countries with the lowest human development have experienced civil war since 1990.[1] It is also widely accepted that underdevelopment is a major cause of conflict, thus giving rise to a vicious cycle in which poverty begets conflict and conflict begets poverty, summarized as "the conflict trap" by Paul Collier and others.[2] Yet the assumption of a straightforward causal relationship between poverty and conflict is oversimple, as indicated by the middle- and high-income areas that suffer conflict—such as Middle Eastern countries, Northern Ireland, the Balkan countries, and the Basque region of Spain—and by very poor areas that avoid conflict, such as Malawi, Tanzania, and Zambia. This chapter explores the economic causes of contemporary civil wars, asking whether it is simply poverty that causes conflict or if more complex situations are involved and identifying policies that might help prevent conflict and its recurrence.

The incidence of conflict has changed over time, as Figures 1 and 2 show. Between 1945 and the late 1980s, there was a steady rise in conflict. After the end of the Cold War, conflict incidence fell off sharply; but since 9/11, that downward trend has stopped, if not reversed.

Africa suffered by far the largest number of major conflicts during the 1990s, with more than 40 percent of the total, but lesser conflicts (those with deaths of twenty-five to one thousand annually and more than one thousand cumulatively) were concentrated in Asia. These numbers show that there is no simple equation between poverty and conflict—poverty at a global level fell

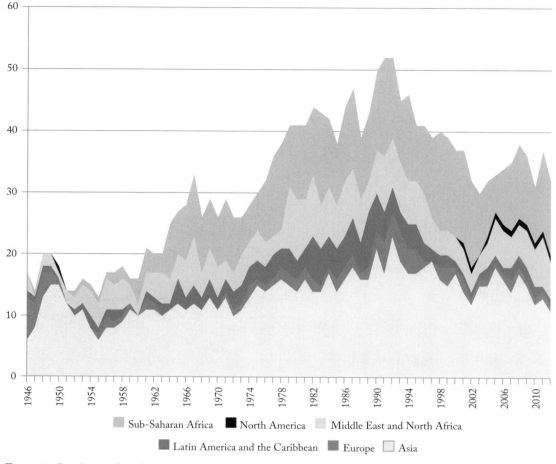

Figure 1. Incidence of conflict by geographic region, 1946–2012

Source: Uppsala/PRIO Armed Conflict Dataset.

proportionately (although it was constant or rising in absolute numbers) during much of the period. However, the incidence of conflict is undoubtedly heaviest among low-income countries. Thus it is estimated that, from 1960 to 1995, 0.5 percent of the population of low-income countries died due to conflict, while the proportion was 0.3 percent among lower-middle-income countries and 0.1 percent among upper-middle-income countries.[3] Econometric analysis also shows that low income per capita is a predisposing factor for conflict.[4]

Not only incidence but also the nature of conflict has shifted during the post–World

War II period. Wars coded as "extra-systemic"—essentially violent decolonization struggles—were largely a thing of the past by the mid-1970s, and interstate conflict has also declined drastically over the past decades; between 2004 and 2010, there were no ongoing interstate wars at all. In contrast, the proportion of civil conflicts that have become "internationalized" has been growing steadily since 9/11. In recent years, around 30 percent of all conflicts were internationalized; even at the height of the Cold War era "proxy wars," this figure rarely exceeded 15 percent and was never more than 20 percent. Hence, while the "conflict trap"

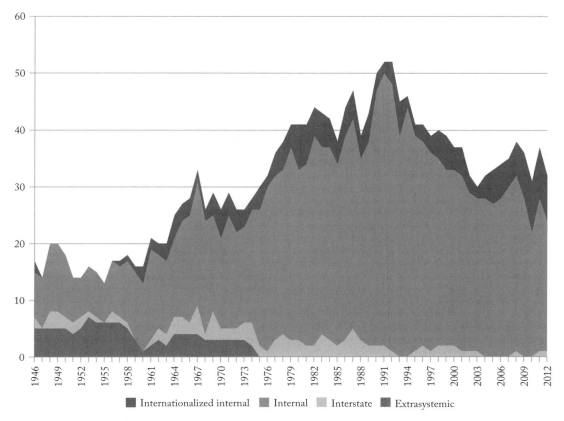

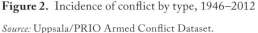
Internationalized internal   Internal   Interstate   Extrasystemic

Figure 2. Incidence of conflict by type, 1946–2012

Source: Uppsala/PRIO Armed Conflict Dataset.

and associated economic arguments explain part of the reason why countries experience civil war, a fuller explanation needs to take political and international dimensions into account, as well as economic motivations extending beyond low incomes.

Any review shows a considerable variety of types of conflicts, distinguished by their ideology and forms of mobilization, the nature of warfare, and the extent of external intervention or influence. Important types of conflicts over the past decades include:

- "Wars by proxy." During the Cold War, the East and the West supported different sides of some locally fought conflicts with funds, arms, and "advisers" in order to capture a particular country for their own side. Examples are the wars in Central America, Vietnam, Mozambique, and Afghanistan. Some of these wars ended with the Cold War, but others gained a life of their own (e.g., Afghanistan). New forms of proxy conflicts are associated with the war against terrorism, such as the current US military-supported counterinsurgency operations in the secessionist Muslim south of the Philippines and support for repression of the Taliban in Pakistan.

- Military "interventions" in domestic conflict by outside powers, generally motivated by political or economic objectives of the intervening country. Since the end of the Cold War particularly, this type of conflict has predominantly been associated with the West. Examples are Kosovo, the 2001 invasion of Afghanistan, and the wars in Iraq. But there are other examples that do not involve the West, such as Vietnam's invasion of Cambodia.

- Revolutionary or ideological wars that aim to overturn the established order. Examples are the wars waged by the Khmer Rouge in Cambodia, the Colombian conflict (especially in its early stages), the Shining Path in Peru, and the Maoists in Nepal. Rebellions aimed at installing democracy in repressive regimes (as in Syria) or at imposing a particular ideology (e.g., to institute sharia law, as in Mali) are also examples.

- Wars fought for regional independence or autonomy, such as the wars in Eritrea (Ethiopia), Biafra (Nigeria), Sri Lanka (the Tamils), Chechnya (Russia), southern Sudan, Kosovo, Spain (the Basques), and the southern Philippines (Muslim separatists).

- Wars fought to gain (or retain) political supremacy by particular groups representing specific cultures (ethnicities or religion). These include the conflicts in Rwanda, Burundi, Northern Ireland, and Uganda. Such wars may be fought primarily by individual groups or by coalitions of groups, as occurred, for example, in the conflicts in the Democratic Republic of the Congo (DRC) and Sierra Leone.

Some conflicts fall into more than one of these categories. Besides the first two categories—which clearly involve external forces—most conflicts have international or regional dimensions; the DRC is a contemporary example, with direct and indirect in-terventions by a number of countries in the region. These international dimensions can complicate or facilitate peacemaking.

Some wars are initiated by the economically deprived and those without political power, and others are initiated by the relatively privileged. The variety and complexity of the typology of conflicts suggest that there is no simple, single causal explanation for war. The next section of this chapter reviews four alternative economic explanations of conflict. The subsequent section provides an account of different dynamics of mobilization and summarizes some of the evidence for and against each explanation. The final section considers policy implications emanating from the conclusions of this review.

ECONOMIC EXPLANATIONS OF VIOLENT CONFLICT

Although some observers attribute contemporary conflicts to fundamental differences arising from ethnicity or religion,[5] such differences are evidently an insufficient explanation; many multiethnic or multireligious societies live peacefully—for example, Ghana and Tanzania—while others are at peace for decades before experiencing conflict. In fact, the vast majority of multiethnic societies are at peace.[6] As Abner Cohen succinctly stated four decades ago:

> Men may and do certainly joke about or ridicule the strange and bizarre customs of men from other ethnic groups, because these customs are different from their own. But they do not fight over such differences alone. When men do, on the other hand, fight across ethnic lines it is nearly always the case that they fight over some fundamental issues concerning the distribution and exercise of power, whether economic, political, or both.[7]

Four economic explanations have dominated recent analysis: the first points to group motives and group inequalities as a source of conflict; the second focuses on individual gains from conflict; the third is derived from a failed "social contract"; and the fourth theorizes that environmental pressures are a major source of conflict ("green war").

Group Motivation

Political conflicts, in contrast to most forms of criminality, consist of fighting between groups that wish to gain independence or take over the state and groups that resist this course of action, aiming to preserve the integrity of the nation or their power.[8] Each group is united under a common banner, with broadly common purposes. These common purposes may be termed "group motives" for conflict. Although individual motivation is also important, group motivation and mobilization underlie many political conflicts.

Groups engaged in internal conflict are often united by a common ethnic or religious identity. Some authors include religious identity under the generic term "ethnicity,"[9] and in many conflicts, opposing groups differ in both ethnicity and religion, and it is difficult to differentiate between the two as prime movers, as in, for example, Bosnia, Sri Lanka, and the middle belt of Nigeria. In other conflicts, one or another identity is clearly the relevant difference, such as ethnicity in Burundi and Rwanda, or religion in Northern Ireland or the Philippines. Moreover, there are differences between ethnic and religious forms of mobilization in organization, mobilization strategies, opportunities for securing external support, and the motives of both leaders and followers that make it relevant to distinguish the two in analysis of conflict motivation and dynamics.[10]

Since 1945, the proportion of conflicts attributable to ethnic or religious differences has been steadily increasing (see Figure 3).

These conflicts are generally presented as either religious or ethnic; these identities provide a powerful source of mobilization and unity. It seems that the proportion of conflicts based on religious differences is increasing: Muslims versus others (e.g., in Mali), Buddhists versus Muslims (e.g., in Myanmar), and many different denominations of Islam in conflicts in the Middle East. Nonetheless, many multiethnic and multireligious societies live relatively peacefully, and in many situations the majority of people do not perceive ethnic or religious identities as being of overriding importance. Hence the need to look beyond religion or ethnicity to find the causes of what are commonly described as "ethnic" or "religious" conflicts.

One plausible hypothesis is that conflict occurs where there are significant underlying differences in access to economic or political resources among ethnic or religious groups, providing both leaders and followers with a strong motive to fight. Ted Robert Gurr terms such group differences "relative deprivation." Frances Stewart defines differences in groups' access to economic, social, and political resources as "horizontal inequalities," in contrast to the traditional "vertical" inequalities that apply to individuals rather than groups.[11] The horizontal inequalities explanation of conflict is based on the view that cultural differences that coincide with economic and political differences between groups can cause deep resentments that may lead to violent struggles. These inequalities may involve regional differentiation, in which case they often lead to separatist movements (as in Aceh, Indonesia, and the Tamil regions of Sri Lanka), or different identities may occur within the same geographic space (such as in Rwanda, Northern Ireland, and Uganda), where political participation and economic and political rights are at stake.

Horizontal inequalities (HIs) are multidimensional, involving access to a variety of resources along economic, social, and political

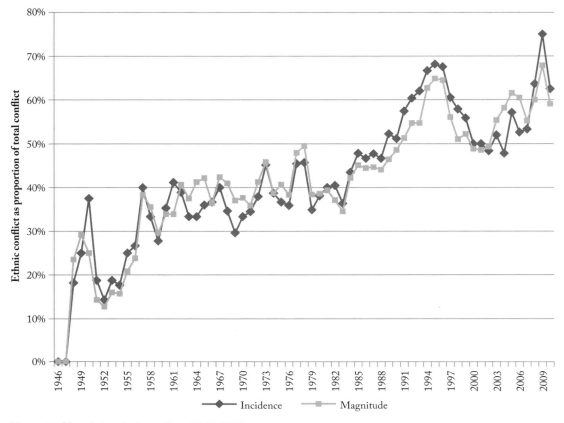

Figure 3. Trends in ethnic conflict, 1945–2009

Source: Monty G. Marshall, *Major Episodes of Political Violence, 1946–2012* (Severn, MD: Center for Systemic Peace), http://www.systemicpeace.org/warlist.htm (accessed August 20, 2013).

vectors or dimensions. Along the economic vector, not only is income important but also access to employment and to a variety of assets (e.g., land, credit, education) comes into play. Along the social vector, access to services (e.g., health care, water) and to assets (e.g., housing) can form relevant HIs. The political vector includes power at the top (e.g., the presidency, the cabinet), at lower levels (e.g., parliamentary assemblies, local government), in the bureaucracy at all levels, and in the army and the police. The relevant HIs are those that matter to people, and this varies across societies. For example, in Zimbabwe unequal access to land is important,

while in Northern Ireland conflict concerned HIs in housing, education, and jobs. HIs seem to be more provocative where they are consistent across the political and economic dimensions. The evidence suggests that economic and social HIs provide the conditions that lead to dissatisfaction among the general population and, consequently, give rise to the possibilities of political mobilization, but political exclusion is likely to trigger conflict by giving group leaders a powerful motive to organize in order to gain support. There is also often a provocative cultural dimension in group mobilization. Examples of cultural issues that give rise to inequalities and resentments are decisions on official languages, religion, or cultural events that favor one group or another; in the presence of other conditions, such cultural events can provoke violence.[12] The Orange marches in Northern Ireland and the adoption of Sinhalese as the official language in Sri Lanka are specific examples.

Although HIs may give rise to political movements, these political movements are not necessarily violent. Whether they become violent depends on whether demands are accommodated by the political system or whether they meet resistance. The violent reaction of those in power to the claims made by opposition groups (who may initially be protesting peacefully) is often the major source of escalation in violence, as indicated by events in Libya and Syria. It is important to note that relatively rich groups may instigate conflict, as well as relatively poor groups. The relatively rich do so mainly to preserve their riches (and/or power) for themselves, while the relatively poor do so out of a sense of injustice with the intention of achieving some redistribution. For example, Sudan's attack on Darfur and, earlier, the South is an example of a richer group aiming to repress a poorer one in order to seize its resources; while the Sri Lankan Tamils' rebellion is an example of a poorer group seeking autonomy.

Empirical evidence that severe HIs constitute a significant cause of violent conflict is accumulating. In the socioeconomic dimension, cross-sectional quantitative analyses have shown a significant relationship between socioeconomic inequality and conflict. Early country-level studies—such as Luca Mancini's analysis of the role of horizontal inequality in explaining regional variation in the wave of communal conflicts that occurred in Indonesia after the fall of Suharto's regime in 1998[13] and Gates and Murshed's finding of a significant relationship between "spatial" HIs (i.e., differentials between geographical regions) and the intensity of the Maoist insurgency in Nepal[14]—have been supplemented by cross-sectional country studies that find HIs a powerful explanatory variable for the incidence of conflict. Using Demographic and Health Survey data, Gudrun Østby and her collaborators found evidence of the impact of ethnic and regional HIs on conflict incidence in Sub-Saharan Africa.[15] Using historical measures of regional gross domestic product, Graham Brown found evidence that the intersection of regional disparity with ethnic distinctiveness accounts significantly for the incidence of violent secessionism.[16] Lars-Erik Cederman et al. use geocoded proxies for wealth and ethnic group location to provide a global analysis that confirms these findings.[17]

There is also substantial case study evidence; for example, Stewart's review of the experiences of nine countries shows not only that an increase in socioeconomic HIs has preceded the emergence of violent conflict but also that reductions in socioeconomic HIs, such as occurred in Northern Ireland during the 1980s, may contribute to the conditions for a peaceful resolution of such conflict. However, the connection between HIs and violent conflict is not an automatic one, and some societies show severe HIs without experiencing conflict (e.g., Bolivia, Brazil, and Ghana). Political inclusiveness is one reason that some societies avoid conflict despite severe economic HIs; Ghana, for example, has included political representation of all major groups in government. Political HIs—the exclusion or underrepresentation of groups within the political structure of a state—can provoke violent conflict when they change abruptly. In Côte d'Ivoire, for example, Félix Houphouët-Boigny avoided significant conflict for three decades, largely due to the policy of balancing representatives of the major groups in positions of importance in the government and bureaucracy. Following Houphouët-Boigny's death and the introduction of multiparty elections in the early 1990s, political leaders sought to mobilize ethnic sentiments to enforce their grip on power; they thus undermined Houphouët-Boigny's careful balancing act, leading to a spiral of ethnicization, xenophobia, and, ultimately, civil war.[18]

Econometric evidence, as well as case studies, shows that violent conflict is most likely when political and socioeconomic HIs exist at the same time.[19] Conflict is likely to erupt in such a situation because the political inequalities motivate leaders to mobilize in order to gain power, while the socioeconomic inequalities provide potential followers with a powerful grievance.

Private Motivation

People who fight have their own private motivations for doing so, as well as loyalty to the group that is fighting. War confers benefits as well as costs on some individuals. Political sociologists such as David Keen and Mark Duffield and economists such as Paul Collier and Anke Hoeffler have emphasized private or individual motivation as the fundamental cause of conflict.[20] The private motivation hypothesis has its basis in rational choice economics, arguing that the net economic advantages of war to some individuals motivate them to fight.[21] In this approach, group identities are regarded not as an independent factor but as instruments, created or accentuated to help fulfill the private motives of those who fight (especially leaders).

Keen lists many ways in which war confers individual benefit on particular categories of people: it permits people, especially uneducated young men, to gain employment as soldiers; it offers opportunities to loot, to profiteer from shortages and from aid; to

trade arms; and to carry out illicit production and trade. Where alternative opportunities are few, because of low incomes and poor employment, and the possibilities of enrichment by war are considerable, wars are likely to be more numerous and last longer. Moreover, conflicts may persist because some powerful actors benefit through the manipulation of scarcity and through smuggling, among other actions, and have no interest in resolving the conflict. An oft-cited case used to support this argument is the role of "conflict diamonds" in the protraction of the civil war in Sierra Leone.[22] Private motivation seems also to be a predominant factor behind the persistent conflict in the DRC, where abundant natural resources offer big rewards to those who control them.

Collier and Hoeffler put forward econometric evidence to support the view that "greed" motivates people to fight, on the basis of the observation that conflict incidence increases as the share of primary products exports in GDP rises (up to a point), which, it is argued, supports the view that conflict is caused by individual greed.[23] However, the share of primary products exports in GDP is a very crude approximation of greed, and the econometric results have been shown to lose significance with alternative specifications.[24] There is stronger econometric evidence that oil resources are associated with conflict, but this, too, depends on the model specification and exclusions of outliers.[25] Case studies suggest that even where natural resources are abundant, private motives are rarely the full explanation. As a study of seven countries in conflict concluded: "Very few contemporary conflicts can be adequately captured as pure instance of 'resource wars.' . . . Economic incentives have not been the only or even the primary causes of these conflicts."[26]

Research into motivation of those who have joined militias or have given them support suggests that people have a variety of motives, including the search for security and escape from traditional hierarchies (particularly in the case of women) and what has been termed the "pleasure of agency."[27]

In some cases, leaders may be motivated by self-aggrandizement, while their followers may not follow maximizing logic but may be coerced into fighting or persuaded to fight by leaders playing up religious or ethnic differences and grievances:

> Grievance is to a rebel organization what image is to a business. In the economist's view of conflict, grievance will turn out to be neither a cause of conflict, nor an accidental by-product of it. Rather, a sense of grievance is deliberately generated by rebel organizations. . . . [Rebel supporters] are gulled into believing the discourse which self-interested rebel leaders promote.[28]

At this point, the group explanation and the individual explanation of conflict come together. It is hard to persuade people to risk their lives for grievances that are not genuine (i.e., unless there is some sort of exclusion or economic horizontal inequality), while it seems that leaders may be, at least in part, motivated by personal ambition in both the HI and the individual maximizing paradigms. In both cases, it is argued that they are motivated by their political exclusion (i.e., political HIs), which denies them access to resources and power.

It is clear that although they are generally not a sufficient explanation of conflict, expected rewards sometimes play a role in the decision to rebel. As Collier notes, citing the cases of Aceh (Indonesia), Biafra (Nigeria), and Katanga (Zaire), separatist rebellion often emerges in resource-rich areas of a country; he concludes that rebellion is "the rage of the rich."[29] Yet there are also examples of separatist movements in regions with poor

resource endowment—for example, the Muslim rebellion in Thailand, the Tamils in Sri Lanka, and Eritrea and Bangladesh. In resource-rich areas, the gains (and motivation) may benefit the individual or group, or both. However, even in many of these cases, the leaders of the rebellions left lucrative and safe positions to instigate rebellion. Hasan di Tiro, for example, left a secure position at the United Nations in New York to lead the Acehnese uprising. In the case of Colombia, often depicted as a greed-motivated conflict, interviews with both leaders and those who were mobilized to fight show that generally their economic position worsened as a result of participating in the conflict; most put forward ideological reasons for fighting, including the issue of land reform.[30] Thus, short-run self-aggrandizement does not seem to be uppermost as a motive for these leaders. Moreover, even the conflicts in the natural resource-rich areas were framed in ethnic terms: the Acehnese in Indonesia, the Igbo in Biafra, and the "authentic" Katanga groups (as opposed to migrant communities) in Zaire. In each, it seems that the objective of promoting political and cultural autonomy for the ethnic group was also an important source of mobilization.

Hence, while individual maximization is certainly part of the story, it is clearly not the whole story. Group identities and group mobilization are also generally present. Although leaders undoubtedly often do sell identities as a way of securing support, they cannot create an identity out of nothing: "The [past] acts as a constraint on invention. Though the past can be read in different ways, it is not any past."[31] A common history, language, culture, or religion is generally required to generate felt identities powerful enough to mobilize people for conflict. Nor can leaders expect support unless there are genuine grievances—political, economic, social, or cultural—among those who follow them.

Failure of the Social Contract

A third explanation of violent conflict points directly to grievances. It derives from the view that social stability is premised on an implicit social contract between the people and the government. According to this (hypothetical) contract, people accept state authority as long as the state delivers services and provides reasonable economic conditions in terms of employment and incomes. With economic stagnation or decline and worsening state services, the social contract breaks down and violence results. Thus, high (and rising) levels of poverty and a decline in state services would be expected to cause conflict; indeed, early social contract theorists such as Thomas Hobbes used precisely such logic to explain the emergence of a social contract, albeit one that he thought would be absolutist in nature.[32] High vertical inequality might also be associated with such a failure, unless accompanied by populist measures to compensate the deprived. Conversely, political institutions that are able to channel and respond to socioeconomic discontents strengthen the social contract and thus reduce the risk of conflict.

Considerable evidence from econometric studies shows that conflict incidence is higher among countries with lower per capita incomes, life expectancy, and economic growth.[33] Many analyses have found an inverted U curve relationship between the extent of democratization in a country and the risk of conflict, whereby the incidence of conflict in both consolidated democracies and extreme authoritarian regimes is lower than in those countries that fall into categories in between. The usual interpretation of this trend is that "stable" democracies are indeed able to avert violent conflict through a strong social contract, whereas strongly authoritarian regimes are able to suppress potential conflict in the manner of a Hobbesian

Leviathan.[34] Recent attention has focused on the process of democratization as a time of particular vulnerability to the emergence of conflict. Jack Snyder argues that the process of democratization can be hijacked by ethnonationalist mobilization.[35] With Edward Mansfield, Snyder also argues that early democracies may be more belligerent internationally as well, because ethnic and nationalist rhetoric is invoked where institutions are weak.[36] Marta Reynal-Querol suggests that it is the particular type of democracy—whether it has a presidential system, and whether the outcomes of votes are majoritarian, winner-takes-all or involve proportional representation—that affects the propensity for conflict, rather than the level of "democracy" per se.[37]

"Green War" (Environmental Scarcity)

A fourth explanation of violent conflict, associated with the work of Thomas Homer-Dixon, is the "green war," or "environmental scarcity," argument.[38] The essence of this perspective is that the contest for control over declining natural resources, often intensified by population pressures, is a major cause of violent conflict around the world. Poorer societies are more at risk because they are "less able to buffer themselves" from environmental pressures.[39] Three dimensions of environmental scarcity may lead to conflict: "supply-induced scarcity," linked to the "depletion and degradation of an environmental resource"; "demand-induced scarcity," linked to population growth and the consequent extra pressures on existing resources; and "structural scarcity," which "arises from an unequal distribution of a resource that concentrates it in the hands of a relatively few people."[40] Writing in the early 1990s, the Toronto Group predicted "an upsurge of violence in the coming decades that will be induced or aggravated by scarcity."[41]

The environmental scarcity hypothesis, in its various manifestations, overlaps substantially with the other hypotheses discussed here. It overlaps with the social contract hypothesis, for instance, in viewing poverty as the root cause of conflict, although it points to specific environmental causes of such poverty. It can also overlap with the group motivation approach, as proponents emphasize that environmental pressures often lead to conflict where there are "groups with strong collective identities that can coherently challenge state authority."[42] Indeed, the "structural scarcity" dimension of the green war approach is very similar to the models of relative deprivation and horizontal inequality, albeit restricted to a particular dimension of inequality. In other manifestations, notably Robert Kaplan's prediction of a "coming anarchy" linking environmental degradation with increasing criminality and lawlessness, the environmental scarcity argument has more in common with the private motivation approach.[43]

The environmental scarcity view has been criticized by James Fairhead, who argues that conflict is associated not with scarcity but with environmental riches, interpreting environmental riches as the presence of valuable natural resources such as those found in the DRC.[44] The environmental riches hypothesis thus overlaps the private motivation/greed hypothesis. In fact, both environmental poverty and environmental riches may cause conflict, for different reasons and in different circumstances.

Other critiques of the green war hypothesis include accusations of a lack of conceptual clarity and concerns about the somewhat fatalistic approach that leaves few policy options open for conflict prevention and resolution.[45] In addition, the decade that has passed since Homer-Dixon and Kaplan predicted an increase in conflict has seen, instead, a significant decline in worldwide conflict. A systematic review of the evidence on climate change and conflict by Ole Magnus Theisen, Nils Petter Gleditsch, and Halvard Buhaug found no strong evidence of a link between the two.[46] It remains to be seen whether the experience of future decades will validate such predictions. Nonetheless, it is clear that although pressures arising from environmental scarcity may play an important role in many conflicts, the environmental scarcity hypothesis is—and really doesn't claim to be more—only a partial theory that contributes toward an understanding of causes of conflict, but not the general conditions under which conflict is likely to arise.

◆ ◆ ◆

These theories of conflict causes appear, in their extreme formulations, to be diametrically opposed—the oft-cited "greed versus grievance" debate being a clear example. But, as seen above, more often than not, proponents of one perspective accept or support in part the insights of others. Some conflicts are neatly explained by one of the explanations, some are explained by others, and some clearly have multiple causes. For example, Keen has described the long conflict in Sudan, which finally ended in the secession of South Sudan, as the product of individual greed as government and soldiers used the war to advance their own economic positions.[47] Yet, the conflict can also be seen as an example of sharp HIs, where southerners rebelled against their exploitation and sought autonomy while northerners sought to preserve their privilege.[48] The rebellion in the south can also be seen as an example of a failed social contract: although provision of services for the country as a whole had been improving, service provision in the south was grossly inadequate, there was no physical security, and there was virtually no advantage to being part of the Sudanese state. Finally, the poverty of Sudanese (in both the south and the west) can be interpreted as partly due to environmental pressures, and the wars can be explained as being green wars. Most contemporary conflicts can similarly be explained in terms of more than one of the four explanations advanced here, although in many cases, one (or two) of the explanations is dominant.

One rather simple conclusion, that qualitative analysts of conflict are mostly aware of but quantitative analysts tend to overlook, is that the broad causal theories discussed involve a degree of oversimplification and excessive generalization. The causes and dynamics of any single conflict are typically complex and sometimes contradictory and involve aspects of many, if not all, of the perspectives discussed. Yet it is important to understand which explanation dominates in a particular case, because that perspective has important implications for policy prescriptions for the prevention and resolution of the conflict.

Financing Conflict

One interpretation of some of the evidence is that the availability of financial or other resources—either to enable governments to suppress potential conflicts or to facilitate rebel activities—determines the incidence and duration of conflict.[49] Governments in relatively rich countries can collect more revenue and consequently spend more on security, making conflict less likely, while the availability of natural resources that are accessible to opposition groups, such as diamonds or timber, in turn finance the activities of these groups, thus explaining the greater propensity to conflict in countries where such resources are available (such as the DRC, Angola, Afghanistan, and Colombia). If this premise is taken as the entire explanation, underlying it is a basic assumption that all societies have a propensity for con-

flict, and that conflict will break out if it is not suppressed and/or the resources to finance rebellion are available. A less extreme position is that financing becomes an issue only when other conflict-causing elements are present.

Jeremy Weinstein takes the latter position and argues that the nature and extent of finance available (for rebels) determines the nature of a conflict: if natural resources are available to finance rebels, then mercenary armies are more likely to emerge, but in the absence of natural resources, conflicts are financed by local populations and are carried out by dedicated voluntary fighters motivated by ideology or ethnic loyalties.[50]

Conflict, Poverty, and Underdevelopment

Where does this leave the "poverty and underdevelopment" explanation of conflict? Each of the explanations intersects differently with poverty and underdevelopment. Table 1 illustrates these intersections, showing the main variables associated with conflict according to the different explanations. As far as group differences and HIs are concerned, relative poverty, not absolute poverty, matters. For the avoidance of civil wars, what matters is sharing resources of all kinds across all communities; shared poverty and underdevelopment do not lead to conflict. Where a society is poor but some groups succeed in securing a disproportionate share of resources, there may be a predisposition to conflict; Nepal is an example, where strong caste and geographic inequality have led to acute relative deprivation in the context of a society that is generally quite poor. Moving to the international dimensions of contemporary conflicts, underdevelopment in the Global South is associated with acute North/South HIs that may be potentially destabilizing. A more specific case is the sharp economic di-

Table 1. Summary of hypotheses and evidence on causal factors in conflict

Economic Variables Associated with Conflict	Evidence of Association with Conflict	Hypotheses
Decline/stagnation in per capita incomes	Cross-country and case study support	Failure of social contract; environmental degradation; low opportunity costs of war—private motive; government lacks finance to suppress conflict
Horizontal inequality	Cross-country and case study support	Group motives for conflict (HIs)
Vertical inequality	Conflicting evidence	Failure of social contract
High poverty	Cross-country and case study support	Failure of social contract; green war; private motives
Reduced government revenue and social expenditure	Case study evidence; limited statistical investigation; no evidence for association with IMF programs	Failure of social contract; weak government ability to suppress conflict—failed state
High levels of natural resources	Support for mineral resources only	Private motives (and financing)
Political Factors Associated with Conflict		
History of conflict	Strong statistical and case study evidence	Persistence of economic conditions giving rise to conflict; memory of conflict acting as mobilizing agent
State expenditure as low proportion of national income	Causal evidence	Weak states
Unequal access to political power among groups	Case study and statistical evidence	HIs
Intermediate political regime	Statistical and case study evidence	Inability to negotiate change or suppress violence

vide between Palestine and Israel, and, more generally between Muslims and non-Muslims, which are a mobilizing factor for Muslims generally—and form an element in current terrorist threats.

For those who emphasize individual maximization and rational choice, poverty and underdevelopment lower the opportunity costs of wars. If people, especially young men, lack employment or fruitful income-earning opportunities, the moderate "riches" conferred by war may offer them an attractive option. Those who argue for the overwhelming importance of individual motivation of this type point to the empirical correlations of conflict incidence with low average incomes and low levels of education. However, this view of conflict is based on the premise that fighting does offer opportunities for enrichment, which is difficult to argue in very poor societies such as Afghanistan and Somalia.

The social contract theory incorporates poverty as part of the explanation of conflict. The social contract fails when the state fails to deliver—in terms of social services, economic opportunities, and physical security. Poverty and underdevelopment are certainly part of this failure; Afghanistan and Somalia are clear examples. Yet there are poor societies where the state succeeds in providing basic services and sharing the limited opportunities. Low average incomes in a society do not necessarily imply a failed social contract. Some poor states—for example, Tanzania—succeed in delivering sufficient, if minimal, social services and physical security and avoid chronic conflict.

The green war hypothesis is certainly in tune with an explanation associated with poverty and underdevelopment, to the extent that poverty is caused by environmental pressures. However, there are many other causes of poverty and underdevelopment, so the green explanation does not provide a general connection between poverty, underdevelopment, and conflict.

Although there are many connections between poverty and conflict, the view that if we could only eliminate poverty we would also eliminate conflict is not supported by either the analysis presented here or by evidence. Recent conflicts in the Arab world, support this view: poverty ratios in Egypt, Libya, and Syria, for example, are low by global standards.[51] On the one hand, absolute poverty might be eliminated, yet conflict could well persist, as long as HIs continue and some groups are excluded politically as well as economically. On the other hand, a poor society can also be a fair and inclusive one and need not be prone to conflict. Conflict may become less likely when development efforts are successful, leading to a lessening of some sources of conflict, as is shown by the econometric evidence. But policies for the prevention of conflict need to go beyond raising average incomes or reducing poverty if they are to be successful.

ECONOMIC, SOCIAL, AND POLITICAL POLICIES AIMED AT PREVENTING CONFLICT

Economic and social policies may contribute in each of the three stages of conflict: preconflict, conflict, and postconflict. In a preconflict situation, where there is no conflict but there is a high probability of one occurring, preventive policies should be aimed at changing the underlying conditions in such a way as to make the outbreak of conflict less likely. When a conflict has broken out, economic and social policies can help protect the economy and the people against some of the costs resulting from the conflict; for example, through food distribution.[52] After a conflict has ended, policies are needed to help reconstruct the economy. This section focuses primarily on preventive policies; these are most relevant to the preconflict situation but are also relevant to the other stages, particularly the postconflict situation, because there is generally a high probability of conflict recurring soon after it has ended,[53] and it is therefore vital to introduce preventive policies. The postconflict stage also requires straightforward reconstruction policies, such as investment to replace destroyed facilities, and measures to integrate the combatants into peaceful activities—policies that are not considered here.

If conflicts are regarded as irrational or caused by unavoidable ethnic clashes, there is little role for policy other than repression or separating people from different groups. But to the extent that conflicts are the outcome of economic causes, preventive policies may be effective in reducing their incidence. Each of the different theories discussed here has implications for preventive policies. Which policies are relevant depends on a country's situation and which theory most closely approximates the situation.

Evidence suggests that the following types of countries are clearly vulnerable to conflict:

- Low-income, low–human development countries, given the fact that at least half of these countries have been in conflict at some time over the past thirty years and that econometric evidence points to low income as a correlate with conflict
- Any country that has been in conflict over the past thirty years, because the evidence shows that previous conflict is the most significant pointer to further conflict
- Any country with high HIs in political or economic dimensions, because such countries are likely to suffer from conflict
- Countries whose political regime is repressive but likely to liberalize, or countries in an "intermediate" state of transition from strong repressive regimes to more democratic regimes because previously suppressed grievances come to the fore as liberalization occurs and governments in such situations are often not accommodating

Three types of policies are needed, directed at the main factors responsible for conflict:

- Policies to address HIs (i.e., aimed at group motives)
- Policies to reduce the functionality of conflict (i.e., to address private motives)
- Policies to promote equitable and sustainable development (i.e., to address social contract failures and environmental pressures)

Correcting HIs

The general direction of policy change to avoid violence must be to reduce group inequalities. To achieve this, politically, economically, and socially inclusive policies are necessary. These include policies to achieve geographically balanced benefits, as well as balance between ethnicities, religions, or races. Politically, this means that all major groups in a society participate in political power (e.g., by becoming members of the administration, the army, and the police). Inclusive economic outcomes require that horizontal inequality in economic aspects (assets, employment, and incomes) be moderate; inclusive social outcomes require that horizontal inequality in social participation and well-being also be moderate. "Moderate" is a loose term. Group equality would be the ideal. "Horizontal equity" describes a degree of horizontal inequality that is acceptable to major groups in society and consequently would be unlikely to provoke conflict. The effect of any measure of inequality on conflict-propensity increases if it occurs systematically over a number of dimensions and grows over time. These are the considerations that should enter into a judgment of what an acceptable degree of horizontal inequality is. The general objective of inclusivity and moderate horizontal inequality will translate into specific policy recommendations differently in particular cases, depending on the relevant groups in the society, the dimensions of importance in the particular society, and if there is substantial horizontal inequality.

Political Inclusivity. The most universal requirement is for political inclusivity because the monopolization of political power by one group or another is often responsible for many of the other inequalities as well as being deeply resented for itself. Yet, achieving political inclusivity is among the most diffi-cult changes to bring about. Political inclu-sivity is not just a matter of democracy, defined as rule with the support of the major-ity, because majority rule can be consistent with the abuse of minorities, for example, in the recent history of Rwanda, Cambodia, and Zimbabwe. As long ago as the 1830s, Alexis de Tocqueville identified the poten-tial problems of the "tyranny of the major-ity."[54] In a politically inclusive democratic system, particular types of proportional representation are needed to ensure partici-pation by all major groups in the elected bodies. For inclusive government, represen-tation of all such groups is essential not only at the level of the cabinet but also in other organs of government. For political inclusiv-ity, moreover, members of major groups need to be included at all levels of the civil service, the army, and the police. An excellent ex-ample of how the institutionalization of in-clusive politics can avert conflict comes from Switzerland, where the 1848 federal consti-tution institutionalized a high degree of power sharing, bringing to an end centuries of intermittent fighting between Protestant and Catholic cantons (albeit the constitution excluded women from voting until 1971).

Political participation can occur at many levels (e.g., central, regional, local), in dif-ferent types of decisions (e.g., defense, eco-nomic, social), and in different institutions (e.g., army, police, civil service). Full politi-cal participation means that significant groups in the population participate across the board and their presence is not just nominal. There are many ways full political participation can be promoted, all of which have been adopted in some form or another in divided societies.[55] Some of the most powerful ways include the following:

- *A federal constitution.* Where groups are mainly separate geographically, a federal constitution can empower

different groups, as in the case of Belgium and Switzerland. Nigeria is an example of how the design of the constitution can affect the propensity to conflict. India is an example of a huge developing country that has maintained peace at a national level, partly due to its federal constitution.

- *The extent and nature of decentralization.* Decentralization, like federalism, can contribute to power sharing. This may have been one reason why Bolivia avoided conflict despite deep HIs. But decentralization does not always work in the intended way; it can replace one set of power brokers with another, which may or may not diffuse group domination.[56] Where groups are geographically concentrated, such decentralization may give greater political power to previously underrep-resented groups, but it can also lead to continued (or even greater) disempow-erment for some (normally minority) groups within the decentralized areas, as is also the case with federalism (e.g., in Nigeria).

- *The voting system.* A proportional repre-sentation (PR) system, or similar voting system, gives more power to minorities, but even with PR, a majority can domi-nate decision making unless a power-sharing system in elected assemblies and other government bodies is also adopted. Such systems are rare in developing countries, although no country with PR has had serious internal conflict.[57]

- *The nature of the elected assemblies.* In a bicameral assembly, it is possible to combine democratic representation in one house of the assembly with geographic (as in the United States) or group representation in the other. In India, for instance, group reservations operate for Scheduled Castes and

Scheduled Tribes in the Lok Sabha lower house, while the Rajya Sabha upper house is organized along regional lines. The voting system within assemblies can also be designed to prevent a single group from dominating (e.g., by requiring a two-thirds majority or by granting veto powers to particular groups).

- *Seat reservation in parliament for particular groups.* This has been adopted in a number of multiethnic societies, such as Burundi and Lebanon, as well as for the unscheduled castes and tribes in India and also for women in a large number of cases.[58] It is an important feature of the new Iraqi constitution.

- *Employment allocations within government.* There can be formal or informal provisions for a fair share of political posts at every level, including the presidency, the cabinet, the senior civil service, the military, and the police. For example, there is provision for three presidents in Bosnia and Herzegovina; postconflict Cambodia had two prime ministers for many years.

- *Citizenship rights.* These can be comprehensive, covering all who live in an area, or highly restrictive, requiring several generations of residence or extended only to "blood" relatives of some "original" inhabitants. Exclusionary citizenship rights can be highly provocative (as in Côte d'Ivoire in the 1990s), but relatively easy access to citizenship rights can also generate local resentment where this is seen as an attempt to "dilute" a regional minority, as in the Malaysian state of Sabah.

- *Constraints on political parties.* When there are no constraints, political parties in divided societies tend to become "ethnic."[59] For this reason,

multiparty elections often provoke violence.[60] Policies toward political parties range from outlawing them altogether (as initially in Yoweri Museveni's Uganda) to requiring them to have multiethnic support (as in Nigeria). Although such policies can prevent or reduce the ethnicization of party politics, they can prove problematic where genuine regional grievances exist. The Indonesian constitution, for instance, bans regional political parties, a major sticking point in the peace negotiations in the Indonesian province of Aceh in 2005.

- *Human rights protection.* Strong protection of civil liberties and human rights does not ensure power sharing, but it does limit the abuse of power and clearly plays an important role. Conversely, some (semi-) authoritarian regimes have used the ethnic diversity of their population to justify limitations on human rights, particularly those relating to freedom of speech and freedom of assembly.

This account briefly touches on the many policies that can be used to ensure political participation of major groups. Many instances can be cited of political systems designed to achieve inclusive and balanced political participation in sharply divided societies struggling to maintain peace and cohesion. Among developed countries, Belgium and Switzerland are prime examples. Many developing countries initially suppressed these problems through authoritarian regimes, but the political issues associated with multiethnic societies are coming to the fore with democratization. The widely recommended formula of majoritarian multiparty democracy is proving inadequate, and postconflict countries have struggled to find alternative, more inclusive models. Nigeria, Fiji, Ethiopia, and Malaysia are examples, having modified their political systems as a consequence of political unrest. It is clear that policies to address political HIs need to accompany economic and social policies if renewed conflict is to be avoided.

Economic and Social Inclusivity. Deciding what "economic and social inclusivity" means is not a straightforward task. Should one aim for equality in opportunities in access to resources or in outcomes? Apparent equality of opportunities may lead to very unequal outcomes because of a variety of implicit practices and past disadvantages of some groups relative to others. The liberal philosophy of "equal opportunities" is at best a necessary condition for advancing group equality. Equality in access to resources is likely to get closer to providing a genuine level playing field, but it may still result in inequalities of outcomes (defined very broadly in terms of health, educational achievements and income per capita) because the disadvantaged group is likely to be less efficient at using a particular set of assets. For equality of outcomes, inequality in access to targetable assets may be necessary, such as with education, land, and capital.

Policies toward achieving greater group equality in economic entitlements can be divided into three types, although the distinctions are not watertight: policies aimed at changing processes that are directly or indirectly discriminatory can be adopted; assistance directed to particular groups; and targets and quotas for education, land distribution, and financial and physical assets.

Policies aimed at changing discriminatory processes may not be so different from policies to promote competition. Anti-discriminatory policies are likely to be the most acceptable type of policy and can have a significant impact. For example, addressing discrimination was a major component of the policy set adopted in Northern Ireland.

The second type of policy concerns the nature and distribution of public funds, often involving a redirection of expenditure across regions or neighborhoods, as well as groups within them. This is in principle within the control of the government, but it may meet resistance from privileged regions or from the government itself to the extent that it represents privileged groups. This type of policy requires careful review of the implications of all public expenditure (and other relevant policies) for the group distribution of benefits. It is noteworthy that such a review does not form an explicit consideration in the public expenditure reviews supported by international donors, or those of most governments.

The third type of policy, pertaining to quotas and targets, is the most controversial and politically provocative. It is this type of policy that many people refer to when they talk of "affirmative action," although affirmative action can be interpreted as including all three types of policies.

If the public sector constitutes a major source of HIs (in education, employment, and infrastructure), much can be achieved through direct action by the government. HIs located in the private sector are more difficult to tackle, though all three types of policies will make a contribution. The growing horizontal inequality in incomes in Guatemala since the Peace Agreements in the late 1990s, despite some government action to correct inequalities, shows the importance of tackling inequalities that originate in the private sector, while in South Africa vertical income distribution has been widening despite explicit policies aimed at reducing racial inequalities.[61]

There are many cases where affirmative action has been adopted in one way or another, pointing to a large range of possible policies.[62] Such policies have been adopted in the North (as in the United States, New

Zealand, and Northern Ireland) and the South (as in Fiji, India, Malaysia, South Africa, and Sri Lanka). They have been introduced in different political circumstances: some by disadvantaged majorities; for example in Fiji (ethnic Fijians), Malaysia (Malays/Bumiputera), Namibia (black population), South Africa (black population), and Sri Lanka (Sinhalese); and others introduced by advantaged majorities for disadvantaged minorities; for example in Brazil, India, Northern Ireland, and the United States. The former, with firmer political support, tends to be more extensive.

Policies that have been introduced to correct group inequalities include:

- *Policies to correct asset distribution.* These include policies to improve the group distribution of land through redistribution of government-owned land, forcible eviction, purchases, and restrictions on ownership (adopted in Malaysia, Zimbabwe, Fiji, and Namibia); policies concerning the terms of privatization (Fiji and Malaysia); and policies regarding credit allocation preferences (Fiji and Malaysia), training and education (Brazil, New Zealand, Malaysia, and the United States), and housing and public-sector infrastructure (South Africa, and Northern Ireland).
- *Policies to correct income and employment distribution.* These include policies concerning employment quotas in the public sector (Malaysia, Sri Lanka, and India) and the requirement for balanced employment in the private sector (South Africa); and policies regarding transfer payments (although there are many cases of age-, disability-, and gender-related transfers, transfers according to ethnicity, religion, or race are rare).

Reductions in sharp HIs may be essential to produce a stable society, but the introduction of policies to this end can be provocative. The most clear-cut example is Sri Lanka, where policies to improve the position of the Sinhalese contributed to Tamil rebellion. In Zimbabwe, land policies, along with other policies, have been introduced in a highly provocative way and can hardly be taken as a model. In Kenya, land settlement policies introduced after independence reduced inequality in land ownership between Africans and Europeans, but at the cost of creating injustices among African ethnic groups, which later led to violence.[63] Although some action is necessary if conflict is to be avoided in the longer run, such policies must be introduced with sensitivity. In Malaysia, which with its New Economic Policy (NEP) instituted arguably the most extensive and comprehensive policy package in history to reduce HIs, the successful implementation of these policies largely depended on acceptance of their political necessity by all groups precisely because of the risk of instability associated with the status quo ante. Nonetheless, Chinese discontent with the NEP strengthened in the mid-1980s, when the spectacular growth of the previous decade stalled, suggesting that such policies are best implemented in an economic environment that is otherwise favorable.[64] Generally, opposition to affirmative action tends to grow over time, especially if the inequalities have been substantially reduced. This happened in the United States and in Northern Ireland as well as in Malaysia. Consequently, it is important to devise an "exit" strategy from the start.

Reducing Private Incentives

For conflict prevention, it is helpful to introduce policies aimed at reducing the functionality of conflict. One important aspect of such policies is to increase people's peace-time economic opportunities by extending their access to education and other assets and through a dynamic peacetime economy that offers people employment and earnings opportunities, so the gains that may be made during conflict (e.g., through theft, smuggling, and looting) are less attractive.

Much of the profiting from war arises because of general lawlessness—where a weak state has little control over criminality. Strengthening the state can be an important aspect of preventive policies, yet the policy agenda today tends to weaken the state through the strong push toward the market, cutbacks in government expenditure, the increasing use of nongovernmental organizations (NGOs) for service delivery, and moves toward decentralization of government, as for example in El Salvador. Governance reforms demanding greater transparency and accountability, aimed at improving the integrity and efficiency of the state, may not strengthen the state in the way required.

Expanding employment opportunities for young men is generally important in preventive policy, and especially for postconflict societies. High male unemployment is frequently associated with outbreaks of conflict—for example, in Sri Lanka and Algeria—while lack of opportunities in general is a common feature of many countries when conflict breaks out, including, for example, in the preconflict situation in Sierra Leone.

Another set of policies commonly recommended to reduce the private incentives for war, as well as the financing of it, aims at reducing the "rents" arising from natural resources.[65] These consist partly of domestic reforms, such as greater transparency and competition in the production and marketing of natural resources, and partly of international policies that may reduce trade in war commodities, such as diamonds and drugs. As with the policies discussed earlier, what is appropriate differs from country to country.

Restoring the Social Contract

Policies to restore the social contract have two important aspects. One is to generate equitable and sustainable economic growth. The other is to ensure that the government provides essential services—including health care, education, economic infrastructure, and security—that form an essential part of the social contract.

Although it is universally agreed that equitable and sustainable development would make conflict less likely, this is difficult to achieve in conflict-prone countries. Many such countries have recently experienced conflict, with all the adverse implications for development that conflict entails. Moreover, even in peace, it is difficult to generate sustained development in poor countries with weak human capital, especially those heavily dependent on primary products.

A great deal of analysis has been devoted to delineating the conditions for widely shared growth. Economic growth requires sustained investment in physical and human capital, political stability, and a fair international system, including flows of aid to poor countries, modest debt servicing requirements, and stable terms of trade. It also requires a reasonably responsible and effective government. Equitable growth requires a fair distribution of assets, especially land; a comprehensive educational system; a robust employment situation; and a variety of safety nets for those who are unable to participate fully in the economy. In practice, very few poor countries meet these requirements, particularly those falling into the "vulnerable to conflict" category.

In addition, the universal and effective provision of basic services is a critical requirement of the social contract, and one that is clearly not being fulfilled in many developing countries.[66] Yet this aspect of the contract is probably the easiest to achieve because the cost of basic services is just a fraction of the national income, even in poor countries.

Taken as a whole, these form an ambitious set of policies. Particularly challenging is the aim of achieving equitable and sustainable growth, especially for low-income countries that have recently suffered conflict—the most vulnerable category of countries. One reassuring aspect is that the policies relevant to the different types of causes are in general consistent with one another. Indeed, some are complementary or even the same. For example, policies that promote horizontal equality will also generally improve vertical income distribution, and the converse is likely to be true. Policies that promote inclusive and equitable growth are also likely to reduce the incentives for low-income people to become fighters because they will generate jobs and other income-earning opportunities. Policies that help fulfill the social contract, by extending basic services to everyone, will also help promote economic growth because of the critical importance of human capital for growth. Policies that improve the physical security of a country are likely to help attract investment and thereby promote growth. Thus the policies reinforce one another. Moreover, they are generally desirable policies even without considering their conflict implications, as they lead to a fair and prospering society.

Policy change, however, is particularly difficult to achieve in the context of a country prone to violence, especially one with a history of conflict. In this context, there are inherited memories and grievances, entrenched group identities, and intergroup animosities. The government is rarely broadly based, often representing only a subset of the groups potentially involved in conflict. It would be naive to think that the government even invariably wants to promote peace, given the prevalence of state-instigated violence. In the case of Uganda, for example, the governments of Idi Amin and Milton Obote were responsible for much of the violence. The same is true in Sudan.

Hence the context for introducing policy change must be recognized as structurally unfavorable. Nonetheless, some governments give high priority to promoting peace (e.g., Nelson Mandela in South Africa; Yoweri Museveni when he first came to power in Uganda; and, arguably, the Maoist government in Nepal) and are willing to promote inclusive policies; in other cases, the majority group constitutes the relatively deprived one and is therefore keen to correct HIs (e.g., Malaysia and South Africa). In Nigeria, the entire population wanted to avoid a recurrence of the highly damaging civil war (1967–70) and therefore agreed on changing the constitution so that it would be more inclusive, but the government did not take corresponding action to address socioeconomic inequalities, which provided fertile ground for new conflicts.

The role of the international community is therefore important. Yet despite this, and the fact that peace-promoting policies contribute to development, it is surprising the extent to which such policies are *not* the bread and butter of the international community's policy agenda. A review of donor policies toward countries that had ended long conflicts and were clearly vulnerable to their renewal concluded that the leading economic institutions—the International Monetary Fund (IMF) and the World Bank—gave major emphasis to recommending macropolicies, market-oriented policies to promote competition and efficiency, and poverty-reduction policies, but largely ignored policies aimed at horizontal equality and, for the most part, vertical inequality.[67] This created a dissonance between the policies recommended and those likely to sustain peace; for example:

- IMF insistence on the normal macro-budgetary requirements tends to impede the expenditures needed for infrastructure investment and social sector recovery; for example, in El Salvador and Nicaragua.[68]
- Policies rarely support the revenue-raising needed to extend social services and often involve reductions in trade taxes; for example, in Rwanda, where government revenue was only 10 percent of GNP, and in Guatemala.[69]
- The objective of correcting HIs (or increasing inclusivity) is often recognized but implementation is rare. The need for inclusive development is mentioned in World Bank documents, but in most cases no specific policies are recommended for this, nor are the policies extended beyond the immediate postconflict situation to vulnerable countries generally.[70] Analysis of Mozambique's postconflict situation, dominated by international agencies, shows the limited efforts devoted to correcting HIs—indeed, in Mozambique, economic postconflict policies, including aid distribution, worsened HIs—while the political system virtually disenfranchised major groups.[71]

Poverty reduction strategy papers supported by the World Bank sometimes acknowledge the importance of reducing exclusion but rarely recommend explicit policies.[72] Similarly, the political dialogue conducted by the international community with developing countries generally stresses the need for multiparty democracy rather than the need for inclusive government.

Preventive policies of the types just reviewed must become part of development policy toward vulnerable societies.

A notable exception to the above trend is Nepal in the postconflict period from 2006. Before the insurgency, the international community adopted its normal policy set, but donor policy shifted remarkably following the escalation of the Maoist insurgency in 2001. Whereas previously the World Bank and other major donors emphasized macroeconomic reforms, after the conflict ended they addressed socioeconomic exclusion as an important element of their country assistance strategy.[73] Donors generally have not yet addressed *political* exclusion, however.[74]

THE NEW INTERNATIONAL SECURITY ENVIRONMENT AND CONFLICT IN POOR COUNTRIES

The globalized nature of most conflicts has increased in many respects—in the nature of the conflicts and the support they get, in military interventions, and in finance and restrictions over finance—although it is easy to exaggerate the change. Almost everything one says about global connections could have been said before, but there has been a change in degree if not in kind.

In the post–Cold War environment, East-West conflicts have been replaced by a variety of types of conflict, including location-specific conflicts, often with an ethnic or religious dimension; conflicts motivated by the objective of instituting democratic forms of government; and global tensions and violence associated with a divide between Muslims and others.[75] Each type is frequently associated with underlying HIs. This section considers how each of the four underlying socioeconomic causes of conflict—HIs, private motivations, failed social contracts, and green war—have played out at the global level, particularly in recent years.

For the world as a whole, inequalities between countries have been falling, mainly due to the rapid growth of China and India.[76] The politicization of global inequalities, however, has increased. At a general level, this is exemplified by dissatisfaction with the role and governance structures of global financial institutions and the initiation of regional and bilateral alternatives. More serious is that inequalities are high and increasing along the most significant cultural fault line—between Muslims and others—both at a cross-country level and within countries in both the North and the South. For example, there are big and growing economic gaps between Israelis and Palestinians, between Western countries and the Middle East, and between Muslim populations within particular countries (e.g., the United Kingdom and France and many developing countries). Each of these inequalities feed into political mobilization at both local and global levels.

As the HI hypothesis suggests, this dimension of inequality is particularly dangerous because it falls along culturally distinct lines and makes mobilization along those lines more likely. Even moderate, broadly pro-Western Muslim leaders such as former Malaysian prime minister Abdullah Ahmad Badawi have interpreted the "war on terror" and the associated global insecurity in such terms: "Muslims see ourselves as a collective *ummah* [global community of the faithful]. . . . This is why Muslims who are not affected by poverty or have nothing to do with Palestine feel strongly about this issue. This is why without addressing the root causes, the war against terrorism will not succeed."[77]

With the growth of international migration and of global media connections, groups increasingly consider not just their local relative position but also their international one—where identities cross nations—and mobilize and provide support for conflicts across borders. This is most evident in Muslim countries, where international connections, finance, and fighters move from one locality to another. For example, fighters from Afghanistan have moved to Algeria and to Iraq; Muslims in the Philippines and Thailand receive support internationally; and British and French Muslims move to Iraq and Afghanistan. The globalization of perceptions of inequality means that the inequalities in some countries—such as those faced by Muslims in Europe relative to non-Muslims—provoke not only conflict in those countries but also support for conflict against the West elsewhere. Similarly, the inequalities between Palestinians and Israelis are used to justify and stimulate conflict in many other places. Global interventionism, especially of Western countries fighting and providing finance for conflicts involving Muslim populations, feeds into such perceptions.

Governments in developing countries are able to classify rebellions as "terrorist" and thus to cash in on the war on terror, gaining military equipment and financing. This trend extends beyond conflicts involving Muslim populations; for example, the Philippine, Sri Lankan, Nepalese, Colombian, and Pakistan governments have gained various types of support for what they now define as their wars against "terrorists."

In terms of the private motivations hypothesis, globalization has extended to the international arena possibilities of profiting from conflict as well as gaining financing for it.[78] For example, "conditions of armed conflict boost narcotics production and enable insurgents to become involved in the drug trade to finance their struggle," thereby creating a "crime-terror nexus." Notable examples are Afghanistan and Colombia.[79] Nonetheless, the involvement of relatively rich Muslim individuals and groups in terrorist incidents and Muslim insurgency demonstrates the limitations of the private motivations hypothesis in accounting for many contemporary conflicts from a Muslim perspective. Yet Western interventions have been attributed to the expectation of commercial profits from natural resources (especially oil) and from "reconstruction" of postwar economies (well exemplified by the case of Iraq), gives some credence to the hypothesis that private motivations play an important role in some of the Western motivation underlying the war against terror.

It is more difficult to employ the failed social contract hypothesis to explain the new international security environment, because there is no clear "international social contract" in the absence of global government. This approach, however, brings attention to the failure of major Western countries and international institutions, such as the United Nations and the Bretton Woods institutions, to achieve development and security for all. The enduring poverty in some parts of the world breeds discontent and resentment, makes local conflict and political disintegration more likely, and provides some sort of "haven" for global "terrorists" and a location for the illegal movement of goods and funds to finance global conflicts.

The relationship between resource scarcity/distribution and the new international security environment is an important area for investigation. Even before the invasion of Iraq, scholars and political commentators were noting that "the determination to ensure US access to overseas supplies of vital resources . . . [and] the protection of global resource flows is becoming an increasingly prominent feature of the American security policy."[80] Oil is not the only global resource that is linked to the international security environment. Control of water resources has been linked in particular to the Israeli occupation of Palestinian territory, a claim that long predates the current transformation of international security.[81] Empirical research has found some evidence linking water resources to international conflict, although the causality is not clear.[82]

It was argued earlier that preventive policies toward conflict need to address the underlying causes, including inequality, unemployment, and poverty. This remains true in the new environment, although it is now necessary to consider not just domestic inequality but also global inequality. Yet the global remedies adopted to date have not been of that kind; they have consisted of the provision of military support and aid to improve the repression of rebellion and support for the interdiction of financial flows that might fund such rebellions. Similarly, dialogue with developing countries facing conflict has focused on repression rather than development, while military resource transfers to vulnerable countries, such as Pakistan, greatly exceed development support.

Economic and technological globalization has brought enhanced globalization of motives for, and finance of, conflict. A new security agenda has emerged aimed at suppressing terrorism globally, but it has not been accompanied by the type of social, economic, and political policies needed for sustained conflict prevention.

CONCLUSION

Although much contemporary conflict seems to be about political, ethnic, or religious differences, in fact these conflicts generally have an economic and a political basis. HIs form one fundamental economic and political cause. Others include poor economic opportunities and deficient social services leading to a failed social contract, environmental degradation, and the potential enrichment that accompanies some conflicts. These motives have global as well as domestic dimensions.

Appropriate policies depend on the specific situation; notably, which of these underlying causes is most applicable. Hence, careful analysis of the local situation is essential. For prevention, it is imperative to address political as well as economic inequalities. Many of the policies needed for conflict prevention and for the protection of people during war differ from the policies currently advocated (and often required) by the international development community, especially by the international financial institutions. The new security environment has increased the global nature of conflicts and supported governments' capacity to repress rebellions, but it has not addressed the underlying economic, social, or political causes.

NOTES

We are grateful for extremely helpful comments from the editors of this volume.

1. Human development data taken from the United Nations Development Programme (UNDP) dataset at http://hdr.undp.org/. Conflict data taken from the Uppsala/PRIO Armed Conflict Dataset, available at http://www.pcr.uu.se/research/ucdp/datasets/ucdp_prio_armed_conflict_dataset/.

2. Paul Collier et al., *Breaking the Conflict Trap: Civil War and Development Policy* (Washington, DC: World Bank; Oxford: Oxford University Press, 2003).

3. Frances Stewart and Valpy Fitzgerald, eds., *War and Underdevelopment: The Economic and Social Consequences of Conflict* (Oxford: Oxford University Press, 2001), table 4.3.

4. Juha Auvinen and E. Wayne Nafziger, "The Sources of Humanitarian Emergencies," *Journal of Conflict Resolution* 43, no. 3 (1999): 267–90.

5. For example, see Samuel P. Huntington, "The Clash of Civilizations?" *Foreign Affairs* 72, no. 3 (1993): 22–49.

6. James D. Fearon and David D. Laitin, "Explaining Interethnic Cooperation," *American Political Science Review* 90, no. 4 (1996): 715–35.

7. Abner Cohen, *Two-Dimensional Man: An Essay on the Anthropology of Power and Symbolism in Complex Society* (Berkeley: University of California Press, 1974), 94.

8. Ted Robert Gurr, *Minorities at Risk: A Global View of Ethnopolitical Conflicts* (Washington, DC: United States Institute of Peace Press, 1993); and Donald L. Horowitz, *Ethnic Groups in Conflict* (Berkeley: University of California Press, 1985).

9. "Ethnic groups are defined by ascriptive differences, whether the indicum is color, appearance, language, *religion*, some other indicator of common origin, or some combination thereof." See Horowitz, *Ethnic Groups in Conflict*, 17 (emphasis added).

10. Frances Stewart, "Religion versus Ethnicity as a Source of Mobilization: Are There Differences?" in *Understanding Collective Political Violence*, ed. Yvan Guichaoua, (London: Palgrave Macmillan, 2012), 196–221.

11. Ted Robert Gurr, *Why Men Rebel* (Princeton, NJ: Princeton University Press, 1970); Gurr, *Minorities at Risk;* and Frances Stewart, "Horizontal Inequalities: A Neglected Dimension of Development," in A. B. Atkinson et al., eds., *Wider Perspectives on Global Development* (Basingstoke: Palgrave Macmillan, 2005), 101–35.

12. Anna Dimitrijevics, "Integrating Patterns of Conflict Resolution: A Group-Oriented Approach to the Study of the Genesis and Dynamics of Conflict" (DPhil thesis, Oxford University, 2004).

13. Luca Mancini, "Horizontal Inequality and Communal Violence: Evidence from Indonesian Districts," CRISE Working Paper no. 22 (Centre for Research on Inequality, Human Security and Ethnicity, Oxford University, Oxford, 2005).

14. Scott Gates and Mansoob S. Murshed, "Spatial-Horizontal Inequality and the Maoist Insurgency in Nepal," *Review of Development Economics* 9, no. 1 (2005).

15. Gudrun Østby, *Do Horizontal Inequalities Matter for Civil Conflict?* (Oslo: Centre for Study of Civil War/International Peace Research Institute Oslo, 2004); and Gudrun Østby, Ragnhild Nordås, and Jan Ketil Rød, "Regional Inequalities and Civil Conflict in Sub-Saharan Africa," *International Studies Quarterly* 53, no. 2 (2009): 301–24.

16. Graham K. Brown, "The Political Economy of Secessionism: Identity, Inequality and the State," Bath Papers in International Development, Working Paper no. 9 (Centre for Development Studies, University of Bath, 2010).

17. Lars-Erik Cederman, Nils B. Weidmann, and Kristian Skrede Gleditsch, "Horizontal Inequalities and Ethnonationalist Civil War: A Global Comparison," *American Political Science Review* 105, no. 3 (2011): 478–95; and Lars-Erik Cederman, Kristian Skrede Gleditsch, and Halvard Buhaug, *Inequality, Grievances and Civil War* (Cambridge: Cambridge University Press, 2013.

18. Arnim Langer, "Horizontal Inequalities and Violent Group Mobilisation in Côte d'Ivoire," *Oxford Development Studies* 33, no. 1 (2005): 25–45.

19. Gudrun Østby, "Inequalities, the Political Environment and Civil Conflict: Evidence from 55 Countries," in *Horizontal Inequalities and Conflict: Understanding Group Violence in Multiethnic Societies*, ed. Frances Stewart (London: Palgrave Macmillan, 2008); and Cederman et al., "Horizontal Inequalities and Ethnonationalist Civil War."

20. David Keen, *The Economic Functions of Violence in Civil War* (Oxford: Oxford University Press, for the International Institute of Strategic Studies, 1998); Mark R. Duffield, "The Political Economy of Internal War: Asset Transfer, Complex Emergencies and International Aid," in *War and Hunger: Rethinking International Responses to Complex Emergencies,* Joanna Macrae and Anthony Zwi, ed. (London: Zed, 1994); and Paul Collier and Anke Hoeffler, "Greed and Grievance in Civil War," *Oxford Economic Papers* 56 (2004): 563–95.

21. Jack Hirshleifer, "The Dark Side of the Force," *Economic Inquiry* 32, no. 1 (1994): 1–10.

22. Paul Collier, *Economic Causes of Conflict and Their Implications for Policy* (Washington, DC: World Bank, 2000), 5.

23. Collier and Hoeffler, "Greed and Grievance in Civil War."

24. James D. Fearon, "Primary Commodity Exports and Civil War," *Journal of Conflict Resolution* 49, no. 4 (2005): 483–507. See also the other papers on the subject in this special issue.

25. James D. Fearon and David D. Laitin, "Ethnicity, Insurgency and Civil War," *American Political Science Review* 97, no. 1 (2003): 75–90; and Macartan Humphreys and Ashutosh Varshney, "Violence Conflict and the Millennium Development Goals: Diagnosis and Recommendations," CSGD Working Paper Series (Columbia University, New York, 2004).

26. Karen Ballentine and Jake Sherman, *The Political Economy of Armed Conflict: Beyond Greed and Grievance* (Boulder, CO: Lynne Rienner, 2003), 259–60.

27. Elisabeth Jean Wood, *Insurgent Collective Action and Civil War in El Salvador* (Cambridge, Cambridge University Press, 2003); Luisa Maria Dietrich Ortega, "Gendered Patterns of Mobilization and Recruitment for Political Violence: Experiences from Three Latin American Countries, in *Understanding Collective Political Violence*, ed. Yvan Guichaoua (London: Palgrave, 2012), 84–104; Yvan Guichaoua, "The Making of an Ethnic Militia: The Oodua People's Congress in Nigeria," CRISE Working Paper no. 26 (Centre for Research on Inequality, Human Security and Ethnicity, Oxford University, Oxford, 2006); Yvan Guichaoua, "Introduction: Individual Drivers of Collective Violence and the Dynamics of Armed Groups," in *Understanding Collective Political Violence,* ed. Yvan Guichaoua (London: Palgrave: 2012), 1–20; and Francisco Gutiérrez Sanin, "Criminal Rebels? A Discussion of Civil War and Criminality from the Colombian Experience," *Politics and Society* 32, no. 2 (2004): 257–85.

28. Collier, *Economic Causes of Conflict,* 5.

29. Ibid., 10.

30. Gutiérrez Sanín, "Criminal Rebels?"

31. Anthony D. Smith, "The Nation: Invented, Imagined, Reconstructed?" *Millennium: Journal of International Studies* 20 (1991): 353–68.

32. Tony Addison and Mansoob S. Murshed, "Post-Conflict Reconstruction in Africa: Some Analytical Issues," in *Post-Conflict Economies in Africa,* Paul Collier and Augustin Kwasi Fosu, ed. (London: Palgrave, 2005); and E. Wayne Nafziger and Juha Auvinen, "The Economic Causes of Humanitarian Emergencies," in *War, Hunger and Displacement: The Origin of Humanitarian Emergencies,* vol. 1, ed. E. Wayne Nafziger, Frances Stewart, and Raimi Väyrynen (Oxford: Oxford University Press, 2000).

33. Collier and Hoeffler, "Greed and Grievance in Civil War"; Ibrahim Elbadawi and Nicholas Sambanis, "How Much War Will We See? Estimating the Incidence of Civil War in 161 Countries," *Journal of Conflict Resolution* 46, no. 3 (2002): 307–34; and Nafziger and Auvinen, "Economic Causes of Humanitarian Emergencies."

34. See, for example, Tanja Ellingsen, "Colorful Community or Ethnic Witches' Brew? Multiethnicity and Domestic Conflict during and after the Cold War," *Journal of Conflict Resolution* 44, no. 2 (2000): 228–49.

35. Jack Snyder, *From Voting to Violence* (New York: W. W. Norton, 2000).

36. Edward D. Mansfield and Jack Snyder, *Electing to Fight: Why Emerging Democracies Go to War* (Cambridge MA: MIT Press, 2007).

37. Marta Reynal-Querol, "Political Systems, Stability and Civil Wars," *Defence and Peace Economics* 13, no. 6 (2002): 465–83.

38. Thomas Homer-Dixon, "On the Threshold: Environmental Changes as Causes of Acute Conflict," *International Security* 16, no. 2 (1991): 76–116; Thomas Homer-Dixon, "Environmental Scarcities and Violent Conflict: Evidence from Cases," *International Security* 19, no. 1 (1994): 5–40; and Val Percival and Thomas Homer-Dixon, "Environmental Scarcity and Violent Conflict: The Case of South Africa," *Journal of Peace Research* 35, no. 3 (1998): 279–98.

39. Homer-Dixon, "Environmental Scarcities and Violent Conflict," 6.

40. Percival and Homer-Dixon, "Environmental Scarcity and Violent Conflict," 280.

41. Homer-Dixon, "Environmental Scarcities and Violent Conflict," 6.

42. Percival and Homer-Dixon, "Environmental Scarcity and Violent Conflict," 280.

43. Robert Kaplan, "The Coming Anarchy: How Scarcity, Crime, Overpopulation and Disease Are Threatening the Social Fabric of Our Planet," *Atlantic Monthly,* February 1994, 44–74.

44. James Fairhead, "The Conflict over Natural and Environmental Resources," in Nafziger, Stewart, and Väyrynen, *War, Hunger and Displacement.*

45. Nils Petter Gleditsch, "Armed Conflict and the Environment: A Critique of the Literature," *Journal of Peace Research* 35, no. 3 (1998): 381–400; and Marc Levy, "Is the Environment a National Security Issue?" *International Security* 20, no. 2 (1995): 35–62.

46. Ole Magnus Theisen, Nils Petter Gleditsch, and Halvard Buhaug, "Climate Change and Armed Conflict," in *The Elgar Handbook of Civil War and Fragile States*, ed. Graham K. Brown and Arnim Langer (Cheltenham, England: Edward Elgar, 2012.

47. David Keen, *The Benefits of Famine: A Political Economy of Famine Relief in Southwestern Sudan, 1883–1989* (Princeton, NJ: Princeton University Press, 1994).

48. Alex Cobham, "Causes of Conflict in Sudan: Testing the Black Book," *European Journal of Development Research* 17, no. 3 (2005): 462–80.

49. Ian Bannon and Paul Collier (2003). *Natural Resources and Armed Conflict: Options and Actions* (Washington, DC: World Bank, 2003); and Philippe Le Billon, Wars *of Plunder, Conflicts, Profits and the Politics of Resources* (New York: Columbia University Press, 2012).

50. Jeremy M. Weinstein, *Inside Rebellion: The Politics of Insurgent Violence* (Cambridge: Cambridge University Press, 2007).

51. The most recent data from the World Bank's World Development Indicators shows that for Egypt, the $1.25 head-count poverty rate was 2.0 percent in 2005, while the $2.00-a-day rate was 18.5 percent and for Syria in 2004, the $1.25 poverty rate was 1.7 percent and the $2.00 a day was 16.9 percent.

52. For exploration of policies during the war stage, see Stewart and Fitzgerald, *War and Underdevelopment.*

53. Astri Suhrke, and Ingrid Samset (2007). "What's in a Figure? Estimating Recurrence of Civil War." *Journal of International Peacekeeping* 14, no. 2: 195–203.

54. Alexis de Tocqueville, *Democracy in America*, vol. 1 (New York: Vintage, 1954).

55. See Frances Stewart, "Policies towards Horizontal Inequalities in Post-Conflict Reconstruction," CRISE Working Paper no. 7 (Centre for Research on Inequality, Human Security and Ethnicity, Oxford University, Oxford, 2005), appendixes A2 and A3.

56. Vedi R. Hadiz, "Decentralisation and Democracy in Indonesia: A Critique of Neo-Institutionalist Perspectives," *Development and Change* 35, no. 4 (2004): 697–718.

57. A possible counterexample here is Israel, which practices proportional representation, although the conflict with the Palestinians is not an "internal" conflict per se.

58. According to Mona Lena Krook and Diana Z. O'Brien, "The Politics of Group Representation: Quotas for Women and Minorities Worldwide," *Comparative Politics* 42, no. 3 (2010): 252–72, over a hundred countries have quotas for the representation of women, and over thirty for the representation of minorities.

59. Horowitz, *Ethnic Groups in Conflict*.

60. Snyder, *From Voting to Violence*; and Frances Stewart and Meghan O'Sullivan, "Democracy, Conflict and Development: Three Cases," in *The Political Economy of Comparative Development into the 21st Century: Essays in Memory of John C. H. Fei*, vol. 1, ed. Gustav Ranis, Sheng-Chen Hu, and Yu-Peng Chu (Cheltenham, England: Edward Elgar, 1999).

61. Corinne Caumartin and Diego Sanchez-Ancochea, "Explaining a Contradictory Record: The Case of Guatemala" in *Horizontal Inequalities and Post-Conflict Development,* ed. Arnim Langer, Frances Stewart, and Rajesh Venugopal (London: Palgrave, 2012); Servaas van den Berg and Megan Louw, "Changing Patterns of South African Income Distribution: Towards Time Series Estimates of Distribution and Poverty," *South African Journal of Economics* 72, no. 3 (2004).

62. Stewart, "Policies towards Horizontal Inequalities," appendix A1.

63. Frances Stewart, "Horizontal Inequalities in Kenya and the Political Disturbances of 2008: Some Implications for Aid Policy," *Conflict, Security and Development* 10, no. 1 (2010): 133–59.

64. Graham Brown, "Balancing the Risks of Corrective Surgery: The Political Economy of Horizontal Inequalities and the End of the New Economic Policy in Malaysia," CRISE Working Paper no. 20 (Centre for Research on Inequality, Human Security and Ethnicity, Oxford University, Oxford, 2005).

65. Collier et al., *Breaking the Conflict Trap*; and United Nations Development Programme, *Human Development Report 2005* (New York: United Nations, 2005).

66. United Nations Development Programme, *Human Development Report 2004* (New York: United Nations, 2004).

67. Langer, Stewart, and Venugopal, eds., *Horizontal Inequalities and Post-Conflict Development*.

68. Tilman Brück, Valpy Fitzgerald, and Arturo Grigsby, "Enhancing the Private Sector Contribution to Post-War Recovery in Poor Countries," Queen Elizabeth House Working Paper no. 45 (Queen Elizabeth House, Department of International Development, Oxford University, 2000).

69. James K. Boyce, *Investing in Peace: Aid and Conditionality and Civil Wars* (London: International Institute for Strategic Studies, 2002).

70. Collier et al., *Breaking the Conflict Trap*.

71. Stewart, "Policies towards Horizontal Inequalities."

72. S. Fukuda-Parr, "Correcting Horizontal Inequalities as a Development Priority: Poverty Reduction Strategy Papers (PRSPs) in Haiti, Liberia and Nepal," in Langer, Stewart, and Venugopal, *Horizontal Inequalities and Post-Conflict Development*, 84–107.

73. Graham Brown, "Nepal: First Steps towards Redressing HIs?" in Langer, Stewart, and Venugopal, *Horizontal Inequalities and Post-Conflict Development*, 256–96.

74. Frances Stewart and Graham Brown, "The Implications of Horizontal Inequality for Aid" CRISE Working Paper, no. 36 (Centre for Research on Inequality, Human Security and Ethnicity, Oxford University, Oxford, 2006).

75. Frances Stewart, "Global Aspects and Implications of Horizontal Inequalities: Inequalities Experienced by Muslims Worldwide," in *Global Governance, Poverty and Inequality,* Jennifer Clapp and Rorden Wilkinson ed. (London: Routledge, 2010), 265–94.

76. Xavier Sala-i-Martin, "The Disturbing 'Rise' of Global Income Inequality," Working Paper 8904 (National Bureau of Economic Research, Cambridge, MA, 2002); and Branco Milanovic, "Half a World: Regional Inequality in Five Great Federations," World Bank Policy Research Working Paper 3699 (World Bank, Washington, DC, 2005).

77. Abdullah Ahmad Badawi (speech at the Oxford Centre of Islamic Studies, Magdalen College, Oxford University, 2004).

78. Mark R. Duffield, *Global Governance and the New Wars: The Merging of Development and Security* (London: Zed, 2001).

79. Svante E. Cornell, "The Interaction of Narcotics and Conflict," *Journal of Peace Research* 42, no. 6 (2005): 751–60.

80. Michael T. Klare, *Resource Wars: The New Landscape of Global Conflict* (New York: Henry Holt, 2001), 6.

81. See, for example, Sharif S. Elmusa, "The Land-Water Nexus in the Israel-Palestinian Conflict," *Journal of Palestine Studies* 25, no. 3 (1996): 69–78.

82. Nils Petter Gleditsch et al., "Conflict over Shared Rivers: Resource Wars or Fuzzy Boundaries?" *Political Geography* 25, no. 7 (2006).

13

CRIME-WAR BATTLEFIELDS

Vanda Felbab-Brown

Military conflicts around the world increasingly conjoin political violence, organized crime and illicit economies. In many regions, domestic law enforcement responses to organized crime resemble warfare. Government suppression of urban crime and rural instability in Latin America and South Asia, for example, progressively merges police and military operations. In Mexico, Brazil, and Central America, clashes between criminals and the authorities often have the intensity of intrastate urban conflict.

Modern militaries were not designed or trained to deal with illicit economies and organized crime. Nonetheless, the frequency and intensity of international military action at the nexus of violent conflict and crime have increased since the 1990s. Training police forces and devising responses to rising crime have been a key feature, and deficiency, of the counterinsurgency effort in Afghanistan. NATO works alongside the Chinese and Saudi militaries in antipiracy patrols off the coast of Somalia, in what would normally be regarded as law enforcement operations.

Although criminals and militants often interact with illicit economies in the same way, it is rare for such groups to merge into a homogenous, monolithic entity. Rather, when a crime-terror or crime-insurgency nexus emerges, their interactions will be unstable. Accordingly, countering domestic crime that threatens national security, or resolving military conflicts that involve criminals and illicit economies, requires a complex, nuanced, and carefully calibrated response.

URBAN AND LOW-INTENSITY WARFARE

An example of extraordinarily destructive crime that threatens national security is drug trade violence in Mexico, which has claimed almost 50,000 lives since 2006, including over 12,300 in 2011 and over 9,100 in 2012.[1] More than 25,000 people in Mexico have disappeared since 2006.[2] The country's drug-trafficking organizations engage in bloody territorial disputes over smuggling routes and corruption networks, and have made gun battles and murders common occurrences in some Mexican cities. These groups show a determination to fight Mexican law enforcement and security forces, and a burgeoning ambition to control other illicit and informal economies in the country, including the extortion of legal businesses. In parts of Mexico, criminal gangs dominate the lives of entire municipalities and their reach extends to state governments.[3] Some analysts have described this conflict, which has spread into Central America, as a "criminal insurgency," a label the Mexican government angrily rejects.[4]

In many parts of the world, not only remote rural peripheries but also prominent urban areas are becoming crime-war battlefields.[5] Criminal violence in Karachi resembles low-intensity warfare, and can even be regarded as a microcosm of a complex civil war, with hundreds to thousands of casualties per year. Conflict in the city combines terrorism, ethnic militancy, and political mobilization with mafia fights and territorial disputes. It is also intricately linked to major political actors in Pakistan who pursue their agendas by exploiting ethnic tensions and manipulating criminal groups. Political parties benefit from the violence by demanding votes and money from the city's residents, and Inter-Services Intelligence, the country's intelligence directorate, often uses the conflict to justify its interference with government affairs.[6]

Operations combating this kind of urban violence increasingly resemble military action. In cities such as Medellín, Kingston, Rio de Janeiro, and Ciudad Juárez, the authorities have deployed heavily armed police or military forces to retake territories in urban slums largely governed by criminal or insurgent groups. Brazil received international attention for its pacification policies in the shanty towns of São Paulo and Rio in the 2000s.[7] In Rio, the Brazilian government pioneered the Unidade de Policía Pacíficadora (Police Pacification Unit) program, which entailed the forced takeover of territories and their subsequent handover to community police forces in the city's poor and crime-ridden favelas, inhabited by 1.2 million of its 6 million residents.[8] Program outposts were established in the slums, particularly near World Cup 2014 and Olympics 2016 venues, and

major transport arteries. Policies in both Rio and São Paulo drew from a similar earlier program entitled Grupamento de Policiamento em Áreas Especiais (Group Policing of Special Areas), which was implemented with varied success in Rio in 2000.[9] All of these policies have sought to break with Brazil's past marginalization and isolation of poor communities through the construction of walls around shanty towns, which resulted in violent and highly repressive police raids on gang-controlled territories that were ineffective in the long term.

Former Mexican president Felipe Calderón deployed regular army troops in law enforcement roles in Ciudad Juárez, Tijuana, and other cities affected by intense drug-related violence. His strategy was based on the premise that corruption and a lack of resources prevented the police from adequately dealing with the violence or reducing the power of drug-trafficking organizations. The plan also called for the reform and retraining of the police, who would resume their duties after the military ensured that such groups were no longer a threat to national security. Ciudad Juárez's municipal police returned to their posts following a 2-percent drop in criminal violence (from its peak in autumn 2011) and significant reductions in military deployment in 2010 and federal police deployment in 2011. Significantly, troops were withdrawn more because of public dissatisfaction with their behavior than because of their effectiveness in reducing violence and criminality.[10] Ultimately, the Sinaloa Cartel's takeover of large portions of the city's criminal markets and smuggling routes, combined with new initiatives by the police, such as hotspot policing, meant that in winter 2012 murder rates had declined by 40 percent from peak levels in 2009–10.

The counterinsurgency and law enforcement policies implemented in Medellín in the 2000s followed a similar pattern. In 2002, former Colombian president Álvaro

Uribe initiated Operatión Orión, which deployed the military to retake the city's poor *comunas* (communes), ruled by the Revolutionary Armed Forces of Colombia (FARC). Orión defeated the FARC in Medellín but allowed Diego Murillo "Don Berna" Bejarano, a crime lord and paramilitary leader, to consolidate his control of the city's criminal markets. Bejarano's rule of the *comunas* and a panoply of criminal rackets in the city resulted in a significant drop in homicides in 2000–10, and Medellín mayors Sergio Fajardo and Alonso Salazar took advantage of the city's improved security to develop infrastructure in these impoverished areas. However, Bejarano's imprisonment and extradition to the United States in May 2008 precipitated new violence in Medellín as various criminal groups fought for control of drug smuggling and distribution, prostitution, extortion, and gambling in the city.[11] This period of violence subsided only when Oficina de Envigado (The Office), the crime group that Maximiliano Bonilla "Valenciano" Orozco inherited from Bejarano, won the battle. His arrest in November 2012 set off another succession conflict between his organization and rival group Los Urabeños (those from Urabá), although, so far, it has not escalated to the levels seen in 2008–09.

The Tivoli Gardens area of Kingston has been ruled by drug gangs linked to Jamaican political parties for several decades, and was controlled by drug lord Christopher "Dudus" Coke from the 1990s and until 2010. After finally yielding to US pressure to arrest and extradite Coke in 2010, then-Jamaican prime minister Bruce Golding sent a heavily armed force to Tivoli Gardens in an operation that also resembled urban warfare more than a standard arrest. Golding later promised to implement community policing and social development programs in the area but failed to do so.

Increasingly, perceptions of public safety and the state's effectiveness and accountability are determined by how well it responds to crime and insecurity in urban areas. Yet in many of the world's major cities, law enforcement and social development programs have not been adequately adapted to increases in population. There is a deep and growing divide between developed and reasonably safe sectors of economic growth and social advancement, and slums mired in poverty, marginalization, and violence. Addressing such violence and improving these areas will be a major challenge for many governments.

COMPETITIVE STATE BUILDING

Effective public safety and internal security policies addressing intensely violent crime need to be thought of as competitive state building between the government and nongovernmental actors rather than as strategies for suppressing aberrant social behavior. Extensive criminality and illicit economies pose many threats to states and societies. They undermine democratic processes by allowing criminal organizations to gain political influence. Political entrepreneurs, who enjoy the financial and political resources generated through their connections to illicit economies, are frequently successful in securing official positions and wielding influence from behind the scenes. Moreover, the success of one such entrepreneur encourages other politicians to act in the same way and may lead to endemic corruption at both the local and national levels. Afghanistan, Guatemala, El Salvador, and Haiti are cases in point.

The spread of illicit economies run by traffickers also undermines the effectiveness of, and may corrupt, the police and judiciary. Where crime is unpunished, the credibility and deterrent effects of law enforcement, the judiciary, and government authority are diminished. To discourage prosecution, powerful traffickers frequently resort to murdering or bribing prosecutors, judges, and witnesses.

Late-1980s Colombia and present-day Mexico have shown how extensive criminal networks may corrupt and paralyze law enforcement and high levels of violent crime may harm the judiciary. The Guatemalan government accepted assistance from the International Commission against Impunity in Guatemala, a UN body created to help reconstruct the country's legal system and combat organized crime and state corruption, after Guatemala's judiciary virtually collapsed as a result of infiltration by criminal groups.

Illicit economies also have large, complex effects on the legal economy. Drug cultivation and processing, for example, often create employment for poor rural populations and may even improve their social mobility. In Afghanistan, the drug trade generates around 20–30 percent of the country's GDP, and directly and indirectly employs around 20 percent of the populace.[12] The illegal sector can have powerful microeconomic spillover effects that boost overall economic activity, such as in the Mexican state of Sinaloa, where drug smuggling has driven demand for goods and services, and indirectly improved the livelihoods of poor populations. The drug trade is estimated to provide 20 percent of Sinaloa's contribution to GDP, and may have an even more significant impact on some of the country's southern states.[13]

The negative effects of a burgeoning drug trade may include increased inflation, which can harm tourism and exports. It can also encourage real estate speculation, undermine currency stability, and displace legitimate production. Because the drug trade is more profitable than legal production and has lower transaction and sunk costs, local populations are frequently uninterested, or unable to participate, in legal economic activity. The presence of a large-scale illicit economy can therefore lead to stagnation in other core economic sectors because it increases land

and labor costs. Although US firms continue to invest in Mexico, drug violence in the country has not only undermined public safety but also decreased tourism in areas such as Acapulco.[14]

CRIME AND HUMAN SECURITY

The relationship between crime and wider society is often highly complex. For many marginalized people in areas of weakened state influence and institutional capacity, informal or illegal economies provide the only means of survival and social advancement, despite the threat they may pose to individual and national security. A state's absence or inability to provide public services increases the likelihood that communities will become dependent on, and supporters of, criminal or militant groups tied to illegal economies. Particularly important to this relationship are public safety, suppression of street crime, access to justice, infrastructure, health care, education, and legal employment. The damage caused by state failure to provide such services is particularly apparent in areas affected by violent conflict.

Participation in illicit economies may therefore allow belligerent groups to gain significant political capital in the support of local populations, whose livelihood they protect from government attempts to suppress illegal trade.[15] They also obtain such capital by protecting producers (such as drug-trade farmers) from brutal and unreliable traffickers, driving out foreign competitors and investing in social services, goods, and infrastructure.[16] In Brazil, for example, this type of investment has allowed drug gangs to dominate many poor urban areas. Ironically, criminal groups often provide what little security there is in these territories by regulating violence and suppressing particular kinds of crime, such as theft, robbery, and rape.[17] Organizations such as São Paulo's Primeiro Comando da Capital (First

Capital Command) even resolve disputes, establish courts, and enforce contracts.[18]

Nonstate actors often recognize that accruing political capital may cause grateful communities to withhold intelligence from state officials investigating their activities. Such intelligence is frequently vital to the success of counterterrorism, counterinsurgency, and law enforcement efforts. These actors challenge the government by becoming alternate providers of political-economic regulation and public goods and services, and may establish effective alternative governance, including even self-rule in some territories.

STATE RESPONSES
TO ORGANIZED CRIME

To reduce crime in areas dominated by the illicit economies of nonstate actors, governments need to engage in state building that strengthens their relationship with local communities. This approach requires governments to address the causes of popular support for illegal activity. Such initiatives need to ensure not only that crime is punished but also that laws are consistent with local needs and can be seen as legitimate by the populace.

States always need to respond to pervasive crime with law enforcement initiatives, and usually with accompanying measures in other areas. A lack of public safety and effective enforcement of rules and agreements will weaken socioeconomic approaches to crime, hamper legal economies with violence, reduce local investment, and damage social capital. Effective law enforcement strategies may include establishing a permanent police presence and developing local forces; adopting approaches such as problem-oriented and community policing; quickly enacting schemes to combat street crime or train specialized interdiction units and comprehensive institutional reform. Governments need to carefully assess local conditions to decide

the order in which aspects of such strategies are implemented.[19]

Effective responses to crime need to include well-designed socioeconomic policies that address the causes of criminality. Generating legal alternatives to economically motivated participation in crime requires a development strategy that addresses the structural drivers of illegal economic production. A comprehensive approach to combating crime also requires that the state provide stable property rights, access to microcredit, inclusive education and health care, and effective major infrastructure.[20]

INTERNATIONAL MILITARY FORCES

Modern militaries have both fought against and, occasionally, employed criminal groups. Japanese forces occupying China during World War II had to battle the powerful Green Gang, a criminal group led by Du Yuesheng, for control of Shanghai.[21] Acting on assistance and intelligence from the Mafia was an integral part of the US campaign in Sicily in the same war.[22] Many twentieth-century insurgencies, including, famously, Mao Zedong's Long March, involved illicit economies.[23] Since the 1990s, international military forces have increasingly encountered illicit economies and criminal actors in humanitarian interventions (Somalia) and peacekeeping in civil wars (Sierra Leone), and in dealing with terrorism and failed states. The wars in the Balkans in the early to mid-1990s involved extensive smuggling operations and illicit economies that developed in response to international sanctions and embargoes.[24] Prior to his deposal in 2003, former Iraqi president Saddam Hussein frustrated international efforts to isolate his regime by using sanctions as a basis for a lucrative illicit economy.

In the 1990s, the end of the Cold War and the overwhelming victory of the United States in Operation Desert Storm produced a widespread belief that the era of interstate warfare was largely over. Analyzing genocide in Rwanda, rebellion in Chechnya, and intensifying civil war in Colombia, scholars such as Mary Kaldor and Mark Duffield described contemporary war as internal, disorganized, and blurring the line between civilians and combatants.[25] Paul Collier, Mats Berdal, David Keen, and other analysts argued that wars were increasingly driven by economic motives rather than ideology or political grievances, and created their own systems of rents rather than destroying economic order altogether.[26] Al Qaeda's attacks on 9/11, returned ideology to the center of thinking about world politics, but the new focus on nonstate actors and territories in which state presence was weak remained a preoccupation of many military and foreign policy strategists.

This preoccupation with the relationship between illegal economies and political violence is reflected in the way in which counterterrorism, counterinsurgency, and state building in Afghanistan is tied to policies for dealing with the country's narcotics trade. It is also shown in recent anti-crime initiatives such as the anti-piracy patrols off the coast of Somalia previously mentioned. The stability of, and fate of democracy in, Libya and Egypt following the Arab Spring will be determined by the success with which the countries' governments combat rising crime and prevent law enforcement agencies from being used for political oppression.

In dealing with illicit economies, international peacekeepers and intervention forces face difficult dilemmas. Criminal actors, including warlords and local officials, may spoil peace processes begun by the intervening powers. For such initiatives to succeed, these actors must therefore be placated or removed through new political arrangements or the use of military force (although the latter may require more resources than

the intervening powers are willing to offer). Forcibly removing such actors is further complicated if they provide critical intelligence or military support. In Afghanistan in 2001–02, for example, US forces relied on intelligence and military assistance from warlords, many of whom were or became major drug traffickers.[27] ISAF (International Security Assistance Force) troops in the country continue to rely on power brokers involved in criminal activity.[28]

Elsewhere, political entrepreneurs with extensive criminal connections have prolonged military conflicts for financial gain. Former Liberian president Charles Taylor's schemes for acquiring diamonds in his country and Sierra Leone may be the most notorious examples of this type of corruption.[29] The empowerment of such actors through cooperation with international forces or inclusion in postintervention or postconflict political systems may result in governance that is both unpalatable to the intervening powers and regarded as discriminatory, predatory, and exclusionary by the local populace. Postintervention political structures linked to illicit economies are likely to be as unstable as the system of governance they replaced.[30] Yet removal of an illicit economy on which large segments of populace depend may be equally destabilizing, and is likely to increase distrust of international forces.

THE STATE AS MAFIA BAZAAR

Although illicit economies are longestablished features of postwar states, such environments have seen significant recent changes to the types of illegal activity that occur, the distribution of power in criminal markets, and the effect of crime on political structures.[31] Criminal and political systems in these settings frequently originate in patronage, corruption, and rent networks that precede recent conflicts.

The quantity of drugs trafficked through West Africa, especially cocaine from South America en route to Europe, has increased dramatically over the past decade.[32] Driven by rising demand for cocaine in Western Europe, falling demand for the drug in the United States, and pressure on smuggling from interdiction operations in the Caribbean, a quarter of all cocaine consumed in Europe is now transported through the region.[33] Countries such as Guinea-Bissau are rife with drug-related violence and political instability, and many analysts argue that organized crime poses a significant threat to the rule of law and quality of governance in the region.

Many institutional networks and illicit economies in West Africa are well-established and predate intensive drug trafficking in the region. Indeed, various economies of this kind are deeply integrated into national political systems. Political competition in the region has often focused on using the state to gain access to major sources of revenue, such as control rents from a range of legal, semi-illegal, and illegal economies.[34] These include human trafficking (Mali, Togo, and Ghana) and trade in precious metals, stones, and timber (Sierra Leone and Liberia); crops (Côte d'Ivoire); oil (Nigeria); and fish (often by international fleets). In essence, governance in the region has often been regarded as a means to personal wealth.[35]

Yet it is wrong to assume that the burgeoning drug trade in West Africa will create political instability by threatening the established political order. External drug traffickers may destabilize states by forming alliances with domestic opponents of a regime (such as current or former rebels, or new challengers seeking social mobility in an exclusive system) but they may also ally with and enrich governing elites. In the latter scenario, drug traffickers would benefit from illicit government protection, and while this would threaten democratic processes and the institutional development of the country, political stability may be maintained.[36] In many parts of the world where foreign actors pursue military, counterterrorism, humanitarian, or peacekeeping objectives, domestic governance is closely tied to criminal enterprises and ruling elites allow their clients and patronage networks to operate outside of legal constraints.

Whether West Africa's growing drug trade will foster international terrorism largely depends on local conditions and the skill of terrorist groups. The effectiveness of law enforcement in combating illegal economies will critically influence the development of a regional nexus of crime and terror. It is important to avoid inadvertently driving criminal and terrorist groups into partnerships in which they share networks, tactics, intelligence, and logistical operators. The formation of nexuses of crime and terror can be prevented, and those that exist are unstable. Indeed, relations between such groups are often characterized as much by violent internal conflict as by cooperation.[37] At most, such relationships are tactical alliances of convenience. The success with which international terrorist groups exploit illicit economies in new territories depends on their ability to gather intelligence, adapt to local culture, and understand complex national relationships between politics and crime.

DEALING WITH CRIME IN VIOLENT CONFLICTS

International forces that encounter illicit economies in violent conflicts must devise policies that are highly specific to local institutions and culture. Nonetheless, important lessons can be drawn from past conflicts in which crime has played a major role.

International peacekeeping forces need to operate on the premise that the weakening of a legal economy will strengthen the illicit economy that underpins it. Prominent military and political actors in the region, such as those connected with regionally recruited intervention forces, may also be deeply involved in the illicit economy and gain power and influence from their ability to use it to provide for the needs of the local populace. The way in which intervention forces engage with such actors will have profound effects on the structure of, and power distribution within, the illicit economy, and on the country itself. By interacting with influential local figures, such forces are able to alter the balance of power in the illicit economy and, accordingly, the political environment.

Rushing to destroy an illicit economy on which the populace relies without providing alternative sources of income or resources will hamper international peacekeeping and counterinsurgency efforts. Moreover, international forces will have limited success in suppressing illicit economies without a strong troop presence on the ground. Regardless of the methods used, anticrime initiatives will not be effective unless security has been established throughout the territory in which they are implemented. States must be strengthened and conflict ended for such initiatives to work.

The more limited the scope of an intervention, the greater the constraints on international forces in suppressing or restructuring nexuses of crime and conflict. Operations limited to aerial or naval bombardment will have difficulty tackling local illicit economies. Local proxies of international forces will have a higher chance of capturing not only political power in the postintervention phase but also the country's criminal markets. In such limited, arms-length interventions, establishing a relatively peaceful state controlled by proxy criminal groups may be the best that international forces can hope for.

Combating corruption and illicit economies in peacekeeping operations requires international forces to have a robust presence on the ground and a very detailed understanding of the connections between local crime, conflict, politics, and socioeconomic structures. Expanding the traditional role of peacekeeping forces to include anticrime initiatives therefore demands continual intelligence gathering to monitor how changes to illicit economies affect stability, development, and the distribution of political and economic power in the country. Peacekeepers need to be given strong intelligence and analytical support that includes experts on politics, economics, agriculture, anthropology, and crime.

Intervention forces rarely have a good understanding of local illicit economies and patronage networks, and often lack the capacity to combat organized or street crime (either directly or by training local police). Rises in street crime are often the first and most direct way that local populaces experience postintervention insecurity. Such crime may alienate the population from the state and intervention forces, increase popular support for the previous regime, strengthen extralegal power brokers, and even precipitate a wide-reaching criminal order. Military law enforcement and counterinsurgency operations are inadequate substitutes for traditional community-oriented policing. A determined, systematic effort to develop police forces capable of tackling street crime would therefore greatly enhance the effectiveness of international interventions.

States that decide to promote good governance and combat crime as part of an intervention need to plan such initiatives before taking action and implement them early in the operation. The period following the completion of initial military objectives is best suited to shaping a country's political and criminal environment. This is the phase of the operation in which local power brokers are most uncertain about the future and show restraint in challenging intervening states. Their networks of power have often been weakened by the collapse of the previous order and they will not have had time to reestablish control.

During this period, the local populace is also likely to work with intervening states in establishing a new order. In ideal circumstances, they will have disapproved of the previous political regime and be hopeful about the future. Locals who oppose the intervening state are likely to be uncertain about the extent of its power and fearful of actively resisting it. The longer intervention forces delay state building, the harder it becomes: new military opposition to the intervention may emerge, local power brokers may regain control, and the populace may become pessimistic about the future. Undoing such negative trends becomes harder with time, and renewing the support of the population is especially difficult. The window of opportunity closes rapidly and may never reopen. It is important to recognize, however, that the presence of peacekeeping forces is temporary. The suppression of illicit economies will only be sustained by providing the populace and government with economic and political incentives to support such action.

◆ ◆ ◆

It is unlikely that outside policy interventions will remove the majority of organized crime groups and illicit economies in postconflict environments, and the intervening powers need to identify which criminal networks must be combated first. These include organizations that have strong links to international terrorists, are most disruptive to the development of a fairer state, and fund and empower exclusive elites. Identifying the most important targets among such groups may occasionally be difficult, and could create significant policy challenges. When choosing a course of action, the likelihood that they will be successfully removed needs to be consid-

ered alongside the severity of the threat they pose to local society and the wider world.

It is important to recognize that indiscriminate law enforcement can have undesirable outcomes. Firstly, by removing the weakest criminal groups such an approach may inadvertently empower the stronger organizations that remain. Secondly, it may push criminal groups into alliances with terrorists. Both outcomes have often occurred in various regions of the world as a result of opportunistic, nonstrategic drug interdiction and law enforcement policies. Finally, in determining whether and how to combat crime, international forces need to analyze the potential indirect effects of their policies. For example, is illegal poppy cultivation more harmful in Afghanistan than in Pakistan, and should efforts to prevent such activity in the former be maximized? Will antipiracy efforts off the coast of Somalia merely push piracy from the Gulf of Aden into the wider Indian Ocean, and is this a better outcome? Will the imposition of international sanctions lead to new smuggling enterprises in the countries they affect, and who will profit from them?

Such questions do not have easy answers, and states are loath to contemplate them. By failing to analyze how illicit groups and economies could adapt to new policies, however, governments may make dealing with violent conflict all the more challenging.

NOTES

This chapter was originally published as Vanda Felbab-Brown, "Crime-War Battlefields," *Survival: Global Politics and Strategy* 55, no. 3 (June-July 2013): 147–166. Copyright © 2013 The International Institute for Strategic Studies, reprinted by permission of Taylor & Francis Ltd, www.tandfonline.com on behalf of The International Institute for Strategic Studies.

1. These figures are taken from *Reforma*, a Mexican newspaper that until November 30, 2012, reported statistics on drug-related homicides on a weekly basis. The government of Mexico often provided higher estimates, such as over sixty thousand killed in drug-related violence since 2006, with more than 16,600 deaths in 2011 alone. See Alfredo Corchado, "Violence Levels Off in Some Parts of Mexico, but Spreads to Others," *Dallas Morning News*, February 4, 2012, http://www.dallasnews.com/news/nationworld/mexico/pathofdestruction/20120204-violence-levels-off-in-some-parts-of-mexico-but-spreads-to-others.ece.

2. Ana Laura Magaloni Kerpel, "La Revisión del Pasado," *Reforma*, December 15, 2012, http://aristeguinoticias.com/1612/mexico/la-revision-del-pasado-articulo-de-ana-laura-magaloni/.

3. Vanda Felbab-Brown, *Calderón's Caldron: Lessons from Mexico's Battle against Organized Crime and Drug Trafficking in Ciudad Juárez, Tijuana, and Michoacán* (Brookings Institution, Washington, DC, September 2011), 24–30, 34–36, http://www.brookings.edu/~/media/Files/rc/papers/2011/09_calderon_felbab_brown/09_calderon_felbab_brown.pdf. For an analysis of the latest developments in Mexico and President Enrique Peña Nieto's efforts to reform the country's security policy against organized crime, see Vanda Felbab-Brown, *Peña Nieto's Piñata: The Promise and Pitfalls of Mexico's New Security Policy against Organized Crime* (Brookings Institution, Washington, DC, February 2013), http://www.brookings.edu/~/media/research/files/papers/2013/02/mexico new security policy felbabbrown/mexico new security policy felbabbrown.pdf.

4. John P. Sullivan, "Future Conflict: Criminal Insurgencies, Gangs, and Intelligence," *Small Wars Journal*, May 31, 2009, http://smallwarsjournal.com/blog/journal/docs-temp/248-sullivan.pdf.

5. Richard Norton, "Feral Cities," *Naval War College Review* 56, no. 4 (Autumn 2003): 97–106.

6. "Escalation," *Economist*, December 1, 2012, http://www.economist.com/news/21567422-links-between-violent-sectarian-groups-and-pakistani-taliban-are-growing-escalation; "Into the Abyss," *Economist*, August 27, 2011, http://www.economist.com/node/21526919; and Steve Inskeep, *Instant City: Life and Death in Karachi* (London: Penguin, 2011).

7. Jennifer Peirce, "Divided Cities: Crime and Inequality in Urban Brazil," *Paterson Review of International Affairs* 9 (2008): 85–98, http://www.diplomatonline.com/pdf_files/npsia/2009/PDF - Jen Peirce - Crime and Inequality in Urban Brazil.pdf; Ted Goertzel and Tulio Kahn, "The Great São Paulo Homicide Drop," *Homicide Studies* 13, no. 4 (November 2009): 398–410; and Teresa Caldeira, *City of Walls: Crime, Segregation and Citizenship in São Paulo* (Berkeley: University of California Press, 2001).

8. Benjamin Lessing, "Pesquisador: Estado Deve Tomar Cuidado com a Tropa de Elite," *Globo*, December 16, 2010, http://oglobo.globo.com/blogs/favelalivre/posts/2010/12/16/pesquisador-estado-deve-tomar-cuidado-com-tropa-de-elite-349907.asp; and André Gomes Alves, "Segurança Pública e Polícia Pacificadora: A Fruição do Direito a Segurança Pública nas Favelas de Rio de Janeiro" (University of Brasilia, June 2011), http://bdm.bce.unb.br/bitstream/10483/1966/1/2011_AndreGomesAlves.pdf. For background on life in the favelas prior to the policy and the evolution of government responses, see Maria Helena Moreira Alves and Philip Evanson, *Living in the Crossfire: Favela Residents, Drug Dealers, and Police Violence* (Philadelphia: Temple University Press, 2011); and Ben Penglase, "The Bastard Child of the Dictatorship: The Comando Vermelho and the Birth of 'Narco-culture' in Rio de Janeiro," *Luso-Brazilian Review* 45, no. 1 (2008): 118–45.

9. Clarissa Huguet and Ilona Szabó de Carvalho, "Violence in the Brazilian *Favelas* and the Role of the Police," *New Directions for Youth Development* 119 (Autumn 2008): 93–109; and Graziella Moraes D. da Silva and Ignacio Cano, "Between Damage Reduction and Community Policing: The Case of Pavão-Pavãozinho-Cantagalo in Rio de Janeiro's Favelas," in *Legitimacy and Criminal Justice: International Perspectives*, ed. Tom R. Tyler (New York: Russell Sage Foundation Publications, 2007), 186–214.

10. Felbab-Brown, *Calderón's Caldron*; William Booth, "In Mexico's Murder City, the War Appears Over," *Washington Post*, August 20, 2012, http://articles.washingtonpost.com/2012-08-20/world/35492884_1_hector-murguia-cartels-ciudad-juarez. For overall security policy in Mexico, see Eric L. Olson, David A. Shirk, and Andrew Selee, eds., *Shared Responsibility: U.S.–Mexico Pol-*

icy Options for Confronting Organized Crime (Washington, DC: Wilson Center, 2010).

11. Adam Isacson, "Medellín: Two Steps Forward, One Step Back," in *Tackling Urban Violence in Latin America: Reversing Exclusion through Smart Policing and Social Investment* (Washington Office on Latin America, June 2011), 6–9, http://mafiaandco.files.wordpress.com/2011/06/wola_tackling_urban_violence_in_latin_america.pdf; and Vanda Felbab-Brown, "Reducing Urban Violence: Lessons from Medellín, Colombia," (Brookings Institution, Washington, DC, February 14, 2011), http://www.brookings.edu/opinions/2011/0214_colombia_crime_felbabbrown.aspx.

12. Estimates of the size of the drug economy and the number of people it employs greatly vary. For smaller, narrowly based estimates, see "Afghanistan Opium Survey 2011," United Nations Office on Drugs and Crime and Islamic Republic of Afghanistan Ministry of Counter Narcotics, http://www.unodc.org/documents/crop-monitoring/Afghanistan/Executive_Summary_2011_web.pdf; for larger estimates. See also Christopher Ward and William Byrd, "Afghanistan's Opium Drug Economy," Working Paper Series Report no. SASPR-5 (World Bank South Asia, Poverty Reduction and Economic Management Network, December 2004).

13. Manuel Roig-Franzia, "Mexico's Drug Cartels Take Barbarous Turn: Targeting Bystanders," *Washington Post*, July 30, 2008, http://www.washingtonpost.com/wp-dyn/content/article/2008/07/29/AR2008072902106.html.

14. Randal C. Archibold, "Despite Violence, U.S. Firms Expand in Mexico," *New York Times*, July 10, 2011, http://www.nytimes.com/2011/07/11/world/americas/11matamoros.html.

15. Vanda Felbab-Brown, *Shooting Up: Counterinsurgency and the War on Drugs* (Washington, DC: Brookings Institution Press, 2010).

16. Vanda Felbab-Brown, "Human Security and Crime in Latin America: The Political Capital and Political Impact of Criminal Groups and Belligerents Involved in Illicit Economies" (Brookings Institution, Washington, DC, September 2011), http://www.brookings.edu/research/articles/2011/09/latin-america-crime-felbab-brown.

17. For pioneering work on the regulatory and security services provided by organized crime groups, particularly the Sicilian Mafia, see Diego Gambetta, *The Sicilian Mafia: The Business of Private Protection* (Cambridge, MA: Harvard University Press, 1993).

18. Enrique Desmond Arias and Corrine Davis Rodrigues, "The Myth of Personal Security: Criminal Gangs, Dispute Resolution, and Identity in Rio de Janeiro's Favelas," *Latin American Politics* 48, no. 4 (Winter 2006): 53–81. In 2012 the group restarted its murderous campaign against the city's police forces, killing over seventy officers. See Simon Romero, "Alarm Grows in São Paulo as More Police Officers Are Murdered," *New York Times*, October 2, 2012; and Graham Denyer Willis, "What's Killing Brazil's Police?" *New York Times*, December 1, 2012.

19. Vanda Felbab-Brown, "Law Enforcement Actions in Urban Spaces Governed by Violent Non-State Entities: Lessons from Latin America" (Brookings Institution, Washington, DC, September 2011), http://www.brookings.edu/~media/research/files/articles/2011/9/law enforcement felbab brown/09_law_enforcement_felbab_brown.

20. Vanda Felbab-Brown, "Bringing the State to the Slum: Confronting Organized Crime and Urban Violence in Latin America" (Brookings Institution, Washington, DC, December 5, 2011), http://www.brookings.edu/papers/2011/1205_latin_america_slums_felbabbrown.aspx.

21. Brian G. Martin, *The Shanghai Green Gang: Politics and Organized Crime, 1919–1937* (Berkeley: University of California Press, 1996).

22. Joshua Hammer, "In Sicily, Defying the Mafia," *Smithsonian*, October 2010, http://www.smithsonianmag.com/people-places/In-Sicily-Defying-the-Mafia.html; and Alfred W. McCoy, *The Politics of Heroin in Southeast Asia* (New York: Harper and Row, 1972).

23. For a comprehensive list of insurgent and terrorist groups linked to the drug trade, see, Felbab-Brown, *Shooting Up*, appendix A.

24. Peter Andreas, *Blue Helmets and Black Markets: The Business of Survival in the Siege of Sarajevo* (Ithaca, NY: Cornell University Press, 2008).

25. Mary Kaldor, *New and Old Wars: Organized Violence in a Global Era* (Stanford, CA: Stanford

University Press, 1999); and Mark R. Duffield, *Global Governance and New Wars: The Merging of Development* and *Security* (London: Zed, 2001).

26. Paul Collier and Anke Hoeffler, "On Economic Causes of Civil War," *Oxford Economic Papers* 50, no. 4 (October 1998): 563–73; Mats Berdal and David Keen, "Violence and Economic Agendas in Civil Wars: Some Policy Implications," *Millennium: Journal of International Studies* 26, no. 3 (December 1997): 795–818; and David Keen, *The Economic Functions of Violence in Civil Wars*, Adelphi series, no. 320 (Oxford: Oxford University Press for the International Institute of Strategic Studies, 1998).

27. Felbab-Brown, *Shooting Up*.

28. Vanda Felbab-Brown, *Aspiration and Ambivalence: Strategies and Realities of Counterinsurgency and State-building in Afghanistan* (Washington, DC: Brookings Institution Press, 2013).

29. William Reno, *Corruption and State Politics in Sierra Leone* (Cambridge: Cambridge University Press, 1995); and William Reno, *Warlord Politics and African States* (Boulder: Lynne Rienner, 1998).

30. James Cockayne, "State Fragility, Organised Crime and Peacekeeping: Towards a More Strategic Approach" (Norwegian Peacebuilding Resource Centre, September 15, 2011), http://www.peacebuilding.no/var/ezflow_site/storage/original/application/2af427c8039ed02db6fd29fab1144aa8.pdf; and James Cockayne and Adam Lupel, eds., *Peace Operations and Organized Crime: Enemies or Allies?* (Abingdon, UK: Routledge, 2011).

31. The phrase "state as mafia-like bazaar, where anyone with an official designation can pillage at will" was coined by George B. N. Ayittey in *Africa in Chaos: A Comparative History* (New York: Palgrave Macmillan, 1998), 151.

32. "Transnational Trafficking and the Rule of Law in West Africa: A Threat Assessment," United Nations Office on Drugs and Crime, July 2009, http://www.unodc.org/documents/data-and-analysis/Studies/West_Africa_Report_2009.pdf.

33. James Cockayne and Phil Williams, "The Invisible Tide: Towards an International Strategy to Deal with Drug Trafficking through West Africa" (International Peace Institute, October 2009), http://www.ipacademy.org/media/pdf/publications/west_africa_drug_trafficking_epub.pdf; and Joseph Kirschke, "The Coke Coast: Cocaine and Failed States in Africa," *World Politics Review*, September 9, 2008.

34. Semi-illegal economies are those that trade in legal commodities but do so in violation of national or international regulations, such as taxation and licensing.

35. Geoffrey Wood, "Business and Politics in a Criminal State: The Case of Equatorial Guinea," *African Affairs* 103, no. 413 (October 2004): 547–67; and Jean-Francois Bayart, Stephen Ellis, and Beatrice Hibou, *The Criminalization of the State in Africa* (Oxford: James Currey, 1999).

36. Vanda Felbab-Brown and James Forest, "Political Violence and the Illicit Economies of West Africa," *Terrorism and Political Violence* 24, no. 5 (Winter 2012): 787–806.

37. Douglas Farah, "Narcoterrorism and the Long Reach of U.S. Law Enforcement: Testimony before the House Committee on Foreign Affairs Subcommittee on Terrorism, Nonproliferation and Trade," October 12, 2011, http://www.strategycenter.net/research/pubid.259/pub_detail.asp; and Vanda Felbab-Brown, "Narcoterrorism and the Long Reach of U.S. Law Enforcement" (October 12, 2011), http://www.brookings.edu/research/testimony/2011/10/12-terrorism-drugs-felbabbrown.

14

THE IMPACT OF GLOBAL DEMOGRAPHIC CHANGES ON THE INTERNATIONAL SECURITY ENVIRONMENT

Jack A. Goldstone, Hilton Root, and Monty G. Marshall

Demographic changes will pose new challenges to the international order in the first half of the twenty-first century. While the traditional great powers cope with shrinking and aging labor forces, large middle-income countries such as Turkey, Brazil, and Indonesia will emerge as major new players to be integrated into global security institutions. At the same time, across an arc sweeping from Central America to tropical Africa, through the Middle East and into parts of Central and South Asia, rapid population growth and youth surges in relatively weak states will pose challenges to political stability. Indeed, perhaps the most striking risk is that virtually all global population growth up to 2050 will occur in countries that today are rated as having high to extreme state fragility, and thus face difficulty in providing their surging young populations with the education, funds, and social order needed to assume productive roles in the world economy.

Demography has traditionally been seen as important to international security simply through the weight of numbers: other things being equal, larger countries can field larger armies and, at a given level of economic development, will also have larger economies and can afford larger budgets for defense. From the seventeenth century, when infantry formations came to dominate European warfare, up until the twentieth century, land powers were defined mainly by the size of their armies; hence, the dominant powers were countries with large populations. Mercantile and naval powers such as Holland and Great Britain were only partial exceptions; though able to create powerful colonial empires, they could dominate the great power politics of the European continent only through alliances with larger countries.

Since World War II, however, technological prowess and the capacity for complex organization and deployment have become far more important to military might than sheer numbers. Poor countries with large populations have therefore not been major factors in international security. Rather, countries with nuclear arms and missiles to deliver them have been the major powers.

Yet, in the early twenty-first century, we stand at a tipping point, wherein demography again matters, but for very different reasons than in the past. First, the world's major international security threats have shifted. Instead of land battles between major powers—the kind of conflict that NATO forces were designed to deter in Eastern Europe during the Cold War—the main sources of violence and disruptions in the international system are *internal* wars. These conflicts have repeatedly engaged the great powers—whether in the Balkans (Bosnia, Kosovo), in the Caucasus (Chechnya, Abkhazia), in the Middle East and Central Asia (Iraq, Afghanistan, Syria), in Latin America (Nicaragua, Colombia, Haiti), or in Africa (Libya, Mali, Somalia)—both because such wars create humanitarian crises and massive flows of refugees across borders, and because they spawn ungoverned spaces and rebel groups that support international crime and terrorism.[1] Yet the ability of the great powers to prevail in such wars has been limited by the exigencies of asymmetric warfare, in which the numbers, mobility, and local knowledge of partisan fighters can neutralize the technical superiority of foreign intervention forces. In these arenas, the major powers have often found themselves fighting lengthy wars of attrition, in which the high cost of their soldiers places them at a disadvantage. Rapid population growth in poor and poorly governed nations now matters for international security because such growth increases the risks of internal wars, increases the size of the populations subject to becoming refugees, and raises the number of local militia and partisan fighters who must be faced. The populations of many such countries are still exploding as we move toward the middle of this century, and thus these risks are steadily growing.

Second, the populations of the major developed powers in North America, Western Europe, and East Asia are all rapidly aging, and in many cases population growth has slowed or reversed. One-child families are increasingly common, as are childless ones. This presents several new challenges to these nations, as the increasing costs of caring for an aging population start to compete with military spending, and raising troops from shrinking populations and much smaller families becomes more difficult. While the richer countries are responding by putting more emphasis on small, highly trained units of special forces and extending their use of remotely piloted vehicles (drones) to attack targets, it has yet to be shown that either of these methods are effective in dealing with internal wars and providing necessary security and support to stabilization, peacekeeping, and state-building missions.[2]

Third, the economic development of several middle-income countries with very large populations—Brazil, Turkey, Indonesia, Mexico, India—has raised them to the level of major players in the global economy. At the same time, these large and relatively youthful countries also have some of the largest reserves of young men available for military service. Yet they remain outside all the major international security frameworks that developed after World War II, such as NATO (excepting Turkey) and permanent membership in the United Nations Security Council. These countries—all increasingly important for their rising military capabilities and their growing weight in the global economy—are seeking a role in the global international security framework. Yet that role remains unsettled.

Will they join the Western powers in some broader league to defend democracies? Will they shift to favor Asian and Latin American interests against those of North America and Europe? Will they form a bloc of independent nations pursuing their own policy toward Africa, the Middle East, and other key regions? Or will they go separate ways and add to the chaos and breakdown in the new world order? As they continue to grow in population—by 2050, just these five countries will have 2.4 billion people[3]—the question of their relation to international security institutions and alliances will grow ever more acute.

Together, these three changes are creating a new international security environment, with persistent and novel challenges.

DEMOGRAPHY AND DEMOCRATIC PROGRESS

Since the fall of communism in the Soviet Union and Eastern Europe, there has been much enthusiasm for the progress of democracy around the world. Indeed, as Figure 1

Figure 1. Global trends in governance, 1946–2012

Source: Center for Systemic Peace, Polity IV Project, www.systemicpeace.org and Monty G. Marshall and Benjamin R. Cole, *Global Report 2009: Conflict, Governance, and State Fragility* (Arlington, VA: Center for Systemic Peace and George Mason University Center for Global Policy, 2009).

shows, if we simply count the countries that are full or partial democracies, versus those that are dictatorships, there are many reasons to cheer.

From the end of World War II to the 1980s, the number of dictatorships in the world had quadrupled, fed by communist revolutions in Eastern Europe and Asia, the rise of "big men" dictatorships in newly independent states in Africa and the Middle East, and the return of military regimes to Latin America. The number of full or partial democracies, by contrast, increased only slowly, growing by about 20 percent in this period. By 1985, there were 80 dictatorships in the world, and only 43 democracies and 22 partial democracies. Then, from the late 1980s to the first decade of the twenty-first century, this trend sharply reversed. The "third wave" of democratization flowed across Latin America, Eastern Europe, and even parts of Asia and Africa.[4] During a five-year span in the early 1990s, the number of democracies leapt from 46 in 1988 to 75 in 1993; the number of partial democracies rose from 25 in 1988 to 49 in 1993.

Over the following two decades, democracies continued to increase in number. By 2009, the global pattern of the mid-1980s had been completely reversed. Instead of dictatorships being twice as numerous as democracies, the number of democracies (94) was nearly five times the number of dictatorships (20); meanwhile, the number of partial democratic regimes had also more than doubled, to 53. From being far more numerous than full and partial democracies combined in the 1970s, by 2012 dictatorships ruled just 12 percent of the world's nations (among countries with at least 500,000 population in 2012). In recent years, some commentators have noted that gains in the number of full democracies have ceased, and some countries—notably Russia and Thailand—have slipped backward toward autocracy.[5] Yet the major gains in global democracy from

the third wave have been remarkably persistent. For the first time in history, we can say we are living in a predominantly democratic world.

Yet there is more to governance than formal democracy. Many countries that are formally democratic in their selection of leaders are in fact wracked by corruption, internal strife, and economic failure. Nigeria and Pakistan, Kenya and Tanzania, Guatemala and Nicaragua, the Democratic Republic of the Congo and the Philippines—none of them dictatorships—come to mind as countries that have had success in holding competitive elections, but face a host of difficulties in improving the lives of their citizens.

The Center for Systemic Peace and the Center for Global Policy at George Mason University have thus devised a richer indicator of quality of governance: the "State Fragility Index." Although in some ways similar to the Fund for Peace's and *Foreign Policy*'s "Failed States Index," the emphasis in the State Fragility Index (SFI) is on what states are doing *right*. The SFI uses objective published data to score states in four different areas: security, the political system, the economy, and social services. In each of those four areas, scores are derived for the *effectiveness* of state operations and the *legitimacy* of state operations. Effectiveness indicators include, for example, whether there is ongoing conflict or military involvement, the stability and duration of leadership, the level of GDP per capita and economic growth, and human development scores, among others. Legitimacy indicators include the level of human rights violations, political discrimination and exclusion, corruption, and excess infant mortality, among others.[6]

Of these eight dimensions—effectiveness and legitimacy scores for each of security, politics, the economy, and social services—economic performance is scored from 0 to 4 and the others scored from 0 to 3, giving a maximum possible score of 25 (with higher scores indicating *worse performance*). The SFI list of the most fragile states is led by conflict-riven countries such as Somalia (25), Sudan (23), the Democratic Republic of the Congo (23), and Afghanistan (22). Twenty-one states have perfect fragility scores of 0—Japan, South Korea, Taiwan, and most of the EU nations; the United States has a score of 2 (reflecting its current military involvements and responsibility for civilian deaths in Iraq and Afghanistan). The advantages of the SFI are that it focuses on improvements that states can make across a range of areas of governance, that it is wholly transparent because it is calculated from publicly available data, and that because of its sources, we can go back and compute SFI scores for countries from the mid-1990s to the present, to assess changes over time.[7]

If we look at the trend over time in SFI scores around the world, we again see reasons for optimism. From 1995 to 2007, SFI scores have undergone a marked decline in every region, falling on average by more than three points among former socialist countries; by two points in Latin America, Asia, the Middle East and North Africa; and by more than one point in Sub-Saharan Africa. Globally, the total world fragility scores summed over all nations declined by 18 percent over this period. The greatest improvements occurred in the effectiveness and legitimacy of political systems and of social service provision. The least improvement was seen in the legitimacy of economies (reflecting corruption and economic inequality), and the legitimacy of security (reflecting human rights violations). Nonetheless, the overall trends show steady improvement.

While these trends should be reducing conflict—and they are, as we have seen a notable decline in internal wars and violent conflicts from the 1990s through 2005[8]—we need to look to the future and ask what lies ahead. Here, it is less important to count the number of democratic regimes, or to count

country-by-country fragility. What matters is the current *and future* populations likely to be governed by fragile states. After all, many very successful countries are quite small (Denmark, Botswana, Singapore), and moreover have stable or even shrinking populations. At the same time, many still fragile countries are huge and have rapidly growing populations (Nigeria, Pakistan, Ethiopia).

Figure 2 shows the most recent SFI scores for all the countries in the world as a shaded map, with darker countries having worse SFI scores. Troubles and unstable states stretch in a clear arc from Sub-Saharan Africa across the Middle East and into South and Southeast Asia.

While that is hardly news, these trends appear in a different light when they are examined in terms of global population trends, for the countries in the "arc of fragility" include many of the fastest-growing countries in the world. Despite recurrent violence (which, in contrast to past conflicts, has resulted mainly in high levels of displaced populations, rather than in massive death tolls), population is on the rise in countries from Nigeria and Sudan to Yemen and Pakistan. Afghanistan, for example, which has proved a severe military challenge to NATO forces to stabilize, had a 2000 population of 20.6 million, and is projected to have a population of almost 51 million by 2040. Yemen, already a worrying breeding ground for terrorism and civil war, had a population of 17.5 million in 2000; by 2040, with its oil and water supplies diminishing, it is projected to be struggling with over twice that population, or 38.8 million. Nigeria, a critical country for Africa's future, which is now experiencing a wave of violence fueled by the jihadists of Boko Haram, is projected to see its population rise from 160 million in 2010 to 350.7 million by 2040—a population almost as large as all the EU-15 countries combined will have at that time.[9]

In 2011, Tunisia's long-standing dictator, Zine el Abidine Ben Ali, was forced to flee

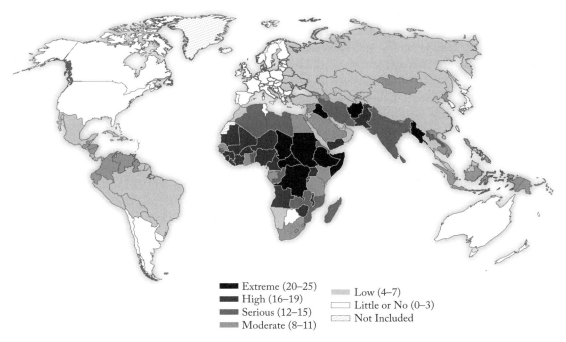

Extreme (20–25)
High (16–19)
Serious (12–15)
Moderate (8–11)
Low (4–7)
Little or No (0–3)
Not Included

Figure 2. State Fragility Index, 2011

Source: Monty G. Marshall and Benjamin R. Cole, *Global Report 2011: Conflict, Governance, and State Fragility* (Vienna, VA: Center for Systemic Peace, 2011).

by protests initiated by youngsters who faced bleak job prospects. Tunisia's regime was in many ways one of the best, not worst, in the arc of fragility. Indeed, its SFI was moderate, based on relatively low levels of violence, a history of long-term political stability, and high levels of income, health, and education for the region. Where Ben Ali failed was in regard to his political legitimacy, which was undermined by a level of crony-centered corruption that led even the middle classes and the military to conclude that he and his family were looting the country. As a result, when protests broke out following the self-immolation of a young man who killed himself to protest against police closing down his vegetable cart, which was the sole means of support for himself and his family, the army stood back and refused to reinforce police in suppressing the crowds. Labor, professionals, and businessmen all joined in the protests to force out Ben Ali and his corrupt inner circle,

hoping to gain a new leader who would foster rather than prey on private business, and share public revenues more widely.

Neighboring Egypt, however, was rated "seriously fragile" in the SFI, and thus it should have come as no surprise that the spark set in Tunisia started an even more vigorous conflagration on the banks of the Nile. Egypt had significant deficits in political and economic legitimacy and effectiveness; and while its provision of security was effective, it was also increasingly illegitimate, reflecting police abuses. All these factors were on display in the grievances and demands of protestors across Egypt.

The basic story line of Tunisia and Egypt—a vast wave of youth coming of age, facing bleak prospects for employment and venting their anger against aging, corrupt regimes—is being repeated throughout Africa, the Middle East, and parts of Asia. Whether there will be sparks to fan further flames, and whether the military and bureaucracy will side with their governments or stand aside, will vary over time and place. Yet the pressures are mounting and increasingly likely to produce turmoil in the many regimes with significant deficits in legitimacy or effectiveness.

It is troubling that the two areas where SFI scores show the least improvement are in corruption and state repression, which undermine regime legitimacy. The growth of China, India, and other developing economies is leading to a boom in commodity sales throughout Africa and Asia. Yet revenues gained from natural resources are notorious for fueling corruption, and corrupt regimes frequently grow more repressive to protect their ill-gotten gains. If the future does indeed present us with increasingly corrupt and repressive regimes in precisely those areas with surging populations and rapidly growing youth cohorts, then even long-stable regimes may become increasingly vulnerable to the kinds of protest just seen in Tunisia, Egypt, Libya, Yemen, and Syria.

Figure 3 shows how much this risk is growing. This graph shows the United Nations'

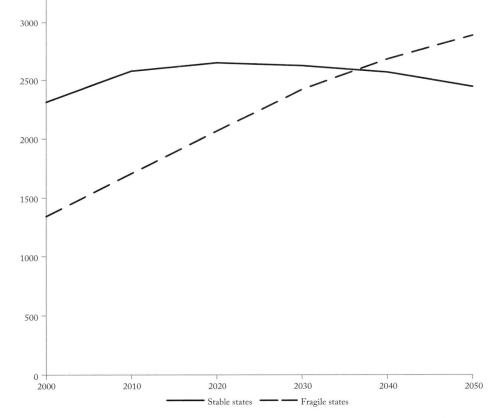

Figure 3. Growth of labor force (ages 15–59) in millions, in stable vs. fragile states, 2000–2050

Source: Data from United Nations, Department of Economic and Social Affairs, Population Division, Population Estimates and Projections Section, "World Population Prospects: The 2012 Revision," http://esa.un.org/unpd/wpp/unpp/panel_population.htm; and Monty G. Marshall and Benjamin R. Cole, *Global Report 2011: Conflict, Governance, and State Fragility* (Vienna, VA: Center for Systemic Peace, 2011).

medium projections for growth in the world's labor force (persons aged 15–59), divided between stable states (countries that have little, low, or moderate SFI scores) and fragile states (those that have serious, high, or extreme SFI scores) as of 2010. From 2000 to 2010, labor force growth was similar in both stable and fragile nations. Yet this has now changed, as labor force growth in the stable countries—including China—has virtually stopped since 2010; indeed, their labor force will decline slightly after 2040. As this graph shows, *all the net global labor force growth in the next forty years will take place in states that currently are highly, seriously, or extremely fragile.*

The implications of this statement for the world economy, and for international security, are staggering. In 2000, almost two-thirds of the global labor force lived in relatively stable states, which were still growing rapidly. Instability in the remaining states was thus a humanitarian problem, and occasionally an economic problem if the violence threatened supplies of key minerals or other commodities. By 2050, however, only 45 percent of the global labor force will live in today's stable states; a majority of the world's working-age population will live in states that are currently highly fragile. Moreover, if all the *growth* in the world's labor force comes, as projected, from fragile countries—states that so far have shown themselves unable to adequately educate their population, or to attract the capital and provide the security necessary for them to become more productive—global economic growth will face immense hurdles.

The problems of large youth cohorts, increasingly educated but with limited economic opportunities, facing corrupt regimes of limited effectiveness and legitimacy, which propelled much of the Middle East and North Africa into turmoil, is thus set to increase dramatically in the coming decades.

THE CHALLENGES OF CONCENTRATED AGING AND CONCENTRATED YOUTH

In recent years, most countries of the world have experienced a sharp fall in fertility, as more education and more work experience leads women to have fewer children. Countries as diverse as Brazil, India, Iran, and even Saudi Arabia have seen substantial fertility declines. These trends have started to reduce the proportion of young people in these societies. Yet in a substantial number of countries, mostly in Sub-Saharan Africa, fertility remains stubbornly high. In these countries, from Nigeria down to Tanzania, with women still having four to five children per family, the median age of the population will remain 20 or younger through 2040.

Such young populations require not only an expansion of education to prepare their youth to be productive, but also capital investments in labor-intensive industries to provide meaningful employment. Such investments, however, require political stability. Easier investments in mining and other commodities, which produce quick gains in output, usually do not provide commensurate increases in employment. In this respect, the recent economic boom in many African countries may be misleading, as much of it is commodity driven. Even Zimbabwe, one of Africa's worst-governed nations, has been experiencing rapid economic growth of late. Yet this growth has been mainly driven by large increases in foreign assistance and raw mineral exports; meanwhile, critical problems such as an inadequate food supply, poor property rights protection, and a bloated government sector remain unresolved.[10] At the same time, Zimbabwe's population continues to grow, from 13 million in 2010 to a projected 26 million in 2050. This doubling of population in one generation, if these broader problems remain unsolved, is likely to produce a generation with unmet needs for employment and stable socialization. Zimbabwe's current economic growth, most of which is benefiting a small state-connected elite (a situation that mirrors what happened in Egypt and Libya in recent years), could thus be storing up more severe future problems.

Today, the skewing of global population growth, with by far the fastest growth occurring in low-income countries, has meant a concentration of youth in the poorest and worst-governed societies. Already, more than half of the world's population under age 15 is growing up in those countries with serious, high, or extreme state fragility. This combination of surging youth cohorts and governments that provide poorly for broad-based, inclusive economic growth tends to produce political crises. A substantial volume of recent research has shown that countries with larger youth cohorts relative to the adult population have more violence and are less able to make a stable transition to consolidated democracy.[11]

At the same time, the populations of the NATO nations, which have taken on the task of coping with fragile states, are expected to stagnate over the coming years. With the exception of Turkey and the United States, none of the NATO states will have significant population growth in the coming decades, and even Turkish and US growth will be much slower than it has been in the last half century. As a result, the population of NATO countries—indeed, the population of all the world's stable countries with relatively low SFI scores—will be flat, while that of the unstable, high-SFI countries will be rapidly increasing.

Most NATO countries and the United States' Asian allies also face very rapid aging. In Germany, the largest country in Europe, the median population age already reached 44 in 2010 and will exceed 50 by 2040. South Korea and Japan are on a similar trajectory, with their median age expected to

hit 50 and 53, respectively, by that year. Even the United States, whose population has been continually renewed by immigration, is projected to reach a median age of 40 by 2040; and this may rise higher, because the rate of immigration into the United States seems to be falling with slower economic expansion.[12]

This concentrated aging in the rich countries also bears on international security, insofar as the prime labor force years are also the years for potential military service. The number of people aged 15 to 59 is projected to grow by nearly a billion between 2020 and 2050 in today's highly fragile states, while that age group in countries that today are stable is projected to *decrease* by almost 200 million. The ability to finance and recruit military forces in the rich nations of Europe, North America, and Far East Asia (Japan and South Korea) will be adversely affected by the need to devote ever-more resources to pensions and health care for aging populations, not to mention the paucity of young people of military age. This "graying of the great powers" will constrain their ability to put "boots on the ground" in military operations.[13]

With such a shift, the ability of the more stable countries to intervene with sufficient force to resolve conflicts in fragile states will be far more challenging than it is today. To take one striking example of the changes that are under way: In 1980, the population of Europe (excluding Russia) was still 15 percent greater than the population of all of Africa. Today, some thirty years later, the population of Africa is 75 percent larger than Europe's; and thirty years hence, according to the UN Demographic Division, the population of Africa will be *more than three times as large* as that of Europe. The ground is rapidly shifting beneath us.

To point out one more vital issue: Europe and America have of late struggled with large waves of foreign immigrants, propelled by a combination of flight from turmoil in their own countries and greater economic opportunities in the West. What will happen to international migration pressures in the coming decades, with the populations of Africa and Asia and parts of Latin America continuing to surge, if turmoil in these regions grows worse and opportunities for jobs and education continue to lag behind the aspirations of their people?

Of course, the lines in Figure 3 do not have to follow those trajectories, nor need the two lines cross. The population figures are unlikely to change (most people alive in 2050 have already been born). What will be crucial is to shift some of the larger and fastest-growing countries—Nigeria, Ethiopia, Pakistan, India, Bangladesh, the Philippines, the Democratic Republic of the Congo, Kenya, Uganda, Tanzania, Sudan, Iran, Afghanistan, Iraq—out of the condition of fragility, and to have them follow countries such as Indonesia, Vietnam, Colombia, and South Africa into the ranks of stable states. If those fourteen large and fast-growing countries were to become stable by 2050, that would shift 2.2 billion people aged 15 to 59 out of the conditions of fragile countries, and create a world in which the lines of Figure 3 essentially reverse, as the labor force in stable countries would more than double and that in fragile countries would be halved, compared to the levels today.

Nation building is hard and may often appear unrewarding work. It may be easier to simply applaud the growth in the number of the world's formal democracies, and conclude that rich countries should simply walk away from trouble in faraway places. But that would be to ignore the current trends in state fragility and population growth, which paint a stark choice: between a world in which all of tomorrow's additional workers grow up in countries where they will fail to become productive, and in which a majority of the world's potential soldiers will be in

highly fragile states, or a world in which large and fast-growing countries are able to attain stability, so that by 2050 three-quarters or more of the world's workers are living in countries with stable, effective, and legitimate governments, where they can develop their potential and contribute to global peace and prosperity, rather than threaten it.

WHAT IS TO BE DONE?

The rapid growth of youth cohorts in states with weak or illegitimate governments and highly uneven economic growth, taking place in many of the largest and fastest-growing countries in the world, suggests that major security dilemmas lie ahead. The policy of the United States and Western powers, accepting, or even supporting, increasingly troubled and illegitimate regimes—from Saudi Arabia and Afghanistan to Uganda and Chad, among others—in the hope of forestalling future disorders seems increasingly wrongheaded.

At this moment, as Europe and the United States struggle to pull out of recession, it may seem unimportant to invest in improving governance in unstable regions of the world. But there could hardly be any more important investment for our future. It is vital to keep our eye on where future economic and population growth is likely to occur. The workforce in developing countries, many of which are still highly fragile, will be far more important to the global economy in the future than it has been in the past or is today.

Still, we have learned that fragile countries cannot be stabilized simply by external intervention, and that even long-lived and apparently stable regimes may be far more fragile than they appear. So what can the richer countries do?

At present, there is no viable international framework that is capable of managing the security risks posed by hundreds of millions of young people being added to the population of countries with fragile governments. Indeed, in many ways the growth of China, Brazil, India, and other emerging economies has made the situation more difficult. Their demands for natural resources have created increased opportunities for corrupt regimes to cooperate in looting their countries; these new emerging powers have increasingly sought to weaken the influence of the Atlantic powers and project their own policies; and China's own model of authoritarian growth has attracted admirers and emulators. The world is thus threatened with the prospect of fracturing into a competitive asymmetric multipolarity—with regional powers such as Brazil, India, China, and Turkey seeking their own advantage, while the Atlantic and Far Eastern economies are weakening—at precisely the time that a broader framework of global cooperation is vitally needed to head off the risks of increased turmoil in many fast-growing but fragile states.

It is therefore vital to enlist the support of the fast-growing, populous, but politically more stable countries—Brazil, Turkey, Mexico, Indonesia—for new projects of global governance and regional security. The "older" developed nations are becoming older quite literally, as their populations age. The creation of the G20, inviting these fast-growing, stable countries to take their place among global economic leaders, was long overdue; as of 2012, Brazil, Mexico, Indonesia, and Turkey were respectively the world's seventh, eleventh, fifteenth, and sixteenth largest economies (in terms of purchasing power parity–adjusted GDP). Yet this should be just a beginning. However difficult it may be, remodeling NATO and the UN Security Council to give these fast-growing countries a key role is vital for the energy, legitimacy, and effectiveness of the institutions of global governance and security.

Of course, gaining international cooperation to strengthen fragile states will be enormously difficult. China, India, Brazil, Turkey, and other regional powers are suspicious of interventions in other countries, and of the motives of Western nations. Enlisting their assistance will require marked changes in strategy.

First, the Atlantic powers will have to recognize that emerging nations will not simply follow in their footsteps or adopt their views. Even the large emerging democracies, which Goldstone has dubbed the "TIMBI" countries[14]—Turkey, India, Mexico, Brazil, and Indonesia—have their own views of the world, and their own local and regional priorities. The project of global strengthening of fragile regimes thus cannot and should not be presented as a project of spreading Western institutions and values. Rather, it should be presented in terms of attractive goals—greater prospects for regional stability, economic growth, and increased trade—the pursuit of which will generate widespread benefits.

Moreover, strengthening fragile states should not be sought simply through calling for more elections and more democracy. All too often, elections prompt more conflict and radicalism if prior agreements do not exist among elites to tolerate opposition, accept election outcomes, and respect basic human rights.[15] In states as diverse as Brazil, South Korea, Indonesia, Ukraine, and now Egypt and Tunisia, people will themselves try to seize opportunities to move toward democracy when they have achieved some level of security and seek to rid themselves of excessively corrupt leaders. The best way to avoid sudden shocks and collapses will be to rely on building consensus around existing international agreements and organizations that focus on basic human rights, the rule of law, and combating corruption, such as the UN conventions, the Organization for Security and Cooperation in Europe, the World Bank, and the World Trade Organization. It will be crucial to strengthen the role of emerging powers in these organizations and to expand their membership, while at the same time increasing the responsibility and accountability of member-nations to abide by these agreements. Supporting freedom of speech and media and fighting crony-centered corruption are in the interests of all the capitalist trading democracies, and are standards that should be demanded of all states engaged in global trade. Where such rights gain strength, democracy is likely to follow; but without such rights, democracies are brittle and breed conflict.

Second, where states are fragile, rather than relying mainly on government to eventually tackle the problems of inclusive economic growth and opportunity, it is crucial to give every possible encouragement and reward to entrepreneurs—social as well as economic entrepreneurs. Publicity for their accomplishments, help in raising capital, and support in defending their enterprises from corruption can advance their efforts and encourage emulation of their success. Without successful entrepreneurship, fragile countries will not make the gains in jobs and opportunities they need for their populations, nor will they generate the internal leadership they need to right themselves.[16]

Disorder in fragile nations can be avoided or at least diminished by providing rewarding jobs for young men and women. Efforts to stimulate economic growth must focus not just on increasing GDP but also on creating large numbers of jobs. This will require an emphasis on manufacturing, commercial agriculture, and services, rather than mining and commodity production; and on vocational training rather than just university education. Supporting legal and economic reforms to improve transparency of finance, availability of credit, the start-up of new firms, and foreign investment should be priorities. Moreover, one should not simply expect that increasing educational spending and enrollment will create fertile conditions for increased employment. Rather, education

must be tailored to providing skills and experience that will fit into the jobs likely to be available. Otherwise, the overproduction of educated graduates creates "educational bubbles," which increase the conditions for mass organization, identity politics, protest, and instability.[17]

Finally, a more muscular and better-funded standing international regime for dealing with humanitarian and local security issues is vital to head off the conditions that destroy resources and breed continued instability. One of the defining characteristics of fragile states is that they have difficulty responding to natural disasters and humanitarian catastrophes, as well as being prone to internal conflicts. It is clear from the sustained crisis following Haiti's earthquake and the slow mobilization of international aid for the victims of floods in Pakistan in the same year that the global institutions for recovery and reconstruction assistance are woefully weak, lacking the coordination and standing authority of, for example, the World Health Organization. It is unfair to point only to failures, and not laud success. International support and brokering of internal agreements, such as occurred in Sudan, the Democratic Republic of the Congo, and Kenya have been vital in creating breathing spaces for change after the fires of war. In addition, multilateral aid has helped ravaged economies such as those of Ethiopia, Mozambique, and East Timor to take significant steps forward. Yet these were the result of ad hoc interventions, not responses by a reliable arm of the international community.

In sum, we risk being lulled into a false sense of security by simply counting the number of regimes that have transitioned to democracy, or by recent improvements in many countries' economies and governance. While these are certainly positive trends, the world is, in fact, at risk of becoming more dangerous in the coming decades. With virtually all the world's labor force growth to

2050—adding over a billion young people—occurring in states that today are severely fragile, the prospects of political and economic stability are not encouraging. In addition, with the demographic and economic resources of the Atlantic powers diminishing in relative terms, the ability of those powers to lead (and pay for) efforts to maintain global order is bound to decline.

The new global order thus calls for renewed efforts to create international institutions that can help strengthen fragile states and respond to crises in them, not for the abandonment of those efforts. It is true that the Western powers, and especially the United States, have made significant errors in recent undertakings in this regard. We can accept that fact and still have confidence that if we learn from those errors, we can have greater success in the future.[18] In fact, given the global trends that are already under way, we have no choice but to try and do so.

NOTES

1. John T. Picarelli and Louise Shelley, "The Diversity of the Crime-Terror Interaction," *International Annals of Criminology* 43½ (2005): 51–81.

2. See the debate on drone warfare between Daniel Byman ("Why Drones Work: The Case for Washington's Weapon of Choice") and Audrey Kurth Cronin ("Why Drones Fail: When Tactics Drive Strategy") in *Foreign Affairs* 92, no. 4 (July/August 2013): 32–54.

3. Unless otherwise indicated, all demographic data and projections in this chapter are from the United Nations, Department of Economic and Social Affairs, Population Division, Population Estimates and Projections Section, "World Population Prospects: The 2012 Revision," http://esa.un.org/unpd/wpp/unpp/panel_population.htm.

4. Samuel P. Huntington, *The Third Wave: Democratization in the Late Twentieth Century* (Norman: University of Oklahoma Press, 1991).

5. Joshua Kurlantzick, *Democracy in Retreat: The Revolt of the Middle Class and the Worldwide Decline of Representative Government* (New Haven,

CT: Yale University Press, 2013); and Arch Puddington, "The Freedom House Survey for 2012: Breakthroughs in the Balance," *Journal of Democracy* 24, no. 2 (2013): 46–61.

6. For complete details on how the SFI is composed, and country scores from 1995 to 2013, see Monty G. Marshall and Jack A. Goldstone, "Global Report on Conflict, Governance, and State Fragility 2007," *Foreign Policy Bulletin* 17 (Winter 2007): 3–21; and Monty G. Marshall and Benjamin R. Cole, "Global Report on Conflict, Governance, and State Fragility 2008," *Foreign Policy Bulletin* 21 (Winter 2008): 1–26. The SFI is produced annually by the Center for Systemic Peace (www.systemicpeace.org) and featured in the *Global Report* series; annual SFI data is posted on the INSCR Data page.

7. The SFI is only one such index, of course. In addition to the Fund for Peace/*Foreign Policy* "Failed States Index," there is the Swedish Quality of Government Institute's basic dataset; the World Bank's governance indicators and its Country Policy and Institutional Assessment; Carlton University's Country Indicators for Foreign Policy list of fragile states; and the Global Peace Index compiled by Vision of Humanity, among others. For a profile of these and other sources, see "Measuring Fragility" by the Governance and Social Development Resource Centre (GSDRC) at http://www.gsdrc.org/go/fragile-states/chapter-3–measuring-and-assessing-fragility/measuring-fragility. Each ranking has its own set of indicator variables and schemes for weighting them, but with few exceptions they agree on identifying the most troubled and poorly governed states and world regions. Thus the argument in this chapter would be supported by almost any choice of index to identify fragile states.

8. Human Security Report Project, *Human Security Brief 2007* (Vancouver: HSRP, 2008).

9. The projections for Afghanistan, Yemen, Pakistan, and Nigeria are the United Nations' medium estimates, which assume a *decline* in fertility from current levels at historic rates; if one assumes that today's fertility levels persist, then projected populations would be still higher. The population projection for the EU-15 (Austria, Belgium, Denmark, Finland, France, Germany, Greece, Ireland, Italy, Luxembourg, Netherlands, Portugal, Spain, Sweden, and United Kingdom) is from Eurostat (the EU statistical agency), *Europe in Figures—Eurostat Yearbook 2006–07*, http://epp.eurostat.ec .europa.eu/cache/ITY_OFFPUB/KS-CD-06 -001-01/EN/KS-CD-06-001-01-EN.PDF.

10. Craig J. Richardson, "Zimbabwe: Why Is One of the World's Least-Free Economies Growing So Fast?" Policy Analysis No. 722 (Cato Institute, Washington, DC, March 18, 2013).

11. Henrik Urdal, "Youth Bulges and Violence," in *Political Demography: How Population Changes Are Reshaping International Security and National Politics*, ed. Jack A. Goldstone, Eric P. Kaufmann, and Monica Duffy Toft (Boulder, CO: Paradigm, 2012), 117–32; Richard Cincotta and John Doces, "The Age-Structural Maturity Thesis: The Impact of the Youth Bulge on the Advent and Stability of Liberal Democracy," also in *Political Demography*, 98–116; Elizabeth Leahy, Robert Engelman, Carolyn Gibb Vogel, Sarah Haddock, and Tod Preston, *The Shape of Things to Come: Why Age Structure Matters to a Safer, More Equitable World* (Washington, DC: Population Action International, 2012); Hannes Weber, "Demography and Democracy: The Impact of Youth Cohort Size on Democratic Stability in the World," *Democratization* 20, no. 2 (2013): 335–57; and Tim Dyson, "On Demographic and Democratic Transitions," supplement, *Population and Development Review* 38, no. S1 (2013): 83–102.

12. D'Vera Cohn, "Census Bureau Lowers U.S. Growth Forecast, Mainly Due to Reduced Immigration and Births," *PEW Social Trends*, December 14, 2012, http://www.pewsocialtrends.org /2012/12/14/census-bureau-lowers-u-s-growth -forecast-mainly-due-to-reduced-immigration-and -births/.

13. Mark L. Haas, "America's Golden Years? U.S. Security in an Aging World," in Goldstone et al., *Political Demography*, 49–62; Richard Jackson and Neil Howe, *The Graying of the Great Powers: Demography and Geopolitics in the 21st Century* (Washington, DC: Center for Strategic and International Studies, 2008); and Jennifer Dabbs Sci-

ubba, "A New Framework for Aging and Security: Lessons from Power Transition Theory," in Goldstone et al., *Political Demography*, 63–77.

14. Jack A. Goldstone, "Rise of the TIMBIs," *Foreign Policy*, December 2, 2012, http://www.for eignpolicy.com/articles/2011/12/02/rise_of_the _timbis.

15. Snigdha Dewal, Jack A. Goldstone, and Michael Volpe, "Forecasting Stability or Retreat in Emerging Democracies," *Democracy and Governance* 1 (2013): 32–47; Jack A. Goldstone et al., "A Global Model for Forecasting Political Instability," *American Journal of Political Science* 54, no. 1 (2010): 190–208; Philip Keefer and Razvan Vlaicu, "Democracy, Credibility and Clientelism," *Journal of Law, Economics and Organization* 24, no. 2 (2008): 371–406; and Edward D. Mansfield and Jack L. Snyder, "Democratic Transitions, Institutional Strength, and War," *International Organization* 56, no. 2 (2002): 297–337.

16. Wim Naudé, "Entrepreneurship, Developing Countries, and Development Economics: New Approaches and Insights," *Small Business Economics* 34 (2010): 1–12; and Zoltan J. Acs and Nicola Virgill, *Entrepreneurship in Developing Countries* (Boston: Now Publishers, 2010).

17. Matthew Lange, *Educations in Ethnic Violence: Identity, Educational Bubbles, and Resource Mobilization* (New York: Cambridge University Press, 2011).

18. Promising guides for improving interventions to strengthen failed states include Ashraf Ghani and Clare Lockhart, *Fixing Failed States: A Framework for Rebuilding a Fractured World* (New York: Oxford University Press, 2008); Francis Fukuyama, *State-Building: Governance and World Order in the 21st Century* (Ithaca, NY: Cornell University Press, 2004); Seth D. Kaplan, *Fixing Fragile States: A New Paradigm for Development* (Westport, CT: Praeger, 2008); and Organization for Economic Cooperation and Development, *Supporting Statebuilding in Situations of Conflict and Fragility: Policy Guidance* (Paris: OECD, 2011).

15

MISPERCEPTION, OVERCONFIDENCE, AND COMMUNICATION FAILURE BETWEEN RISING AND STATUS-QUO STATES

Deborah Welch Larson

The main risk of conflict today derives from dynamic power change and uncertainty, especially in Asia, combined with cultural differences. New powers—China, India, Indonesia, South Korea—are rising as part of the inevitable shift of economic production to the East.[1] The rising powers are joining major powers already in the region, such as Japan and Russia, which are unwilling to give up their position. Never before have China, India, and Japan been great powers at the same time, nor do they have any experience in dealing with each other as equals.

Adding to the risk of conflict is uncertainty about the extent of China's future ambitions. The Chinese would like to play a larger role in East Asia, but whether this will be at the expense of the United States is not yet clear.[2]

Despite increasing economic interdependence, there is a risk of a military conflict in the region that could draw in the United States as a result of conflicting claims to territory and maritime rights. Increasing the risk that overlapping claims could lead to war are tensions derived from China's rise to great power status, historical memories, and resistance by smaller states in the region to China's potential dominance. China, for its part, has demonstrated the normal desire of a rising power to receive external recognition, compounded by a strong drive to restore Chinese honor and dignity after "one hundred years of humiliation," beginning with losses in the Opium Wars with Britain and France in 1839–42 (resulting in the cession of Hong Kong) and 1856–60 (including the burning of the imperial summer palace), followed by defeat by an upstart Japan in 1894–95 and subjugation to Japanese imperialism in 1931 and 1937–45.[3] The combination of Chinese emotions, aroused by nationalist sentiment, and Western uncertainty about Chinese intentions suggests the need for remedies beyond conventional prescriptions for confidence-building measures and step-by-step agreements. Psychological biases and overreactions to perceived humiliations could interfere with Beijing's ability to act on a hardheaded assessment of China's interest in maintaining peace in the region.

To understand what is at stake today in Asia, it is useful to draw on more general knowledge derived from historical eras when changing relationships among the major powers generated uncertainty, fears, and status competition. When the relative balance of power among states is changing, two types of misperceptions are likely: first, that the established powers will view the rising power's status aspirations as a guise for expansionist aims, and second, that the rising power will overestimate its capabilities. The established powers generally tend to respond to a rising power with efforts at containment or engagement. Containment of a rising power, however, may lead to a conflict spiral, with each side responding to the other, and a ratchet effect, with ever-increasing levels of tension. A ratchet is a mechanical device that once engaged allows motion in only one direction, as in a car jack. This chapter examines how this basic pattern is playing out in regard to potential flashpoints in the South and East China Seas, as well as the reaction of other states in the region and of the United States. The chapter concludes with some generalizations about the underlying dynamics of relations between rising and established powers.

DYNAMIC POWER RELATIONSHIPS AND STATUS CONCERNS

Uncertainty and changing power relationships can lay the basis for conflict among states over their relative position in the world.[4] Rising powers typically want more prestige and influence to go along with their increased military and economic capabilities.[5] But an improvement in the rising power's prestige usually means a decline in the position of one or more of the established powers. If everyone has high status, then no one does. Loss of status is painful, not only to leaders but also to the population of a country, undermining collective esteem and morale.[6] Consequently, declining or stagnating powers are likely to delay accepting the status claims of a rising power, if it would mean accepting a loss in their own standing.

Added to the inherent competition for position between rising and declining powers are two types of misperception that can increase the likelihood of conflict. First, a rising power's desire for greater recognition and status may be misperceived by others as hegemonic aims. Partly this is because a state cannot simply declare that it wants more status; showing too great an interest in status is demeaning. But, in addition, many of the policies that states use to enhance their status can be interpreted as efforts at power aggrandizement, such as modernizing the military or acquiring blue-water naval capabilities, including aircraft carriers.

Would-be great powers are likely to assert their right to be consulted on issues in smaller neighboring states, to have a *droit de regard*, but such claims are likely to threaten others, particularly medium-sized states that do not want to be part of a sphere of influence. China believes that it is entitled to be the dominant power of Asia because of its history for thousands of years as the Middle Kingdom, to which smaller tributary states such as Korea, Vietnam, Burma, and Siam paid tribute by bearing gifts to the Chinese emperor and receiving gifts in return.[7] Indonesia and Vietnam, however, do not wish to be treated as smaller, subordinate states to the Chinese hegemon.

Despite the difficulty, it is important to distinguish power from status motivations to avoid unnecessary conflict. Some US observers believe that China's "Anti-Access Area Denial" strategy is aimed at preventing the United States from coming to the aid of its allies, in particular, Taiwan.[8] However, if China is mainly trying to act as a great power in neighboring waters, US overreaction could cause conflict and tensions to escalate. From the Chinese perspective, the South China Sea is equivalent to the Caribbean and the Gulf of Mexico for the United States, which asserted the Monroe Doctrine.[9] Many Chinese also believe that establishing a naval presence in coastal seas is essential to restoring China's status after a "century of humiliation" in which imperialist depredations came from the ocean,[10] beginning with the 1839–42 Opium War, when British steam-powered paddle-wheel boats easily overpowered Chinese junks.[11]

The other type of misperception involves the biased processing of information to preserve self-image. Officials of higher-status states are particularly likely to downplay or misinterpret information that suggests their state's relative standing is declining.[12] Such perceptual blinders increase the likelihood that established powers will be insensitive to the status aspirations of rising powers.

Conversely, officials of an aspiring power are apt to denigrate the superior state's resolve—casting the other as a "paper tiger" or "soft"—to rationalize dismissive estimates of its capabilities. Supposedly, the rising state's superior spirit, morale, and élan will carry the day against the established state's power.[13] For example, in 1941, once the Japanese military believed that war with the United States was inevitable, they inferred that the United States would surrender quickly after its fleet was destroyed at Pearl Harbor in Hawaii. Wishful thinking prompted Japanese military planners to ignore information that the United States could outproduce Japan in strategic materials and weapons by ten to one.[14]

This sort of biased information processing can easily lead to overconfidence.[15] Officials play up their areas of superiority while downplaying areas of inferiority.[16] Overconfidence could encourage offensive action by the rising power in response to anger over perceived humiliations or slights. Such incidents could occur unintentionally, as a result of the established powers' defensive efforts against the threat posed by the rising power.

POLICY RESPONSES TO RISING POWERS

Conventional wisdom and standard balance-of-power theory prescribe that external powers should hedge against the risks posed by a rising power's increased military capabilities through some form of containment—either a military buildup in the region or the formation of alliances. For example, some analysts have called for containment of China.[17] The purpose of containment is to deter the emerging power from engaging in aggressive expansion. The rising power, however, is likely to misinterpret containment as an attempt to prevent it from achieving its rightful place. Lower-status states believe that higher-status ones want to keep them down, just as established business firms try to discourage competitors.

Denial of a rising power's status aspirations provokes anger and an offensive reaction.[18] Under the influence of strong emotions, the state is likely to assert its claims forcefully. Strong nationalism and the presence of emotions may block calculations of relative power and considerations of future influence. Before World War I, for example, Germany would have been much better off if it had refrained from aggressive behavior and waited for the power balance to continue shifting in its direction due to its population growth, capable military, and industrial expansion.[19] Fighting to uphold one's dignity and honor, though, is not a matter of rational choice.[20] An example of a status-driven conflict is Russia's 2008 incursion into Georgia. Russia invaded to assert its right to a sphere of "privileged interest" in the former Soviet Union territories and to deter Georgia and Ukraine from joining NATO.[21] Although Russia succeeded in these aims, the war was costly to the Russian economy, precipitating a 46 percent decline in the benchmark Russian Trading System index and capital flight.[22] It is noteworthy that some Chinese naval analysts have cited Russia's incursion into Georgia as a potential model for China in the South China Sea—to assert China's rights and deter further challenges.[23]

Anger and vengefulness help restore an actor's dignity and self-esteem.[24] Although it may be satisfying, such assertive behavior only confirms the original suspicions of status-quo powers and is likely to provoke further efforts at containment in the form of alliance building, arms racing, and military maneuvers. Further military measures will, in turn, confirm the rising power's suspicion that the established powers are determined to prevent its rise. A spiral of conflict may result, with each side responding to the actions of the other, and a ratchet effect.

The alternative policy usually proposed, engagement, entails trying to integrate the rising power into international institutions while using a combination of rewards and punishments to induce it to accept the rules of the system. While engagement is often effective with prospective regional powers such as Brazil, Turkey, or Indonesia, a state that aspires to great power status is unlikely to appreciate being given carrots and sticks as if it were a donkey.[25]

In the nuclear age, with high levels of economic interdependence, it is unlikely that the major powers will deliberately choose to initiate war. States are concerned with security and with increasing their wealth as well as status, so that conflict between rising and declining states is not inevitable. The potential for escalation and substantial economic costs, though, might not prevent an inadvertent military conflict. This could result from adventurist or opportunistic local commanders crossing a border or seizing control of disputed territory. Another possible source of conflict would be military accidents, such as the inadvertent shooting down of a plane or collision between submarines. In 2001, the collision of a US Navy EP-3 spy plane with a fighter jet over China caused a major diplomatic incident.[26] Surveillance activities by status-quo states may be interpreted by the rising power as attempted aggression in its airspace or national waters. For example, in March 2009, five Chinese vessels confronted the USNS *Impeccable*, an unarmed surveillance ship seventy-five miles to the south of Hainan Island in international waters and engaged in risky maneuvering to force it out of the area. The Chinese government protested illegal spying by the United States, claiming that other states must obtain Chinese permission to send military ships inside its two-hundred-mile Exclusive Economic Zone, an interpretation of international law accepted by few other states.[27] The Chinese had stepped up their efforts at interception beginning in 2000 in response to increased US surveillance to monitor China's military modernization.[28] Such incidents may provoke nationalistic fervor on both sides and unwillingness to compromise.

These general observations about the potential for conflict in the confluence of aspiring great powers, status concerns, and changing power distributions apply in particular to China's territorial disputes in the South and East China Seas.

POSSIBLE FLASHPOINTS

China's growing assertiveness in the aftermath of the 2008–9 financial crisis helped precipitate the US "pivot to Asia" announced in November 2011. Increasing incidents in the South China Sea and East China Sea exemplify the influence of status concerns for both rising and declining powers, and the risk of spiral dynamics in confrontations between them.

The South China Sea: Escalating Territorial and Maritime Conflict

Islands and coral reefs in the South China Sea, where the surrounding waters are likely to be rich in oil, gas, and other resources, are claimed by Indonesia, Brunei, Taiwan, Vietnam, Malaysia, and the Philippines, as well as China. China's claims are based on first discovery, historical use, and administration by Chinese governments beginning with the Han dynasty in the second century BCE. Such historical claims are not recognized by international law, which favors states that can show continuous and effective occupation. China was unable to occupy these territories in the nineteenth and twentieth centuries due to domestic instability and foreign intervention. Nevertheless, China claims "indisputable sovereignty" over the South China Sea islands and adjacent waters.[29] Recovering these territories is part of the Chinese leadership's drive to restore China's dignity and status after "one hundred years of humiliation."[30]

In the past, Beijing has deliberately stirred up popular nationalism to achieve foreign policy objectives while distracting attention from domestic problems such as corruption and inequality. Once aroused, popular nationalism can become a constraint on the options of the Chinese leadership, especially given the proliferation of popular media and Internet users.[31] The People's Liberation Army may also be playing up the US role in the dispute to justify the need for higher defense expenditures. Retired military officers have inflamed Chinese nationalists by calling for forcible action to preserve Chinese rights, although this is not necessarily the opinion of the higher leadership.[32] Other Chinese bureaucratic agencies, not under the control of the Foreign Ministry, such as the Bureau of Fisheries Administration, China Marine Surveillance, and local governments, also have their own interests at stake, which do not necessarily coincide with China's national interests.[33]

At stake are fishing rights, oil and gas reserves, and maritime security. The area is prime fishing ground, especially as stocks in nearby areas have dwindled. It may also hold substantial oil and natural gas reserves—how much is unknown because of the difficulty of exploration and competing national claims. Finally, ships with energy and raw materials destined for China and Japan that pass through the Malacca Strait transit the South China Sea. Apart from the Paracels, which it controls, China occupies only some reefs and shoals in the sea, while the other islands are under the administrative control of other claimants. The leading disputants are Vietnam and the Philippines, in addition to China.[34]

Beginning in 2009, China adopted more aggressive tactics toward Vietnam and the Philippines while postponing negotiations with ASEAN countries on a "code of conduct" for the South China Sea.[35] In May 2009, in response to claims from Malaysia and Vietnam, China for the first time submitted to an international organization, the UN Commission on the Limits of the Continental Shelf, a map with a nine-dashed line encompassing at least 80 percent of the disputed waters.[36] Although the line first appeared on Kuomintang maps in 1947, Chinese officials have refused to clarify what they mean—even after six decades—or the extent of Chinese claims. Uncertainty and ambiguity increase anxiety in the region over the scope of China's demands. By one interpretation, China regards the entire area as its "historic waters," a claim that would be in violation of international law.[37] China has also extended the duration of a unilateral fishing ban, increased maritime security patrols (conducted by the Chinese Fisheries Administration Bureau), used various forms of political and economic pressure, and conducted naval exercises in the area.[38]

Partly in response to pressure from Vietnam and other regional states, the United States, which had formerly maintained a position of neutrality on the territorial claims, inserted itself into the conflict at the July 2010 meeting of the Association of Southeast Asian Nations (ASEAN), when Secretary of State Hillary Clinton announced that the United States had a national interest in "freedom of navigation" in the South China Sea and in peaceful resolution of the territorial disputes. Clinton offered the services of the United States in holding multilateral talks on the issue.[39] Surprised and taken aback, the Chinese foreign minister Yang Jiechi delivered a blistering diatribe against outside involvement in the South China Sea issue, which he claimed would only increase tensions. He menacingly reminded the assembled Southeast Asian nations that "China is a big country. Bigger than any countries here."[40] The virulence and emotionality of China's reaction to Clinton's proposal suggests that deep-rooted issues of Chinese identity and self-esteem were aroused by the US decision to take a more active role.

Tensions peaked in spring 2011, when the Philippines joined Vietnam in increasing its economic activity in the area. In March 2011, two vessels operated by the Chinese Marine Surveillance Force, a civilian law enforcement agency, expelled a Philippine vessel conducting a seismic survey in a Philippine exploration block near Reed Bank. In May 2011, China escalated the level of violence by cutting the cable of a Vietnamese seismic survey ship that was operating 120 nautical miles off the coast of Vietnam, and a month later, did the same to a Norwegian ship that was surveying an exploration block off the coast of southern Vietnam.[41] The Chinese foreign ministry claimed that a Chinese fishing boat net was inadvertently entangled in the cables of the Vietnamese vessel, and after being dragged for an hour, the Chinese fishermen cut the cable to separate the two vessels.[42]

By some accounts, the decision by the Obama administration to divert resources from the Middle East to the Far East, the "pivot to Asia," was stimulated by concern over Chinese assertiveness in the South China Sea. The "pivot," or "rebalancing," as it was later called, was announced on President Barack Obama's November 2011 trip to Honolulu, Australia, and Indonesia. As part of the policy shift, President Obama declared his support for a Trans-Pacific Partnership (TPP), a trade and investment organization based on transparency, intellectual property rights, labor rights, environmental protection, and so on—principles that China does not support. (China was not among the initial group of countries asked to participate.) The United States also joined the East Asia Summit. In addition, President Obama signed an agreement with Australia to rotate 2,500 US Marines in Darwin, the point of Australia that is closest to the South China Sea.[43] In 2012, Defense Secretary Leon Panetta announced that the balance of warships between the Middle East and East Asia would shift from 50–50 to a 40–60 distribution by 2020.[44]

The official Chinese response to the US "rebalancing" has been restrained, but most Chinese analysts believe that the United States is trying to prevent the rise of China as a potential rival and is escalating tensions in the region by encouraging other states to challenge China's territorial claims.[45] The United States, however, perceives that its previous passivity and preoccupation with Iraq and Afghanistan has contributed to Chinese overconfidence, and is now trying to redress the balance.[46]

Why are the Chinese making an issue of their claims in the South China Sea at this time? China's recent assertiveness has undone many of the achievements of the "charm offensive" it launched toward Southeast Asia beginning in 1997, to undermine perceptions that China's rise constituted a threat.[47] Previously, Chinese policy for the South China Sea as announced by Deng Xiaoping was to postpone dealing with territorial claims in favor of joint development of the resources.[48] China's recent assertiveness reflects an improved assessment of its relative status due to the humbling of the United States by the 2008–09 financial crisis, which originated on Wall Street. Since the financial crisis, China has recovered relatively rapidly, while the United States has experienced continuing economic stagnation, largely due to political deadlock.[49] In other words, China's forward policy owes as much to psychological factors as to its improved naval capabilities.

And yet the Chinese are *overconfident*, because the US Navy is far superior in firepower, submarines, and aircraft carriers.[50] Nevertheless, if incidents escalate, the United States could be trapped into fighting over islands because of its alliance commitments. The United States is allied with the Philippines and is increasingly cooperating militarily with Vietnam.

Adding to the difficulty of resolving the conflict are the global implications for the US-Chinese rivalry, including the supposed decline of the United States, containment of China, and China's alleged desire to have an exclusive sphere of influence. The dispute over the South China Sea is viewed as emblematic of competition between a rising power, determined to have sway over an area, and a global power trying to preserve its presence in the region.[51] China is now suspicious of ASEAN efforts to resolve the conflict, perceiving that the United States is manipulating the member states.[52]

After undertaking a more moderate approach in mid-2011 to repair relations with other states in the region, China renewed its assertive policies, confronting Vietnam and the Philippines more vigorously. In April 2012, the Philippines sent a warship to arrest eight Chinese fishing boats with large illegal hauls of protected species of giant clams, coral, and live sharks near a disputed island, called Scarborough Shoal by the Philippines and Huangyan Island by the Chinese. Before the Philippine ship could act, however, the Chinese sent two maritime surveillance ships. When the Philippine government replaced the warship with coast guard ships, hoping to deescalate the conflict, a two-month standoff ensued. China retaliated economically by delaying inspection of Philippine bananas, threatening the livelihood of two hundred thousand Filipino farmers, and by canceling tourism to the Philippines, ostensibly on the grounds of safety.[53] President Benigno Aquino negotiated an agreement with Beijing for a mutual withdrawal of ships. After the Philippine vessels left, however, Chinese fishing boats and government ships returned. The Chinese vessels remain, preventing the Filipinos from entering an area where generations have fished, one that is 130 miles off the coast of the Philippines' largest island, Luzon, and more than 500 miles from the southern tip of China's Hainan Island. The Chinese have hung a rope across the lagoon. Some Chinese military analysts have referred to this as the Scarborough Shoal model, advocating the use of a Chinese law-enforcement presence to prevent other claimants from infringing on China's rights in the South China Sea.[54]

China's more forceful assertion of its rights has been part of an interactive dynamic with the Philippines and Vietnam, but China has not reacted proportionally, often escalating to create new facts or deter future challenges. Moreover, the emotionality of China's response and its refusal to negotiate over its sovereign rights suggest that deeper forces are driving its policy.[55]

The East China Sea: Rivalry between a Rising and Declining Power

Even more dangerous is the conflict between Japan and China over the Senkaku (Diaoyu) Islands in the East China Sea. The dispute is escalating in intensity, and the causes of the conflict appear to be symbolic rather than material. As a declining power, Japan does not want to give up any territory, whereas as a rising power, China believes that it is entitled to recover any territories that were lost in the "century of humiliation."[56] It is unclear what value—if any—these five rocky, unoccupied islands possess. During the Ming dynasty (1368–1644), the islands were a bridge between China and Okinawa, a tributary state that traded with the mainland. The Japanese claim that the islands were unoccupied in 1895, when they annexed them, and hence appropriately returned to Japan in 1971. But the Japanese annexation took place after Japan's 1895 defeat of Qing China, which also resulted in their taking possession of Taiwan.[57] The real significance of the islands lies in their symbolism of the rivalry between "Asia's two economic giants, one rising and the other in what many see as a slow decline."[58] Infusing the territorial dispute with added emotion is China's outrage and sense of entitlement over Japan's imperialism in the 1930s and recent backtracking on apologies for its imperialist behavior.

As in the South China Sea dispute, the Chinese have become more vigorous about asserting their claims to the East China Sea islands since the 2008–09 financial crisis. In September 2010, China pressured Japan to release a Chinese fishing captain who was arrested for ramming a Japanese coast guard vessel near the disputed islands. China cancelled ministerial-level talks, curtailed Chinese tourism to Japan, arrested four Japanese construction employees, and announced an embargo of rare-earth minerals, which are vital to Japan's electronics and auto industries. In light of the economic threat, Japan had little choice but to back down.[59]

Tensions flared again in the fall of 2012 when the Japanese government purchased three of the islands from a private owner to prevent the ultranationalist former governor of Tokyo from annexing them. The Chinese foreign ministry denounced the action as "illegal and invalid." Anti-Japanese protests erupted in dozens of Chinese cities, with destruction of Japanese-owned shops and factories. Japanese products were boycotted by Chinese consumers. Chinese tourism to Japan was canceled. Even more significant, on the same day that Japan announced that it was purchasing three islands, China declared a territorial baseline around all the islands, which formally placed them under Chinese administration, justifying Chinese action to prevent intrusion of Japanese Self-Defense Force vessels into the area.[60]

Alarmed, the United States sent a delegation of four high-level members of the US foreign policy establishment—including Stephen Hadley who was the national security adviser under President George W. Bush, and James Steinberg who was Hillary Clinton's number two at the State Department—to warn the Chinese that an attack on the islands was covered by the US mutual defense treaty with Japan.[61]

Undeterred, the Chinese repeatedly sent surveillance ships in December, and a month later, when Japan scrambled fighter jets to intercept a Chinese plane flying near the islands, the Chinese sent their own fighter jets. In February, the Japanese government charged that a Chinese naval frigate used its missile-directing radar to "lock" onto a Japanese naval destroyer, a charge that the Chinese denied.[62] In April 2013, China sent eight patrol ships near the islands, the largest number at one time since the dispute began the previous summer.[63] With increased military activity comes a risk of unauthorized exchange of fire or accidental collision, either at sea or in the air.[64]

As the Chinese have stepped up their naval presence around the islands, Prime Minister Shinzo Abe has pledged to increase Japan's defense budget for the first time in eleven years. With US assistance, a thousand-man unit is being trained to make helicopter and amphibious landings to defend the Senkaku Islands.[65] Abe has compared the Chinese naval intrusions into Japanese-controlled waters to the 1982 Argentine invasion of the Falkland Islands (Malvinas), which sparked a brief military conflict with Britain, suggesting that Japan is defending the principle of rule of law, as did Margaret Thatcher.[66] With such an attitude, a compromise solution appears unlikely.

There is a risk that Japan will be emboldened by the US security guarantee to take more provocative actions in defense of the islands, and that China will blame Japan's newfound assertiveness on interference by the United States. The Japanese have been spurred to stimulate their economy, to reverse their country's slow decline. One of the principal motivations for Abe's attempt to revive the Japanese economy through loose monetary policy, fiscal stimulus, and deregulation is concern over Japan's decline relative to China, and its replacement by China as the world's number two economy.[67] In a February 2013 speech in Washington, Abe asserted that "in order for us, Japan and

the US, to jointly provide the region and the world with more rule of law, more democracy, more security and less poverty, Japan must stay strong."[68] Abe is less inclined to apologize for Japan's past imperialism and more favorable toward visits of high-level officials and lawmakers to the Yasukuni Shrine in Tokyo, where the buried dead include convicted war criminals, a sore point for Chinese and South Koreans.[69]

While a stronger Japanese economy would be beneficial to the world, a more nationalistic Japan that refused to accept its responsibility for World War II would be a menace to other states. But the apparent consistency of China's policy in the South and East China Seas, across the area, and in different countries contributes to the image of an aggressive rising power, an impression that the Chinese leadership wants to avoid.

CONCLUSION

In sum, claims to increased status by rising powers, misperception, and overconfidence could lead to military conflict despite economic interdependence and globalization. Regional economic integration increases incentives for cooperation on shared problems such as piracy, overfishing, congested navigation, pollution, and terrorism. While tensions over islands in the South and East China Seas may wane, the larger problem of competitive dynamics between a rising power and an established one remains.

Neither the realist call to preserve US primacy in the Pacific nor a liberal emphasis on multilateralism addresses the problems raised by uncertainty, shifting power relationships, and regional status aspirations. Ironically, increased regional economic integration has encouraged nationalism and competing sovereignty claims.[70] Fundamental issues include how to recalibrate the relative status of states in the region and how to undermine mistrust. Mistrust arises from uncertainty about a rising power's intentions, which, in turn, provokes efforts by established states to protect against the possibility of future aggression—for example, by strengthening their alliance ties and acquiring new weapons. But such defensive measures are perceived by the rising power as an attempt to keep it from achieving its rightful place. The aspiring power will respond emotionally and assertively to perceived rejection of its status aspirations, which confirms the original suspicion of the leading powers that the emerging state has expansionist intentions. This can lead to a spiral of conflict with a ratchet effect that will be difficult to check or reverse once it is set in motion. The rising power and the established state may become geopolitical rivals even if the two states' aims are not incompatible.

Similar dynamics took place at the beginning of the twentieth century, as Britain's fear of Germany's rising power and increased naval spending contributed to a British search for geopolitical supporters, which in turn fed Germany's sense of being encircled and encouraged its subsequent truculence, creating conditions conducive for the outbreak of World War I.[71]

While insisting that the Chinese use diplomatic means to achieve their ends, the United States also has to be sensitive to China's historically rooted status goals and identity. It is natural for China as a rising power to assert its naval predominance in neighboring waters. With changing power relationships and associated status aspirations, uncertainty, and heightened sensitivity to slights, the established power has to walk a fine line between deterring aggression and provoking anger. The United States must reassure others that it intends to maintain its presence in East Asia to avoid contributing to Chinese perceptions of US relative decline. If the Chinese believe that China is already the leading state in East Asia, then they may miscalculate the US reaction to

bullying, enhancing the risk of inadvertent military conflict. In this regard, the US "pivot to Asia" was prudent. But the United States must also tamp down hostile rhetoric and try to avoid giving the impression that it wants to contain China or prevent its rise. As Chinese president Xi Jinping observed at the Sunnylands summit with President Obama, "The vast Pacific Ocean has enough space for the two large countries of China and the United States."[72]

NOTES

1. National Intelligence Council, Office of the Director of National Intelligence, "Global Trends 2025: A Transformed World" (November 2008), 1–3, 23–36; and National Intelligence Council, "Global Trends 2030: Alternative Worlds" (December 2012), 15–18.

2. For discussion of alternative views of the implications of China's rise, see Alastair Iain Johnston, "Is China a Status Quo Power?" *International Security* 27, no. 4 (Spring 2003): 5–56; Aaron L. Friedberg, "The Future of U.S.-China Relations: Is Conflict Inevitable?" *International Security* 30, no. 2 (Fall 2005): 7–45; Thomas M. Christensen, "Fostering Stability or Creating a Monster? The Rise of China and U.S. Policy toward East Asia," *International Security* 31, no. 1 (Summer 2006): 81–126; Alastair Iain Johnston, "How New and Assertive Is China's New Assertiveness?" *International Security* 37, no. 4 (Spring 2013): 7–48; and Kevin Rudd, "Beyond the Pivot: A New Road Map for U.S.-Chinese Relations," *Foreign Affairs* 92, no. 2 (March/April 2013): 9–15.

3. Peter Hays Gries, *China's New Nationalism: Pride, Politics, and Diplomacy* (Berkeley: University of California Press, 2004), 43–53.

4. See A. F. K. Organski, *World Politics* (New York: Knopf, 1958); A. F. K. Organski and Jacek Kugler, *The War Ledger* (Chicago: University of Chicago Press, 1980), which employ power transition theory; Robert Gilpin, *War and Change in World Politics* (Cambridge: Cambridge University Press, 1981), which employs hegemonic stability theory; and Charles F. Doran, *Systems in Crisis: New Imperatives of High Politics at Century's End* (Cambridge: Cambridge University Press, 1991), which employs power cycle theory.

5. Andrew Hurrell, *On Global Order: Power, Values, and the Constitution of International Society* (Oxford: Oxford University Press, 2007), 45.

6. Daan Scheepers, Naomi Ellemers, and Nieska Sintemaartensdijk, "Suffering from the Possibility of Status Loss: Physiological Responses to Social Identity Threat in High Status Groups," *European Journal of Social Psychology* 39 (2009): 1075–92. For recent scholarship on the importance of status to states, see Richard Ned Lebow, *A Cultural Theory of International Relations* (Cambridge: Cambridge University Press, 2008); Randall Schweller, "Realism and the Present Great Power System: Growth and Positional Conflict over Scarce Resources," in *Unipolar Politics: Realism and State Strategies after the Cold War*, ed. Ethan B. Kapstein and Michael Mastanduno (New York: Columbia University Press, 1999), 28–68; Yong Deng, *China's Struggle for Status: The Realignment of International Relations* (Cambridge: Cambridge University Press, 2008); William C. Wohlforth,"Unipolarity, Status Competition, and Great Power War," *World Politics* 61, no. 1 (January 2009): 28–57; Deborah Welch Larson and Alexei Shevchenko, "Status Seekers: Chinese and Russian Responses to U.S. Primacy," *International Security* 34, no. 4 (Winter 2010): 63–95; and Thomas J. Volgy et al., eds., *Major Powers and the Quest for Status in International Politics: Global and Regional Perspectives* (New York: Palgrave Macmillan, 2011). For a review see Allan Dafoe, Jonathan Renshon, and Paul Huth, "Reputation and Status as Motives for War," *Annual Review of Political Science* (forthcoming).

7. David Shambaugh, *China Goes Global: The Partial Power* (New York: Oxford University Press, 2012), 53–54; and David C. Kang, *East Asia before the West: Five Centuries of Trade and Tribute* (New York: Columbia University Press, 2010).

8. James R. Holmes and Toshi Yoshihara, "History Rhymes: The German Precedent for Chinese Seapower," *Orbis* 54, no. 1 (Winter 2010): 27; and Michael D. Swaine, *America's Challenge: Engaging a Rising China in the Twenty-First Century* (Washington, DC: Carnegie Endowment, 2011), 159–60.

9. Toshi Yoshihara and James R. Holmes, "Can China Defend a 'Core Interest' in the South

China Sea?" *Washington Quarterly* 34, no. 2 (2011): 48; and Marvin Ott, "Southeast Asia's Strategic Landscape," *SAIS Review* 32, no. 1 (2012): 122.

10. Carnes Lord, "China and Maritime Transformations," in *China Goes to Sea: Maritime Transformation in Comparative Historical Perspective*, ed. Andrew S. Erickson, Lyle Goldstein, and Carnes Lord (Annapolis, MD: Naval Institute Press, 2009), 447.

11. Jonathan D. Spence, *The Search for Modern China* (New York: W. W. Norton, 1990), 157–58.

12. B. Ann Bettencourt, Kelly Charlton, Nancy Dorr, and Deborah L. Hume, "Status Differences and In-Group Bias: A Meta-Analytic Examination of the Effects of Status Stability, Status Legitimacy, and Group Permeability," *Psychological Bulletin* 127, no. 4 (2001): 520–42.

13. For examples from Russian history, see William C. Fuller Jr., *Strategy and Power in Russia 1600–1914* (New York: Free Press, 1992).

14. Michael A. Barnhart, "Japanese Intelligence before the Second World War: 'Best Case' Analysis," in *Knowing One's Enemies: Intelligence Assessment before the Two World Wars*, ed. Ernest R. May (Princeton, NJ: Princeton University Press, 1984), 450–55.

15. Dominic D. P. Johnson, *Overconfidence and War: The Havoc and Glory of Positive Illusions* (Cambridge, MA: Harvard University Press, 2004).

16. For supporting psychological evidence, see Henri Tajfel and John C. Turner, "An Integrative Theory of Intergroup Conflict," in *The Social Psychology of Intergroup Relations*, ed. William G. Austin and Stephen Worchel (Monterey, CA: Brooks/Cole, 1979), 33–47. For experimental evidence, see Naomi Ellemers and Wendy Van Rijswijk, "Identity Needs versus Social Opportunities: The Use of Group-Level and Individual-Level Identity Management Strategies," *Social Psychology Quarterly* 60, no. 1 (March 1997): 52–65; and Naomi Ellemers, Wendy Van Rijswijk, Marlene Roefs, and Catrien Simons, "Bias in Intergroup Perceptions: Balancing Group Identity with Social Reality," *Personality and Social Psychology Bulletin* 23, no. 2 (1997): 186–98.

17. John J. Mearsheimer, *The Tragedy of Great Power Politics* (New York: W. W. Norton, 2001), chap. 10; and Aaron L. Friedberg, *A Contest for*

Supremacy: China, America, and the Struggle for Mastery in Asia (New York: W. W. Norton, 2011).

18. Henri Tajfel, "Achievement of Group Differentiation: Studies in the Social Psychology of Intergroup Relations," in *Differentiation between Social Groups: Studies in the Social Psychology of Intergroup Relations*, ed. Henri Tajfel (London: Academic Press, 1978), 96–97; Rupert J. Brown and Gordon F. Ross, "The Battle for Acceptance: An Investigation into the Dynamics of Intergroup Behavior," in *Social Identity and Intergroup Relations*, ed. Henri Tajfel (Cambridge: Cambridge University Press, 1982), 155–78; Diane Mackie, Thierry Devos, and Eliot R. Smith, "Intergroup Emotions: Explaining Offensive Action Tendencies in an Intergroup Context," *Journal of Personality and Social Psychology* 79, no. 4 (October 2000): 603, 606, 613; and Reinhard Wolf, "Respect and Disrespect in International Politics: The Significance of Status Recognition," *International Theory* 3, no. 1 (2011): 126–32.

19. Paul Kennedy, *The Rise and Fall of the Great Powers: Economic Change and Military Conflict from 1500 to 2000* (New York: Random House, 1987), 210–13.

20. Andrei P. Tsygankov, *Russia and the West from Alexander to Putin: Honor in International Relations* (Cambridge: Cambridge University Press, 2012).

21. Eugene Rumer and Angela Stent, "Russia and the West," *Survival* 51, no. 2 (April 2009): 94. "Privileged interest" was the term used by President Dmitry Medvedev in an interview with Russian television channels after Russia's war with Georgia, August 31, 2008, http://www.kremlin.ru/eng/speeches /2008/08/31/1850_type82912type82916_206003. shtml.

22. Andrew E. Kramer, "Russia Stock Market Fall Is Said to Imperil Oil Boom," *New York Times*, September 13, 2008; and Andrew E. Kramer, "Russia Halts Stock Trading as Indexes Decline," *New York Times*, September 18, 2008.

23. Lyle Goldstein, "Chinese Naval Strategy in the South China Sea: An Abundance of Noise and Smoke, but Little Fire," *Contemporary Southeast Asia* 33, no. 3 (December 2011): 338–39.

24. Philip Shaver, Judith Schwartz, Donald Kirson, and Cary O'Connor, "Emotion Knowl-

edge: Further Exploration of a Prototype Approach," *Journal of Personality and Social Psychology* 52, no. 6 (June 1987): 1078.

25. Robert Jervis, "The Challenges of Coercive Diplomacy," *Foreign Affairs* 92, no. 1 (2013): 113.

26. Gries, *China's New Nationalism*, 108–13.

27. Kathryn Hille, "China Hits Out at US 'Illegal' Intrusion," *Financial Times*, March 11, 2009; "Naked Aggression: China and America Spar at Sea," *Economist*, March 14, 2009, 45; Michael D. Swaine and M. Taylor Fravel, "China's Assertive Behavior—Part Two: The Maritime Periphery," *China Leadership Monitor*, no. 35 (September 21, 2011): 10, Hoover Institution, http://www.hoover .org/publications/china-leadership-monitor/article /93591; and David Rosenberg, "Governing the South China Sea: From Freedom of the Seas to Ocean Enclosure Movements," *Harvard Asia Quarterly* 12, nos. 3–4 (Winter 2010): 10–11; "China Says U.S. Naval Ship Breaks International, Chinese Law," Xinhua, http://news.xinhuanet.com/ english/2009-03/10/content_10983647.htm.

28. Swaine and Fravel, "China's Assertive Behavior," 11.

29. Li Guoqiang, "The Formation of China's Sovereignty over the South China Seas Islands and the Origins of the South China Sea Dispute," *Qiushi Journal* (English edition) 3, no. 4 (October 2011), http://english.qstheory.cn/international /201112/t20111229_132736.htm; Ian Storey, "China's Bilateral and Multilateral Diplomacy in the South China Sea," in *Cooperation from Strength: The United States, China, and the South China Sea*, ed. Patrick M. Cronin (Washington, DC: Center for a New American Security, January 2012), http://www.cnas.org/southchinasea, 54.

30. Michael D. Swaine, "China's Maritime Disputes in the East and South China Seas," testimony before the US-China Economic and Security Review Commission, April 4, 2013, Carnegie Endowment for International Peace, http://carn egieendowment.org/files/Michael_Swaine_-_ Testimony.pdf.

31. Susan L. Shirk, *China: Fragile Superpower* (Oxford: Oxford University Press, 2007), 62; and Suisheng Zhao, "Foreign Policy Implications of Chinese Nationalism Revisited: The Strident Turn," *Journal of Contemporary China* 22, no. 82 (2013): 544–45.

32. International Crisis Group (ICG), "Stirring Up the South China Sea (1)," Asia Report no. 223, April 23, 2012, 11, 28, 33. See also the discussion in Goldstein, "Chinese Naval Strategy in the South China Sea," 320–47.

33. ICG, "Stirring Up the South China Sea," 8–10.

34. Ibid.

35. "Choppy Waters: China's Assertiveness at Sea," *Economist*, January 23, 2010, 41–42; "Shoal Mates: The South China Sea," *Economist*, April 28, 2012, 44; "Roiling the Waters: The South China Sea," *Economist*, July 7, 2012, 39–40; and "Divided We Stagger: ASEAN in Crisis," *Economist*, August 18, 2012, 35–36.

36. "Note from the People's Republic of China to the Secretary-General of the United Nations, May 7, 2009," http://www.un.org/depts/los/clcs_new/submissions_files/mysvnm33_09/chn_2009re_mys_vnm_e.pdf.

37. M. Taylor Fravel, "China's Strategy in the South China Sea," *Contemporary Southeast Asia* 33, no. 3 (December 2011): 294–95; and Storey, "China's Bilateral and Multilateral Diplomacy, 54."

38. Fravel, "China's Strategy in the South China Sea," 303–5; and Swaine, *America's Challenge*, 161.

39. Mark Landler, "Offering to Aid Talks, US Challenges China on Disputed Islands," *New York Times*, July 24, 2010; Andrew Jacobs, "Stay Out of Island Dispute, Chinese Warn the US," *New York Times*, July 27, 2010; and ICG, "Stirring Up the South China Sea," 22–23.

40. Jeffrey A. Bader, *Obama and China's Rise: An Insider's Account of America's Asia Strategy* (Washington, DC: Brookings Institution Press, 2010), 105–6.

41. Fravel, "China's Strategy in the South China Sea," 306–7.

42. "Foreign Ministry Spokesperson Hong Lei's Remarks on Vietnamese Ships Chasing away Chinese Fishing Boats in the Waters off the Nansha Islands," Ministry of Foreign Affairs (China), June 9, 2011, http://www.fmprc.gov.cn/eng/xwfw/s2510/t829427.htm.

43. Geoff Dyer, Richard McGregor, and David Pilling, "Obama Shifts Foreign Policy Focus to Asia-Pacific," *Financial Times*, November 16, 2011; Ian Johnson and Jackie Calmes, "As U.S.

Looks Toward Asia, It Sees China Everywhere," *New York Times*, November 15, 2011; and Martin S. Indyk, Kenneth G. Lieberthal, and Michael E. O'Hanlon, *Bending History: Barack Obama's Foreign Policy* (Washington, DC: Brookings Institution Press, 2012), 57–60.

44. "Pivotal Concerns," *Economist*, May 11, 2013, 59.

45. Michael Swaine, "Chinese Leadership and Elite Responses to the U.S. Pacific Pivot," *China Leadership Monitor*, no. 38 (August 6, 2012), Hoover Institution, http://www.hoover.org/publications/china-leadership-monitor/article/124546; and Shambaugh, *China Goes Global*, 77. See, for example, Zhong Sheng, "Goals of US 'Return-to-Asia' Strategy Questioned," *People's Daily* (English edition), October 18, 2011, http://english.people daily.com.cn/90780/7620216.html; Wang Fan, "Commentary: U.S. Should Back up its Proclaimed 'Good Intentions' in Asia-Pacific with Action," Xinhua, June 6, 2012, http://news.xinhuanet.com/english/indepth/2012-06/03/c_131628241.htm.

46. Shawn Brimley and Ely Ratner, "Smart Shift: A Response to 'The Problem with the Pivot,'" *Foreign Affairs* 92, no. 1 (January/February 2013): 177–81.

47. David Shambaugh, "China Engages Asia: Reshaping the Regional Order," *International Security* 29, no. 3 (Winter 2004–05): 64–99; and Shambaugh, *China Goes Global*, 60–61.

48. Fravel, "China's Strategy in the South China Sea," 312.

49. Kenneth Lieberthal and Wang Jisi, *Addressing U.S.-China Strategic Distrust*, John L. Thornton China Center Monograph Series (Washington, DC: Brookings Institution Press, 2012), vii–viii, 10; Shambaugh, *China Goes Global*, 22–23, 51–52; and Ott, "Southeast Asia's Strategic Landscape," 121.

50. Swaine, *America's Challenge*, 173–74, 177–78.

51. Brantly Womack, "The Spratlys: From Dangerous Ground to Apple of Discord," *Contemporary Southeast Asia* 33, no. 3 (December 2011): 375–76.

52. ICG, "Stirring Up the South China Sea," 22.

53. "Shoal Mates," 44; Jane Perlez, "Dispute between China and Philippines over Island Becomes

More Heated," *New York Times*, May 11, 2012; David Pilling, "The Nine Dragons Stirring Up the South China Sea," *Financial Times*, May 17, 2012.

54. Zhao, "Foreign Policy Implications of Chinese Nationalism," 550; Barbara Demick, "In a Disputed Reef, Philippines Sees Face of Chinese Domination," *Los Angeles Times*, May 14, 2013; and ICG, "Stirring Up the South China Sea," 8–9.

55. Swaine, "China's Maritime Disputes," 4.

56. International Crisis Group, "Dangerous Waters: China-Japan Relations on the Rocks," Asia Report no. 245, April 8, 2013.

57. David Pilling, "Why China and Japan Are Oceans Apart," *Financial Times*, November 11, 2010; and "Narrative of an Empty Space," *Economist*, December 22, 2012, 53–55.

58. Martin Fackler, "In Shark-Infested Waters, Resolve of Two Giants Is Tested," *New York Times*, September 23, 2012.

59. Martin Fackler and Ian Johnson, "Japan Retreats in Test of Wills with the Chinese," *New York Times*, September 25, 2010; and "Bare Anger: Rocky Relations between China and Japan," *Economist*, November 6, 2010, 53–54.

60. ICG, "Dangerous Waters," 10–11.

61. Gideon Rachman, "The Shadow of 1914 Falls over the Pacific Ocean," *New York Times*, February 5, 2013.

62. "The Drums of War," *Economist*, January 13, 2013, 43–44; Martin Fackler, "Japan Says China Aimed Weapons-Targeting Radar at Ship near Islands," *New York Times*, February 6, 2013; and Chris Buckley, "China Denies Directing Radar at Japanese Naval Vessel and Copter," *New York Times*, February 9, 2013.

63. Martin Fackler, "Old Sore Spots Flare Up in China-Japan Disputes," *New York Times*, April 24, 2013.

64. ICG, "Dangerous Waters," 45–49.

65. Martin Fackler, "Japan Shifting Further Away from Pacifism," *New York Times*, April 2, 2013.

66. Chris Buckley, "China Trades Sharp Words with Japan over Islands," *New York Times*, March 1, 2013.

67. Martin Fackler, "Japan's New Optimism Has Name: Abenomics," *New York Times*, May 21, 2013.

68. David Pilling, "China and the Post-Tsunami Spirit Have Revived Japan," *Financial Times*, May 9, 2013; and "Japan and Abenomics," *Economist*, May 18, 2013, 24–26.

69. "Japan's Master Plan," *Economist*, May 18, 2013, 13; and Fackler, "Old Sore Spots."

70. Rosenberg, "Governing the South China Sea," 4, 7, 12.

71. See, for example, Jonathan Steinberg, *Yesterday's Deterrent: Tirpitz and the Birth of the German Battle Fleet* (London: Macdonald, 1965); and Ivo Nikolai Lambi, *The Navy and German Power Politics, 1862–1914* (Boston: Allen and Unwin, 1984).

72. The White House, "Remarks by President Obama and President Xi Jinping of the People's Republic of China before Bilateral Meeting," news release, June 7, 2013, http://www.whitehouse.gov/the-press-office/2013/06/07/remarks-president-obama-and-president-xi-jinping-peoples-republic-china-.

PART III

ACTORS AND INSTITUTIONS

16

THE PICCOLO, TRUMPET, AND BASS FIDDLE
THE ORCHESTRATION OF COLLECTIVE CONFLICT MANAGEMENT

Chester A. Crocker, Fen Osler Hampson, and Pamela Aall

A rapidly changing conflict management environment in the post–Cold War era has challenged the international community to develop a unified response to security problems. However, in the place of formal alliances and intergovernmental bodies, a new relatively unstructured approach has come to the fore. Collective conflict management (CCM) is an emerging phenomenon of multiagency behavior in international relations in which state, intergovernmental, and nonstate actors band together to deal with security challenges, to diminish or end violence, and to improve conditions for sustainable peace. This chapter suggests that CCM has arisen as a response to a vacuum in global consensus, offers a definition of CCM, identifies requirements for CCM to work, and examines the motivation of CCM participants.[1]

This chapter presents three examples of CCM. The first, the effort to combat piracy off the Somali coast, is based on strong shared interests among the participants to shore up their own security and to provide governance in the waters off of Somalia. This effort, although still ongoing, seems to be successful; the coalition is holding and takes effective action on a regular basis. The second case dates to the early 2000s and documents an attempt to help end a low-level but potentially destabilizing war in the Philippines. This effort did not succeed but laid the groundwork for the peace agreement of 2014. The third CCM case involves the Special Court for Sierra Leone, which deals with accountability issues arising out of the ten-year civil war in Sierra Leone. This ongoing effort has been successful in prosecuting and trying those charged with war crimes. All these cases involve the cooperation of a wide range of third-party actors in addressing threats to security, using both coercive and noncoercive instruments to advance their respective interests. Whether or not these cases point to a sustainable future for CCM is an open question.

MANAGING SECURITY OR MANAGING CONFLICT?

One of the vexing problems today is the lack of international consensus on security threats and challenges to conflict management. The long post–Cold War period is still in search of a name, especially in the realm of security. Although there are many candidates—"post–Cold War," "global war on terror," "rise of China and India," "decline of the United States," "age of fragile and failing states"—none captures the essence of the period and gives a sense of direction to the security problems that exist today. Without an agreed-upon definition of what the security problems are, it is difficult to craft a unified—or even somewhat coordinated—response. Even categorizing the challenges the international community faces is a problem. Are weak states security risks or development failures? Do repressive governments threaten regional security by denying universal freedoms and essential human rights, or are they guarantors of stability in turbulent places? What are the roots of terrorism—social injustice or a desire for power? Are these security or conflict management challenges? Does this distinction matter?[2]

Historically, academics and practitioners have made a distinction between international or national security and conflict management. International and national security are concerned with the security of the state and the international system against threats to stability and the capacity to govern. The nation-state lies at the heart of the definition. This objective still is a potent force in world dynamics, illustrated by both the time and the attention given to transnational threats to state security such as terrorism, international crime, interstate disputes, and refugee flows. The aim of national and international security is to provide a relatively predictable international environment in which threats to security can be contained, managed, or counteracted on a national or global basis.

But since 1990 and the end of the Cold War, the international environment has changed greatly. In some regions, borders have been reshaped and new states have proliferated. Although many of these new states have made relatively peaceful transitions to independence, at least half of them were born out of violent conflict or have seen periods of serious conflict since independence. Thus, while these transitions may be positive for security in the long run, in the immediate moment they are often destabilizing and pose threats to regional and global security. Transitions within long-established states and states that emerged during the heyday of European decolonization, such as Tunisia, Libya, Egypt, Somalia, Pakistan, and Syria, can also undermine regional security as societies struggle over leadership and legitimacy battles.

More destabilizing has been the persistent weakness of states in crisis—for example, Afghanistan, Pakistan, Iraq, Sudan, South Sudan, Congo, Ethiopia, and Haiti. All these countries are in the top twenty of the Fund for Peace's 2013 Failed State Index, and all have been in or near conflict in recent years.[3] The first five in that top twenty are critical to US national security, and the other fifteen—including Somalia, Chad, Zimbabwe, Côte d'Ivoire, Yemen, and Burma—have a high potential for causing violent regional instability and providing conditions in which conflict entrepreneurs, criminal behavior, and terrorism can thrive.

Managing conflict in these situations engages a variety of actors—the United Nations, regional organizations, nongovernmental organizations (NGOs), and states. The objective of these conflict management ventures is to prevent or end the fighting and put societies, states, and regions back together after they have been rent apart by conflict. Although these conflicts may play out in remote places, their ramifications for global and regional security can be profound. The United States' experience in Iraq and Afghanistan has clearly illustrated the extent to which managing conflict and shoring up national security have overlapped in the last ten years.

The term *conflict management* is sometimes used narrowly to describe the peaceful resolution of disputes through negotiation and other "soft power" instruments. It is distinguished from traditional security management, which relies on "hard power" and the use of force to advance key national interests. In its broader usage, however, conflict management covers the use of both hard and soft power instruments to address both traditional and nontraditional security threats and conflict challenges. (These conflict management techniques include, for example, the employment of various diplomatic, legal, judicial, policing, and economic instruments in conjunction with the use of force.)

Given the growing overlap between security and conflict management, there might be an expectation that there would be a growing international consensus on the causes of conflict and effective ways to respond to it. In fact, the opposite seems to have happened. The major powers, caught up in cascading economic crises, give sporadic attention to persistent conflicts and are caught by surprise by significant events, shown, for example, in the slow reaction to the 2010 street protests in North Africa and the Middle East. The United Nations plays a relatively muted role on the world stage, at least in comparison to the role it played in the 1990s. Regional organizations in some areas have moved to fill the security gap, but in others, the security/conflict management vacuum allows conflicts to fester and burn.[4]

NGOs, although willing to play a role, are in most circumstances too weak to have much impact when acting by themselves. And for all these institutions, the question of how to characterize, analyze, and respond to conflagrations continues to bewilder. Yet, while there has been a breakdown in global consensus on what is the problem, what is the appropriate response, and who should take the lead in responding, a persistence of low-level conflicts threatens security in various parts of the globe. The problem will not go away just because no one seems to have an answer.

COLLECTIVE CONFLICT MANAGEMENT: DEFINITIONS AND TYPOLOGIES

CCM describes an emerging phenomenon in international relations in which individual states, coalitions and alliances, international institutions, and nonofficial bodies address potential or actual security threats by acting together to (1) diminish or end the violent conflict; (2) offer mediation or other assistance to a negotiation process or negotiated settlement; (3) help resolve political, economic, and/or social issues associated with a conflict; and/or (4) provide monitoring, guarantees, or other long-term measures to improve conditions for a sustainable peace.

CCM is related to, but distinct from, collective defense and collective security. The North Atlantic Treaty Organization (NATO) is a classic example of collective defense, an arrangement wherein

> The Parties agree that an armed attack against one or more of them . . . shall be considered an attack against them all; and consequently they agree that, if such an armed attack occurs, each of them in exercise of the right of individual or collective self-defense recognized by Article 51 of the Charter of the United Nations, will assist the Party or Parties

so attacked by taking forthwith, individually and in concert with the other Parties, such action as it deems necessary, including the use of armed force, to restore and maintain the security of the North Atlantic area.[5]

It is a formal arrangement based on a treaty ratified by the legislative bodies of the member states, binding on the signatories, and relatively clear as to rights and responsibilities. Collective security—exemplified by the United Nations—is also treaty based, but it is broader ranging than collective defense, being universal in scope and incorporating members' agreement that they will not attack each other in addition to pledging to work together on what to do if a member is the object of attack.[6] Regional groups such as the African Union apply this principle regionally. Both collective defense and collective security arrangements involve long-term relationships among the members, formal decision-making structures, and an expectation that action under the arrangement could be activated by a variety of threats, including ones unforeseen by the original treaty drafters.

CCM arrangements may coexist and overlap with collective defense and security activities, but they differ from them in a few important ways:

- CCM arrangements are not necessarily the result of a formal treaty or membership in an organization; they can be the result of an informal agreement to act jointly to resolve a conflict.
- CCM arrangements do not involve an enduring relationship among the collaborating organizations, but can be either ad hoc or part of a collective mission statement.
- CCM arrangements may be organized around a single conflict and be disbanded once that conflict is resolved.

- Membership in a CCM arrangement may include both official and non-official organizations.
- Interventions undertaken by CCM arrangements can occur even if the target country does not invite help (especially if NGOs are involved in the CCM).

Collaboration in conflict management efforts is not a new trend, and there are several examples of collaboration that brought together different institutions in peace processes. The war in Bosnia saw the collective action by the United States, NATO, and the Organization for Security and Cooperation in Europe (OSCE). More recently, the African Union and the United Nations have shared the space in Sudan. Quite often, however, these examples of collective action turn out to be sequential engagements rather than cotemporaneous responses, meaning that one institution hands off responsibility to another, rather than the two acting together simultaneously.

The addition of NGOs to collaborative arrangements is also not new. Sant'Egidio, a lay Catholic charity organization, led the mediation in Mozambique in the early 1990s. In this case, the NGO was supported in an informal sense by three regional and five external powers, which lent heft to the process and provided guarantees. Although this is an early example of an informal network, its form was still fairly traditional. The principal lead—albeit an NGO—acted alone and in a leadership role, rather than as part of a group of institutions that shared responsibility for the mediation.[7]

There are no membership rules associated with CCM. A CCM engagement might encompass international organizations (the United Nations), regional organizations, countries acting in concert, and coalitions of official and nonofficial organizations. Because CCM is a relatively new "system," with no organizational center or universal rules, its practice may vary depending on who is practicing it and the circumstances of the conflict.

Categories of CCM Engagement

CCM engagement can be grouped into three major categories: operational or functional cooperation; cooperation for mediation; and normative cooperation. Operational or functional cooperation focuses on solving a specific problem or set of problems that directly affects CCM coalition members. The action is initiated by the outside third parties, and there is generally broad consensus on how to resolve the issue at stake. These coalitions are usually led by a powerful entity (or entities) that calls the shots, and the costs of the coalition are generally shared according to the ability to pay. In these CCM operations, each member benefits from the collective action.

CCM in support of mediation may arise because third parties decide to help a peace process along or because the parties to the conflict want a broadly representative body associated with the peace process. These coalitions are generally more fragmented than functional CCM groupings, and consensus on the problem and the solution may or may not be present. The lead in mediation CCM varies and depends in part on the preferences of the parties to the conflict, and thus may change as party preferences change. At times, the entity that bears the costs is different from the lead CCM actor (e.g., Norway is often willing to fund third-party processes in which it is not involved). The direct beneficiaries of a successful mediation CCM effort are generally the parties and societies involved in the conflict, although the CCM members may also benefit in terms of increased regional or global security and boosts to their own reputations as skillful managers of contentious processes.

Normative CCM cooperation arises because groups within the conflict area or external groups endorse intervention (political, legal, or military) in support of human rights or humanitarian norms, for instance, the responsibility to protect (R2P). Although there may be consensus about the problem and the solution among the CCM actors, their ability to act is often constrained, putting a strain on the CCM coalition. The lead actor is often a prominent person or an institution acting on behalf of the United Nations or the international community. The beneficiaries of a successful normative CCM process are generally the aggrieved parties or target population, although some generalized benefit may be conferred by removing direct threats to security and through deterrence of future threats. CCM members may benefit from the application of norms, especially if there is broad domestic or international support for the norm in question.

Motivations for Collaboration

Each of these CCM arrangements offers different benefits to their memberships. Collaboration means that costs can be shared, leverage can be gained from partners, and more issues can be covered. A CCM arrangement augments these benefits. Operational CCM offers the most direct benefits to members, but mediation CCM and normative CCM cooperation also bring some benefits. However, it is important to remember that collaboration in a conflict management effort changes the benefit equation for all members of the collective. Collaboration comes with costs. Joint analysis, planning, and execution are difficult unless institutions have well-practiced habits of coordinating, as the arduous interagency process in the United States (and elsewhere) shows. If the bulk of a mediator's time is spent negotiating with his or her foreign ministry or in the interagency environment, adding partners to the decision-making process only magnifies the complexities.[8] Sharing the costs does not always mean that costs are shared equally or even proportionally (to size or to decision-making weight). What, then, drives entities to collaborate in conflict management ventures?

Understanding the dynamics of collective action has been the focus of much study in both economics and political science. Since Mancur Olsen's seminal work, *The Logic of Collective Action*, many people have explored why collectivities arise, why entities join them, who bears the costs, what determines the outcome, and how effective these arrangements are.[9] In the international relations/conflict management field, topics have ranged from defense or security alliances to cooperation on natural resources.[10] However, a basic assumption behind these examinations of collective behavior is that the actors act in their own self-interest—that each will benefit in direct ways from the coordination effort. The benefits are often tangible—that is, more security or a more equitable access to scarce resources—but there are also many cases in which the benefits may be intangible, for instance, an enhancement of one's reputation in the eyes of the larger community or the potential avoidance of future costs. Some collaborative ventures are driven by altruism, as in the case of international efforts to assist victims of major natural disasters.

The tangible benefits to a third party of participating in a conflict management exercise are usually less direct than the benefits realized through alliances. This is not to say that the benefits are not real. They may involve greater general security across a region or a better environment for international trade. The intangible benefits may be more direct, revolving around the reputation and legitimacy of the third-party actor. Norway's engagement in active third-party peacemaking sharpened that country's pro-file as a force for good on the international stage. The work of the Carter Center in numerous conflicts has also enhanced that organization's reputation.[11]

There seem to be five kinds of motivations to become engaged in a CCM exercise: security needs; more generalized governance concerns growing out of the challenges of dealing with the anarchy of ungoverned places; the impetus provided by a belief in conflict management approaches; reaction to the pressure of domestic interests and politics; and the requirements of organizational mandates.

Similar to collective defense arrangements, CCM based on security needs springs from a common vision of the problem and of the solution. Members of the coalition engage in a joint assessment of the security threat and arrive at a mutually acceptable means to divide tasks associated with the response and a willingness to share the costs of the security arrangement in some equitable arrangement.[12]

CCM action may also arise from concerns about the risk that ongoing conflict—especially in weak states—presents in terms not only of destabilizing regional security and promoting terrorists networks but also of encouraging illicit drug networks and other criminal behavior. The normative exigency to respond in positive ways to conflict can be found in the increasing activity of groups of like-minded states such as the European Union and of individual states such as Norway and Switzerland to offer leadership, funding, and/or support to peace processes. This action is not based on immediate self-interest, but may be based on a bond between the third party and one of the parties to the conflict. American official engagement with the Philippines was based not only on security interest in isolating regional terrorist groups that might be in contact with the Moro Islamic Liberation Front but also on the long involvement of the United

States in the Philippines' history and development.

A third motivation—the preference for stopping the fighting rather than allowing conflicts to continue indefinitely—reflects an emerging consensus on the need for international conflict management. The fact that since the end of the Cold War roughly one-third of all conflicts have been settled, at least temporarily, through a process of negotiation, generally with the assistance of third parties, underscores this emergent norm in international relations.

Domestic politics can also push a government or even private groups to become more active in a collaborative peace process. This is apparent in cases in which the third-party state does not have sufficient resources or political will to lead a process by itself. Domestic politics in France, Britain, and other European states incline these countries to seek a visible role with other actors in Middle East conflict issues, while in the United States, a confluence of activist interest groups played a decisive role in prompting the government to become a leading player in the quest for peace in Sudan (and between it and South Sudan), acting in coordination with African and European states and the African Union.

Finally, organizational mandates—the way that organizations define their tasks and justify their existence—can serve as a powerful motivating influence to join a CCM venture. An organizational mandate is often the foundation of NGO engagement in conflict management and provides a sturdy platform for NGOs as they engage with larger, more powerful but less flexible organizations. The United Nations is also driven by an organizational mandate to respond to the request of member states or the Security Council to engage in conflict management, whether or not it has the financial and human resources to undertake such a mission.

CASES OF COLLECTIVE CONFLICT MANAGEMENT

Table 1 shows three cases of international engagement in internal conflicts as examples of the different types of CCM. The first is cooperation against piracy in the Horn of Africa and Western Indian Ocean (the Somali piracy case), which is an example of operational or functional CCM. The second is a facilitation effort in the Philippines as an illustration of CCM for mediation. The third is the Special Court for Sierra Leone as an example of normative CCM.

Table 1 indicates the strength or weakness of a cooperative endeavor depending on the type of CCM initiative, the motivation of the actors, and the effectiveness of the CCM effort ("capacity").

This section examines these three cases, looking at who are the actors, why CCM emerged, what CCM activities were undertaken, and how effective the efforts were. The section closes with a discussion of the CCM members' motivations.

Cooperation against Piracy in the Horn of Africa/Western Indian Ocean

Escalating attacks by Somali pirates on tankers, fishing boats, and merchant vessels crossing the Gulf of Aden, Arabian Sea, and Western Indian Ocean have generated an unusually broad-based conflict management response. This example of CCM has featured a rare blend of hard power actions and coordinated diplomatic initiatives, paralleled by private-sector measures and judicial assistance to bring captured pirates to justice. Although it remains ad hoc, CCM against piracy rests on a strong legal and institutional foundation, reflecting the fact that piracy has been long established as a "crime of universal jurisdiction" (meaning that any state can take action against it).

Table 1. Differing motivations and capacities in different types of CCM

TYPE OF CCM	MOTIVATING FACTORS				
	National Interest/Security Concerns	**Governance/ Instability Concerns**	**Conflict Management Imperatives**	**Domestic Politics**	**Organizational Mandates**
Operational or Functional CCM	Strong—Somali piracy case	Intermediate motivation/ weak to intermediate capacity	Intermediate motivation/ intermediate to strong capacity	Strong motivation, strong capacity	Strong motivation, weak to intermediate capacity
CCM for Mediation	Intermediate— Philippines	Intermediate motivation/ weak to intermediate capacity	Intermediate motivation/ weak to intermediate capacity	Weak to intermediate motivation, weak to intermediate capacity	Strong motivation, weak to intermediate capacity
Normative CCM	Weak—Sierra Leone Criminal Court	Intermediate motivation	Intermediate motivation/ weak to intermediate capacity	Intermediate to strong motivation/ weak to intermediate capacity	Strong motivation, weak to intermediate capacity

Who Are the Primary CCM Actors? A combination of intergovernmental, regional, state, and private actors has mounted a collaborative effort to address the threat. Naval action against pirates got into high gear in 2008 as participating states coordinated laterally at sea via NATO; the US Central Command, or CENTCOM (US Fifth Fleet at Bahrain); and EU channels. The effort was accompanied by a series of UN Security Council resolutions. Pursuant to UNSC Resolution 1851, a Contact Group on Piracy off the Coast of Somalia was created on January 14, 2009. The resolution explicitly called for a voluntary, ad hoc international forum to encourage countries, organizations, and industry groups with an interest in combating piracy to do so. Forty-nine countries and seven international bodies participate (the African Union, the League of Arab States, the European Union, INTERPOL,

the International Maritime Organization, NATO, and the UN Secretariat), as well as two major maritime industry groups—the Baltic and International Maritime Council (BIMCO, an independent shipping association founded in 1905, with a membership comprising ship owners, managers, brokers, agents, and many other stakeholders) and the International Association of Independent Tanker Owners (INTERTANKO). The International Maritime Bureau, a specialized unit of the International Chamber of Commerce, acts as an informational clearinghouse. Representatives of this contact group meet periodically in New York to exchange information, but many of its substantive measures are developed by four working groups:

- Military and Operational Coordination, Information Sharing, and Capacity

Building—chaired by the United Kingdom
- Judicial Issues, chaired by Denmark
- Strengthening Shipping Self-Awareness, chaired by the United States
- Public Information and Stratcom, chaired by Egypt[13]

Although there is no unified command structure among the three regularly deployed naval contingents and autonomous national naval units discussed below, there has been extensive coordination at the tactical level in dealing with Somali pirates. Some of the military/naval entities include:

- Combined Maritime Forces Task Force 151 (rotating command, hosted by US Naval Forces in Bahrain, formed by the United States in January 2009 for security in the Gulf of Aden).
- NATO's Operation Ocean Shield, which began in August 2009, replacing NATO's previous operation, Operation Allied Provider.
- National naval missions launched by China, India, Japan, Russia, Yemen, Saudi Arabia, South Korea, Malaysia, Singapore, and Thailand (these states are referred to by partners as the "independent deployers"). South Korea and Thailand have also shared rotating command of Task Force 151 with the United States, the United Kingdom, Pakistan, and Turkey.
- EUNAVFOR Somalia ("Operation Atalanta"), which was created by the European Union on December 13, 2008, initially to protect World Food Program vessels delivering food to Somalia; its mandate was broadened to address the protection, prevention, and repression of all acts of piracy against vulnerable vessels off the coast of Somalia. The first EU naval operation, EUNAVFOR's mandate was extended through December 2014. Twenty-one EU members and several nonmembers have participated in EUNAVFOR operational efforts, including coordination and shared awareness initiatives with other naval operations (national, regional, and multinational).[14]

Why Has CCM Emerged in This Case?
The relatively robust CCM response in the case of Somali piracy reflects the level of serious interests affected by the threat. These interests are political, security (especially related to energy and, potentially, counterterrorism), and commercial and financial. The high seas off Somalia and in neighboring waters (the Gulf of Aden, the Arabian Sea, the Western Indian Ocean) represent—like Somalia itself—an ungoverned space. The threat of maritime anarchy has attracted a governance response in the form of an ad hoc "neighborhood watch" initiative composed of an improvised but rules-based coalition.

Piracy has been recognized as a crime in customary international law for centuries and has been recognized as a crime of universal jurisdiction in conventional international law since at least the late nineteenth century (the 1889 Montevideo Treaty on International Penal Law); more recently, it was codified as a crime in the 1958 Geneva Convention on the High Seas, the 1982 UN Convention on the Law of the Sea, and the 1988 Convention for the Suppression of Unlawful Acts of Violence Against the Safety of Maritime Navigation. This strong legal basis—confirmed by a number of Somalia-specific Security Council resolutions under Chapter VII—is complemented by the powerful commercial interests of the shipping and insurance industries and the vital trading interests of the many nations whose maritime commerce transits these waters. States have been attracted to CCM because of its voluntary character: no participant is obliged to do anything inconsistent with its perceived interests.[15] Commercial groups and industry associations are attracted because piracy imposes a heavy burden on them in the form of the operating cost of increased precautionary measures, mounting ransom demands to liberate ships and crew, and soaring insurance rates.

What CCM Activities Have Been Undertaken? CCM activities in the Somali case fall into several major categories: deterrence, prevention, shared awareness of threats (information sharing), development of best practice doctrines (on maritime navigation), prosecution and judicial action (to handle captured pirates), and capacity building (by the European Union and other donors to strengthen training and facilities for the judicial authorities in Kenya and Seychelles). Maritime shipping lanes, backed by the convoy escort service of naval units, have been identified in the Gulf of Aden. Specific examples of such activity include:

- The formation and operation of a Shared Awareness and Deconfliction (SHADE) mechanism hosted by the headquarters of US Fifth Fleet in Bahrain. Participants share deployment and patrol schedules and agree on who will go where and do what. SHADE is cochaired by EUNAVFOR and Coalition Maritime Forces (CMF) Task Force 151. The command of CMF at Bahrain rotates among participating countries. The innovative nature of this ad hoc activity has been underscored by a senior US official, who noted that it was unprecedented for such diverse actors as NATO, Russia, China, India, Japan, Singapore, Thailand, Indonesia, and the European Union to operate as a single coordinating naval force.[16]
- The production of a guide called *Best Management Practices* by the shipping

industry that details how ship owners and captains can prepare and maneuver to avoid being boarded by pirates. The state-based International Maritime Organization (a UN specialized agency) and the London-based International Maritime Bureau (a unit of the International Chamber of Commerce) are partners in this effort; the International Maritime Bureau provides a real-time, state-of-the-art Piracy Reporting Centre.[17]

- The creation and operation of a reporting hub for pirate activity and a communications hub for multinational naval forces operating in the area. These are provided by the UK Royal Navy's Maritime Security Centre-Horn of Africa at Northwood (established in December 2008 as part of Operation Atalanta) and the UK Maritime Trade Office in Dubai.

How Effective Is This Activity? At one level, the impact of counterpiracy CCM off Somalia's coasts has become increasingly effective. But the process of countering this form of armed criminality took several years to develop and mature. Reports in early 2010 pointed to a mixed picture, with numerous piracy attempts thwarted, scores of pirates captured and turned over to littoral state authorities, and numerous pirate craft destroyed or disabled. Yet the threat persisted, and the cost of CCM operations grew as officials came to recognize the scope of the challenge.

A Gulf of Aden "transit corridor" was set up in 2009; patrolled by naval forces, this action created a zone of relative security. Success in the Gulf of Aden initially pushed pirate activity into the Arabian Sea and far out into the western Indian Ocean. As pirates took commercial targets and converted them into mother ships, their range of operations grew exponentially. Former French Education and Culture minister Jack Lang (at the time Special Adviser to the Secretary-General on Legal Issues Related to Piracy off the Coast of Somalia) described how an "artisanal" pirate economy had grown to become an "industry" run like a mafia and remarked that a mere 1,500 pirates might become "masters of the Indian Ocean." The industry yielded hundreds of millions of dollars, much of it laundered and invested elsewhere by the piracy "machine." Because of the "porosity" of relationships in Somalia, he warned, piracy revenues could be expected to leak into the hands of political actors, some of them with links to terrorist groups.[18]

Other troubling indicators included the taking of ever-larger vessels, the rising ransoms being demanded (and paid), the expansion of the dangerous waters to an area twice the size of Europe, the killing of some hostages, and the capture of some forty to fifty ships and more than eight hundred hostages as of 2010. One observer saw the emergence on land of a pirate "culture" in Somalia's Puntland area fuelled by multi-million dollar ransoms parachuted by ship owners to celebrating young Somalis who enjoyed—at least temporarily—a life of glamour and plenty.[19]

By 2013, the maritime piracy picture was dramatically different. A sharp drop in hijacking attempts occurred in 2012: according to the International Maritime Bureau, piracy incidents fell from 237 in 2011 to 75 in 2012 and only 10 in the first nine months of 2013. Why was CCM so effective? One factor was the self-interest of the shipping industry, which adopted a series of best practices for thwarting pirates and began to use private security units to protect ships from attack, a significant innovation in civilian maritime shipping. Naval coordination improved, and drones and other intelligence resources were deployed to enable more effective intercept and interdict operations. In addition to more aggressive defensive measures, cooperating states stepped up the capture and prosecution of pirates, hampering recruitment and impacting the business model of piracy chieftains who had previously enjoyed a lucrative enterprise.

Despite the enormous progress at sea, the root of the problem is on land, and joint naval operations are ultimately no substitute for greater efforts to tackle the sociopolitical and economic challenges within Somalia. Perhaps the greatest of these challenges is organized criminal networks dominated by some of the same senior figures who earlier organized piracy operations. Control of pirating easily morphed into trade links up the coast to Yemen, Oman, the Emirates, and Iran, with Somali militants in the terrorist Al Shabab group importing illicit arms and exporting massive amounts of charcoal. This pattern of trade denudes the countryside, empowers factional warlords, and sustains conflict.[20] Despite successes in the struggle against piracy, the UN Security Council found it necessary in 2012 to further bolster its support for the African Union's AMISOM peacekeeping operation, calling on all member states to "take the necessary measures to prevent the direct or indirect import of charcoal from Somalia."[21]

Motivations. CCM in the case of Somali piracy is a robust and evolving response to a severe governance challenge—terrestrial and maritime anarchy. This situation produced some unprecedented examples of complex, improvised coordination. The motivations behind the effort run the gamut in the typology presented in Table 1: there are strong national security as well as commercial reasons for protecting the safety and security of international shipping and for checking the rise of organized criminal activity on the high seas; CCM participants seek an innovative and effective yet voluntary response that brings some measure of governance to an anarchic zone; the endeavor is backed by solid normative and legal foundations; domestic commercial and financial interest groups exert strong pressure on national governments to act; and the diverse participating entities have strong individual mandates for action that, in turn, have motivated them to turn to the UN Security Council for explicit authorizing mandates.

Cooperation for Mediation in the Philippines: The Philippines Facilitation Project

Collaborative efforts for conflict management may arise as a result of the request of the principal parties involved in a peace process—either the conflict parties themselves or a third-party mediator. This broadening of the process by bringing in other institutions has occurred twice in recent years in the peace negotiations between the Government of the Republic of the Philippines (GRP) and the Moro Islamic Liberation Front (MILF). The case discussed here examines the Philippines Facilitation Project (PFP), an early CCM effort that started in 2003 and ran to 2007.

The conflict in the Philippines between the government and the Muslim population of Mindanao has deep roots, reaching back to the Spanish colonial period and continuing through the period of American colonization.[22] The issues are many, but principally center around disagreement about whether the Muslim islands in the southern Philippines—sovereign sultanates until they were conquered by the Spanish in 1542—should be an integral part of the Philippines nation-state, an autonomous part of the nation-state, or entirely independent from the nation-state. Muslim leaders have claimed independence throughout Philippines history, and made direct pleas to the US government to respect those rights

when the United States took possession of the Philippines from Spain at the end of the Spanish-American War in 1899. These claims were ignored by the United States and have been ignored by the government of the Philippines since the country became independent in 1946.

Mindanao is fertile island that lies outside the Pacific typhoon belt, unlike most of the Philippines. It is relatively rich in natural resources, including lead, zinc, iron ore, copper, and gold. For a variety of reasons, in the 1930s the Manila government began a program of resettlement that brought thousands of people from other parts of the Philippines to Mindanao. Hostility largely based on land ownership and displacement issues arose between Muslims and Christians and broke out in sustained violent conflict in the early 1970s. After a few failed peace agreements, the GRP and the Moro National Liberation Front (MNLF) signed a "final peace agreement" in 1996, granting the MNLF autonomy over the oddly shaped and often noncontiguous Autonomous Region of Muslim Mindanao. MILF, a militant group that broke away from the MNLF, has continued armed violence as well as participating in peace talks since then.

Who Were the Actors?   The principal actors in this instance of CCM were the US State Department, the United States Institute of Peace (USIP), and the government of Malaysia. When USIP entered the field, a few institutions were already playing a peace-making role in the conflict. The official mediator was the government of Malaysia, which had been involved in the process since 2001. As a member of the Organization of Islamic Conference, Malaysia had a good deal of legitimacy in the eyes of the MILF, the Islamic breakaway group, but had more difficulty engaging with the government in Manila, which viewed Malaysia's activities with suspicion.[23] A number of international

NGOs had also been active over time, including the Asia Foundation, whose focus included social and economic development and conflict resolution. Several local peacemaking efforts were also active, as were official aid agencies such as the US Agency for International Development, the Australian Agency for International Development, and Official Development Assistance from the Japanese Ministry of Foreign Affairs.

Why Did CCM Emerge in This Case? In 2003, the US State Department was approached by both parties to the conflict—the government and the MILF—and asked to step into a third-party role. Since the terrorist attacks of September 2001, however, the State Department had been apprehensive of direct contact with the MILF because of reports that MILF members had connections with Al Qaeda or Al Qaeda affiliates. Thus, the State Department asked USIP, a congressionally funded independent organization whose president, Richard Solomon, had been the US ambassador in Manila, to take a third-party role in its stead. USIP undertook the assignment with the support and funding of the State Department. Close ties between the State Department and USIP were further encouraged by the choice of Eugene Martin, a retired foreign service officer who had been deputy chief of mission in Manila, to lead USIP's Philippines Facilitation Project (PFP).

What Were the CCM Activities? The immediate challenge to USIP was to carve out a place for itself in this universe. According to Martin, the mandate from the State Department was vague.[24] In addition, an important element of the CCM group, the Malaysian government—the official mediator in the process—did not want American involvement in the mediation, despite the fact that both parties to the conflict had asked for American aid. In the end, the mandate for USIP amounted to little more than an invitation to engage in activities that furthered the peace process.

The official peace process covered three areas: economic development for conflict-affected areas in the Philippines; security issues; and issues revolving around the establishment of an autonomous homeland for the Moro people, referred to in the negotiations as "ancestral domain." Because many of the issues surrounding economic development and security had been worked out in previous peace talks, the PFP decided to concentrate on ancestral domain. With the help of experts from around the world, the PFP expanded the understanding of different models of managing contested claims for territory. It brought GRP and MILF officials together to develop common understandings between the two parties on the issue. It wrote analytical papers that became part of the supporting documentation for the official negotiating panels.

The PFP focused on two additional areas. The first was building a constituency for peace among the wider community in Mindanao and in the Philippines as a whole through educational and mass media activities. The second was helping to encourage an intra-Moro dialogue on contested issues growing out of land disputes, clan antagonisms, and political strife. These intra-Moro divides intersected at several points with the larger GRP-MILF conflict, especially in the tensions between the MILF and the MNLF over differing visions of the future. Working with the Institute for Bangsamoro Studies in Cotabato City, the PFP facilitated a number of workshops for young Moro leaders in the hopes of helping to build a better understanding in the next generation of Moro leadership of the complexities of governance.

How Effective Was This Activity? The PFP lasted from 2003 to 2007; during that time, it accomplished a fair amount in terms of broadly supporting the peace process. It helped refine negotiation options, identify solutions to disagreements on ancestral domain, and shore up domestic constituencies for peace.[25] However, the reluctance of Malaysia, the official mediator, to work with the USIP team hampered USIP's effectiveness. In addition, a change in the American ambassador in 2005 and a consequent shift in US perspectives on the conflict resulted in a slow withdrawal of State Department support in the last two years of the PFP. The project came to an end at the request of the State Department, which signaled a preference to take over direct negotiations with the parties based on the USIP work. However, the lack of State Department action in pursuing direct negotiations seemed to indicate instead a drop in the State Department's willingness to engage directly with the MILF.

Motivations. The US government's motivations seemed to grow in part out of the historical ties with the Philippines, but were more strongly identified with security objectives stemming from the global war on terrorism. In October 2003, as Manila ratified the complete set of UN counterterrorism conventions, the United States designated the Philippines as a major non-NATO ally.[26] The Department of Defense's International Military Education and Training program in the Philippines was the largest such program in Asia, and US military aid to the country in the years 2001–05 topped $145 million.[27]

USIP's motivations for becoming engaged were largely based on institutional mandate. The USIP Act, passed by Congress in 1984, states that the purpose of the institution is to "serve the people and the Government through the widest possible range of education and training . . . to promote international peace and the management and resolution of conflict." The legislation makes it clear that USIP's area of operation is overseas, and that conflicts within the United States are outside its remit. In 1996, the organization started working overseas, launching peacebuilding programs in Bosnia. By 2003, it was also operational in the Middle East and Africa; the Philippines initiative, although larger and more directly tied to a third-party mediation role than previous activities, seemed to fit USIP's expanding role in direct peacebuilding operations on the ground.

This facilitation effort is an illustration of CCM's strengths and weaknesses. The initial close collaboration between the State Department and USIP gave the PFP the capacity to undertake the assignment. However, the vagueness of the assignment and the resistance of the Malaysians to USIP activities undercut that capacity. Although USIP's motivation stemmed from an organizational mandate for conflict management, the State Department's motivation grew out of an ever-evolving objective to fight terrorism and strengthen security in the region. When the State Department's assessment of the best way to accomplish that mission changed, the CCM arrangement came to an end.

Additional CCM in the Philippines through the International Contact Group Effort. A CCM process is again playing a role in the Philippines. After USIP disengagement, the GRP and the MILF agreed on a historic Memorandum of Agreement to handle issues of ancestral domain, a direct result of USIP's work. However, the Memorandum of Agreement was blocked by the Philippines Supreme Court in October 2008. Violence renewed at that point and continues today, but there has been significant forward movement toward agreement since the inauguration in 2010 of President Benigno Aquino. The GRP and the MILF requested that a number of countries and organizations establish an informal collaborative body to support the peace talks. The resulting CCM effort, the International Contact Group (ICG), has an assignment that has been spelled out only in the broadest terms by the parties: to assist the Malaysian-led mediation process, building trust between parties, helping to monitor compliance with agreements, and providing expertise in and conducting research on matters of interest to the peace talks. The state members of the ICG include the United Kingdom, Japan, and Turkey. The Organization of Islamic Conference (OIC), although not a member of the ICG, has ties to this group through Turkey. OIC member Malaysia leads the mediation, while fellow OIC members Brunei and Libya are participating in the International Monitoring Team, which monitors the ceasefire between the GRP and the MILF. The GRP and the MILF also asked two NGOs, the Asia Foundation and the Centre for Humanitarian Dialogue (HDC), to join the contact group. HDC provides the secretariat for the ECG. Although the ongoing Philippines-Mindanao peace process remains a work in progress and faces important challenges, its composite mediation structure helped produce a series of striking interim agreements in 2012–2014. The CCM architecture combines governments and NGO as formal members, a first in peace negotiations.

Special Court for Sierra Leone

Who Are the Primary CCM Actors? The Special Court for Sierra Leone was established jointly by the Government of Sierra Leone and the United Nations pursuant to UN Security Council Resolution 1315 of August 14, 2000, with a mandate to try those who bore greatest responsibility and were in violation of international humanitarian law and the criminal laws of Sierra Leone for Sierra Leonean acts committed in the territory of Sierra Leone since the civil

war in that country began.[28] However, the list of actors involved extends well beyond the United Nations and Sierra Leone. The creation of the court was supported by the people of Sierra Leone, various human rights NGOs, and the African Union. Some forty other countries have been involved in helping to finance and support the operations of the court on a voluntary basis. The government of Nigeria subsequently played a key role in handing over President Charles Taylor, the highest profile figure in the court's docket, to UN and Liberian authorities so that he could stand trial for his role in supporting rebel groups in Sierra Leone's brutal civil war. Taylor left Liberia for supervised exile in Nigeria in 2003 as a result of military reverses in the Liberian civil war and mounting external pressures from leading African regional organizations, the US government, and—not least—the Special Court, which had unsealed its indictment against him shortly before his departure.

Why Has CCM Emerged in This Case? The establishment of the Special Court for Sierra Leone provides an interesting example of CCM at work in supporting and advancing international norms concerning international humanitarian law, crimes against humanity, and the protection of civilians. The Special Court for Sierra Leone was established in 2000 following the termination of Sierra Leone's civil war—a war lasting ten years that claimed more than one hundred thousand lives and saw the mutilation of thousands of people, including many women and children, whose limbs were hacked off by Revolutionary United Front (RUF) rebels. Initially, the 1999 Lomé Peace Agreement, which ushered in a temporary end to the fighting, granted an amnesty for crimes committed by all parties and the establishment of a truth and reconciliation commission. However, following the arrest of several rebel leaders, including RUF leader Foday

Sankoh, the government of Sierra Leone asked the United Nations to establish an independent court to try the rebels because it feared that a national trial would be divisive and lead to further escalation of the conflict. The Special Court was the outcome of that request.

What Are Its Activities?   The Special Court has the power to prosecute persons who have committed crimes against humanity, including "widespread or systematic attack against any civilian population." It also has the power to prosecute persons who committed or ordered the commission of serious violations of Article 3 common to the Geneva Convention of August 12, 1949, for the Protection of War Victims and the Additional Protocol II of June 8, 1977. The Special Court can also prosecute persons who committed serious violations of international humanitarian law, such as intentionally directing attacks against the civilian population; intentionally directing attacks against personnel, installations, material, units, or vehicles involved in a humanitarian assistance; and conscripting or enlisting children under the age of fifteen into armed forces or groups.

The Special Court's jurisdiction also covers those who committed various crimes under Sierra Leonean law (i.e., offences relating to the abuse of girls under the Prevention of Cruelty to Children Act of 1926, and offences relating to the wanton destruction of property under the Malicious Damage Act of 1861). Interestingly, the Special Court and the national courts of Sierra Leone have concurrent jurisdiction. However, the Special Court has primacy over the national courts of Sierra Leone. What this means is that at any stage of the procedure, the Special Court may formally request a national court to defer to the Special Court.

The appointment of judges to the Special Court is made jointly by the government of Sierra Leone and the United Nations:

The Chambers shall be composed of not less than eight (8) or more than eleven (11) independent judges, who shall serve as follows: (a) Three judges shall serve in the Trial Chamber, of whom one shall be a judge appointed by the Government of Sierra Leone, and two judges appointed by the Secretary-General of the United Nations (hereinafter "the Secretary-General"); and (b) Five judges shall serve in the Appeals Chamber, of whom two shall be judges appointed by the Government of Sierra Leone, and three judges appointed by the Secretary-General.[29]

The Special Court is the first international criminal tribunal to be funded entirely by voluntary contributions from governments. It has received contributions from more than forty states, including Canada, the Netherlands, Nigeria, the United Kingdom, and the United States.

How Effective Is This Activity?   Thirteen indictments were issued by the prosecutor in 2003 (two of which were subsequently withdrawn). Among those indicted were the three former leaders of the Armed Forces Revolutionary Council (AFRC), two members of the Civil Defence Forces, and three former leaders of the RUF. The highest profile figure on trial has been the former Liberian president Charles Taylor, whose trial concluded in The Hague in 2011. He allegedly sponsored and provided support to RUF rebels by selling diamonds, buying arms, and allowing them to use Liberian territory for the insurgency. His trial was moved to the Netherlands for fear of fresh instability in Sierra Leone and Liberia.

Although Taylor was initially given political asylum in Nigeria in order to end Liberia's civil war, he was accused by various human rights groups of breaking the terms of his asylum because he allegedly continued to interfere in Liberian politics. The Nigerian government refused to extradite him to

Sierra Leone, but indicated that it would send him back to Liberia after a two-year transitional period if the new government of Liberia made a formal request to do so. Liberia president Ellen Johnson-Sirleaf made such a request for extradition shortly after she assumed office in January 2006. The Nigerian government agreed to extradition, but Taylor disappeared. He was subsequently recaptured and handed over briefly to Liberian authorities, and then immediately sent on to Freetown, Sierra Leone, to stand trial; shortly thereafter, Taylor was extradited to The Hague, where his trial before the Special Court for Sierra Leone lasted three years.

The court rendered its verdict on April 26, 2012, convicting Taylor of aiding and abetting the commission of serious crimes, including rape, murder, and destruction of civilian property committed by the RUF and AFRC forces in Sierra Leone from November 30, 1996, to January 18, 2002. Taylor was also found guilty of planning an attack on Freetown, the capital of Sierra Leone. He was sentenced to a jail term of fifty years on May 30, 2012. Taylor's conviction was upheld by the Appeals Chamber judges of the Special Court for Sierra Leone in its own verdict, which was rendered on September 26, 2013. His request to serve his sentence in Sierra Leone was denied, and he will serve out his sentence in a British jail. Britain was the only country that offered to accommodate him.[30]

Until Taylor's arrest and subsequent prosecution, perceptions of the court's performance were mixed. As one observer of the court's work noted:

> Domestic and international perceptions on the impact of the Court vary and are, to some extent, in tension. Although the Court enjoys support in Sierra Leone, there is a domestic perception that its mandate is too narrow, partly because only eleven persons were indicted, and because four of the most high-

profile accused were long unavailable for trial (two have died, whereas two more, including Charles Taylor, remained at large [at the time]). The Special Court has been able to counter these perceptions by running an effective outreach program, but these concerns remain. Internationally, the Court's credibility hinges on its ability to complete its core mission in a focused and efficient manner. Its narrow mandate is widely hailed as a new model and has been followed by the International Criminal Court, but a significant challenge to its overall credibility was the continued absence of former President of Liberia Charles Taylor, until his arrest on 29 March 2006.[31]

Motivation. The political trigger that led to the subsequent creation of the court was a formal request from the government of Sierra Leone to the United Nations for assistance in trying captured rebel leaders. The request was motivated by the very real fear on the part of the government that there would be a renewed escalation of the country's civil war if RUF leaders were tried by local authorities. The reason behind the decision to allow the court to hold its proceedings in Sierra Leone (with the exception of the trial of Charles Taylor) was to allow the victims and the people of Sierra Leone to see justice at work. The court's work, however, was also premised on and informed by evolving norms in international humanitarian law and the prosecution of those involved in war crimes. These included the precedent-setting International Criminal Tribunal for the Former Yugoslavia (ICTY) and the International Criminal Tribunal for Rwanda (ICTR). At the same time, the court's work and jurisdiction were informed by Sierra Leone's own national laws. As Michael Scharf explains in a 2000 analysis:

> the Special Court's subject matter jurisdiction extends (in addition to war crimes and

crimes against humanity) to certain crimes under Sierra Leonean law, including abusing a girl under 14 years of age, abduction of a girl for immoral purposes, and setting fire to dwelling-houses or public buildings. But unlike the ICTY and ICTR, the Special Court does not have jurisdiction over the crime of genocide, since there was no evidence that the mass killing in Sierra Leone was at any time perpetrated against an identifiable national, ethnic, racial or religious group with the intent to annihilate the group as such. Despite these differences, the Special Court is to be guided by the decisions of the appeals chamber of the Yugoslav and Rwanda Tribunals, and to apply the Rules of Procedure of the ICTR, though the judges have the power to amend or adopt additional rules, where a specific situation is not provided for.[32]

The overarching motivation for the creation of the Special Court was the strong desire of leading states to contribute to an African-led process that had the prospect of seeing that justice was done and accountability was established for one of the most horrific civil wars of the 1990s.

CONCLUSION

The cases discussed in this chapter lead to some practical conclusions about the role of CCM member motivations in determining the effectiveness of the CCM venture. Where CCM participants have direct interests in the outcome, as in the Somali piracy and the Sierra Leonean court cases, an informal coalition is more likely to stay together. Where the interests are more diffuse, as in the PFP, the coalitions are more likely to fall apart. One key to successful CCM ventures is to create coalitions in which different parties have strong interests in a successful outcome even if those interests are not identical or congruent.

It is clear that the changing geopolitical context is relevant to all three types of CCM—operational, mediation, and normative. However, it is also important to note a common denominator among the three cases: CCM is more likely in circumstances in which everyone would like to see conflict ended or problems solved, but no single nation or organization wants to bear responsibility for making it happen. This means that CCM arises in situations where there is no natural "owner" of the process—where no one state or organization that can handle the problem alone is capable or prepared to assume the risks of playing a leadership role.

International intervention in Syria illustrates the difficulties of organizing a joint response—whether under the auspices of the United Nations or in a more unstructured CCM initiative—even when in support of universally acknowledged human rights abuses. A large number of outside states and institutions have become involved in Syria. In 2011, the Arab League approached the United Nations Security Council asking for a resolution calling on President Assad of Syria to step down. In early 2012, Russia and China vetoed this resolution. The Friends of Syria initiative was a regionally inspired, collective response to the deadlock in the UN Security Council over Syria. Some sixty countries attended a hastily convened meeting of foreign ministers and representatives of international organizations in Tunis in late February 2012 in a bid to increase the pressure on Syria's al-Assad regime.[33] As the conflict has progressed, however, the collective response represented by the Friends of Syria has decreased from scores of countries to a core group of eleven, including those motivated by a combination of security needs and strong governance concerns: Egypt, France, Germany, Italy, Jordan, Qatar, Saudi Arabia, Turkey, the United Arab Emirates, the United Kingdom, and the United States.[34] In another collective effort dating from the

Russian and Chinese veto of the UN resolution, the Arab League and the United Nations jointly appointed former UN secretary-general Kofi Annan as special envoy. He served only from February to August 2012, however, resigning in frustration over the lack of cooperation from the parties and the evident divisions in the Security Council and, more broadly, in the international community. Annan was succeeded by Lakhdar Brahimi in that same month.[35] These efforts signal the difficulty of keeping together CCM coalitions—preserving collective action and maintaining resolve.

The uncertainty of if and how CCM will evolve in the future remains. If the amount of the ungoverned space—global commons, outer space, cyberspace, failed states—increases (or does not decrease), the need for a collective response will only grow. A fundamental issue is whether CCM responses will remain ad hoc and individualized—will every country or organization respond as it wishes and participate as its own interests, however defined, determine, or will pressures rise to impose some rules and standards to govern CCM ventures? The answer will hinge on the lessons drawn by leading states (and by their domestic constituencies) in all regions from experience with cases such as Syria. Current trends (viewed from the perspective of 2014) toward normative and geopolitical fragmentation, on the one hand, and uncertain appetite or capacity for global leadership, on the other hand, suggest that CCM may be around for a while.

NOTES

1. This chapter builds on the authors' article "Collective Conflict Management: A New Formula for Global Peace and Security Cooperation?" *International Affairs* 87, no. 1 (2011): 39–58.

2. For a discussion of these issues, see, for example, Patrick Stewart, *Weak Links: Fragile State, Global Threats, and International Security* (New York: Oxford University Press 2011).

3. The Failed States Index 2013, http://ffp.statesindex.org/rankings-2013-sortable, accessed December 27, 2013.

4. For regional perspectives on regional capabilities for conflict management, see Chester A. Crocker, Fen Osler Hampson, and Pamela Aall, eds., *Rewiring Regional Security in a Fragmented World* (Washington, DC: United States Institute of Peace Press, 2011).

5. The North Atlantic Treaty, Article 5, http://www.nato.int/cps/en/natolive/official_texts_17120.htm, accessed March 14, 2011.

6. United Nations Charter, Chapter VII, Articles 42 and 43, http://www.un.org/en/documents/charter/index.shtml, accessed March 14, 2011. See also University of Colorado's International Online Training Program on Intractable Conflicts, http://www.colorado.edu/conflict/peace/treatment/collsec.htm, accessed August 27, 2009.

7. Although there have been many instances—from the Balkans to Burundi—in which third parties have attempted to encourage conflict prevention or negotiated settlements, most of the operations have been competitive rather than collaborative. See the case study chapters in Chester A. Crocker, Fen Osler Hampson, and Pamela Aall, eds., *Herding Cats: Multiparty Mediation in a Complex World* (Washington DC: United States Institute of Peace Press, 1999).

8. Richard H. Solomon and Nigel Quinney, *American Negotiating Behavior: Wheeler-Dealers, Legal Eagles, Bullies, and Preachers* (Washington, DC: United States Institute of Peace Press, 2010), 123–56.

9. Mancur Olsen, *The Logic of Collective Action: Public Goods and the Theory of Groups,* revised edition (Cambridge, MA: Harvard University Press, 1971).

10. See, for example, on collective action through alliances, Kenneth N. Waltz, *Theory of International Politics* (Reading MA: Addison-Wesley, 1979); and Stephen M. Walt, *Origins of Alliances* (Ithaca, NY: Cornell University Press, 1987). On collective action on conflict management, see the papers from the "International Workshop on Collective Action, Property Rights, and Conflict in Natural Resource Management" (organized by CGIAR Systemwide Program on Collective Action and Property Rights, June 28–July 1, 2010), http://www.capri.cgiar.org/wks_0610.asp, accessed March 6, 2011.

11. A recent example of the Carter Center's reputational reach was reported by Ria Novosti when Venezuelan president Hugo Chavez suggested that Jimmy Carter join his possible mediation effort in Libya, http://en.rian.ru/world/20110305/162870330.html, accessed March 6, 2011.

12. Chester A. Crocker, Fen Osler Hampson, and Pamela Aall, eds., *Taming Intractable Conflicts: Mediation in the Hardest Cases* (Washington, DC: United States Institute of Peace Press, 2004), 21–43.

13. "International Response: Contact Group," US Department of State, http://www.state.gov/t/pm/ppa/piracy/contactgroup/index.htm, accessed February 13, 2011.

14. "Key Facts and Figures," EU NAVFOR Somalia, http://eeas.europa.eu/csdp/missions-and-operations/eu-navfor-somalia/pdf/factsheet_eu navfor_en.pdf, accessed December 20, 2013. See also "European Union Naval Force Somalia Operation Atalanta," European Union External Action, http://eunavfor.eu/key-facts-and-figures/, accessed December 20, 2013.

15. In Resolution 1851 (2008), the UN Security Council authorizes and endorses—in everything but name—the voluntaristic, neighborhood watch characteristics of the ongoing response to the Somali piracy challenge. Specifically, it calls upon "States, regional and international organizations that have the capacity to do so, to take part actively in the fight against piracy and armed robbery off the coast of Somalia." It also invites "all States and regional organizations" engaged in the fight to conclude special arrangements with countries surrounding Somalia to allow for the embarking of "ship riders" to facilitate the detention and prosecution of detainees. In addition, it urges the creation of an "international cooperation mechanism to act as a common point of contact between and among states, regional and international organizations on all aspects of combating piracy . . . at sea off Somalia's coast." Finally, it encourages UN member states to "enhance the capacity of relevant states in the region to combat piracy, including judicial capacity." In a sweeping illustration of the new normative environment, the resolution urges member states to collaborate with the shipping and insurance industries and the International Maritime Organization in developing "avoidance, evasion, and defensive best practices and advisories to take when under attack or when sailing in waters off the coast of Somalia."

16. US Department of State, interview with Donna Hopkins, US Coordinator for Counter Piracy and Maritime Security, December 3, 2010, http://fpc.state.gov/152316.htm, accessed February 13, 2011.

17. See http://www.icc-ccs.org/home/imb, accessed March 8, 2011.

18. Jack Lang, press conference, January 25, 2011, http://www.unmultimedia.org/tv/webcast/2011/01/press-conference-jack-lang-special-adviser-to-the-secretary-general.html, and Lang's report to the Security Council of the same date at S/2011/30.

19. Jeffrey Gettleman, "The Pirates Are Winning!" *New York Review*, October 14, 2010. He also writes, "Pirate weddings are elaborate two- or three-day affairs, stretching deep into the night, with bands—and brides—flown in from outside Somalia and convoys of expensive 4x4 trucks. The prettiest young women in pirate towns dream of a pirate groom; little boys can hardly wait until they are old enough to sling an AK-47 over their shoulder and head out to sea. In these places, the entire local economy revolves around hijacking ships, with hundreds of men, women, and children employed as guards, scouts, cooks, deckhands, mechanics, skiff-builders, accountants, and tea-makers."

20. See Margaret Coker and Costas Paris, "Somali Pirates Shift Course to Other Criminal Pursuits," *Wall Street Journal*, November 1, 2013.

21. UN Security Council, Resolution 2036, February 22, 2012, http://www.un.org/en/ga/search/view_doc.asp?symbol=S/RES/2036%282012%29, accessed December 20, 2013.

22. For an excellent overview of this case, see Eugene Martin and Astrid Tuminez, *Toward Peace in the Southern Philippines: A Summary and Assessment of the USIP Philippines Facilitation Project 2003–2007*, Special Report no. 202 (Washington, DC: United States Institute of Peace, 2008).

23. This uneasy relationship continues to characterize the ongoing peace process. In late 2010, the GRP objected to Malaysia's continuation in the third-party mediating role. Although this attempt to "fire" the mediator did not lead to change, it highlights the difficulties of a reaching a mediated settlement when one of the parties resists the third party's involvement.

24. Interview with Eugene Martin, February 17, 2011.

25. Martin and Tuminez, *Toward Peace in the Southern Philippines.*

26. "US Relations with the Philippines," US Department of State, Bureau of East Asian and Pacific Affairs, October 29, 2010, http://www.state.gov/r/pa/ei/bgn/2794.htm, accessed March 3, 2011.

27. "Between 2001 and 2005, the Philippines received $145.8 million in Foreign Military Financing and another $11.5 million in military training aid, for a total of more than $157.3 million." Frida Berrigan and William D. Hartun, with Leslie Heffel, *US Weapons at War 2005: Promoting Freedom or Fueling Conflict? US Military Aid and Arms Transfers Since September 11* (World Policy Institute Special Report, June 2005), http://www.worldpolicy.org/projects/arms/reports/wawjune2005.html#10, accessed March 3, 2011.

28. Statute of the Special Court for Sierra Leone, http://www.sc-sl.org/DOCUMENTS/tabid/176/Default.aspx, accessed December 30, 2013.

29. "Statute of the Special Court of Sierra Leone," art. 12, para. 1, http://www.sc-sl.org/LinkClick.aspx?fileticket=uClnd1MJeEw%3D&.

30. On the trial of Charles Taylor, see Open Society for Justice Initiative, "The Trial of Charles Taylor," http://www.charlestaylortrial.org/. Also see Owen Bowcott, "War Criminal Charles Taylor to Serve 50-Year Sentence in British Prison," *Guardian*, October 10, 2013, http://www.theguardian.com/world/2013/oct/10/former-liberian-president-charles-taylor-british-prison/print.

31. Tom Perriello and Marieke Wierda, *The Special Court for Sierra Leone under Scrutiny* (International Center for Transitional Justice, New York, March 2006).

32. Michael P. Scharf, "The Special Court for Sierra Leone" (American Society for International Law, October 2000).

33. PBS Newshour, "In Tunisia, 'Friends of Syria' Call for Ceasefire, Assad to Step Down," February 24, 2012, http://www.pbs.org/newshour/bb/world/jan-june12/syria1_02-24.html, accessed December 29, 2013.

34. Steven Lee Myers, "Nations Press Halt in Attacks to Allow Aid to Syrian Cities," *New York Times,* February 24, 2012, http://www.nytimes.com/2012/02/25/world/middleeast/friends-of-syria-gather-in-tunis-to-pressure-assad.html, accessed December 29, 2013; and US Department of State, "Communiqué of the London 11," Media Note, Office of the Spokesperson, October 22, 2013, http://www.state.gov/r/pa/prs/ps/2013/10/215729.htm, accessed December 29, 2013.

35. A quotation from his resignation statement illustrates the point: "without serious, purposeful and united international pressure, including from the powers of the region, it is impossible for me, or anyone, to compel the Syrian government in the first place, and also the opposition, to take the steps necessary to begin a political process." Rick Gladstone, "Resigning as Envoy to Syria, Annan Casts Wide Blame," *New York Times*, August 3, 2012, http://www.nytimes.com/2012/08/03/world/middleeast/annan-resigns-as-syria-peace-envoy.html, accessed December 29, 2013.

17

Practical Sovereignty and Postconflict Governance

David A. Lake

Some observers see problems in the world today as following from "too much" sovereignty. Consolidated states are overly reluctant to cede authority to supranational institutions designed to deal with global policy problems such as climate change. Weak states exploit juridical sovereignty to immunize themselves against external challenges.[1] In this view, sovereignty interferes with efforts to create effective order in "ungoverned spaces" at all levels. Others see problems arising from "too little" sovereignty, which both permits intervention into the internal affairs of weak states and prevents those states from consolidating control over their territories. In this view, unimpeded national governance is the most effective mechanism for realizing the aspirations of diverse peoples through democratic means and should be protected by enhanced observance of norms of nonintervention.[2]

Yet, sovereignty is a political principle, not a political fact. The principle has never been realized in pure form. Rather, it has been and continues to be a rhetorical weapon used in political battles within states to consolidate public authority against a variety of internal competitors and between states to limit unwanted interference. The actual structure of authority within and between societies is always contested and dynamic. Within societies, it is negotiated between the state, various private authorities, and private citizens, producing, as I explain below, more or less well-consolidated states with different realms of legitimate power. Authority is also negotiated within the community of states, with notions of acceptable state practice and acceptable intervention in states' "internal" affairs varying widely over time and space.

Sovereignty in practice is very different from sovereignty in principle. Appeals to the principle of sovereignty are often (if not always) simply a strategy of self-interested actors pursuing their own objectives. These two insights allow us to reimagine postconflict governance in the twenty-first century. International interventions in states are neither new nor a violation of sovereignty in practice. The international community's responsibility to protect (R2P) and neo-trusteeships, though rare, are not and should not be understood as "exceptions" to a rule that has never been honored. International

293

interventions designed to improve governance in now-ungoverned spaces should not be inhibited by undue respect for a seldom-respected principle.

At the same time, state building is not a simple process. There is no "state in a box" that can be purchased abroad and assembled at home with easy-to-follow instructions printed in multiple languages. Civil wars arise and states fail for a reason. Typically, failed states have dysfunctional internal political systems in which strong private authorities, often clans or other lineage groups, block the consolidation of public authority at the center. To rebuild a state requires not just providing public services that will create greater public support and legitimacy. Rather, it requires that the fledgling state itself provide these services and produce social order better than those private authorities who prevented consolidation in the past, have often grown stronger during conflict, and would be displaced by the creation of new state authority. Would-be state builders must always recognize that their creations must outperform other authorities in the same political space.

The first part of this chapter examines the tension between the principle and practice of sovereignty, and argues that we ought to ground policy in the latter not the former. The second part surveys the variety of international hierarchies in the world today, showing that sovereignty has always been compromised, and that international trusteeships and interventions based on human rights and R2P are consistent with past practice. The third part argues that the balance between public authority (the state) and private authorities is critical to both state consolidation and state failure, and examines the problems of state building in light of strong private authorities. The argument is illustrated in the case of Somalia. The fourth part, by way of conclusion, develops the implications of this analysis for postconflict governance.

SOVEREIGNTY IN PRINCIPLE AND PRACTICE

Although often misunderstood and sometimes believed to possess mystical qualities, sovereignty is merely a statement about how political authority should be (in principle) or is (in practice) organized within and between polities. The principle of sovereignty asserts that public authority is indivisible and culminates in a single apex in each territorially defined state. The practice of sovereignty—that is, how authority is actually distributed—is quite different from this principle.

The modern concept of sovereignty is said to have been established in the Peace of Westphalia (1648), itself composed of the Treaties of Münster and Osnabrück. The conclave and associated treaties ended the Thirty Years' War between the "universalist" Habsburg dynasty, in league with the pope in Rome, and the nascent "particularistic" states seeking to escape from imperial hegemony.[3] In affirming the principle of *cuius regio, eius religio* (whose kingdom, his religion) first articulated in the Peace of Augsburg (1555), the victors gathered at Westphalia are widely believed to have elevated secular rulers to positions of ultimate authority in their realms and secured the dominance of political authority over other possible authorities, especially that of the universal church. As described by Leo Gross, Westphalia is the "majestic portal" through which the age of sovereign states supposedly arrived.[4]

The principle of sovereignty is commonly understood to possess three primary components. First, the sovereign possesses ultimate or final authority over the people and territory of a given realm. As argued by Jean Bodin in his *Six Books of the Commonwealth*

(1576), the first major treatise on the subject, "persons who are sovereign must not be subject in any way to the commands of someone else and must be able to give law to subjects, and to suppress or repeal disadvantageous laws and replace them with others—which cannot be done by someone who is subject to the laws or persons having power of command over him."[5]

Second, external actors are excluded from possessing or exercising authority over the people and territory governed by the sovereign. This is a corollary to the first component. If to be sovereign means that one is the ultimate authority in a given domain, it necessarily implies that no one else can exercise authority in that same area or over the same people. By extension, no other power can intervene legitimately in the "internal" affairs of a sovereign state. Stephen Krasner describes this principle of exclusion as the primary trait of "Westphalian" sovereignty.[6]

Third, sovereignty is indivisible—of a single piece, a whole that cannot be disaggregated, shared, or divided between different authorities. Wherever ultimate authority is vested—be it in a king (e.g., the sovereign) or the people (i.e., popular sovereignty)—there can be only a single or definitive wielder of that authority within any political community. The idea of indivisible sovereignty also originates with Bodin, who concluded that if sovereignty was absolute, it could not be divided between branches or levels of government or between different actors. Sovereignty by its very nature, he claimed, could be vested only in a single person or institution within a political community.[7] This view was echoed by other jurists including Hugo Grotius, the Dutch legal theorist whose classic *De Jure Belli ac Pacis* (1625) was the first major work of international law, who wrote that "sovereignty is a unity, in itself indivisible."[8] Along with the first two components, the assumption of indivisibility implies that

authority must culminate in a single apex at the level of the state—indeed, it is this apex that defines the state.

This classical view of sovereignty is much disputed. Revisionist scholars have searched in vain for Gross's mythic gateway to the modern world.[9] Even the Treaties of Münster and Osnabrück themselves contained numerous violations of the nascent principle of sovereignty. It is now clear that what was actually agreed to at Westphalia and codified in the treaties is substantially different from the received wisdom. Whether the princes at Westphalia intended to establish principles of international order is a topic of continuing debate, but the record makes plain that they did not intend to create the specific principle of sovereignty as we know it today. The treaties were incremental, not revolutionary, and did not wholly settle the so-called religious conflicts of the seventeenth century. Nor were the powers of the princes at Westphalia completely enumerated. Most important, perhaps, any rights and obligations asserted by the leaders at Westphalia still needed to be legitimated by the subjects to whom they would be applied. Westphalia was less a "majestic portal" through which the modern world arrived and more a step in the continuing struggle over who has authority over whom for what. Yet, subsequent observers and practitioners have nonetheless interpreted Westphalia as creating—by design or not—a particular conception of sovereignty that has now been passed down through generations. It is the myth of Westphalia, rather than Westphalia itself, on which today's understanding of the principle of sovereignty rests.

In practice, sovereignty is not fixed and exogenous nor conferred on states by tradition. Rather, it is negotiated and constituted by the interactions of public authorities, private authorities, and occasionally the masses. Ultimate authority is not vested in the state exogenously, but is the product of political struggle. Would-be state builders have always appealed to the principle of sovereignty to consolidate and expand public authority at the expense of private authorities. Political philosopher Thomas Hobbes wrote to justify locating authority in the sovereign at the expense of private authorities, especially the church. John Austin, the founder of modern legal theory, aimed to privilege the state, arguing that it was the repository of ultimate authority within a territorially bounded realm.[10] Decolonization and the doctrine of juridical sovereignty that followed were an attempt to shift authority from the metropole to the new state, and to increase the authority of the state while reducing the authority of various private actors, primarily clans, chiefdoms, and other precolonial forms of private authority.[11] Today, state building in "failed" states likewise tries to consolidate authority in the state and reduce the authority of private religious or clan rulers and "warlords." In no case, however, has the modern state-building project—even in its most extreme, totalitarian versions—completely squeezed out private authority.

Private authorities play a major role in social and political life throughout the world. Families, clans, and other lineage groups, corporations, labor unions, religious institutions, and some civic associations all legitimately regulate various actions of their members. Westphalia did not secure the supremacy of public authority over the daily lives of individuals. Rather, in practice, what might be called the "Westphalian compromise" requires only that all other authorities may not adopt rules that directly contradict rules established by public authorities. Despite the supposed sovereignty of the state, private authorities can still issue commands for their members that are more restrictive than those of the state. For instance, all food products sold in most advanced democracies must meet certain basic health and sanitary requirements, and producers and retailers must comply with these standards or risk punishment for breaking public law. Some religious groups, however, require their members to eat only certain foods prepared in certain ways, and only some products or retailers can be certified by religious leaders as meeting their requirements (e.g., kosher or halal). Public authority does not require everyone in, say, the United States to eat kosher foods, but it does not prohibit Jewish authorities from requiring Jews to do so or from specifying the standards that must be met to be certified as "kosher." Similarly, public authorities regulate some conditions of employment—such as minimum wages, hours of work, and safety conditions—but corporations have broad authority over how they use the labor of their employees within their internal operations. Private authorities cannot require that which the state prohibits, but this does not prevent private authorities from requiring behaviors that the state does not, even in areas not regulated by the state at all. Only "outlaws" of various types, such as rebel militias or criminal gangs and networks, violate the Westphalia compromise by permitting and even encouraging behaviors prohibited by the state—and thus, earning their nickname. Despite the principle of sovereignty, private authorities still have substantial leeway to issue legitimate commands that apply to and are followed by their members.

The Westphalian compromise is even deeper than this "noncompetition" clause, however. State authority is itself shaped by the needs and desires of private authorities to legitimately regulate the behavior of their members. Sometimes private authorities seek and succeed in getting their private restrictions enacted into public law, thereby harnessing the legal and police powers of the state to their private ends. Laws promoted by religious groups regulating access to family planning services are a good example; where religious leaders might confine themselves to prohibiting contraception and abortion by their followers, they sometimes seek to impose their own religiously inspired practices on others. More important, however, private authorities directly through their representatives and indirectly through their constituent members shape the areas of social life in which the state can legitimately exercise power. Freedom of religion was not only an abstract principle held philosophically by the founding fathers in writing the First Amendment to the US Constitution but also a principle that was itself the product of the powerful influence of diverse religious groups in the United States who helped ensure that public authority would not infringe on their own authority over their members. Having secured their authority over followers, in turn, the various churches and their adherents are stalwart defenders of religious freedom even today. Any threats to religious "autonomy" are quickly and forcefully countered not only by religious leaders but also by their parishioners, who are simultaneously the constituents of their elected representatives.

Understood in this second, deeper way, it is difficult to conclude that public authority is actually paramount or superior to private authority. Private authority is not just a "residual" category, filling the spaces left to private actors by default. Nor does it exist only at the sufferance of the state. Private and public authorities continuously shape and reshape one another, co-constituting one another on an ever-evolving basis. So conceived, it is impossible to say that one trumps the other. Rather, a wide range of private authorities exist in the world today who are every bit as "sovereign" as the negotiated authority of the state. In short, public authority is often what private authorities make of it, and vice versa.

If we accept this variegated authority as not only possible but affirmed through re-

peated practice, the first pillar of the principle of sovereignty—ultimate authority vested in the state—dissolves, as does the corollary that external actors must necessarily be prohibited from exercising authority within its delimited territory. Many private authorities are, indeed, transnational. The Catholic Church is perhaps the longest-standing example, exercising authority over its members in virtually every country in the world. Multinational corporations that wield authority over their workforces, organizing production into tight, geographically distributed but integrated processes, are a modern form. Many clan and lineage groups span national borders. Even states exercise authority over other states today, controlling more or less of their security and economic policies in forms of postcolonial international hierarchy, and supranational organizations are wielding increasing authority over states as well, in areas of trade and production (behind the border barriers to trade), human rights, nuclear proliferation, and more (see below).

The principle of indivisibility, in turn, has been criticized as unrealistic since its inception. Indeed, Grotius, after agreeing with Bodin on its indivisible nature, immediately acknowledges that when discussing sovereignty, "a division is sometimes made into parts designated as potential and subjective." He then enumerates several examples where the conferral of sovereignty was not absolute but, in fact, divided. Most important, Grotius recognizes that unequal treaties can, in practice, lead to a division of sovereignty that favors the superior party: "He who has the vantage in a treaty, if he is greatly superior in respect to power, gradually usurps the sovereignty properly so called." Although based in power, Grotius also recognizes that unless the weaker party resists, over time "the part of the weaker passes over into the right of ruling on the part of the stronger. . . . then either those who had been allies become subjects, or there is at any rate a division of sovereignty."[12] Even from its inception, as implied in Grotius's own writings, the principle of indivisibility was inconsistent with observed reality.

Other legal theorists repeated and amplified Grotius's practical observation, especially when they were forced to confront the variety of authority relationships that lay outside Europe. Focusing on the circumstances of the British Dominions, Arthur Berriedale Keith observed "that sovereignty can be divided, and that in any country both internal and external sovereignty may be shared by various authorities." Claiming that "international law has suffered for a long time from the theory of the indivisibility of sovereignty," Hersch Lauterpacht likewise maintained that "from the point of view of international law, sovereignty is a delegated bundle of rights . . . and therefore divisible, modifiable, and elastic."[13] As noted by these legal theorists, sovereignty is in reality readily divisible.[14]

The divisible nature of sovereignty is important because it implies that there can be—and likely are—multiple "ultimate" authorities within any polity. Rather than the state dominating society at a single apex of authority, multiple authorities may exist, each sovereign in its own realm and continuously renegotiating the extent of its authority. Thus, states and corporations, for instance, have separate and autonomous realms of legitimate power over members, but contest the authority of the state to regulate certain business practices. Similarly, states and religious institutions have different sets of authority over citizens who are simultaneously congregants, and struggle over whether the former can impose laws on the latter that are inconsistent with their beliefs. States also compete more directly with certain "traditional" forms of authority, such as clans and other lineage-based groups; both aspire to be more encompassing authorities, and the

state-clan divide is often fraught. As explained below, competition between the state and such private authorities is an important source of state weakness.

The principle and practice of sovereignty diverge sharply. Appeals to principle serve political projects pursued by self-interested leaders and their followers. Like all institutions, sovereignty is not neutral in its effects. Leaders promote sovereignty for particular political purposes, mainly to consolidate authority within the state and to exclude others from interfering with their rule. Policymakers who believe in and adhere to the principle will be caught by surprise by other actors following established practice and exploited as politically "naive."

THE INTERNATIONAL PRACTICE OF SOVEREIGNTY

Just as sovereignty in practice within states is negotiated and variable, sovereignty between states is socially constructed and contested. In one form of international sovereignty in practice, states have always exercised more or less authority over other states, despite the principle of sovereignty. Classic diplomacy recognized large variations in status, ranging from semi-sovereign states to protected independent (and dependent) states, guaranteed states, vassal states, administered provinces, autonomous colonies and dependencies, and members of imperfect unions.[15] The authority exercised by dominant states covered both the subordinate's external relations and internal practices and policies. This authority was sometimes codified in so-called unequal treaties, such as those between European states and China, Japan, the Ottoman Empire, and Siam. More often, though, the authority rested on informal practices of domination. Jack Donnelly has usefully consolidated the types of restrictions on sovereignty into four categories:

- *Rights of protection or guarantee*, which grant the protecting/guaranteeing state powers to assure that the subordinate acts to retain a particular internal status or external alignment (e.g., United States–Federated States of Micronesia and Republic of the Marshall Islands; India-Bhutan)
- *Rights of economic and financial control*, including supervision of customs houses and priority claims over state resources (e.g., United States–Dominican Republic, 1904–41; United States–Ecuador and other countries that have "dollarized" their economies)
- *Rights of servitude*, requiring the subordinate to allow foreign armies to transit territory, provide access to rivers and other waterways, maintain free cities, create demilitarized zones, and adopt neutrality (e.g., United States–Japan regarding military base rights)
- *Rights of intervention*, permitting the dominant state to act to preserve the balance of power, rights of its nationals and so forth, but recently extended to humanitarian practices (e.g., United States–Panama)[16]

Today, various forms of international hierarchy continue to exist in which authority is held by another entity over the foreign and domestic policies of states normally regarded as sovereign (e.g., members of the United Nations). Three main categories are evident, defined by the nature of the external authority. First, states exercise authority over other states.[17] As suggested by the examples above, the United States possesses varying degrees of authority over the foreign policies of countries around the world, but especially over those in Latin America, Europe, and Northeast Asia. From the late nineteenth century on, the United States has maintained a sphere of influence within its hemisphere in which subordinate coun-

tries have been prohibited from allying with powers outside the region; first articulated in the Monroe Doctrine of 1823, this authority really only became effective with the Roosevelt Corollary pronounced in 1904. In Central American and the Caribbean, US authority has been even more extensive, with Washington also requiring regimes to be friendly to its wishes and role in the region. In Europe and Northeast Asia after World War II, the United States imposed at least a sphere of influence in which the subordinate states were either neutral or actively allied with it in the Cold War against the Soviet Union. In some states, notably West Germany and Japan, Washington also required more active forms of security cooperation in housing and actually supporting large numbers of American forces on their soil that, in turn, restricted their foreign policy autonomy. This authority held by the United States is not always imposed, although it may have been in its initial stages in Central America and the Caribbean. Rather, this state-to-state hierarchy has more often emerged as the result of an exchange in which the United States provides a local security order of value to the subordinate state, which in return yields the minimum of its sovereignty necessary to the production of that order. US-European relations after 1945, for instance, have been accurately described in these terms by Geir Lundestad as an "empire by invitation," a system of authority that was co-constituted and even welcomed by many in the subordinate states.[18]

Second, private authorities are active in the world today, especially in areas of international standards and regulation. The International Accounting Standards Board, for instance, wields broad authority over accounting practices, including how firms are valued and, thus, how much their shares are worth on stock exchanges around the world.[19] Through various certification programs and in response to consumer demand, environmental NGOs are setting standards for "green" behavior by corporations around the globe that govern their production practices.[20] More actively, credit reporting agencies exercise authority directly over states through their sovereign debt ratings.[21] States that do not meet accepted standards of fiscal and monetary rectitude suffer downgrades in their ratings and, in turn, sharply higher interest rates on their bonds and loans.

Finally, many supranational authorities with powers to regulate economic exchange have emerged in recent decades, most clearly in the cases of the European Union and World Trade Organization. Most relevant for postconflict governance, the United Nations remains the premier international authority on peace and security. The UN Security Council can authorize the use of coercive force to police peace agreements and cease-fires, and even to impose cease-fires on reluctant parties. The UN human rights regime also reaches far into the internal affairs of states, specifying acceptable and unacceptable relations between governments and their citizens. This human rights regime has been enforced by community-based sanctions against egregious violators and now through the International Criminal Court or other ad hoc tribunals. Importantly, under the emerging principle of R2P, the human rights regime is evolving to include not only negative injunctions against state abuse but also positive injunctions that states must provide for the security and safety of their populations. Independent of R2P but invoking it on occasion, the United Nations also authorizes states or coalitions of states to govern others in a form of neo-trusteeship.[22] Typically authorized only in clearly "failed" states, neo-trusteeships are temporary transfers of sovereignty from a state to a trustee responsible for maintaining security and rebuilding state capacity. Neo-trusteeships have not been especially successful, but this

has not yet led to a decline in or even reform of the nascent practice.[23]

Although R2P and neo-trusteeships may be relatively recent innovations, they are also a continuation of long-standing practices that restrict the sovereignty of states. State-to-state hierarchies, private authorities, and supranational authorities have always existed and have always limited the authority of states over their citizens or in their policies. Westphalian sovereignty has always been a myth, more a political project than a description of the complex reality of international authority. States have never possessed ultimate or exclusive authority over their territories. Rather, authority has been shared with other external actors who regulate their foreign policies and internal conduct. These "violations" of sovereignty are not simply one-off anomalies that occasionally intrude on the practices of states. They are consistent patterns of behavior in which authority is divided between states and other international actors. Current neo-trusteeships and interventions based on R2P are simply continuations of established practice. Although some states at the United Nations continue to oppose international humanitarian interventions and R2P for fear that they will further erode the sovereignty of target states, there is far less new under the sun than these critics and defenders of the principle of sovereignty suppose.

THE DOMESTIC PRACTICE OF SOVEREIGNTY

Within any country, authority is held by a range of private actors, not just the state. One can simultaneously be a citizen under the authority of the state, a child (or even an adult) under the authority of parents who expect adherence to family duty, an employee under the authority of a corporation that controls your labor, a member of a union that has the authority to negotiate wages on your behalf and call strikes if necessary, and an adherent to a faith that determines what you can eat or wear and when and how you can have sex with whom. The state is not the only entity that exercises authority over individuals in their daily lives. Indeed, compared to the full range of authorities that regulate our actions, the state may not even be the most important.

The pattern of authority in any polity at any moment is a bargain between individuals, the state, and private actors. All authority is negotiated. No leader—public or private—has inherent authority, and must earn legitimate power from both her or his subordinates and other authorities within the society. Leaders acquire authority over members in an exchange of order for compliance.[24] Leaders, with the support of their followers, then negotiate with other authorities over whose rules will apply when, where, for whom, and for what issues or behaviors. As with any bargain, leaders bring their resources to bear: the number and strength of their members, allies they can recruit in support of their position, normative and rhetorical justifications, and more. Stronger leaders will increase the range of behaviors they can legitimately regulate, while weaker leaders will eventually have to forfeit some of their legitimate power. Authority is always contingent and dynamic.

It is through this bargaining process that private authorities balance public authority, public authority checks private authorities, and individuals struggle to protect personal autonomy. Religions defend the separation of church and state against public encroachment, states prevent religious leaders from abusing the faithful (e.g., outlawing polygamy even when sanctioned by the church), and individuals rally to defend reproductive freedom from both. Corporations defend "free market" principles, even as states—with the support of voters—attempt to regulate corporate practices that produce large negative externalities. Unions defend collective bargaining, corporations seek to impose "right to work" rules, and individuals seek to control their labor, often negotiating personal contracts with employers that allow for "flextime" or greater autonomy on the job. It is the entire tapestry of interwoven and intricately balanced authority that matters to society, its prosperity, and its level of individual freedom.

In most countries, the balance between public and private authority is healthy. Because they can more easily solve their collective problems than "mass" groups within society, private authorities are necessary to maintaining limited states. Indeed, with too little private authority, leaders incline toward abusive and possibly totalitarian governments. At the same time, too much private authority prevents a state from consolidating, stimulates conflict between rival authorities, and causes the state to "fail." A variety of euphemisms are used to refer to states with weak to nil public authority. Fragile states, countries of limited statehood, failed states, or whatever they may be called lack sufficient public authority to provide social order in some or all of their territory. Unable to "broadcast" legitimate power, in Jeffrey Herbst's phrase,[25] greater or lesser areas within the nominal states are ungoverned or "lawless." Though sometimes treated as a disease that befalls unsuspecting victims, state weakness is commonly endogenous, with private authorities—primarily clans, tribes, or sectarian groups—remaining the locus of social, economic, and political life. Either state authority was never consolidated because of these preexisting private authorities, as in Afghanistan throughout most of its history and in many postcolonial African states, or state authority dissolves because political entrepreneurs reactivate ethnic or religious cleavages that had waned or been suppressed, as during the breakup of the former Yugoslavia. Where public authority is weak, the state is unable to provide basic services to the population, including security. As a result, internal competitors in the market for violence arise to challenge the state, substituting for government and thereby further weakening the state and sometimes stimulating rebellions or secessions. Illicit criminal gangs also arise that operate outside the state and in contravention of its rules, undermining its foundations and weakening its ability to deliver safety and security to its citizens. External competitors such as transnational terrorist groups may also take up residence in the interstices of public authority, a problem of increasing concern to the international community. As competitors expand, the state's monopoly on the legitimate use of violence begins to fray; the state becomes "fragile," and when it dissipates completely, the state "fails."

States are fragile or fail for many reasons. To paraphrase Leo Tolstoy's famous opening line in *Anna Karenina*, every unhappy state is unhappy in its own way. In addition to the abuses of political power found in totalitarian states, states can also fail to establish a monopoly on the legitimate use of force because private authorities are too strong and prevent the center from consolidating politically. Here, strong private authorities block efforts to build a central state that could constrain their own powers over their communities. The weak state, in turn, is unable to offset the centrifugal forces within the polity. This path to failure is more common in postcolonial Africa, where "quasi-states" that enjoy international juridical sovereignty but not domestic sovereignty exist in large numbers.[26] African politics today are often described as a struggle between center, by which is meant public authority, and periphery, or prior "pre-state" private authorities.[27] Particularly contentious have been land rights, a traditional prerogative and source of the political power

of chiefs in rural areas.[28] Lack of authority over property, in turn, has ensured that Africa's states remain unconsolidated and weak. Sometimes, states have won and consolidated power, especially when leaders have been willing to use coercion to repress social forces in general and private authorities in particular, or when private authorities could be co-opted by the center. But oftentimes strong private authorities limit the state and, even if repressed, linger under the surface only to rise again when political or other crises arise.

Somalia

Although often overused as an exemplar of the fragile state, Somalia is a near perfect, if somewhat extreme, illustration of the problem of overly strong private authorities preventing state consolidation. Always a weak state, Somalia has failed twice for this reason. Somalis are often understood to be a relatively homogenous people, sharing a common heritage, language, and culture.[29] Yet, clans remain the dominant force in people's everyday lives. Somalis are organized into clans, subclans, and dia-paying groups. The last is the basic unit of Somali society, consisting of groups of two hundred to two thousand related families "whose members are unified by virtue of the collective obligation to pay or receive compensation or blood money for homicide and other injuries."[30] The dia-paying groups also recognize an obligation to support their members in times of emergency.[31] Dia-paying groups rarely have single leaders but are egalitarian and led by a council of elders. These groups survive through their mutual aid obligations, but identity also provides the glue that holds the group together and limits free riding. More generally, the clans are the primary vehicles for making political demands on the state. By funneling resources through the clan structure, the state has strengthened the hold of these groups on Somali society, even in urban areas.[32]

Rather than the development of an effective and consolidated state, the period after independence saw a rapid rise in centrifugal forces in Somalia. British Somaliland never accepted its integration into Somalia, and was one source of strident opposition to a strong centralized state.[33] Indeed, Somaliland used the second failure of the state in 1991 to set up an autonomous, de facto independent government in its territory.[34] The clan structure also led to a proliferation of political parties, with more than sixty contesting the last democratic election in March 1969—meaning that Somalia had more political parties per capita than any democratic state except Israel.[35] Corruption was rampant. As the political system was spinning out of control after the election in 1969, General Mohammed Siad Barre, then the highest-ranking officer in the army, seized power, leading to the first failure of the state. Demonstrating that irregular transfers of power can be legitimate, the coup was greeted with "joy" by many Somalis.[36]

Allying with the Soviet Union, Barre embarked on a form of "scientific socialism" that promised to reduce corruption and increase equality for Somalis, with some initial success.[37] Over time, however, Barre soon became increasingly predatory, repressive, and corrupt. One of his first moves was to consolidate power by outlawing clans and all references to clans in public life. Despite this move, Barre nonetheless favored his own clan and effectively played divide and conquer with others who might have displaced him.[38] Under the aegis of scientific socialism, he also consolidated state control over the economy, especially the banking system, driving most borrowers to rely even more heavily on their fellow clan members. Barre demonstrates how, in the face of strong private authorities, leaders willing to use enough coercion can stay in power without legitimacy for a substantial period of time. His doing so, however, distorted the economy, gutting farming and other private economic activities. When famine again struck in 1990 and a major drought swept the region, the clans proved their resilience and were resurrected to protect their members and press new claims upon the state. Barre's attempt to repress opposition and consolidate public authority also increased the value of controlling the state, calling forth new competitors as his regime began to weaken. Under Barre, massive military aid, from first the Soviet Union and later the United States, supported his repressive apparatus. Economic aid, funneled by donors through the state, accounted for 50 percent of government spending in the mid-1980s.[39] Both of these trends made the state a rich prize for those who might control it and an object of competition between clans. Opposition groups began to organize, with the Somali National Movement formed in 1981 by business, religious, military, and intellectual leaders from the Isaaq clan, and the United Somali Congress formed in 1987 from members of the Hawiye clan (later split by subclan).[40] As the famine spread, fighting broke out in October 1990, and Barre fell in 1991.

The second failure of the state, which followed Barre's demise, reinforced the clans as central providers of public goods to their members. Acutely insecure, members retreated into their clans for protection and basic necessities, invoking the emergency provisions of their dia-paying groups, although pretty much everyone faced the same extreme conditions. Some clan groupings, previously egalitarian, became more hierarchical as warlords with access to weapons, and thus stolen food, dominated the scene. Reified by the crisis, the clans have so far blocked a consolidated state from reemerging. This, in turn, has permitted a range of criminal and terrorist organizations to set up shop within and operate from Somalia, further undermining attempts to rebuild the state. Any consolidation of public authority would greatly weaken the warlords, who not only gain authority from protecting their followers but also benefit from numerous illicit activities such as piracy that flourish in the absence of public authority. Equally, the clans have become ever more important authorities; in the absence of a state, whatever public goods and services are provided in the country are provided by them. Their role has expanded to fill the vacuum created by the state's failure, and any new public authority would undermine their expanded roles. Even the Somali business community, which would undoubtedly gain from a well-governed state, prefers the status quo to the uncertainties of a new regime and the likely violence that would be entailed in any transition.[41]

Today, in a Somalia of strong private authorities and virtually no public authority, there are few expectations of significant change. Indeed, with private authorities substituting for public authority in large blocks of the country, the quality of life today is no worse than, and in some ways may be improved from, the last years of Barre's predatory rule.[42] Although Somalia, through its decentralized structure, may be one of the sovereign polities best able to cope with the absence of a state, the larger point is that the continued vibrancy of private authorities and their further entrenchment into society continues to prevent the consolidation of the Somali state.

Political Islam has found fertile ground in the anarchy of Somalia.[43] The country is, of course, not the only regional state to undergo an Islamic awakening. Nonetheless, the resurgence of Islamic courts in various parts of the country, and the stability that followed in their wake, initially received widespread support from the population. The Union of Islamic Courts (UIC) emerged and consolidated its authority over most of southern Somalia in 1999–2000. In February 2006, a warlord-controlled alliance supported by the United States challenged the UIC, which fought back through its own militias. Gaining control over Mogadishu in June 2006, the UIC may have been one of the best hopes for consolidating the state and returning stability to Somalia.[44]

As an Islamic organization, however, the UIC was swept up into the global war on terror.[45] At the request of the Somali Transitional Federal Government (TFG), and with air support from the United States, Ethiopia invaded Somalia in December 2006, driving the UIC from power. This invasion, in turn, further radicalized the Islamists, leading to the transformation of Al Shabab into a full-scale guerilla movement.[46] A purported Al Shabab attack on tourists led Kenya to invade Somalia in October 2011, to which Al Shabab retaliated with a deadly attack on a shopping mall in Nairobi in September 2013. The cauldron of violence and unrest in Somalia and the region continues to bubble fiercely.

In the wake of the Ethiopian invasion, an African Union peacekeeping force was formed to support the TFG. With its backing, the TFG evolved into the new Federal Government of Somalia (FGS), established in August 2012. In January 2013, the United States recognized the FGS as the government of Somalia, the first since 1991. But the regime remains weak. Government troops, fighting alongside an African Union force and Ethiopian soldiers, have gained control over several key towns previously controlled by Islamist insurgents. This is significant progress, but in the past, similar steps forward have often been accompanied by later steps back. The struggle between various public and private authorities for their respective powers within Somalia is likely to continue down a halting path whose ultimate destination remains unknown.

Afghanistan after the US-led invasion is similar in many ways to Somalia. Clans dominate the political landscape. Fearful of losing their position and of losing out in any new coalition that forms at the center, they block efforts at consolidation. President Hamid Karzai has not helped matters by his blatant favoritism to his own family and clan and his widespread corruption. US aid—and the prospect of continued aid after the scheduled withdrawal of troops in 2014—nonetheless means that the weak state is a substantial prize still worth fighting for, promoting further clan-based competition. With or without US troops, the prospects for consolidation of public authority in Kabul are also grim.

Lessons

As these examples suggest, rebuilding states requires addressing the critical role of private authorities that are "too strong," whether these be clan and lineage groups, religious organizations, and professional bodies or guilds operating within the law, or militias and criminal organizations operating outside it. One view advocates "power-sharing" political institutions that seek to broker compromises between segments of society as represented by various elites, often but not always embodied in separate political parties.[47] This model promises success because different elites can speak for agreements and enforce them on their members—precisely because these groups are private authorities.[48] The model is now understood, however, as flawed or at least inappropriate in many cases because it reinforces and strengthens these same private authorities over the long term. A second view promotes "power-dividing" political institutions that aim to create and mobilize individuals with cross-cutting cleavages in society into omnibus or

"catchall" parties.[49] This is a Madisonian solution to the problem of private authorities, which seeks not to displace them but to prevent society from being dominated by one central cleavage along which groups can mobilize. Evidence suggests that power-dividing institutions do lead to more effective post–civil war settlements.[50] Thus, it appears that successful postconflict state building may require weakening rather than enhancing "civil society," and especially the private authorities within it.

Yet, the importance of private authority is undertheorized in the academic and policy literatures on state building in at least two ways. First, as we now also know, rebel groups build their own authority by providing services to their supporters.[51] State builders are not competing against an anarchy in which services are completely lacking, but against often well-established private groups that have consolidated their own authority, as in Somalia and Afghanistan. The new state must provide not just any service but better services than these private authorities, who are themselves strategic and often recognize they are competing against the state. Postconflict polities are not *terra nullius*, but already well populated with private authorities who, as in the broader state-building discussion, see state consolidation as a threat to their own positions.

Second, although providing services is potentially effective in building legitimacy for the state at the local level, we simply do not know whether it will scale up to the national level, especially after the stabilizing hand of external patrons is removed. Broadly distributed services by the external patron or a state supervised by an external patron are all well and good. But once on their own, private authorities, unless almost entirely displaced, will still struggle over the distribution of services from the center. Each village may gladly accept a newly dug well, but when the question shifts to how to allocate always-scarce resources across the country and between groups, private authorities are likely to mobilize their supporters to demand greater shares and thereby reignite competition between groups. Unless they believe they will be hegemonic within the new regime, these private authorities will likely block the consolidation of state authority, as they have in the past. Current models of state building largely ignore the question of entrenched private authorities that mobilize supporters for struggles over goods and authority at the state level. Indeed, external patrons often find it easier to work through rather than around local private authorities, thus reinforcing their position. To the extent that external powers push interim or nascent governments to build political coalitions that give all mainstream "factions" a seat at the governing table—as has the United States in Iraq and Afghanistan—they are also protecting and bolstering private authorities and their hold on their followers, preserving these competitors to the state they are ostensibly seeking to rebuild.

The principle of sovereignty implies that authority is concentrated in the state. Focusing on this principle, many would-be state builders expect that authority will naturally and perhaps easily drift "upward" toward a single apex in the sovereign. In practice, where authority is located is an open issue contested by the many private authorities in every polity. Accommodating private authorities is a necessary—but too seldom recognized—part of any state-building process.

IMPLICATIONS FOR POSTCONFLICT GOVERNANCE

Strict adherence to the principle of sovereignty impedes effective postconflict governance. Weak and, especially, fractured states have great difficulty rebuilding themselves. The international community can—if permitted—play an essential role in postconflict reconstruction.

Although state consolidation is a necessary part of postconflict reconstruction, the assumption by both locals and the international community that public authority automatically trumps (or should trump) private authority too often mistakes a contested ideal for reality. The legitimacy of a regime is not conferred by the principle of sovereignty, no matter how fervently believed or supported. Rather, states must earn their authority by providing a better, more attractive social order for their citizens than their private competitors, who will seek to undercut new public authority at every possible turn. States must also negotiate their areas of authority with private authorities, and must typically accommodate the needs and aspirations of these social actors. As always, authority is negotiated and continually contested, not conferred by principle.

The bargain between the state and various private authorities must also be credible—that is, it must ultimately be self-enforcing. Most important, state consolidation creates at least the potential for the abuse of public authority by subsequent rulers. The ability to use state power to create an effective social order is also the ability to turn that power for the leader's self-serving ends, whether this be preserving his rule beyond established limits or acquiring private rents for himself and his family. For private authorities to give up their ability to govern members autonomously, there must be clear and enforceable limits to state power. Absent such limits, private authorities will continue to resist effective state rule, and conflict will endure or recur. The international community likely erred in the immediate post–Cold War era in assuming that democracy and free markets were a panacea for postconflict governance,[52] with the race to early elections stimulating fears of minority group exclusion. But democracy and free markets are among the most effective means of restraining state power, and, along with guaranteed minority representation, may be necessary pillars of any credible bargain between rulers and ruled.

In turn, the international community is likely necessary for stable and effective postconflict governance. The international community has long resisted approving in principle intervention into the internal affairs of member states. Weak states, in particular, oppose intervention as a violation of sovereignty, at least in part to protect themselves from such interference in their own "internal" affairs. Rather than seeing the international community as a bulwark against possible state failure, national leaders seek to affirm the principle of sovereignty to protect themselves against international efforts to restrain their autonomy and avarice. Perhaps as a result of the costly and not entirely successful efforts at state building in Iraq and Afghanistan, the enthusiasm of the international community, and especially the United States, for state building is rapidly waning. Due to this confluence of constraining principle and decreasing interest, we are likely to see far fewer state-building efforts in the decade ahead. This would be an unfortunate mistake.

The international community in general and individual states in particular can play an essential role in postconflict governance. External actors can facilitate the transition to a new, more legitimate regime by providing neutral "peacekeeping" services that ensure a level playing field for formerly antagonistic groups. The external power is typically stronger than any of the remaining social forces, and able to wield force more effectively than most. By bringing new resources to bear, the external power can create the "political space" in which rival groups can resolve their differences.

In addition, and perhaps even more important, the external power can credibly commit to the creation and maintenance of a specific

political order and its attendant governance structures as negotiated by the parties to conflict themselves. In the wake of internal conflict, the problem of "cycling" looms large in any polity. As first demonstrated by Kenneth Arrow, in any political system with multiple decision makers and multiple options, the potential exists for individuals or factions to coalesce around one of two alternatives, only to be displaced by a different coalition around another set of alternatives, only to be displaced by a third coalition around another set, ad infinitum. Political institutions are a partial solution to this problem, as they "induce" an equilibrium by privileging some coalitions or alternatives.[53] Yet, to the extent that political institutions matter for policy, they too are subject to cycling or, in jargon, are endogenous.[54] Instead of one policy option displacing another, one set of institutions simply displaces the alternatives with the same effect. Rather than cycling through policies, a political system can cycle through institutions that determine policy. Moreover, after a major internal conflict, there are likely to be few surviving institutions, except in those cases where a majority defeats a minority challenger. Without established institutions, the problem of cycling will be particularly acute. This is where external powers can play a crucial role. By committing to the preservation of a specific political order, and not some other order, the external power can establish expectations around which social order congeals, solving the problem of potential cycling between alternatives. Given the weakness of the state, this may be the most important contribution an external power can make to the rebuilding of legitimate state authority. The external power can also provide and coordinate foreign aid to rebuild the country's economic infrastructure and political institutions. By solidifying expectations about which set of rules will prevail, and using well-placed aid to encourage buy-in from previously warring parties, external actors can assist in setting a new and hopefully more robust equilibrium in weak or failed states.

Yet, respect for the principle of sovereignty directly interferes with this effort. Sovereignty has never been what it pretends to be. As explained above, in practice, violations of the principle have been so numerous and pervasive that Krasner rightly describes it as an "organized hypocrisy."[55] In protecting the principle, states currently insist on approving interventions through some international body, typically the United Nations but open to occasional forum shopping, and limiting the scope and duration of the mission. Such limits, however, directly undermine the external power's ability to guarantee the negotiated governance structure and undercut the credibility of the agreement. Without an open-ended international commitment to the current political order, local parties to the conflict will not expect the current governance structure to "stick," they will not invest in the proposed political institutions and accommodate themselves to their rules, and thus the agreement is likely to unravel. In trying to protect the principle of sovereignty, the international community virtually guarantees that the state-building effort, bolstered by its own international efforts, will fail.

NOTES

1. Robert H. Jackson, *Quasi-States: Sovereignty, International Relations and the Third World* (New York: Cambridge University Press, 1990).

2. Christopher J. Bickerton, Philip Cunliffe, and Alexander Gourevitch, eds., *Politics without Sovereignty: A Critique of Contemporary International Relations* (London: UCL Press, 2006).

3. Andreas Osiander, "Sovereignty, International Relations, and the Westphalian Myth," *International Organization* 55, no. 2 (2001): 251–87.

4. Leo Gross, "The Peace of Westphalia, 1648–1948," *American Journal of International Law* 42, no. 1 (1948): 20–41.

5. As quoted in Chris Brown, Terry Nardin, and Nicholas Rengger, eds., *International Relations in Political Thought: Texts from the Ancient Greeks to the First World War* (New York: Cambridge University Press, 2002), 273.

6. Stephen D. Krasner, *Sovereignty: Organized Hypocrisy* (Princeton, NJ: Princeton University Press, 1999), 20–25.

7. Edward Keene, *Beyond the Anarchical Society: Grotius, Colonialism and Order in World Politics* (New York: Cambridge University Press, 2002), 43.

8. Quoted in Keene, *Beyond the Anarchical Society*, 44.

9. Stephen D. Krasner, "Westphalia and All That," in *Ideas and Foreign Policy: Beliefs, Institutions, and Political Change*, ed. Judith Goldstein and Robert O. Keohane (Ithaca, NY: Cornell University Press, 1993), 235–64; and Osiander, "Sovereignty, International Relations, and the Westphalian Myth."

10. Brian C. Schmidt, *The Political Discourse of Anarchy: A Disciplinary History of International Relations* (Albany: State University of New York Press, 1998).

11. Jackson, *Quasi-States*.

12. Quoted in Keene, *Beyond the Anarchical Society*, 44–45, 49.

13. Quoted in ibid., 108.

14. Jack Donnelly, "Sovereign Inequalities and Hierarchy in Anarchy: American Power and International Society," *European Journal of International Relations* 12, no. 2 (2006): 139–70.

15. Edwin DeWitt Dickenson, *The Equality of States in International Law* (New York: Arno Press, 1972); and W. W. Willoughby and Charles G. Fenwick, *The Inquiry Handbooks*, vol. 16 (Wilmington, DE: Scholarly Resources, 1974), 5–13.

16. Donnelly, "Sovereign Inequalities," 149–51.

17. David A. Lake, *Hierarchy in International Relations* (Ithaca, NY: Cornell University Press, 2009).

18. Geir Lundestad, *The American "Empire"* (New York: Oxford University Press, 1990), 54.

19. Tim Büthe and Walter Mattli, *The New Global Rulers: The Privatization of Regulation in the World Economy* (Princeton, NJ: Princeton University Press, 2011).

20. Jessica F. Green, *Rethinking Private Authority: Agents and Entrepreneurs in Global Environmental Governance* (Princeton, NJ: Princeton University Press, 2014).

21. Timothy Sinclair, *The New Masters of Capitalism: American Bond Rating Agencies and the Politics of Creditworthiness* (Ithaca, NY: Cornell University Press, 2005).

22. William Bain, *Between Anarchy and Society: Trusteeship and the Obligations of Power* (New York: Oxford University Press, 2003); James D. Fearon and David D. Laitin, "Neotrusteeship and the Problem of Weak States," *International Security* 28, no. 4 (2004): 5–43; and Stephen D. Krasner, "Sharing Sovereignty: New Institutions for Collapsed and Failing States," *International Security* 29, no. 2 (2004): 85–120.

23. David A. Lake and Christopher Fariss, "International Trusteeship: External Authority in Areas of Limited Statehood," *Governance* (forthcoming), doi: 10.1111/gove.12066.

24. Lake, *Hierarchy in International Relations*; and David A. Lake, "Rightful Rules: Authority, Order, and the Foundations of Global Governance," *International Studies Quarterly* 54, no. 3 (2010): 587–613.

25. Jeffrey Herbst, *States and Power in Africa: Comparative Lessons in Authority and Control* (Princeton, NJ: Princeton University Press, 2000).

26. Jackson, *Quasi-States*.

27. Catherine Boone, *Political Topographies of the African State: Territorial Authority and Institutional Choice* (New York: Cambridge University Press, 2003).

28. Herbst, *States and Power in Africa*.

29. Ioan M. Lewis, *Making and Breaking States in Africa: The Somali Experience* (Trenton, NJ: Red Sea Press, 2010), 6–9; Mary Harper, *Getting Somalia Wrong? Faith, War, and Hope in a Shattered State* (New York: Zed, 2012), 35–43; and Afyare Abdi Elmi, *Understanding the Somalia Conflagration: Identity, Political Islam, and Peacebuilding* (London: Pluto Press, 2010), chap. 3.

30. David D. Laitin and Said S. Samatar, *Somalia: Nation in Search of a State* (Boulder, CO: Westview, 1987), 30.

31. Ismail I. Ahmed and Reginald Herbold Green, "The Heritage of War and State Collapse in Somalia and Somaliland: Local-Level Effects, External Interventions and Reconstruction," *Third World Quarterly* 20, no. 1 (1999): 114; and Lewis, *Making and Breaking States in Africa*, 8–9.

32. Laitin and Samatar, *Somalia*, 46.

33. Ahmed and Green, "Heritage of War," 115–16.

34. See Mark Bradbury, *Becoming Somaliland* (London: Progressio, 2008).

35. Laitin and Samatar, *Somalia*, 69; and Lewis, *Making and Breaking States in Africa*, 61.

36. Laitin and Samatar, *Somalia*, 77; and Lewis, *Making and Breaking States in Africa*, 66.

37. David Laitin, "The Political Economy of Military Rule in Somalia," *The Journal of Modern African Studies* 14, no. 3 (1976): 449–68.

38. Peter T. Leeson, "Better Off Stateless: Somalia Before and After Government Collapse," *Journal of Comparative Economics* 35, no. 4 (2007): 694.

39. Matthew Bryden, "Somalia: The Wages of Failure," *Current History* 94, no. 591 (1995): 146; and Leeson, "Better Off Stateless," 694.

40. Ahmed and Green, "Heritage of War," 118–19.

41. Harper, *Getting Somalia Wrong?* chap. 4.

42. Ken Menkhaus, "State Collapse in Somalia: Second Thoughts," *Review of African Political Economy* 30, no. 97 (2003): 405–22; Ken Menkhaus, "Governance without Government in Somalia: Spoilers, Statebuilding, and the Politics of Coping," *International Security* 31, no. 3 (2006): 74–106; Leeson, "Better Off Stateless"; and Benjamin Powell, Ryan Ford, and Alex Nowrasteh, "Somalia after State Collapse: Chaos or Improvement?" *Journal of Economic Behavior and Organization* 67, nos. 3–4 (2008): 657–70.

43. See Elmi, *Understanding the Somalia Conflagration*.

44. Ibid., 82–85; and Harper, *Getting Somalia Wrong?* 170.

45. Harry Verhoeven, "The Self-Fulfilling Prophecy of Failed States: Somalia, State Collapse, and the Global War on Terror," *Journal of Eastern African Studies* 3, no. 3 (2009): 405–25.

46. Harper, *Getting Somalia Wrong?* 172–73; and Elmi, *Understanding the Somalia Conflagration*, 82–88.

47. Arend Lijphart, *The Politics of Accommodation: Pluralism and Democracy in the Netherlands* (Berkeley: University of California Press, 1968).

48. James D. Fearon and David D. Laitin, "Explaining Interethnic Cooperation," *American Political Science Review* 90 (1996): 715–35.

49. Philip G. Roeder and Donald Rothchild, eds., *Sustainable Peace: Power and Democracy after Civil Wars* (Ithaca, NY: Cornell University Press, 2005).

50. Ibid.

51. Eli Berman, et al., "Can Hearts and Minds Be Bought? The Economics of Counterinsurgency in Iraq," *Journal of Political Economy* 119,

no. 4 (2011): 766–819; and Jennifer Keister, "States within States: How Rebels Rule" (PhD diss., University of California, San Diego, 2011).

52. Roland Paris, *At War's End: Building Peace after Civil Conflict* (New York: Cambridge University Press, 2004).

53. Kenneth A. Shepsle, "Institutional Arrangements and Equilibrium in Multidimensional Voting Models," *American Journal of Political Science* 23, no. 1 (1979): 27–59.

54. William H. Riker, "Implications from the Disequilibrium of Majority Rule for the Study of Institutions," *American Political Science Review* 74, no. 2 (1980): 432–46.

55. Krasner, *Sovereignty: Organized Hypocrisy.*

18

THE UN SECURITY COUNCIL AND CRISIS MANAGEMENT
STILL CENTRAL AFTER ALL THESE YEARS

Bruce D. Jones

One year and a day after the 9/11 Al Qaeda attacks on the United States, then US president George W. Bush made an impassioned speech at the United Nations. The stakes were extraordinarily high. After the 9/11 attacks, the United States had turned its military might to the overthrow of the Taliban regime that had allowed Afghanistan to serve as a base for Al Qaeda. Now, Washington was turning its sights on Iraq, and Bush sought UN support for the action. He built an argument by pointing to evidence that Iraq was flaunting the requirements of UN Security Council (UNSC) resolutions and, by doing so, undermining the credibility of the body. Bush stressed that the United Nations was not just a talk shop; the Security Council, he argued, is most essentially a body with both the capacity and the obligation to uphold core principles of collective security. In his estimation, this common security had come under threat from terrorism and from rogue regimes that ignored their international commitments—of which Iraq was a prime example.

The atmosphere surrounding the speech was redolent of the famous highlights of the United Nations' early years: the rapt attention when audiences worldwide listened by radio to Israel's storied ambassador Abba Eban appeal for UN support for Israel's independence; the drama when Soviet premier Khrushchev banged his shoe on his General Assembly desk to protest the speech of British prime minister Harold Macmillan; the dueling speeches by US ambassador Adlai Stevenson and Soviet ambassador Valerian Zorin during the Cuban missile crisis. In the middle of President Bush's speech was the essential passage. The tension in the chamber was palpable when he turned from challenging Iraq to challenging the United Nations itself: "All the world now faces a test and the United Nations a difficult and defining moment. Are Security Council resolutions to be honored and enforced or cast aside without consequence? Will the United Nations serve the purpose of its founding or will it be irrelevant?"[1] The implication was stark: pass a resolution authorizing a US war in Iraq, or the United States will ensure that the Security Council is made irrelevant in international crisis management.

Bush's speech was brilliantly crafted, well delivered, and favorably received. And it utterly failed to accomplish its objectives. The Security Council famously did not pass a resolution authorizing military enforcement against the Iraqi state, but nor did the United States follow by striving to make the Security Council irrelevant or even marginal. The subsequent six years of the Bush administration saw two things that his speechwriters clearly did not anticipate. First, they did not anticipate an uncharacteristic flood of foreign ministers and even prime ministers and presidents into the body, signaling the intent of allies and adversaries alike to shore up the United Nations in the face of an American threat to sideline it. Second, and perhaps even more surprising to Bush's first-term staff, was strong American support for the largest-ever increase in Security Council roles in crisis management and transnational security issues. When George Bush took office in 2000, there were 37,000 uniformed UN peacekeeping personnel in the field; when he left, there were over one hundred thousand.[2] And the Bush administration gave the Security Council new roles on terrorism and nuclear proliferation, as well as limited but important political roles in Afghanistan and later in Iraq. In short, one of the legacies of the Bush administration was to move the Security Council closer to the center of international politics.

Did President Bush make the UNSC the "central motherboard"[3] of international crisis management? Not quite. He was not wrong to point to the unique legal authority of the UNSC. The UN Charter, encoded into American law and the law of every other member state, gives the Security Council the sole authority in international relations to use force, excepting the right of countries to engage in self-defense. If law is legitimacy, then the UNSC has unique legitimacy too, and many governments still hold that to be true. But the law is one thing; practice is another. In actual crisis management and the use of force, as distinct from the law thereof, the Security Council has never been quite as central as the UN Charter proposes.

THE SECURITY COUNCIL AND THE MAJOR POWERS

The reason for this is simple. The deepest crises in international politics are, by definition, those that engage the core interests of the greatest powers. And those that generate the most heat are those in which the interests of the great powers diverge. In those circumstances, from Kosovo to Crimea to Syria, the simple fact of divergent interests between the great powers means that the UNSC has rarely been central to the management of the most important crises.

For exactly the same reason, the UNSC matters more than its critics allow. Time and again, we've seen variants on a pattern. In the first phase of a crisis, divides between the Permanent Five (P5) members of the UNSC mean that the essential work of crisis management, whether it be in negotiations between the parties or deployment of troops for enforcement purposes, happens outside the UN framework. That may take the form of unilateral military action, diplomatic management by informal or semiformal groupings, or NATO action. Then, one of two things happens, or often both. When the most acute phase of the crisis has passed, the powers return to the UNSC to authorize UN action for the second phase—as they did in passing a council resolution that both legalized the ongoing US military presence in Iraq and authorized the establishment of a UN political office in Iraq, the UN Assistance Mission in Iraq (UNAMI). It's a pattern we saw in Kosovo, where divides over NATO's role took negotiations out of the UNSC, but when a basic agreement was reached in the G8 talks at Rambouillet, the powers rapidly returned to the council to encode the terms of the end of hostilities, legalize an ongoing NATO (as well as Russian) presence, and establish a UN transitional authority to run the country until such time as a nascent government could be established.[4] Alternatively (or additionally), we have frequently seen the Security Council find a second-tier crisis around which to unify, even as differences over a first-tier crisis linger—as it did by unifying around UN action in southern Lebanon soon after the clashes over the Iraq war; by agreeing on responsibility-to-protect action in Côte d'Ivoire, right after the divides over Libya; and by issuing mandates for action in Mali, even while clashes over Syria continued.

This raises a second point: that crises can *unify* the interests of the great powers, just as they can divide them. The P5 differ in many respects, but they share a series of profound preferences: a bias toward preserving and protecting sovereignty (notwithstanding differences, as we shall see, over exceptions to the sovereignty norm); a strong interest in protecting themselves and the global economy against threats by non-state actors, especially transnational terrorist organizations and movements; and a favoring of stability over chaos, all things being equal. Thus, they share interests, in broad terms, in tamping down levels of violence and instability in just about every region—something they have voted to do on several hundred occasions since the end of the Cold War.[5]

And so the UNSC *has* become the most important platform for crisis management in second-tier crises—"second tier" being defined purely by the centrality of the crisis to great-power interests. It so happens that during the Cold War, most of the world's civil wars and battle deaths took place in countries in these "second-tier" crises—and in those countries, UN-mandated and UN-managed actions have formed an essential part of the equation in the dramatic reductions in both the number and severity of wars. In 2009, the number of conflicts was one-third less than its post–Cold War high in 1992.[6] Over that time, there were a record number of peace agreements.[7] This was in part an effect of the end of the Cold War. But the explosive growth of mediation and peacekeeping operations played a critical role; scholarship shows with increasing confidence that peace agreements are more likely to endure in situations where a peacekeeping operation is mandated than where none exists.[8] Since 1990, the Security Council has put more than fifty peacekeeping operations and political missions in place, along with considerable mediation activities. Peacekeeping operations have failed, as in the appalling cases of Rwanda and Angola. But they have also recorded notable accomplishments, among which is their role in facilitating countries' transitions out of civil war and into the early stages of establishing stable governance.

This empirical account of the Security Council's activity responds to two forms of excess critique. The first is the account of skeptics, often American, who typically highlight instances of council inaction or division to reinforce preexisting notions about the fallibility of the United Nations or the impossibility of global governance—defined in exaggerated terms that could never be lived up to.[9] Much of this is simply an exercise in selective use of evidence. The second critique is similar but launched from a different perspective, by adherents of a robust approach to global governance who expect the UN Security Council somehow to transcend the core interests of its most important members; they look to the council—to the body, not to its members—to act in ways that uphold the highest principles of the UN Charter. Thus, we hear European and Indian and Arab voices blaming the UNSC for failing to restrain the United States from invading Iraq, or for failing to take action to respond to the Israeli-Palestinian crisis, despite US objections. The evident unrealism of this perspective warrants no further comment—it should be axiomatic that there is no such thing as effective multilateralism that is not aligned with, and usually built on, the policies or actions of the still-leading power, the United States, or by some rough alignment between the United States and the other P5 powers.

The reality of the UNSC is that it is first and foremost a tool of the great powers—and that it's *supposed* to be so. Its essential purpose is to limit the risks of a crisis between the great powers themselves—and anyone who believes that a focus on great-power tensions precludes or constrains a focus on human security should think back to the barbarism and human misery of the period of disorder and conflict between the powers from 1914 to 1945. It so happens, thankfully, that in the post–Cold War era, both the distribution of power in the international system and the interests of the powers themselves enabled the huge expansion of responses to situations of crisis that we've come to expect—and that have saved probably millions of lives over the past two decades. And so while the UNSC may not have been the "central motherboard" for the most strategic crises, it has been an essential platform for collective action by the powers and by a huge range of members (more than one hundred governments have contributed

forces to UN operations) to tamp down conflict and protect lives.

But will these patterns continue?

A BRIEF LOOK BACK: GREAT POWERS AND THE SECURITY COUNCIL DURING THE COLD WAR

A brief historical digression is warranted here. Most readers will assume that the great powers' use of the Security Council as a tool to limit or repair the tensions between them over crises has been limited to the post–Cold War era. That's not entirely the case.

Council lore has it that the body was sidelined during the Cold War, as a function of US and Soviet vetoes cancelling each other out, impeding any kind of action. There was one regional exception to this, a surprising one: the Middle East. Over the course of its first forty years, the UNSC was used on several occasions in the Middle East to tamp down crises that risked triggering great-power proxy war or worse. At the birth of Israel in 1946, during the Suez crisis in 1956, at the onset of the 1967 war, and again in the Yom Kippur War in 1973—in other words, at every major crisis juncture in the region—the UNSC was used by the superpowers to de-escalate crises on the Arab-Israeli front.[10]

The wording is precise: "used by the superpowers." Accounts of the role of the UNSC often suffer from a basic misunderstanding about multilateral institutions—that they have agency beyond the will of the great powers. The most important thing to understand about the UNSC is that it is an instrument of great-power politics, by practice and by design. Observers, and even states that are elected to the ten nonpermanent seats in the body, are often surprised by the extent to which the permanent members dominate its workings; but the whole point of the UN Security Council was to provide a mechanism whereby the great powers could navigate or negotiate at least some set of their security differences, and manage crises so as to avoid escalation that could entangle the great powers in direct conflict.

This is precisely how the UNSC was used in Arab-Israeli crises from 1946–79.[11] The Arab-Israeli wars cannot be treated precisely as proxy wars, but US backing of Israel and Soviet backing of the Arabs, at various junctures, meant that Arab-Israeli crises took on a proxy war dimension, and escalation risked pulling the superpowers into direct conflict in the Middle East. To avoid this outcome, the United States and the Soviets, in each crisis juncture, would engage in shuttle diplomacy and work to articulate the terms of cease-fires or cessation-of-hostilities agreements.[12] These terms would then be brought to the United Nations for ratification and P5 and UNSC endorsement. Moreover, on each of these occasions, the UNSC then mandated the creation and/or use of a variety of mediators, observers, multinational stabilization forces, and peacekeeping operations. Indeed, almost the entire panoply of modern crisis management tools—including the refugee machinery—was born in the Middle East as instruments of US-Soviet crisis management in the Arab-Israeli theater.[13]

Outside the Middle East, the UNSC's engagement in crisis diplomacy *was* exceedingly episodic. In one famous episode in 1960, UN Resolution 143 mandated a huge peacekeeping operation to help the Congolese government suppress the Katanga secession effort. Among other notable facts about that operation: fulfilling a promise made by President Roosevelt in 1945, the US Air Force provided free transport for the UN peacekeepers to the Congo. To this day, there are still UN diplomats who speak proudly of the large, sophisticated operation deployed by the United Nations at that juncture, complete with its own air force, twenty

thousand troops, and civilian staff ranging from public administration to health to education. That the regime that followed the UN operation was one of the most corrupt and dysfunctional in modern African history tends not to be mentioned—an early example of a developing pattern of focus on short-term crisis suppression, not longer-term state building or governance results.

Returning to the Arab-Israeli theater: when that region began its long (and incomplete) shift from serial war-making to iterant peace process with the Camp David Accords, the notion of a UN peacekeeping force to monitor the peace was again mooted—by Israel. And it was overwhelmingly rejected in the General Assembly—by the Arab group. How the world has changed. Not until 2006 would the United Nations once again be asked to take on an important crisis management operation in the wake of another episode of Arab-Israeli crisis (in southern Lebanon, after the Israeli-Hezbollah war, with a major retooling, remandating, and reinforcement of the UN Interim Force in Lebanon, or UNIFIL). With the decision not to deploy a force to observe the Camp David Accords, the UNSC fell into a fallow period.

THE UNITED NATIONS AND REGIONAL ORGANIZATIONS

During such fallow periods, regional organizations are often thought to compete with the Security Council for centrality in crisis management. The numbers tell a very different story.

Based on scale of deployment under their authority, there is no discernible trend toward regional organizations. From the late 1990s to the present, UN peacekeeping operations grew from 10,000 to over 80,000 troops in the field; personnel in UN missions totaled over 100,000 in 2011. In contrast, regional organizations' deployment of peacekeepers decreased from a high in the late 1990s of over 40,000 to 17,000 in 2011. The average UN mission in 2011 was nearly 8,000 personnel, with the largest, UNAMID in Darfur, topping out at over 27,000 personnel, whereas regional organizations fielded missions on a considerably smaller scale, on average 2,500 personnel.[14]

The chart in Figure 1 shows the number of troops deployed globally by all regional organizations combined, plotted against the number of troops deployed by the UNSC, from 2002 to 2012. The graphic speaks for itself.

The relative weight of the UN deployments versus those of regional organizations is even clearer when we remove the NATO mission in Afghanistan (International Security Assistance Force, or ISAF) from the equation (Figure 2).[15]

Although regional organizations, including the African Union (AU) and Economic Community of West African States (ECOWAS), have deployed peacekeeping missions on a number of occasions, these missions have had limited force strength and have often been launched with consid-

erable international backing, as with French support for the ECOWAS mission in Côte d'Ivoire (ECOFORCE/ECOMICI) in 2003. They are commonly absorbed into larger Security Council–authorized missions, as was the case with the ECOWAS mission's incorporation into the UN Operation in Côte d'Ivoire (UNOCI) in 2004; the 2004 AU Mission in Sudan (AMIS); and its 2007 successor, the AU/UN Hybrid Operation in Darfur (UNAMID). In fact, there are currently very few UN operations where the United Nations is the sole actor—85 percent feature joint action, in various forms, with regional organizations.[16] But, in many cases, regional organizations make only a token contribution to the missions.

It is worth noting that in many settings, when the United Nations undertakes an operation, substantial portions of its troop deployments come from the region itself. In this sense, the boundaries between UN and regional operations blur slightly. But there are reasons why the UN gets involved: it provides P5 political engagement, critical assets from nonregional contributors, and logistics and financial support, which some regions cannot themselves provide. This is particu-

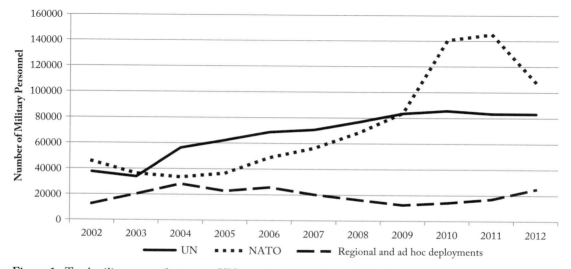

Figure 1. Total military contributions to UN peacekeeping and non-UN military operations, 2002–12

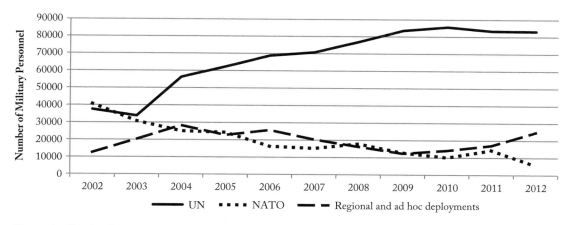

Figure 2. Total military contributions to UN peacekeeping and non-UN military operations, excluding ISAF, 2002–12

larly true when it comes to African operations, where the composition of UN forces is often heavily African (though frequently from other parts of the continent than that where the deployment is centered); to date, African regional organizations have neither the bureaucratic nor financial nor logistical capacity to mount and sustain multiple, large operations.

The only other organization of similar scale and importance is NATO. The character of NATO's crisis management role is quite different from that of the United Nations. NATO is a bit player in the second-tier crises that make up most of the workload of the world's crisis management machinery, but a big player in first-tier ones—from Bosnia to Kosovo to Afghanistan. Nevertheless, for most of the post–Cold War period, the UNSC was overseeing more personnel on the ground than NATO. The deployment of NATO troops increased toward the end of the Afghanistan operation, though, and by 2011 NATO had 145,000 military personnel in the field, largely concentrated in Afghanistan.

Of course, the NATO presence in Afghanistan, its earlier presence in Bosnia, its training presence in Iraq, and its actions in Libya were all authorized by the UNSC.

Only NATO's military action against Serbia was undertaken without Security Council authorization; even its follow-on presence in Kosovo was authorized by UNSC Resolution 1244. The fact of Security Council authorization may not have been a decisive feature of these operations from Washington's point of view, but it was no mere formality for the NATO allies. After divides over the US invasion of Iraq, and alongside debates within NATO about its mission and mandate in the absence of a credible Russian threat to mainland Europe, several NATO allies have adopted laws that require their parliaments to authorize NATO out-of-area operations, and several of those laws, in turn, make reference to UNSC authorization. For example, in the lead-up to NATO action in Libya, the Norwegian, Danish, and Swedish parliaments all authorized the action and did so making explicit reference to the fact that the operation had been authorized by UNSC Resolution 1973. The attitudes of Scandinavian parliaments may seem marginal to NATO operations, but between them, Norway, Sweden, and Denmark flew more than 70 percent of the sorties during the Libya operation. And the Scandinavians are not alone: no one in London or Washington has forgotten the tortuous debates about whether or not the United Kingdom could legally use force in Iraq in the absence of a UNSC authorization.

UNSC authorization for multinational force (MNF) action is, in fact, an understudied and, I would argue, underutilized tool. It provides some of the same advantages of UN Blue Helmet operations: the legal authority and political legitimacy of UNSC authorization, and the ability to blend troop capabilities from multiple regions. However, because in MNF operations—which were used in 1995 in the eastern DR Congo, and in Timor-Leste in 2000—member states rely on their own logistical capacities rather than those of the United Nations, they can deploy substantially more quickly than Blue Helmets (provided the MNF is composed of advanced militaries, as has always been the case). An intriguing variation of this model was the reconfiguration of UNIFIL in southern Lebanon in the summer of 2006, after the end of the Israel-Hezbollah war: UK, French, German, Italian, and Indian troops all deployed into theater within a two-week period, in a mode characteristic of MNF deployments, but ended up under the command of a UN force commander, supplemented by a strategic military cell at headquarters that expanded the United Nations' normal (rather modest) intelligence and strategic command capabilities.

SECOND-TIER CONFLICTS: THREE CONTINUING CHALLENGES

Huge reductions in the level and number of civil wars in the past two decades do not mean that this mode of crisis management is a completed business for the Security Council. Three factors will contribute to its continued engagement in civil conflicts for the foreseeable future: several missions are still in the wind-down phase; there's a continued risk of relapse in places where the UNSC thought it was finished with peacekeeping;

and, most complicating, there are missions currently on the UN docket—such as the Democratic Republic of Congo and South Sudan—that are likely to be long-running crises, cresting in and out of violence, not transitioning smoothly to a stable peace.

First, the Security Council is now in the late stages of wrapping up operations in such countries as Timor-Leste (closed in late 2012), Liberia (authorized until September 2013), and Sierra Leone (where it retains a peacebuilding presence), while it continues to run operations in Haiti and Côte d'Ivoire. Many of these are follow-on operations, sometimes in the second or third round. The UNSC's engagement in these cases has a different character from its engagement in the peak of civil wars or in the immediate postconflict period, where the job is reducing violence and then beginning political negotiations and implementing peace agreements. In the early part of the implementation of peace agreements, the key tasks are ones that play to UN strengths and that UN special representatives of the secretary-general (SRSGs) directly oversee and add value to. As acute conflict recedes, the challenge becomes that of maintaining long-term security reassurance, fostering long-term political reform and the building of political institutions, spurring economic activity under very difficult circumstances, generating jobs, and cultivating the beginnings of the architecture of the rule of law and order.

It would be a stretch to say that these long-term tasks play to the strengths of the UN system. Indeed, they do not play to the strengths of the international system as a whole. If we look at the major international and regional institutions, as well as the major donors, we see a paucity of the kinds of tools needed to help governments and civil societies grapple with long-term political transformations, security transformations, and even economic transformations, if they occur under conditions of instability.[17] The development community, which phases in as the UNSC phases out, is only beginning to tackle this challenge of "development under the shadow of violence."[18] In all these contexts, the threat of violence remains—for a long time—and the risk of a return to violence is a very significant impediment to investment, to political participation, and to confidence in the system. The United Nations has attempted to grapple with some of these issues, notably through the UN report on civilian capacity,[19] as has the World Bank, through the 2011 *World Development Report*;[20] but both institutions are in the infancy of these processes.

Second, the UNSC is learning that when a country exits the phase of very intense violence or is in the context of a long, unstable peace, it presents a scenario that is very attractive for transnational organized crime. A critical determinant of organized criminal flows is the ability to purchase some degree of security at a very low price, either for the extraction of natural resources or for the transshipment of a variety of goods to other markets. So the challenge, and the threat to the state, posed by organized crime is likely to be a growing problem for many actors, including the Security Council.

Third, some of the remaining cases on the UNSC docket are some of the toughest that it will face. Civil wars fall along a spectrum of difficulty, in part due to a function of scale. Currently, 28 percent of the UNSC's mandated troops are operating in the DR Congo and South Sudan, with approximately 19,000 and 7,000 uniformed personnel respectively. Each of these operations is mandated to cover territory on a massive scale: the Democratic Republic of the Congo is approximately 2,344,858 square kilometers, and South Sudan is 1,861,484 square kilometers. The tools that the Security Council has used with success in smaller contexts, particularly large but static peace-keeping forces, are not applicable given the size and nature of these situations. In a place like South Sudan, to provide the degree of coverage that UN forces provided in Liberia or Sierra Leone or Haiti would take hundreds of thousands of soldiers, and there is no realistic prospect that anyone is going to mandate or supply a presence of that scale. So different approaches—more nimble, more political approaches—are going to be necessary. Those can be combined with flexible military options—again highlighting the need for flexibility, which is far from the United Nations' greatest strength.

In fact, we are seeing interesting evolutionary responses here. Most attention so far has gone to the establishment of an "intervention" brigade in eastern DRC, under the overall command of the ongoing UN peacekeeping operations there, MONUC. It speaks to the lack of institutional memory in the UNSC that the brigade was hailed by several UNSC members, including members of the P5, as a dramatic change in UN modes of operation, the "first time" that the United Nations would be commanded purposefully to counter armed rebels, using robust force. It was, of course, not the first time at all: the UN Assistance Mission in Sierra Leone (UNAMSIL) did this in 1999 when the Revolutionary United Front broke with the peace agreement; UNIFIL did this when it was authorized to use force to "extend the authority of the state" in southern Lebanon, including by disbanding "illegal armed groups" (i.e., Hezbollah); and the UN mission in Haiti deployed decisive force, under Brazilian command, to defeat a gang/rebel movement in Cité Soleil. The intervention brigade in the Congo is an evolutionary, not a revolutionary, change, but still an important development.

All these challenges could more than absorb the capacity of the Security Council and the UN Secretariat, both of which have been overstretched for years. But they have been shunted to the back burner by the rapid pace of events in the Arab world.

THE SECURITY COUNCIL AND THE ARAB SPRING

When President George W. Bush launched the US invasion of Iraq, he did not anticipate that merely five years later, having then launched two costly wars, the US Treasury would be hit by the biggest financial crisis since the Great Depression. Quite apart from the economic costs of the invasion, there were political ones as well. The Iraq war inflamed the sensitivities of emerging economies vying for greater voice and role in international affairs; then the global financial crisis thrust them into the forefront of global politics.

In fact, just over twenty years into the post–Cold War era, the UNSC is grappling simultaneously with several different but interlocking transitions. These include a change in the nature and geography of its most intense workload, namely the Arab Spring; the (related) geographical spread of the perceived Islamic terrorist threat; the growing influence of the emerging powers; and (bringing these all together) reinvigorated debates about sovereignty and the use of force. At the same time, the UNSC continues to expand its engagement in counterproliferation, including the two cases that veer most dangerously toward crisis, North Korea and Iran. Just as in previous eras, the issues both divide and unify the Council. And, as in previous eras, the fact that multiple powers are implicated by and necessary to the work of the United Nations will likely be both the cause of its most important failures and the source of its greatest strengths.

Crises in the core of the Arab world differ dramatically from the second-tier cases that absorbed the bulk of the UNSC's attention during the post–Cold War era, and they do so along two dimensions. First, the majority of the wars to which the UNSC has responded over the past twenty years were in contexts where state authority was weak. The opposite is true in most Arab Spring cases—there, it is precisely the strength (and unresponsiveness) of the state that is the source of the crisis. Second, in the majority of the cases to which the Security Council responded in the post–Cold War era, geopolitical attention was low. No major political actor in Washington, Moscow, Beijing, Delhi, or even Brussels had fundamental stakes in the United Nations' performance in Burundi or Liberia or Timor or Haiti. But those capitals all have deep stakes in the question of how crisis and transition plays out in Egypt and Jordan and Syria—to say nothing of the fundamental stakes in the Gulf. As the United Nations struggles to find a way to respond to the dynamics of the Arab Spring, it does so against the backdrop of high-stakes geopolitics. These are precisely the dynamics, argued above, that tend to limit UNSC action, at least in the first phase of a crisis. Thus, while the United Nations has tried to play roles in the political transitions in Egypt and Bahrain, it has been rebuffed; and, of course, the Security Council is profoundly divided over Syria.

On the other hand, the collapse of authoritarian role in several Arab states has also led to the collapse of those states' not inconsiderable roles in suppressing Islamic terrorism. This has been manifest first in Yemen (three out of five provinces of which are now controlled by Al Qaeda), where the United Nations has played a role in political transition; and then in the Maghreb, where the Security Council has acted, both in Libya and in Mali.

THE SECURITY COUNCIL ON TERRORISM AND PROLIFERATION

The spread of Al Qaeda affiliates into the Maghreb is but one part of a backlash against the economic and political globalization that have been defining features of the post-9/11 response of the UNSC. While globalization has driven trends of deepened integration, this interdependence has not come without costs, particularly the rise of transnational threats. The 9/11 attacks in the United States deepened multilateral cooperation, through formal mechanisms like the Security Council, but also through informal institutions, to address a range of transnational threats.[21] The degree of adaptation to this set of new challenges has differed across issues and bodies, though all major multilateral institutions have initiated reforms.[22]

Not just an arena for great-power deconfliction or a tool of great-power interests, the Security Council also has a role in norm creation and diffusion.[23] On transnational threats, the council has mobilized an international response to shared threats, allowing states to take action on common interests to preserve international security. To do so, the UNSC has adapted a set of critical normative and legislative tools against transnational threats like terrorism and piracy. The use of these tools has helped foster a minimum of cooperation by the emerged and emerging powers, although this may not necessarily translate to deepened cooperation on active crises.

This has been most significant with counterterrorism norms. The Security Council has undertaken significant adaptation of the counterterrorism architecture. In conjunction with steps taken by the UN General Assembly, particularly the 2006 "General Assembly Counterterrorism Strategy," this has hastened a shift in normative attitudes around member state cooperation to address common threats, reinforcing attitudes that states are required to act to address conflicts and tackle underlying issues that lay the groundwork for the popular backing of terrorism.[24]

Among the various conventions and protocols the Security Council has adopted—

including the imposition of directed financial sanctions against Al Qaeda, the Taliban, and other affiliates in 1999, and again in expanded form after 9/11—one key resolution has placed considerable obligations on states to combat terrorism: UNSC Resolution 1373, adopted directly following 9/11. It requires that states augment domestic legislation, improve border monitoring, coordinate at the executive level, and refocus attention on cooperative measures to address the threat of terrorism. It also established the Counter-Terrorism Committee (CTC). Resolution 1373 broke new ground in counterterrorism architecture by mandating that all member states comply with its provisions; previous agreements were binding only on those member states that became party to the accords. The resolution incorporated language from previous agreements that did not enjoy universal backing, including the UN Terrorist Financing Convention.

These measures, in an action without precedent, impose consistent obligations on *all* states, not just a target state, requiring them to take domestic steps and to cooperate with one another to combat forms of transnational terrorism and disruption. The Security Council's decision to "legislate" these measures has been controversial, both because of the nature of the resolution's provisions and the role of the council itself. Member states have voiced concerns about UNSC resolutions that dictate their domestic behaviors without considered discussions on the practices. The council's decisions on counterterrorism have spurred calls for "reform" of the body's methods and membership. But while other multilateral, regional, and subregional mechanisms have put measures in places to address transnational terrorism, only the Chapter VII Security Council resolutions are legally binding on all UN member states, and commit states to assisting one another to combat terrorism.[25]

In related adaptations, the Security Council has also taken far-reaching steps to combat the transnational threat of piracy off the coast of Somalia, facilitating cooperation with, and support to, an extremely weak Somali government that is unable to secure the country's borders. Recent resolutions adapt the regime from an existing body of customary international law, foremost the 1958 Convention on the High Seas and the 1982 United Nations Convention on the Law of the Sea (UNCLOS). A series of four resolutions, all passed in 2008, were agreed to under Chapter VII of the UN Charter, making them legally binding on all states.

Developing norms against terrorism is one thing; mounting operations against terrorist organizations is quite another. Most observers would assume that the UNSC has not done this; but, in fact, it has. In the aftermath of the short Israel-Hezbollah war in 2006, the UNSC retooled its operation in southern Lebanon (UNIFIL) to give it both a new mandate and new power. The mandate incorporated the concept of "extending state authority" in the south of the country and the dismantlement of "all illegal armed groups." Neither the words "terrorist" nor "Hezbollah" appear in the text of the resolution, but the target of the action was clear. This was an important precedent for UN action in the far fringe of the Arab Spring, namely Libya, and subsequently Mali.

The UNSC has taken an equally interesting approach on proliferation questions. Along similar lines to UNSC Resolution 1373, the Bush administration pushed the United Nations to adopt Security Council Resolution 1540, which requires all states to hold back from furnishing any type of assistance to non-state actors that seek to develop, obtain, transport, or use any type of chemical, biological, or nuclear weapons. Resolution 1540 also established a Security Council committee to monitor compliance and implementation of its requirements, and

appealed to states to assist those without the required capacity to implement the resolution's provisions in meeting its mandate.

More important still have been UNSC actions on Iran and North Korea. Here we see again the themes introduced at the start of this chapter, of issues of great-power unity and divergence being managed simultaneously in informal settings and the United Nations. There are differences between the two cases. For most of the period since North Korea withdrew from the Non-Proliferation Treaty in 2003, the bulk of diplomatic action has been carried by the Six-Party Talks, a multinational diplomatic forum delinked from the United Nations. The UNSC role was modest, consisting of occasional condemnations when North Korea behaved in ways that annoyed even Beijing, which otherwise protected North Korea from far-reaching UNSC action. The UNSC did pass sanctions resolutions in 2006 and again in 2009 following North Korean nuclear tests; but they were watered-down sanctions. In 2013, there was a shift: a series of provocations by North Korea resulted in the United States and China, after three weeks of intensive negotiations, acting together to prepare and pass UNSC Resolution 2094—the furthest-reaching resolution to date, imposing substantial sanctions on North Korean financial institutions, sanctions that were rapidly implemented by China.

The diplomacy of sanctions involving Iran has been more closely tied to the Security Council. Although the main diplomatic mechanism for dealing with Iran is technically outside the UNSC, the P5+1 (the UNSC's five permanent members plus Germany) is by design and nomenclature closely aligned to the UNSC itself, and there has been frequent interaction between the UNSC and the P5+1. Several rounds of sanctions have been adopted by the UNSC. As with many other sanctions regimes, UN sanctions have been amplified by regional and US unilateral sanctions. All these resolutions have been passed unanimously—expect for one, which saw two "no" votes by Turkey and Brazil, who were elected members in 2010 and tried to secure a negotiated deal with Tehran, only to be rebuffed by the United States and, more strikingly, by Russia and China—both of whom voted for a new round of sanctions almost immediately after Brazil and Turkey announced Iran's signature on their Tehran Accord.

The "no" votes by Brazil and Turkey had no particular effect on the resolution, although they did weaken the unity of the message; but more important, they were a harbinger of tougher fights within the UNSC between the West and the broader set of powers now exerting themselves on the international stage. These tensions played out most dramatically in Libya.

THE SECURITY COUNCIL AND THE RESPONSIBILITY TO PROTECT

In 2011, a Libyan uprising began to challenge Colonel Gaddafi's longtime oppressive rule. It quickly turned bloody as Gaddafi sought to suppress the opposition with force. The United States, after some dithering, and under pressure from other Arab states and from the United Kingdom and France, decided to lead a coalition of states to stop Gaddafi's forces as they prepared for a major crackdown in Benghazi. And to do so, the United States invoked the evolving principle of the "responsibility to protect" (R2P). The debate over the responsibility to protect has been and remains one of the most important in shaping the nature and function of the Security Council.

While the notion of the "responsibility to protect" found its fullest expression only in 2005, and was implemented for the first time fully only in 2011, UNSC resolutions had, in fact, begun to erode the hard wall of sovereignty as early as 1990, with the council's first post–Cold War resolutions, on Iraq. When Saddam Hussein invaded and occupied Kuwait, US president George H. W. Bush decided to use American power to reverse the action. While multiple interests (regional stability, oil) were at stake, prominent in his rhetoric about the action was the notion of defending the principle that one state should not subjugate another. In Bush's words at the outset of the war, "No nation will be permitted to brutally assault its neighbor."[26]

Perhaps more important in terms of subsequent developments was another principle articulated in the aftermath of the reversed occupation. Once Saddam's armies returned from Kuwait, they turned on restive populations inside Iraq itself. Famously, the Bush administration decided not to fight Saddam all the way to Baghdad and depose the regime, leaving a variety of Iraqi minority groups undefended against the wrath of a humiliated army. With one exception. In northern Iraq, the United States and its allies imposed a no-fly zone and started cross-border humanitarian operations designed to protect Iraqi Kurds who were being subjected to outrageous treatment by Saddam's army, including the use of chemical weapons. It did so with the legal backing of the UN Security Council, which passed a landmark resolution (UNSCR 668) that declared that the Iraqi government's repressive measures against its own people constituted a direct "threat to international peace and security." By invoking that terminology, the Security Council did two things: practically, it authorized coercive measures to stop the atrocities; and fundamentally, for the first time in the post–World War II era, the United Nations deviated from the notion that what happens inside the borders of a state is a matter for its government alone.

As newly influential actors exert themselves on the global diplomatic stage, these issues of self-determination and human rights are becoming more controversial. This may seem odd; as formerly colonized states, countries like India and Brazil have long spoken out in defense of downtrodden states and anticolonial policy. But as victims of Western military intervention or economic/financial pressure, they have also long opposed the use of coercive tools that violate other countries' sovereignty. The notion that what happens inside a country's borders is a matter of concern to governments outside those borders is a notion that sits uneasily in Brasília or Delhi, let alone in Beijing.

This debate about values, and the institutional arrangements in which they are embedded, have come together most prominently over the issue of Security Council–mandated interventions in the Maghreb. By chance, four leading aspirants for permanent seats on the council—Brazil, India, Germany, and South Africa—all held short-term elected seats as the Arab Spring's shockwaves reverberated across the region, giving them a platform for their views on Libya and beyond, and previewing future debates.

In this critical test of international principles, the reaction of the rising powers was confused. At first, China, Russia, Brazil, India, and South Africa all voted in favor of three actions by the Security Council: referring Gaddafi to the International Criminal Court; imposing sanctions (no minor step for India and Brazil, both of whom historically opposed the use or threat of sanctions); and, most impressive of all, invoking for the first time the responsibility to protect, implicitly threatening coercive action should Gaddafi fail to stop the bloody crackdown. Then, when the situation worsened and the United States moved toward military action, the semipowers were more or less united, but in a kind of odd fence-sitting: Brazil and India, together with China and Russia, abstained on the UN vote, neither blocking nor endorsing. (Brazil and India both argued for more time, stating that they didn't know what has happening on the ground and seeking more information from an African Union mediator who had been dispatched to try to talk Gaddafi out of the attack.) South Africa broke with the rest and voted in favor of the resolution, while the Western camp saw a similar defection as Germany abstained.

Of course, we shouldn't fail to acknowledge that the Western powers have been deeply inconsistent in their willingness to use force to protect civilians. In the past two decades, they were indifferent to mass slaughter in Rwanda, Burundi, and other cases, but in recent years their willingness to help prevent mass atrocities has increased. And it's true that during the Arab Spring, while Gaddafi's crackdown was being met by UNSC-authorized force, a firm crackdown in Bahrain—where vital US energy and regional security interests were at stake—was met with mild cautionary statements and continued US arms sales to the regime. There are critical differences of scale, though: Bahrain's crackdown, using Saudi forces, killed hundreds; in Libya, there were fears for tens of thousands being killed; and in Syria, at the time of writing, more than eighty thousand have been killed.

The UNSC has also invoked and acted on the responsibility to protect outside the Maghreb. Much ignored between the drama of Libya and the tragedy of Syria was a decision by the UNSC to invoke the R2P concept in authorizing French military action in Côte d'Ivoire. The action had a twofold purpose: to uphold the results of democratic elections undertaken under UN auspices; and to prevent an erosion of stability and a return to bloody civil war. Mere weeks after the divides in the UNSC over the second vote in Libya, the vote for the Côte d'Ivoire operation was unanimous, with China, Russia, India, and Brazil voting with the Western powers and the rest of the Security Council to authorize the actions.

(The crises in Libya and, more recently, in Mali—a long, slow-burn conflict that deteriorated in 2010 and again after the operation in Libya—have spurred a return to the debate about the comparative merits and relative legitimacy of the United Nations and regional organizations in crisis management. Over the intervention in Libya, regional organizations such as the Arab League have served as important "gatekeepers" by playing a role in shaping the political discourse around crisis situations in the Security Council.[27] The Arab League has also been critical of the council's limited response to Syria, although this has not spurred greater action. The African Union focused on bringing about a diplomatic solution in Côte d'Ivoire, pushing against the Security Council, and sought a mediation role in Libya, to the frustration of members of the NATO-led intervention. Regional organizations and regional powers often possess deeper political relationships for mediation in their neighborhood than UN counterparts, giving them added value in this regard. But in the final analysis, they have limited operational capabilities to bring to bear in the field, particularly in peace operations.)

CONCLUDING THOUGHTS: STRENGTHS AND WEAKNESSES OF THE SECURITY COUNCIL

Just as in previous eras, the issues facing the UN Security Council both divide and unify the major powers. Normative divisions over the responsibility to protect are present but less pervasive than some have assumed, as the unified decision to mount an R2P operation in Côte d'Ivoire showed. Deeper geopolitical concerns divide the council over the countries at the core of the Arab Spring, as well as the wider cast of powers important to that region. And—just as in previous eras—it's precisely this fact of multiple powers being central to the

United Nations' work that is simultaneously the source of its weakness and its most important strength.

These are not the only strengths and weaknesses of the United Nations; there are others, and they factor in at the margins.

As a conflict-management mechanism, the Security Council has a unique advantage in the UN Secretariat, which can magnify and channel the disparate capacities of individual member states. As one of the six "principal organs" of the United Nations established by Article 7 in the UN Charter, the UN Secretariat plays the role of an international civil service for the Security Council and other parts of the UN system; its influence is channeled through the secretary-general, though its powers are considerably more far-reaching. While much maligned, the Secretariat adds considerable value. In its personnel, the secretary-general's staff, it has a core reserve of talent that has considerable field experience and practical experience in political negotiations. While the UN system can, at times, function to constrain the role that these staff members play, the Secretariat has considerable institutional and practical knowledge to leverage in the service of the UN system's activities.

As a tool for aggregating capabilities—a force multiplier—the Security Council is unique. Consider its role in peacekeeping: the UN Secretariat manages more than 100,000 UNSC-mandated troops in fifteen different operational locations on four continents. It has more troops under active service than any other actor apart from the US government.[28] Most of the governments participating in UN crisis management operations have no capacity to transport their troops beyond their region, and regional organizations do not provide that capacity—only the United Nations allows Indian troops to operate in the DR Congo or Nepali troops to contribute to stability in Liberia.

Further magnifying these capabilities, the United Nations is a unique actor in the field of humanitarian operations, and its role has only grown in an era in which crises often have both a military and a humanitarian dimension. The post–Cold War era has seen the proliferation of a range of institutions and mechanisms to promote and carry out humanitarian agendas. Considerable adaptation has taken place in the United Nations in a short period of time, with the UN Department for Peacekeeping Operations and the Office for the Coordination of Humanitarian Affairs established little more than twenty years ago. Previously, humanitarian operations were spearheaded by the UN High Commissioner for Refugees (UNHCR) and the International Committee of the Red Cross (ICRC), functioning with considerably less funding, fewer staff, and a smaller caseload as compared to the current humanitarian architecture.

The United Nations' operational and coordination capabilities are unmatched by any other actor; it alone has humanitarian response capabilities that it can mobilize on a massive scale. Reaching back to 1991, when the General Assembly passed Resolution 46/182, the basis of the United Nations' role in humanitarian affairs, the UN system has taken leadership of coordinating international responses to humanitarian disasters and emergencies. Today, there are a number of different agencies and elements of the United Nations' humanitarian architecture, and humanitarian teams in some twenty countries reached 62 million people in 2012, at an annual cost of nearly US$9 billion. The numerous agencies involved in humanitarian operations—including OCHA (Office for the Coordination of Humanitarian Affairs), UNHCR, UNICEF (United Nations Children's Fund), and WFP (World Food Program)—have made coordination between actors a challenge, a problem that mechanisms like the Inter-Agency Standing Committee (IASC) have had only limited success addressing.[29]

On the other side of the ledger, the Security Council's core weaknesses hamper its operational effectiveness across the crisis management spectrum. The United Nations plays a critical role in the peacebuilding field, but it needs to deepen its work with other relevant actors. While the Security Council has, in recent years, mandated more peacekeeping operations that have elements of the peacebuilding agenda, the council still lacks robust relationships with international financial institutions (IFIs) like the World Bank and regional development banks, which are necessary to coordinate critical political-financial linkages in the postconflict recovery process.[30] The Peacebuilding Commission is charged with fostering coherence in the peacebuilding architecture, but its efforts have yielded only limited successes and goals for establishing complementary programming between the UN system and IFIs. The challenges of coordination with IFIs are all the more important to address in the context of the debate around the post-2015 development agenda, where conflict issues are likely to loom larger than they did in the Millennium Development Goals—because somewhere north of 50 percent of the world's poor will soon live in conflict-affected, fragile states.

But here, the United Nations has recently caught a break. Theories of international relations pay scant attention to the personalities of secretaries-general, but they do matter.[31] One of Ban Ki-moon's institutional legacies may be fixing the UN-World Bank relationship. Whether it is because of a shared Korean heritage (as some senior UN officials have suggested) or for other reasons, the fact is that, as president of the World Bank, Kim has been far more willing than his predecessors to join forces with the UN secretary-general, even to the point of traveling together with him (notably, to the

Great Lakes in 2012) and pledging World Bank support for agreements brokered by the United Nations.[32] At the time of drafting (March 2014), this has not yet translated into deeper collaboration between the two institutions; but it does mark a shift in relations between these two top multilateral officials.

In the final analysis, though, relations between the powers is what matters. It's all too easy to see this as a fundamental weakness of the United Nations, especially amid the unfolding tragedy of Syria. The simple fact of the matter is that the United Nations is the only body dealing with matters of peace and security in which all the major powers reside. Regional organizations and informal and ad hoc mechanisms, by their very nature, exclude some major powers. While this can be efficient in terms of building the political capacity to mount an operation in a crisis situation, it neglects important dimensions of crisis management. The Security Council, unique among other mechanisms, functions to minimize diplomatic tensions between the great powers. And it alone has the aggregate capabilities to undertake large-scale crisis response activities, pooling the capacities of great powers, middle powers, and neighbors alike.[33]

When the great powers have aligned interests, as on counterterrorism or avoiding the security repercussions of failed states, cooperation in the Security Council can be robust, and council members are willing to adapt the international architecture to tackle new challenges. Very recently, this has taken on a new form of blending counterterrorism and peacekeeping operations, using established UNSC tools in new and innovative ways. But the Security Council's most important role remains the prevention of conflict between the great powers. In crises that divide the great-power interests, the council functions as a forum to share information, air grievances, and ratchet down tensions, to keep the major powers from clashing indirectly or directly. It is this model of action—or rather, a type of inaction—that is the council's most critical function.

With the increased role of the emerging powers, the issue of Security Council membership reform raises questions anew about the council's future effectiveness. Rising powers and established ones alike voice dissatisfaction about their limited role in the council's ultimate decision-making processes. They longer this dissatisfaction persists, the greater the frustration at the increasing divide between the distribution of power among states and the distribution of power in the Security Council. Controversies around its membership have tarnished perceptions of its legitimacy. This will eventually need to be addressed through UNSC expansion. In the meantime, the council continues to function as the main actor on international crisis management, not in spite of the constraints placed on it by the major powers, but because it is designed to be responsive to major-power interests.

In some situations, this condition dramatically limits the role that the Security Council can play in crisis management. It has always been thus, and it presents risks. If Russia and China adopt a posture of blocking UNSC action on a consistent basis, as they have over Syria, this has the potential to shift attitudes around first-order crises. Under such a scenario, we could witness a shift back to the politics of the late 1990s, when NATO and ad hoc groupings acted outside the UNSC structure, or worse, to the 1980s, when US-Soviet tensions blocked creative engagement in many important civil conflicts.

The Russia-EU crisis over Ukraine, which has dragged in the United States (at least economically and politically, if not yet militarily), makes this scenario more likely. The crisis caused a serious deterioration in US-Russia relations, already deteriorating after

Putin's return to power and the US decision not to attend the Sochi Olympics at a high level. At the time of writing, the situation continued to be highly unstable, as Ukraine signed an association agreement with the European Union, and Russia continued to engage in asymmetric destabilization efforts in eastern Ukraine. Should US-Russia relations enter a deep freeze, the implications for UNSC action could be substantial.

At the time of writing, though, a different pattern appears to be holding—one consistent with the arguments in this chapter. British and other diplomats at the Security Council report the situation to be one of deep tensions over Ukraine and Syria, and sustained, relatively easy cooperation over second-tier crises from Mali to the Democratic Republic of Congo to Somalia. A pattern of insulation appears to be taking hold—that is, diplomats and state leaders on both sides are insulating their joint efforts on crises where they have shared or overlapping interests from tensions over crises where their interests diverge or clash.

Once again, where great power politics diverge, the best the Security Council can do is to serve as a firebreak for those tensions. But where other crises continue to align the interests of the great powers, the Security Council can take more robust, more ambitious action.

NOTES

1. George W. Bush, speech to the UN General Assembly, New York, NY, September 12, 2002.

2. As of December 2008, that included about 80,000 military personnel, just over 11,000 police, and over 18,000 UN civilian staff, not to mention further tens of thousands of UN staff deployed in humanitarian operations by the UN Secretariat. "United Nations Peacekeeping Operations" (background note, United Nations Peacekeeping, December 31, 2008), www.un.org/en/peacekeeping/archive/2008/pkfactsheet2008.zip. See also CIC

Annual Report on Global Peace Operations, 207-2012; and Glyn Taylor et al., "The State of the Humanitarian System, 2012 Edition" (report, ALNAP, London, July 2012), alnap-sohs-2012-lo-res.pdf.

3. The phrase is from the volume editors, who posed to the author the question of whether the UNSC would remain the central motherboard in international crisis management in the period to come.

4. At the time of writing, the United States and the UN Secretariat are developing contingencies for a Security Council–authorized multinational force and UN operation to help restore stability if and when the current phase of civil war and authoritarian repression in Syria breaks.

5. Since the end of the Cold War, the Security Council has established more than fifty peacekeeping operations and political missions, and most of these require consent of the council to be renewed on a six-month or annual basis. Most of these renewals are routine—which is part of the point. Sometimes renewals become the moment for renegotiation of the terms or structure of a mission.

6. Human Security Report Project, *Human Security Report 2012* (Vancouver: Human Security Press, 2012), 161.

7. Peter Wallensteen and Patrik Johannson, "Security Council Decisions in Perspective," in *The UN Security Council: From the Cold War to the 21st Century*, ed. David M. Malone (Boulder, CO: Lynne Rienner, 2004), 17–33.

8. Virginia Page Fortna, *Does Peacekeeping Work? Shaping Belligerents' Choices after Civil War* (Princeton, NJ: Princeton University Press, 2008); and Michael J. Gilligan and Ernest J. Sergenti, "Do UN Interventions Cause Peace? Using Matching to Improve Causal Inference," *Quarterly Journal of Political Science* 3, no. 2 (2008): 89–122.

9. For a classic of the genre, see Naazneen Barma, Ely Ratner, and Steven Weber, "The Mythical Liberal Order," *National Interest*, no. 124 (March/April 2013), which highlights divisions in the UNSC, inflates the importance of the UNSC to the overall international order, and conveniently neglects myriad instances of UNSC cooperation, including on R2P operations in both Libya and Côte d'Ivoire.

10. Bruce D. Jones, "The Security Council and the Arab-Israeli Wars," in *The United Nations Security Council and War*, ed. Vaughan Lowe, et al. (Oxford: Oxford University Press, 2008), 298–323.

11. Bruce Jones and Andrew Hart, "Keeping Middle East Peace?" *International Peacekeeping* 15, no. 1 (2008): 102–17.

12. Brian Urquhart, *A Life in Peace and War* (New York: Harper and Row, 1987).

13. Kati Marton, *A Death in Jerusalem* (New York: Pantheon, 1994).

14. Data from the Center on International Co-operation (New York University), *Annual Review of Global Peace Operations 2012* (Boulder, CO: Lynne Rienner, 2012).

15. Graphics using data from Bruce Jones et al., "Building on Brahimi: Peacekeeping in an Era of Strategic Uncertainty," NYU Center on International Cooperation, April 2009.

16. *Annual Review of Global Peace Operations* (see note 14).

17. Camino Kavanagh and Bruce Jones, "Shaky Foundations: An Assessment of the UN's Rule of Law Support Agenda," NYU Center on International Cooperation, November 2011.

18. Bruce Jones and Molly Elgin-Cossart, "Development in the Shadow of Violence: A Knowledge Agenda for Policy," NYU Center on International Cooperation, September 2011.

19. Report of the Secretary-General, "Civilian Capacity in the Aftermath of Conflict," A/67/312–S /2012/645, August 15, 2012.

20. World Bank, *World Development Report 2011: Conflict, Security and Development* (Washington, DC: World Bank, 2011).

21. Eric Rosand and Sebastian von Einsiedel, "9/11, the War on Terror, and the Evolution of Multilateral Institutions," in *Cooperating for Peace and Security: Evolving Institutions and Arrangements in a Context of Changing U.S. Security Policy*, ed. Bruce D. Jones, Shepard Forman, and Richard Gowan (Cambridge: Cambridge University Press, 2010), 143–65.

22. Bruce Jones, "Making Multilateralism Work: How the G-20 Can Help the United Nations," Stanley Foundation, policy analysis brief, April 2010.

23. Michael Barnett and Martha Finnemore, "Political Approaches," in *The Oxford Handbook on the United Nations*, ed. Thomas G. Weiss and Sam Daws (Oxford: Oxford University Press, 2007), 41–57.

24. Bruce Jones, Carlos Pascual, and Stephen John Stedman, *Power and Responsibility: Building International Order in an Era of Transnational Threats* (Washington, DC: Brookings Institution Press, 2009), 206–33.

25. Eric Rosand, "Security Council Resolution 1373, the Counter-Terrorism Committee, and the Fight against Terrorism," *American Journal of International Law* 97, no. 2 (2003): 333–41.

26. President George H. W. Bush, "Address to the Nation Announcing Allied Military Action in the Persian Gulf," January 16, 1991.

27. Alex J. Bellamy and Paul D. Williams, "The New Politics of Protection? Côte d'Ivoire, Libya and the Responsibility to Protect," *International Affairs* 87, no. 4 (2011): 825–50.

28. Jones et al., "Building on Brahimi."

29. Jones, "Making Multilateralism Work."

30. "Taking Stock, Looking Forward: A Strategic Review of the Peacebuilding Commission" (International Peace Institute and NYU Center on International Cooperation, April 2008).

31. Ian Johnstone, "The Secretary-General as Norm Entrepreneur," in *Secretary or General?* ed. Simon Chesterman (New York: Cambridge University Press, 2007), 123–38.

32. World Bank, "Jim Yong Kim, Ban Ki-moon Make Historic Joint Visit to Africa's Great Lakes Region," (video), http://www.worldbank.org/en /news/video/2013/05/24/world-bank-group-presi dent-jim-yong-kim-and-un-secretary-general-make -historic-joint-visit-to-africa-great-lakes-region.

33. Teresa Whitfield, "Groups of Friends," in *The UN Security Council*, ed. David Malone (Boulder, CO: Lynne Rienner, 2004), 311.

19

REGIONAL ARRANGEMENTS AND THE USE OF MILITARY FORCE

Paul D. Williams

It is difficult—and perhaps unwise—to generalize about the world's regional organizations. The United Nations Charter fails to define what it calls "regional arrangements," and indeed the world's regional institutions come in many different sizes, serve a wide variety of purposes, rarely offer transparency in their decision-making processes, and often contain overlapping memberships. Thus, there is no uncontested "gold standard" against which a regional organization should be measured, although some regional arrangements have explicitly sought to mimic aspects of the European Union's common foreign and security policy. Nevertheless, in some parts of the world, regional arrangements are playing major roles in international peace and security issues and conflict-management initiatives.

Regional arrangements vary in their approaches to conflict management across at least six dimensions: they see different types of conflicts as security challenges; they accord different levels of significance to conflict-management initiatives; they differ

in the relative emphasis they give to particular parts of the conflict-management enterprise (e.g., prevention, mitigation, reconciliation, or postwar peace building); they utilize different types of institutional frameworks for dealing with conflict issues; they vary in terms of the instruments and techniques they prefer to use as part of their conflict-management repertoire; and the geographic scope of their activities is highly uneven, with most staying within their own region but a few operating "out of area."[1]

The scholarly literature has offered four sets of explanations for this regional variation but has not come to a consensus on the relationship between them. The first set of explanations focuses on the exercise of political power, especially the roles played by internal and external hegemons.[2] The second cluster emphasizes domestic factors, particularly the ways in which the political character of regimes can affect regional choices, and domestic coalitions can shape regional preferences.[3] A third set of explanations points to ideational factors, particularly the ways in which regional approaches to conflict management are shaped by shared security cultures that predispose their members toward certain actions and policies.[4] The fourth set revolves around collective capacity issues, since regional organizations can conduct conflict-management initiatives only if they have relevant resources and capabilities.[5] Hence, organizations populated by richer states with more developed power-projection capabilities are more likely to be proactive and engaged in managing conflicts than poorer, less well-equipped states. Future regional approaches to conflict management are likely to be heavily influenced by the outcome of debates in three areas: the perceived relationship between democracy or good governance and regional security; the "responsibility to protect" agenda and civilian protection issues; and the extent to which regional arrangements engaged with actors within civil society or remained statist in their modes of operation.

This chapter focuses on how regional arrangements have approached one crucial part of the conflict-management equation, namely the threat and use of military force. It does so by first analyzing why some regional arrangements choose not to use military force collectively, and then summarizing the justifications and postures that regional arrangements have adopted with regard to the use of force in the post–Cold War era. It then examines the extent to which the activities of regional arrangements challenge or consolidate the existing international order and the traditional rules governing the use of force under the UN Charter system.

Along the way, the chapter advances the following arguments. First, there is no single or simple process of regionalization occurring across the globe. Rather, the patterns of regional engagement in conflict-management activity are highly uneven and frequently involve interregional and UN-regional collaboration. Second, regional arrangements vary in their approach to

military force, but issues related to self-defense and civilian protection appear to be the crucial factors in shaping regional positions in this area. Third, the regional arrangements that have added military force to their repertoire (practically or hypothetically) have not fundamentally challenged the rules on the use of force embedded within the existing UN Charter system. However, some regional arrangements have played a "gatekeeping" role which has influenced how the UN Security Council responds to particular crises. This is particularly evident in relation to questions of governance, especially the perceived connections between liberal forms of governance and regional order/security and humanitarian issues, notably how to implement the "responsibility to protect" principle and respond to civilian protection challenges. In both these areas, the rules on the use of military force are evolving, and some regional arrangements are playing significant roles in that process. Finally, the recent past suggests that the central policy debate going forward will revolve around how to develop optimal "partnerships"—between regional arrangements, between regional arrangements and the United Nations, and between regional arrangements and a variety of other actors (most notably external donors and relevant private contractors).

THE USE OF MILITARY FORCE: CHOICES, JUSTIFICATIONS, AND POSTURES

Among the emerging regional frameworks for the use of force, the principal distinction lies between those that have either deployed or envisage military force as part of their conflict-management repertoire, and those that have ruled it out for reasons related to efficacy, appropriateness, and/or capacity. A small but significant subset of regional arrangements have now either used military force collectively or devised rules to govern their organization's collective use of military force in certain hypothetical scenarios. The principal arrangements in this regard comprise states from Europe, North America, and Africa, specifically the North Atlantic Treaty Organization (NATO),[6] the European Union, the Economic Community of West African States (ECOWAS), the Southern African Development Community (SADC), the African Union, and the Commonwealth of Independent States (CIS). Tables 1–3 list thirty-six military operations conducted or authorized by regional arrangements in the post–Cold War era, 1990–2013.

Table 1. UN-authorized military operations conducted by regional arrangements, 1990–2013

Mission	Location	Duration	Deployed Size
IFOR (NATO)	Bosnia & Herzegovina	1995–96	60,000
SFOR (NATO)	Bosnia & Herzegovina	1996–2005	36,179
KFOR (NATO)	Kosovo	1999–present	45,000
AFOR (NATO)	Albania	1999	5,500
ISAF (NATO 2003–present)	Afghanistan	2001–present	130,000
ECOMICI (ECOWAS)	Ivory Coast	2002–04	1,500
ECOMIL (ECOWAS)	Liberia	2003	3,600
Op. Artemis / IEMF (EU+)	DR Congo	2003	2,205
EUFOR Op. Althea	Bosnia & Herzegovina	2004–present	6,500
EUFOR RD	DR Congo	2006	2,275
AMISOM (AU)	Somalia	2007–present	22,126
EUFOR-Chad	Chad	2008–09	3,700
Op. Unified Protector (NATO+)	Libya	2011	Unclear
AFISMA (AU- and ECOWAS-authorized)	Mali	2012–13	9,600
MISCA (AU)	Central African Republic	2013–present	5,000

Table 2. UN-recognized military operations conducted by regional arrangements, 1990–2013

Mission	Location	Duration	Deployed Size
ECOMOG 1 (ECOWAS)	Liberia	1990–99	12,040
CPKF (CIS)	Tajikistan	1993–2000	32,000
CPKF / CPFOR (CIS)	Georgia (Abkhazia)	1994–present	2,500
ECOMOG 2 (ECOWAS)	Sierra Leone	1997–2000	14,000
ECOMOG 3 (ECOWAS)	Guinea-Bissau	1998–99	750
Op. Sovereign Legitimacy (SADC-authorized)	DR Congo	1998–2001	15,500
Op. Essential Harvest, Amber Fox, Allied Harmony (NATO)	Macedonia, FYR	2001–03	4,400
FOMUC (ECCAS)	Central African Republic	2002–08	380
Op. Concordia (EU)	Macedonia, FYR	2003	400
AMIB (AU)	Burundi	2003–04	3,250
AMIS (AU)	Sudan	2004–07	7,700
RCI-LRA (AU-authorized)	Central Africa	2011–present	5,000
MISSANG-GB (CPLP-authorized)	Guinea-Bissau	2011–12	200
ECOMIB (ECOWAS)	Guinea-Bissau	2012–present	629

Table 3. Non-UN military operations conducted by regional arrangements, 1990–2013

Mission	Location	Duration	Deployed Size
South Ossetia Joint Peacekeeping Force (CIS)	Georgia / South Ossetia	1992–present	1,500
Op. Boleas (SADC-authorized)	Lesotho	1998–99	3,850
Op. Allied Force (NATO)	Kosovo/Serbia	1999	Unclear
CEN-SAD Peacekeeping Force in CAR	Central African Republic (CAR)	2002	300
AMISEC (AU)	Comoros	2006	1,260
Op. Democracy in the Comoros (AU)	Comoros	2008	450
MICOPAX (ECCAS)	CAR	2008–13	730

Other regional arrangements, however, have not used collective military force in the post–Cold War era because they consider it undesirable, ineffective, or practically impossible. Such arrangements include the Association of Southeast Asian Nations (ASEAN), the Organization of American States (OAS), the Arab Maghreb Union (AMU), the Organization of Islamic Cooperation (OIC), the Intergovernmental Authority on Development (IGAD), the Organization for Security and Cooperation in Europe (OSCE), and the South Asian Association for Regional Cooperation (SAARC). There are several explanations for such a posture. First, an organization might simply lack the relevant collective military capabilities; hence, military instruments do not form part of its conflict-management toolkit. Alternatively, some arrangements might rule out the use of military force because they are skeptical about its utility as a tool of conflict management compared to more peaceful approaches such as mediation, arbitration, and other peacemaking initiatives.[7] A third factor might be the lack of consensus within a regional arrangement about the political purposes for which force might be deployed. Regions that lack deep consensus over political values are unlikely to develop regional arrangements that will regularly resort to the collective use of military force. The Middle East and South Asia—the two regions thought most likely to trigger major, broader instability—are cases in point.

The following analysis, therefore, pertains only to a subset of the world's regional arrangements, those that see a role for the collective use of military force as part of their conflict-management repertoire. Specifically, it addresses two issues: How have regional organizations justified their actual or potential use of military force in the post–Cold War era? And what practical postures have these organizations adopted to carry out such action?

Regional Justifications

Since 1990, regional arrangements have justified the collective use of military force with reference to self-defense, humanitarian military intervention, and civilian protection issues.

The first justifications relate to the inherent right to self-defense, which is acknowledged and reiterated in Article 51 of the UN Charter. Although it seems that no regional arrangement has actually used collective military force as a direct response to an attack upon its members, several organizations specify their commitment to use force in such a scenario. Perhaps the closest case occurred in the aftermath of the 9/11 terrorist attacks on the United States when NATO offered to deploy its forces under Article 5 of the Washington Treaty as part of the subsequent invasion of Afghanistan. As it turned out, the George W. Bush administration turned down NATO's offer on the basis that while NATO's support was useful politically, the United States preferred to operate militarily with a smaller, ad hoc coalition of partners.

A related variant of this approach has been reference to collective self-defense, that is, where regional arrangements have deployed troops to support a government under attack from insurgents.[8] There are numerous examples of this type of activity. In the 1990s, the ECOWAS operation in Liberia (1990) started as an attempt to defend Samuel Doe's regime from Charles Taylor's rebellion, while the ECOWAS mission in Sierra Leone from 1997 supported the embattled regime of President Ahmed Tejan Kabbah.[9] Two further examples are the operations conducted by factions within the SADC during 1998: Operation Boleas, conducted by South Africa and Botswana in Lesotho; and Operation Sovereign Legitimacy, carried out by Zimbabwe, Angola, and Namibia in the Democratic Republic of the Congo (DRC).[10] In the twenty-first century, examples include the African Union's Operation Democracy in the Comoros, conducted in 2008 by Tanzanian and Sudanese troops (with logistical support from Libya and France) in support of the de jure authorities, and the African-led International Support Mission to Mali (AFISMA) deployed to support the incumbent regime against a variety of insurgent groups in the north of the country. In some instances, these missions have turned into lengthy counterinsurgency operations, as in the ongoing efforts of NATO's International Security Assistance Force in Afghanistan (2003–present) and the AU Mission in Somalia, AMISOM (2007–present). Sometimes, these types of operations have seen regional arrangements authorize the deployment of missions to reform the security forces of the target state. Examples include the European Union's ongoing training missions in Somalia and Mali, or the security-sector-reform missions deployed to Guinea-Bissau by both the European Union and Angola (the latter in 2011 with the endorsement of the Community of Portuguese Language Countries, the CPLP).

Another related scenario is the explicit focus on using collective military force to counter terrorism within an organization's member-states. This is the rationale behind the Collective Security Treaty Organization's (CSTO) Rapid Deployment Forces of the Central Asian Region, as well as the coordination training being conducted by the armed forces of the Shanghai Cooperation Organization (SCO).[11]

A third justification for military force is collective enforcement operations—more colloquially, "invasions"—to enforce the will of the organization upon the target. In the post–Cold War era, regional enforcement operations have been justified with reference to not only collective self-defense (described above) but also the doctrine of "humanitarian military intervention" (i.e., the use of military force by external actors without host state consent, aimed at preventing or ending genocide and/or mass atrocities) and the "responsibility to protect" (R2P) principle.[12] In all, five regional organizations have established provisions for humanitarian intervention in their respective charters: NATO, the European Union, the Economic Community of West African States (ECOWAS), the African Union, and the Economic Community of Central African States (ECCAS).[13] However, the only practical example of such a humanitarian intervention authorized and conducted by a regional arrangement is NATO's Operation Allied Force in Kosovo/Serbia in 1999. In March 2011, however, the League of Arab States (LAS), the Gulf Cooperation Council (GCC), and the Organization of Islamic Cooperation (OIC) all called on the UN Security Council to impose a no-fly zone and conduct operations to protect civilians in Libya. These decisions were crucial in facilitating the passage of UN Security Council resolution 1973, the council's first-ever humanitarian military intervention against a functioning state government.[14] Of course, it is important to note that the stated (humanitarian) justification behind such calls for military intervention may not always be the principal driving force behind the decision. NATO's intervention in Kosovo/Serbia, for example, was also widely seen as being related to the credibility of the alliance and its desire to punish Serbian President Slobodan Milosevic for his repeated intransigence, and anti-Gaddafi sentiments were commonly thought to be at the heart of the push by the GCC and LAS for a military response to Libya's crisis in 2011.[15] These and other examples attest to the conclusion that when it comes to so-called "humanitarian military intervention," the motives behind the decisions of states and international organizations are always mixed.[16]

A third set of cases in which regional arrangements have used military force involves attempts to implement various civilian protection mandates. These types of operations have blurred the lines between the traditional concepts of peacekeeping and peace enforcement. While they operate with the consent of the host state at the strategic level—and consequently do not count as humanitarian military interventions as defined above—at the operational and tactical levels they may well engage in offensive military activities, usually under the authority of Chapter VII of the UN Charter. Recent examples of civilian protection operations include the European Union's Operation Artemis in the DRC (2003) and its mission

in Chad/Central African Republic (2008–09); the AU Mission in Sudan, AMIS (2004–07); and the ECCAS Mission for the Consolidation of Peace in the Central African Republic (MICOPAX), deployed since 2008.[17] Until mid-2013, when it adopted a new civilian protection strategy, the AU Mission in Somalia (AMISOM) had been in the odd position of being tasked with protecting certain very important civilians (i.e., certain members of Somalia's Transitional Federal Government) but not Somali civilians more generally.[18]

Regional Postures

Important distinctions have also been evident in the practical postures that regional organizations have assumed with regard to military force. First, there have been cases where a regional arrangement has become the delegated instrument of the UN Security Council to undertake some kind of enforcement action.[19] These include the NATO-UN dual key relationship during the Bosnian war (1992–95); and the European Union's Operation Artemis (2003) and EUFOR RD Congo mission (2006), the former deployed to protect civilians in the Congolese town of Bunia, and the latter to ensure the security of the Congolese presidential elections. More recently, in March 2011, a coalition consisting of NATO and several supporting states was authorized by the UN Security Council to use military force to protect civilians in Libya, while in October 2012, UN Security Council resolution 2071 authorized a variety of regional arrangements (including ECOWAS, the African Union, and the European Union) to deploy troops as part of an international military force "in order to restore the authority of the State of Mali over its entire national territory, to uphold the unity and territorial integrity of Mali and to reduce the threat posed by AQIM [Al Qaeda in the Islamic Maghreb] and affiliated groups" (paragraph 9). This ultimately resulted in the deployment of the African-led International Support Mission to Mali (AFISMA) in the first few months of 2013.

A second set of cases has occurred in which a regional arrangement has itself authorized and conducted a military operation without prior authorization from the UN Security Council. Examples include NATO's Operation Allied Force in Kosovo/Serbia (1999), the ECOWAS Monitoring Group operation in Liberia (1990–96), and the SADC missions in Lesotho and the DRC in 1998. While the ECOWAS and SADC operations in Liberia, Lesotho, and the DRC were conducted under the legal cover of collective self-defense, NATO's bombing campaign in Kosovo/Serbia was an illegal use of military force, albeit one carried out in the name of civilian protection.[20]

A third posture has seen regional organizations call on other actors to undertake enforcement measures. Examples of this type of action include the calls made by the LAS, GCC, and OIC in early 2011 for the United Nations to impose a no-fly zone and civilian protection measures in Libya, primarily because they did not have the requisite military capabilities to conduct such operations themselves. Two other examples involve the African Union. First, in November 2011, the African Union authorized the Regional Cooperation Initiative for the Elimination of the Lord's Resistance Army (RCI-LRA).[21] Second, in late 2012, the African Union and SADC called for the deployment of a neutral international force in the DRC in response to the rise of the M23 rebellion in the east of the country.[22] This resulted in the UN Security Council authorizing, in late March 2013, a new "intervention brigade" to operate under the auspices of the UN peacekeeping force already on the ground. According to UN Security Council resolution 2098 (March 28, 2013), the brigade would be based around three infantry battalions from SADC member-states and be authorized to protect civilians, neutralize armed groups, and monitor the implementation of the arms embargo. By November 2013, the brigade had played a major role in the capitulation of the M23 rebels.

A fourth posture involves regional arrangements in Africa working in partnership with the United Nations and other organizations—notably the Group of Eight (G8), the European Union, and NATO—to build their capacity to project military power in order to conduct peace operations.[23] The UN's ten-year capacity-building program for the African Union, authorized in 2006, is unique in this regard.[24] This program has facilitated collaborative efforts between the United Nations and African Union in relation to several military operations in the Sudan, the Comoros, Somalia, CAR, and Mali.[25] This partnership posture is exemplified by the AU Mission in Somalia (AMISOM), where the United Nations, the African Union, the European Union, and a range of bilateral donors have worked together to deliver a large-scale peace enforcement operation. In this case, the mission was initially created by the African Union (in 2007) after an earlier attempt by IGAD to establish a peace operation in Somalia had failed; it was subsequently endorsed by the UN Security Council, and paid for by the troop-contributing countries (Uganda and Burundi) and their bilateral supporters, principally the United States, the United Kingdom, and France. Later, in 2009, the United Nations created an unprecedented logistical support package for the operation (the UN Support Office for AMISOM, UNSOA), which was paid for using UN-assessed contributions and the AMISOM Trust Fund. The same year, another regional arrangement, the European Union, agreed to use its African Peace Facility to pay the allowances of the AU troops, which by 2012 numbered approximately seventeen thousand and rose to over twenty-two thousand by the end of 2013.[26]

Finally, some regional organizations have devised rules governing the use of military force but have yet to test those rules in a practical case. These include the African Union and its concept of humanitarian intervention as set out in Article 4(h) of the African Union's Constitutive Act, and the ECCAS Protocol Relating to the Establishment of a Mutual Security Protocol in Central Africa (2000).[27]

◆ ◆ ◆

The preceding analysis highlights the complex patterns of regional activity with respect to military force. Not only do the active participants in these activities represent only a small subset of the world's regional arrangements but they are clearly engaged in complex patterns of interregional and global-regional collaboration. It is therefore unhelpful to conceptualize these patterns as simply a process of "regionalization" wherein the regions are rising and the global center collapsing. Second, the regional arrangements that are engaged in military operations have framed the majority of their activities in terms of either self-defense or civilian protection.

EXISTING RULES ON THE USE OF FORCE: REGIONAL ARRANGEMENTS AS CHALLENGERS, SUPPORTERS, OR GATEKEEPERS?

To what extent do these emerging regional justifications and postures challenge or consolidate the existing international rules governing the use of force? Overall, they do not amount to a fundamental challenge to the existing international order. Instead, the emerging rules and practices of regional arrangements point to widespread consensus that the core principles on the use of mili-

tary force embedded within the UN Charter system remain legitimate, although there is clearly scope for their continued evolution in response to changing circumstances and interpretations of what counts as a threat to international peace and security. The major issue in that regard is the extent to which military force is justified as an instrument of civilian protection.

Why is this? First, the most active regional arrangements with regard to the use of force in the post–Cold War era are NATO and the European Union, and neither is interested in undermining the current world order. Moreover, where NATO has pushed beyond the current international legal boundaries (namely in Kosovo/Serbia), it has done so in the name of advancing liberal norms. To the extent that NATO forces facilitated the overthrow of Gaddafi's regime in Libya in 2011, this was also done in the name of advancing liberal governance in Libya. Of course, these dynamics possess a significant material dimension inasmuch as global-force-projection capabilities remain heavily concentrated among the United States and its core allies.[28] It is therefore unsurprising that the use of military force by such actors generally supports rather than challenges the existing international order and pushes it in directions aligned with their strategic interests. The preponderance of relevant capabilities in Western states also helps account for two further trends. The first is that NATO and the European Union are the only regional organizations to deploy military forces outside their own neighborhoods.[29] The second is that the United States has been at the helm of many of the most controversial uses of military force in the post–Cold War period. Arguably the most controversial of these US-led missions have been the establishment of the no-fly zones in Iraq in the aftermath of Operation Desert Storm, aided by France and the United Kingdom (1991); NATO's Operation Allied

Force in Kosovo/Serbia (1999); and the invasion of Iraq (2003). All of these operations took place without explicit authorization in a UN Security Council resolution.

A second observation is that with the odd exception, the rules and practices developed by regional arrangements relating to the use of force have broadly conformed to the core principles governing this issue set out in the UN Charter system. As yet, there has been only one case—NATO's Operation Allied Force in Kosovo/Serbia (1999)—where a regional arrangement fundamentally challenged the UN Charter rules on the use of military force by invading Serbia without explicit authorization from the Security Council. Every other instance of military force conducted by a regional organization in the post–Cold War era conforms to the basic tenets of the UN system which state that the use of military force should be limited to cases of self-defense (including collective self-defense) or where it is explicitly authorized by the UN Security Council. That said, there is a related but distinct debate over the extent to which NATO and other foreign forces overstepped the boundaries of the civilian protection mandate granted by UN Security Council resolution 1973 concerning the crisis in Libya.

Outside the Western world, it is in Africa where states and organizations have been most actively engaged in debates about developing international rules on the collective use of force. Although Africa's new peace and security architecture remains a work in progress, the African Union's practices to date also suggest that it is unlikely to challenge the core norms of the existing international/UN Charter order.[30] Its relevant conventions emphasize the need to respect the territorial integrity of states, international law, and state sovereignty. Moreover, the two principal exceptions where the African Union is trying to make sovereignty even more conditional are in line with es-tablished liberal norms of human rights and "good governance." The first is its ongoing efforts to prevent unconstitutional changes of government on the continent. Here, the various elements of the African Governance Agenda are pushing AU members toward—not away from—liberal governance.[31] The second exception is Article 4(h) of the AU Constitutive Act which permits the union to undertake a humanitarian military intervention in one of its member-states in "grave circumstances," namely, genocide, crimes against humanity, and war crimes. This does appear to be a direct challenge to the UN Security Council's authority and Article 53 of the UN Charter. In practice, however, this mechanism has not been invoked by the African Union to sanction a military intervention, and its more recent statements appear to indicate that such an intervention would not take place without prior authorization by the UN Security Council.[32]

A third, and related, point is that some regional organizations have also been at the forefront of the UN Security Council's evolving practice of broadening the definition of what counts as a threat to international peace and security, and hence the cases where the use of military force is legally permissible. Some of them—notably NATO, the European Union, and the African Union—have also been heavily involved in the development of civilian protection mandates for peace operations which involve the use of military force at the operational and tactical levels. In a number of recent cases where military force was debated as a hypothetical option to protect civilians (e.g., Darfur in 2004–06, Burma/Myanmar in 2008, Somalia in 2008–09, Côte d'Ivoire in 2010–11, Libya in 2011, and Syria in 2011–), the relevant regional organizations played a sort of gatekeeping function that influenced the Security Council's emerging practice on the use of force. In this sense, they have contributed to strengthening the United

Nations' ability to respond to this type of challenge.

While some regional arrangements have become important military actors in their own right, of perhaps greater significance is their emerging role as "gatekeepers"— influencing which issues get debated in the UN Security Council, how they are framed, and the range of possible Council responses. Gatekeeping is not a new phenomenon, since the United Nations has always generally preferred to act in concert with the wishes of the relevant regional arrangement(s). But as more regions try and assert their own values, procedures, and methods, it does appear to have become more prominent in the response to a variety of international crises. This is because gatekeepers can facilitate access to particular regional crises. Recall, for example, SADC's role in defining appropriate international responses to Zimbabwe's crisis (2002–present), or the importance of ASEAN's position on how best to engage with the junta in Burma/Myanmar. But gatekeepers are not in total control; they could conceivably be overridden by the Security Council or bypassed by other external actors, as was the case with the African Union in relation to the Libyan civil war in 2011.

Such gatekeeping is the logical outcome of two complementary factors: the UN Security Council's preference for acting in conformity with the policies of the relevant regional arrangements rather than against them; and the desire of regional arrangements to exercise considerable autonomy over responding to crises in "their" region. The Security Council's position is sensible because international responses to protection crises are most effective when there is strong partnership between the United Nations and relevant regional organizations. The regional position is appropriate because subsidiarity is a sensible principle to follow in relation to issues of multilayered governance.

Examples of regional gatekeeping have thus become increasingly common.[33] For example, in Côte d'Ivoire's constitutional crisis in late 2010 and early 2011, the position of African regional arrangements was a critical determinant of UN Security Council action, especially because it seems unlikely that China and Russia would have overruled Laurent Gbagbo's attempts to steal the election without prior regional support. Similarly, in the Libyan case in early 2011, the LAS in particular played an important gatekeeping function. Specifically, before the LAS resolution calling for the imposition of a no-fly zone and safe areas to protect civilians in Libya, British and French diplomats believed it was highly unlikely that the Security Council could be persuaded to authorize enforcement action, and the United States remained distinctly frosty to the idea of military intervention. Without the LAS statement, it is unlikely that what became resolution 1973 would ever have been tabled for a vote. Whatever the reasons behind the LAS decision, it changed dynamics at the Security Council: it made opposition to enforcement more difficult; it brought the United States onboard, which enhanced the feasibility of the military option; it helped persuade the three African members of the Security Council; and, ultimately, it pushed the remaining skeptical members toward abstention.

But gatekeeping also brings challenges. First, the Libya case illustrated the dilemma of which regional organization the UN Security Council should support when two or more organizations can legitimately claim the mantle of "gatekeeper" with respect to a particular crisis. In adopting resolution 1973, the council—and not only those members that supported the resolution—privileged the attitudes of the LAS over the African Union, which had adopted a policy of mediation without military intervention.[34] Particularly significant in this regard was the decision of the three African members of the Security Council (Nigeria, Gabon, and South Africa) to support resolution 1973 rather than abstain. Had two of the three African members reflected the AU position in their voting, resolution 1973 would have fallen short of the required nine affirmative votes. If regional gatekeeping continues, questions about which organizations the Security Council should prioritize and the potential for "forum shopping" will come to the fore.

A second potential problem is that while regional gatekeepers can facilitate robust international responses to crises, they can also block military or other decisive action. Thus, while the LAS facilitated intervention in Libya, the same organization initially stymied the UN Security Council from even condemning violence against civilians in Syria. In the debates over intervention in the case of Darfur, Sudan, in 2004–06, the African Union repeatedly urged other external actors not to act without the cooperation of the regime in Khartoum. Similar dynamics were on display in relation to the United Nations' stance on Zimbabwe's governance crisis, which largely followed the preferences set out by SADC and the African Union, and how to respond in the aftermath of Cyclone Nargis in Burma/Myanmar in 2008, which followed the preferences expressed by the ASEAN.

In sum, although only a subset of the world's regional arrangements have added the collective use of military force to their conflict-management repertoire (practically or hypothetically), those organizations that have done so have not fundamentally challenged the rules on the use of force embedded within the existing UN Charter system. However, some regional arrangements have played a significant "gatekeeping" role, which has influenced how the UN Security Council responds to particular crises. Moreover, the most prominent area in which the international rules on the use of force are evolving, namely the area of civilian protection, has been heavily influenced by the policies of regional arrangements.

CONCLUSION: PARTNERSHIPS AS THE WAY FORWARD?

Looking forward, it appears that whether and how regional arrangements use military force to manage conflicts will remain an important part of international debates. This issue has a much longer pedigree than the post–Cold War period and certainly longer than the uprisings across the Arab world. Debate will continue because it is far from clear that any regional arrangement has found the optimal balance between peaceful approaches to conflict management and the threat and/or use of military force. Regional arrangements at both ends of the spectrum can at best point to a mixed record of success for their initiatives.

For those organizations that have made collective force part of their toolkit, the central policy debate will revolve around how to utilize military instruments as part of an effective political strategy of conflict resolution and how to develop optimal "partnerships"—between regional arrangements, between regional arrangements and the United Nations, and between regional arrangements and a variety of other actors (most notably external donors, individual states, and relevant private contractors). In this respect, the AU Mission in Somalia, or AMISOM, is a particularly important operation because it is likely to be viewed as the litmus test for how complex global-regional partnerships are judged. At present, "the AMISOM model" is being increasingly lauded as the best way forward, with similar approaches and divisions of labor being adopted to deal with crises in Mali and the Central African Republic. Although "the AMISOM model" can be interpreted in several different ways, the mission now embodies a complex division of labor whereby African states provide the majority of personnel, the United Nations provides the logistical support (in conjunction with a wide range of private contractors), the European Union pays the peacekeepers' allowances, and various bilateral supporters help train and equip the African troop-contributing countries as well as the Somali national security forces. If this model really is the shape of things to come in the DRC, Mali, the Central African Republic, and perhaps elsewhere, then it should be subjected to far more scrutiny than it has received so far.

NOTES

1. Paul D. Williams and Jürgen Haacke, "Regional Approaches to Conflict Management," in *Rewiring Regional Security in a Fragmented World*, ed. Chester Crocker, Fen Osler Hampson, and Pamela Aall (Washington, DC: United States Institute of Peace, 2011), 49–74.

2. See, for example, Peter J. Katzenstein, *A World of Regions* (Ithaca, NY: Cornell University Press, 2005); and Amitav Acharya, "The Emerging Regional Architecture of World Politics," *World Politics* 59, no. 4 (2007): 629–52.

3. See, for example, Benjamin Miller, *States, Nations, and the Great Powers* (Cambridge: Cambridge University Press, 2007); and Amitav Acharya and Alastair Iain Johnston, eds., *Crafting Cooperation: Regional International Institutions in Comparative Perspective* (Cambridge: Cambridge University Press, 2007).

4. See, for example, Michael C. Williams, *Culture and Security: Symbolic Power and the Politics of International Security* (London: Routledge, 2007); and Williams and Haacke, "Regional Approaches," 63–65.

5. See, for example, David A. Lake and Patrick M. Morgan, eds., *Regional Orders: Building Security in a New World* (University Park: Pennsylvania State University Press, 1997).

6. I have included NATO in this analysis despite the fact that it is officially defined as a collective alliance because in the post–Cold War era it has taken on a range of conflict-management roles beyond those associated with the direct self-defense of its members.

7. See, for example, Ibrahim Sharqieh's discussion of the OIC's notion of "moral power" in "Can the Organization of Islamic Cooperation Resolve Conflicts?" *Peace and Conflict Studies* 19, no. 2 (2012): 162–79.

8. Katharina P. Coleman has labeled these operations "solidarity deployments" (i.e., military support of embattled governments). See her "Innovations in 'African Solutions to African Problems': The Evolving Practice of Regional Peacekeeping in Sub-Saharan Africa," *Journal of Modern African Studies* 49, no. 4 (2011): 526–31.

9. For more details, see Herbert M. Howe, *Ambiguous Order: Military Forces in African States* (Boulder, CO: Lynne Rienner, 2001), chap. 4.

10. The text refers to "factions within" SADC rather than SADC itself because it appears that both operations were launched without following the organization's internal rules of procedure. The same could also be said of the ECOWAS Monitoring Group mission in Liberia, established in 1990. See Katharina P. Coleman, *International Organisations and Peace Enforcement* (Cambridge: Cambridge University Press, 2007), chaps. 3–5.

11. To date, the CSTO reaction force has not been used in a real operation. See Oksana Antonenko, "Russia and Central Asia," in Crocker et al., *Rewiring Regional Security*, 328–32.

12. As set out in the 2005 UN General Assembly World Summit Outcome Document, the "responsibility to protect" principle affirms that each UN member-state has "the responsibility to protect its populations from genocide, war crimes, ethnic cleansing and crimes against humanity," as well as "their incitement" (para. 138). Moreover, should any state be found to be "manifestly failing to protect their populations" from these four crimes, the world's governments committed themselves "to take collective action, in a timely and decisive manner, through the Security Council, in accordance with the Charter" (paragraph 139). UN document A/60/L.1, October 24, 2005.

13. Although the SADC Protocol on Politics, Defence and Security Cooperation (2001) gives

the organization a role in responding to intrastate conflict in southern Africa, including in cases of "genocide, ethnic cleansing and gross human rights violations" (Article 11.2b.i), it also states that no enforcement action will be taken without the prior authorization of the UN Security Council as stipulated in Article 53 of the UN Charter (Article 11.3d).

14. For details, see Paul D. Williams and Alex J. Bellamy, "Principles, Politics, and Prudence: Libya, the Responsibility to Protect, and the Use of Force," *Global Governance* 18, no. 3 (2012): 273–97.

15. See, for example, Michael McGwire, "Why Did We Bomb Belgrade?," *International Affairs* 76, no. 1 (2000): 1–23; and Michael Theodoulou, "Qaddafi Considered 'Most Unpopular Arab Leader,'" *The National* (UAE), April 3, 2011, http://www.thenational.ae/news/world/middle-east/qaddafi-considered-most-unpopular-arab-leader.

16. See Nicholas J. Wheeler, *Saving Strangers: Humanitarian Intervention in International Society* (Oxford: Oxford University Press, 2000).

17. AMIS was subsequently transformed into the AU/UN Hybrid Operation in Darfur (UNAMID). Although a joint operation at the strategic political level, UNAMID is funded by the UN peacekeeping budget, and its personnel wear the UN's blue helmets.

18. See Paul D. Williams, "The African Union Mission in Somalia and Civilian Protection Challenges," *Stability: International Journal of Security and Development* 2 (2013), http://www.stabilityjournal.org/.

19. For background, see Danesh Sarooshi, *The United Nations and the Development of Collective Security* (Oxford: Oxford University Press, 2000).

20. See Independent International Commission on Kosovo, *The Kosovo Report* (Oxford: Oxford University Press, 2000).

21. This initiative involves the armed forces of four central African states on whose territory the Lord's Resistance Army has been operating: the Central African Republic, the DRC, the Republic of South Sudan, and Uganda. It is made up of a Joint Coordination Mechanism located in Bangui; a Regional Task Force comprising some five thousand troops from the affected countries with a headquarters in Yambio, South Sudan; and a Joint

Operations Center, which provides planning and monitoring functions for the Regional Task Force. The Regional Cooperation Initiative was endorsed by the UN Security Council in June 2012.

22. Although early SADC proposals suggested the neutral intervention force might operate independently from the UN stabilization mission (MONUSCO), this option was rejected in favor of integrating the force into MONUSCO.

23. For an overview and discussion, see Linnéa Gelot, Ludwig Gelot, and Cedric de Coning, eds., *Supporting African Peace Operations* (Uppsala, Sweden: Nordic African Institute, 2012).

24. See the declaration on "Enhancing UN-AU Cooperation: Framework for the Ten Year Capacity Building Programme for the AU" (UN document A/61/630), signed on November 16, 2006, by the UN Secretary-General and the Chairperson of the AU Commission.

25. See Paul D. Williams and Arthur Boutellis, "Partnership Peacekeeping: Challenges and Opportunities in the United Nations-African Union Relationship," *African Affairs* 113, no. 451 (2014).

26. See Paul D. Williams, "AMISOM," *RUSI Journal* 157, no. 5 (2012): 32–45.

27. There is also the converse example of the Intergovernmental Authority on Development (IGAD), which despite not having explicit provisions for conducting military operations in its founding conventions, authorized in 2004 the deployment of a peace-building force to Somalia, IGASOM. (Advocates argued that Article 7[g] of the Agreement Establishing the IGAD [1996] provided the legal basis for such an operation.) Although this was nominally a peace-building operation, it was to be conducted by soldiers and, given the situation on the ground in and around Mogadishu, it was highly likely that these troops would have ended up using force, if only in self-defense. In the event, IGASOM never materialized.

28. See International Institute for Strategic Studies, *The Military Balance 2013* (London: Taylor & Francis, 2013).

29. On paper at least, the African Union has declared an aspiration that the African Standby Force might operate beyond the continent. See *Harmonized Doctrine for Peace Support Operations*, AU document, October 2006, chap. 5, para. 12c.

The Collective Security Treaty Organization has made a similar declaration. Article 6 of the treaty states that "Armed Forces can be used beyond the territory of the States Parties exclusively in the interests of international security in strict compliance with the Charter of the United Nations and the legislation of the States Parties to this Treaty."

30. See Paul D. Williams, *War and Conflict in Africa* (Cambridge: Polity, 2011), chaps. 8 and 10.

31. Arguably the most significant convention in this regard is the African Charter on Democracy, Elections and Governance, which entered into force in February 2012.

32. See *Roadmap for the Operationalization of the African Standby Force*, African Union document EXP/AU-RECs/ASF/4(I) (Addis Ababa: March 22–23, 2005), 5.

33. This paragraph draws from Alex J. Bellamy and Paul D. Williams, "The New Politics of Protection? Côte d'Ivoire, Libya and the Responsibility to Protect," *International Affairs* 87, no. 4 (2011): 825–50.

34. For a discussion of the African Union's position on Libya, see Alex de Waal, "African Roles in the Libyan Conflict of 2011," *International Affairs* 89, no. 2 (2013): 365–79.

20

CIVIL SOCIETY AND CONFLICT MANAGEMENT

Thania Paffenholz

War and peace have traditionally been understood as state affairs, in which diplomats and parties in armed conflict meet to negotiate a peace agreement. The few international nongovernmental organizations (NGOs) that have played prominent peacemaking roles, such as the Quakers or the Community of Sant'Egidio, were considered exceptions on the scene. This view has changed radically since the mid-1990s, as it has become clear that contemporary conflict management is of a collective nature and requires broader participation, involving a multitude of local and international actors. Supporting and strengthening civil society is now a key priority for policymakers and donors alike. The role of civil society in the Arab Spring has reconfirmed its relevance in political transitions. This shift in focus, particularly within the donor community, was clearly highlighted by the World Bank already in 2007: "Today the main question in the international debate is no longer 'whether' civil society has a role to play in peacebuilding, but 'how' civil society can best realize its valuable contributions."[1]

However, in policy circles, there persists resistance to involve civil society in track one negotiations, due to the fear that enhanced participation challenges the consensus-building process, making it more difficult to reach a peace agreement. It was only in 2009 that the UN secretary-general highlighted the importance of involving broad-based and widely respected civil society groups into official mediation processes.[2]

Interestingly, the policy and research communities offer opposing assessments. The policy community allocates civil society an overwhelmingly positive and constructive role in long-term peacebuilding and state building, though skepticism remains for its role in short-term conflict management. The research community's findings vary between positive and very critical on the achievements of civil society actors in long-term peacebuilding, while their findings are largely positive on the role of civil society in short-term conflict management, arguing that broader participation ensures sustainable peace agreements.[3]

The objective of this chapter is to unpack these puzzling findings by taking a closer look at how international and local civil society actors can contribute to ending wars, sustaining peace, and managing political transitions in the area of collective conflict management. The chapter aims to clarify the various functions played by both international and local civil society actors, present different models for including these actors in high-level negotiations, and determine the challenges and dilemmas associated with their involvement.

The chapter is structured around four main questions: *Who* is civil society? *What* can they contribute to collective conflict management? What *challenges* will they likely encounter along this path? And *how* can they be best involved in conflict management processes?

The first section explores the "who" question by elucidating our understanding of civil society and the differences or similarities to NGOs by clarifying the terminology and providing an overview of differing debates in various contexts. The second section addresses the "what" question by presenting constructive roles for civil society in conflict management. The third section discusses challenges and dilemmas, while the fourth addresses the "how" question, presenting models for involving civil society in track one negotiations in war-to-peace or authoritarianism-to-democracy transitions. The chapter ends with summations of the present and future of civil society in collective conflict management.

THE "WHO" QUESTION: UNDERSTANDING CIVIL SOCIETY

Prior to engaging in any debate about the role of civil society in collective conflict management, it is important to clarify what one is talking about. Hence, this chapter first explains what is understood by "conflict management" in this chapter by emphasizing which distinct phases and types of con-

flict management are discussed here. Second, the chapter provides a definition of "civil society" and explain why that term is preferred over the term "NGOs" in this chapter.

Conflict management is an umbrella term covering various types of collective interventions carried out in order to end armed conflict or negotiate political transitions in the short, medium, or long term. What civil society can contribute to conflict management varies depending on these different phases. One thus has to distinguish between its role in short-term (often referred to as "peacemaking") and long-term conflict management (mostly referred to as "peacebuilding" or "state building," the latter being used in political transitions).

Civil society is generally understood as the arena of voluntary, collective actions of an institutional nature around shared interests, purposes, and values that are distinct from those of the state, family, and market. Civil society consists of a large and diverse set of voluntary organizations and comprises non-state actors and associations that are not purely driven by private or economic interests, are autonomously organized, show civil virtue, and interact in the public sphere.[4]

In the literature, the terms "civil society organizations" (CSOs) and "nongovernmental organizations" (NGOs) are often used interchangeably. In recent years, the term "civil society" has entered mainstream research and policy discourse, and is now more commonly used to describe both local and international organizations.[5] Yet the NGO terminology remains in some of the conflict management literature, as it is often used to refer to INGOS (international nongovernmental organizations) and their local partner NGOs specializing in international conflict management and conflict resolution,[6] or to modern, mostly Western NGOs working on humanitarian or development service delivery (see further differentiations below).

It is also important to note that civil society is not a homogenous actor solely comprising the "good society" that contributes to dialogue and democratization.[7] Rather, research has found that inclusive, civic, bridging, and pro-peace organizations often work alongside exclusivist, sectarian, and occasionally xenophobic and militant groups.[8]

In light of these clarifications, it is possible to identify the following—non-mutually exclusive—categories of civil society actors:

- *Special interest groups* (for example, trade unions; professional associations for teachers, farmers, and journalists; minority and women's organizations; and veterans' associations)
- *Faith-based organizations* (for example, churches and Islamic associations)
- *Traditional and community groups* (for example, youth groups, councils of elders, women's and mother's groups, radio listener's clubs, and user groups)
- *Researchers and research institutions* (for example, local and international think tanks, universities, and individual researchers)
- *Humanitarian or development service delivery organizations* (which include both local and international "modern," "traditional," or religious organizations, like humanitarian aid NGOs, churches, or Islamic charities)
- *Human rights and advocacy organizations* (which can also be clustered under special interest groups)
- *Conflict resolution and peacebuilding NGOs and INGOs* (which might also be advocacy or training service organizations, depending on their mandate)
- *Social and political movements* (which can take the form of broad-based public movements around a common cause, such as the Arab Spring; or longer-term movements, like the

environmental, women's, or peace movements)
- *Business associations* (for example, associations of entrepreneurs or journalists, independent of their profit-making side of business)
- *Networks* (which generally represent a larger number of organizations from any of the categories specified above, such as a network of religious councils)

Islamic charities are a good example of how these categories sometimes overlap. They can be both faith-based organizations and provide development or humanitarian services to the poor.

One important debate in the civil society discourse concerns its origins and its developments in different geographical contexts. A closer look into the history of civil society also sheds light on some current terminological debates. Historically, the notion of civil society has been an almost purely Western concept, tied to the political emancipation of European citizens from former feudalistic ties, monarchy, and the state during the eighteenth and nineteenth centuries. This has given rise to a debate as to whether the concept of civil society is transferable to non-Western context.[9] Nevertheless, there has always been some form of civil associations in all geographical and historical contexts. In this respect, a number of context-specific discourses can be observed.

In Latin America, for instance, the concept of civil society gained momentum in the fight against military dictatorships at the end of the 1960s. Social movements contributed to organized resistance against authoritarian regimes but failed to take on a major role once democracy had been restored.[10] To make a living, many of them transformed from movements into service delivery NGOs and hence became less political.[11]

On the question of whether the concept of civil society is applicable in Africa, a number of different viewpoints can be found in the literature. David Lewis, for example, states that due to the historical developments caused by colonial rule (fostering a small urban elite in cities while oppressing a large majority of the population in rural areas), Africa knows only traditional associations and has no space for a civil society.[12] Nelson Kasfir and Kwadwo Appiagyei-Atua, however, see little problem in applying the concept of civil society to Africa. They opt for a wider understanding of civil society in the African context, to include traditional associations, voluntary organizations, youth groups, elders and chiefs.[13]

In Eastern Europe, as well as in Central Asia and the Caucasus, most countries faced a threefold transition: (1) a political transformation from dictatorship to democracy; (2) an economic transformation from a state to a market economy; and, in some cases, (3) a state transformation due to the disintegration of the Soviet Union.[14] As a result, the emergence of civil society became linked to the empowerment of dissident opposition movements to counter suppressive regimes.[15] Later on, some of these opposition movements even assumed a political role.[16] At the same time, civil society organizations based on the communal concept of informal ties (clan, family, or neighborhood) or neopatrimonial structures persisted. In the case of Georgia and Armenia, the church continues to play an important role in helping nurture those ties.[17] A common strand among countries in Asia is that civil society is still not protected, as the state continues to be the central, and often the most repressive, actor in the region.[18]

With regard to the Middle East and North Africa, the literature generally has identified the weakness of civil society to counter strong authoritarian regimes. However, during the Arab Spring, civil society movements have been in the forefront of political change and the overthrow of authoritarian rule. In the immediate aftermath of the recent "revolutions," civil society is divided along secular/religious and rural/urban lines, as well as between unstructured movements and organized groups. Groups have yet to define their future role within the transitions. In the Arabic language, "civil society" translates either as *al-mujtama al-madani* or as *al-mujtama al-ahlī*. The former is used for "modern," mostly secular NGOs, while the latter refers to primordial solidarities and is used for kin-based organizations and religious charities, Muslim and Christian alike. In many countries in the region, this distinction between *madani* and *ahlī* also reflects the group's political positioning, particularly since the reinforcement of political Islam, which enhanced a feeling of marginalization on the part of "modern," secular NGOs.

In sum, when it comes to conflict management, both terms, "NGOs" and "civil society," still prevail. However, the latter has now become mainstream terminology. This chapter therefore mostly uses "civil society" rather than the narrower term "NGOs." The term "NGO" is used, however, when referring to peacebuilding/conflict management or development/humanitarian organizations.

THE "WHAT" QUESTION: CIVIL SOCIETY FUNCTIONS IN CONFLICT MANAGEMENT

In the literature we find, various roles and functions are attributed to civil society in conflict management. The following seven functions present the most comprehensive overview. These functions are what civil society can contribute: protection, monitoring, advocacy, socialization, social cohesion, facilitation, and service delivery.[19]

Each function is discussed below in more detail.[20]

Protection

Protection of citizens and communities against the despotism of the state is highly necessary in any situation. However, during and after an armed conflict, protection becomes almost a precondition for fulfilling other functions, as civil society actors are substantially hindered from taking up conflict management roles when threatened by armed groups. This is particularly true because states weakened by armed conflict cannot properly fulfill their protection function. The main protection-related activities are international accompaniment, watchdog activities, creation of "zones of peace," and human security initiatives like demining.

In terms of impact, protection initiatives by local grassroots organizations were effective in their immediate constituency. The longer a conflict endures, the more likely that people will revert to clans, communities, families, and religious entities. Such groups begin to take on the responsibility to protect their members. For example, in Afghanistan and Somalia, clans played this role; in Guatemala, it was the Catholic Church; and in Northern Ireland, it was family groupings that tended to protect members from paramilitary violence.

Protection by specialized protection NGOs like Peace Brigades International have been more effective when they were systematically combined with monitoring and advocacy campaigns, and when there is cooperation between international and local CSOs. During Nepal's civil war, for example, a number of local human rights organizations monitored human rights violations by the army and the Maoists, and systematically channeled all information to the National Human Rights Commission, the media, and to Amnesty International (AI). AI, in suit, used the data to successfully lobby at the international level for the establishment of a UN monitoring mission.

Monitoring

Monitoring is, in general, a precondition for the protection and the advocacy functions. Monitoring is highly relevant to holding governments accountable and putting pressure on the conflict parties. International and local groups monitor the conflict and human rights situation, and issue recommendations to decision makers or provide human rights and advocacy groups with information. Supervising and verifying the implementation of peace agreements are also key elements of monitoring activities, but they have often been neglected. For example, in the context of the Israel-Palestine conflict, no monitoring initiative was ever set up for the Oslo process during the 1990s. This would have had considerable bearing, especially because the parties were criticized for not fulfilling their promises.

The impact of monitoring has been greater when activities were designed to reinforce protection and advocacy initiatives. For example, the International Crisis Group (ICG) monitors the situation in conflict countries and provides political analysis and recommendations to decision makers. Due to ICG's high profile, high quality of analysis, and international network and media coverage, it has become an influential monitoring institution. In Afghanistan under the Taliban, the Cooperation Center for Afghanistan managed to submit coded reports to international human rights organizations, and the country remained on the international agenda. In Nigeria, ongoing human rights reports have sustained international attention for human rights abuses in the Niger Delta.

Advocacy

Advocacy is a core function for civil society. The strongest form of advocacy is public mobilization, when masses of people go to the streets to demand the end of authoritarian rule or armed conflict, as recently seen in the Middle East and North Africa, or in Nepal in 2006. The main activities within this function are agenda setting by CSOs, such as bringing themes to the national agenda in conflict countries (road map projects, awareness workshops, public campaigns); lobbying for civil society involvement in peace negotiations; and applying public pressure (e.g., mass mobilization demanding peace negotiations, protesting against the recurrence of war, or supporting the proper implementation of peace agreements). Also important are global international advocacy campaigns that lobby, for example, against land mines, blood diamonds, or the abuse of children as soldiers.

The impact of advocacy initiatives is increased when organizations have campaigning know-how, base their advocacy on results of monitoring initiatives, and know how to use the media for their cause. International attention additionally enhances their impact. For example, in Northern Ireland, civil society groups managed to successfully lobby for the integration of human rights provisions into the peace agreement. Women's groups in Nigeria played a successful advocacy role for the protection of women and ethnic minorities. In Afghanistan under the Taliban, an NGO anti–land mine campaign convinced Mullah Omar to issue a fatwa banning the use of landmines.

Socialization

Socialization is a key civil society function that supports the practice of democratic and peaceful values within society, realized through the active participation of citizens in various associations, networks, or movements. Socialization takes place only within groups, not between former adversary groups (which is social cohesion, discussed below); it focuses on strengthening in-group bonding ties. For example, more and more international NGOs are working on each side of the Israel-Palestine conflict separately in order to strengthen each group in their peace efforts and understanding.

Every national or local association that practices peaceful coexistence contributes to this function. International NGOs often support local groups through peace education via different media (radio or TV soap operas, street theater, peace campaigns, schoolbooks, poetry festivals, etc.), but also through conflict resolution or negotiation training.

With regard to impact, socialization initiatives have been less effective overall, because many of them have engaged only in short-term projects with actors and institutions that do *not* have the power to socialize people. For example, many NGOs dedicated to international conflict resolution provide training to local NGOs. However, the key institutions in society that influence how people learn democratic and conflict behavior are families, schools, religious groups, secular and cultural associations, and the workplace. Yet, in most conflict countries, these socialization spaces tend to reinforce existing divides. In Israel, for example, education in schools reinforces the Jewish and Zionist identity and, to a lesser extent, liberal democratic values. In Cyprus, youths have been educated along nationalist lines, which tends to disregard the needs and fears of the "other." Greek Cypriots are inculcated with the idea that the island was and will always be Greek, whereas Turkish Cypriots learn that the island is Turkish and should go back to Turkey. Under these circumstances, a few training programs, directed mainly at like-minded local NGOs, do not have sufficient change potential.

However, in-group socialization of marginalized groups has often been effective. For example, the in-group education of the Maya in Guatemala by the Catholic Church helped empower a generation of civic leaders. The experience of war and widespread violence allowed for the construction of a pan-Maya identity across the twenty-four distinct language groups.

Intergroup Social Cohesion

Social cohesion is an important civil society function in conflict management, aimed at (re)building "good" social capital that was destroyed during war. Therefore, it is crucial to build "bridging ties" across adversarial groups rather than "bonding ties" within specific groups.[21] The objective is to help these groups learn to live together in peaceful coexistence.

The impact of social cohesion initiatives has been limited overall. As explained in the discussion of socialization above, divided societies have many strong socialization institutions, including families, schools, and religious organizations. When these institutions preach hatred and formulate enemy images over a long period (usually generations), the existence of few social cohesion initiatives cannot be very effective. In Somalia, for example, clan-based organizations worked to reinforce social cleavages and to weaken national cohesion. Moreover, divided communities by definition live segregated lives. In Northern Ireland, for example, the Protestant and Catholic communities live in different parts of towns, and any form of daily interaction is limited. In addition, problem-solving workshops tend to select English-speaking elites as representatives, people who are often already "converted" to the idea of positive images of the other group. Evidence of this was found in an evaluation of a series of work-

shops in Cyprus that assessed attitudes of participants prior to and after the program. The evaluation revealed that most participants already had a positive attitude toward the other group prior to the workshops.

However, social cohesion initiatives can have an impact when there is a low level or an absence of violence, or when they aim at bringing people together to work for a common cause (e.g., joint water management instead of a reconciliation-only focus). Long-term systematic initiatives have been more effective than short-term scattered ones, especially when they have focused on a wide range of societal cleavages and also bridged difficult groups.

Facilitation

Civil society can function as a facilitator to help bring parties together in a peace or transition process. Facilitation takes place both on the local and the national level. For example, in Afghanistan during Taliban rule, traditional mediation was the only resource for facilitating peace between the Taliban and the various Afghani communities. The Tribal Liaison Office helped organize local peace *jirgas* with religious and local leaders to explore options for peacebuilding. On the national level, facilitation is often done by prominent civil society leaders. In Nigeria, the government nominated a Catholic priest as chief mediator between Ogoni groups. In Nepal, each side of the conflict nominated two well-respected civil society leaders as facilitators. In South Africa, Desmond Tutu played this role.

The impact of facilitation is largely contingent on the context and often depends on the existence of eminent civil society leaders and their legitimacy vis-à-vis the conflict parties. It is therefore difficult to come up with generalizable results with regard to facilitation's success.

Service Delivery

During armed conflict, the provision of aid services through civil society actors (mainly NGOs, but sometimes associations as well) increases tremendously as state structures are either destroyed or weakened. There is no doubt that this function is extremely important to help the war-affected population and to support reconstruction of the state and society at large. However, service delivery can have an impact on conflict management only if agencies create entry points for other functions such as protection and social cohesion, especially when large-scale violence ends. For example, in Somalia, the total absence of a state for almost two decades made service delivery *the main* activity performed by civil society; Islamic charities were especially successful in creating entry points for peacebuilding by extending networks across clan and regional lines.

CHALLENGES AND DILEMMAS

Civil Society as a Mirror of Society at Large

Civil society is part of the larger society and mirrors its characteristics. Consequently, it is not surprising that civil society organizations are also divided along lines of power, hierarchy, ethnicity, and gender, and they display moderate as well as radical images and behaviors. In general, civil society organizations are dominated by male leadership from influential groups within society, with the exception of women's and minority organizations. Hence, civil society can be "uncivil,"[22] as exclusivist, sectarian, and occasionally even xenophobic and militant groups work alongside inclusive, civic, bridging, and pro-peace organizations.[23] During the Sri Lankan peace process, popular mobilization often took place along nationalist and even racist lines. Some Sinhalese organizations interpreted negotiations with the

Tamil militants as a way to undermine the unity and sovereignty of what they view as a holy Buddhist country. Buddhist monks staged frequent demonstrations against peace negotiations. Overall, Sri Lankan civil society protested more against than in support of peace initiatives.

Moreover, in conflict areas, high emotional salience is attached to group identity. Civil society organizations that represent only one group are common. In most cases, in-group socialization reinforces members' shared identity at the expense of developing cross-ethnic ties. Northern Ireland (e.g., the Orange Order), Israel (e.g., right-wing Jewish religious groups), and Bosnia (e.g., the Serb Movement of Independent Associations) offer good examples of this tendency.

Changing Relevance and Impact of Civil Society Functions

A four-year research project on the relevance and impact of civil society in peacebuilding found that in many instances, the functions that were relevant in a particular phase were not necessarily performed by civil society.[24] Protection is always necessary during violent phases of conflict, but only a few civil society initiatives took place. Monitoring, advocacy, and facilitation are always relevant. While advocacy and facilitation were performed regularly (though mostly with little international support), monitoring was starkly underperformed. Service delivery was always performed, but generally not with an eye to conflict management. Socialization and social cohesion are mainly relevant in periods with low levels of violence or after the end of large-scale violence, but they were performed throughout all phases of conflict management, despite low impacts. The overwhelmingly performed activities included training in conflict resolution and transformation, dialogue, and peace education initiatives.[25] For example, in Sri Lanka, when war broke out again and the government decided on a military solution to the conflict, training in peace journalism was still supported, even as many journalists were being killed or imprisoned. It took the donor community a while to realize that protection of journalists was needed instead of peace education.

The reasons why certain functions are favored over others are manifold and complex. They include the availability of funds; the often reactive mode of changing donor priorities; poor planning procedures on the part of NGOs that do not factor the likelihood of changing context into the design of initiatives; a limited set of theories of change (impact assumptions) on what works and what does not work in conflict management, which has led to more competencies in some areas (e.g., peace education, dialogue) than in others (protection, monitoring); and the lack of linkages between human rights (i.e., protection) and peace-related work.[26]

Differing Impact Potential of Civil Society Actors

International and local NGOs can be particularly effective in providing protection and in conducting targeted advocacy campaigns. However, mass-based organizations such as unions or other professional associations as well as schools and families have far greater potential to promote socialization and social cohesion than NGOs—even though their performance remains low and often counterproductive. Traditional and local entities (like elders or spiritual leaders) can be effective in facilitation and protection, while eminent civil society leaders and conflict management NGOs can be effective in preparing the ground for national facilitation and in helping parties break out of a stalemate in negotiations. Women's groups have performed well in support of gender and minority issues, and can be effective in bridging

existing divides. Yet it also seems clear that broader change requires the uniting of all available multiple change-oriented mass movements. Aid organizations—if they are aware of their conflict management potential and make systematic use of it—can further support protection, monitoring, and social cohesion.[27]

International Donor Support and the "NGOization" of Civil Society Groups

Due to administrative needs, Western donors have a preference for supporting international and local NGOs over membership-based civil society groups and associations. To get access to these funds, social movements and other civil society organizations transform themselves into professional service delivery NGOs. In many cases, this has limited their conflict management potential because they become less political and often more accountable to the donor than to their own peace constituency.[28] Moreover, NGOs have a weak membership base and naturally cannot change the attitudes and values of their members.

Context Matters

The main context factors that enable or disable civil society's impact on conflict management are the level of violence, the behavior of the state, the performance of the media, the behavior and composition of civil society itself (including diaspora organizations), and the influence of external political actors and donors.[29] In short, the higher the level of violence, the more reduced the space for civil society to act; the more repressive the state, the more it limits the space for action; the more state institutions fulfill traditional functions like protection and service delivery, the more civil society can concentrate on other functions; the more the mass media play a constructive role, the more space is created for civil society to act for peace; the less polarized civil society is, the more it can unite for a common cause; the more regional states and key international actors support a peace or transition process, the greater the impact local initiatives will have on the peace or transition process.

THE "HOW" QUESTION: EIGHT MODELS OF CIVIL SOCIETY PARTICIPATION IN CONFLICT MANAGEMENT

On the question of how to involve civil society in conflict management, this section presents eight models of inclusion; they focus primarily on the short-term conflict management phase and look at means to broaden participation in track one negotiations.[30] The eight models—ranging from the most direct representation to the least direct—are as follows:

1. *Direct representation*, either as additional delegations to the negotiations or as part of official delegations
2. *Observer status*: direct presence during the negotiations
3. *Official consultative forums*, parallel to the official negotiations and endorsed by the mediators and negotiators
4. *Consultations*, including less formal consultations without official endorsement from all the stakeholders prior to during or after official negotiations
5. *Post-agreement mechanisms*, such as the participation of civil society in implementation and monitoring provisions of the agreement
6. *High-level civil society initiatives*: unofficial facilitation initiatives in the prenegotiation phase or parallel to official negotiations, following a problem-solving approach
7. *Third-party facilitation*, in which international NGOs are linked to the con-

flict parties or mediators and represent the interests of local groups
8. *Public participation*, involving the broader population via mass action, public decision making (elections), campaigns, referenda, public hearings, or opinion polls

The different models are discussed in greater detail below, supplementing the theoretical description of each model with case illustrations and offering a short assessment of each model's validity for conflict management.

Model 1: Direct Representation at the Negotiations

Civil society representatives can be a direct party to negotiations, either on their own or as part of another actor's delegation. These options constitute the most direct form of participation as they give civil society the same status as the main conflict parties. However, the greater the number of groups present at the table, the more complex and challenging it becomes to reach an agreement. To decrease this problem, mediators in the 1999–2002 Inter-Congolese Dialogue resorted to sub-working groups as a way to break up great numbers of participants.[31] The UN mediators brought together the Kinshasa government, the armed groups, and the unarmed opposition, but insisted also on the participation of civil society representatives (*les forces vives*) to ensure broad societal consensus in the negotiations. A similar multi-stakeholder negotiation is currently taking place in Yemen for the National Dialogue Conference under UN mediation.

What are the achievements of direct participation? In the (few) cases with direct participation, the legitimacy of the negotiations was enhanced. This was particularly relevant in cases where the armed groups did not enjoy sufficient legitimacy among the people. Moreover, civil society groups were able to add important issues to the negotiation agenda that would have otherwise not been debated. Moreover, peace agreements with civil society participation were more sustainable compared to those that were negotiated without broader participation.[32]

Model 2: Observer Status at the Negotiations

Civil society groups or international and local NGOs can be granted an observer status. This happened in Liberia (2003), Sierra Leone (1996), the Solomon Islands (1991), and Burundi (1996–98). In the Burundi peace process, women's groups actively lobbied the chief mediator, Julius Nyerere, for their direct participation in the talks. As the parties did not agree to include women, Nyerere offered them observer status instead.

What have civil society groups achieved as observers? In all the above cases, the attending civil society actors were well informed about the negotiation agenda. As a result, they were able to play a critical watchdog function, advise the conflict parties and the mediators, and form alliances with other observers to facilitate the agreement. In the case of Liberia, the groups with observer status inside the negotiations cooperated closely with groups outside the talks. They passed along critical information that allowed the outside groups to put public pressure on the parties.

The main challenge associated with observer status is the exclusive choice of groups. As only a few groups will be granted observer status, careful selection is crucial for making their participation meaningful.

Model 3: Official Consultative Forums Parallel to Negotiations

Civil society forums can act as a consultative body to the negotiation process, provided the mediator and the conflict parties officially endorse them. The forums' mandate can be specified by the mediator, the conflict parties, or by civil society itself. In most cases, the consultative forum follows the same agenda as the official negotiations, but it can also add issues to the negotiation agenda.

This model of participation has both advantages and disadvantages. On the one hand, conducting an official forum avoids the problem of multiplying the number of actors at the main negotiation table, while including a broad set of perspectives that gives the process more legitimacy. It can also help facilitate the discussion on difficult issues and provide an alternative channel for negotiations if the official talks stall. On the other hand, it comes at the cost of more distance from the negotiation table. Despite its mandate, a forum can be ignored, sidelined, or dismissed by the principle negotiators. Another danger is the possibility that the forum will be co-opted by the main negotiators seeking to use civil society to promote their own negotiation agendas. Moreover, in order to ensure civil society input, regular communication has to take place between the mediation/facilitation teams of the official negotiation and the civil society forum.

What have consultative forums achieved? Successful forums took place during the UN-led mediations in Guatemala (1994–96) and in Afghanistan (for one week in December 2001). In both cases, civil society groups were able to bring crucial issues to the negotiation agenda that would have otherwise been left out. In Guatemala, this especially concerned the rights of indigenous people and issues related to land and women. Eighty percent of all civil society proposals were incorporated into the peace agreement.

Model 4: Formal and Informal Consultations

While not officially part of the negotiations, formal and informal consultations with civil society actors can still meet the objectives of making diverse voices from the population heard and informing civil society about the negotiation process. They allow the mediation team not only to get a better understanding of the conflict context and the critical issues for the agreement but also to gain insights into people's needs, ideas, and visions. Consultations also help the mediation team understand who needs to be involved in shaping the post-agreement agenda, thus increasing the sustainability of the agreement, and begin an ongoing exchange of information and ideas. However, in comparison with an official consultative forum, these consultations involve a greater distance from the negotiations, as well as a more limited use of civil society's potential. In Kenya in 2008, when Kofi Annan failed to persuade the conflict parties to agree to an official civil society consultative forum to negotiate a peace agreement for the post-election violence, he and his team opted to engage directly with a broad array of civil society actors over the entire period of the negotiations. Part of these consultations involved separate meetings with Kenyan women's groups.

Could these more informal consultations achieve something? They certainly achieved less than the official forums. Nevertheless, as the Kenyan case demonstrates, the involved civil society groups took up important advisory roles. The Kofi Annan team was able to discuss critical proposals with the groups and get their opinion on how these proposals would be accepted (or not) by a broader set of actors.

Model 5: Inclusion in Post-Agreement Mechanisms

The inclusion of civil society into various post-agreement mechanisms aims at strengthening democratization as well as the sustainability of the agreement. The main function of this model is monitoring. Many peace agreements include provisions for the inclusion of civil society in implementation mechanisms, ranging from general to very specific.[33] Some peace agreements also include provisions for civil society to create awareness about the agreement among the population. In Somalia, for example, the 1993 agreement included a provision stipulating that civil society delegations would travel to all parts of the country to drive up awareness of the agreement. In Colombia, the peace talks between the government and the FARC from 1999 to 2002 established a national committee tasked with consulting widely with the population. Some agreements even provide seats for civil society representatives in national legislatures, as was the case in Liberia in 2003, Burundi in 2000, and the Philippines in 1996. General provisions are rarely effective. In cases where provisions were specific, civil society groups had taken an important role already during the negotiations. These findings confirm the need for space during the negotiations to discuss the details of the implementation and monitoring provisions.[34]

As the case of Liberia shows, participation of specialized civil society groups (e.g., for human rights monitoring) in post-agreement mechanisms has enhanced the quality of monitoring and put more pressure on the parties to comply with the agreement.

Model 6: High-Level Civil Society Initiatives

Problem-solving workshops or private facilitation initiatives aim at strengthening the impact of negotiations, providing facilitation, and, depending on the case, advocating for specific issues to be included in the agreement.

Problem-solving workshops are not official and generally not publicly known. They bring together representatives close to the leaders of the conflict parties and offer them communication channels without pressure to reach agreement.[35] Such initiatives can last up to several years and are generally organized and facilitated by INGOs or academic institutions.

The Schlaining Process in the Georgian-Abkhaz conflict demonstrates the use of these workshops. Between 2000 and 2007, the Schlaining Process involved twenty dialogue workshops gathering over one hundred Georgian and Abkhaz interlocutors. Named after the Austrian town in which the workshops were initially held, they were facilitated and organized by a British INGO and a German INGO in partnership with a range of Abkhaz and Georgian NGOs. The main objective was to provide a secure, confidential space for influential actors on either side of the divide to engage with one another. Participants analyzed all key issues in the formal negotiation process, enabling them to test ideas, and the potential reception of those ideas, in ways that could feed into the political negotiations and make them more effective. Communication channels existed with the mediators of the formal process, and the facilitators met regularly with the Special Representative of the UN Secretary-General and other senior UN staff in Tbilisi and Sukhumi. Though the Schlaining Process came to an end in 2007, it fostered the generation of ideas and communication channels across the conflict divide.

Model 7: Third-Party Facilitation

In this model, an international actor, generally an international conflict resolution or mediation NGO, represent the interests of local civil society organizations vis-à-vis the main conflict parties. This model has recently been applied in the Philippines. Indeed, the self-determination conflict in Mindanao, which has pitted government forces against the Moro Islamic Liberation Front (MILF), is believed to be on the right track to reach sustainable peace. This is so because the peace process reached an important breakthrough in October 2012 as the parties signed the Framework Agreement on the Bangsamoro. Two international NGOs, the London-based Conciliation Resources and Geneva-based Centre for Humanitarian Dialogue, played a third-party facilitation role within the International Contact Group (ICG) by providing mediation support to the official Malaysian facilitator of the peace talks between the government and MILF and by reaching out to regional civil society networks through sustained dialogue on the Mindanao conflict. The ICG is the first mechanism of its kind: it is a novelty, as international NGOs get the opportunity for the first time to work alongside diplomats. The ICG has efficiently helped promote peace and legitimacy of the process by ensuring the inclusion of the voices of civil society groups into the Framework Agreement, and has offered creative ways forward when negotiations reached a stalemate.

Model 8: Public Participation

Public participation is more than a normative attempt to democratize the negotiation process; it can also be a very powerful instrument to put pressure on the conflict parties. Public participation can take a number of different forms, such as mass action, campaigns, referenda, opinion polls, public hearings, and public decision making via elections.[36] It is hoped that such a buy-in into a track one elite pact will also contribute to enhanced sustainability of the agreement.

Overall, mass mobilization may create a general pro- or anti-peace agreement atmosphere or involve targeted advocacy campaigns for the inclusion of relevant issues into the peace agreement. In Nepal in 2006, three months of mass demonstrations to end the war and authoritarian rule paved the way for a comprehensive peace agreement. In contrast, the street agitation against the 2002–06 peace negotiations in Sri Lanka had a greater influence on the conflict parties' peace-process strategies than on those of the pro-peace camp. Mediators can also increase their understanding of the population's needs and expectations by conducting referenda, public hearings, and opinion polls.

Different forms of public participation have achieved public buy-in, as well as greater national legitimacy for and international acceptance of fragile peace agreements. When negotiation parties can demonstrate that the majority of people understand and accept an agreement, the implementation of the agreement is facilitated and its sustainability strengthened.

CONCLUSIONS

Contemporary conflict management requires broad participation of a multitude of local and international actors. The presence of international and local civil society organizations in conflict management has therefore become normal. Civil society organizations have played important roles in protecting people from violence, monitoring human rights abuses, or advocating for the ending of wars or authoritarian rule. Moreover, sufficient evidence from research shows that involving civil society into track one peace negotiations enhances the sustainability of peace agreements. However, the debates and examples discussed in this chapter have highlighted a number of important issues that will determine the future relevance of civil society's role in conflict management.

First, simply funding more civil society activities does not automatically bring us closer to more effective conflict management. It is crucial to understand who in civil society should be involved and in which function, depending on the particular needs and phase of a given process. What different actors in civil society (both international and local) can contribute to conflict management differs considerably and is also dependent on a set of context-specific factors, such as the level of violence, the role of the state, and the role of the media, as well as on the behavior of powerful regional actors.

Second, civil society organizations are not always the "good" constructive actors they are believed to be; rather, they act as a mirror of the larger society, providing peace support as well as, in some cases, obstructing the peace process by preaching hate and polarizing adversary groups. It is therefore not simply a normatively good move to involve a broad set of actors, but a sensitive and delicate process.

Third, track one mediators and conflict parties are still far away from routinely engaging civil society in track one negotiations. The dominant perception in track one circles is that additional actors will enhance the complexity of the process and thus reduce the effectiveness of reaching an agreement. However, this perception will slowly change with increased awareness of the advantages of broader participation and different models of how to practically engage civil society in these processes.

Fourth, civil society will continue to be active in peace and transition processes with or without the support of donors, and it will demand increased participation in decision making. As the Arab Spring has demonstrated, the important role of civil society is not necessarily sustainable. International support that is provided to groups in a context-sensitive manner and combined with political action can therefore help create more space for civil society in conflict management.

NOTES

1. World Bank, "Civil Society and Peacebuilding: Potential, Limitations and Critical Factors," Report no. 36445-GLB (World Bank, Washington, DC, 2007).

2. UN Security Council, "Report of the Secretary-General on Enhancing Mediation and Its Support Activities," UN document S/2009/189, April 8, 2009, UN High Commissioner for Refugees, http://www.unhcr.org/refworld/docid/49e6f2880.html.

3. Desirée Nilsson, "Anchoring the Peace: Civil Society Actors in Peace Accords and Durable Peace," *International Interactions* 38, no. 2 (2012): 243–66; and Anthony Wanis-St. John and Darren Kew, "Civil Society and Peace Negotiations: Confronting Exclusion," *International Negotiation* 13, no. 1 (2008): 11–36.

4. Christoph Spurk, "Understanding Civil Society," in *Civil Society and Peacebuilding: A Critical Assessment*, ed. Thania Paffenholz (Boulder, CO: Lynne Rienner, 2010), 3–28.

5. Jenny Pearce, "From Civil War to 'Civil Society': Has the End of the Cold War Brought Peace to Central America?" *International Affairs* 74, no. 3 (1998): 587–615; Thomas Carothers, "Civil Society: Think Again," *Foreign Policy*, no. 117 (Winter 1999–2000): 18–29; Roberto Belloni, "Civil Society in War-to-Democracy Transitions," in *From War to Democracy: Dilemmas of Peacebuilding*, ed. Anna K. Jarstad and Timothy D. Sisk (Cambridge: Cambridge University Press, 2008), 182–210; Camilla Orjuela, "Building Peace in Sri Lanka: A Role for Civil Society?" *Journal of Peace Research* 40, no. 2 (2003): 195–212; Beatrice Pouligny, "Civil Society and Post-Conflict Peacebuilding: Ambiguities of International Programmes Aimed at Building 'New' Societies," *Security Dialogue* 36, no. 4 (2005): 495–510; Paffenholz, *Civil Society and Peacebuilding*; and World Bank, "Civil Society and Peacebuilding."

6. Pamela Aall, "The Power of Nonofficial Actors in Conflict Management," in *Leashing the Dogs of War: Conflict Management in a Divided World*, ed. Pamela Aall, Chester Crocker, and Fen Osler Hampson (Washington, DC: United States Institute of Peace Press, 2007), 477–94; Diana Chigas, "Capacities and Limits of NGOs as Conflict Managers," in Aall et al., *Leashing the Dogs of War*, 553–82; and Andrea Bartoli, "NGOs and Conflict Resolution," in *SAGE Handbook on Conflict Resolution*, ed. Jacob Bercovitch, Victor Kremenyuk, and I. William Zartman (London: Sage, 2009), 392–412.

7. Orjuela, "Building Peace in Sri Lanka," 210.

8. Roberto Belloni, "Civil Society and Peacebuilding in Bosnia and Herzegovina," *Journal of Peace Research* 38, no. 2 (2001): 163–80; Augustine Ikelegbe, "The Perverse Manifestation of Civil Society: Evidence from Nigeria," *Journal of Modern African Studies* 39, no. 1 (2001): 1–24; Orjuela, "Building Peace in Sri Lanka"; and Thania Paffenholz et al., "Enabling and Disenabling Factors for Civil Society Peacebuilding," in Paffenholz, *Civil Society and Peacebuilding*, 414–20.

9. David Lewis, "Civil Society in African Contexts: Reflections on the Usefulness of a Concept," *Development and Change* 33, no. 4 (2002): 569–86.

10. Robert Pinkney, *Democracy in the Third World* (Boulder, CO: Lynne Rienner, 2003), 102–3.

11. Pearce, "From Civil War to 'Civil Society.'"

12. Lewis, "Civil Society in African Contexts," 567–77.

13. Nelson Kasfir, "Civil Society, the State and Democracy in Africa," *Commonwealth and Comparative Politics* 36, no. 2 (1998): 123–49; and Kwadwo Appiagyei-Atua, "Civil Society, Human Rights and Development in Africa: A Critical Analysis," *Peace, Conflict and Development*, no. 2 (December 2002), University of Bradford, http://www.bradford.ac.uk/ssis/peace-conflict-and-development/issue-2/CivilSocietyAfrica.pdf.

14. Wolfgang Merkel, *Systemtransformation: Eine Einführung in die Theorie und Empirie der Transformationsforschung* (Opladen, Germany: Leske and Budrich, 1999), 377.

15. Babken Babajanian, Sabine Freizer, and Daniel Stevens, "Civil Society in Central Asia and the Caucasus," *Central Asian Survey* 24, no. 3 (2005): 212.

16. M. Holt Ruffin and Daniel Waugh, eds., *Civil Society in Central Asia* (Baltimore, MD: Johns Hopkins University Press, 1999), 27–31.

17. Babajanian et al., "Civil Society in Central Asia and the Caucasus," 214.

18. For more information on civil society in different geographical and historical contexts, see Spurk, "Understanding Civil Society," 9–17.

19. Thania Paffenholz and Christoph Spurk, "Civil Society, Civic Engagement and Peacebuilding," Conflict Prevention and Reconstruction Paper no. 36 (Social Development Papers, World Bank, Washington, DC, 2006), 27–33; and Paffenholz and Spurk, "A Comprehensive Analytical Framework," in Paffenholz, *Civil Society and Peacebuilding*, 65–76.

20. In the text that follows, most of the examples given to illustrate the functions are taken from Paffenholz, *Civil Society and Peacebuilding*, parts 2 and 3. More details can be found there.

21. Robert Putnam, *Bowling Alone: The Collapse and Revival of American Community* (New York: Simon and Schuster, 2000).

22. Spurk, "Understanding Civil Society," 18–19.

23. See note 8 above.

24. Paffenholz, *Civil Society and Peacebuilding*.

25. Ibid., 381–404.

26. Thania Paffenholz, "International Peacebuilding Goes Local: Analysing Lederach's Conflict Transformation Theory and Its Ambivalent Encounter with 20 Years of Practice," *Peacebuilding* 2, no. 1 (2014): 11–27.

27. Paffenholz, *Civil Society and Peacebuilding*, 381–403.

28. Orjuela, "Building Peace in Sri Lanka," 255; Mary Kaldor, *Global Civil Society: An Answer to War* (Cambridge: Polity Press, 2003), 79; Kasfir, "Civil Society, the State and Democracy in Africa"; Pouligny, "Civil Society and Post-Conflict Peacebuilding"; Belloni, "Civil Society and Peacebuilding in Bosnia and Herzegovina"; Belloni, "Civil Society in War-to-Democracy Transitions"; and Paffenholz, *Civil Society and Peacebuilding*, 425–30.

29. Paffenholz et al., "Enabling and Disenabling Factors," 405–24.

30. Thania Paffenholz, "Civil Society and Peace Negotiations: Beyond the Inclusion-Exclusion Dichotomy," *Negotiation Journal* 30, no. 1 (2014): 69–91.

31. Wanis-St. John and Kew, "Civil Society and Peace Negotiations," 17–18.

32. Nilsson, "Anchoring the Peace."

33. Christine Bell and Catherine O'Rourke, "The People's Peace? Peace Agreements, Civil Society, and Participatory Democracy," *International Political Science Review* 28, no. 3 (2007): 293–324.

34. David Lanz, "Who Gets a Seat at the Table? A Framework for Understanding the Dynamics of Inclusion and Exclusion in Peace Negotiations," *International Negotiation* 16, no. 2 (2011): 275–95.

35. Ronald Fisher, "Interactive Conflict Resolution," in *Peacemaking in International Conflict: Methods and Techniques*, rev. ed., ed. I. William Zartman (Washington, DC: United States Institute of Peace Press, 2007), 227–72.

36. In other publications by the author this model is divided into three different models: public decision making, public participation, and mass action. See Paffenholz, "Civil Society and Peace Negotiations."

21

PEACE AND SECURITY IN THE TWENTY-FIRST CENTURY
UNDERSTANDING THE GENDERED NATURE OF POWER

Chantal de Jonge Oudraat and Kathleen Kuehnast

The US National Intelligence Council (NIC) in its *Global Trends 2025* report highlighted women as agents of geopolitical change and predicted that the "economic and political empowerment of women could transform the global landscape."[1] However, neither the NIC report nor any other strategic forecast has articulated how and under which conditions women's empowerment would transform the global landscape. More generally, they have failed to recognize that gender (that is, the socially constructed roles ascribed to women and men in societies) is a key explanatory variable of societal dynamics—including dynamics that determine peace and security. As such, these reports fail to fully understand the dynamics that will shape the future and hence leave policymakers empty-handed when trying to address problems of conflict and postconflict reconstruction.

Numerous studies in the development field have clearly shown that women's empowerment is key to obtaining many health, education, and related development objectives. The World Bank has documented how countries that invest in the promotion of the social and economic status of women tend to have lower poverty rates.[2] Academic research has demonstrated that the welfare and education of children is strongly correlated to the mother's education and socioeconomic status.[3] Former UN secretary-general Kofi Annan argued that "there is no tool for development more effective than the empowerment of women." He also asserted that empowering women is the most effective policy action both in preventing conflict and in achieving reconciliation after a conflict has ended.[4]

Indeed, during the 1990s, women's civil society organizations increasingly demanded to be heard in peace negotiations. The fourth World Conference on Women, held in Beijing in 1995, highlighted the impact of war on women's lives and explicitly recognized the importance of women's empowerment in establishing and maintaining international peace and security. The notion of women as agents of change and the importance of including women in peacebuilding efforts were both key messages of the groundbreaking United Nations Security Council Resolution (UNSCR) 1325, adopted in October 2000.[5] Unfortunately, the momentum generated by UNSCR 1325, as well as by related and energized initiatives, such as the responsibility to protect, dissipated in the wake of the terrorist attacks of 9/11, when the attention of the security community focused almost exclusively on the US-proclaimed "Global War on Terror" and the wars in Iraq and Afghanistan.[6]

The role of women specifically, and the larger context of the role of gender, in peacebuilding have long been grossly neglected in mainstream international relations and security studies, despite strong empirical evidence of linkages between the security of women and the security of states.[7] This lack of attention by the academic, think tank, and policy communities is all the more surprising given that in the late 1990s, as Cold War security preoccupations with nuclear deterrence faded, and those communities started to call attention to the security of individuals and groups within states (human security) as opposed to the security of territory and borders (state security). Indeed, the formidable challenges posed by intrastate conflicts changed the way in which policymakers and experts started to think about war and its impacts. General Rupert Smith, the UN commander in Bosnia in 1995, defined twenty-first-century wars as "wars amongst the people," a "reality in which the people in the streets and houses and fields— all the people, anywhere—are the battlefield."[8]

Regrettably, the failure to integrate gender—that is, the socially constructed roles

of men and women—as an analytical concept in the study of war and peace, as well as the failure to follow up on UNSCR 1325, has left both academics and policymakers unable to understand how to deal effectively with violent conflicts and their aftermaths; it has stunted international and national approaches to peacebuilding, to conflict management, and to conflict resolution.

The lack of attention to gender in the analysis of conflict has also limited many well-intentioned policy initiatives, such as the 2013 G8 initiative to prevent and deal with sexual violence in conflict. As a result, many policy initiatives have a tendency to inadvertently reinforce gender stereotypes and present polarized and limited understandings, whereby men are seen as perpetrators and women as victims, and gender equality programs are seen exclusively in terms of women empowerment programs.

What is lacking in many of these initiatives is a nuanced understanding of the multiplicity of roles that both men and women play during armed conflict as well as in peace. Violent conflict alters not only the individual and household roles of men and women in society but also the institutions that govern them. Violent conflict exacerbates and relaxes the norms about existent inequalities simultaneously. The result is a muddled set of altered relationships between men and women that do not correspond to previous determined sociocultural roles. Failure to recognize these changing social dynamics will lead to missed policy opportunities and appropriate programming, and, ultimately, the failure to establish stable and secure postconflict societies.

This chapter argues that just as there is often no clear dividing line between peace and war, nor should the roles of men and women in conflict and postconflict societies be seen as binary opposites. The chapter proposes that scholars and policymakers see the world through a lens that recognizes the multiplicity and dynamic nature of gender roles in the complex dimensions of war and peace—not only at individual levels but also at national and global systemic levels.

The global political shift of the twenty-first century not only involves the dispersal of power from central institutions to smaller units but also features men and women changing and exchanging a multiplicity of social roles. Hence, conflict managers would do well to consider the complex roles and relational dynamics between men and women in societies undergoing violent conflict and transition. They also need to be more attentive to the gendered nature of security institutions and their often static, limited, and gender-ignorant approaches to conflict resolution.

More specifically, analysts and policy makers need to begin to recognize that gender roles are a reflection of power dynamics within societies and are continuously redefined and renegotiated.[9] A rebalancing of gender roles will require express policy actions to favor women. However, they will also require a reconceptualization of what it means to be a man in a society coming out of conflict. If manhood and masculinity continue to be defined in terms of a man's ability to provide material support for his family, many men in postconflict and fragile states will fall short, because jobs in postconflict and fragile states are few and far between, and many men may not find jobs that would allow them to provide for their families.[10] The outcome of narrow social notions of manhood may be to resort to violence, including sexual violence, or apathy and emasculation, neither of which is an ingredient for the development of stable and democratic communities or states. In sum, policy and conflict analyses must capture the changing roles and expectations among men and women and acknowledge that they may en-

tail a reconceptualization of power and its attributes. The effects of these conceptual shifts will ultimately have a positive effect on economic and political stability in societies.

This chapter is divided into three parts. The first part examines three issues that bedevil many conflict analyses: the lack of a correct understanding of the gendered nature of peace and security institutions; the confusion between gender balancing and gender mainstreaming; and the lack of strong empirical data about the complex interactions of men, women, and security. The second part focuses on the issue of sexual violence in conflict and postconflict settings. Despite the increased international recognition of the serious impact that sexual violence in conflict and postconflict settings poses to security and peace, initiatives to prevent or mitigate violent acts have continued to fall short, because they have failed to examine the underlying causes of sexual violence and how such violence often attempts to perpetuate existing power dynamics within societies. The chapter thus debunks some of the conventional wisdom related to sexual violence as it examines international policy responses. The third and final part of the chapter presents a number of policy recommendations designed to overcome the current lack of understanding of the role of gender in peace and security.

THE GENDERED NATURE OF PEACE AND SECURITY

Gender is not about women or men as actors, but about the dynamic power relations in society between men and women, as well as preordained division of labor peace and conflict settings. Power relations shape the roles and expectations of men and women in societies and are amplified in institutional and ideological (gender) norms and behaviors.[11] International relations are also gendered, made up of a complex web of power, inequities, and arrangements operating between and across the spectrum of gender and within and among states.

Conflict and postconflict situations either push gender relations to extremes, such as when notions of hyper masculinity lead to extreme violence, including sexual violence, or allow for shifts in those relations, such as when women move into positions of power and when new institutions are created to govern relations between members of society based on different principles and power (hierarchical) distributions. It is important to note that national and international structures and institutions are not gender neutral; rather, they are vehicles of values, norms, and types of behavior previously defined and mostly developed to accommodate men's work and activities, with specific processes to define and maintain societally relevant definitions of masculinity. The gendered nature of institutions, structures, and many national and international postconflict demobilization and reintegration programs, including women empowerment programs, predetermines not only who participates in those programs or is targeted but also what norms and behaviors are transmitted or addressed.

When intervening in conflict or postconflict situations, international actors need to be attentive to the gendered nature of the societies in which they intervene and to understand how their actions may advance or set back an emancipatory agenda and peace. For example, all too often peace negotiations and peace processes intended to stop violent conflict focus on those groups who control the guns, and exclude those who do not. Indeed, it is often assumed that those engaged in violent conflict are the key actors, and the only ones who can stop it.[12] UNSCR 1325 challenges this assumption and posits that, in order to establish lasting peace, international actors should reach out to those who have demonstrated a commitment to nonviolence and peace, as well as to those who can mitigate conflict, including community leaders, and particularly women community leaders.

International actors also need to have a more finely grained understanding of the behavior of men. Indeed, research points to evidence that violent behavior is often a coping strategy to deal with feelings of vulnerability and a loss of status, power, and identity. For example, a survey in the very violent eastern part of the Democratic Republic of the Congo (DRC) revealed that 65 percent of men believed that women should accept partner violence to keep the family together. That same survey also revealed that 75 percent of the men felt ashamed to face their families because of their lack of employment.[13] These survey findings suggest a correlation between violent behavior and loss of status and identity. It follows that conflict resolution initiatives in such situations must include more than programs to protect and empower women; they must also address the particular underlying causes and motivations for the violent behavior of men, including the visual and mediated notions of a hyper sense of masculinity

The lack of a full-spectrum gender analysis that examines the roles and positions of both men and women limits understanding about the short- and long-term consequences of international actions that may further victimize those groups who might be potential allies in conflict resolution and peacebuilding. For example, when the international community imposes sanctions to change the behavior of warring factions, it will often make sure that the sanctions do not target basic needs, such as imports of grain, so as not to hurt the population at large. Yet, in the 1990s, in the first years of the UN embargo on Iraq, prenatal vitamins and baby milk were not considered basic needs. Hence, the sanctions inordinately affected women and young babies, who were surely not the groups whose behavior international actors were trying to alter.[14]

In addition, in postconflict situations, national and international efforts often reinforce traditional division of labor between men and women, with the former being assigned the provider role and the latter ascribed the caregiver role. Rarely do national and international programs question such traditional designations; consequently, they reproduce gender norms that no longer contribute productive and resolute approaches to society and escalate social tensions and, in some cases, violence.[15]

Gender Balancing and Gender Mainstreaming

Two powerful ideas are at the heart of UNSCR 1325 and notions of gender equality: gender balancing and gender mainstreaming. Gender balancing has to do with equal rights and rebalancing the number of women and men engaged in implementing international peace and security policies. To this end, UNSCR 1325 stresses the importance of women's "equal participation and full involvement in all efforts for the maintenance and promotion of peace and security, and the need to increase their role in decision-making with regard to conflict prevention and resolution."

Gender mainstreaming has to do with operational realities and ultimately operational effectiveness. Programs, policies, or initiatives in which gender has been mainstreamed recognize and identify the extent to which those programs, policies, or initiatives have impacted men and women differently and ensure that they do not perpetuate existing inequalities.[16] For example, a program aimed at demobilization and reintegration of armed militias needs to make sure that it targets not only adult men bearing

arms but also women, as well as young boys and girls who may have been recruited to perform other tasks for the militia. The program also needs to recognize that sexual abuse is often rampant but not restricted to women or girls.[17] Proponents of gender mainstreaming—including the authors of UNSCR 1325—argue that a better understanding of the gendered (and socially constructed) nature of societal relations and roles of men and women leads to better policies for furthering peace and security, and hence contributes to the maintenance and promotion of international peace and security.[18]

Many in policy circles and the institutions that promote gender assume that there is an intrinsic relationship between gender balancing and gender mainstreaming, whereby progress in one automatically leads to progress in the other. However, research about the nature of this relationship is nascent, and hence inconclusive. Thus, policymakers and other international actors must take care not to mistake gender balancing for gender mainstreaming, or to conflate policies aimed at one or the other but not both. It is critical that policies go beyond "just adding women" through quotas or other gender balancing means; those are incomplete approaches to gender mainstreaming.

Real gender mainstreaming should also involve an analysis of the situations and roles of men, and recognize that they may have specific vulnerabilities and may have to be engaged not only as the locus of trouble but also as a force to enact social change. The attitudes of men can and do change over time.[19] Norway is one the few countries that has instituted gender equality policies and tracked their results over time—and discovered that those policies have notably lowered rates of violence and enhanced quality of life.[20] The constructive engagement of men in conflict and postconflict situations is essential to establish lasting peace.

Reshaping the Analysis to Yield Inclusive Data Sets

As has been argued elsewhere, research on the gendered nature of peace and security and the relationship between gender balancing and gender mainstreaming remains on the margins of international relations and lacks inclusive analytical frameworks and strong empirical data. Further, the lack of sex-disaggregated data is an important obstacle to effective policies toward implementing UNSCR 1325 and, more generally, policies aimed at gender equality.

Former US secretary of state Hillary Clinton was keenly aware of the data gap. At the launch in July 2012 of Data 2X, an initiative aimed at increasing the collection of sex-disaggregated data and closing the gender data gap, she observed that

> we have strong evidence that women play roles in all kinds of things, and in particular in peacekeeping and conflict prevention. They raise issues in these kinds of negotiations, like human rights and human security that are fundamental to forging a lasting and sustainable peace. But we need more internationally comparable data to examine how women's contributions affect conflict regions. And only then can we really create frameworks for making sure they are included. . . . We have neither invested enough in collecting gender-sensitive data nor in quantifying how increasing gender equality yields benefits to societies.[21]

But it is not enough to count men and women in their respective "jobs" or "roles"; what is needed is qualitative data that captures the changing nature of societies coming out of war, and the critical dimensions of improved human rights and equal opportunities afforded to all.

Greater attention to the importance of data collection by national and international policymakers is a welcome development. Researchers and academics are important change agents in ensuring that the data sets are consistent and that the right inferences are drawn from that data. For example, Erik Melander and Elin Bjaregard, in their study on political representation and the decline of civil wars in East Asia, illustrate that "political representation of women is not necessarily a valid measurement of a society's general level of gender equality."[22] In 2012, the *Human Security Report* posited that, because the number of violent conflicts and the number of battle deaths had declined, the number of sexual assaults and rapes during wartime must also have decreased.[23] However, many experts were quick to expose this misguided inference, as there is no known correlation between battle deaths and sexual violence. As David Brooks pointed out in his *New York Times* column, "Data creates bigger haystacks, but the needle we are looking for is still buried deep inside."[24] Big population surveys are needed, but they are not a silver bullet—at most they can serve as a signpost pointing in the direction of more carefully targeted qualitative research or research that might lay bare causal relations. Such research also needs to be fully gendered; that is, it needs to examine both men and women in their dynamic relational roles.

The Example of Sexual Violence in Conflict and Postconflict Settings

The way sexual violence in conflict and postconflict settings is understood is a prime example of why a gendered framework is necessary to fully comprehend the complexity of this phenomenon. Understanding sexual violence as being at the intersection of gender identity and power relations was a central theme of an international symposium, "The Missing Peace Symposium 2013: Sexual Violence in Conflict and Post-

Conflict Settings," held at the United States Institute of Peace in Washington, D.C., in February 2013. As one of the participants noted, this was the first international dialogue that "mainstreamed men" in its deliberations, and whose participants recognized that policies and strategies dealing with sexual violence cannot be developed without understanding the full continuum of experiences of both men and women. The current predominant approach in expert and policy circles that focuses on women as the victims of sexual violence and men as the perpetrators fails to recognize that there are also strong correlations between men as victims (including as witnesses) of sexual violence and their own perpetration of violence.[25] Effective preventive strategies need to address not just the issue of impunity for perpetrators but also the causes of sexual violence. Focusing only on women as victims prevents the development of a rich understanding of the complex dimensions of the phenomenon and the most promising ways of tackling it.

Sexual violence in war is a subset of "gender-based violence," an umbrella term for any harm that is perpetrated against a person's will and that results from power inequalities based on gender roles. Around the world, gender-based violence almost always has a greater negative impact on women and girls than on men. For this reason, the term "gender-based violence" is often used interchangeably with the term "violence against women." Gender-based violence, however, is not perpetrated only against women. As the academic, practitioner, and policy communities increasingly recognize, in conflict situations men and boys are also subject to sexual violence.

Sexual violence includes but is not limited to rape, sexual mutilation, sexual humiliation, forced prostitution, and pregnancy. The relationship between sexual violence in times of "peace" and conflict-related violence is complex. It is known that sexual violence in

the immediate aftermath of a peace settlement is often very high and related to sexual violence perpetrated during the war. One school of thought thus sees sexual violence as on a time continuum.[26] Another school of thought emphasizes the differences between conflict-related sexual violence and nonconflict-related sexual violence.[27] Wartime sexual violence and rape are often more brutal and public than nonconflict sexual violence and generally involve multiple perpetrators. In addition, some evidence suggests that "the lived experience of war" pushes some people to become perpetrators of sexual violence, including rape.[28] Finally, some scholars have suggested that wartime sexual violence has longer-term societal consequences than nonconflict-related sexual violence.[29] According to this view, wartime sexual violence is one of the invisible wounds of war that, unless addressed, will perpetuate conflict or at best hold back postconflict reconstruction efforts and the transition to peace.

International concern with sexual violence in conflict became codified in UNSCR 1325 and subsequent UN Security Council resolutions, most notably UNSCR 1820.[30] In 2013, the United Kingdom made the prevention of sexual violence in war a major initiative of the G8.[31] Such increased international attention to the issue of sexual violence is to be applauded, but some observers have warned that the current attention to sexual violence can make people lose sight of the gender dimensions involved. An unintended consequence of this focus is to confirm gendered stereotypes of women as sexual victims and sexual objects.[32]

In addition, much of the attention to sexual violence by policymakers is focused on legal recourse and punitive measures. The emphasis on prosecution has a tendency to lull some into the belief that the problem is being fully addressed through legal channels, when in fact most countries in which conflict-related sexual violence is an issue have little or no legal capacity to prosecute, much less to house, offenders.[33] The emphasis on prosecution and punitive measures reinforces the notion that sexual violence is just a problem involving a few bad actors.[34] Similarly, as pointed out by Samel Abdelnour, a researcher at the London School of Economics, the international community's embrace of fuel-efficient stoves as an answer to sexual violence has a tendency to transform "an overwhelming social and political issue into a resolvable technical problem." The idea that women were assaulted when looking for fuel and water outside camps or villages gradually took root. It led to a vast expansion of "clean stoves" programs, not just in the name of health and environmental concerns but also as a measure that could reduce "the personal security risks" faced by women. "The logic that stoves can prevent sexual violence is a media friendly dead end. It raises public awareness of global sexual violence, but masks the root causes of the phenomenon."[35]

Rape and sexual assault should be seen not just as horrific crimes committed by and against individuals, but also as an instrument and tactic of war, and a manifestation and symptom of patterns of domination and criminal activity, or even a type of terrorism within a given society or country. A response that focuses solely on the technical, physical, and psychosocial aftermaths of sexual violence or that allows only for redress and accountability, is not sufficient. The underlying causes of sexual violence need to be confronted, both in the context of conflict and postconflict settings, and years later, when a society has forgotten the day-to-day impacts of war but bears their lasting imprint in the form of the normalization of sexual violence as a tool of power, rank, and intimidation.

Misconceptions about Sexual Violence

Most scholars agree that there are many misguided assumptions regarding sexual violence in war, assumptions that, unfortunately, are often perpetuated in public discourses. A report by Elisabeth Wood, Dara Cohen, and Amelia Hoover Green published in February 2013 identified five of these major assumptions.[36]

First, the authors debunk the common notion that wartime rape is inevitable. Public discourse often focuses on the "testosterone argument," which presumes that men have uncontrollable sexual desires that are kept in check only by learned societal norms. As this argument goes, in times of war, those norms break down and men revert to a state of "nature." Feminist scholars, for their part, often emphasize more structural factors such as gender inequality and patriarchy. They focus on how war amplifies gender inequalities and pushes gender relations to extremes. That said, the research of scholars such as Wood, Cohen, and Hoover Green shows that conflict-related sexual violence varies greatly in terms of type, prevalence, and target.[37] Wood also rejects the structural patriarchy argument. Indeed, she has discovered that in many conflicts there are asymmetric patterns of rape—where one group engages in patterns of rape and other groups do not. Patriarchy may be a necessary condition, but in and of itself it does not explain sexual violence in war. In explaining variation in sexual violence within and between conflicts, recent research has also focused on armed groups and their institutions, rather than on national and cultural differences. This research has found that government forces are more likely to be perpetrators of rape than rebel groups,[38] and that groups that recruit by abductions are also more likely to resort to rape than those who recruit on a more voluntary basis.[39]

A second misconception, as mentioned above, is that sexual violence affects only women. Recent research by a new generation of scholars on sexual violence, has uncovered that while women are mostly affected, men and boys are also victims of sexual violence, but the question was simply not asked. This is another example of why gender must be an inclusive analytical tool and cannot be focused on only one sex. In addition, recent research has uncovered that females may also perpetrate sexual violence in the context of conflict as a form of group initiation and hazing rituals. In the DRC, Haiti, and Rwanda, a significant number of women have engaged in sexual violence.

A third misconception, particularly popular among current policymakers in international discourse, is that widespread sexual violence is always a strategy of war. In many instances, however, sexual violence is not so much ordered as it is tolerated, which undermines the idea that sexual violence only occurs due to explicit wartime strategy. In most cases, sexual violence is more of an expression of dominance and power than it is an overt wartime strategy. This nuance, of course, does not make such violence any less of a problem, but it does mean that responses to it will have to be different and tailored to precipitating factors.

A fourth misconception is that conflict-related sexual violence is chiefly a recent and African problem. However, history is replete with instances of widespread sexual violence in war, from that described in Homer's *Iliad*, to the accounts of the 1915 Armenian genocide, the Japanese assault on Nanjing in 1937, the partition of India and the creation of Pakistan, and the Bangladeshi war of independence in 1971. Recent research has also shown that sexual violence has proportionally been more of a problem in Eastern Europe than in Africa. That is, between 1980 and 2009 State Department data reported a higher level of rape in conflicts in

Eastern Europe than in conflicts in Africa.[40] Unfortunately, sexual violence is a problem that is encountered across history, diverse societies, and continents.[41]

A fifth misconception is that sexual violence is increasing. In reality, no one is sure if it is increasing or not. What is known is that reports of sexual violence have increased,[42] but more reports do not necessarily equate to higher levels of violence.

POLICY RECOMMENDATIONS AND TASKS FOR THE FUTURE

International efforts to tackle sexual violence in conflict and postconflict settings must acquire a more nuanced understanding of the nature, variety, and causal elements of such violence. Sexual violence is a subset of gender-based violence, and any response to or understanding of these phenomena should take that into account. There is no such thing as a gender-neutral approach. The gendered nature of institutions, structures, and many national and international programs not only predetermines who participates in or is targeted by the violence but also affects how problems are articulated and how solutions are envisaged. The political discourse on sexual violence always seems to be prone to intellectual shortcuts and has a tendency to perpetuate widely held erroneous beliefs; these shortcuts and misconceptions can render policy responses inadequate or, worse, may actually aggravate the situation.[43]

If the international community is to craft more effective responses, it needs to build on the spirit of UNSCR 1325. UNSCR 1325 is not a resolution about women or gender per se, but a resolution about how best to establish and maintain international peace and security. Through this resolution, members of the UN Security Council recognized that they needed to be more attentive to the effects of their policies on different groups in societies. The member states recognized that they needed to be smarter when using their policy tools, whether coercive, such as the use of force and economic sanctions, or cooperative, such as peacekeeping, humanitarian relief, and postconflict reconstruction assistance.

Being smarter means recognizing that policy tools may have different effects on different groups in society, and particularly on men and women. Violent conflict and wars alter gender relations, needs, and capacities; policymakers and civil society actors in those environments need to recognize these changes. Failure to do so may mean that a given policy or action falls flat or, worse, backfires.[44] While this may seem self-evident, the conceptual tools for understanding international relations often take issues at face value and presume that events occur in a gender-neutral rather than a gendered environment.

Building a better understanding of gender relations in conflict will involve accomplishing a series of important tasks by a wide range of actors. The first of these tasks is to "mainstream" research on gender and UNSCR 1325 within the broader international relations and security studies research agendas. All long-term security projections acknowledge that empowerment and gender equality are going to be key factors for peace and stability in the twenty-first century. Thus, if scholars of international relations and security studies want to remain relevant, gender analysis in peace and security must become better understood and integrated in curriculum and practice.

A second task is to consider each of the four pillars of UNSCR 1325—prevention, participation, relief and recovery, and protection—when reflecting upon international intervention strategies in Afghanistan, Syria and the Middle East, the DRC, and Mali, to name but a few of the current pressing international crises. The increasing number of countries (fifty-five, as of this writing) that have developed national action plans to implement UNSCR 1325 provide additional opportunities to cooperate in this regard.

The third task is to gather more refined gender data and to undertake more research that can better illuminate the need to understand gender as a dynamic force in our conceptions of the peace and security field. Researchers have a unique opportunity to help shape and drive national and international efforts to collect more rigorous sex-disaggregated data. Policymakers and practitioners alike recognize the paucity of data collection efforts thus far. In launching Data2X, Hillary Clinton emphasized that "data not only measures progress, it inspires it." She added that "once you start measuring problems, people are more inclined to take action to fix them."[45] There is currently a rare window of opportunity for researchers to contribute directly and immediately to policy debates by actively engaging in discussions on gaps and areas for expansion in data collection. In addition, more qualitative research that allows for contextualization and that is action-oriented is needed. There are still too many gaps in the knowledge base about what works under which conditions.

A fourth task is to develop collaborative partnerships across North and South and among researchers, practitioners, and policymakers to bridge divides and develop more innovative approaches to this issue. Sexual violence in conflict and postconflict settings is a multidimensional problem that requires the engagement of many different stakeholders at many different levels. Only then can the issue be addressed effectively.

Lastly, researchers and academics need to approach the multidimensional nexus of gender, peace, and security with more imagination. UNSCR 1325 is a unique and potentially transformative international instrument. It recognizes that the gap between men and women and the violence against women and men in preconflict, conflict, and postconflict situations are indicative of dysfunctional and disruptive patterns of state domination and that they make interstate and intrastate aggression more likely.[46] No task is more noble and pressing than helping to uncover the conditions under which this is so, and thus contributing to a more peaceful and secure international order.

NOTES

Parts of this chapter are based on Kathleen Kuehnast, Chantal de Jonge Oudraat, and Helga Hernes, eds., *Women and War: Power and Protection in the 21st Century* (Washington, DC: United States Institute of Peace Press, 2011); and Chantal de Jonge Oudraat, "UNSCR 1325: Conundrums," *International Interactions* 39, no. 4 (2013): 612–19.

1. The report posited: "Although data on political involvement are less conclusive than those regarding economic participation, political empowerment of women appears to change governmental priorities. Examples as disparate as Sweden and Rwanda indicate that countries with relatively large numbers of politically active women place greater importance on societal issues such as healthcare, the environment, and economic development. If this trend continues over the next 15–20 years, as is likely, an increasing number of countries could favor social programs over military ones. Better governance also could be a spin-off benefit, as a high number of women in parliament or senior government positions correlates with lower corruption." See *Global Trends 2025: A Transformed World* (Washington, DC: National Intelligence Council, November 2008), 16.

2. See the World Bank's website, http://www.worldbank.org/mdgs/gender.html. The idea that gender equality has importance for society more broadly, and that the empowerment of women can change policy choices and make institutions more representative of a range of voices, was also echoed in the *2012 World Bank Development Report on Gender Equality and Development*.

3. See, for example, Valerie M. Hudson, Mary Capriolo, Bonnie Ballif-Spanvill, Rise Mc-

Dermott, and Chad F. Emmet, "The Heart of the Matter: The Security of Women and the Security of States," *International Security* 33, no. 3 (Winter 2008–2009): 27.

4. Remarks by Kofi Annan, quoted in *UN Daily News*, February 28, 2005, http://www.un.org/apps/news/story.asp?NewsID=13478&Cr=commission&Cr1=women. See also the remarks by Kofi Annan on March 8, 2006, SG/SM/10370. For a nuanced view of women empowerment and economic development, see Esther Duflo, "Women Economic Empowerment and Economic Development," *Journal of Economic Literature* 50, no. 4 (2012): 1051–79, http://dx/10.1257/jel.50.4.1051.

5. The adoption of UNSCR 1325 was the result of active mobilization of civil society groups—particularly women's groups—as well as recognition by international policymakers that approaches for dealing with violent conflict in the post–Cold War era had important shortcomings. It emphasized the importance of including women at peace negotiating tables and recognized the inordinate effects of war on women. The resolution also focused international attention on the issue of sexual violence in conflict and the need for greater protection for women. For more, see Sanam Anderlini, *Women Building Peace: What They Do and Why It Matters* (Boulder, CO: Lynne Rienner, 2007); and Carol Cohn, "Mainstreaming Gender in UN Security Policy: A Path to Political Transformation?" Working Paper no. 204 (Boston Consortium on Gender, Security and Human Rights, Boston, MA), www.genderandsecurity.umb.edu?Cohn%20Working%Paper.pdf.

6. The responsibility to protect (R2P) resulted from the work of the International Commission on Intervention and State Sovereignty (ICISS), established in September 2000. It released its report *The Responsibility to Protect* in December 2001.

7. See Hudson et al., "Heart of the Matter," 7–45. In this article the authors show that the relative position of women in society is a good bellwether for peace and security. See also Valerie Hudson, Bonnie Ballif-Spanvill, Mary Capriolli, and Chad F. Emmett, *Sex and World Peace* (New York: Columbia University Press, 2012).

8. See Rupert Smith, *The Utility of Force: The Art of War in the Modern World* (New York: Knopf, 2007).

9. Realist and liberal approaches to international relations are focused on a level of analysis that tends to ignore agency and gender. Even constructivist analysis of international affairs, with its heavy focus on agency (i.e., actors), has mostly ignored the gender and the gendered nature of relationships among the actors it studies. Feminist scholars have focused on gender, but for many of them this was to offset a mostly male-dominated field and linked to a clear policy and advocacy agenda of women's empowerment. All camps seem to be set up for zero-sum games, whereby the gain of one is the loss of the other.

10. See, for example, Marc Sommers, *Stuck: Rwandan Youth and the Struggle for Adulthood* (Athens: University of Georgia Press, 2012).

11. For a further discussion, see Carol Cohn, "Women and Wars: Toward a Conceptual Framework," in *Women and Wars,* ed. Carol Cohn (Cambridge: Polity Press, 2013), 1–30.

12. This is a point frequently underscored by Sanam Anderlini. See, for example, Anderlini, *Women Building Peace.*

13. The same survey also. See Henny Slegh, Gary Barker, Benoit Ruratotoye, and Tim Shand, *Gender Relations, Sexual Violence and the Effects of Conflict on Women and Men in North Kivu, Eastern Democratic Republic of Congo: Preliminary Results from the International Men and Gender Equality Survey (IMAGES)* (Cape Town, South Africa: Sonke Gender Justice Network; Washington, DC: Promundo-US, 2012).

14. Quoted in Laura Sjoberg and Sandra Via, "Introduction," in *Gender, War and Militarism: Feminist Perspectives,* Laura Sjoberg and Sandra Via, ed. (Santa Barbara, CA: Praeger, 2010), 6.

15. See, for example, Gary Barker et al., *What Men Have to Do with It: Public Policies to Promote Gender Equality* (Washington, DC: International Center for Research on Women; Rio de Janeiro: Instituto Promundo, 2009). See also "The Involvement of Men in Gender Equality Initiatives in the European Union" (report prepared for the European Institute for Gender Equality, Vilnius, 2012); and the research of Marc Sommers on youth in Rwanda.

16. In 1997, the United Nations Economic and Social Council (ECOSOC) defined gender mainstreaming as "the process of assessing the implications for women and men of any planned action, including legislations, policies or programmes, in any area and at all levels. . . . The ultimate goal of mainstreaming is to achieve gender equality."

17. Gender mainstreaming ultimately has as its aim gender equality. In mainstreaming gender, policies or programs need to be cognizant of not reproducing gender stereotypes.

18. On gender mainstreaming, see also Theodora-Ismene Gizelis, "Gender Equality and Post-conflict Reconstruction: What Do We Need to Know in Order to Make Gender Mainstreaming Work?" *International Interactions* 39, no. 4 (2013): 425–34.

19. In this regard, it is also important to underscore that there is no one universal form of masculinity (as there is no one form of femininity).

20. See Oystein Gullvag Holter, Helge Svare, and Catherine Egeland, *Gender Equality and Quality of Life: A Norwegian Perspective* (Oslo: Nordic Gender Institute [NIKK], 2009).

21. See US Secretary of State Hillary Clinton, "Remarks on Evidence and Impact: Closing the Gender Data Gap, July 19, 2011" (US State Department, July 19, 2012). The initiative involves major international institutions—including the United Nations, the World Bank, the OSCE, PARIS21, and Gallup—and aims to increase the collection of sex-disaggregated data.

22. See Erik Melander and Elin Bjaregard, "Revisiting Representation: Communism and the Decline of Civil War in East Asia," *International Interactions* 39, no. 4 (2013): 558–74. See also Anita Schjolset, "Data on Women's Participation in NATO Forces and Operations," *International Interactions* 39, no. 4 (2013): 575–87.

23. Human Security Report Project, *Human Security Report 2012, Sexual Violence, Education and War: Beyond the Mainstream Narrative* (Vancouver: Human Security Research Group/Human Security Press, 2012)

24. David Brooks, "The Philosophy of Data," *New York Times,* February 4, 2013.

25. See Slegh, et al., *Gender Relations, Sexual Violence and the Effects of Conflict on Women and Men in North Kivu.*

26. See, for example, Jelke Boesten and Melissa Fisher, "Sexual Violence and Justice in Postconflict Peru," Special Report no. 310 (Washington, DC: United States Institute of Peace, June 2012).

27. See, for example, Elisabeth Wood, "Armed Groups and Sexual Violence: When Is Wartime Rape Rare?" *Politics and Society* 37, no. 1 (2009): 131–61.

28. Elisabeth Wood, "Variation in Sexual Violence during War," *Politics and Society* 34, no. 3 (2006): 323.

29. Ibid.

30. In the run-up to UNSCR 1325, three different situations and events served to focus international attention on sex crimes in war: the war in the former Yugoslavia and the reporting on rape camps; the coming forward of the Korean "comfort women" for Japanese soldiers during World War II; and the 1995 "Fourth World Conference on Women" in Beijing.

31. More specifically, the UK G8 initiative seeks to: shift the balance of shame from survivors to perpetrators; increase the number of perpetrators brought to justice; strengthen national efforts to prosecute; and support states in building national capacities. The United Kingdom has also created a team of rapidly deployable teams of experts in conflict and postconflict situations. These teams are composed of doctors, forensics experts, and others who can help with investigation and prosecution as well as care of victims. In 2013, the UK team deployed in Turkey on the border with Syria and was involved in a training mission in Mali.

32. This was also a theme throughout "The Missing Peace Symposium 2013."

33. There are some eerie similarities with the international response to war in the Balkans in the 1990s and the idea that the establishment of an international criminal tribunal for Yugoslavia would help deter further crimes in the Balkans. But then and now, there is little evidence that this type of deterrence actually works.

34. Gina Heathcote has in this regard been critical of the "naming and shaming" approach adopted in UNSCR 1960. She has argued that shaming has little effect when targeted at nonstate actors, who have little respect for the institution that shames.

35. See Samer Abdelnour, "Is Sexual Violence Being Efficiently Addressed in Global Conflict Zones?" *Risk and Regulation* (Spring 2013): 10–11.

36. See Dara Cohen, Amelia Hoover Green, and Elisabeth Wood, "Wartime Sexual Violence: Misconceptions, Implications, and Ways Forward," Special Report no. 323 (Washington, DC: United States Institute of Peace, February 2013). This report was commissioned by the organizers of the symposium "Missing Peace: Sexual Violence in Conflict and Post-Conflict Settings." Indeed, the organizers of Missing Peace (the United States Institute of Peace, SIPRI North America, the Peace Research Institute Oslo, and the Human Rights Center of the University of California at Berkeley) were of the view that these misperceptions were widely held and turned to three of the most innovative researchers in the field.

37. Ibid.

38. Wood, "Variation in Sexual Violence during War." See also Elisabeth Jean Wood, "Rape Is Not Inevitable during War," in *Women and War: Power and Protection in the 21st Century,* ed. Kathleen Kuehnast, Chantal de Jonge Oudraat, and Helga Hernes (Washington, DC: United States Institute of Peace Press, 2011), 37–63.

39. Cohen et al., "Wartime Sexual Violence," 8.

40. Wood, "Rape Is Not Inevitable during War," 37–63.

41. See also Ragnhild Nordås, "Preventing Conflict-related Sexual Violence," PRIO Policy Brief 02-2013 (Peace Research Institute Oslo, 2013); Dara Kay Cohen and Ragnhild Nordås, "Sexual Violence by Militias in African Conflicts: Not a Question of 'Delegation' by States," PRIO Policy Brief 01-2012 (Centre for the Study of Civil War, Peace Research Institute Oslo, 2012); Dara Kay Cohen and Ragnhild Nordås, "Sexual Violence in African Conflicts, 1989–2009: What the Data Show," PRIO Policy Brief (Peace Research Institute Oslo, 2012); and Ragnhild Nordås, "Sexual Violence on the Decline? Recent Debates and Evidence Suggest 'Unlikely,'" CSCW Policy Brief 03-2012 (Centre for the Study of Civil War, Peace Research Institute Oslo, 2012).

42. The 2012 *Human Security Report* argued that the number of sexual assaults in time of war had decreased. They based their argument on the fact that the number of violent conflicts and battle deaths had decreased. However, there is no known correlation between battle deaths and sexual violence.

43. For more on these "myths," see Cohen et al., "Wartime Sexual Violence."

44. Erik Melander and Elin Bjaregard express concern about the instrumentalization of UNSCR 1325 and the notion that gender balancing (gender equality and representation) is promoted as an effective instrument for establishing and maintaining international peace and security rather than as "issues of justice, in their own right." Melander and Bjaregard also argue that claims for greater women's representation in peace negotiations "may reinforce, rather than eliminate, gendered stereotypes by essentializing women and nurturers, having a pacifying effect on peace negotiations and decision-making at large." We would argue that, as compelling as the moral-and-justice argument may be, the effectiveness argument, particularly if backed up by solid evidence, will trump the justice argument and allow a broader coalition of actors to start paying attention. In addition, a UNSCR 1325 stated objective is the restoration and maintenance of international peace and security—we would not know of a more important objective.

45. See Clinton, "Remarks on Evidence and Impact."

46. See also Hudson, *Sex and World Peace.*

PART IV

THE TOOLS AND USE OF CONFLICT MANAGEMENT

22

THE TOOLS OF NEGOTIATION

Fen Osler Hampson and I. William Zartman

> The term "negotiation" means the art of handling the affairs of state. . . . However negotiation is not limited to international affairs. It takes place everywhere where there are differences to conciliate, interests to placate, men to persuade, and purpose to accomplish. Thus, all life could be regarded as a continual negotiation. We always need to win friends, overcome enemies, correct unfortunate impressions, convince others of our views, and use all appropriate means to further our projects.
> —Fortune Barthélemy de Felice, *Dictionnaire de justice naturelle et civile*

Aesop tells of the wager between the Sun and the Wind as to who can make a man remove his coat.[1] When the Wind blustered, the man only drew his coat more tightly around him. When the Sun shone brightly, the man took it off. Negotiators have many ways of talking, sometimes tough and blustery sometimes sweet and sunny.

Power is resources plus will and skill. Resources, especially military power, stand behind their expression, but the way they are wielded is what makes the effect, and that way is through words. Talking needs reality behind it, but the reality of resources is brutish. The world is what it seems, not what it is, and talk shapes that perception. If that were not evident throughout history, it hits us between the eyes in the twenty-first century as we watch the world rattled to its foundations by financial crises, the Arab Spring, WikiLeaks, and Edward Snowden's revelations about Internet eavesdropping by the US National Security Agency.

Words can be used in many ways, but just because they are words and not the resources on which words sit, they should not be taken as something soft and flabby, as opposed to the iron men who prove their mettle with their muscles. Talk is the way words are loaded and fired, and it can come out as smoke, as buckshot, or as a rifle bullet, among other forms. These forms can be named and discussed, so as to identify the ways and times they can be used effectively and the traps to avoid.

This chapter describes the different ways that negotiators can talk to parties who are in conflict. We argue that there is more than one way to negotiate and that effective diplomacy begins with a proper understanding of the different tools that are in a negotiator's toolkit. Yet, we must emphasize that good negotiation strategy does not rely exclusively on one set of tools. One does not use a lathe to hammer a nail or a screwdriver to loosen a rusty pipe fitting. Good diplomacy, like good construction, means using the right tools for the right task at the right moment. It also means having a well-conceived plan of action before starting work.

THE NEGOTIATOR'S TOOLKIT

There are a baker's dozen different ways to negotiate. *Tough Talk* expresses firm position, threats, and sanctions. It is talk that is usually backed by military firepower or economic clout and muscle. *Straight Talk* means telling things as they are, particularly in regard to alternatives. Straight Talk is sober and honest discussion about what the present course bodes and what must be done to rectify a bad situation. *Sweet Talk* contains a vast array of inducements, from references to higher values (flattery), to promises of solid inducements (bribery), to soothing words that ease feelings of hurt and damaged pride (solace). *Happy Talk* emphasizes a better future, building castles on the horizon for the parties to share. It is the kind of talk that tries to get the parties to see the possibilities of building a better world for themselves and their constituents. *Small Talk* focuses on the details of getting to a better place—the proverbial "who does what, when, where, and how" under a set of negotiated commitments, principles, and formulas—where the devil is said to reside and whose neglect has led many good dreams to be drowned. *Right Talk* is wordsmithing, editorial diplomacy, choosing that special right word to convey an idea when apparent synonyms do not express quite the same thing. *Trash Talk* is a put-down, occasionally useful if deployed at the right moment in the right way. Humiliating or denigrating rivals is sometimes a necessary tool of diplomacy—especially if the rivals misbehave or are way out of line—but Trash Talk is mostly something to be saved for those rare occasions when friendly negotiation is not an option.

These kinds of talk are the major tools of diplomacy. They are the "cutting" or "moving" tools of negotiation, which push, coax, or seduce parties from their entrenched positions. They are tools that have to be used as part of a long-term plan of action to achieve a definable set of political goals. There are also other kinds of negotiation tools of a procedural nature, which can be used to bind, shape, and fasten the parties to a negotiation process much like a welding iron or rivet gun. And any negotiator, like a construction worker, sometimes has to don protective gear on an extremely hazardous work site.

Sticky Talk makes the negotiating encounter part of a process, and is often needed to keep the conflicting parties at the job of making peace and away from the alternative of making war. Like a rivet gun, Sticky Talk binds the parties to talks and agreements and makes it difficult for them to break free or walk away from the negotiating table when the discussion gets tough and concessions become costly. *Safe Talk* is like protective gear that takes a negotiation out of the harsh glare of a damaging media spotlight. Safe Talk is critical when the secrecy of a private conversation is the key to building trust and getting agreement. It is the operative part of "open covenants, secretly arrived at," to amend Woodrow Wilson's words. Safe Talk can be useful when simply being seen in the company of sworn enemies or recognizing their claims can blow up a peace process.

Timely Talk is talk that takes place before the parties have started to throw bricks at each other. It is talk directed at getting the parties to commit to a political as opposed to a violent solution to settle their differences, by seizing the ripe moment in the conflict or making the moment ripe when the conflict dynamics have not done so. *Street Talk* seeks to generate public support for a peace process before formal negotiations begin or when they are stalled. It can also be used after a formal political settlement is concluded to get buy-in from the public.

Just as clear, effective, and timely communication between workers is important on a work site, any diplomatic venture requires the establishment of proper and effective channels of communications. *Triple Talk* is mediated negotiation, where direct two-party talks have become impossible for various reasons that the mediator must overcome. It includes shuttle diplomacy, for example, where the mediator becomes the telephone, creatively carrying messages between the conflicting parties.

Most construction jobs require more than one kind of tradesperson. On any site, surveyors, heavy equipment operators, framers, bricklayers, roofers, electricians, and carpenters all must work together as a team to get the job done. Likewise, modern diplomacy requires different kinds of "tradespeople" who bring different capabilities and resources to the negotiating table. Some are equipped to do the heavy lifting in negotiations because they are well endowed with reward or coercive power. That is to say, they can back up Sweet Talk by offering positive inducements to the parties, and when they resort to Tough Talk, they are credible because they have the military or sanctioning capacity to provide pressure. Others are more suited for Straight Talk or Happy Talk roles because they are extremely knowledgeable about the issues and/or have good relations with the parties, so that when they speak the truth or paint a rosy picture of the future, they are credible interlocutors. Still others may act as a go-between, ferrying messages between the parties because they can be trusted to keep secrets, not distort the message, or play fast with the truth.

Most diplomatic undertakings require more than one kind of negotiator or interlocutor. *Team Talk* is the process of bringing different parties—sometimes even rivals—together in a shared enterprise so that they work effectively as a team and do not undermine a negotiation by freelancing or talking at cross purposes. *Stop Talk* is the threat of bringing diplomacy to a halt, by turning off the power switch and letting the parties stew in their own juice.

◆ ◆ ◆

There are many ways to handle the substance of a political dispute or a problem. Some of them emphasize how bad the current situation is and therefore the need to get out of it; others emphasize how good the future could be and ways to get into it. Tough, Straight, Trash, and Stop Talk fall into the first category; Sweet, Street, and Happy Talk are in the second; and Small and Timely Talk bridge the two. Each deserves a fuller, illustrated discussion.

TOUGH TALK

Richard Holbrooke, the US negotiator who helped bring an end to the brutal wars on Europe's doorstep in the Balkans in the early to mid-1990s, was known as a tough talker, which is why he was chosen to talk to Serbia's leader Slobodan Milosevic, Bosnia's Muslim leader Alija Izetbegovic, and Croatia's Franjo Tudjman about the status of Bosnia in the mid-1990s, and then again to Milosevic about the status of Kosovo in the late 1990s. His assignment came after previous envoys, including former British foreign minister David Owen and former US secretary of state Cyrus Vance, were not able to talk sweetly enough in selling a plan for peace and government in Bosnia to the same antagonists.

In the Middle East, Secretary of State John Kerry talked tough as he edged the two sides to revive the Israeli-Palestinian talks toward a two-state solution in 2013, and threw in Timely Talk and a Stop Talk deadline to reinforce the toughness. President Jimmy Carter was known to be a tough talker if the moment required. He leveled with Egyptian president Anwar al-Sadat and Israeli prime minister Menachem Begin at the Camp David Mideast Peace Summit in 1978. Secretary of State James Baker was legendary for his directness and toughness. He posed "serious conditions" and "unforeseen consequences"[2] to Prime Minister Yitzhak Shamir to force him to attend the Madrid Conference in 1991—something Shamir was loathe to do because the leader of the Palestine Liberation Organization, Yasser Arafat, was going to be there. President Bill Clinton was occasionally a tough talker, but he didn't always get the timing right. He talked tough to the Palestinians only after the Camp David meetings broke down in 2000. Tough Talk during the actual negotiations could have made a difference by keeping Arafat, who allegedly "never missed an opportunity to miss an opportunity," properly engaged.[3] President George W. Bush shied away from Tough Talk altogether in his various visits to the Middle East in 2008 because he did not want to offend Israel, although Tough Talk by an American president to both sides, Israelis and Palestinians, would have accelerated the peace process.

Tough Talk need not be hostile, although sometimes hostility is needed to make the point. "Never get angry, except on purpose," said the US diplomat Harlan Cleveland.[4] But it does take persistence, insistence, repetition, and rephrasing. One's own needs and views are frequently not obvious to other parties, nor are they always in harmony with other parties' interests, needs, and views. "The secret of negotiation is to reconcile the interests of the parties," wrote François de Callières to the young French King Louis XV three hundred years ago. "The two principal purposes of a negotiator are to do the business of his master and to discover that of the other."[5]

Tough Talk serves as the bookends of any negotiation. If tough and clear words are appropriate at the beginning of negotiations, as the parties make their needs and interests

known, they also are called for at the end, as the parties move closer to agreement. The endgame of any negotiation is not the time to go soft, but rather the moment to press toward a goal in sight, with insistence on the principles and details that make an outcome solid. In between, a party can relax the sharpness of the tone in order to give the other party leeway to think creatively of a way out of the conflict or impasse. Similarly, content has a relation to its bearer; when the other side is talking tough, it is sometimes necessary to call its bluff by retorting in kind, lest it begin to feel it can bully its way through. The United States does this regularly with North Korea, alone and in concert. Often bullies are stopped only by momentary counterbullying to show that this kind of tactic will lead nowhere, to be relaxed when the other party changes its tone.

STRAIGHT TALK

Negotiation begins with a clear exposé of one's positions and, behind them, one's interests—that is to say, what "really" matters. This diagnosis phase of negotiation is the time when one party must make sure the other side understands what the stakes are.

Clearing the way to frank exchanges in search of a remedy to a problem frequently requires letting the other "know how much I hurt and how much you are the cause of my hurting." In effect, one is saying "if this situation continues, we will never resolve our problems." As Jan Egeland, the former state secretary in the Norwegian Ministry of Foreign Affairs who helped facilitate the Oslo peace process recalls:

The two teams were determined to break away from the tradition set by earlier Israeli-Palestinian talks and most Jewish-Arab discussions and agreed not to dwell on the past. I remember both sides saying during the very first meetings: "If we are to quarrel about the historic rights to these holy lands, about who was there first, or about who betrayed whom and when, we will sit here quarreling forever. We must agree to look to the future."[6]

Straight Talk is also a way to expose a lie and show a cheater to be what he or she is. An ambassador is often thought of as someone sent abroad to lie for his country. But as François de Callières observed, "the use of deceit in diplomacy is of necessity restricted, for there is no curse which comes quicker to roost than a lie which has been found out."[7] In the Strategic Arms Reduction Talks (START), the US negotiators gained an edge and surprised the Soviets by revealing information about the Soviet arsenal that some of the Soviet negotiators did not know. In July 1983, the United States went public with the revelation that US intelligence had detected a large early-warning radar system being constructed near the city of Krasnoyarsk in Siberia. Because the installation was more than 800 kilometers away from the nearest Soviet border, it was deemed to be in violation of the Anti-Ballistic Missile Treaty the two countries had signed in 1972 that mandated that radars had to be located on the national periphery of each country and be oriented outward.

One of the boldest uses of Straight Talk came during the Cuban Missile Crisis, when US Ambassador to the United Nations Adlai Stevenson, waving aerial photos, gained an enormous point before a world audience by telling the Soviet ambassador that "I will wait till hell freezes over for you to admit that you lied about missiles in Cuba."[8] Straight Talk does not necessarily mean telling *all* the truth, but it does mean being truthful in what one tells.

Straight Talk is more than not lying, however. It is making the parties face unpleasant facts in a search for a solution. It is a cool look at the conflict as a painful mess in which the parties have caught themselves and that

threatens to get worse. Sometimes negotiating parties need to be brought up against the hard facts of the situation so that they can focus on real solutions to real problems instead of hiding in fantasy. In 1997, when the Carter Center's negotiating team was working to develop a deal among the three "presidents" of Congo-Brazzaville, two of whom were in exile but thought themselves still rightly in office, one of the mediators took the risk of offending Pascal Lissouba by saying, "Mr. President, Let me remind you: you are no longer in office nor in Brazzaville, but Sasso Nguesso is!" Lissouba's tone suddenly changed, and he turned to the problem at hand.[9]

Straight Talk is particularly useful in bringing out real alternatives to a negotiated solution, known as security points or BATNAs (Best Alternatives to a Negotiated Agreement). "If you don't like what we're doing, and you think you can get the Golan back in any other way, then go ahead and get it back," Secretary Baker snapped at President Hafez al-Assad as he worked to set up the 1991 Madrid Conference. "Assad and I made eye contact," Baker recalls. "He seemed to sense that we had reached a certain unhealthy threshold" and gave in.[10]

Alternatives are perhaps the major source of power in negotiation: If one's security point is high (close to a potential negotiated outcome), the negotiator is strong and can be tough, but if it is low (much worse than a possible negotiated solution), the negotiator is in a weaker position. Negotiations often take place between alternatives rather than between positions; parties try to weaken each other's alternatives or strengthen their own. This means telling it like it is, pointing out to the other party that its alternative is not as good as it appears, using Straight Talk.

When is the right time to talk straight? The context should decide: when the point to be made is firm and important, it is necessary to say so. And when the position of the other side is fixed and unrewarding, it is time to say so, too. Negotiation, as has been noted, is giving something to get something; parties too often tend to think of the getting without considering the giving, and Straight Talk is often necessary to make them think about the compensation that is required to get the rewards they want from an agreement.

SWEET TALK

"I think that you and I, with our heavy responsibilities for the maintenance of peace, were aware that developments were approaching a point where events could have become unmanageable. So I welcome this message and consider it an important contribution to peace," wrote President John F. Kennedy to Chairman Nikita Khrushchev, after the Soviet Union had embroiled the world in a fast-moving crisis by installing atomic missiles in Cuba and had been dissuaded by careful, deliberate, restrained US diplomacy. Recognizing the other side's constructive contribution to securing an agreement, even if undeserved, is an important ingredient of sound diplomacy.

Looking ahead to other kinds of cooperative endeavors is important, too, especially if relationships are to be put on a sounder footing. Kennedy went on to discuss in his letter how the United States and Soviet Union could work more closely together toward the common goal of global disarmament:

> Mr. Chairman, both of our countries have great unfinished tasks and I know that your people as well as those of the United States can ask for nothing better than to pursue them free from the fear of war. . . . I agree with you that we must devote urgent attention to the problem of disarmament, as it relates to the whole world and also to critical areas. Perhaps now, as we step back from

danger, we can together make real progress in this vital field.[11]

"Don't crow!" is a key piece of advice that diplomats give to each other and to politicians. However, Kennedy needed no such instructions. As his brother Robert Kennedy recounted:

> After it [the Cuban Missile Crisis] was finished, he made no statement attempting to take credit for himself or for the Administration for what had occurred. He instructed all members of the Ex Comm and government that no interview should be given, no statement made, which would claim any kind of victory. He respected Khrushchev for properly determining what was in his own country's interest and what was in the interest of mankind. If it was a triumph, it was a triumph for the next generation and not for any particular government or people.[12]

Agreements must be bought: If you can't take it, you have to buy it, and negotiation is the means of setting the price. Hagglers in a bazaar know this. In the more sophisticated world of diplomacy, the method is known as compensation, that is, promising the other party items that he or she values in exchange for items the first party values. In the Cuban Missile Crisis, the agreement with the Soviets was "bought" with the promise that the United States would remove its nuclear-armed Jupiter missiles from Turkey in a secret deal that was worked out between Robert Kennedy and Soviet ambassador Anatoly Dobrynin.[13] However, diplomats and politicians often forget the need for exchange, because they focus on the items they value, forgetting that the other party is looking for items it values in order to clinch the deal. It is fair game, and sometimes necessary, to bring additional items into the discussion in order to make a mutually satisfactory deal.

In the late 1970s, President Carter launched an initiative to win independence for South West Africa, telling South Africa, the colonial occupier, that it had a moral obligation to leave and would get nothing (not even praise, because it would remain the apartheid state) in exchange. The attempt failed. Under President Ronald Reagan, Assistant Secretary of State Chester Crocker assured South Africa of positive treatment if it would withdraw its troops from South West Africa (and also from neighboring Angola) and, as part of the bargain, the United States would secure the withdrawal of Cuban troops from Angola (whose presence was South Africa's excuse for having its own troops there). Sweet Talk was backed by rewarding action.

HAPPY TALK

"What we are trying to do is to show North Korea that there is a better way to achieve security than excessive armament, and that is to join the security arrangements of the international community," is how US undersecretary Christopher Hill laid out the alternatives to Pyongyang, showing a better way to achieving its goals.[14] Happy Talk is the complement of Straight Talk. The purpose of negotiation is to work out a more pleasant future to replace the unpleasant present. No negotiation will succeed if the parties do not feel that they are better off when the negotiation is over. But "better off" is a comparative concept. Each party must be aware of the alternative that the other party has in mind. A party that may be hurting now may have an eye on a glorious day in the future when all will be golden again: "Next year in Jerusalem." Or it may be focusing on its current condition, seeking a way out of present pain. Obviously, an agreement will have to be more promising in the first case than in the second. But whatever the reference point, the agreement must be presented as attractive to the other side, not just to one's own side.

As the quotation from Ambassador Hill indicates, positive outcomes need to be couched in terms defined by the other side as attractive, but they can come in several forms. This can be done in one of three ways: compromise, compensation, or construction. Compromise is the riskiest, because it is essentially zero sum—"what you get I lose"—and means that each side gives up a bit of the contested item as they both move toward a midpoint. A stark example is found in the intense debates at Camp David (2000) and elsewhere between Palestinians and Israelis over the percentage of the West Bank and Jerusalem that would constitute (along with Gaza) the Palestinian state. Compensation means giving something else to get something, and is based on the premise that the stakes can be divided into those that matter more to one side and less to the other, and that a satisfying exchange can take place. A happy example is the case of South West Africa/Namibia between Angola and South Africa, mentioned above. Construction involves redefining the issues into a common goal that can benefit both sides. Under the assistance of hemispheric mediators, Peru and Ecuador overcame the zero-sum legal boundary dispute by turning to the goal of the development of the border region, which required the cooperation of both parties. The same idea was offered by Shimon Peres in his plan for "the New Middle East," but the idea was stillborn and failed to shake the parties from their zero-sum view of the conflict.

SMALL TALK

The devil is in the details, as every negotiator knows. After the parties have agreed on a formula outlining the terms of trade or the basic principles of justice or the identification of the problems and its solution, they then turn to fleshing out this general agreement with its application in fine print. Each party must make sure that the specific distribution of outcomes fits the general formula and then that each detail is satisfying in itself. Which 93 percent or 96 percent of the West Bank will constitute the Palestinian state, which settlements will remain where, what additional 7 percent or 4 percent will come out of Israel? Israel's talks with Syria broke down over a piece of Galilean shoreline, and almost broke down in 1974 over three small hills around Quneitra, even though the general principles underlying the agreements were already accepted.

RIGHT TALK

Right Talk is a special feature of negotiation. Agreement often hangs on just the right word, none other will do, and the negotiator becomes a wordsmith. The right word symbolizes some particular idea or formula in the parties' minds, and synonyms will not suffice. Finnish president Martti Ahtisaari picked up the Aceh negotiations in 2005 and devised the term, "self-government" for the new status, which worked when the previous concept, "special autonomy," had failed. The difference between the two terms was almost indistinguishable but crucial. In the 1995 negotiations in Chiapas, the stalemate buster was the suggestion of "free determination" in the place of "self-determination," which acceptably filled the space between independence and autonomy. Tatarstan signed an agreement with Russia in 1994 defining its status as a state "united with" but not "within" the Russian Federation, and the dangers of a Chechnyan-type conflict was dissolved. When UN secretary-general Kofi Annan went to Baghdad in search of an agreement on terms of inspection, Saddam Hussein refused to have an "ambassador" accompany the inspectors; Annan came up

with the term "senior diplomats," which was accepted.

Sometimes, Right Talk is quite the opposite: many words instead of one, to muddy things appropriately. Saddam Hussein objected to "inspections" and wanted "visits," as more respectful of Iraqi state dignity; Annan suggested "initial and subsequent entries for the performance of tasks mandated."[15] All these are examples of wordsmith diplomacy, where agreement hung on Right Talk.

TRASH TALK

Trash Talk is another way of taking aim at adversaries by dragging their names through the mud and letting them know how one really feels about them. It is talk that can express a wide range of emotions, from barely concealed contempt to outright anger and rage. Such talk may be a prelude to a declaration of war. It is talk that is typically directed at strengthening public resolve when dealing with foreign despots and dictators. It is also the kind of talk that is not tempered by the usual nuances and niceties of everyday diplomacy. "If Hitler invaded hell I would make at least a favorable reference to the devil in the House of Commons,"[16] Churchill famously said of Britain and America's alliance with Soviet dictator Joseph Stalin after the Nazis invaded the Soviet Union. When President George W. Bush lumped together Iran, Iraq, and North Korea in an "axis of evil" in his 2002 State of the Union speech, he was, in effect, saying that the United States had reached a crisis point in its relations with all three countries.

Trash Talk does have its uses, as Churchill knew. He used it skillfully to attack Hitler and bolster the resolve of the British people in their hour of peril. Reagan identified the USSR as an evil empire, but at the same time offered inducements to repent. Stepping on the plane to attend the opening ceremonies of the 2008 Olympics in Beijing, George Bush chided the Chinese over their human rights policies: "America stands in firm opposition to China's detention of political dissidents and human rights advocates and religious activists," he stormed. This was careful Trash Talk tempered by the subsequent actions of the speaker. By attending the opening ceremonies, the US president was sending a strong message that the United States was not only willing to do business with China but also recognized its entry onto the world stage as host of the games. Beijing, in return, was deeply appreciative of the president's attendance over the objections of many members of Congress. A Chinese foreign ministry spokesman rejoindered with the usual mantra that China strongly opposed "using human rights and other issues to interfere in the other countries' internal affairs," but went out of his way to say that Sino-American relations "have kept a sound momentum of development over the past years" as a result of "effective dialogue, exchanges and cooperation in extensive bilateral fields and major international and regional issues."[17]

Such talk can be used to rally support in a diplomatic face-off. In a keynote speech he delivered in Abu Dhabi on January 15, 2008, while touring some states in the Persian Gulf, President Bush accused Iran of being "the world's leading state sponsor of terror" because "it sends hundreds of millions of dollars to extremists around the world while its own people face repression and economic hardship at home." The president also alleged that "Iran's actions threaten the security of nations everywhere. So the United States is strengthening our long-standing security commitments with our friends in the Gulf and rallying friends around the world to confront this danger before it is too late."[18]

But when used clumsily, Trash Talk can be counterproductive. In the aftermath of Bush's State of the Union speech, US allies worried openly that the United States was opening a new front in its war against terrorism. Such fears were warranted. The United States attacked Iraq a little more than a year later, leading to speculation about whether or not Iran or North Korea was next on the hit list.

Iran's leaders are no strangers to the use of Trash Talk, beginning with branding the United States as "the Great Satan" after Iran took the US diplomatic mission prisoner in 1979. On June 11, 2008, just prior to a meeting between the American president and German chancellor Angela Merkel, President Mahmoud Ahmadinejad told thousands of supporters in central Iran that America was powerless to strike Iran and that Mr. Bush's "era has ended." "This wicked man [Bush] desires to harm the Iranian nation," Ahmadinejad sneered, as his audience chanted "Death to America."[19]

As the WikiLeaks diplomatic revelations indicate, diplomats in "private communication" may resort to Trash Talk in reporting to their superiors about wayward behavior of leaders and officials in other countries. Such communications are the normal stuff of diplomacy. Although the revelations have been embarrassing in some instances to US interests, they are not part of deliberate strategy of negotiation that is intended to discredit other parties. In fact, the revelations have prompted a great deal of Safe Talk by American officials to smooth ruffled feathers and limit the political fallout.

There are other procedures for talking beyond simple two-party, face-to-face communication. Getting the other party's attention to focus on a search for ways out of the dispute or problem may be the biggest challenge of all. Sticky, Safe, Timely, Street, Triple, Team, and Stop Talk are some of the most important procedural devices.

STICKY TALK

This is the kind of talking that simply will not let go. When Secretary Richard Holbrooke wanted to get an agreement on Bosnia out of the three leaders of the Yugoslav republic, he locked them in Wright Air Force Base at Dayton and would not let them out. When President Carter wanted to get a peace agreement out of Begin and Sadat, he holed them up in the cloistered hills of Camp David and would not let them out. There were special circumstances in both cases: The issue was a major violent conflict, and the mediator with the key was a (or the) superpower. Yet, in any negotiation, the conflicting or problem-ridden parties need to be kept at the job or the job will not get done, even though they often would like to go home and leave things for another day.

When the door cannot be physically locked, Sticky Talk must be imposed from the inside or outside: the problem will not go away and so the parties must be convinced to face it. Patience, persuasion, and persistence are the marrow of negotiation, the soft core that carries the blood and nerves of the communication. Too often, conflicting parties get together, by themselves or through the work of a mediator, agree on what they can agree on, and go home to live with their problem or continue their conflict, perhaps in a slightly altered form. The list is endless, from the fifteen incomplete peace agreements signed among the warring factions in Liberia between 1990 and 1997 to the hurriedly signed peace agreements in Angola in 1991, 1992, and 1994 that failed to end hostilities between government and opposition forces, to the hurriedly mediated Abuja agreement between Sudan and one of the Darfur factions that left the others free to continue the war.

The counterlist contains impressive cases of successful Sticky Talk negotiations. It took six years of painstaking prompting and cajoling and preparing for a ripe moment by Assistant Secretary of State Crocker before he was able to extract an agreement that put an end to the war in South West Africa, brought independence to Namibia in 1988, and paved the way to the end of the apartheid regime in South Africa. It took many months of hard slogging and endless rounds of diplomacy to end the civil and regional conflict in Cambodia in the early 1990s. The Good Friday Agreement in 1998, which provided the blueprint for the peace process in Northern Ireland, was reached only after talks that arguably began seven years earlier with the launch of the multiparty talks in Belfast in 1991. The Middle East disengagement agreements of 1974–75 were designed to be unstable and "fall forward" toward a final Israeli-Egyptian peace treaty, marking the nature of the step-by-step process.

SAFE TALK

Safe Talk is the diplomacy of the corridors and cafes, the woods and wharves, and the bar at the hotel or conference center where negotiations are taking place. President Woodrow Wilson was lost in idealism when he said just prior to the peace conference at the end of World War I, "Open covenants openly arrived at."[20] The delicate exchanges of negotiation require closed doors and breaks away from the table where people can talk as people, not as formal delegations. These breaks have resulted in some of the most productive moments in important negotiations.

The so-called walk in the woods is a famous episode when the United States and the Soviet Union almost clinched an agreement to stop the nuclear arms race in Europe. For almost two years, the United States had negotiated with the Soviets to reduce intermediate-range nuclear forces (INF) on both sides to the lowest equal levels, ideally zero. Both sides came close to an agreement when, in June 1982, the chief US negotiator, Paul Nitze, and his Soviet counterpart, Yuli Kvitsinsky, secretly decided to take a long walk in the woods on an outing near Geneva, Switzerland, where the talks were being held. During their walk, they agreed to a formula that would limit each side to specified number of missile launchers and long-range aircraft. Both the White House and the Kremlin initially rejected the gambit because neither side felt the need to make concessions. However, some years later, on December 8, 1987, President Reagan and General Secretary Mikhail Gorbachev did sign the INF Treaty banning intermediate-range and shorter-range missiles from Europe.

The "walk on the wharf" is a less well-known example of the value of Safe Talk. In January 1983, the United States and the Soviet Union launched the Stockholm Conference to begin a negotiation that would lead to the adoption of a comprehensive, mutual set of confidence-building measures that would cover the continent of Europe by opening military activities to greater levels of transparency by sharing information and strengthening communications. The negotiations had to deal with thorny issues of asymmetry in geography and differences in the structure and training of NATO and Warsaw Pact forces. A walk on the wharf along Stockholm's magnificent harbor front led to a productive exchange of views between the US and Soviet delegation heads. During their walk, they came up with the idea of a new and complementary principle of equivalence— Soviet agreement to confidence- and security-building measures in exchange for US commitment to a "no first use of force" (NFU) declaration. The suggestion was conveyed to President Reagan, who included it in a speech he delivered to the Irish parliament in June 1984, which not only broke the impasse but also quickened the pace for the rest of the negotiations.

Whole sessions held in secrecy and suffused with informality provide the best example of the opportunities offered by Safe Talk. The groundbreaking agreements between Israelis and Palestinians known as the Oslo Accords were the direct result of secret and informal negotiations that took place over an eight-month period in 1993 in a Norwegian farmhouse with the assistance of a handful of Norwegian facilitators. The Norwegians were able to open up a confidential back channel to the ongoing formal and public Washington-led negotiations that involved high-level, direct face-to-face negotiations between Israeli and Palestinian officials. The nongovernmental partner in these negotiations provided academic camouflage that gave the parties much-needed deniability, and the Norwegians' ability to deflect media attention allowed parties to take risks without fear of exposure. A small country such as Norway was able to play the role of third-party facilitator precisely because it was perceived by the parties as neutral and impartial. In this instance, Safe Talk under Norwegian cover helped change the political architecture of the Middle East in the 1990s by bringing together bitter enemies who became, in the words of one of the Norwegian facilitators, Jan Egeland, "each other's legitimate counterpart in peaceful negotiations."[21] Among great power efforts, the secrecy with which Secretary Kerry shrouded his Israeli-Palestinian mediation efforts in 2013, while fending off a prying press with careful statements of his own, is a good example.

Of course, the first part of Wilson's proposition still holds true: the results of Safe Talk must be made public so that parties do not find themselves tied down later by privately given commitments. Such secret agreements were correctly seen by Wilson as a major cause of World War I. Although secret agreements have generally been avoided because of the World War I experience, lesser secret commitments still occur; they are often the necessary payment to lock in an agreement, but they can cause problems later. Henry Kissinger promised the Israelis that the United States would not talk to the Palestinians without prior notification, which did not constrain US diplomacy excessively, but Carter unfortunately changed the promise from notification to prior permission. Secret or open, the commitment would have caused a problem, but secret at the time it was made, it had a double-negative effect—in its limitation and its revelation. Secret negotiations have their downsides, but when properly used as a breather during more formal talks, they allow for trial balloons and explorations without commitment and let negotiators use their most productive approach: "What if . . . ?"

Timely Talk

Negotiations led by a third party can sometimes prevent the outbreak of violence or further escalation of a conflict. Before violence occurs and positions have hardened, parties may be able to see the dangers ahead and consider a search for solutions led by mediators. Such mediated or Timely Talk interventions are directed at lengthening the "shadow of the future" by dramatizing the long-term costs of violence and other costs to the parties if negotiations fail. Once a conflict is under way, such interventions typically become more difficult and harder to sustain because conflicting parties' attitudes and perceptions have usually hardened and they are not prepared seriously to explore the negotiation option. The low-key manner in which the High Commissioner on National Minorities in the Organization for Security and Cooperation in Europe (OSCE) tackled the problem of national minorities in Central and Eastern Europe and areas of the former Soviet Union in the 1990s underscores the value of Timely Talk. By maintaining an

arm's length relationship with the OSCE, and ironically by eschewing the formal language of mediation, the commissioner at the time, Max van der Stoel, was able to gain entry into conflicts in ways that a formal mediation approach could not have because it would have raised the political stakes and limited the flexibility of the parties to make concessions.

When the conflict is not prevented, Timely Talk means sensing when to mediate and seize the moment, to recognize that the parties need to feel locked in a painful impasse where military escalation is not an option. Ripe moments need to be seized, for although they are only subjective perceptions, they are necessary to opening negotiations. If the parties cannot feel the moment (which may indeed be fleeting), Triple Talk must come into play to help them, as discussed below. When the moment is simply not present, Timely Talk is needed to ripen it for negotiations to take place.

Ripeness is the key to most successful negotiations, including the Cuban Missile Crisis, the Haitian restoration, the Namibian settlement, the Oslo Agreement, and the Middle East (Sinai) disengagement, and its absence helps explain the failure of negotiations between Israel and Palestine, India and Pakistan, and rebels and government in Syria, among others.

Street Talk

One of the key challenges in a peace process is to build support for negotiations within the society at large and to address the needs of local communities that bear the deepest scars of the conflict. Peacemaking is a multifaceted enterprise, and in today's world, it must actively involve citizens themselves if the enterprise is to succeed. Track two and its multiple variations use unofficial discussions for problem solving, at best in coordination with official efforts. As assistant secretary of state for the Middle East during Camp David I, Hal Saunders, who has been a pioneer of engaging citizens in sustained dialogues in public peace processes around the globe, argues: "There are some things that only governments can do, such as negotiating binding agreements; there are other things that citizens can do, such as change human relationships."[22] Street Talk is a form of dialogue that, in Saunders' words, "engages representative citizens from the conflict parties in designing steps to be taken in the political arena to change perceptions, stereotypes, to create a sense that peace may be possible and to involve more and more of their compatriots."

One of the most famous instances of Street Talk comes from the Cold War era. The Soviet-US Dartmouth Conference was the longest continuous bilateral exchange between leading US and Soviet citizens; it began in 1960 at the behest of US president Dwight Eisenhower and Soviet leader Nikita Khrushchev. After the Cold War, the Kettering Foundation, which financially and administratively supported the Dartmouth Conference, put its efforts into the Tajik Dialogue under Saunders. The dialogue provided a second track to conflict resolution, parallel to official discussions, leading to the end of five years of conflict (1993–97) in the former Soviet republic, and it still continues, recently celebrating its fiftieth anniversary.

The peace process in Guatemala, which began with a meeting in Oslo organized by the Lutheran Church, continued until the Contadora Declaration of August 1995 and concluded with a settlement in 1996 that was negotiated under UN auspices. This is another illustration of a Street Talk initiative that engaged civil society and public participation. The Civil Society Assembly, which was launched with the assistance of the United Nations, contributed to the national dialogue and provided input into the negotiations and subsequent terms of the peace settlement

that ended one of Central America's most brutal civil wars. However, the political situation almost twenty years later remains fractured and tenuous, largely because of continued fragmentation of civil society, a lack of accountability to the country's populace by the country's leaders and political institutions, and a weak and biased media that have made it difficult to debate issues and criticize the government.

TRIPLE TALK

Negotiation is an exchange of contingent agreements: "I will do this if you do that." As such, it is a very delicate job of making sure that both contingent promises are kept, and that parties—particularly enemy parties seeking to overcome their enmity—are wary of being caught in even a semblance of a commitment before the other side has made a similar and balancing commitment. Even direct meetings (or even intimations that negotiations are going on) may be the first step toward entrapment. For this reason, parties often can talk only without looking like they are talking, and frequently that can be done only by talking to someone else—a mediator. Triple Talk is required.

A mediator (by that or any other name— "facilitator," "good offices," "third party," and so forth) therefore becomes necessary to get parties talking. Conflicting parties may need and hope for a negotiated solution to their conflict, but they do not trust the opponent; that is part of the conflict. In that case, they need a surrogate for trust, a third party whom each party can rely on. That third-party mediator may carry trustworthy messages, or bring new ideas, or even sweeten the pot of the agreement to make it more attractive. In whatever form—as communicator, formulator, manipulator—parties in conflict need help, and that help must respond to the particular obstacle that keeps them from seeking and finding an agreement. But it is not solutions that are lacking; it is a vehicle of trust between the two parties, a crutch to help them walk, a way out of their "prisoner's dilemma" in game theory terms.

When the parties simply cannot talk to each other, the mediator acts like a secure telephone, carrying messages from one party to the other when direct contacts would be deemed compromising. The job is to convey a clear and accurate message. This is the minimal role of communicator or facilitator, guaranteeing the bona fides of the communication but nothing more. It is often done at arm's length, by shuttling between parties who never meet. The facilitator uses no pressure, adds no content, and lets the momentum of the mediated exchanges carry the negotiations forward. This is what presidents Clinton and Bush did for most of their tenures in office, mainly what the Norwegians did at Oslo, and what Kissinger also did to get talks started before moving on to the next step.

When facilitating or communicating is not enough, the mediator must put some of himself or herself into the exchange, in the form of some ideas and pressures toward an agreement. The third party must help formulate new ways out of the conflict, or concessions to be made, or compensation to balance a one-sided concession, or a new way of framing the dispute, or the right words. Disputes that are impervious to facilitation because the parties cannot think creatively beyond their fixed position need mediator involvement as a formulator.

But maybe ideas are not enough; the obstacle is simply that the stakes are such that the prospect of peace is not enough to draw the parties out of their conflict. In this case, the mediator needs to act as a manipulator, a term that emphasizes the deep involvement and risks that the role carries. If taking on that role exposes the mediator to greater involvement than he or she wants,

then the mediator must decide if hanging back and letting the conflict fester meets his or her own interests. Kissinger, often a formulator, became a manipulator in negotiations between Israel and Egypt over the Sinai, and it brought success.

The progressive moments in the Middle East peace process were made possible only by the active participation of a mediator: the United States as third party was the inventor of the peace process. When there was no committed involvement of a third party or there was only involvement that was poorly targeted on the problem, such as Reagan's 1983 plan or Bush's Annapolis initiative or Clinton's Camp David II, there was no progress in the process. Even a committed and sharp-eyed mediator, however, may not be enough, especially when a sense of pain in a deadlocked conflict is not acute enough to bring the parties to the negotiating table and conclude an agreement. Some Middle East hands maintain that the United States even in the present day should stay out of the area's conflict and let the parties handle conflict themselves, but those observers are not considering both the one-to-one correlation and the cost that the Middle East conflict imposes on the outside world. The closest things to participant solutions to Middle East conflicts have been Oslo and the Jordanian-Israeli peace treaty; Oslo (delicately facilitated by the Norwegians) reverted back to the conflict-ridden status quo, and the Jordanian treaty made peace where there was already little conflict.

Mediators can be found all over the world. In many cases, what is necessary is not muscle but clever thinking, careful massaging, dignified authority, trustful relations, and no visible interest involved, all operating under propitious circumstances—especially where the parties themselves want to end their conflict under acceptable terms but just can't do it by themselves. Martti Ahtisaari, the former president of Finland and a trusted UN mediator, pulled the rabbit of an agreement out of the hat in the Aceh conflict in Indonesia in 2007, in a civil war that had proved remarkably resistant to any kind of negotiated settlement. He did so right after the 2007 tsunami, when there was a sudden willingness on the part of all sides to bury the hatchet. The office of the Vatican mediated a bitterly fought dispute over the bitterly cold Beagle Channel in 1984, after the December 1983 revolt had removed the bellicose Argentine junta. The Catholic lay organization Sant'-Egidio mediated an end to the Mozambican civil war in 1990–92 after a terrible drought had weakened both sides. The United Nations mediated an end to the Soviet Afghan occupation in 1986–88 as the Soviet Union was heading for a change of leadership and collapse.

When it comes to longstanding, intractable disputes of a serious nature not involving superpowers directly, the United States is perhaps the only capable mediator, and it must become deeply involved. Without the United States and the resources, leverage, and clout it brings to the table, no settlement is possible. Facilitation and communication are not enough; the United States cannot just carry messages and let the process flow forward on its own momentum. The momentum will only turn into a boxing match. The world's hegemon needs to be involved up to its elbows, if not up to its waist, carrying ideas and alternatives back and forth between the parties as a formulator or carrying incentives and inducements as a manipulator. There is no alternative, and anything short will fail, as the historical record has shown. "The US has the vocation to mediate," wrote Ambassador Stephen Low in 1985.[23] That is no less true now that the United States is the last remaining superpower than it was when there were two.

TEAM TALK

Not only are conflicts no longer bilateral in today's world but the bystanders who seek to do some good, pull the warring parties apart, and bring peace to a region are frequently numerous and just as diverse in their interests as are the warring parties themselves. They do have a common interest, however, in bringing the conflict under control, and they often have to do it while handling an undermining opposition at home. This situation arguably constitutes the toughest challenge for negotiation—to build "teams of rivals" to manage regional crises.

"In negotiation," wrote Jean Monnet, the leading architect of the European Coal and Steel (and eventually Economic) Community, "the parties should not sit across the table facing each other but should sit on the same side facing the common problem."[24] France and Germany had been in a deadly boxing match for centuries, repeatedly doing mortal damage to each other, most recently twice in the first half of the twentieth century. They emerged from World War II with the same attitudes until, a decade after its end, the same two leaders who had continued to carry the hatred, said, "Let's stop doing each other—and ourselves in the bargain—harm, and let's do something together larger than ourselves, like building a Europe." Their conversion took place in a remarkably short time, a few years.

There are examples of Team Talk having a profound effect on major negotiations. In the early 1990s, the five permanent members of the UN Security Council (the P5), plus the neighboring countries as the Association of Southeast Asian Nations (ASEAN), had rather divergent and even contradictory interests over the future of Cambodia. The United States skillfully brought these many countries together into an agreed solution. In much of the first decade of the 2000s,

North Korea singlehandedly held off a group of world leaders as it pursued its nuclear security objectives. But the five most concerned nations with often diametrically opposed interests were brought together in the Six-Party Talks by China and the United States, playing very different roles, to produce some basic documents necessary for progress. Going back to the 1960s, the leading countries of the old (colonial) and new (Cold War) world order overcame their differences to negotiation in a momentary solution to the beleaguered position of Laos. In an even earlier era, in 1830–33, the leading powers of the Concert of Europe eventually overcame a stalemate among opposing positions to produce a stable status to the new state of Belgium that has lasted to this day (even if with some breaches and maybe not much longer). Looking ahead, stability in the Asian heartland will be achieved only when the most important of Afghanistan's immediate and distant neighbors—Pakistan, India, China, Iran, Russia, and the United States—take a hard look at their long term shared interests, and negotiate a regional entente.

Building negotiating teams is not a task confined to the warring parties themselves. Deliberate efforts to widen the coalition of mediators or interlocutors by bringing influential parties into the club can multiply the impact of the third-party collective effort. Here it is important to remember that leverage may or may not consist of material means to induce the parties to the dispute to change their behavior or attitudes. The four countries—Argentina, Brazil, Chile, and the United States—that served as guarantors of the 1942 Rio Protocol between Peru and Ecuador were able to work together to help resolve the boundary dispute that escalated into full-scale warfare between the two countries in 1995. The guarantors were the only channel of communications between the two countries, and no negotiation would have been possible without them.

The point of all these examples is that when conflicting parties have the wisdom to realize the costs of the conflict and the ability to identify a common problem or project that they can attack as a team, they have benefited mightily. There are two lessons in this realization. One is the enormous advantage to the parties of deciding to tackle a problem jointly, even when reduced by the cost involved in getting there. The other is that this type of negotiated process and outcome does not automatically fit any problem or conflict. Not all conflicts are replaceable by a common project, and even when they are, the project is often not easily identifiable. It takes work, creativity, imagination, and inventiveness to find an appropriate subject for teamwork to overcome historic enmity. Parties often hold incompatible positions because they themselves are incompatible, and it takes long and assiduous efforts to overcome images of irreconcilable differences that underlie differences in policies. The two communities of Northern Ireland arrived at an unlikely compromise in 1998 to manage their conflict, but they still are not fully reconciled. Ethiopia and Eritrea agreed to a divorce in 1993, but their mutual dislike is sharper than ever, as their murderous war in 1998–2000 all too tragically underscored. The repeated failure of Israeli-Palestine negotiations has convinced many on both sides of the bad faith of the other and the impossibility of ever reaching an agreement. Teamwork is a rare prize, worth seeking, but not always available.

STOP TALK

If negotiations are getting nowhere, it sometimes helps to let the parties know that one party is ready to leave. Parties can negotiate for a number of reasons other than finding solutions, including delaying resolution or preparing for more conflict, and if they are using negotiations as a cover for something else, it is best to call the game and go home. Or parties may be unwilling to move to a point where problem solving and conflict resolution are possible, and they need to be faced with the choice of compromise or failure. Former secretary of state Baker, recalling his efforts to get the Mideast parties to the Madrid Conference in 1991, has said that the most helpful tactic in the process was the "dead cat effect":[25] no one wanted the "dead cat" of being responsible for conference failure on its doorstep. A threat to leave is sometimes a powerful goad.

The qualifier "sometimes" relates to a particular condition: the third party must not want to leave more than the negotiating parties do and the parties being threatened must not want the third party to leave. In general, a threat to do something the threatened party wants done anyhow is not much of a threat. A common problem arises when sanctions are threatened, only to be withdrawn when those imposing sanctions feel more hurt by the sanctions than the party being sanctioned. The same is true when a mediator that the parties would rather not have around threatens to leave, or a negotiator threatens to cut off negotiations that a party would already like to see severed: such threats are not likely to galvanize the party into action. When the United States and the Western Contact Group (comprising the United States, the Federal Republic of Germany, France, Canada, and the United Kingdom) were trying to get South Africa out of its South West African colony, they threatened in 1978 to end mediation and apply sanctions if South Africa did not agree to liberating terms. The threat to cut off negotiations was quite acceptable to South Africa, and the threat of sanctions was withdrawn by Secretary of State Vance as more harmful to the United States and allies than to South Africa.

However, when Senator George Mitchell threatened to leave his mediation and chair-

ing of the peace talks in Northern Ireland in early 1998 if the parties did not get serious and move toward agreement among themselves (i.e., the moment was now or never), the parties capitulated. They recognized that Mitchell's principled leadership was necessary if they were to reach an agreement, and so they went back to work and brought him with them. The Good Friday Agreement was the result. And at Dayton in 1994, Secretary Warren Christopher and Assistant Secretary Holbrooke packed their bags and were ready to call the negotiations a failure, but for an agreement of the three parties to continue their efforts toward an agreeable solution. At Camp David in 1975, the parties also packed their bags, ready to leave and out of ideas; President Carter, the mediator, pleaded with them to think of the consequences, and so they returned to draw up the Camp David Agreements.

Threats by one of the parties to call off the mediation or negotiation, or to focus heightened conflict on the parties, are the ultimate tactics of talk power, inducing a return to negotiation by a threat to stop it.

KEEP TALKING

In this chapter, we have discussed the different ways of talking, which, in essence, are different ways to negotiate with friends, enemies, and strategic rivals as well as with the parties in a conflict who are incapable of raising their sights beyond the battlefield to consider an alternative vision of the future. There is an enormous richness and variety in these different tools of statecraft. However, the challenge for diplomacy is not simply to make use of these tools, but to use them adroitly and skillfully in different kinds of situations and above all to keep talking—at least most of the time. Effective diplomacy depends not just on grabbing the right tools out of the negotiation toolbox, but on timing, coordination, calibration, careful planning, and leadership. Effective negotiation also depends on having a diplomatic strategy that is informed by a clear sense of one's own strategic interests. As different kinds of problems are encountered along the road to securing a political settlement or diplomatic solution, negotiators must make use of more than one set of negotiation tools while being familiar with all of them so as to make the right choices.

NOTES

Epigraph. Fortune Barthélemy de Felice, *Dictionnaire de justice naturelle et civile* (Yverdun 1778), trans. in *The Practical Negotiator* I. William Zartman and Maureen R. Berman, (New Haven, CT: Yale University Press, 1982), 238.

1. This chapter is based on Fen Osler Hampson and I. William Zartman, *The Global Power of Talk: Negotiating America's Interests* (Boulder, CO: Paradigm, 2012), chap. 3.

2. James A. Baker III, "The Road to Madrid," in *Herding Cats: Multiparty Mediation in a Complex World,* ed. Chester A. Crocker, Fen Osler Hampson, and Pamela Aall (Washington, DC: United States Institute of Peace Press, 1999), 187.

3. The quotation is attributed to Abba Eban, the Israeli diplomat and politician, who was also quoted as saying "the Arabs never miss an opportunity to miss an opportunity"; available at http://en.wikiquote.org/wiki/Abba_Eban.

4. Harlan Cleveland, *Nobody in Charge: Essay on the Future of Leadership* (San Francisco: Jossey-Bass, 2002), 224.

5. François de Callières, *The Art of Diplomacy* (Lanham, MD: University Press of America, 1994), 81–82.

6. Jan Egeland, "The Oslo Accord," in Crocker et al., *Herding Cats,* 533.

7. De Callières, *Art of Diplomacy,* 22.

8. "United Nations: Until Hell Freezes Over," *Time,* November 2, 1962, http://www.time.com/time/magazine/article/0,9171,874589,00.html. Also quoted in Robert F. Kennedy, *Thirteen Days: A Memoir of the Cuban Missile Crisis* (New York: W. W. Norton, 1969), 54.

9. Recollection of I. William Zartman, who was a member of President Carter's negotiating team.

10. Baker, "The Road to Madrid," 203.

11. Department of State Telegram Conveying President Kennedy's Reply to Chairman Khrushchev, October 28, 1962, available at http://www.jfklibrary.org/jfkl/cmc/cmc_correspondence.html.

12. Kennedy, *Thirteen Days,* 105–6.

13. See, for example, Thomas Blanton, "Annals of Blinksmanship," *Wilson Quarterly* (Summer 1997), http://www.gwu.edu/~nsarchiv/nsa/cuba_mis_cri/annals.htm.

14. Quoted in *Current Issues Briefing* (Washington, DC: United States Institute of Peace, September 28, 2005).

15. Nicholas Berry, "Why Saddam Hussein Approved UN Inspections," *Foreign Policy Forum* (September 17, 2002), http://www.foreignpolicyforum.com/view_article.php?aid=19.

16. John Petrie, "Collection of Winston Churchill Quotes," http://jpetrie.myweb.uga.edu/bulldog.html.

17. Jane Macartney, "President Bush Condemns China Human Rights Record on Eve of Olympics," *Sunday Times,* August 8, 2008, http://www.timesonline.co.uk/tol/news/world/asia/article4476593.ece.

18. Paula Wolfson, "Bush Warns Gulf States of Iran Threat," *Voice of America* (January 13, 2008), http://www.globalsecurity.org/wmd/library/news/iran/2008/iran-080113-voa01.htm.

19. Harry de Quetteville, "Iranian Leader Mahmoud Ahmadinejad Taunts 'Wicked' President George W. Bush," *Telegraph,* June 11, 2008, http://www.telegraph.co.uk/news/worldnews/middleeast/iran/2111093/Iranian-leader-Mahmoud-Ahmadinejad-taunts-wicked-President-George-W-Bush.html.

20. President Wilson's Fourteen Points, Delivered in Joint Session, January 8, 1918, http://wwi.lib.byu.edu/index.php/President_Wilson%27s_Fourteen_Points.

21. Jan Egeland, "The Oslo Accord: Multiparty Facilitation Through the Norwegian Channel," in Crocker et al., *Herding Cats,* 530.

22. Harold H. Saunders, "Prenegotiation and Circum-negotiation: Arenas of the Peace Pro-

cess," in *Managing Global Chaos: Sources of and Responses to International Conflict,* ed. Chester Crocker, Fen Hampson, and Pamela Aall (Washington, DC: United States Institute of Peace Press, 1996), 419–32.

23. Ambassador Stephen Low, "The Zimbabwe Settlement, 1976–1979," in *International Media-tion in Theory and Practice,* ed. Saadia Touval and I. William Zartman (Washington, DC: Johns Hopkins University, SAIS, Foreign Policy Institute, 1985), 93.

24. Jean Monnet, *Memoirs* (New York: Doubleday, 1978), 216.

25. Baker, "The Road to Madrid," 188 and 196.

23

THE DIPLOMACY OF ENGAGEMENT IN TRANSITIONAL POLITIES

Chester A. Crocker

Engagement is a term that often causes confusion when used to describe diplomacy. Much of the confusion stems from the term being used to mean very different types of diplomacy. Some commentators use "engagement" as foreign policy shorthand for simply talking to another government or as a synonym for "normal" diplomacy." Others wield "engagement" as a weapon of advocacy or rhetorical attack: "We've tried military intervention, it's time for a policy of engagement"; or "We tried engagement with Iran and it failed so we need to keep all options on the table." These, however, are crude and imprecise uses of the term. Properly understood, the purpose of an engagement strategy is to change the target's perception of its own interests and, hence, to modify the target's policies and behavior. An engagement strategy can be applied to a wide variety of target governments, in a range of contexts, and using an assortment of tools and techniques—for example, negotiation or mediation, coercive measures such as sanctions and threats, diplomatic promises, and conditional offers.[1]

One of the contexts for such a strategy is the subject of this chapter: managing conflict and coping with the challenges that arise during political crises and violent transitions when regimes melt down. The turmoil sweeping the Middle East and North Africa since the start of this decade offers dramatic examples of such transitions, but the problem of coping with violent transitions is neither new nor confined to that region. To set the stage for analyzing the strategy of engagement in such scenarios, it is useful to recall how transitional conflicts have unfolded—and sometimes been managed—in the past. This chapter explores—chiefly from a US perspective—some of the tools of influence available to support an engagement strategy and the considerations that should be in the minds of those who use the tools to manage transitional conflict environments.

Two clarifications are needed at the outset. Even the most creative and powerful conflict managers cannot impose durable political order on transitional societies unless those managers are prepared to occupy and administer those societies indefinitely. In a world where the norm of self-determination prevails, the citizens of transitional societies are unlikely to accept such a notion. They are the ones who pay the price of violent transitions, and it is they who will ultimately shape their course.

Yet, the decisions taken by powerful actors such as the United States can make a significant difference, especially at critical junctures in a transition process. This reality places an onus on the shoulders of powerful actors: their interventions (political as well as military) may shape who comes out on top; by the same token, a decision not to intervene may shape the outcome by letting the best-armed local protagonist prevail.

A UNIVERSE OF TRANSITIONS

A range of possible outcomes of violent transitions can be identified:

- A "revolution" in which a more or less coherent new order sweeps away the old as a result of violent struggle (e.g., Russia, 1917; Ethiopia, 1974; Uganda, 1986)
- A velvet revolution, in which the regime collapses amid a mixture of street power, external pressure, and leadership splits (e.g., Philippines, 1986; the Soviet Union, 1991; Egypt and Tunisia, 2011)
- Bloody, broken-back regime change following prolonged strife as regime elements defect and leaders arrange their exit or are killed (e.g., Ethiopia, 1991; Yemen, 2011; Libya, 2011)
- Successful repression using scorched-earth tools so that the opposition is defeated (e.g., Peru, 1992–2012; Zimbabwe, since 2000; Sri Lanka, 2009)
- Drawn-out political stalemate followed by "negotiated revolution" (e.g., South Africa, 1992–94; Burma, since 2010)

- Prolonged, bloody strife that prompts coercive external intervention and an imposed peace (e.g., Bosnia, 1995)
- Prolonged strife that prompts powerfully backed, externally led negotiations leading to an internationally monitored transition period and elections (Namibia, 1966–90; Mozambique, 1976–94; El Salvador, 1979–94; Liberia, 1989–2005)

These outcomes might be one stage in a longer transition process whose subsequent stages are unclear. Prolonged stalemate could evolve into a de facto partition of the state into ethnic, regional, or confessional enclaves as the regime arms its core supporters and the central state loses control of much of the territory (e.g., Somalia, the Democratic Republic of the Congo). The Egyptian example suggests that velvet revolutions can morph into directions that remain unpredictable for some time, while bloody regime change in Libya has been followed by ambiguous signs and incoherence. Successful engagement could produce autonomy arrangements that partially decentralize power while the now more-constrained state remains intact (e.g., Aceh in Indonesia, Mindanao in the Philippines).

If outside states attempt to freeze power relations or to entrench political-military groups in open-ended power-sharing structures, they will likely sow seeds of future conflict and distort the chances for organic political development (e.g., Lebanon and Bosnia). Powerful local actors—the men with the guns—often try to game the arrangements that flow from negotiated peace deals and use the trappings of democracy to seize and hold onto power, as in Cambodia, Sudan/South Sudan, and Angola. Too often, such negotiations simply reflect the balance of coercive forces on the ground at the moment they take place and lead to the marginalization of unarmed civilians. Avoiding this outcome requires that outside interveners maintain a high level of commitment to peacebuilding during and beyond the immediate transition period.

CHALLENGES OF ENGAGEMENT

Engagement in transitional polities is fraught with strategic challenges. Outside powers must navigate between competing priorities as they consider whether, when, and how to bring their influence to bear. A "peace at any price" approach might respond to immediate humanitarian imperatives, but it could also entrench the wrong actors, prolonging rather than resolving the society's problems. Thus, a central issue is the timing of cease-fires and the extent to which the act of engagement is motivated primarily by a concern to preempt or stop the violence.[2]

The timing of third-party engagement has far-reaching implications. It affects the central issue of deciding how much of the existing state apparatus can serve as an institutional base for the transition and future governance. A related issue concerns the fate of people associated with the government during the previous period of misrule. The task here is to mesh the quest for desirable change with the necessity of achieving some measure of continuity—both to reassure the incumbents' core constituencies and their allies and to avoid a descent into chaos. Timing and sequencing are of critical importance in order to avoid "wasting" finite leverage resources by premature action, on the one hand, and delaying so long that the "ripe" moment for intervention is lost, on the other hand. The United States and other "friends of Syria" wrestled with this challenge during the first three years of that country's civil war (2011–13).

The greatest challenge facing outsiders is their overarching responsibility to avoid making an already troubled society (and region) even worse. The test of statesmanship in such transitions is to define the least bad outcome.

This requires a very careful assessment of local and regional players. The bad guys may be evident, but good guys may be hard to find. If so, the best option is to help foster a credible transition process rather than to select winners.

DEFINING DIPLOMATIC ENGAGEMENT

As noted at the beginning of this chapter, confusion surrounds the term "engagement" in the practice of statecraft. Engagement is not about sweet talk. Nor is it based on the illusion that problems can be solved if only people would talk to each other. Although talk is required, the purpose of engagement is not simply getting involved, showing concern, or reaching out to another party. The purpose of engagement is not normalization or improved relations, although better relations might be the ultimate result. The engager's purpose is to change the target's behavior toward more cooperative and constructive policies. Engagement is a process that involves exerting pressure by raising questions, probing assumptions, and exploring hypothetical possibilities. Above all, it involves testing how far the target might be willing to go. Properly understood, the diplomacy of engagement places the ball in the target's court.

Diplomatic engagement can be used in relations with adversaries (e.g., the US approach toward the Soviet Union during the final chapters of the Cold War), pariah states (e.g., Barack Obama's administration's policy toward Myanmar), and so-called rogue states. An illustration of the last type occurred in the early 2000s as the George W. Bush administration worked with the British to mount a strategy of engagement with Libya that led to the elimination of that country's programs to develop weapons of mass destruction. Clearly, different types and amounts of power or leverage are called for depending on the context and the targets. But engagement is generally about exploring the possibility of an understanding, defining a road map for future relations, and trying to find terms under which the target takes certain steps and the engager reciprocates with moves of its own. At times, engagement diplomacy can be based on "pure" negotiated procedures, but it can also be backed by raw (if diplomatically worded) exercises of coercive influence (deterrence, compellence, sanctions, vetoes, or offers of assistance or the promise or denial of membership in an institution or formal relations).

Engagement diplomacy can be applied in a variety of contexts.[3] Mediation is a case in point. It was used by Americans to dampen regional violence and promote political solutions in Southern Africa in the 1980s.[4] Former Finnish president Martti Ahtisaari engaged in mediation with the Indonesian government and an Acehnese rebel movement to negotiate an autonomy deal in 2005, ending decades of violence in Aceh.[5] Algerian diplomat Lakhdar Brahimi, operating under a joint UN-Arab League mandate starting in 2012, sought to engage the Syrian regime and opposition groups in a mediation effort with the support of states in the Friends of Syria group.

Another context for engagement is in counterterrorism strategy. For example, in the case of Egypt's political turbulence, the rationale for early engagement with the Muslim Brotherhood and a range of Salafi parties was to pursue dialogue, clarify positions, identify redlines, lay down markers, and understand intentions while agendas were still fluid. Writing in mid-2012, Daniel Byman and Zack Gold noted that a central message in this engagement diplomacy was to underscore that "continued U.S. aid depends on Egypt remaining a U.S. ally on counterterrorism, not breaking the peace treaty with Israel and other important strategic issues."[6]

Violent political transitions are a third arena for engagement diplomacy. This is the main focus of the remainder of this chapter. The next section identifies the tools of influence available to outside conflict management actors in transitional polities. Some of these tools may be relevant to engagement diplomacy in other contexts such as conflict prevention.

THE TOOLS OF ENGAGEMENT

The diplomacy of engagement requires selecting a mixture of tools appropriate to each specific case. It requires leverage, and leverage comes from power, both actual and potential. Direct military intervention may be the most compelling but also the least flexible form of power for use in support of engagement in violent transitions. To paraphrase Colin Powell in the Iraq context, if we break the target state and disrupt its social fabric, we may end up owning the result. Another problem, as Samuel Huntington observed in commenting on the poor record of most small, incremental interventions, is that military forces are "not primarily instruments of communication to convey signals to an enemy; they are instead instruments of coercion to compel him to alter his behavior."[7] In other words, military force is a blunt instrument, difficult to calibrate. Furthermore, military intervention, even if justified on largely humanitarian grounds, involves taking sides.

Analyzing the so-called values cases of the 1990s, where US national security interests were not directly involved—Haiti, Somalia, Bosnia, and Rwanda—Richard Betts makes a persuasive case that "impartial" intervention is a delusion. To intervene militarily is to decide who rules the target state—a reality both when outsiders arrive and when they leave.[8] But nonintervention by a powerful actor such as the United States raises another dilemma because the option to intervene did exist: inaction could deliver the society to those who are best armed and organized. In other words, inaction is a way to decide who rules. The first principle has been at work in Afghanistan since 2001; the second principle has been in place in the Great Lakes region of Africa since 1994. These examples of the use and the nonuse of direct military instruments by a powerful state underscore the importance of an integrated analytic approach by policymakers so that the relevant instruments of power can be understood in a realistic context.[9]

The United States and its allies hold many tools of leverage and influence. One such tool is economic sanctions designed to wear down and isolate the target regime. But broad trade and investment sanctions are also blunt instruments that tend to hurt civilians first and foremost. This explains the increasing recourse to targeted financial, travel, and other sanctions tools focused on the regime itself.[10] Another tool is humanitarian aid to mitigate the suffering of affected populations. Such assistance is seldom viewed as impartial and is almost always perceived as "intervention" by the incumbent regime, which then seeks to control the channels through which the aid is distributed. Alternatively, humanitarian assistance can be employed as an openly acknowledged act of solidarity with opposition elements, as was the case with the relief and humanitarian assistance program employed by the United States from Pakistan into Afghanistan and the cross-border feeding program from Sudan into the Tigray and Eritrea areas of Ethiopia, both during the 1980s. In cases such as these, humanitarian and strategic purposes were joined, and the goals included creating pressure for negotiations.

Another tool in an engagement strategy is the provision of lethal assistance to opposition forces in hopes of leveling the playing field and thereby accelerating the arrival of a ripe moment for negotiation. Whether supplied through proxies or directly, overtly, or covertly, such external aid serves multiple purposes: it can give the provider a seat at the table in future talks; it sends a signal to the regime's backers that they face competition and their actions will not be cost free; when successfully employed, it can create or strengthen a stalemate. This tool is part of a strategy of ripening the transitional conflict by gradually bleeding the regime. Of course, there are downsides. The ultimate destination of weapons is hard to control in a civil war. Lethal intervention could become a slippery slope leading to pressure for additional decisions. The provision of such support requires a choice to be made about recipients, or "good guys," when, in reality, the "good guys" may be a mixed bag of good and bad. Above all, the conflict manager needs to keep eyes fixed on the broader goal of backing a successful transition process.

The Syrian civil war that started in 2011 sadly illustrates all these points. Backing "the opposition" in order to level the playing field in support of a negotiated settlement becomes much more complex when the opposition is deeply fragmented and includes undesirable elements. Using military tools to support a negotiated outcome raises serious geopolitical issues when other powerful states are backing the current regime. Yet, such tools may be the only way to get attention and neutralize regime advantages. A further policy conundrum underscored by the Syrian case is that once an external power such as the United States engages in transitional diplomacy, the domestic political stakes get higher. After months of mounting political pressure to take a clear stand against the regime, President Obama used an August 2011 visit by Turkish prime minister Recep Tayyip Erdogan to declare that "the time has come for President Assad to step aside." But this statement did not amount to a policy, and it only accentuated pressure for decisions to back up the words with action. The diplomacy of engagement in the Syria case raised three domestic political dilemmas: the slippery slope of providing lethal aid; the question of how to select and characterize opposition elements worthy of support; and the ever-present need to explain why it may be necessary to work with elements of the very regime that "must go" in order to achieve a negotiated outcome. In many cases, the tools discussed above—by themselves—are unlikely to produce a successful outcome. They are too narrowly conceived and too unilateral in scope. The remedy lies partly in finding sources of borrowed leverage and credibility. Neighboring states, regional hegemons, and major powers associated with the regime are the most obvious sources of leverage. Close behind them are regional organizations, alliances, and the United Nations. A few examples illustrate the argument:

- US negotiators found leverage by engaging with the backers of all factions in the complex Cambodia diplomacy of the early 1990s. This strategy worked because of broader geopolitical dynamics and the ability to exploit the appetite for exit in the key "patron" capitals.
- In Liberia in 2003, US officials brought minimal military presence (mainly offshore) to bear, but the main action was to catalyze the military and diplomatic support of Nigeria, Ghana, and the Economic Community of West African States (and then the UN secretariat) to shape a two-year transition plan that removed Charles Taylor from office and introduced a UN peacekeeping operation, set up a transitional regime, and paved the way for elections.
- The United States acquired leverage and the benefits of de facto partnership with skilled UN mediators and Central American leaders in the diplomatic efforts preceding the 1992 El Salvador settlement, snatching success from the jaws of a domestically controversial quagmire.

- UN credibility and diplomatic skill provided the backdrop to sustained US efforts that ultimately succeeded in a 1988 agreement ending the colonial regime in Namibia and the major Cuban military presence in Angola with the help of leverage borrowed from African neighbors, US allies, the Cubans, and the Soviets.
- French and UN forces, along with rhetorical support from the African Union, enabled Washington to play a firm but quiet back seat role in removing a stubborn tyrant from office in Côte d'Ivoire in 2011.

The practice of recruiting groups of "friends" or "contact groups" around the leading conflict managers is another example of the search for leverage. The motives and interests involved can vary widely: for example, acquiring relevant partners in hopes of gaining added leverage with one of the conflict parties; surrounding the conflict parties with a united front in order to limit end runs and forum shopping; and legitimizing a UN-based negotiating process by making it more inclusive of interested states.[11] Practitioners need to be aware, however, that borrowed leverage is often accompanied by complexity and even confusion, adding substantial burdens of coordination and lateral diplomatic legwork. The balance sheet of multilateral conflict management requires careful accounting.[12] The motives and interests of those who are recruited also need to be taken into account: for example, joining (and being seen to join) a negotiating process for reasons of domestic politics or diplomatic prestige; gaining access to "inside" information and a seat at the table in order to obstruct progress or simply to support one side in the conflict situation. Some recruits could bring more confusion or unintended consequences than they are worth.

DIPLOMACY WITH REGIMES AND REBELS

Borrowing leverage is the essence of good diplomacy. But it is not the only diplomatic tool in the arsenal, especially not in the case of a major power such as the United States. If the troubled regime is a friendly one at some level—as, for example, the Philippines under Ferdinand Marcos was friendly to the United States in terms of military and diplomatic cooperation—Washington has the option of withdrawing or reducing its support. If the target is a rogue, warlord, or unfriendly regime, US diplomacy can facilitate a leader's exile by speaking to those who might accept him, as Washington did successfully in Liberia in 2003. An unheralded but brilliant example of arranging a soft landing occurred in Ethiopia in 1991, when rebel forces were on the outskirts of Addis Ababa. The Soviet-backed thug Mengistu Haile Mariam and his coterie escaped to Zimbabwean exile in a carefully orchestrated exit just before the Tigrayan rebel chieftain Meles Zenawi and his forces entered the city. That diplomacy was conducted by US officials using one of the most powerful modern diplomatic weapons: a cell phone. As this example of tradecraft illustrates, diplomatic engagement is carried out by individual diplomats using their wits, imagination, and capacity to connect with the right people at the right time, and it is done in the field as well as in major capitals.

Calibrating relations with regimes and rebels or civilian-led opposition groups requires clear thinking about basic objectives, as a transition unfolds. Conflict management requires choices on issues such as public distancing and pressures, channels and levels for engaging oppositionists, and what forms of tangible support to withdraw or provide. These choices depend on the conflict manager's purpose: is the goal to help insurgents replace the regime, to warn them against unacceptable behavior, to curry favor with them in case they come out on top, to send a message to the regime's backers, or simply to have a seat at the table and keep options open as events unfold? Even more basic issues lie behind these questions. Does the conflict manager seek a negotiated transition in which there are elements of continuity as well as elements of change?

The most important choices involve:

- When to reach out to local opposition parties as a regime begins to run into trouble
- If and how to engage with armed actors, including those that may engage in acts of terror or other forms of criminal activity
- What roles armed opposition movements and their civilian-led counterparts will play in negotiating the transition

The political context shapes the answers. In the case of a previously friendly regime that is sliding into political crisis—Iran under the Shah, the Philippines under Marcos, Côte d'Ivoire under Laurent Gbagbo, Egypt under Mubarak—the act of engaging opposition groups sends a powerful signal of distancing and hedging. That may be its primary initial purpose. Diplomatic support and institution-building aid may follow. (Lethal assistance to rebels confronting a friendly regime would not make strategic sense.) Even in relatively peaceful settings where the goal is to hedge and broaden contacts in the society, engaging with opposition movements should not be viewed as a gift to them. Engagement is not making nice; it is a test that could open the door to a possible road map for relations. It may also be undertaken to protect future equities and avoid estrangement from a future leadership. In any event, engagement should be undertaken early in the process, ideally before political conflict ripens into crisis.

The picture gets more complicated once the crisis facing a previously friendly regime crosses the line toward violence. At this point, state institutions, and the people running them, may be at risk. This makes it important to assess the pros and cons of working toward a relatively soft landing versus sweeping away the old order. As regime brutality converts protesters into rebels (often as the result of provocation aiming for precisely this result), conflict managers need to know more about the armed groups that emerge. These groups may be led by patriots or warlords; the leadership may be pragmatic or ideologically rigid; its agenda may be homegrown or shaped by those who arm and fund it; that agenda may be driven by principle or by a raw quest for power; the armed opposition may be cohesive or fragmented and doomed to a future of fratricidal strife as the old order crumbles. Armed groups may or may not respect the rights of innocent civilians.

In sum, a deep dive into the granular details of a specific scenario is required in order to get some answers. Early engagement is called for, not as an act of solidarity with future good guys but in order to send warnings, clarify positions and interests, ask tough questions, and obtain information. As the old regime goes down, it becomes increasingly important to avoid wearing rose-colored glasses when viewing likely successors: there are no Nelson Mandelas in most scenarios, especially violent ones.

Engagement with armed groups has become an increasingly fraught undertaking. If a group has managed to get itself on the US, UN, or EU list of proscribed entities because of terrorist acts, officials may be deterred by the risk of political controversy or, in the case of US officials, legally prohibited from contact with them in the absence of special waivers—a relatively recent development that severely complicates peacemaking in conflict zones. Since the June 2010 US

Supreme Court decision in *Holder v. Humanitarian Law Project,* nonofficial organizations have also been directly constrained in their dealings with armed groups that are on US terrorism lists. This prohibition can be interpreted as criminalizing mere training, advising on political solutions, and providing humanitarian aid. US legislation, court decisions, and executive branch regulations severely undercut US diplomatic reach and represent a form of unilateral diplomatic disarmament. The net effect is to require that communication with such armed groups take place through private, non-US intermediaries, and to place excessive reliance on intelligence channels or on friendly third parties that are free from such self-defeating inhibitions.[13]

These legal and legislative developments compound an already complex environment for engaging armed actors. Contact with armed groups operating in friendly states such as Spain, Colombia, the Philippines, Yemen, and Northern Ireland is highly sensitive politically. Key exchanges typically take place in the utmost secrecy, often conducted by nonofficial bodies. If conflict managers are to engage successfully in transitional polities, they need sufficient flexibility to deal with the major political forces emerging during violent transitions, and the earlier they have that flexibility, the better. In places as diverse as South Africa, El Salvador, Kashmir, the Palestinian territories, Nepal, and Afghanistan, it is hard to imagine how outside powers could have exerted influence for constructive change without being able to engage these emerging forces, challenging them to operate as political rather than as violent actors.

The purposes of engaging armed actors are several. First, conflict managers want to support moderate voices and undercut the rabid extremists and greediest warlords. They also want to make clear the limits of what can be achieved by the gun and to encourage a return to politics. By debating, arguing from experience elsewhere, and opening the eyes of blinkered militants, the goal is to raise doubts by asking awkward questions—a classic tool of good diplomacy. A third purpose may be to split the leadership or entice it to think and act politically so that a negotiated transition can have a chance. The most basic message is this: terrorism and armed struggle cannot get you what you say you want, but politics can.[14] This approach prevailed as successive British governments and international mediators grasped the Northern Ireland nettle. This is also the approach pursued almost invisibly by various third parties, including nonofficial groups, that have successfully pushed the Euskadi Ta Askatasuna (ETA) to abandon the violent pursuit of Basque national aspirations.[15]

This logic applies equally to violent transitions that threaten unfriendly regimes with which conflict managers have difficult or strained relations. Policy toward such places as Cambodia, Zimbabwe, Burma, Angola, Sudan, and Kosovo required a similar calculus about how much and what kinds of support to offer opposition groups. In Cambodia and Angola, US officials had few illusions about the character and conduct of the Khmer Rouge and the National Union for the Total Independence of Angola (UNITA), respectively, and they did not entertain ideas of achieving an outright military "win." Where they have faced both armed and nonviolent groups, as in Kosovo, US officials have made an effort to walk a balanced line—recognizing the critical role played by the people with the guns but taking steps to include those relying on nonviolent methods. Trying to exclude relations with armed groups marginalizes the conflict manager more than the armed groups.

Yet, what roles armed groups are permitted to play in an eventual negotiation process does matter very much. Unless they are somehow defeated or marginalized by civilian leadership, armed groups will assert the right to be at the table on matters affecting security, cease-fires, external military monitoring, future force configurations, and disarmament. These are the topics on which armed groups have a direct "professional" stake and on which their buy-in is essential. Furthermore, armed groups are unlikely to cooperate unless they get credible answers to their priority security concerns: Who will guarantee an agreement and assure that others respect their commitments? What remedies will be available to one faction if others cheat? The case of post-Gaddafi Libya illustrates what can happen when there is no authoritative, binding understanding about the intricate process by which a successor regime achieves a monopoly on the use of armed force.

Having recognized their role in the negotiation of security issues, however, it is imperative that armed groups not be given the opportunity to dominate the agenda of a negotiated transition. Issues such as election monitoring, refugee return, freedom of assembly and speech, economic reconstruction, and the administration of justice and postconflict accountability mechanisms are, or should be, in the purview of civil society actors and political parties at the negotiating table. To be realistic, this is easier said than done when contending armed forces are in a position to intimidate or coerce.

Negotiating a political transition is a process in which issues need to be sequenced. Giving militarized groupings—especially ones organized on regional or sectarian lines—a direct role in shaping the terms of political change and writing a new constitution poses dangers for the future. It encourages armed actors to permanently entrench their positions and block the emergence of a civil order. The experience of Bosnia after the Dayton agreement illustrates the pitfalls of guaranteeing sectarian or nationalist militants a power base from which to make political demands. The lesson here is to detach the immediate transition arrangements in which power is inevitably shared from the next phase, in which political roles are defined constitutionally.

WHAT TO DO WITH THE STATE?

It may be, as Dirk Vandewalle has argued, that Libya's post-Gaddafi elites are benefitting from the fact that he destroyed any institutions he inherited and essentially left none behind when he was murdered.[16] In most cases, however, the transitional polity will feature a range of still-operative administrative institutions as well as an inevitably politicized security cluster of agencies, forces, and services. Their fate and the fate of the personnel who staff them will be important subjects of transitional negotiation. If a chaotic, Iraq-style vacuum is to be avoided, those issues need to be negotiated with representatives of the existing state. Thus, the role of externally led diplomacy is to seize the window of opportunity created by the changing balance of military forces and to support a negotiated transition. Diplomacy and military power must work hand in glove—they are not opposites or alternatives.

When contested transitions reach their culminating point, incumbent leaders make choices. Scorched-earth leaders meet Gaddafi's fate or face the prospect of trials at the International Criminal Court. When the walls close in and power shifts toward the challengers, some leaders opt to flee and accept the uncertainties of exile, as in Haiti, Ethiopia, Iran, Liberia, and the Philippines. This is one end of the spectrum of regime transitions. At the other end are Burma and South Africa, where open warfare was preempted by far-sighted leaders capable of negotiating and managing change. Just as there are no Mandelas in the truly violent scenarios, there are also no F. W. de Klerks or Thein Seins capable of seeing what is best for their country and what serves the long-term interests of their core constituency.

Viewed in this light, a negotiated transition is not necessarily an alternative to battlefield victory. It may be the way to exploit and follow up on military success and the creation of a coherent political opposition. To be sure, negotiations do not always succeed, and their successes are often short lived. Conflict managers are hard pressed to keep things on track and to sustain the parties' interest in finding common ground. It is ambitious to devise credible external guarantees, to sustain outsiders' interest and commitment to providing peacekeepers and political support so that the parties receive necessary assurances as the transition unfolds. Each political settlement may be nothing more than another chapter in a continuing narrative of instability.

Engagement in transitional polities is not without risks. Decision makers who seek to help manage such conflicts face criticism for seeking to arrange soft landings and power-sharing compromises. Purists identified with one side or another demand a clear alignment with the good guys (even where these are in short supply) and decry any evidence that the conflict manager is attributing "moral equivalence" to the conflict parties. Engagement with odious political actors (in the regime or the opposition) is attacked as conferring legitimacy on them. If an emerging political settlement leaves elements of the old regime and its administrative apparatus in place, voices are raised demanding regime change and a complete overthrow of the old order.

Other risks arise once the conflict manager enters the negotiating arena in transitional polities. The conflict parties will test each other and the peacemaker by pronouncing a series of preconditions that others must meet before talks can begin. Such demands need to be answered or—better yet—set aside so that serious talks can begin. The most difficult risks arise after relationships have evolved to the point that the parties respond seriously to the conflict manager's tests and probes. The conflict manager needs to reflect on what to do if the parties "bite": what do they get if they say yes to the challenge of a compromise deal. The greatest risk of engagement diplomacy is that it will work and thereby force the engager to make decisions as well.

NOTES

1. Robert Jervis, "Getting to Yes with Iran: The Challenges of Coercive Diplomacy," *Foreign Affairs* 92, no. 1 (January–February, 2013): 105–15, explores the application of promises, threats, rewards, and pressures.

2. Silvie Mahieu, "When Should Mediators Interrupt a Civil War? The Best Timing for a Ceasefire," *International Negotiation* 12, no. 2 (2007): 207–28.

3. See the discussion of engagement diplomacy in Fen Osler Hampson and I. William Zartman, *The Global Power of Talk: Negotiating America's Interests* (Boulder, CO: Paradigm, 2012), 89–116.

4. See Chester A. Crocker, "Peacemaking in Southern Africa: The Namibia-Angola Settlement of 1988," in *Herding Cats: Multiparty Mediation in a Complex World,* ed. Chester A. Crocker, Fen Osler Hampson, and Pamela Aall (Washington, DC: United States Institute of Peace Press, 1999), 207–44.

5. See Martti Ahtisaari, with Kriistina Rintakoski, "Mediation," in *The Oxford Handbook of Modern Diplomacy,* ed. Andrew Cooper, Jorge Heine, and Ramesh Thakur (Oxford: Oxford University Press, 2013): 337–51.

6. Dan Byman and Zack Gold, "The Salafi Awakening," *National Interest,* no. 120 (July–August 2012): 27–37.

7. I am indebted to Fen Hampson for bringing this argument to my notice (referred by Fareed Zakaria) at https://www.google.com/search?q=zakaria+Chances+are+small+the+U.S.+will+achieve+its+aims+in+Syria++&ie=utf-8&oe=utf-8&aq=t&rls=org.mozilla:en-US:official&client=firefox-a). Huntington's argument first appeared in *American Military Strategy,* Policy Papers in International Affairs no. 28 (Institute of International Studies, University of California, 1986), 15–16. See also Karin von Hippel, *Democracy by Force: US Military Intervention in the Post–Cold War World* (Cambridge: Cambridge University Press, 2000).

8. Richard K. Betts, "The Delusion of Impartial Intervention," *Foreign Affairs* 73, no. 6 (November–December 1994): 20–33.

9. To be sure, UN peacekeepers have intervened in the Democratic Republic of the Congo, but seldom has peace enforcement been attempted in this vast country. In 2013, the Security Council deployed a well-resourced combat brigade to stop the mayhem.

10. David L. Asher, Victor D. Comras, and Patrick M. Cronin, *Pressure: Coercive Economic Statecraft and US National Security* (Washington, DC: Center for a New American Security, 2011).

11. For a comprehensive treatment of this practice, including case studies, see Teresa Whitfield, *Friends Indeed? The United Nations, Groups of Friends and the Resolution of Conflict* (Washington, DC: United States Institute of Peace Press, 2007).

12. Chester A. Crocker, Fen Osler Hampson, and Pamela Aall, "Conclusion," in Crocker et al., *Herding Cats,* 665–700.

13. For a discussion of the pros and cons of these developments in the American legal and regulatory context, see Veronique Dudouet, "Mediating Peace with Proscribed Armed Groups," Special Report no. 239 (United States Institute of Peace, Washington, DC, May 2010); and Teresa Whitfield, *Mediation Practice Series: Engaging with Armed Groups* (Geneva: Centre for Humanitarian Dialogue, 2010). See also Robert Ricigliano, ed., *Choosing to Engage: Armed Groups and Peace Processes.* (London: Conciliation Resources Accord Series, 2005.)

14. I. William Zartman and Guy Olivier Faure, "Introduction: Why Engage and Why Not?" in *Engaging Extremists: Trade-Offs, Timing, and Diplomacy,* ed. I. William Zartman and Guy Olivier Faure (Washington, DC: United States Institute of Peace Press, 2011), 1–19.

15. On the Northern Ireland process, see Jonathan Powell, *Great Hatred, Little Room: Making Peace in Northern Ireland* (London: Bodley Head, 2008). On the Basque example, see Teresa Whitfield, *Endgame for ETA: Elusive Peace in the Basque Country* (London: C. Hurst and Co., 2014).

16. Dirk Vandewalle, "After Qaddafi: The Surprising Success of the New Libya," *Foreign Affairs* 91, no. 6 (November–December 2012): 8–15.

24

BUILDING INTERESTS, RELATIONSHIPS, AND CAPACITY
THREE ROADS TO CONFLICT MANAGEMENT

Pamela Aall

A central challenge for peacebuilding is to design activities that persuade conflict parties to move from war to peace, to give up fighting and move to social and political processes. Having some basic and reliable assumptions about what makes people stop fighting is critical to developing effective conflict management strategies, but a lot less attention has been paid by researchers to discovering why fighting stops than to explaining why wars end. And yet it is the objective of stopping violence, of "stopping the killing," as Roy Licklider has put it, that animates a good deal of conflict management work.[1] What are the strategies that peacemakers use to end fighting and why do they think those strategies work?

This chapter argues that the strategies that conflict managers use fall into three major groups. The first group consists of activities aimed at creating a common interest in peace through building common economic, social, and political interests.[2] The strategy

starts with the assumption that this web of interests will increase the costs of war while increasing the benefits of peace. The second group comprises activities that build personal relationships between and among conflict parties. Here, the assumption is that at least part of the problem lies in the parties' ignorance of each other's wants and needs. Once a personal relationship is established, it will be harder for any one individual or group to behave violently toward another. The third group focuses on increasing the capacity within the conflict parties or conflict societies to resolve their own problems. Building this capacity may entail any number of activities, from strengthening democratic institutions to providing new textbooks for teaching history. Whatever the activity, increased institutional and personal capacity will allow conflict societies to resolve their problems politically rather than through violence.

These strategic approaches can and often do overlap. Projects based on finding common interests often aim also to build or improve relations between parties. Projects based on building relationships may do so through capacity-building workshops. In fact, as this chapter concludes, conflict management efforts are most powerful when they intentionally involve all three approaches. In order to understand what this entails, the chapter looks in turn at the approaches—building interests, building relationships and building capacities—and examines the pros and cons of each. It then charts how the approaches can be used to address the four types of conflict raised in the first chapter of this book (conflicts arising from legitimacy battles, from weak states, and from existential threats, and interstate wars). The chapter concludes with a plea to strengthen coordination among institutions and approaches in order to stop wasting effort and to make conflict management more effective.

WHY DO CONFLICT PARTIES MAKE PEACE?

Why combatants stop fighting in cases of outright victory or an imposed peace is fairly straightforward as a question; the war is over and they have won, lost, or been suppressed.[3] In a negotiated agreement, however, there is not a clear victory and no clear winners and losers. Persuading parties to lay down arms in those circumstances is difficult. Many experts believe that conflict parties do not want to give up the options of using violence until all of their resources and capabilities are exhausted.[4] In their view, the job of the conflict manager—whether it is a powerful state, the United Nations, a regional organization, a nongovernmental organization (NGO), or a private person—is to recognize when these conditions prevail or to work to make them materialize. Other experts believe that conflict is the result of fear of the "other" and perceived inequality of access to goods and resources, and the only way to get parties to

move toward peace is to build relationships between groups and address their underlying fears, needs, and concerns. Still others believe that parties can recognize the advantage of peace well before the exhaustion period but may not have the skills and institutions to support the move away from violence. The job of the conflict manager in this scenario is to help conflict societies build the capacity to support the peace process.

Programs reflecting these three basic assumptions abound in the practice of responding to conflict. While originally peacebuilding was a small subfield populated largely by academics and humanitarians, today it is an expansive discipline that shapes the policies and practices of governments, international institutions, NGOs, and, occasionally, private enterprises.[5] The multi-institutional engagement reflects the recognition that conflicts are complex systems and that all parts of the complexity must be addressed in order to move from war to peace. While thirty years ago it was possible to congratulate oneself for a job well done if the parties signed a peace agreement, today the task of managing conflict has expanded to include the creation of new institutions, new social patterns, new economic structures, and, at times, new states. Success is measured not by the end of violence but by the viability of new institutions and the participation of previously marginalized groups (such as women) in the political process.

These new measures of success call for a multifaceted approach to conflict management. This tough task has been made tougher by the recent drop in the political appetite to engage in conflict zones. International involvement in the Afghanistan transition is a case in point. In early 2014, Afghanistan faced uncertainty in nearly every sector of its society. Politically, its government had relatively little legitimacy, as it struggled to deliver basic services, especially in the area of security. Although warlords had evolved from strongmen who use physical force to defend their interests to strongmen who used economic and political tools to get what they want, they still derived their power from their ability to call up their militias. Economically, Afghanistan depended on infusions of foreign cash; a good proportion of the population was unemployed, corruption was high, and foreign investment was scarce. Socially, its patchwork of ethnic groups was still a battlefield on which those groups vied for prominence. There was no common vision of what the country should strive to become, and the social cohesion needed to transform the state was lacking. To compound all these problems, a culture of violence had settled on the country after twenty-five years of war. The general public regularly carried arms for self-defense. Score settling, disguised as ethnic targeting, was a common means of resolving disputes.

Afghanistan's conflicts were too deeply imbedded in this complex fabric to be easily resolved. Afghanistan needed a process of conflict transformation that could deal with the underlying causes of conflict as well as the specific issues at hand.[6] To help get this transformation started, hundreds of foreign and domestic institutions launched aid and reconstruction programs, working on every aspect of the difficulties mentioned above.[7] They restructured political institutions, encouraging economic and social development, opening educational access, developing professional exchange programs, and providing training in technical skills and in conflict management. They engaged in diverse activities from educational programs in rural districts to working with female political figures in Kabul in order to help the country get back on its feet and allow it to establish the foundation for a stable, democratic, postconflict society. That they are still far from achieving this goal underscores the difficulty of the process.

However, because postconflict needs were so urgent, conflict management organizations

rarely had to deal with the question of *why* they believed that their particular activities would help to convince conflict parties to stop fighting. In part, this was due to the tendency among assistance organizations to react to immediate need, rather than engage in conflict analysis.[8] As a result, most programs were designed to meet basic human needs and at the same time address the conflict dynamics, correct the wrongs of the past, establish effective institutions, and establish a more open and transparent political environment. Relatively little systematic thought was given to how the different conflict management methods these programs used— political and social restructuring, institutional reform, economic development, transformation of educational systems, people-to-people exchange, mediation, facilitation, training, and even coercive measures, such as sanctions and robust peacekeeping—actually change attitudes and behaviors of conflict parties.

Recently, a number of scholars and practitioner institutions have tried to fill in this gap, incorporating theories of change into their research and practice of evaluation.[9] A theory of change provides the missing link to answering the question of why parties stop fighting, and gives conflict managers a road map to persuade parties to alter their behavior from pursuing war to pursuing peace. As they build their theory of change, conflict management institutions establish metrics that allow them to assess whether their work has impact.[10] These theories, however, are context-specific, meaning that they grow out of the specific circumstances of individual conflict cases. Building on that specific situation, theories of change may suggest approaches that might prove effective in some other conflicts, but approaches that would be applicable across *all* conflicts have yet to emerge.[11] Over time, testing hypotheses for theories of change may lead to larger, more robust theory, but in the interim, it is useful to focus on what conflict managers—whether they are powerful states or relatively power-less NGOs—*think* they are doing. The activi-ties they choose to endorse reveal underlying assumptions about changing behavior. Are they aware of these assumptions? Do patterns emerge in these assumptions? Can under-standing those assumptions lead to improve-ments in the practice of conflict management?

BUILDING INTERESTS

Building shared interests in resolving a com-mon problem has a long history in conflict pre-vention and containment. Governments and intergovernmental institutions, also known as the track one community, often employ an interest-based strategy in efforts to resolve disputes or conflicts. For instance, most bilat-eral and multilateral agreements, from trade deals to alliances, rest on this objective, and a good deal of diplomatic energy is spent iden-tifying common interests around contested issues. In these interest-based agreements, the common problem may be specific—determining who has rights to a resource such as oil or water, for example—or it may deal with more general issues, such as how politi-cal power is distributed in a postconflict set-ting. The nonofficial world—the track two community—has also contributed to the de-velopment of a problem-oriented approach to conflict management through such mecha-nisms as promoting dialogue and interactive conflict resolution.[12]

Whatever the issue is, it must be presented in ways that allow the antagonists to analyze the problem, identify their interests in find-ing a solution, develop options that would settle the issues, find a process by which they can negotiate a settlement, and arrive at an implementable solution. Most negotiation in the corporate and legal worlds is based on this functional approach to conflict resolution. Parties usually enter this kind of negotiation attempting to maximize their own gains, but they often find that compromises and

"giving to get" allow them to realize much of what they seek. In order to work, this type of win-win negotiation is heavily dependent on agreed-on laws or rules that can guide discussion.[13] In the world of violent conflict, however, gains are often seen as indivisible: one party's gain represents another's losses. In addition, disputes and problems are com-pounded by an absence of basic rules for managing conflict or by disagreement on or disregard for those basic rules. Among other objectives, interest-based conflict manage-ment, which focuses on developing a com-mon interest in an end to violence and a postconflict settlement, attempts to address this deficit.

One approach is to foster economic or political bonds between and among antago-nists. This approach has its roots in theories of functionalism and neofunctionalism.[14] These theories hold that the creation of shared interests on one project or in one sec-tor produces shared interests in other areas through a spillover effect. It was this theory and belief in spillover that lay behind the creation of the European Coal and Steel Community, the first institution of the cur-rent European Union. The European Union has been extremely successful as a conflict management mechanism. Turning their backs on almost a millennium of bloody conflict, EU members have seen sixty years of peace, and the development of a culture of collabo-ration that makes war in the EU space highly unlikely. The success of this venture was rec-ognized globally in 2012, when the Euro-pean Union received the 2012 Nobel Peace Prize for its contribution "to the advancement of peace and reconciliation, democracy and human rights in Europe."[15]

Although the recent tensions arising over the European Monetary Union and other matters have fueled the debate over the future of the European Union, this debate centers not on whether the European Union has kept the peace in Europe but on its effectiveness and political legitimacy as a democratic entity.[16] Although the institution has grown far beyond its early collaborative ventures, the objective that lay behind those early ventures—to tie Germany economically and politically to the rest of Europe so as to make war between them unthinkable—remains at the heart of the European experiment.

The European Union is a pragmatic, interest-based venture, and its success in Europe raises the question of why it has not been replicated—to the same extent—elsewhere.[17] One reason is the strong desire in most areas of the world for countries to preserve their sovereignty over both domestic and foreign policies. While other regions have established regional conflict management patterns, none have matched the European Union in the amount of power that individual countries cede to a central mechanism. Few other regions in the world have been willing to take on the financial and political costs of establishing joint political institutions, legal systems, and financial structures. Latin American countries, which have created a number of conflict-resolving mechanisms, prefer treaties and other law-based approaches. The members of the Association of Southeast Asian Nations (ASEAN) favor nonbinding, consensus-based initiatives. The African Union, while adopting a strong profile on peacekeeping and peace enforcement exercises, has been less enthusiastic about pushing other common functional interests among its membership.[18] However, the success of the European Union—shaky as it is in moments of crisis—remains the strongest argument for a pragmatic, interest-based approach to conflict management.

This approach lies behind other international agreements and institutions, too, including the United Nations' International Telecommunication Union, the UN Convention on the Law of the Sea, and countless other multilateral and bilateral treaties and entities dealing with issues ranging from collective security to trade. It is also found in nonofficial conflict management strategies that aim to build resistance to conflict through economic or social ties. A study by Ashutosh Varshney found that associational ties between different ethnicities seem to play a fairly powerful role in explaining outbreaks of violence—or rather the lack thereof—in several cities in India.[19] These associational ties built on common interests included "business associations, professional organizations, reading clubs, film clubs, sports clubs, festival organizations, trade unions, and cadre-based political parties."[20] It was these associational ties, rather than daily interactions between members of the different ethnic groups, that seem to prevent the outbreak of rioting and communal conflict in select urban areas. Cities of similar ethnic makeup that lack opportunities for associational ties experienced more violence. The Varshney study highlights the enduring relationships that have formed from associational ties and, for that reason, also has strong links to the relationship-building approach to conflict management. However, what is striking about this example is that the ties are built on common interests. The relationships are the result of the shared interests rather than the other way around; the common interests are the glue that cements the relationships together.

Building common interests underlies economic approaches to peacebuilding through business, finance, and commerce. Business practice, particularly in the area of natural resource development, has been linked to conflict, and this link has brought attention to the role that extractive industries play (often unintentionally) in promoting conflict.[21] But because there is a potent link between money, resources, and conflict, policymakers and practitioners have tried to build positive incentives for peace through business and commercial life. Often, the focus is largely on corporate social responsibility (CRS) issues such as human rights protection,[22] but some efforts have broadened CRS approaches to include peacebuilding efforts.[23] Smaller-scale efforts encourage the participation of women in local enterprise or involve local economic actors, such as agricultural extension agents, in conflict management initiatives.[24]

Another pragmatic approach to conflict management and resolution is through working groups and other fora that revolve around developing a common interest in resolving tangible problems among interested parties.[25] An example is the informal working group on the South China Sea convened in the 1990s by Hasjim Djalal, a former Indonesian minister for the law of the sea, and Ian Townsend-Gault, a Canadian academic. This effort consisted of a series of nonofficial workshops to discuss a range of joint scientific, environmental, and legal issues pertaining to the South China Sea. Participants included officials—acting in a nonofficial capacity—from states with claims on the South China Sea area, and the proceedings complemented a series of ongoing bilateral negotiations at the official level. These workshops encouraged dialogue and developed ideas for joint cooperation. They reduced tensions by addressing issues in an informal way and stressing the shared interests of the participants in solving common problems.

Successful as this process was, it also serves to highlight the limitations of the interest-building approach to conflict management. While participants were willing to discuss problematic issues, such as dealing with piracy in the region, the fundamental issue of rival claims over the territory was never addressed.[26] Indeed, two decades later, territorial disputes over the area are still active. In 2012, President Benigno Aquino III of the Philippines required his government's agencies to use the name "West Philippine Sea" when referring to the area, as a way of recognizing his country's claim to the Spratly Islands, also claimed by China, Vietnam,

and Taiwan. There are also conflicting claims about the Paracel Islands and the Scarborough Shoal, among others, and these territorial disputes are at the core of talks held in the ASEAN Plus Three (China, Japan, and South Korea) process. Does this mean that the South China Sea informal working group process was a failure? Making a direct link between the earlier 1990s working group process and today's official talks is difficult, but the ongoing attempts to resolve the disputes through diplomatic means arguably dates back to this effort.

Coercive conflict deterrence strategies, such as sanctions and the threat of or use of force, also fall into the interest-building category. Their purpose is to change the perception of the value of one course of action over another; in other words, to change the cost-benefit calculations of fighting and making peace. They build interest in peaceful strategies by increasing the costs of bellicose ones. Criticism has been lobbed at the use of these coercive strategies, because they are generally fairly blunt in their application and often bring suffering to the general population, rather than to the leadership responsible for promoting conflict. However, the use of targeted sanctions increases the ability to influence individual leaders. And as sanctions expert George A. Lopez points out, lifting those sanctions can become "astute rewards for other concessions."[27]

Among the three strategies, interest-building approaches are the easiest to assess as they often deal in matters that can be measured: land for peace, renegotiation of treaty terms, or access to resources, for example. However, the concrete nature of this approach is also its limitation, especially in those cases in which the concrete thing is tied up with strong perception or identity issues. For instance, people often have deep cultural attachments to land. In these cases, land is not only a tangible, divisible item but also a mark of personal or group identity. The conflict between the Moro Islamic Liberation Front and the government of the Republic of the Philippines was partly over land, but it was expressed in terms of "ancestral domain"; that is, what the historic claims to this land were, not what its economic worth was. Building interests in this case goes far beyond the ability to assign an economic or political worth, and has to incorporate a measure of mutual acknowledgement and respect, values that are difficult to produce from a cost-benefit strategy. Powerful as this strategy is, it can rarely be used alone, without the aid of the other two strategies.

BUILDING RELATIONSHIPS

A serious cost of conflict, particularly long-term social conflicts, is the loss of contact between or among the various parties. Conflict disrupts normal social connections. The danger of random or targeted violence, heightened animosity and distrust, desire to protect one's own group, and/or physical separation, break down communication among antagonists and make relationships distant, constrained, or nonexistent. The amount of exchange between Greek and Turkish Cypriots, for instance, was virtually nil from the mid-1970s to the mid-2000s, a thirty-year gap that promoted anger and resentment rather than contact and compromise. While negotiations did take place between the Greek and Turkish Cypriot leaders at a number of junctures during those thirty years, the general population had little incentive to learn about the other side, or to participate in peacebuilding exercises. The absence of any public buy-in may have led to the rejection of a UN plan for peace by Greek Cypriots in a 2004 plebiscite.

Relationships are severed in other ways. Sometimes, contact drops off because parties simply avoid one another. A case study on cattle-raiding dynamics among tribes in northern Kenya notes that "the conflict be-

tween the Turkana and the Pokot has been going for so many decades that most interviewees were unable to remember when they had last met with the other group."[28] Researchers of the Israeli-Palestinian conflict have found that the same dynamic holds, even in Jerusalem, a city shared by both groups.[29]

Conflict management strategies that address this isolation aim to build relationships that can form the basis for reconciliation.[30] These relationships do not have to be close or friendly. They do have to incorporate an element of respect and willingness to hear the other side out. It was this goal that Harold Saunders and his colleagues had in mind as they launched the Inter-Tajik Dialogue process, a non-official effort to prepare Tajik civil society to play an active role in the official UN–led peace process in 1993. While the effort was indeed intended to increase negotiating capacity among these civil society actors, Saunders notes that in deeply divided societies, "the real problem is how to start a political process that can change relationships and lead to the end of violence, to peace, and to reconciliation."[31] In this case, Saunders and his colleagues were focused on rebuilding relationships, using a capacity-building approach to do so. The same rationale underlies the work of local peace committees (LPCs). The LPCs' purpose is to provide a "local infrastructure for peace," where problems can be discussed and defused before they boil over into widespread violence. This methodology has been employed with positive effect in South Africa, Northern Ireland, and other conflict zones, using the establishment of local relationships across lines to solve problems.[32]

Relationship-building strategies are usually associated with non-official third parties or track two efforts, although a number of government-sponsored education and exchange programs—such as the US embassy's Bicommunal Support Program, which works to bring together Greek and Turkish

Cypriots—also have this objective in mind. A number of organizations specialize in "people-to-people" approaches, programs that convene representatives of the conflict groups "to interact purposefully in a safe, co-equal space to forge trust and empathy."[33] Examples of these programs include Seeds of Peace (SOP), an organization that conducts summer camps in Maine for youths from both sides of the Israeli-Palestinian conflict. The camps focus on dialogue led by facilitators. SOP maintains ties with former participants through the publication of a student-run newspaper, by bringing back former participants to assist with summer camps, and by networking within students' home countries. Since 1993, SOP has established International Camps that parallel the Maine camp and has focused on working with educators as well as students.[34]

Another example is the community relations work undertaken in Northern Ireland. Initially sponsored by the British government, the program distributes money through the Central Community Relations Unit, which reports to the Northern Ireland Civil Service. Community councils sponsor community relations events (one-off events that highlight the need for further contact, such as a "peace tree planting ceremony") and long-term projects (such as the formation of inter-communal sports teams and brass bands). Community councils also sponsor focused community relations projects, such as conferences and workshops that explicitly address community relations.[35]

Other efforts target improving the quality and salience of the conversation once the group is together, helping participants overcome limitations imposed by the past relationships. These limitations may include a refusal to talk, avoidance of sensitive issues, an inability to move beyond mutual recrimination, and the deployment of various delaying or derailing tactics. Sustained dialogue (SD)

"is a process for transforming the relationships that cause problems, create conflict and block change. SD is not a problem-solving workshop but a sustained interaction that develops through a sequence of meetings over months or years. The process moves through five recognizable phases: deciding to engage; mapping relationships; probing problems and relationships; scenario-building; and acting together."[36] The Inter-Tajik Dialogue, mentioned above, is an example of SD, as is the work of the South African local peace committees that promoted communication between former antagonists as the country made its transition from apartheid to multiracial democracy.[37]

Problem-solving workshops are another example of an effort to produce productive dialogue among conflict parties. Harvard professor Herbert Kelman's problem-solving workshop approach brings together influential individuals who represent the various parties to a conflict. The objective of the workshop is to increase understanding of each party's position and circumstances and to identify acceptable solutions to the conflict. As the participants return to their own communities, they carry with them their new insights and suggestions for action and feed these into the political process.[38] In some ways, this methodology is similar to the spill-over effect that was the basis for neofunctionalism, and like that phenomenon it has met with some success and some challenges in transferring positive experiences in one sector or venue to another. However, the problem-solving workshops that Herbert Kelman and Nadim Rouhana ran in the early 1990s between Israeli and Palestinians have been credited with building the relationships critical to the Oslo Accords negotiations and with helping develop negotiating relationships in other protracted conflicts.[39]

There is a flip side to relationship building. When the parties believe that relations are beyond repair, they may opt for partition and separation rather than attempting to build or rebuild relationships. While this is often the goal of at least one party to the conflict, the solution has a mixed record in preventing or managing conflict. Pakistan's separation from India has not prevented the two countries from constant political (and sometimes physical) warfare and a protracted stand-off in Kashmir. South Sudan's separation from Sudan, while still in its early days, shows many signs of deteriorating into armed conflict between the two countries over the border regions.

Dealing with the human aspect of conflict through addressing relationship issues is critical to the success of conflict management. As important as it is, however, there are limitations to what it can achieve. While there is evidence that building relationships among individuals or specific groups can lead to attitudinal change, there is also evidence that change may be temporary and/or tied to specific issues in specific circumstances.[40] Changes in the relationships between individuals may not be significant enough to change group attitudes and in fact may put those individuals at risk within their communities. Even in those cases where leaders and other influential persons develop a better sense of understanding through relationship-building strategies, there is no guarantee that their constituents will support their changed attitudes. Making sure that supporters continue to back them can put strong constraints on leaders, and make it difficult for them to achieve change across society. Changing views or behaviors at the local level is difficult enough. Expanding that effort to produce attitudinal change throughout the conflict parties takes a level of effort equivalent a massive national rebuilding project. In other words, in order for relationship building to work, it too has to be used in conjunction with other strategies.

STRATEGIES BASED ON HOW: BUILDING CAPACITY

The capacity-building approach to conflict management has roots in human development theory, which focuses on building individual capability as a means to generate economic and social growth, and in democratic peace theory, which is built on the premise that fully democratic countries do not go to war with each other.[41] The fundamental objective of capacity building is to improve the effectiveness and accountability of governments, institutions, and individuals so that they can function better and resolve conflict through peaceful means. Capacity building is not primarily associated with any one set of institutional actors. Both official and nonofficial institutions sponsor capacity-building activities. And although it is not new, its usage has risen dramatically as a conflict management and resolution technique over the past twenty years. In 1992, then UN secretary-general Boutros Boutros-Ghali introduced the concept of peacebuilding, defined as "action to identify and support structures which will tend to strengthen and solidify peace in order to avoid a relapse into conflict."[42] Over the intervening years, many programs have been developed to support the structures Boutros-Ghali refers to. In this context, the term "capacity building" is often used to cover a wide variety of activities aimed at increasing the capacity of local, host-country nationals to prevent and resolve their own conflicts. These activities range from small training programs in conflict management, negotiation, and civil society activism to the reform of whole sectors of society; for example, the police, the educational system, or the judicial system. There are also strong proponents—especially in the military services—for using capacity building as a way to improve security or to avoid conflicts. US secretary of defense Robert Gates helped to reorient American defense policies through his call for "building partner capacity" as a strategic goal for the armed services. He put it bluntly: "In these [current conflict] situations, the effectiveness and credibility of the United States will only be as good as the effectiveness, credibility, and sustainability of its local partners."[43]

Capacity building has been strongly associated with the postconflict phase, with the rebuilding of societies and political structures that can address their own rifts and resist the return to conflict, as noted in the Boutros-Ghali definition. The United Nations Development Programme notes in the introduction to its 2010 report on capacity building in postconflict societies that the content focuses on "coherent and well coordinated early action to support post-conflict governments to build core state capacities that will help to restore legitimacy and effectiveness."[44] The unstated assumption in this formulation is that legitimacy and effectiveness will produce a more democratic, more inclusive, and, at the same time, more efficient means of making policy and resolving differences, a tall order even in the most stable of circumstances.

It is this underlying idea that drives the movement toward capacity building. According to the movement's proponents, the heightened ability to govern will not only allow states to make the transition from war to peace but also enable them to resolve disputes in an equitable way. This approach to managing conflict extends far beyond the institutions and mandates traditionally associated with the field. It may engage development agencies, law-based NGOs, education and training specialists, management consultants, and/or corporations. The areas of focus might include the reform of the civil service, legal reforms in the area of criminal and civil law or of economic accountability, training of parliamentarians, inclusion of women in the political process, civic education, and de-

velopment of civil society. The list is almost endless.[45]

On the official side, one of the more interesting and controversial experiments in the area of capacity building for conflict management has been the development, in the Iraq and Afghanistan wars, of provincial reconstruction teams (PRTs). PRTs were temporary arrangements conceived by the State Department and staffed by an interagency team (composed of both government officials and private citizens), representing different competencies: health, transportation, justice, security, and so forth. The purpose of these teams was to "diminish the means and motivations for conflict, while developing local institutions so they can take the lead role in national governance (provide basic services, foster economic development, and enforce the rule of law)."[46] In other words, the intention in creating the PRTs was to improve the capacity of local institutions, which would lead to greater local government legitimacy and therefore greater capacity to exert authority and manage conflict. The controversy lies not in the PRTs' intentions but in how well they worked in practice.

Other official efforts to increase conflict-handling mechanisms through capacity building have been quite diverse. The European Union has capacity-building programs aimed at shoring up the legitimacy and effectiveness of the African Union, particularly in the area of conflict prevention.[47] Its training mission in Mali goes beyond civilian capacity building and includes engaging Mali's military on countering the challenges in the north of the country. OneWorld, an NGO that increases communication in developing countries, notes that its efforts are aimed at "capacity building in our respective countries . . . [which] will guarantee peace and security, and make it possible to attain high growth rates."[48] A number of institutions link capacity building among women as being a critical element in addressing conflict. The United

Nations, the European Parliament, and many NGOs make explicit connections between developing capacity in women and strengthening peace and security.[49] The same link surfaces across many sectors—strengthening the capacity of institutions (or civil society, or local groups) and increasing conflict prevention and resolution capabilities. Some of these projects try to combine changing social attitudes with capacity building, a combination often seen in tandem in efforts to reform curricula or revise how material is taught. A number of these curriculum reform efforts have been successfully introduced into school systems.[50]

It is the almost infinite incarnations that capacity building can take that makes the capacity-building approach to conflict management difficult to define, conceive, and assess. If everything is important to the conflict management process, what are the priorities? The task of setting priorities is made more difficult by the fact that most of the institutions involved in capacity building do not regard themselves primarily as conflict resolvers. From their point of view, they are playing an important role in helping the country or society in question come up to the mark in one critical area, such as law or security. They are not engaged in a communitywide effort to provide a holistic solution to an impending or ongoing conflict. Building peace, in other words, comes as a result of the success in another area, almost as an unintentional consequence of better education and training in a host of areas, such as civil society development or community policing.

In addition, world history shows that peaceful behavior is not necessarily a corollary of more capable practice. Building capacity can also build proficiency in war fighting, as the AFRICOM (US Command for Africa) found when some soldiers it had trained in Mali defected to join the northern Islamic rebels; human rights organizations accused other soldiers of killing many noncombatants

and worsening tensions in the country as part of the military campaign against the northern rebels.[51] As this example shows, capacity building as an approach to conflict management can be a doubled-edged sword. In the right hands and circumstances, it can bring new capabilities to a peacemaking or transitional effort. In the wrong hands or at the wrong time, it can give spoilers or other opponents of negotiated agreements tools that they can use for their own ends.

MATCHING APPROACHES TO CONFLICTS

Deciding which of the three approaches to management conflict—interest building, relationship building, or capacity building—would work best on which conflict is difficult because a large part of the success of these approaches depends as much on the conflict environment and the personalities of the participants involved in the efforts as on the approach itself. Moreover, these approaches are not the only means to successful conflict management. For instance, when addressing an intractable conflict, surprising progress can occur if the leadership is ready for a bold step, as was Egypt's Anwar Sadat when he became the first Arab leader to visit Israel and, later, when he signed the Camp David Accords with the Israeli prime minister Menachem Begin in 1978 and the Egypt-Israel Peace Treaty of 1979. In fact, if you ask a practitioner what works when, you are likely to get a fairly stock response: "It depends," meaning it depends on the timing, actors, moments of opportunity, unforeseen circumstances, and (it seems) phases of the moon.

Rather than arguing which approach is best, it may be more productive to identify how each approach might contribute to managing different kinds of conflicts. The introductory chapter of this book suggests there are four different types of conflict that characterize the current global security environment:

conflicts over legitimacy, conflicts caused by state weakness and fragility, conflicts based on existential rivalries, and conflicts that arise from interstate power rivalries. Table 1 matches some of the conflict management strategies discussed above to some of the major conflict types. For example, in conflicts based on legitimacy disputes, an interest-building conflict management approach would concentrate on shoring up programs or elements that both (or all) parties would find attractive (such as agreeing on power-sharing or revenue-sharing arrangements), while the relationship-building approach would focus on bringing groups together so that they could discuss (and perhaps resolve) their disputes. The capacity-building approach might target the reform of institutions (such as those within the security sector and educational system) that provoke or exacerbate the legitimacy dispute.

The purpose of Table 1 is not to take a stand on what strategy best suits which type of conflict but to demonstrate that none of the three approaches is necessarily strong enough in and of itself to effect change in a conflict situation. While these categorizations are helpful to tease out primary assumptions behind the answer to the question of why conflict parties make peace, many conflict management strategies combine elements from all three approaches. The conflict manager who focuses on interests as the most promising avenue to resolving conflict issues may in fact also encourage better relationships between parties, through training as a means to a peacebuilding end. For instance, when the United States Institute of Peace (USIP) engaged with the conflict between Serbs and Kosovar Albanians in 1998–2000, the focus was on building a common vision for the future of Kosovo, or in other words, the focus was on interests. However, getting to the common vision entailed a good deal of relationship building within the Kosovar

Albanian community, which was torn by partisan fighting. Another aspect of reaching a common vision was USIP's program of negotiation training offered to both Serbs and Albanians. Only the Albanians accepted this capacity-building support, but without it the primary goal of a common vision would have been much more difficult to reach.[52]

The Kosovar conflict, of course, did not end through the negotiation of a common vision among unified parties. Shortly after the USIP project held its first meeting, NATO bombed Belgrade, providing a show of force that immediately altered the situation on the ground. The NATO campaign focused on changing the interests, raising the costs to the Serbs of continuing to fight, and making the benefits of stopping the fight more compelling. The NATO strategy was not concerned with building relationships or negotiating capacity. The NATO campaign was successful in stopping the violence in the short run, but did little to lay the foundation for building a functioning relationship between the parties in the long run. The USIP strategy, ineffective in stopping the fighting, may well have helped to build reconciled relationships over a longer term. At the time, however, these conflict management efforts operated independently of each other, so the opportunity for synergies between them was absent.

NEED FOR COORDINATION

This last point—the need for institutions to work in concert on conflict management strategies in order to achieve a noticeable impact—highlights a critical challenge to any and all approaches to peacebuilding. The need for coordination has received a great deal of attention over the past decade, but the problems remain the same: different institutional approaches to the same problem; lack of leadership; dissipation of effort; and the tendency of the parties to the conflict to "forum

Table 1. Illustrative conflict management strategies by conflict type

Type of conflict	Conflict management approach		
	Interest building	Relationship building	Capacity building
Legitimacy disputes	Coalition building; negotiation; power sharing arrangements; mediation; isolation and/or engagement strategies	Efforts to build relationships between disputants, and between civil society groups; problem-solving workshops on disputed issues; sustained dialogue initiatives	Constitutional, electoral, and institutional reform; education; training and mentoring; support to parties to build up legitimacy
State (or institutional) weakness	Coalition building around common objectives among civil society and official institutions; aid; trade	Coalition building; facilitation; dialogue	Support for strengthening and reforming government institutions; support for establishing and/or strengthening civil society institutions; economic and political accountability reform; education; training and mentoring
Existential rivalries	Negotiation; mediation; confidence-building measures; agreements based on benchmarks and monitoring; aid and trade; power-sharing arrangements; establishing or strengthening ties over common interests; expansion of pie	Efforts to change attitudes among leaders and citizen groups; sustained facilitated dialogue	Reforming and strengthening official and civil society efforts in addressing issues; education and training on democracy, tolerance, "living with the other"; strengthening conflict resolution capacity of dominant and marginalized groups (women, youth, etc.)
Interstate power rivalries	Negotiated understandings and agreements; diplomatic pressure (engagement and isolation); concert-based (as in Concert of Europe) strategies of negotiation; forging and strengthening economic ties; institutional arrangements based on common interests	Facilitated dialogue to surface issues related to perceived threats or lack of respect in the official relationships; citizen exchange; collaborative problem-solving workshops	Support for institutional cooperation; education; training and mentoring

shop," moving from one would-be peace-builder to another as it suits the party's narrow interests.[53]

Even bringing up the topic of coordination can raise hackles. "Coordination" is a term that can sound like "management-speak." It may also seem like a heavy-handed approach to the task at hand, with visions of one insti-

tution at the top of the hierarchy being in charge and issuing orders to the other "coordinated" institutions. The institution that most naturally assumes this role is the military, but military approaches to conflict management may sometimes be inappropriate or counterproductive to a political or social process. As the example of the PRTs illustrates, civilian government agencies do collaborate among themselves and will coordinate with the military in specific settings, but these coordinated bodies take a high degree of energy to maintain and often suffer in microcosm from the same institutional dysfunction that marks the overall coordination effort. NGOs are often excluded from these official coordinating bodies, even though they are often the implementing agencies for government development agencies and ministries and for multilateral development banks.

This lack of coordination means that even when these different institutions are taking the same approach to a problem—for instance, a capacity-building effort for security sector reform—they may use very different tactics to achieve their ends. One set of institutions may work on creating the capacity for dialogues between local community leaders and local police as a grassroots peacebuilding measure that might reach upward to affect the elites. Another set of institutions might work directly with government officials and policymakers to institute widespread reforms in the army, justice system, and police, with the aim of increasing democracy in the security sector. Both are important tasks, but it is likely that they will take place in isolation from each other; and it is just as likely that the institutions will criticize the approach taken by the other set of institutions. While not subverting one another's work, neither are they building on each other's efforts. Addressing this problem is not easy, as it often awakens a defensiveness growing out of the desire to protect institutional autonomy and the requirements of the institutions' mandates.

Another challenge is in the assessment of these efforts. Institutions may take different approaches to help resolve the problems that they find in conflict situations, but the reasons that they choose these strategies are complex. Part of the choice lies in understanding what the institution is good at, be it negotiation, contact opportunities, or training programs.

Another element, as noted above, lies in the theory of change to which the institution subscribes. Conflict, however, is such a complex system that it is hard to isolate the impact of one aspect of an intervention over another. Impact may be the result of well-planned projects, carefully designed and implemented over time, and measured at the end to assess the degree of impact. It rarely comes from a number of loosely related projects that may all be excellent efforts in their own right but do not build a unified whole. These projects generally lack impact and, worse still, they may distract and dissipate valuable energy, both for the organization that undertakes the project and for the people who stand to benefit from it. If a golden rule for the development world is "do no harm," taken from the Hippocratic oath, a golden rule for the conflict management field should be "do not compete." A more precise version might read, "do not distract, overlap, duplicate, subvert, or undermine the other's initiative out of institutional rivalry and cultural dissonance."

While the field waits for better methodologies and better metrics, there are steps that institutions and actors can take to heighten the chances that their interventions will cause more good than harm: careful assessments, deliberate design based on an understanding of the relevant theory of change, joint education and training opportunities, collaborative action with other conflict management institutions, careful collection of data, and realistic interpretation of results. In addition, there need to be greater professional incentives for lateral thinking and teamwork across institutional and process divides. Instead of insisting on the supremacy of one or the other approach, conflict management actors need to recognize, understand, and validate all three approaches, and work for better collaboration among those practitioners and institutions that bring different strengths and experiences. Until conflict managers and peacebuilders do this, the effectiveness of their efforts will continue to be determined largely by luck.

NOTES

With thanks to Sarah Graveline, currently a Boren Fellow in Tanzania and formerly a research assistant at the United States Institute of Peace, for her help in researching some of the cases for this paper.

1. Roy Licklider, *Stopping the Killing: How Civil Wars End* (New York: New York University Press, 1995).

2. For ease of reference, this chapter uses the shorthand term "conflict manager" to refer to all institutions and persons who engage in conflict management and peacebuilding. This list includes foreign ministries and development agencies of a number of large and small countries, international organizations, NGOs, peace initiatives led by internationally eminent persons, civil society organizations, militaries engaged in peacekeeping missions, and other activities designed to encourage movement away from violence and toward peace.

3. The same dynamics may also be at work in some cases of global systemic change (such as the fall of the Berlin Wall in 1989), especially when one party benefits from the change. However, systemic change can also raise uncertainty for all parties, making them unsure about their relative status and fearful that the changes will leave them worse off. Both dynamics were at work in Eastern and Southeastern Europe at the end of the Cold War. In most countries, democratic forces were the victors over the former repressive regimes. In the former Yugoslavia, however, the systemic change raised the level of interethnic competition and fear, ripe circumstances for ambitious nationalist leaders who preferred to achieve their ends through war rather than negotiation.

4. See I. William Zartman, "Ripeness: The Hurting Stalemate and Beyond," in *International Conflict Resolution after the Cold War*, ed. Paul C. Stern and Daniel Druckman (Washington, DC: National Academies Press, 2000), 225–50. For a different view, see Edward N. Luttwak, "Give War a Chance," *Foreign Affairs* 78, no. 4 (July/August 1999).

5. Louis Kriesberg, "The Growth of the Conflict Resolution Field," in *Turbulent Peace: The Challenges of Managing International Conflict*, ed. Chester A. Crocker, Fen Osler Hampson, and Pamela Aall (Washington, DC: United States Institute of Peace Press, 2001), 407–26.

6. John Paul Lederach, *Preparing for Peace: Conflict Transformation across Cultures* (Syracuse, NY: Syracuse University Press, 1995).

7. Afghanistan Research and Evaluation Unit, *The A to Z Guide to Afghanistan Assistance*, 10th ed. 2012), 199–341, http://areu.org.af/Uploads/Edition Pdfs/1208E-A%20to%20Z%202012.pdf, accessed October 12, 2013.

8. This practice is changing, albeit slowly. Recently, a number of studies have concentrated on what the intervention or conflict management strategy is trying to achieve: security, a responsive political system, a robust legal structure, a functioning economy, healthy social institutions, etc. See Beth Cole et al., *Guiding Principles for Stabilization and Reconstruction* (Washington, DC: United States Institute of Peace Press, 2009).

9. Ilana Shapiro, "Theories of Change," in *Beyond Intractability*, ed. Guy Burgess and Heidi Burgess (Boulder: Conflict Research Consortium, University of Colorado, Boulder, January 2005), http://www.beyondintractability.org/essay/theories_of_change/, accessed July 23, 2013. See also the work of CDA Collaborative Learning Projects, the Organization for Education and Cooperation in Europe; and Eileen Babbitt, Diana Chigas, and Robert Wilkinson, with Amex International, "Theories and Indicators of Change Briefing Paper: Concepts and Primers for Conflict Management and Mitigation" (briefing paper, US Agency for International Development [USAID], Washington, DC, January 2013).

10. There is a rich literature on evaluation of peace, conflict management, and peacebuilding projects. For example, a seminal project by the Collaborative for Development Action (CDA) in 1999, Mary B. Anderson, *Do No Harm: How Aid Can Support Peace—Or War* (Boulder, CO: Lynne Rienner, 1999), examined the link between development, peace, and conflict. This effort was followed by another path-breaking study by Mary Anderson and Lara Olson, "Confronting War: Critical Lessons for Peace Practitioners" (report, Collaborative for Development Action, Cambridge, MA, 2003). This work has been continued by CDA under its Reflecting on Peace Practice program. The Organisation for Economic Co-operation and Development (OECD) has also been very active in this area. See http://www.eldis.org/vfile/upload/1/document /1201/hoffman_handbook.pdf, http://web.idrc.ca/ uploads/user-S/10533919790A_Measure_of_Peace. pdf, and http://www.oecd.org/countries/angola/351 14211.pdf. See also Mark Hoffman, *Peace and Conflict Impact Assessment Methodology* (Berlin: Berghof Research Center for Constructive Conflict Management, 2004); and Lisa Schirch, *Conflict Assessment and Peacebuilding Planning: Toward a Participatory Approach to Human Security* (Boulder, CO: Kumarian; Lynne Rienner, 2013).//www.berghof-handbook.net.

11. Babbitt et al., *Theories and Indicators*, 2–3.

12. Ronald J. Fisher, "Methods of Third-Party Intervention," in *Berghof Handbook for Conflict Transformation II.*, ed. M. Fischer, H. Geismann, and B. Schmelzle (Berlin: Berghof Research Center for Constructive Conflict Management, 2010), 157–82.

13. Roger Fisher, William Ury and Bruce Patton, *Getting to Yes: Negotiating Agreement Without Giving In*, 2nd ed. (New York: Penguin Books USA, 1991).

14. See David Mitrany, *The Functional Theory of Politics* (New York: St. Martin's, 1975); and Ernst Hass, *The Uniting of Europe*, (Stanford, CA: Stanford University Press, 1958). Neofunctional theory took the European experiment as its principal case study, and its fortunes as an explanatory theory have waxed and waned with the institution itself.

15. The Norwegian Nobel Committee announcement of the 2012 Nobel Peace Prize, at http://no belpeaceprize.org/en_GB/laureates/laureates-2012 /announce-2012, accessed February 17, 2013.

16. See Johan Galtung and Larry Siedentop, *Democracy in Europe* (Harmondsworth, England: Penguin, 2000); and Andrew Moravcsik, "In Defence of the 'Democratic Deficit': Reassessing Legitimacy in the European Union," *Journal of Common Market Studies* 40, no. 4 (2002): 603–24. There continues to be a lively debate over whether neofunctionalism was one of the causes of the Euro-crisis of 2012–13. See Thomas M. Dunn, "Neo-Functionalism and the European Union," for *e-International Relations*, November 28, 2012, http://www.e-ir.info/2012/11/28/neo-functional

ism-and-the-european-union, accessed February 17, 2013.

17. Much has been written on this topic. See, for example, Joseph S. Nye, *Peace in Parts: Integration and Conflict in Regional Organization* (Boston: Little, Brown, 1971); Joaquin Roy and Roberto Dominguez, eds., *The European Union and Regional Integration: A Comparative Perspective and Lessons for the Americas* (Miami, FL: University of Miami Press, 2005), http://www.as.miami.edu/eucenter/books /The%20EU-Regiional-text+cover-final.pdf, accessed December 15, 2013; Benoit Mayer, "The 'European Model' of International Law and Its Significance for Asia: Some Critical Reflections," Working Paper no. 7 (EU Centre in Singapore, June 2012), http://www.eucentre.sg/wp-content/uploads /2013/06/WP07.EuropeanModelofInternational Law.pdf, accessed December 15, 2013.

18. Chrysantus Ayangafac and Jakkie Cilliers, "Assessing the Capacity of African Peace and Security Architecture," in Chester A. Crocker, Fen Osler Hampson, and Pamela Aall, eds., *Rewiring Regional Security in a Fragmented World* (Washington, DC: United States Institute of Peace Press, 2011), 215–48.

19. Ashutosh Varshney, *Ethnic Conflict and Civic Life: Hindus and Muslims in India* (New Haven, CT: Yale University Press, 2002); "Ethnic Conflict and Civil Society: India and Beyond," *World Politics* 53 (April 2001): 362–98.

20. Varshney, *Ethnic Conflict and Civic Life*, 1.

21. Ian Bannion and Paul Collier, *Natural Resources and Violent Conflict* (Washington, DC: World Bank, 2003).

22. See, for example, the work of the UN Global Compact, which has put together informal codes of conduct for institutions, including corporations, working in troubled areas. These "codes" cover a number of different areas from human rights protection to anticorruption measures.

23. For example, the Business for Peace Foundation (Norway) honors several business leaders every year for their peacebuilding work (see http:// businessforpeace.no, accessed August 29, 2013). While this is an area of growth in the conflict management field, data is hard to come by. For instance, it is clear that corporations are actively working to increase transparency and fight corruption—over seventy large oil, gas, and mining companies belong to the Extractive Industries Transparency Initiative (EITI; an international initiative that certifies the revenue transparency compliance of natural resource-rich countries), according to the EITI website, http://eiti.org/eiti, accessed July 29, 2013. However, it is difficult to develop figures on a direct correlation between their initiatives and the reduction or prevention of conflict. See Ans Kolk and François Lenfant, "MNC Reporting on CSR and Conflict in Central Africa," *Journal of Business Ethics* 93, no. 2 (2010): 241–55.

24. A small-scale project of the US Department of Agriculture (USDA) and USIP, run in 2011–12, revolved around training agricultural extension agents working in conflict areas. Agricultural extension agents are government employees whose function is to improve agricultural practice in their area of responsibility. They interact with farmers, farm suppliers, and other local players in the agricultural marketplace. In some cases, they are mistrusted because of their connection with government, but in others they are seen as a legitimate interlocutor and beneficial resource. The USIP-USDA project was meant to increase their conflict-handling skills so that they could prevent or resolve local conflicts before they escalated into widespread violence. The project was premised on the assumption that farmers were interested in increasing their productivity, and on the ability of the agricultural agent to convince them that violence or protracted conflict would impede their efforts to reach that new level of productivity.

25. Teresa Whitfield, *Friends Indeed? The United Nationals, Groups of Friends and the Resolution of Conflict* (Washington, DC: United States Institute of Peace Press, 2007).

26. Hasjim Djalal and Ian Townsend-Gault, "Managing Potential Conflicts in the South China Sea: Informal Diplomacy for Conflict Prevention," in *Herding Cats: Multiparty Mediation in a Complex World*, ed. Chester A. Crocker, Fen Osler Hampson, and Pamela Aall (Washington, DC: United States Institute of Peace Press, 1999), 107–34.

27. Quoted in Howard LaFranci, "If Sanctions Worked with Iran, Would They Work with Rogue States?" *Christian Science Monitor*, November 27, 2013, http://www.csmonitor.com/World/Security -Watch/2013/1127/If-sanctions-worked-with-Iran -will-they-work-with-rogue-nations, accessed December 10, 2013.

28. Janpeter Schilling, Francis E. O. Opigo, and Jürgen Scheffran, "Raiding Pastoral Livelihoods: Motives and Effects of Violent Conflict in North-western Kenya," in Janpeter Schilling et al., *Pastoralism: Research, Policy and Practice* 2, no. 25 (2012), accessed February 25, 2014, http://www .pastoralismjournal.com/content/2/1/25.

29. See, for example, Bernard Wasserstein, *Divided Jerusalem: The Struggle for the Holy City* (New Haven, CT: Yale University Press, 2001); and Jon Calame and Esther Charlesworth, *Divided Cities: Belfast, Beirut, Jerusalem, Mostar, and Nicosia* (Philadelphia: University of Pennsylvania Press, 2012).

30. John Paul Lederach, *Building Peace: Sustainable Reconciliation in Divided Societies* (Washington, DC: United States Institute of Peace Press, 1997), 23–35.

31. Harold H. Saunders, "Prenegotiation and Circum-negotiation," in *Turbulent Peace: The Challenges of Managing International Conflict*, ed. Chester A. Crocker, Fen Osler Hampson, and Pamela Aall (Washington, DC: United States Institute of Peace Press, 2001), 485.

32. Andries Odendaal, *A Crucial Link: Local Peace Committees and National Peacebuilding* (Washington, DC: United States Institute of Peace Press, 2013).

33. USAID, *People to People Peacebuilding: A Program Guide* (report prepared for USAID, Bureau for Democracy, Conflict, and Humanitarian Assistance, Office of Conflict Management and Mitigation, Washington, DC, January 2011), http://transi tion.usaid.gov/our_work/cross-cutting_programs /conflict/publications/docs/CMMP2PGuidelines 2010-01-19.pdf, accessed March 3, 2013.

34. Ned Lazarus, "Evaluating Peace Education in the Oslo-Intifada Generation: A Long-Term Impact Study of Seeds of Peace 1993–2010" (PhD dissertation, American University, 2011).

35. Colin Knox and Joanne Hughes, "Crossing the Divide: Community Relations in Northern Ireland" *Journal of Peace Research* 33, no. 1 (February 1996): 83–98.

36. Bettye Pruitt and Philip Thomas, "Democratic Dialogue: A Handbook for Practitioners" (commissioned by the Canadian International Development Agency, International, the Organization of American States, and the United Nations Development Programme, 2007).

37. Harold H. Saunders and Randa Slim, "The Inter-Tajik Dialogue: From Civil War towards Civil Society," *Accord 10* (2001), http://www.c-r.org/accord-article/inter-tajik-dialogue-civil-war-towards-civil-society, accessed July 30, 2013. See also Harold H. Saunders, *Sustained Dialogue in Conflicts: Transformation and Change* (New York: Palgrave MacMillan, 2012). For other examples of dialogue work, see David R. Smock and Daniel Serwer, eds., *Facilitating Dialogue: USIP's Work in Conflict Zones* (Washington, DC: United States Institute of Peace Press, 2012). For a review of local peace committees' work in South Africa, Northern Ireland, and Kenya, see Andries Odendall, *A Crucial Link: Local Peace Committees and National Peacebuilding* (Washington, DC: United States Institute of Peace Press, 2013).

38. Herbert C. Kelman, "The Interactive Problem-Solving Approach," in *Managing Global Chaos: Sources of and Responses to International Conflict*, ed. Chester A. Crocker and Fen Osler Hampson with Pamela Aall (Washington, DC: United States Institute of Peace Press, 1996), 501–19.

39. R. J. Fisher, "Interactive Conflict Resolution," in I. W. Zartman, ed., *Peacemaking in International Conflict* (Washington, DC: United States Institute of Peace Press, 2007), 237.

40. Knox and Hughes, "Crossing the Divide," 85–86.

41. On human development, see Amartya Sen, *Development as Freedom* (New York: Knopf, 1999); and the UN Development Program's annual *Human Development Report*. On democratic peace, see, for example, Michael W. Doyle, *Ways of War and Peace* (New York: W. W. Norton, 1997); Edward D. Mansfield and Jack Snyder, *Electing to Fight: Why Emerging Democracies Go to War* (Boston: MIT Press, 2005); and Bruce Russett, *Grasping the Democratic Peace* (Princeton, NJ: Princeton University Press, 1993).

42. Boutros Boutros-Ghali, *An Agenda for Peace: Preventive Diplomacy, Peacemaking and Peace-keeping* (UN Document A/47/277, Report of the Secretary-General pursuant to the statement adopted by the Summit Meeting of the Security Council on January 31, 1992), http://www.un-documents.net/a47-277.htm, accessed September 2, 2013.

43. Robert M. Gates, "Helping Others Defend Themselves: The Future of U.S. Security Assistance," *Foreign Affairs* 89, no. 3 (May/June 2010): 2–6.

44. Jago Salmon and Eugenia Piza-Lopez, "Capacity Development in Post-Conflict Countries" (Global Event working paper, UN Development Programme, Washington, DC, 2010), 3. http://www.undp.org/content/dam/aplaws/publication/en/publications/capacity-development/capacity-development-in-post-conflict-countries/CD%20in%20post%20conflict%20countries.pdf, accessed February 18, 2013.

45. There has been a proliferation of training materials aimed at building capacity in conflict management. These materials are often aimed at an inclusive audience, underscoring both the breadth of reach and the unfocused approach of these efforts. See, for example, the UN Public Administration Network's training manual, "Developing Capacity for Conflict Analysis and Early Response," which is aimed at "Funders, Middle level policy makers, Advocacy Organisations, Pressure Groups, Non-governmental Organisations in development and peace building, Conflict Parties and other Stakeholders," http://unpan1.un.org/intradoc/groups/public/documents/un/unpan011117.pdf, accessed February 24, 2013.

46. According to the Center for Army Lessons Learned at Fort Leavenworth, the mark of success of these programs is to increase "the legitimacy of the government and its effectiveness as perceived by the local population and the international community; [t]he perceived legitimacy of the freedoms and constraints placed on the force supporting the government"; and "[t]he degree to which factions, the local population, and other actors accede to the authority of the government and those forces supporting the government." Center for Army Lessons Learned, "PRT Playbook: Tactics, Techniques, and Procedures," *CALL Handbook,* no. 7-34 (September 2007), 1–2.

47. http://ec.europa.eu/europeaid/where/acp/regional-cooperation/peace/capacity_building/capacity_building_en.htm, accessed March 2, 2013.

48. http://uk.oneworld.net/guides/capacity-building, accessed March 2, 2013.

49. See, for example, UN Security Council Resolution 1325 and the UN Population Fund, http://www.unfpa.org/women/index.html, accessed March 2, 2013.

50. Another example is the Department of Education for Northern Ireland (DENI) effort, started in 1991, to mandate "education for mutual understanding" (EMU) in all schools in Northern Ireland. This programming recommends interschool contact and mandates that curricula address concepts of prejudice and conflict. Most EMU programming is carried out by volunteers.

51. "Mali Crisis: US Admits Mistakes in Training Local Troops," BBC, January 25, 2013, http://www.bbc.co.uk/news/world-africa-21195371, accessed July 31, 2013.

52. Daniel Serwer and George Ward, "Kosovo: Promoting Ethnic Coexistence," in *Facilitating Dialogue: USIP's Work in Conflict Zones,* ed. David R. Smock and Daniel Serwer (Washington, DC: United States Institute of Peace Press, 2012), 45–66.

53. See, for example, Bruce Jones, "The Growing Challenge of Strategic Coordination," in *Ending Civil Wars: The Implementation of Peace Agreements,* ed. Stephen John Stedman, Donald Rothchild, and Elizabeth M. Cousens (Boulder, CO: Lynne Rienner, 2002). Ten years after this piece was published, the theme of the coordination/collaboration was the focus of a three-day conference, "Managing Complexity and Working across Silos." The conference was organized by the Alliance for Peacebuilding, an umbrella association of major peacebuilding NGOs, and the conferees suggested that some progress had been made over the past decade, but major gaps still remained. For a differing contemporary view, see Thomas G. Weiss, *Humanitarian Business* (Cambridge: Polity, 2013).

25

DETERRENCE GONE ASTRAY
CHOICES IN COERCION FOR CONFLICT MANAGEMENT

Richard K. Betts

Deterrence isn't what it used to be. In the second half of the twentieth century it was the backbone of national security, the essential military strategy behind containment. Its purpose, logic, and effectiveness were well understood. It was a crucial ingredient in winning the Cold War without a World War III. Since then, the time-honored strategy has gone astray, and US defense policy is the worse for the change.

In some cases the United States has gotten the strategy backward. It has clung to deterrence where it should not, aggravating conflict with Russia, while elsewhere it has rejected deterrence where it should rely on it, at the price of one unnecessary and disastrous war with Iraq and the risk of another with Iran. In the third and potentially most important case, where miscalculation will be most dangerous—China—Washington is confused and indecisive about whether to apply the strategy. Mistakes in choices about deterrence have come from faulty threat assessment, forgetfulness about history, inat-

tention to the concept itself, and short-sighted policymaking.

WHEN DOES DETERRENCE MATTER?

Deterrence is passive coercion, a strategy for combining two competing goals: countering an enemy threat while avoiding war. Academics have explored countless variations and nuances of deterrence theory.[1] The basic concept grasped by policymakers, however, is quite simple: the enemy will refrain from attacking if faced with the defender's capability to defeat the attack, or threatened with unacceptable damage from retaliation even if the attack succeeds. Simple as it is, officials sometimes mix up why, how, and when the idea should underwrite policy.

Military deterrence is for coping with an enemy threat, preventing a potential attack. A threat, in turn, should be understood in terms of a simple equation: $T = C \times I$. That is, Threat equals Capability times Intention. Policy debates swirl around disagreements about how to measure capabilities and intentions, and which are most important. No matter how dangerous an opponent's capability or intention to attack may be, however, neither can be the sole focus of concern; if either one is zero, the threat is zero.

If only capabilities mattered, Washington would have to worry mightily about deterring Britain, whose nuclear weapons could incinerate several dozen American cities. But no one worries about the British threat because we "know" that their intention to attack us is zero. On the other hand, if only hostile intentions mattered, Washington would have had to worry about deterring Hugo Chavez, but US leaders lost no sleep over the Venezuelan threat because Chavez lacked much capability to hurt the United States.

Deterrence is not a strategy for all seasons. If there is no threat, deterrence is unneeded. At best, applying deterrence when it is unneeded wastes resources, and at worst it may provoke conflict rather than hold it in check. Careful consideration of intentions is important because deterrence is only relevant against an enemy who might otherwise be tempted to attack; it is superfluous or counterproductive against mild adversaries who might like to see the United States taken down a peg but who have no incentive to go to war.

Where it is needed, however, deterrence may not necessarily work automatically. Whatever capabilities or hostile intentions may be, deterrence may not be effective against an enemy who is suicidal or invulnerable to counterattack. Thus it is more useful against governments, which have a return address and want to survive, than against terrorists who cannot be found or who do not fear death. (Much of Americans' unwillingness to rely on deterrence against Iran comes from careless blurring of the difference between the targetable regime in Tehran and anonymous terrorists.) Deterrence may also be unworkable against many threats in the ever more important realm of cybersecurity, where the attribution problem—the technical inability

to be absolutely sure who the source of a cyber attack is—remains unsolved.

Where deterrence is relevant, it should not be applied loosely. If the matter in dispute is definitely something we are willing to fight over, the deterrent warning should be loud and clear, lest subtlety allow the target to misread it. John Foster Dulles used to convey inflexible warnings in a way that liberal critics saw as crudely unintelligent, but he did so for a good reason: to avoid the possibility that Moscow or Beijing would misunderstand flexibility and press their luck.[2] Deterrence should be ambiguous, if ever, only when it is a bluff, and Washington would actually be unwilling to go to the mat. What is particularly dangerous is the reverse situation, where Washington fails to declare deterrence in advance, but then decides to fight when an unexpected attack comes. This confusion caused two wars for the United States, over Korea and Kuwait.

Although deterrence does not guarantee success, it must be measured against what its alternatives can guarantee. Where it is not counterproductive, it provides an option between aggression and appeasement. There are risks in relying on it, but also in rejecting it where the alternatives may be worse. US policy needs a better grip on when and where deterrence should be applied or held back.

DETERRENCE OUT OF PLACE

Russia's annexation of Crimea in 2014 was inexcusable but understandable. The crisis over Ukraine followed two decades in which the West cut Russia down to size and pushed it around, with NATO expansion, war in Kosovo, and, in 2014, the European Union's attempt to force Ukrainian integration with the West and the toppling of the Russia-friendly Yanukovich regime finally producing forceful pushback from Moscow. Now the West has to deter Russia from further intervention in Ukraine, but consider how a less demanding approach might have avoided the crisis.

For more than twenty years after the Cold War, deterrence lived on where it was obsolete, in a low-key way, yet complicating relations with Russia. Few US leaders talked openly about deterrence of Russia, but some did, and most others passively accepted policies on North Atlantic Treaty Organization (NATO) expansion and nuclear arms control that implied it and that undercut a "reset" of relations. Continued deterrence may seem natural in this case because of long habit—its accoutrements were institutionalized for half a century. At best this deterrence from inertia retarded progress from the Cold Peace that has followed the Cold War. At worst it risked embroilment in potential conflicts where Moscow's stakes were much higher than Washington's, as in Ukraine.

In the Cold War, deterrence was serious business because the Soviet threat appeared to be huge. Moscow's capabilities included 175-odd mobilizable divisions aimed at Western Europe and close to forty thousand nuclear weapons. The Soviet Union's intentions were much debated, but officially assumed to be very hostile. Formation of NATO and deployment of ample military counterpower was the Western response—and it worked. For more than forty years deterrence held until the Soviet Union gave up. Doves doubted that much deterrence was necessary, but hawks could be reassured that deterrence never failed. Despite tense crises over Berlin and Cuba, and proxy conflicts in the Third World, Moscow never dared unleash its military capability directly against the West.

◆ ◆ ◆

The Cold War ended long ago, but deterrence of Moscow did not. NATO morphed from a military alliance first and foremost to a political club for Western democracies, and its military actions have been directed out of area, to the Balkans, Afghanistan, and Libya. Yet the alliance retained a residual deterrence posture toward Russia. Although forces stationed in Europe were reduced after the Cold War, as of 2014 US combat units still remained there. Although arms control negotiations with Moscow are no longer the big business they were decades ago, they are still one of the main arenas of strategic interaction. Mitt Romney was only channeling the continuing instincts of many in the mainstream when he said that Russia is still the United States' "number one geopolitical foe." These continuities would make sense only in relations between serious adversaries.

Adversaries we remain, but hardly serious adversaries who might go to war with each other. Until Crimea, the problems were abrasions due to Moscow's failure to keep up its progress toward democracy after the Soviet empire's collapse, snippy backbiting between Putin's regime and Washington, and simple inertia from the institutionalized confrontation of the Cold War. Keeping NATO oriented to deterrence was gratifying to the organization's newest members, such as Poland, but for the alliance as a whole such inertia was a drag on the consolidation of peace. It did less to protect against a threat than to feed suspicions that worsen political conflict.

The Ukraine crisis, which might have been avoided by accepting a Russian sphere of influence, now requires deterrence, but of the weaker sort that NATO can stomach for a nonmember: economic sanctions. Otherwise, neither capabilities nor plausible intentions make a case for deterrence. In dramatic contrast to the Cold War, it is now hard to make the case that Russia is more a threat to NATO than the reverse. First, the East-West balance of military forces, which was favorable to the Warsaw Pact or at best even, has not just shifted dramatically to NATO's advantage; it has become utterly lopsided. Russia is now a fraction of what the old Warsaw Pact was. It not only lost its old Eastern European allies, but those allies are now arrayed on the other side, in NATO. Russia itself is scarcely more than half of what the old Soviet Union was, and the lost parts of the union are now in NATO too, or nonaligned.

The result is a tectonic shift in the balance of resources and forces. Leave aside the Western technological advantage in weaponry, which has persisted. The ratio of defense spending between NATO and the Warsaw Pact in 1985, the mid-point of the Reagan presidency, was about 1.3 to 1, but in 2011 the ratio between NATO and Russia was a crushing 20 to 1. The ratio of men under arms was about even in 1985; in 2011 it was well over 2 to 1 in NATO's favor. The total population imbalance for the two sides quadrupled, from 1.6 to 1 to 6.6 to 1. The ratios for GNP/GDP doubled, from less than 9 to 1 to more than 18 to 1.[3] In 1985, hefty Soviet forces were deployed in the middle of Germany, within striking distance of the English Channel; today they are much smaller and huddled hundreds of miles further back.

The one capability that keeps Russia militarily potent is its nuclear force. This, however, is useful only as a deterrent against NATO. There is no way that Moscow's nuclear weapons could be used for aggression, except as a backstop for a conventional offensive—for which NATO's capability is now the greater. If either side has reason to fear the other's capabilities today, which side is it?

Relative capability is low, but do hostile intentions make Russia a threat? Putin and company are distasteful characters, but they have no plausible reason to think that a military attack on the West could serve their interests. In the twentieth century there were clear conflicts of interest between the two sides, including over territory in each other's core security zones (West Berlin and Cuba). Most of all, there was a titanic struggle over which of their ideologies would come to dominate social organization throughout world. Russia today is recalcitrant in political reform, but it no longer aspires to be the vanguard of a globe-spanning revolutionary ideal.

Unresolved territorial issues today are ones that engage Russia's interests far more than the West's. Before Ukraine the danger was highlighted by the 2008 mini-war between Russia and Georgia over the latter's secessionist regions. These are territories on Russia's doorstep—indeed, territories that used to be *inside* the Soviet border.

Did the lopsided imbalance of capabilities between NATO and Russia mean that Russian interests need be of no concern and we could continue to rub the Russians' noses in their inferiority with impunity? No. Russia is still a major power whose future policies and alignment matter. The gross imbalance with the West does not negate this fact but obscures it, simply because the West is such a behemoth; NATO and the European Union (EU) have close to half the wealth in the world. If recovering Russia were to combine with rising China, however, the strategic implications for the United States are not trivial; as it is, we worry more and more about China alone. Too many blithely assume that Sino-Russian antagonism is an inevitable feature of international politics, all the while that NATO in Europe and the United States and Japan in the Pacific are giving both countries incentives to put aside their differences and make common cause against pressure from the West.

It is clear that NATO governments do not want to contest Ukraine militarily. The best solution would be to "Finlandize" the country. This would give a higher priority to peace with an uncongenial regime than to absolute support for smaller neighbors, a pragmatic compromise of idealistic exploitation of US primacy in favor of a calmer modus vivendi based on balance of power. Keeping a deterrent stance truncated the resolution of the Cold War despite the collapse of serious threat to the West, looks more like an aggressive threat than a defensive one to its target, and unnecessarily pushes Russia to join forces with a bigger potential threat.

WHERE IS DETERRENCE WHEN WE NEED IT?

In contrast to excessive deterrence of Moscow, the most dangerous change from the Cold War era was the rejection of deterrence where it should be applied—as a strategy for coping with nuclear proliferation, and most immediately, Iran. Instead policymakers moved to a preference for preventive war—not in those words, but unmistakably in effect—as if deterrence is too weak a counter to dangerous countries. They forgot that the exact purpose of deterrence is to cope with dangerous adversaries, not wimpy ones. The eclipse of deterrence by preventive war was especially dubious because it happened in the face of lessons from long and hard experience with Iraq.

Deterrence played no role in the run-up to the first major conflict after the Cold War, the 1991 Persian Gulf War. But that war was a stunning success at remarkably low cost as wars go, so few Americans were troubled that it might have been avoided. Saddam Hussein's assault on Kuwait was also widely misread as showing that he was "undeterrable." It showed no such thing, however, because the United States *had not tried* to deter him. Had Saddam known that invading Kuwait would bring the United States to launch a decisive war against him, he almost certainly would have refrained.

In the fateful meeting with Saddam before the invasion, US Ambassador April Glaspie was not instructed to make any such threat. The dictator was left free to miscalculate. This eerily repeated the mistake of forty years earlier. At the beginning of 1950, Secretary of State Acheson and General MacArthur made public statements that excluded South Korea from the US defense perimeter in the Pacific, only to have President Truman turn around and send American forces against the North Korean invaders when Kim Il Sung took Washington at its word.

If Bush the Elder could have focused on the question before the 1990 crisis, he might well have decided to warn Saddam that the United States would fight if he struck. Bush was understandably not prepared for the Kuwait contingency, because, as in 1950, it came out of left field. Bush the Younger did not have the same excuse a dozen years later. He deliberately chose not to handle a dangerous Iraq with containment and deterrence, as presidents had handled the more dangerous Soviet Union and China for almost half a century during the Cold War. Instead the second Bush chose to start a war immediately in order to avoid a possible war eventually.

Administration spokesmen mistakenly called the US invasion of Iraq "preemptive"—a politically insidious conceptual corruption. Preemption assumes that the enemy is already preparing an attack, and simply beats him to the draw. Preventive war only assumes that the enemy might decide to strike sometime in the future, a far more uncertain threat. Thus preemption is much easier to justify. But Saddam was not preparing an imminent attack in 2003.

Presidents considered preventive war against Stalin in the 1950s and Mao in the 1960s but rejected the option, even though the communist tyrants then seemed even more fanatical, reckless, and aggressive than Saddam Hussein, Mahmoud Ahmadinejad, or Supreme Leader Ali Khamenei. Mao made notorious statements that the prospect of nuclear war "is not a bad thing," because the world could afford to lose two-thirds of its population if capitalism would be defeated.[4] Rhetoric that alarming is still unmatched by anything yet heard from Tehran.

Truman, Eisenhower, and Kennedy refrained from preventive war against the United States' most dangerous adversaries for many reasons, but one was the fear of communist retaliatory power, something the second Bush did not have to worry about in 2003. However, there is now the benefit of hindsight and knowing that relying on deterrence in the Cold War obviously turned out to be the better option, even if a more aggressive alternative to it had been feasible. If a preventive war against the Soviet Union or China could have been brought off without direct damage to the United States, it would still have been an unnecessary catastrophe.

The result of preventive war against Iraq in 2003 was a lesser catastrophe, but it still cost far more in blood, treasure, and American standing in the world than whatever benefit it produced. The experiment to see whether the alternative of relying on deterrence to keep Saddam in his box would have produced a bigger disaster, as the instigators of the war asserted, cannot be run. There is no evidence, however, that Saddam could not have been deterred indefinitely. He indulged in aggression against Iraq in 1980 and Kuwait a decade later, but only when he had reason to believe he faced no daunting counter-power. He was a reckless bully but, like most bullies, not suicidal. He never attacked in the face of a US threat to respond, nor did he even use his chemical and biological weapons when the incentive to take risks was highest, in defense against the US assault in 1991.

IS WAR SAFER THAN DETERRENCE? THE BALANCE OF RISKS

Considering the awful miscarriage of strategy in Iraq after 2003, and the positive result from Cold War containment, one might have expected deterrence to gain in appeal as a fallback strategy if Iran could not be dissuaded from developing nuclear weapons. But once again the fanaticism of enemy leadership led

Israeli and American statesmen to fear that Tehran might one day use nuclear weapons for aggression despite facing the threat of devastating retaliation. Once again, however, there was no evidence that Iranian leaders have any interest in national suicide. (Consider as well that Islamist suicide bombing has so far been almost entirely a Sunni phenomenon, while Iranians are Shiite.)[5] Iran has engaged in terrorism and sub rosa violence, claiming to respond against Israeli and US covert warfare, but however aggressive its motives, it has not initiated regular military attacks against its enemies.

Nevertheless, rather than handle a prospective Iranian nuclear arsenal with a deterrent threat, both Israel and the United States preferred preventive war in principle. The official hope has been to prevent Iran's production of nuclear weapons through diplomacy, sanctions, or covert coercion, but not to live with it if peaceful prevention fails. As Iran's uranium enrichment efforts progressed closer to producing fissionable material, voices favoring a strategy of deterrence as the lesser evil were cries in the wilderness. The effective range of debate about what to do if Tehran moves to produce nuclear weapons was not about whether to attack, but when. Obama differed from Netanyahu only on matters of timeline and red-line. President Obama went out of his way to declare firmly that he did "not have a policy of containment," but "a policy to prevent Iran from obtaining a nuclear weapon."[6] Secretary of Defense Panetta reiterated this in Israel. As Ambassador Martin Indyk put it, "The more the Israelis threaten, the more we respond by showing them that we will take care of the problem if it comes to that."[7] State Department spokeswoman Victoria Nuland declared, "The president has said, again and again, unequivocally, that we will not allow Iran to obtain a nuclear weapon. . . . We are absolutely firm about the president's commitment."[8] So not only the Israeli government but the United States as well explicitly refused to accept the possibility of eventually living with Iranian nuclear weapons by relying on deterrence to block their use.

The logic behind rejecting deterrence is that it could fail, and Tehran might somehow decide to use nuclear weapons despite being threatened with devastating retaliation.[9] Why Iran poses more of such risk than other nasty regimes who developed nuclear weapons has not been demonstrated, but of course some risk exists. Refusing to accept an iota of such risk, however, ignores the big risks from the alternative of initiating war.

Leave aside the danger of being blindsided by unanticipated forms of resistance or reprisal—say, biological weapons. The well-recognized risks include immediate Iranian retaliation by overt military means against US forces in the region, or delayed retaliation by covert means against assets outside the region. The disastrous results of the initially successful assault on Iraq in 2003 are a reminder that wars we start will not necessarily end when and how we want. Indeed, the record of American and Israeli wars suggest that both countries underestimate the prospective costs of wars they enter far more often than not. Washington happily paid fewer costs than it counted on in one case, the first Persian Gulf War, but faced a far higher bill than anticipated in Korea, Vietnam, Kosovo, Afghanistan, and the second war against Iraq. Israel got out of the Six Day War in 1967 better and more cheaply than expected, but was badly surprised by the price of the October War in 1973, the 1982 Lebanon War, and the 2006 war against Hezbollah in Lebanon.

◆ ◆ ◆

The diplomatic and political costs of launching a war against an Iran that has not yet attacked another country would have spillover effects on U.S. security. Attacking without immediate provocation would fracture the international coalition that stands behind sanctions against Iran. It would be seen throughout the world as another case of arrogant American aggression against Muslims.

This might all seem an acceptable price if it dissuades other countries from attempting to get their own nuclear deterrents, but it might just as well energize such efforts. Bush's war to prevent Iraq from getting nuclear weapons did not dissuade North Korea, which went on to test its own a few years later, nor did it turn Iran in the other direction. The invasion of Iraq may have induced Muammar Gaddafi to surrender his nuclear program, but a few years later his reward from Washington turned out to be overthrow and death. What should that example suggest to other American enemies about the wisdom of renouncing nuclear weapons?

All these risks might be considered an acceptable price for eliminating the Iranian weapons of mass destruction (WMD) threat. But attacking Iran does not do that, short of invasion and occupation, and may well have the reverse effect.[10] As even proponents admit, air attack alone can only delay Iran's pursuit of nuclear weapons, not end it. If the answer then is maintenance bombing—striking Iran's facilities every couple of years—three questions about capabilities and intentions discredit the wisdom of starting the preventive war project.

First, what reason is there to believe that Iran will cooperate with maintenance bombing by reviving its program in ways and places subject to reliable detection or vulnerable to effective targeting? Although bomb-making might be forced into less efficient modes, the problem hawks fear is not just a big, sophisticated Iranian nuclear arsenal, but even a handful of shaky bombs.

Second, what reason is there to bank on the indefinite willingness of future presidents to keep making war? It is strategically foolish to bank on a solution whose success requires agreement by authorities not yet known.

Third, and most salient, what effect will attacking Iran's capabilities have on its intentions? If capabilities are temporarily degraded but incentives to use future capabilities are inflamed, attack may increase the threat rather than diminish it. If the reason to start a war is the fear that Iran would eventually launch nuclear weapons without provocation and without regard for suffering retaliation, one can only assume that striking such a bloodthirsty and irrational regime will incite it even more to unleash whatever nuclear or biological weapon it develops at the earliest opportunity. Is such a fear overwrought? Probably—but then the diagnosis of Tehran's undeterrability collapses.

A nuclear-armed Iran is an alarming prospect. There is no definite evidence, however, that it is more alarming than the nuclear capability of several other countries with which we have learned to live. The most telling example is North Korea. Although the public paid far less attention (at least until the regime's hyperbolic threats to launch nuclear attacks in 2013), Pyongyang's record of fanatical belligerence and terrorist behavior over the years is far worse than Tehran's. There is no sure solution to some dangers, and this challenge presents a strategic choice between different risks. There is simply no real evidence to underwrite confidence that incomplete suppression of Iranian capability at the price of dramatic provocation will yield any more safety than handling a new Iranian nuclear capability with good old deterrence.

INDECISIVE DETERRENCE: IGNORING RISKS

The most dangerous risk for the longer term lies in the failure to decide one way or the other about policy toward China: to treat it as a threat to be contained or a power to be accommodated. Washington has so far been trying to have it both ways. Such incoher-

ence is common in the real world of complicated cross-pressures, avoids big costs in the near term, and can work as long as no catalyst brings contradictions to a head. It is ultimately unrealistic, however, unless China decides to act indefinitely with more humility than any other rising power and less sense of entitlement than the United States has itself.

In one influential but faltering view, deterrence is a nonissue for US-PRC relations because economics makes military competition passé: cooperation is natural because of mutual interest in avoiding disruption of profitable interdependence. In this view, military conflict is nonsensical, so preparing for it risks making conflict a self-fulfilling prophecy. The opposing view, that China's rising power is a threat that must be countered militarily, has been gaining, but has not been turned into explicit policy. The declared "pivot" or "rebalancing" of American military power toward Asia has not been accompanied by any clear signal of intent about where, when, why, or how US armed forces would or would not be sent into combat against China, nor is there a clear operational rationale for the change in capabilities that most symbolizes the pivot—sending a US Marine contingent to Australia.

Meanwhile, conflicts brew, such as the revival of tensions between China, the Philippines, and Japan over disputed islands, and Washington ignores the question of when Beijing's long patience about resolving the Taiwan question could end. Preoccupied with other strategic challenges, the United States is drifting toward unanticipated confrontation, without a clear decision about the circumstances in which it would be willing to go to war with China.

This distraction and hesitancy prevent clear warnings to Beijing of the red-lines for avoiding war. Indeed, it is unclear that the US government has decided for itself what the red-lines are. Continuing lack of clarity increases the risk of inadvertent crisis, miscalculation, and accidental escalation. The problem in this crucial case is not that deterrence has been inappropriately rejected or embraced, but that it is muddled.

Chinese and Philippine maneuvers over islands in the South China Sea in mid-2012 were a wake-up call, and subsequent jockeying by Japan and China over the more dangerous issue of which owns the Senkaku/Diaoyu chain brought the confusion into focus. Washington's response to the latter dispute was a disturbing set of utterly contradictory statements. The State Department announced, "We don't take a position on the islands, but we do assert that they are covered under the [U.S.-Japan defense] treaty."[11] A couple weeks later, during a trip to Asia, Secretary of Defense Panetta affirmed that the United States would not take sides in regional disputes over territory, claimed that US strategic rebalancing toward Asia is more than rhetoric, yet also claimed that it was not a threat to China.[12] All this is ambivalent deterrence, rhetorical bobbing and weaving rather than solid strategic planning.

Ambivalent deterrence is dangerous. Crossed signals can be diplomatically useful as long as contestants are not near coming to blows, but can be disastrous when they are. In this case, they project provocation and weakness at the same time. Indecisive deterrence tells China not to take the various islands but does not threaten to block them from doing so, even while telling Japan that the United States is treaty-bound to defend them. Subsequent developments or secret statements to either capital might mitigate the contradiction, but even if so, the public posture subverts US credibility. It invites Beijing to see the United States as hesitant, a paper tiger who will fold in an escalating crisis. In such a crisis, however, under the pressure of events for which it has not thoroughly prepared in

advance, Washington might act as it did in June 1950 and August 1990.

◆ ◆ ◆

There are two logical but opposite alternatives to this risky confusion, and one phony but possibly useful one. One is to make a US commitment to containment of China clear. This sounds precipitous, because Beijing sees containment as an aggressive threat, so it would best be done with euphemistic rhetoric. But containment in the proper literal sense is no more than defensive action to keep China from expanding, from taking control of more territory by either military action or political coercion. The benefit of this alternative would be to make deterrence harder to mistake and more effective, involving brighter red-lines that would reduce the odds of an unanticipated chicken game producing a war neither side wants. But the cost would be big: a new Cold War, and disruption of potentially advantageous cooperation on many issues. There is yet no consensus among either American voters or the foreign policy elite for such a decisive shift, which would amount to a red light.

If containment is unnecessary or too costly, the second, opposite alternative is accommodation—in effect, a green light. Critics would call it appeasement, an idea discredited since the 1930s. It would make sense if Beijing's ambitions are limited (unlike Hitler's) and will stay limited, if its growing power is not derailed, and if disregard of the interests of US allies is preferable to growing conflict with an emerging superpower—all very big "ifs." Accommodation would recognize that as China becomes a superpower it will naturally feel entitled to prerogatives of a superpower—most obviously, disproportionate influence in its home region—and can expect disputes over minor issues such as the present unresolved territorial claims to be settled on its terms rather than those of weak neighbors. The big obstacles to this alternative would be Japan, a powerful rather than weak neighbor, and Taiwan, a far bigger stake than the uninhabited rocks disputed in 2012. Americans are far from a consensus favoring anything with the odor of appeasement—yet also far from a consensus on willingness to go to war for either the Senkakus or Taiwan.

Given the unattractiveness of either alternative, it is no surprise that Washington finesses the question. Incoherent compromise is a common and sometimes sensible diplomatic strategy. In Asia, however, it underestimates the risks of drift and indecision if Chinese power continues to grow and Chinese restraint about outstanding claims declines. US policy now amounts to a yellow light, a warning to slow down, short of a firm requirement to stop. Yellow lights, however, tempt some drivers to speed up.

The third alternative is a variant of accommodation with less of the appearance of appeasement: insistence on resolving the ownership of disputed islands through international arbitration or judgment by some multilateral mechanism like the World Court. This is a phony alternative except in the unlikely event that the contending parties were to accept the adjudication. It might get the United States off the hook of overtly choosing deterrence or retreat over the minor stakes in the near term, but it would not resolve the long-term issue of Taiwan.

There is no pain-free solution on China. Confusion to date reflects the unpalatable nature of the choice. Muddling is the path of least resistance and may work for a long time, avoiding the cost of a new Cold War, but only as long as Chinese forbearance lasts. At that point, if a crisis is fraught enough, ambivalent deterrence may cause conflict rather than prevent it. It may prove too weak to make Beijing swerve first, but strong enough to keep Washington from swerving either, thus causing collision. The solution is necessary but unlikely: a clear decision for grand strategy about whether to accept China's full claims as a superpower when it becomes one, or to draw clear red-lines before a crisis comes.

WHY THE DISARRAY?

Inappropriate inertia in applying deterrence to Russia followed from failure to go all the way from the end of Cold War hostility to a new Concert of Europe, in which Russia would have been drawn into the West, becoming a member of the community covered by NATO and the European Union. That possibility may always have been fanciful, no more appealing to Moscow than to the West, but the alternative was necessarily a Cold Peace. It was still possible to take military confrontation out of the relationship more thoroughly than has happened. Western instinct and habit, demands of liberated East European members of the old Warsaw Pact, and Moscow's unpleasant political development all abetted the inertia of deterrence. It was off-handed deterrence, however, and did as much to prompt Russia's reassertion of its interests in its traditional sphere of influence as to discourage it.

The quite different problem of failing to exploit deterrence when it should be used is due primarily to two epochal changes. One is in the international distribution of power. The United States owes the inclination to replace deterrence with preventive war to the simple fact that it can get away with it. Despite flirtation with the alternative of rollback, containment and deterrence came to be the strategy of choice in the Cold War by default—the alternatives were too costly to contemplate. *Mutual* deterrence was imposed by bipolarity.

In a unipolar world, in contrast, most assume that Washington need not worry about devastation occurring inside the United States if it elects preventive war against Iran. True, compared to the Cold War the threat is low, but confidence in immunity is still complacent. If Iran's leaders are so fanatical that they might launch an unprovoked nuclear attack despite facing devastating retaliation, it is foolish not to worry that they will find a way to strike back strenuously when they *are* provoked. Iran might not have to wait until it recovers and rebuilds a nuclear capability to do something awful. There is no reason for confidence that Iran could not use biological weapons at an earlier date or that such retaliation could not reach the interior of the US homeland. If that idea sounds outlandish, it is certainly less so than the idea that Iran would detonate nuclear weapons for aggressive purposes in the face of deterrence.

The second reason deterrence has lost appeal is that its most potent form—the threat to annihilate the enemy's economy and population in retaliation—is no longer legitimate. In 1945 hardly any Americans objected to the incineration of hundreds of thousands of Japanese civilians, and throughout the Cold War few objected to the doctrine that threatened to do the same on an even greater scale if we suffered Soviet attack. But times have changed. Today evolving norms and Pentagon lawyers have put the idea of deliberately targeting civilians thoroughly out of bounds for war planners. It would be difficult for the US government to declare that if one Iranian nuclear weapon is detonated somewhere, the United States will kill millions of Iranians in return.

That inhibition should hardly be a reason to prefer starting a war, nor does it cripple deterrence. First, a variant of deterrence would be a threat not to annihilate Iran's population, but to annihilate its regime—to strike back with any and all instruments that would destroy the leaders, organizations (such as the Quds Force and Republican Guard), and assets of the government. Such an effort pursued to the fullest would actually inflict much collateral damage against innocents, but it could still be much more easily promulgated in principle. It could be supplemented by a threat

to guarantee extermination of the regime by invasion, as in Iraq, a price that would be far more reasonable to pay after an Iranian nuclear strike than it was in 2003. Second, even if the United States may no longer threaten massive retaliation against civilians, Israel certainly can. These separate but mutually reinforcing threats—that the fruits of the Iranian revolution or Iranian society in general would cease to exist—would be a powerful restraint on Tehran.

Deterrence was not a disastrous danger when applied unnecessarily to Russia, but it did have negative effects. It is not a sure thing against Iran, but it beats starting a war. Deciding for or against it in the face of a larger policy dilemma, as with China, is not an easy choice, but avoiding the choice makes the dilemma ever more dangerous if unresolved claims are not resolved peacefully. Reducing future risks requires paying some immediate costs.

To fix any of these strategic problems, it will help to get the question of deterrence back into focus. In the Cold War, it was so ingrained and pervasive an element of US strategy that deterrence became a buzzword, used to justify everything in defense policy. In recent years, however, it has almost vanished from the vocabulary of strategic debate. US strategy will gain from more discrimination, increasing and reducing emphasis on deterrence in different circumstances. The alternative of continued inattention or confusion will not matter only until it does. That would be in a surprise crisis, something that tends to happen to the United States more often than we ever expect, and figuring out what to do on the fly proves not the best way to avoid disaster.

NOTES

A condensed version of this chapter appeared as "The Lost Logic of Deterrence," *Foreign Affairs* 92, no. 2 (March/April 2013). Reprinted by permission of FOREIGN AFFAIRS, (volume 92, no. 22, 2013). Copyright © 2013 by the Council on Foreign Relations, Inc.

1. General surveys include Lawrence Freedman, *Deterrence* (Cambridge: Polity, 2004) and Patrick Morgan, *Deterrence Now* (Cambridge: Cambridge University Press, 2003).

2. Michael A. Guhin, *John Foster Dulles: A Statesman and His Times* (New York: Columbia University Press, 1972), 149–55.

3. *The Military Balance 1985–1986* (London: International Institute for Strategic Studies [IISS], Autumn 1985); *The Military Balance 2012* (London: IISS, March 2012). Ratios are NATO:Warsaw Pact for 1985, NATO:Russia for 2011. Military manpower figures include active and reserve forces and count Russia as having two million usable reserves (those within five years of service).

4. "We have no experience in atomic war. . . . The best outcome may be that only half of the population is left and the second best may be only one-third. When 900 million are left out of 2.9 billion, several five-year plans can be developed for the total elimination of capitalism and for permanent peace. It is not a bad thing." Mao Zedong (Second Speech to the Party Congress, May 17, 1958), quoted in "Mao and Terror," http://www.worldfuturefund.org/wffmaster/Reading/Quotes/maoterror.htm.

5. Robert A. Pape and James K. Feldman, *Cutting the Fuse* (Chicago: University of Chicago Press, 2010), 32, 47, 106.

6. "Remarks by the President at AIPAC Policy Conference" (White House press release, March 4, 2012).

7. *New York Times*, August 2, 2012, A3.

8. *Wall Street Journal*, September 11, 2012, A6.

9. A different argument offered is that Iran would not launch nuclear attacks without provocation but would use nuclear capability as a shield to enable conventional aggression. The proper preparation for that scenario, however, is not preventive war but deterrence by denial—clear capacity for conventional defense and retaliation against any such Iranian venture.

10. This argument is elaborated in Richard K. Betts, *American Force* (New York: Columbia University Press, 2012), chap. 6.

11. Victoria Nuland, quoted in *New York Times*, September 4, 2012, A4.

12. *New York Times*, September 20, 2012, A12.

26

DEALING WITH PROLIFERATION
THE NUCLEAR ABOLITION VISION VERSUS PRACTICAL TOOLS FOR TODAY'S EXTREMIST STATES

Michael O'Hanlon

This chapter considers two major questions: What are the prospects for a nuclear-free planet at some point in the future? What are the means for limiting proliferation—or handling proliferation by extremist states, once it has occurred—in the near term?[1]

THE NUCLEAR ABOLITION DEBATE

A discussion of how to stop individual states from pursuing the bomb tends to devolve into a litany of specific challenges in a given region. Should Iran's nuclear facilities be bombed? Should strong economic sanctions be used against Iran, or North Korea, to pressure the regime into reassessing the merits of pursuing the bomb? How can regional allies of the United States be protected, and themselves be discouraged from seeking nuclear weapons if their neighbors do so first?

These kinds of questions are also posed in this chapter. But before delving into what might be termed the micropolicy of counter-proliferation, it is useful to consider the broad strategy, or the big-picture vision. Especially in light of President Barack Obama's decision to elevate the objective of a nuclear-free planet to a major goal of his presidency, at least in rhetorical terms as reflected in his Prague speech of 2009, this chapter begins by considering the plausibility and advisability of an effort to eliminate nuclear weapons from the planet. Virtually everyone acknowledges that this goal will take decades to achieve; in his Prague speech of 2009, Obama doubted that he would see the aspiration realized in his own lifetime. But that need not make it irrelevant, even for near-term policy. Does such a goal make sense, and if so, on what terms?[2]

Put differently, can humans "uninvent" the nuclear bomb and rid the world of the greatest military threat to human species and the survival of the planet? Logic may seem to say no. But the president of the United States and a number of key foreign policy dignitaries are on record as saying yes. They acknowledge that a world free of nuclear weapons is a vision that is not immediately attainable and perhaps not achievable within the lifetimes of most contemporary policymakers. But they also believe that the vision needs to be made visible, vibrant, and powerful.

Since 2007, when former secretaries of state George Schultz and Henry Kissinger, former defense secretary Bill Perry, and former senator Sam Nunn wrote a newspaper column in advocating a nuclear-free world, a movement to attempt that has been gaining in strength. Prominent scholars have lent their voices to the idea.[3] Notably, convening in Paris in December 2008, a group of one hundred signatories (not including the above four) established Global Zero, a movement whose goal is to rid the world of nuclear weapons by 2030 through a multilateral, universal, verified process. The group wants negotiations on a global zero treaty to begin by 2019.[4]

Calls for eliminating the bomb are as old as the bomb itself, and bursts of energy have been devoted to the disarmament cause at various moments in the past, such as the early to mid-1980s.[5] But the pace of activity, including the organization of a movement, has accelerated greatly in recent years. The movement now has a strategy for moving forward—not at some distant time, when miraculous new inventions might make nukes obsolete, but within the next ten years, when a treaty might be written, even if another ten years would be needed to put it into effect.

Will President Obama really pursue such an idea? Will he go beyond the inspiring speech he gave in Prague in 2009, the modest cuts in deployed forces he and Russia agreed to in the New START Treaty, and the modestly lowered profile of nuclear weapons set out in his April 2010 Nuclear Posture Review?[6] These steps are not insignificant, but they are basically a continuation of past policy and result in a world very far from nuclear disarmament.[7] The much-heralded Nuclear

Security Summit in April 2010 in Washington, D.C., was worthwhile, as was a follow-up meeting in Seoul a couple years later. However, they were primarily notable not for progress toward eliminating all nuclear weapons but for the promotion of actions to reduce the risks of nuclear theft, accident, and terrorism. For example, Mexico agreed to convert a research reactor from highly enriched uranium (usable in bombs) to lower-enriched uranium (not usable); Ukraine agreed to eliminate its stocks of highly enriched uranium within two years; and the United States and Russia recommitted to eliminating an excess stock of plutonium.[8] These steps, as well as the Obama administration's request for a 25 percent increase in funding for global nonproliferation activities (to $2.7 billion in the fiscal year 2011 budget), are sensible.[9] In fact, these steps could end up being huge if, by better securing existing materials, they prevent a nuclear terrorist act that could kill tens of thousands. But they are less fundamental strategically and therefore less controversial than the pursuit of a nuclear-free world. They essentially involve helping countries that do not have nuclear weapons ambitions adopt safer practices in how they produce power or conduct scientific research.

A bold new push by President Obama on nuclear issues seems dubious. These tools, to cut to the heart of the questions in this chapter, are more relevant for reducing nuclear dangers in countries with no interest in the bomb than for dealing with extremist states that may pose proliferation problems.

Some observers consider the idea of a nuclear-free world utopian. Indeed, it may be a bridge too far. But as this American president realizes, the motivation for the idea of abolishing nuclear weapons is neither utopian nor futuristic. Indeed, some of the original designers of nuclear weapons were catalysts for the first abolition movement—right after the bomb was invented, in the form of the Baruch project and related efforts that sought either to "disinvent" the technology or to put it entirely under UN control.

Nor is the motivation for nuclear disarmament simply to deny extremist countries the excuse of getting the bomb because others already have it.[10] Rather, it is to put significant pressure on them if they pursue such weapons. With leaders in Tehran, Pyongyang, and elsewhere bent on obtaining nuclear weapons and charging US policymakers with double standards in their insistence that the United States can have the bomb but they cannot, President Obama's ability to galvanize a global coalition to pressure Iran and North Korea (and perhaps others) into slowing down their weapons programs may depend on regaining the moral high ground. And that in turn may require a US commitment to work toward giving up its own arsenal—once doing so is verifiable and once others agree to do the same.

How to rid the world of nuclear weapons as well as bomb-ready fissile materials? And how to do so safely? A nuclear abolition treaty could constructively contribute to global stability if done right. But it could be hazardous if done wrong. Among other things, countries that currently depend on US military protection could decide to seek nuclear weapons of their own. If the Turkeys and Saudi Arabias and Japans and Taiwans of the world interpret the US debate over nuclear disarmament to imply that they can no longer rely on the United States as a dependable strategic partner (a formal ally in the cases of Turkey and Japan, an informal but still trusted friend in the cases of Saudi Arabia and Taiwan), serious consequences could result. The Global Zero movement could wind up sparking the very wave of nuclear proliferation and instability it hopes to prevent. Sam Nunn (not an advocate of the Global Zero movement, because of its near-term schedule to pursue a disarmament treaty) uses the image of nuclear disarmament as a mountain—with the summit beyond reach and perhaps out of

sight. He advocates moving from the current position to a higher base camp (meaning deeper disarmament and related measures) to determine if the summit can in fact be reached at some point.[11] That image makes sense—but the United States and its allies must stay safe on the way to the new base camp and avoid committing to a particular route to the top too soon.

The impediments to the pursuit of a nuclear-weapons-free world are potentially more complex than many nuclear disarmament advocates have acknowledged to date. What if a dangerous country is suspected of having an active nuclear weapons program and verification cannot resolve the matter? What if a country develops an advanced biological pathogen with enormous potential lethality—and perhaps even an antidote to protect its own people? It is hard to see why nuclear deterrence would not be appropriate against such a capability—itself also an indiscriminate weapon of mass destruction, and perhaps comparably lethal someday to nuclear weapons, depending on the course of microbiological research. Would nuclear deterrence truly be irrelevant or inappropriate as a means of addressing such problems?

There are practical problems, too. Russia, with a declining population, extremely long land borders, and a burgeoning Chinese nation to its immediate south (as well as NATO to its west), may not feel it can ever afford to give up nuclear weapons even if verification and related technical issues can be solved. Israel may feel similarly about its place in the Middle East. Pakistan may see the bomb as its only equalizer vis-à-vis archrival India.

Many, if not most, advocates of nuclear disarmament consider the abolition of nuclear weapons the moral equivalent of the abolition of slavery—and imply that, just as with slavery, once eliminated, nuclear weapons should be gone for good (absent a blatant violation of the treaty by a country that chooses to build a nuclear arsenal in the future). This is a dangerous way to portray the vision of disarmament, however, for it would deprive the United States of deterrent options that may be needed someday given the unpredictable course of human history. In other words, even once nuclear weapons are eliminated, they may not be eliminated forever. At a practical level, the world will likely be full of nuclear power plants as well as all the nuclear waste that nuclear bomb and energy programs have generated. The knowledge of how to make nuclear weapons will not disappear, and neither will relevant nuclear materials.

I argue for a middle-ground position on the idea of nuclear disarmament—and the pace at which it can be pursued. Moving to nuclear disarmament soon by trying to write a treaty in the next few years is not realistic. But dropping the subject for now and waiting for the twenty-second century or some other distant date is not viable either.

In addition to possibly spooking US allies who worry about how they will ensure their security in a dangerous world, there are two problems with trying to abolish nuclear weapons too soon. Deterrent arrangements that are working today but that are somewhat fragile could be disrupted; and states disinterested in nuclear disarmament might be encouraged to build up arsenals in the hope that their nascent nuclear power might grow as the existing nuclear powers build down. The main problem, though, is that the nuclear disarmament notion lacks credibility in a world in which even some existing nuclear powers clearly have no interest in denuclearizing anytime. Absent a serious process for moving toward zero, declaration of ambitious but arbitrary and unattainable deadlines for action is more likely to discredit the initiative than to advance it.

The problem with putting off debate about nuclear disarmament is that existing powers remain in a weak position to pressure would-be proliferators to abstain from the pursuit of nuclear weapons, and a false sense of complacency about the supposed safety of living with the bomb is perpetuated. What is needed is a prudent form of urgency. Neither haste and impetuousness nor indefinite postponement of the issue will suffice.

The United States should endorse a nuclear-free world with conviction, as President Obama did in his 2009 Prague speech. But it should not work to create a treaty now and should not sign any treaty that others might create for the foreseeable future. The right time horizon for seriously pushing a new nuclear accord is when most of the world's half-dozen or so major territorial and existential issues involving major powers are resolved—and this cannot be set to a calendar as precisely as the Global Zero movement would like. Such issues include the status of Taiwan, the issue of Kashmir, political relations between Russia and the key "near-abroad" states of Georgia and Ukraine, and the state of Israel. Nuclear crises involving Iran and North Korea also need to be addressed, although the beginnings of a move toward nuclear disarmament might not have to await their complete resolution. Once these contentious matters are largely resolved, the plausibility of great-power war over any issue that one can identify today will be very low. That will in turn make the basic structure and functioning of the international political system stable enough to risk moving toward a nuclear-free world—a process so radical as to be inherently destabilizing and thus prudent to pursue only when the great powers are in a cooperative mode and undivided by irredentist territorial issues.

Some will argue that there is no foreseeable period of great-power peace and thus no prospect of the preconditions required for moving to a denuclearized world. They believe for the most part that the prospects of great-power war in the future will be as, or nearly as, great as they were in the prenuclear eras. Such individuals often call themselves realists and imply that ideas such as global zero are too utopian to be within reach. But as argued below, this so-called realist argument is also problematic—history, particularly of the nuclear age to date, makes it hard to believe that nuclear weapons will never be used if they continue to occupy a central role in international politics. If realism means that nuclear war likely will occur someday, how can such a worldview be called prudent— indeed, how can it even be called realist, with all the connotations of prudence and pragmatism that the term implies?

That said, my vision for nuclear disarmament is one of dismantling nuclear warheads— a vision that should not be confused with their permanent abolition, a term favored by some. The desire to eliminate forever such weapons is understandable, given their incredible and largely indiscriminate destructive power. But it is war itself that is most inhumane, and targeting civilians is the fundamental moral blight that the international community should be trying to eliminate. Forms of highly lethal biological weapons that attack with advanced pathogens, large-scale conventional conflict, and wars that include genocide may be as inhumane as a nuclear attack. Outlawing nuclear weapons in a way that increases the prospects of other types of immoral warfare would be no accomplishment at all. Therefore, even as the international community strives to dismantle nuclear weapons, it needs practical options for rebuilding them should other perils present themselves—not only suspected pursuit of nuclear arms by a country bent on violating an accord but perhaps also the development of advanced biological pathogens (a threat considered by the Obama administration's 2010 Nuclear Posture Review[12]) or an especially threatening conventional military buildup by an extremist state. That is the broad, strategic argument in favor of preserving options for reconstitution even after a nuclear disarmament treaty is signed and implemented.

Any disarmament treaty must therefore allow a country like the United States the right of temporary withdrawal from such a treaty not only for obvious nuclear weapons violations by a threatening state but even for suspected nuclear weapons violations—as well as for advanced biological pathogen programs and especially threatening conventional military buildups. This list of exemptions is far longer than most nuclear zero proponents favor or are even willing to countenance. But the nature of international relations, and of modern weaponry, leaves little choice in the matter. The terms by which the right of temporary withdrawal could be exercised must be as clearly stated as possible, and a burden of proof must be placed on any state or group of states exercising the right. Giving the UN Security Council the ultimate say in whether or not temporary nuclear weapons reconstitution is allowable would not be a sound idea, because the veto of a single unfriendly state could prevent a rearmament process that might in fact be vitally important. That said, the council should have an opportunity to hear the argument of a country that believes it must rearm in response to the belligerent actions of another.

In addition, there should be a contact group of states with varying political perspectives, able to hear and discuss sensitive intelligence for each country that might consider the option of rearming. The contact group would not have veto power, but it would be able to offer independent assessments on whether a defensive form of rearmament is warranted. For the United States, such a group might include not only traditional close allies but also independently minded countries like India and Brazil, the views of which could go far toward persuading skeptical countries that the United States is on reasonable ground in a decision to suspend its compliance with a nuclear disarmament accord if that proves necessary.

There is a technical reason to view reconstitution as a real future policy option. Simply put, nuclear weapons will always be within reach of humans. Even as they improve, verification methods will not be capable of fully ensuring that all existing materials are dismantled or destroyed. The existence of the nuclear power industry makes it likely that bomb-grade materials will be salvageable from nuclear fuel or nuclear waste. In other words, not only is permanent, irreversible abolition unwise, it is impossible. But dismantlement of all existing bomb inventories, in recognition of the fact that the day-to-day role of nuclear weapons in international security is dangerous and ultimately unsustainable, should become the goal, as President Obama has emphasized.

Some might argue that with all these caveats and conditions, a nuclear disarmament treaty, even one that is patiently and prudently pursued, is not worth the trouble. They underestimate both the danger posed by nuclear weapons and the positive power of ideas and ideals in international politics. These weapons are so heinously destructive as to be illegitimate; they are indiscriminate killers; and they have proven to be far harder to build and handle safely than many predicted. More harm could be caused today by moving precipitously to eliminate them than by keeping them. That said, nuclear weapons have no proper role even as visible deterrents in the normal interactions of states, and the United States should aspire to a world—and try to create a world—in which they no longer have such an active, operational role.

THE MOTIVATION OF THE ABOLITION MOVEMENT

Twenty years after the end of the Cold War, people favoring the elimination of nuclear weapons point to several main arguments for this elimination.

First, nuclear weapons are inhumane. They kill indiscriminately and are immensely destructive, and they deserve no place in the national security policies or armed forces establishments of respectable countries. If conventional weapons such as napalm, carpet bombing, and incendiary weapons are no longer used because they are considered immoral, then neither should a type of weaponry with hundreds of times the lethality have a legitimate place in a country's military arsenal.

Second, the logic of the Non-Proliferation Treaty (NPT) seems unsustainable. The NPT was built on double standards—those that apply to the nuclear haves and those that apply to the have-nots. When the NPT was negotiated in the 1960s, after a period of intense Cold War arms racing, the idea that the United States and the Soviet Union would disarm was unrealistic. The only realistic goal for the superpowers seemed to be that they curb their nuclear competition. So the NPT was in that sense a practical response to the world in which it was negotiated. With the Cold War over, the logical inconsistency and political unfairness of an NPT regime in which some countries are allowed nuclear weapons into perpetuity while others are denied them categorically seems increasingly unsustainable.

The NPT itself calls for an end to these double standards, specifically in Article VI, which discusses "general and complete disarmament." That reads like utopianism to many, because the language implies an end to all armed conflict and all organized military forces, not just nuclear abolition.[13] But the NPT review conference of 2000 reaffirmed the goal, making disarmament impractical simply to ignore, because it is now in effect part of the bargain that commits most states not to pursue their own nuclear arms.[14]

Third, abolitionists argue that "loose nukes" remain a serious worry. During the Cold War, when the states possessing nuclear weapons were few and typically strong in their internal controls, this concern was not so great. But with at least nine nuclear powers today, three or four of them subject to internal strife, the danger of theft or confiscation is very high. One should not hyperventilate over the imminence of the threat, as academic John Mueller has rightly pointed out.[15] But to trivialize the destructive force of these weapons, or to assume that no nuclear accident or other disaster will happen in the future because one has not happened in half a century, would be to make a major mistake in the direction of complacency, given the lessons learned from crises ranging from Berlin to Cuba to Kargil. The dangers seem destined to grow as the nuclear club expands—a development that may accelerate with the world's renewed interest in nuclear power, because preparation of nuclear fuel inherently involves many of the same technologies used to produce fissile materials for weapons.

COUNTERARGUMENTS

These abolitionist arguments have merit. But strong counterarguments raise the stakes in the debate. These are difficult to rebut; indeed, any realistic strategy for disarmament needs to face them squarely, as they challenge the nuclear-zero goal. The main argument is that humans may not be able to live safely with nuclear weapons, yet it is not clear how to live safely without them.

Much of the Cold War nuclear literature is filled with discussions of "extended deterrence"—devising credible ways for a nuclear power like the United States to persuade would-be aggressors not to attack its allies. Nuclear weapons had a large role in this debate when the possible enemy was a hypermilitarized Soviet Union abutting key American allies. As Keith Payne points out, in addition to deterring would-be aggressors, American security commitments must also provide positive assurance to friends and allies. That assurance is especially critical when the goal is prevention of nuclear proliferation, because nervous allies may elect to build their own nuclear arsenals to feel secure.[16]

Perhaps the tasks of both deterrence and assurance are easier now that the Soviet Union is gone. And in many ways, these tasks surely are easier for the United States and a large number of its allies. But Russia may feel an even greater need for nuclear weapons now than it did during the Cold War, given Western conventional military superiority.[17] This is a complicating matter in any pursuit of nuclear disarmament, because without the support of other powers for the idea, there can be no worldwide elimination of nuclear weapons.

Even the United States and its allies face complications in this more complex period of multiple nuclear powers that some have called the "second nuclear age."[18] To take one example, is Japan really confident it will never need nuclear weapons to deter a rising China? And if Japan gains nuclear weapons, what will South Korea, then surrounded by four nuclear weapons states, choose to do? Will Taiwan really believe that an already indirect American security pledge is reliable enough that it can forgo a nuclear capability of its own? Because China has in the past declared that Taiwanese pursuit of nuclear weapons would be grounds for war, this scenario is very troublesome.

The situation is also difficult in the Middle East. To be sure, Iran is attempting to justify its own nuclear programs by exploiting the alleged hypocrisy of the NPT regime and the established nuclear powers. Depriving Tehran of this excuse for its nuclear ambitions would seem to argue in favor of a nuclear abolition treaty. But few countries really seem swayed by Tehran's arguments. Rather, their commercial interests in Iran, or their inherent belief in positive diplomacy as a tool for improving other states' behavior, or even a desire to frustrate the United States seem to be more important factors limiting their willingness to get tough with the Iranian regime. The world's acute need for Iran's oil further compounds the problem. It is not clear that the double standards of the NPT are the core of the problem.

Iran has made direct and grave threats against Israel in recent years. It has also thrown its weight around quite a bit in the region, in Iraq, Lebanon, and the Persian Gulf, to the point of threatening the stability of ruling regimes. Under such circumstances, US steps toward nuclear disarmament could produce undesired dynamics. Countries like Saudi Arabia that do not have formal security alliances with the United States could be skittish about facing an Iranian nuclear capability without their own deterrent, should Washington join other key capitals in moving toward a nuclear-free world. They may fear that Iran would cheat even after signing such a treaty. Tehran might then try to intimidate its neighbors, who could worry that Iran possesses the bomb even after the United States deprives itself of its own arsenal. In recent work at Brookings, Martin Indyk and others suggest that in response to Iran's apparent ambitions, the United States might need to increase rather than diminish the robustness of its nuclear guarantees to key regional friends if it is to discourage them from acquiring nuclear weapons of their own.[19] In addition, reports continue to appear of possible arrangements under which Pakistan would provide Saudi Arabia with nuclear weapons in a crisis situation if need be.[20]

Some observers argue that, with the Cold War over and US military preponderance clear to all, nuclear umbrellas are no longer needed to ensure deterrence. Overwhelming conventional military superiority can suffice, they say—even if an adversary might have chemical or biological arms or a secret nuclear bomb program. But this argument is facile. Conventional military dominance is harder to attain, and sustain, than many acknowledge; in many cases, translating that dominance into rapid and decisive victories can be equally difficult. In the aftermath of the Iraq and Afghanistan wars, it is impossible

to know just how willing Americans will be to use force to defend faraway allies—especially if adversaries might use or threaten to use weapons of mass destruction. As I have argued, along with others, for years, trends in military technology are not making the task of deploying decisive military force to distant regions radically easier. Even classic defensive missions can be hard to conduct with conventional arms alone. In other words, situations like the Iraqi invasion of Kuwait in 1990, or Serbian attacks on Kosovar Albanians in 1999, cannot be confidently prevented, and rolling back such aggressions, especially by a more advanced state, can be hard. Of course, nuclear deterrence will often be of dubious relevance to such scenarios too, but it may be helpful in certain egregious cases; the possibility cannot be dismissed.[21]

Some observers also hope that missile defenses may improve enough that offensive nuclear weapons will fade in significance and defenses will become dominant in many key regions of the world. The United States, for example, has now deployed advanced radars, together with thirty long-range interceptor missiles—the latter in California and Alaska—that could destroy incoming offensive nuclear warheads in flight. To date, test results suggest that each individual interceptor missile could have a likely success rate of perhaps 50 percent, plus or minus a fairly wide margin of error, depending in part on the technology employed by the attacker. Yes, missile defense can lower the odds of successful attack, especially by lesser powers with small missile arsenals of limited sophistication. But a reliable missile defense against advanced threats is challenging to imagine. If the day ever arrives when such a defense is possible, it will be far in the future. Currently, missile defenses would do well to intercept a few warheads launched without advanced countermeasures from a predictable location. Larger attacks, surprise attacks, and sophisticated attacks will probably be capable of punching through available defenses for a long time to come.

Then there is the problem of verification. Nuclear arms control agreements to date have limited large objects, such as intercontinental ballistic missile silos and heavy bombers; the agreements have indirectly constrained missile warheads, air-launched cruise missiles, and the like by counting the launchers that carry them. The world today is full of additional bombs, a great deal of additional bomb material, and nuclear waste and energy facilities in dozens of countries that contain materials that could be diverted to weapons purposes. Sometimes the country holding relevant material does not know the exact amounts in its possession. Fissile materials can be shielded well enough that physical emissions are apparent only to detectors within a few dozens of meters of their locations. In other words, their characteristic signatures are not easily noticed. Even centrifuge facilities, and other possible technologies for uranium enrichment, can be well hidden. Arms control protocols allowing inspections of suspected sites can help—but they work only if outsiders can articulate their suspicions with enough precision to allow inspectors to target the right locations. This usually requires having defectors or spies inside a country able to develop leads on illicit programs. Gaining such tip-offs in timely fashion cannot be taken for granted. As writers like James Acton and George Perkovich explain, some argue that in the future, changes in global morality will make it much more likely that "societal verification" could unearth a bomb program from within a state bent on cheating. This assumption seems optimistic given the long history of states being able to convince or coerce their own citizens to remain silent even in the face of enormous atrocities committed by governments against their own people or their neighbors.[22]

Biological pathogens are another complicating factor. If a modified form of smallpox,

perhaps genetically joined with a contagious influenza-like organism, could be developed and then employed against populations, millions could die. The attacking country, knowing more about the properties of the pathogen it developed than anyone else, might be able to inoculate its own citizens against the disease in advance. Perhaps even more plausibly, it might claim it has such an antidote and then threaten to unleash the biological agent on other countries if they do not accede to its demands of one type or another. How could such attacks—or perhaps other types of mass casualty attacks that currently cannot be foreseen—be deterred absent nuclear weapons? A conventional response requiring many months of preparation and combat could be tough to execute if many of the soldiers of the retaliating country are falling ill from a disease that their doctors are powerless to prevent or to cure.

A REALISTIC PATH TO ZERO

In the end, the arguments both for and against nuclear disarmament are extremely strong. How to resolve them?

First, regarding timing, the world is not ready to take even initial steps toward negotiating a global zero treaty. It will not be ready until great-power peace is more firmly established, necessitating progress on key issues in East Asia, South Asia, the Middle East, and Eastern Europe. These matters cannot be set to a calendar, so current aspirations for developing even a notional timeline for pursuing a binding global zero accord are unwarranted. In fact, they are potentially harmful because they convey the sense that somehow the great powers (or some of them) have made nuclear weapons abolition a higher priority than the preservation of great-power peace. That would be a major strategic mistake.

Looking further down the road, this chapter supports the nuclear disarmament agenda—but only by recasting it. Rather than think of an absolute end state, in which nuclear weapons are abolished forever, treaty proponents must be more realistic. They must settle for a world in which all nuclear weapons are disassembled and destroyed—but in which the ability to rebuild a modest arsenal is preserved, technically, politically, and legally. Such an arsenal would be built only in an extreme situation. Ideally, such a reconstitution option would never be invoked, but it is critical that the option be retained. Nuclear zero should not amount simply to de-alerting or disassembling weapons, with stocks of fissile materials at the ready (above and beyond those modest amounts of materials that could be quickly available through the nuclear energy fuel cycle). A world of weapons-grade and bomb-ready highly enriched uranium and plutonium, maintained in significant quantities, would keep nuclear weapons too close to the center of international military planning and global power relationships.[23] But a nuclear disarmament accord should generally permit what cannot be banned verifiably. As such, plans for reconstitution should be fairly robust even if facilities and materials for rebuilding arsenals should not be. Given that the existence of nuclear power plants will give many governments the option of building arsenals within months, even if highly enriched uranium can be eliminated as a fuel and even if plutonium reprocessing is stopped, these plans should be fairly "warm."

Ruling out the option of reconstitution claims more knowledge about the future than anyone can have. Some proponents of abolition recognize this, but others do not, and in most cases, the mechanisms of planning for reconstitution are not given adequate thought. In fact, a central element of any nuclear disarmament regime must be a way to end or at least suspend that regime—in diplomatic, legal, military, and technical terms. Hoping otherwise, and assuming that eliminating nuclear weapons by treaty means abolishing them forever, presupposes a favorable international security environment that may not endure permanently. It therefore runs too high a risk of driving security-conscious states to build nuclear arsenals themselves, and it risks worsening the very proliferation problem that abolition is designed largely to address.

Perhaps the world can get rid of nuclear weapons—as long as states know that they can rebuild them in the event of a sufficiently grave violation of the regime by an aggressive country. Under such circumstances, the international community needs legal and physical mechanisms for deciding whether to rebuild nuclear capability to punish a regime violator. More than just the obvious case of a violating state building nuclear weapons, other possible actions need to be woven into the framework. Suspicion that an aggressive state is building a bomb may suffice to justify others rearming, at least temporarily, even without hard evidence or irrefutable proof. Extremely lethal biological pathogens in the hands of a ruthless regime may also legitimate reconstitution of another country's arsenal, depending on circumstances. Indeed, genocide carried out with conventional weapons may itself be reason enough.[24]

The Manhattan Project was motivated largely by US fears about Germany's bomb program. But replaying the events of World War II in one's imagination, it is hard to argue that the United States should have eschewed nuclear weapons even if it knew full well that Nazi Germany and Imperial Japan could not get them. One can admittedly still debate whether the United States should have used its nuclear weapons, but the argument that it should have made denuclearization a higher priority than ending a war that killed more than 50 million people is far from persuasive.

As I have argued elsewhere,[25] a nuclear disarmament world requires a strategy for reconstitution before a treaty is pursued, to avoid possibly pernicious and counterproductive dynamics as the treaty is negotiated and implemented. From an American perspective, these include:

- Specific clauses in the treaty allowing reconstitution in the event of a direct violation of the treaty by another party.
- More controversially, clauses allowing nuclear reconstitution in the event of the development of a particularly lethal advanced biological pathogen or other highly threatening weapon (including a sufficiently extreme conventional military buildup).
- Clauses allowing a government to bring intelligence information to the UN Security Council if it fears that another government is violating the treaty and wants to respond quickly. In other words, there must be a mechanism for debating violations before they culminate in production, deployment, or use of a bomb.
- A US capacity, including access to facilities at a place such as Los Alamos National Laboratory (and other sites, in case the main site is attacked preemptively), to reconstitute a team of nuclear weapons experts capable of rebuilding a modest number of warheads within months of a decision to do so. Other countries may choose to exercise a similar right.
- A US statement to the effect that, even if the UN Security Council rejects an argument that another country is believed to be building nuclear or advanced biological agents, the United States reserves the right under Article 51 of the UN Charter to rebuild a nuclear arsenal anyway, once a contact group of countries is familiarized with the US case for reconstitution and allowed to comment publicly.

This right would be invoked only in a truly extreme case, should be temporary in its application—and ideally would never be needed. But absent such a statement, the US role as a guarantor of the security of many other countries would be at risk, and the incentives for others to build their own weapons would increase undesirably. The proliferation costs could easily outweigh the benefits; more states rather than fewer might wind up with the bomb.

COUNTERPROLIFERATION STRATEGIES FOR SPECIFIC STATES

Clearly, setting broad parameters about nuclear weapons is crucial as a prerequisite to a successful nonproliferation strategy. Beyond the matter of determining if the goal is a nuclear-free planet, other broad policy matters are central to the issue. They include US national security policy writ large, with its goals of maintaining a stable international order and deterrence as well as reassurance in key regions of the world, and a properly balanced nuclear weapons posture that conveys an adequate degree of resolve without so over-relying on nuclear weapons that it indirectly condones their spread.

Once these broad parameters are put in place, short of actual war-fighting operations, the international community has a number of tools available to address key crises and problems as they might arise. These include economic sanctions, as applied to Iran and North Korea and before that Iraq and Libya; positive incentives, including economic aid, as also offered or denied to most of these states in one form or another (North Korea and Pakistan being good examples); trade restrictions or trade opportunities; flexibility on technology transfers; and diplomatic engagement.

The economic sanctions debate has been particularly prominent of late. As North Korea has expanded its nuclear arsenal, and

Iran has marched toward its own possible bomb, the international community has responded with economic retribution. High-technology assets for Iran's oil industry have been denied, and short-term purchases of Iranian oil have been curtailed. International banking restrictions have been placed on both countries. Key members of each country's ruling circles have been impeded from gaining visas or having access to assets abroad. Trade in military-related technology in general has been severely circumscribed. Arms exports have been precluded in many cases, with Russia's decision to cancel a conventional arms shipment to Iran in recent years a prominent case in point.[26]

This section, however, highlights two specific examples from the recent past that have not received as much attention: North Korea in 2013 and Pakistan in recent decades. These cases illustrate how not only sanctions but also economic incentives, or carrots, can be deployed as tools of crisis management and nonproliferation policy.

North Korea

What could the international community have done in response to North Korea's third nuclear test in early 2013? This led to UN sanctions—and then a round of retribution from North Korea that left the threat of war greater than most international actors were comfortable with. Was there an alternative? Focusing directly on that question helps bring to a head the debate over what tools are available to curtail proliferation and what kinds of debates surround their proper implementation. If there are further tests or other North Korean provocations, this question may need to be revisited.

As of spring 2013, the international community faces a conundrum. North Korea has already been sanctioned intensively; without the support of China, the United States cannot tighten the noose much more. China for its part does not wish to increase the economic pressure on Pyongyang much more, fearing that North Korean instability could result. Moreover, when North Korea has been sanctioned, it has often upped the ante rather than backing down.

There is another dilemma: the possibility that North Korea is producing highly enriched uranium at a secret site. This could give it the capacity to produce up to several bombs' worth of U-235 per year, in theory. As Graham Allison of Harvard and others have warned, such a situation could lead to North Korea selling nuclear materials to the highest bidder—something the United States should, Allison advises, warn North Korea not to do in the strongest possible terms.

There is one more complication, although of a different sort. It has to do with the longer-term prospects for encouraging North Korean reform. Although hope is evaporating that North Korea's new leader, Kim Jong-Un, might be more inclined to consider changes at home, and detente with the outside world, than did his father or grandfather, the United States must keep that option alive. After all, Vietnam and China ultimately reformed even while keeping their communist systems. There is still a chance that North Korea will too—less from a softening of the regime's attitudes than out of economic necessity.

The thirty-year-old Kim is not showing reformist inclinations in the spring of 2013. But it is possible that he feels political pressure internally to establish himself with hardliners before he can pivot to a more reasonable line. This may not be the likely future trajectory, but it cannot be ruled out.

One suggestion on how to handle the situation is that any additional UN sanctions, above and beyond the base that now exists, could be temporary. They could be constructed in such a way as to sunset automatically in a couple years if there is no further nuclear testing in the interim. But they would automatically return if North Korea were to conduct another test, again for two years' duration—or perhaps for three or four years, to avoid any suggestion that this approach is somehow soft or lenient. Continued irresponsible behavior by North Korea would therefore not lead to continued new enticements for better behavior (which some believe is the story of international engagement with Pyongyang over the last two decades), but to ongoing if temporary costs for the North Korean regime.

Such an approach might prove negotiable with Beijing. It could also give Kim Jong Un a chance to reassess his belligerent ways—rather than lock into a permanently hostile dynamic with him.

Any lifting of other, preexisting sanctions, including trade sanctions, would require resolution of the broader nuclear problem. North Korea would have to stop enriching uranium and agree to a long-term plan for gradual denuclearization. Indeed, if it did these things while also gradually making other reforms, outside powers could also offer it the prospect of substantial development assistance.

A road map to a grand bargain and fundamentally improved relationship cannot realistically be pursued. For now, therefore, the goal should be more modest: to provide a firm response to North Korea's unacceptable behavior, but do it in a way that can engender Chinese participation while not closing off the door to a calmer relationship down the road. Making any additional sanctions temporary could achieve this balance and should be considered.

Pakistan

Pakistan reveals the complexities of coping with a multifaceted challenge that cannot be reduced to a primarily nonproliferation concern.

Pakistan has been NATO's primary conduit for logistics supplies reaching Afghanistan. It also helped in the apprehension of several key Al Qaeda figures, including Khalid Sheikh Mohammed, the chief operational planner of the 9/11 attacks, and several others. Al Qaeda's new top leader, Ayman al-Zawahiri, is believed to reside in Pakistan's northern and western tribal regions near the Afghanistan border, and this is the area from which recent attacks or attempted attacks against the United States and other states, such as the 2006 London airplane bombing plot and 2010 Times Square bombing, have emanated. Pakistan is the second-largest Muslim majority nation in the world. It is nuclear-armed and has the fastest-growing nuclear arsenal in the world. It has fought India three times in their brief histories as independent states. It either provoked or contributed to at least three crises with India in the last fifteen years alone (Kargil, 1999; the attack on the Indian parliament by terrorists with ties to Pakistan, 2001; and the Mumbai tragedy of 2008) that could have produced another war—this time between nuclear-armed states. Its economic fragility, high birth and unemployment rates, weak political traditions, unresolved ambitions toward Kashmir, and antipathy felt by most of its citizens and elites toward India make the future prospects of instability foreboding.[27]

Former US deputy secretary of state James Steinberg was surely right when he told Charlie Rose of PBS in June of 2011 that "there is probably no more complex bilateral relationship in the world than the relationship between the United States and Pakistan."[28]

President Obama recognized that, to have any chance of eliciting support from Pakistan for shutting down the Afghan insurgent sanctuaries operating on its soil, more generous US assistance was needed—even as Islamabad sustained a vigorous nuclear weapons production program. The Kerry-Lugar-Berman bill (originally sponsored as well by then-Senator Biden, and supported by then-Senator Obama) began to redress the situation, as did greater amounts of military aid.[29]

Obama appointed the formidable Richard Holbrooke as special representative for Afghanistan and Pakistan, a new position; encouraged his military leaders to expand their contacts in Pakistan; and asked Secretary Clinton and Secretary Gates to lead a strategic dialogue with their counterparts.[30]

But Obama inherited a tough situation in Pakistan, and progress was bound to be slow and fitful.[31] The Mumbai attacks in late November 2008, after Obama was elected but before he was inaugurated, were linked to the LeT group, which Islamabad had supported in the past. The attacks brought Pakistan and India to the brink of war—and gave rise to the possibility that India would retaliate if attacked again, despite its tradition of restraint.[32] After the assassination of Benazir Bhutto and the decision by General Musharaf to step down from the presidency, Pakistan also gained a new leader in 2008, Asif Ali Zardari, the widower of Bhutto, but, more poignantly, a man known for his corrupt ways in the past. This context made it difficult for Obama to reach out enthusiastically to Pakistan even as some types of support and interaction were increased.[33]

Indeed, the passage of the Kerry-Lugar-Berman bill in 2009, which led to an increase in aid levels to Pakistan (the average of the ensuing years being well over $2 billion), was telling as much for the rancor it caused as for any gratitude or improved relations that resulted. Pakistani critics believed it included too many conditions and demands on their country. Speaking with an ISI official in Rawalpindi, Pakistan in March 2010, I was struck to hear such a well-informed and senior government servant belittle US aid as a "drop in the bucket." Yet, there was a whiff of truth behind the complaints. The legislation itself was solid. But the global economic downturn that began in 2008, largely due to US financial transgressions, swamped the Kerry-Lugar-Berman aid in its magnitude. Pakistani GDP growth that had been averaging almost 7 percent annually in mid-decade fell to just 2 percent in 2008 and again in 2009, and returned only to 3 percent in 2010. US foreign investment in Pakistan also dropped by nearly a billion dollars a year.[34] Measured against a nearly $200 billion economy, this translated into roughly a $10 billion differential in growth—each year—from what Pakistan might have otherwise been expected to enjoy.[35]

Pakistan has tolerated the Quetta Shura Taliban on its territory for years, allowing the Afghan insurgency a virtual sanctuary there. Pakistan also provided insufficient help, at best, in the pursuit of Al Qaeda. It did not turn over Osama bin Laden even as he lived for five years in the town of Abbottabad near Islamabad, an urban area full of military personnel and hosting a military academy.[36] Pakistan was not seen as trustworthy enough to be told about the US raid in advance, out of fear that intelligence might be compromised and bin Laden allowed to escape.[37] This was hardly the first time Pakistanis had told American counterparts less than the full truth about a matter of major significance for US interests.[38] But even so, the possibility that Pakistani officials knew where bin Laden had been yet chose not to inform the United States or take action themselves was hard to accept.

Against this backdrop, what are US and international options for persuading Pakistan to clamp down on its production of nuclear bombs, and perhaps also agree to formalize its inclination not to test nuclear weapons again? Clearly, any nuclear-related incentives need to be woven into a broader policy context. Moreover, punitive steps are difficult to imagine, at a time when Pakistan's assistance (or limited, hedged assistance) is needed in Afghanistan—and when Pakistan itself is "too big to fail."

One suggestion is that the United States and the international community offer Islamabad new incentives, but make them conditional on cooperation in the Afghanistan and the nuclear contexts. The United States could offer a major energy deal, perhaps nuclear related and perhaps not, depending on Pakistan's progress with export controls and its willingness to curb production of nuclear weapons. Another suggestion is a free trade accord. Struggling economically, Pakistan needs a shot in the arm, and with average tariffs on goods from Pakistan at 11.4 percent in the US market, a trade deal could arguably make more of an impact than aid at this point.[39] A third suggestion is debt forgiveness or other balance-of-payments help, partly in recognition of how much of Pakistan's economic mess was exacerbated by the United States with the 2008 financial crisis and ensuing global recession. Such American generosity would be sensible and politically feasible in the US Congress only if Islamabad were to clamp down in general on terror groups operating on its soil, including Al Qaeda and Lashkar-e-Taiba, as well as the insurgent groups operating in Afghanistan, and agree to at least some caps on its nuclear activities. But Washington might consider making clear that it would be inclined toward greater generosity if Pakistan could get off the fence in terms of its policies toward extremist groups.

The United States could also consider providing more aid to civilian, development projects in Pakistan and less to the country's military, as suggested by Bruce Riedel and others. This would not prevent Pakistanis from compensating for the reallocation by using more of their own resources for the military in the future. But it could complicate that kind of effort by the Pakistani armed forces—and it would send a different message than current policy does.[40]

In terms of sticks rather than carrots, it is difficult to imagine trade sanctions or other truly punitive steps. But, as suggested by Bruce Riedel, it is time for a message to Pakistani military and intelligence leaders that

American support for and collaboration with them cannot continue at the previous levels of generosity absent a change in their actions. In other words, the closest thing to a stick is the warning of the withholding of future positive incentives or carrots absent better cooperation.

CONCLUSION

The cases discussed here show that every nonproliferation strategy is context specific and each one must be tailored to the challenges and countries at hand.

This is all the more reason why, to provide thematic consistency and strategic clarity to broader nonproliferation efforts, some degree of broad theory of the case is needed. Pursuit of a nuclear-zero world can help—provided that it is not rushed, oversimplified, or elevated to a higher priority than the still-necessary tasks of deterrence and reassurance.

NOTES

1. Although the specific considerations addressed here may change before readers peruse these pages, I hope that the conceptual framing of the policy choices as of this writing in spring 2013 may have future applicability.

2. "Obama Promotes Nuclear-Free World," *BBC*, April, 5, 2009, http://news.bbc.co.uk/2/hi/7983963.stm.

3. See, for example, Ivo Daalder and Jan Lodal, "The Logic of Zero," *Foreign Affairs* 87, no. 6 (November/December 2008).

4. See "Global Zero," www.globalzero.org/en/getting-zero (accessed April 5, 2010).

5. See, for example, Jonathan Schell, *The Fate of the Earth* (New York: Knopf, 1982), 181–84.

6. Robert M. Gates, *Nuclear Posture Review Report* (Washington, DC: US Department of Defense, 2010). In actual terms, the reductions in deployed long-range warhead counts would be about 10 percent or perhaps slightly more. See Union of Concerned Scientists, "Fact Sheet: New START Treaty" (Cambridge, MA, April 2, 2010),

www.ucsusa.org/assets/documents/nwgs/start-fol
low-on-fact-sheet.pdf (accessed April 16, 2010).

7. For a good argument along these lines, see Peter D. Feaver, "Obama's Nuclear Modesty," *New York Times*, April 9, 2010.

8. The White House, "Highlights of the National Commitments Made at the Nuclear Security Summit," April 12–13, 2010, www.whitehouse .gov/the-press-office/highlights-national-commit ments-made-nss (accessed April 15, 2010).

9. Gates, *Nuclear Posture Review Report*, 11.

10. Some critics of nuclear zero contest the notion that taking away such an excuse could be reason enough to pursue nuclear disarmament—and they are right to do so. See, for example, Douglas J. Feith and Abram N. Shulsky, "The Dangerous Illusion of 'Nuclear Zero,'" *Wall Street Journal*, May 21, 2010, A15; and Bruno Tertrais, "The Illogic of Zero," *Washington Quarterly*, 33, no. 2 (April 2010): 129–30.

11. Sam Nunn, "Taking Steps toward a World Free of Nuclear Weapons," *Daedalus* (Fall 2009): 155.

12. Gates, *Nuclear Posture Review Report*, 16.

13. See, for example, Fred C. Ikle, "Nuclear Abolition, A Reverie," *National Interest*, no. 103 (September–October 2009): 6.

14. United Nations, "2010 Review Conference of the Parties to the Treaty on the Non-Proliferation of Nuclear Weapons (NPT)" (New York: United Nations, 2010), www.un.org/en/conf/npt/2010/back ground.shtml (accessed April 5, 2010).

15. John Mueller, *Atomic Obsession: Nuclear Alarmism from Hiroshima to al-Qaeda* (Oxford: Oxford University Press, 2010), 129–58.

16. Keith Payne, "Evaluating the U.S.-Russia Nuclear Deal," *Wall Street Journal*, April 8, 2010, http://online.wsj.com/article/SB10001424052702 3037206045751695329920779888.html.

17. Alexei G. Arbatov, "Russian Nuclear Posture: Capabilities, Missions, and Mysteries inside Enigmas" (paper presented at "P-5 Nuclear Doctrines and Article VI," Stanford, CA, October 16–17, 2007), 120.

18. For a discussion of the second nuclear age, see Robert P. Haffa Jr., Ravi R. Hichkad, Dana J. Johnson, and Philip W. Pratt, "Deterrence and Defense in 'The Second Nuclear Age'" (Arlington,

VA: Northrop Grumman Analysis Center, 2007), 5–11, www.analysiscenter.northropgrumman.com (accessed September 1, 2009). For another discussion of extended deterrence, see Andrew F. Krepinevich, *US Nuclear Forces: Meeting the Challenge of a Proliferated World* (Washington, DC: Center for Strategic and Budgetary Assessments, 2009).

19. Martin Indyk and Tamara Wittes, "Back to Balancing in the Middle East: A New Strategy for Constructive Engagement," in *Opportunity 08: Independent Ideas for America's President*, ed. Michael E. O'Hanlon (Washington, DC: Brookings Institution Press, 2008).

20. Bruce Riedel, "Pakistan and the Bomb," *Wall Street Journal*, May 30, 2009, online.wsj.com/ article/SB100014240529702036585045741918 42820382548.html (accessed July 2, 2009).

21. Michael O'Hanlon, *Technological Change and the Future of Warfare* (Washington, DC: Brookings Institution Press, 2000), 144–53.

22. James Acton and George Perkovich, "Abolishing Nuclear Weapons," *Adelphi Paper* no. 396 (London: International Institute for Strategic Studies, 2008).

23. For a concurring view on this point, see Sverre Lodgaard, "Toward a Nuclear-Weapons-Free World," *Daedalus* (Fall 2009): 142.

24. Defense against asteroids is a very remote, but not totally absurd, possibility that could lead to a need for a short-term reconstitution of a nuclear capability—if not by a single country, then by the international community writ large. However, it is not at the center of any argument I make here. For a credible and readable account, see Caryn Meissner, "Too Close for Comfort," *Science and Technology Review* (December 2009): 12–14.

25. Michael E. O'Hanlon, *A Skeptic's Case for Nuclear Disarmament* (Washington, DC: Brookings Institution Press, 2010).

26. On these matters, see Jonathan D. Pollack, *No Exit: North Korea, Nuclear Weapons, and International Security* (London: International Institute for Strategic Studies, 2011); Martin Indyk, Kenneth Lieberthal, and Michael O'Hanlon, *Bending History: Barack Obama's Foreign Policy* (Washington, DC: Brookings Institution Press, 2012); Ken Pollack's forthcoming book on Iran; David Albright, *Peddling Peril: How the Secret Nuclear Arms Trade*

Arms America's Enemies (New York: Free Press, 2010); and Bruce E. Bechtol, Jr., *Defiant Failed State: The North Korean Threat to International Security* (Washington, DC: Potomac, 2010);

27. See, for example, Stephen P. Cohen, *The Idea of Pakistan* (Washington, DC: Brookings Institution Press, 2004).

28. Interview with Deputy Secretary of State James Steinberg, *The Charlie Rose Show*, June 24, 2011, http://www.charlierose.com/guest/view/3378 (accessed July 14, 2011).

29. Bruce Riedel, *Deadly Embrace: Pakistan, America, and the Future of the Global Jihad* (Washington, DC: Brookings Institution Press, 2011), 119–25.

30. Huma Yusuf, "US-Pakistan Strategic Dialogue," Atlantic Council, Washington, DC, October 25, 2010, http://www.acus.org/new_atlanticist /us-pakistan-strategic-dialogue (accessed March 5, 2011).

31. David E. Sanger, *The Inheritance: The World Obama Confronts and the Challenges to American Power* (New York: Broadway, 2010).

32. Stephen P. Cohen and Sunil Dasgupta, *Arming without Aiming: India's Military Modernization* (Washington, DC: Brookings Institution Press, 2010), 53–70.

33. Riedel, *Deadly Embrace*, 122.

34. Nancy Birdsall, Wren Elhai, and Molly Kinder, "Beyond Bullets and Bombs: Fixing the US Approach to Development in Pakistan" (Center for Global Development, Washington, DC, June 2011),

29, http://www.cgdev.org/content/publications/detail /1425136 (accessed July 15, 2011).

35. For the GDP figures, see International Monetary Fund, "World Economic Outlook" (International Monetary Fund, Washington, DC, April 2010), 160, www.imf.org/external/pubs/ft/weo/2010 /01/pdf/text.pdf (accessed February 1, 2011).

36. Testimony of Steve Coll, president of the New America Foundation, before the House Committee on Homeland Security Subcommittee on Oversight, Investigations, and Management, June 3, 2011, 5, newamerica.net/sites/newamerica.net/files/ profiles/attachments/Coll_Homeland_Security_ Testimony_June_3.pdf (accessed July 1, 2011).

37. New York Post Wire Services, "CIA Director Leon Panetta Feared Pakistan 'Might Alert' bin Laden of Raid," *New York Post*, May 3, 2011, http://www.nypost.com/p/news/international/raid _director_leon_panetta_feared_qbsU3X5g9934s NNAIdG62O (accessed May 3, 2011).

38. See, for example, Stephen J. Solarz, *Journeys to War and Peace* (Lebanon, NH: Brandeis Press, 2011), 160.

39. See, for example, Riedel, *Deadly Embrace*, 119–44; and Birdsall, Elhai, and Kinder, "Beyond Bullets and Bombs," 27.

40. Michael O'Hanlon and Bruce Riedel, "Slogging Through: The Next President Must Address the Crisis in Afghanistan and Pakistan," in *Campaign 2012: Twelve Independent Ideas for Improving American Public Policy,* ed. Benjamin Wittes (Washington, DC: Brookings Institution Press, 2012).

27

THE FUTURE OF CONFLICT PREVENTION

Paul B. Stares

How one assesses the prospects for conflict prevention in the future hinges on how one judges its record in the past. To some observers, recent efforts to promote peace and tame deadly conflict represent a remarkable success.[1] War between states—long a defining feature of international relations—has become such a rarity that many people now consider it obsolete.[2] The "long peace" between great powers has held for more than six decades.[3] Even intrastate or civil conflict—since 1945 the most common type of organized violence—has markedly declined since its peak shortly after the end of the Cold War.[4] Looking ahead, the commitment of leading international actors to manage and minimize organized violence in the world has arguably never been greater, and there is no immediate or obvious reason to believe that what has been accomplished in the past will be reversed in the foreseeable future.

Yet, to other observers, the judgment is more critical and the outlook is less sanguine. The proclaimed reduction in levels of violence may have little or nothing to do with deliberate conflict prevention efforts, and may instead be the result of policies pursued primarily for other reasons, such as nuclear deterrence, free trade and economic development, and the promotion of democratic forms of governance.[5] Meanwhile, for all the sanctimonious declarations by the international community to curb violence and respond to early warnings of conflict, wars continue to break out with lamentable regularity.[6] Major impediments stand in the way of effective preventive action, and there is no reason to expect that they will not stymie the best intentions in the future. There are ominous signs that the level of violent conflict, or at least the amount of armed confrontation, could ratchet up in various parts of the world. The violence convulsing much of North Africa and the Middle East largely as a result of the Arab Awakening, as well as rising tensions in many parts of Asia that some observers attribute to the reemergence of deep-seated nationalistic sentiments, provide sobering reasons to be concerned, even fearful, of the future.

This chapter takes a middle ground position between these two arguments, starting with a precise definition of the meaning and operational scope of conflict prevention—a term that continues to be employed in varied and inconsistent ways. This chapter acknowledges that conflict prevention efforts have had a mixed record, but contends that the more obvious failures should not obscure some notable successes that cannot be discounted as the serendipitous by-product of unrelated processes. Future progress in averting conflict will depend on how well-committed actors recognize and address the recurring challenges to preventive action in the face of emerging threats to international peace and stability. There will surely be setbacks, and so the overriding goal should be to ensure that attention is directed toward forestalling the most consequential threats that risk a reversal of the gains that have been made thus far. This tactic requires a much more systematic and professional approach to conflict prevention than has been the norm. The concluding section discusses what such an approach could entail.

THE SCOPE OF CONFLICT PREVENTION

Conflict prevention is first and foremost about averting *violent* or *deadly* conflict. It is not about eliminating all tensions and disputes in society, something that most people would acknowledge is an unavoidable fact of life and even an indispensable ingredient to human progress. Preventing the resort to violence in human interactions is therefore the primary criterion for delimiting the scope of conflict prevention. This definition leaves open an enormous array of violent human behavior, ranging from interpersonal to international types of conflict. As a consequence, efforts to further demarcate the scope of conflict prevention typically are based on either who is doing the fighting (states and/or non-state actors), the context or contours of the conflict (whether it is mostly confined within national boundaries or transcends them), and the magnitude or scale of the violence (if it

crosses a specified threshold of fatalities and destruction).

Conflict prevention has been pursued for thousands of years, as early civilizations and then nation states developed governance structures for the purpose of imposing and then maintaining order among their subjects.[7] As the system of states evolved, the challenge of limiting aggression between them became an important focus and the leading reason for the creation of international rules and norms of behavior to regulate their interaction. The most important of these, certainly in the evolution of the Western state system, were enshrined in the Peace of Westphalia of 1648 that effectively ended the Thirty Years' War and established the foundational principles of national sovereignty and noninterference in the internal affairs of states.

Diplomatic conventions and mechanisms were later adopted to promote peaceful state behavior and, in particular, to reduce great power conflict. For example, the Congress of Vienna of 1815, following the conclusion of the Napoleonic wars, established a Concert of Powers with practices recognizable today as conflict prevention measures such as regularized high-level consultations, demilitarized zones, and procedures to resolve international disputes peacefully. This system more or less kept the peace in Europe for the next fifty years. Similar great power accords and various international agreements, which increasingly took on an institutionalized form, did the same from 1871 to 1914 and again between 1919 and 1939. Although both world wars exposed the weaknesses of the arrangements designed to avert such conflagrations, the elements deemed beneficial for peace and stability—notably, the norms of national sovereignty, standing great power consultative bodies, and dedicated judicial mechanisms to arbitrate national disputes—were retained and incorporated into the post–World War II United Nations system that remains in effect today.

Only relatively recently, however, was any of this activity described as "conflict prevention." It was not until 1960, for example, that the term "preventive diplomacy" was coined by UN Secretary-General Dag Hammarskjöld, and it was really only after the end of the Cold War that this term gained currency—and then in the narrow context of preventing large-scale violence *within* states.[8] This imprecise definition had the unfortunate effect of conflating preventive diplomacy and conflict prevention in general with the challenge of managing violence in what are now referred to as "weak and failing" states.

Meanwhile, the task of preventing other forms of violence, such as major interstate war or the threat of terrorism, has been more commonly seen as the purview of something else—typically, diplomacy, deterrence, or national security strategy—even though the core goal is the same as that of conflict prevention. As a consequence of this pigeonholing, conflict prevention has been commonly viewed as a lesser pursuit than "high politics" international diplomacy and strategy.

It has not helped that conflict prevention as a distinct field of endeavor suffers from conceptual confusion about what it actually entails and where in the life cycle of a conflict is it principally directed. Many different definitions have been offered, albeit in variations on the umbrella term.[9] To some, conflict prevention is first and foremost—if not exclusively—about removing or minimizing the root causes of a conflict before it turns violent. These activities are sometimes characterized as upstream or front-end forms of preventive action. To others, however, conflict prevention also includes more downstream efforts to prevent dangerous situations arising that carry the latent risk of violence and to defuse them before they escalate or spread. Some would extend the scope of conflict prevention still further to include peacemaking—bringing an ongoing conflict to an end—and peacebuilding—ensuring

through reconciliation and reconstruction efforts that conflict does not reignite—on the grounds that both activities are essentially preventive in purpose.[10]

Attempts to address the conceptual confusion by differentiating between different kinds of conflict prevention have not been entirely satisfactory. A commonly used typology is to distinguish among three types of conflict prevention: systemic, structural, and operational.[11] Although there are notable inconsistencies in how these terms are defined and used—inconsistencies that reflect the underlying weakness of the typology—these terms are more or less differentiated as follows:

- *Systemic prevention* refers to measures intended to have broad global impact in promoting peace and reducing violence without regard to a specific region or country. They typically include the promotion of rules, norms, institutions, and regulatory regimes with this goal specifically in mind.
- *Structural prevention* is focused on redressing the root causes of conflict at the subnational, national, or regional level. Measures and tactics typically include political, economic, social, and legal efforts to rectify specific grievances and disputes.
- *Operational prevention* entails relatively short-term efforts to forestall incipient or escalating violence, with the parties to the conflict (and, more specifically, their leaders) being the principal target. Political, diplomatic, and, if called for, military measures are viewed as the main tools for this type of preventive action.

These distinctions are not entirely helpful for several reasons. The scope of systemic prevention is too broad. Are there not measures with goals similar to systemic prevention that could be applied to specific countries or regions? Structural prevention is associated almost exclusively with redressing intrastate forms of violence. How relevant, therefore, are the tools commonly used with this approach to prevent other forms of organized violence? Similarly, are "operational" kinds of prevention relevant only for crisis management interventions?

These deficiencies could be rectified with further refinement and definitional elaboration, but a good argument can be made for starting afresh and adopting typologies commonly used in other areas of preventive action, notably in the public health and public safety spheres. Here preventive action is typically distinguished in terms of specific interventions at relatively discrete stages in the emergence, onset, and progression of a disease or criminal act.[12] The three stages and associated preventive interventions are as follow.[13]

- *Primary prevention or risk reduction measures* are initiatives generally understood to help promote peace and stability within and between states. They are the equivalent of following a healthy diet and lifestyle to reduce the likelihood of disease. States that are democratically governed, for example, are widely considered less bellicose—at least toward one another—than nondemocratic ones are.[14] By permitting regular opportunities to change governments through popular suffrage, established democracies are on the whole more stable and peaceful than nonestablished democracies. Those that respect basic human rights—notably, freedom of speech, assembly, religion, and fair trial—are likewise less susceptible to violent conflict. At the same time, considerable evidence testifies to the pacifying effect of commerce and economic development, especially if undertaken equitably and

in an environmentally sensitive fashion. Targeted investment and foreign assistance can be employed to facilitate this. In general, risk reduction measures may be global in application or more narrowly focused on a specific region or state.

- *Secondary prevention or crisis prevention* measures are directed at preventing extant or emerging sources of conflict (again, within and between states) from intensifying and ultimately erupting into violent conflict. The health equivalent is early medical treatment to reverse and ultimately cure a disease, and, if this is not feasible, to inhibit or contain its harmful progression. Depending on the nature of the conflict, a variety of preventive measures can be directed at addressing and resolving the source of the dispute. External mediation and arbitration, for example, have proven useful in many instances for this purpose. If the source of the conflict cannot be resolved, at least in the short term, then preventive measures are best employed in shaping the calculus of the parties in dispute so that a resort to violence is seen as neither attractive nor necessary. Various military, economic, and diplomatic measures can be targeted to constrain or positively influence the motives, means, and opportunities of the parties not to engage in violent behavior. At the interstate level, these range from cooperative-based initiatives, such as arms control and confidence-building measures, designed to reduce mistrust and avoid unintended escalation to unilateral actions intended to deter aggressive behavior through military assistance, security guarantees, and the threat of sanctions for noncompliance. Similar techniques can be used for intrastate disputes to shape the behavior of governments as well as nonstate actors.

- *Tertiary prevention or conflict mitigation* measures entail managing the violent eruption of a conflict to limit further escalation and bring it to an end with or without resolution. Emergency care would be the medical equivalent. Here again, the approach is broadly similar to crisis prevention in that positive and negative inducements are employed to leverage participants in ways that de-escalate the conflict. Coercive de-escalation measures might entail the use of various sanctions (e.g., diplomatic pressure, travel bans, trade embargoes, withholding foreign aid, legal and military threats), whereas consensual de-escalation could involve offering various rewards for compliant behavior (e.g., economic assistance, diplomatic recognition, military support, domestic power sharing). These tactics are not mutually exclusive, and more often than not they are used together (sticks and carrots). Where de-escalation is not immediately feasible, containing the conflict and minimizing the human costs may be the best that can be accomplished.

This typology sets reasonable parameters on the scope of conflict prevention. Just as emergency medical treatment can stop short of initiating remedial solutions to a harmful condition, not to mention postoperative recovery and rehabilitation, so the conflict prevention equivalent falls short of what is commonly known as peacemaking, peacekeeping, and peacebuilding.

TAKING STOCK

As noted above, reaching definitive conclusions about the success or failure of conflict

prevention efforts is difficult.[15] Just as it is notoriously difficult to parse the origins of any given war, so it is a challenge to explain why peace or relatively low levels of violence prevail under certain circumstances and at certain times. Multiple factors are typically at work, and evaluating their individual and relative importance depends on making controlled comparisons across different cases and carrying out extensive counterfactual analysis that by definition is speculative. Nevertheless some broad-brush judgments appear defensible (or at least are not easily refutable) about the efficacy of conflict prevention efforts since 1945. These judgments are based on an assessment of the latent risk of war in certain times and places and a determination if deliberate efforts to avert conflict were made and if it is reasonable to infer that these efforts had an effect on the trajectory of events.

The level of interstate conflict has been low since 1945, especially after the internationalized wars of liberation more or less ended once the process of decolonization ran its course in the mid-1970s.[16] What accounts for this is a matter of some debate.[17] It is hard to prove that the proscriptions on the international use of force enshrined in the UN Charter had a constraining effect on aggressive behavior by states, although such behavior has clearly become delegitimized since 1945, judging by the global opprobrium now associated with it. The norm has arguably also been strengthened through various United Nations-sanctioned collective security operations, notably against North Korea in 1950 and Iraq in 1990. The larger contribution of the UN system—its various consultative bodies, dispute resolution mechanisms, and regulatory regimes—to limiting international conflict is likewise difficult to prove, but at the same time it is hard to imagine that the risk of war would have remained the same had the United Nations not been established and its operational scope had not grown. The same is likely true regarding the expansion of institutionalized cooperation in reducing international mistrust and misunderstanding in virtually every field of human endeavor.

It seems safe to conclude that the progressive spread of democratic governance around the world since 1945 has had a beneficial effect, given the virtual absence of armed conflict between democracies. Yet, it should be acknowledged that "democratic enlargement" as a deliberate conflict prevention strategy was not widely articulated and promoted as a conflict prevention strategy until after the end of the Cold War. Moreover, neither the democratic peace theory nor the similar capitalist peace theory explains the low level of armed conflict with nondemocratic and noncapitalist countries despite substantial mutual animosity, not least during the Cold War. In this case, it is reasonable to assert that secondary and tertiary forms of conflict prevention played a meaningful role.

This argument certainly seems to be true for Europe. From being the primary locus of international strife, Europe is now widely seen as the poster child for a true "peace community" where war between states is virtually unimaginable.[18] This historically unprecedented peacefulness can be attributed to widespread exhaustion from fighting World War II and to the dampening effect of the US and Soviet confrontation on preexisting tensions and rivalries within the superpowers' respective European spheres of influence. Deliberate efforts—certainly in the western half of the continent—were taken to address the root causes of European instability, notably, democratizing Germany (and Italy), constraining Germany's war-making potential, and promoting Franco-German reconciliation and cooperation through the creation of a European-wide economic community that would become the European Union. In the latter case, the architects of European

integration were explicit about their conflict prevention motives and strategy.[19]

To be sure, these efforts could not have succeeded without overarching efforts to prevent the Cold War from turning hot. Although the extent to which the Soviet Union harbored militarily expansionist intentions is a matter of debate, the system of security guarantees offered by the United States to countries perceived to be threatened by communist aggression—in many cases, manifested by the presence of US forces, including nuclear weapons, as well as formal alliance structures—was generally successful in deterring any such moves and, by extension, major war. What crises and armed clashes did occur were usually in places where the boundaries of the conflict were ambiguous or the level of commitment was unclear, such as in Berlin, Korea, and Cuba.

As the Cold War progressed, informal ground rules as well as formal agreements for managing the conflict and avoiding dangerous crisis escalation were developed. These included the tacit acceptance of reconnaissance for strategic reassurance purposes, various arms control agreements to rein in destabilizing military competition and buttress mutual deterrence, and several crisis prevention and management mechanisms to reduce the chance of accidental or unintended war. There were also many instances where both the United States and the Soviet Union acted to restrain and otherwise dampen hostilities between other countries where the risk of superpower escalation existed, notably in the Middle East and, to a lesser extent, South Asia. This cooperation continued to the end of the Cold War and the negotiations surrounding the unification of Germany, which were specifically choreographed and structured to avoid sowing the seeds for future conflict in Europe.[20]

Although the risk of major interstate war receded in the wake of the Cold War, it did not disappear. Several international wars have broken out, notably the 1990 Gulf War, the 1998–2000 Eritrea-Ethiopia border conflict, and the brief Russia-Georgia clash in 2008, all of which can be considered conflict prevention failures. Yet there have also been several cases where diplomatic mediation and third-party crisis management appear to have averted conflict or serious escalation. Examples include multiple efforts to diffuse crises between India and Pakistan and between North and South Korea; and more recent diplomatic interventions in Sudan and the South China Sea.[21] The United Nations can point to several successful mediating efforts in defusing disputes, including those between Turkmenistan and Azerbaijan, Nigeria and Cameroon, and Gabon and Equatorial Guinea.[22]

With regard to intrastate conflict prevention, it is harder to demonstrate success. For most of the Cold War, the UN framework was oriented toward the prevention of interstate conflict; to the extent that its conflict management system engaged in civil wars, the engagement was focused primarily on downstream peacemaking and peacemaking efforts. Meanwhile, the UN support for universal human rights and self-determination lent legitimacy to, if not fueled, much of the intrastate conflict that erupted in the post-1945 world—initially with various wars of liberation from colonial rule and later with numerous secessionist and postcommunist struggles. To its credit, however, the United Nations did not make things worse by supporting a wholesale revision of colonial boundaries as new nations emerged.

At the same time, the two superpowers made little effort to curb emerging civil conflict. To the contrary, in many instances they fomented instability and supported armed resistance as part of their larger strategic rivalry. Thus, it is not an exaggeration to state that for most of the Cold War period, intra-

state conflict prevention was hardly practiced, and certainly not in a strategic and systematic fashion.

With the surge of civil conflicts in the immediate aftermath of the Cold War, international attitudes, and with it policy priorities, started to change. With the publication in 1992 of its report *An Agenda for Peace*, the United Nations began to emphasize the merits of preventive action as it became more engaged and thus more burdened by dealing with the upsurge in violence. The response by the international community—at least initially—was not encouraging. Although the level of intrastate conflict began to decline in the 1990s, this can largely be attributed to efforts to end ongoing conflicts rather than to endeavors to prevent new ones.[23] The onset of new conflicts in this period continued at a rate not significantly different from Cold War levels. These conflicts included multiple wars in the former Yugoslavia as well as the Rwandan genocide, not to mention mass atrocities in neighboring Burundi.

A legitimate argument can be made that the level of violence in the 1990s could have been much worse had it not been for some notable preventive successes. The so-called quiet diplomacy of the Organization for Security and Cooperation in Europe (OSCE) is considered by many to have been effective in quelling ethnic tensions in several Eastern European countries. International actions to prevent the conflict in the Balkans from spilling over into Macedonia—including the deployment of a dedicated UN force along the border with the Federal Republic of Yugoslavia and Albania—is another example. Beyond Europe, pressure from the Organization of American States (OAS) appears to have averted dangerous instability in Peru and Guatemala. And following the mass atrocities in Rwanda, increased attention was given to averting further violence in Burundi.[24]

The failures of the 1990s spurred the United Nations and other international institutions to invest more heavily in conflict prevention efforts and capacities. With "weak and failing" states increasingly identified as the primary source of concern, more attention was given to isolating principal risk factors, such as poverty and poor institutional capacity, and actively mitigating them through development assistance programs. Here the efforts of the European Union, the World Bank, and the Organisation of Economic Co-operation and Development (OECD) led the way.[25] The United Nations and several regional organizations began to develop informal conflict early warning mechanisms and procedures for responding to the threat of internal conflict.[26] The use of special envoys, fact-finding missions, preventive military deployments, and various mediation mechanisms all became more common. Many observers believe that these tactics have been used to good effect over the past decade in many different settings, including Niger, Guinea, Ghana, South Sudan, Kenya, Madagascar, Kyrgyzstan, Nepal, and Iraq (Kirkuk).[27]

It is worth mentioning the growing practice of prosecuting war crimes and crimes against humanity. Although primarily intended to dispense postconflict justice, the prosecution of human rights violations can have a deterrent effect.[28] Similarly, the widespread acceptance by UN states in 2005 of their responsibility to protect civilians threatened by conflict and violent discrimination may facilitate early humanitarian intervention. This view gained currency with the successful NATO intervention to avert the threat of mass atrocities in Libya in 2011, where the responsibility to protect (R2P) principle was invoked, although the subsequent failure to staunch civilian violence in Syria and Egypt subsequently made many people question the power of this norm.

RECURRING CHALLENGES TO CONFLICT PREVENTION

The mixed record of conflict prevention efforts reflects recurring challenges to executing timely and effective policies. Although these challenges are commonly boiled down to early warning failures or deficiencies in early response (typically characterized as a failure of political will), they are actually more varied and complex.

Proactive risk reduction measures (primary conflict prevention) are hard to enact when the putative benefits appear unwarranted, much like weight control and exercise may seem unnecessary to an outwardly healthy person. Some of the measures considered beneficial to peace and stability can take time to have a positive impact. Expending immediate effort and political capital for what appears to be distant rewards is thus unappealing to term-limited policymakers facing more pressing demands on their time and resources. In the case of initiatives that require multilateral endorsement—for example, new international legal measures or international regulatory regimes—the obstacles to gaining the necessary support to make them meaningful multiply.

In contrast, preventing parties already in an adversarial relationship from escalating and resorting to violence (secondary conflict prevention) requires less suspension of disbelief about the latent risks but it has its own set of challenges. Unless the threat of violence is undeniably compelling and, moreover, appears imminent, political leaders and the bureaucracies they nominally oversee are not renowned for taking swift and responsive action. They are typically focused on—and more often than not consumed by—managing the crisis of the moment. The available bandwidth to consider potential crises that by definition may never materialize is thus limited. Even when the danger signs are undeniable, the general tendency is to discount them or to hope for the best. It does not help that there are few if any political or bureaucratic rewards for averting something that cannot be convincingly proven would have happened were it not for the timely intervention. This hurdle is especially hard to overcome when national interest is seemingly not directly imperiled.

All these factors compound the already strong forces of inertia acting on leaders and bureaucracies. The logic of "letting events ripen" and "retaining freedom of action" become common arguments for procrastination. Even when there is a consensus to take early preventive or precautionary measures, the nature of the threat can set limits on what can realistically be accomplished. Efforts to address an emerging source of instability inside a country can be resisted as interference in the domestic affairs of a sovereign state. Mobilizing the attention of an intergovernmental institution that must respect sovereign equality and unanimity of action is difficult for the same reason.

As for managing a crisis where the use of force appears likely or force has already been used so as to prevent further escalation and mitigate the consequence (tertiary prevention), much hinges on accurately identifying the relevant danger signals and conveying that information to decision makers in a timely manner. As various cases of strategic surprise have demonstrated, timely early warning can be impeded by numerous obstacles, including failures to focus intelligence collection efforts on at-risk places, to correctly identify critical signals amid background noise, to counter various analytical biases that can distort the interpretation of relevant information, and to minimize the bureaucratic barriers to the timely alerting of senior decision makers.[29] These challenges have arguably grown more complex and difficult to overcome as the focus of concern has shifted away from monitoring the potentially hostile military intentions of states to discerning signs of societal instability within a country, including the actions of nonstate actors.

By the time a crisis erupts or starts to escalate, the imperatives for preventive action are clearer and more pressing, and the earlier opportunities to defuse the conflict may have narrowed or passed completely, leaving only costly and politically unpalatable choices for decision makers. Generating the necessary political will to act thus becomes a more difficult proposition. And because by this stage, preventive action may necessitate collective international effort, not only to share the burdens but also to legitimize the effort—especially if the action requires breaching principles of sovereignty—achieving a consensus to act and agreement on how to act further compounds the challenge.

LOOKING AHEAD

It is possible to imagine two different but plausible trajectories for violent conflict in the world over the next ten to twenty years: one is a steadily more peaceful world in which the forces and factors that have contributed to the downturn in interstate and intrastate violence continue to exert their pacifying effect; the other sees the reversal of recent gains by a wave of dangerous crises and game-changing events, made worse by structural changes underway in the international system.

Looking at the positive scenario first, there is no reason to believe that the broad processes of globalization—economic development, expansion of trade, commercial interdependence, widening respect for human rights, and functional cooperation on a broad range of issues—will not continue (albeit at varying rates) and exert a broadly beneficial effect in promoting peace and dissuading violence.[30] Demographic trends—principally, aging populations—in several regions are likely to reinforce these tendencies.[31] It is also reassuring that many leading regional and global actors are emphasizing conflict prevention as a policy goal and programmatic priority. For the United States, interest in conflict prevention has much to do with the widespread desire to avoid major new military commitments after more than a decade of fighting since 9/11. The fiscal situation, which afflicts many leading powers active in international conflict management, is another factor supporting the logic of preventive action. For the United Nations, heightened interest has much to do with the frequency with which it has been saddled with the unenviable and costly task of reconstructing countries emerging from the ravages of war. Likewise, the aspirations of regional organizations to play a more prominent role in averting conflict have been growing not only because their members are the principal beneficiaries but also because they have become painfully aware that the support of the outside world cannot be taken for granted, especially when the UN Security Council is often deadlocked.

As for the negative scenario, numerous short-term threats to peace—if poorly managed—as well as longer-term shifts in the distribution of world power, could combine to undermine international peace and stability. In East Asia, the rise of a more powerful and assertive China has raised fears that great power rivalry and even armed confrontation will be rekindled in the region, if not globally. Several territorial disputes pit China against India and against allies of the United States. Various contingencies on the Korean Peninsula could easily ignite a major war. States in the region are hedging against uncertainty through increased investments in military capabilities and greater security cooperation, which can increase, rather than lower, tensions. In Central and South Asia, considerable uncertainty surrounds the effect of the drawdown of US and coalition forces from Afghanistan. It is not hard to imagine how conflict in Afghanistan and Pakistan could spiral upward in the coming years.

Meanwhile, many of the long-standing sources of tension between Pakistan and India remain unresolved.

Much of the Middle East and North America is in turmoil as the effects of the Arab Awakening continue to reverberate in the region. Syria has descended into civil war and could break up, with destabilizing spillover effects on its immediate neighbors, especially Lebanon, Jordan, and Iraq. Iraq seems to be sliding back into major sectarian strife and could also fracture. There is also no guarantee that recent progress in reaching a satisfactory solution to the crisis with Iran over its alleged nuclear weapons program will reach fruition with a permanent deal. Tensions could easily come to a head again with potentially violent and destabilizing consequences for the region. Meanwhile, the situation in Egypt and several countries in North Africa remains highly volatile and could easily descend into more violence, with unpredictable consequences. And finally, no one can assume that the long-standing Israeli-Palestinian conflict will remain relatively quiescent.

Despite notable improvements in many areas, Africa continues to be blighted by conflict in the Great Lakes region, the Horn, and parts of the Sahel, notably Mali and the Central African Republic. After seceding from Sudan in 2011, South Sudan is now riven by ethnic conflict. Several countries in West Africa that have experienced conflict in recent years also remain vulnerable to relapse. As a recent assessment of the US National Intelligence Council (NIC) concluded, "Looking forward, the potential for conflict to occur in Sub-Saharan Africa is likely to remain high even after some of the region's countries graduate into a more intermediate age structure because of the probable large number of ethnic and tribal minorities that will remain more youthful than the overall population."[32] Finally, although the Western

Hemisphere has been one of the most pacific regions, the level of violence related to criminal activity has become a serious and growing problem in several countries, particularly Honduras and El Salvador.

Over the longer term, various discernible developments could undermine international peace and cooperation. One is the *relative* decline of the United States and the emergence of new regional and potentially global actors. Previous power transitions in the international system have been accompanied by instability and major conflict. Access to weapons of mass destruction and long-range delivery systems is projected to grow not only among states but also among nonstate actors, with potentially destabilizing consequences. Military technology is constantly evolving, and one cannot assume that future developments will not undermine international stability. And finally there is the potential impact of environmental change and resource scarcity brought about by global development and population growth that could create dangerous stresses within and between countries.[33]

Whether one or the other of the two scenarios becomes reality will depend on the inclination and effectiveness of committed actors within the international system to promote the former and inhibit the latter through effective preventive policies. Although the apparent commitment of leading actors is certainly increasing, the challenges they face are formidable. Perversely, many of the reasons that make preventive action more appealing at this time can as easily become an excuse for preventive inaction if key actors turn inward and isolationist. As the aforementioned NIC report also warns,

> During the next 15–20 years, the US will be grappling with degree to which it can continue to play the role of systemic guardian and guarantor of the global order. A declining US

unwillingness and/or slipping capacity to serve as a global security provider would be a key factor contributing to instability particularly in Asia and the Middle East. A more fragmented international system in which existing forms of cooperation are no longer seen as advantageous to many of the key global players would also increase the potential for competition and even great power conflict.[34]

It is not inconceivable that several major failures occurring more or less simultaneously could so overburden international willpower and resources that conflict prevention efforts begin to suffer. This could happen for a variety of reasons, ranging from the effect of political recriminations, a loss of confidence, and a rise in mistrust to more mundane issues of limited personnel and organization capacity in the system. In other words, failure could be contagious, with potentially harmful consequences to the otherwise positive forces of globalization.

Given that the first scenario cannot be taken for granted and the second scenario cannot be easily dismissed, several broad considerations should inform conflict prevention efforts in the coming years.

Prioritize Efforts and Focus on the Most Important Threats.

Not all potential conflicts are equally consequential and thus deserving of equal attention and resources. The possibility of renewed rivalry and hostility between great powers—the United States and China and, to a lesser extent, Russia, as well as between India and China—should be the greatest concern even if it appears remote. The reasons are clear: all are nuclear-armed powers, and renewed tensions will raise the stakes of any outbreak of conflict to existential levels. Deep distrust, rivalry, and armed confrontation will undermine the prospects for cooperation on regional threats to peace, not to mention the management of pressing global concerns like climate change. Similar logic applies to emerging regional powers and the need to manage their rise without detriment to peace and security.

Safeguard and Strengthen the Foundational Elements of the International Order.

This action refers to the international rules, norms, institutions, and regimes that regulate state behavior in predictable and peaceful ways.[35] The multifaceted structure of the international order is coming under increasing strain from two directions—the permissible parameters for national self-defense on one hand and humanitarian intervention in the sovereign affairs of a state on the other.

It not hard to imagine how the pressures on states to act militarily across borders to counter emerging threats to national security will grow, especially if existing global controls on the proliferation of weapons of mass destruction weaken and nonstate actors gain increasing access to a variety of deadly or disruptive technologies. Such pressures are already evident from several (overt and covert) counterproliferation and counterterrorism operations that have been carried out in recent years. Pressure to use force or intervene militarily could grow in the face of threats that stem from mass migration, the outbreak of deadly pandemics, and irresponsible environmental behavior. Defining precisely when anticipatory self-defense is permissible is beyond clear legal formulation, and attempts to do so may have the unintended consequence of weakening existing UN Charter-based rules. But just as the legality and legitimacy of humanitarian intervention has grown through the progressive endorsement of state behavior for this purpose, basic principles governing anticipatory self-defense—particularly as they relate to necessity and proportionality—may become acceptable in the future. Waiting for events to drive this process is risky, however, and thus it would be useful for a group of like-minded states to encourage

debate in multilateral forums about how to reconcile the growing imperatives to act preemptively with the need to adhere to the core precepts of the international order.

At the same time, many states—including great powers such as China and Russia—are uncomfortable with and at times resistant to, evolving international norms about how states should treat their citizens, which they view as an infringement of their sovereign prerogatives. The right to intervene for humanitarian reasons—if necessary by forceful means—under an R2P mandate as occurred with NATO military action against Libya that eventually led to the ouster of its leader Muammar Gaddafi, is particularly controversial. Although the protection of civilians is a norm that deserves to be promoted, extreme care needs to be taken that this effort does not come at the expense of international stability. As one scholar has argued,

> A world in which violations of human rights trump the sanctity of borders may turn out to produce more wars, more massacres, and more instability. It may also be less law-abiding. If the history of the past half century shows anything, it is that clear legal norms, the empowering of states and the securing of international stability more generally also serve the cause of human welfare.[36]

This observation suggests not only that efforts to uphold the emerging norm give greater emphasis to early nonmilitary preventive measures but also that when coercive interventions are contemplated, they be considered a last resort and conducted in a way that enjoys broad international legitimacy. The latter is generally viewed as requiring a clear mandate from the United Nations or, if that is not possible, the backing of the regional organization most affected by the humanitarian contingency.

This requirement raises another challenge. The United Nations' universal membership and corresponding legitimacy make it an indispensable actor in the maintenance and evolution of desirable global norms. Yet the composition of the United Nations' governing core—the Security Council—does not reflect the distribution of power in the world today and will be increasingly viewed as archaic if not illegitimate as the structure of the international system continues to evolve. Effort must be made to reform the Security Council—both its membership and its operating rules—to ensure that it remains relevant and representative, or its critical role will diminish. This means enlarging the number of permanent members of the Security Council to broaden regional representation, improving its working methods to improve the transparency of decision making, and modifying the circumstances in which vetoes can be wielded or overridden. There is no guarantee that such reforms would make the United Nations a more effective organization, but they are unlikely to make it less so. Certainly, waiting for a crisis to provide the necessary political will to carry out such reforms is risky. Other global institutions that play a similar, if more indirect role, such as the major international financial institutions, face a similar challenge. They too must be reformed or risk irrelevance.

Beyond efforts to strengthen normative principles, various global and regional regimes that contribute to international stability in different ways must be sustained and where necessary strengthened with appropriate enhancements. A particular area of concern is the regulation of the use of the "global commons"—areas beyond sovereign jurisdiction, essentially the oceans, outer space, cyberspace, and the polar regions—where the risk of international competition is likely to grow in the coming decades as a result of climate change, technological advances that make these areas more accessible, and growing commercial pressures to exploit them.

Expand the Circle of Committed Actors Engaged in Conflict Prevention Around the World and More Effectively Harness the Diverse Efforts of Those Already Involved.

The challenges are too large and complex for the hitherto leading players—principally the Western powers with global influence—to take on alone. Expanding the circle should entail several related initiatives: encouraging emerging powers to play a more active and responsible role, certainly in their immediate regions; bolstering the capacity of regional organizations to carry out various kinds of preventive action; and urging the private business sector, which has much to lose and gain from conflict prevention efforts, to become more actively engaged. At the same time, more effective partnerships must be forged with the growing universe of nongovernmental civil society organizations involved in various aspects of conflict prevention. Too often, these groups are viewed as marginal players in prevention efforts, but numerous cases demonstrate how valuable they can be.

FINAL THOUGHTS

How well those engaging in conflict prevention efforts fare in the future will depend on how they go about it. There is much to be done to improve the praxis of preventive action, starting with a clearer conceptualization of its operational parameters. Drawing on comparable concepts and practices from other types of preventive action offers a way to do this, which in turn should become the basis for developing what the militaries of the world recognize as established operational doctrine or best practice–based guidance for planning and implementation. Generating lists of putatively useful preventive measures or tools at the disposal of policymakers is not a substitute for practical guidance on how and when they should be employed in given situations or phases of conflict.[37] The development of policy guidance should draw on real world experience. Unfortunately, very few countries or organizations make a systematic effort to learn from past cases of preventive action and to adapt their responses accordingly. Not surprisingly, therefore, professional education and training in conflict prevention techniques are generally poor.

All these are necessary improvements to make but alone cannot be considered sufficient. The institutional context and organizational culture are also vital ingredients. Suitably prepared individuals and organizations dedicated to preventing deadly conflict will accomplish little if the system they operate within is not appropriately configured and adequately resourced. Too often, those responsible for assessing and warning of potential instability and conflict are disconnected from the policy planning process or have little role in driving its efforts. Similarly, bureaucratic "silos" can impede collective thinking and collective effort despite the advantages—even imperatives—of cooperation. This fact applies within countries as well as between them. Ensuring that resources can be deployed in a flexible manner is essential. Most of all, a fundamental recognition of the value of preventive action and the need to think and act accordingly must take root. These requirements represent a tall order but not an impossible one.

NOTES

1. See, for example, Steven Pinker, *The Better Angels of Our Nature: Why Violence Has Declined* (New York: Viking, 2011); and Joshua S. Goldstein, *Winning the War on War: The Decline of Armed Conflict Worldwide* (New York: Dutton, 2011).

2. John Mueller, *Retreat from Doomsday: The Obsolescence of Major War* (New York: Basic Books, 1989); John Mueller, "War Has Almost Ceased to Exist: An Assessment," *Political Science Quarterly* 124, no. 2 (Summer 2009): 297–321; and Bruno Tertrais, "The Demise of Ares: The End of War as

We Know It?" *Washington Quarterly* 35, no. 2 (Summer 2012): 7–22.

3. The term "the long peace" was coined by John Lewis Gaddis in "The Long Peace Elements of Stability in the Postwar International System," *International Security* 10, no. 4 (Spring 1986): 99–142.

4. For a discussion of conflict trends since the end of World War II, see Lotta Themner and Peter Wallensteen, "Armed Conflict, 1946–2012," *Journal of Peace Research* 50, no. 4 (July 2013): 509–21.

5. For an excellent discussion of competing explanations of recent conflict trends, see *Human Security Report 2009/2010* (New York: Oxford University Press, 2011), 21–44.

6. A recent Council on Foreign Relations scorecard of efforts to manage armed conflict gave the United States a B-, while the international community received a C+. See http://www.cfr.org/thinktank/iigg/reportcard/armed_conflict.html#report-card.

7. There is broad consensus that levels of violence declined significantly as states began to impose order on the territory they nominally controlled five thousand years ago. See Azar Gat, "Is War Declining—And Why?" *Journal of Peace Research* 50, no. 2 (2012): 150.

8. See Alice Ackermann, "The Idea and Practice of Conflict Prevention," *Journal of Peace Research* 40, no. 3 (2003): 340.

9. For examples, see Peter Wallensteen and Frida Möller, "Conflict Prevention: Methodology for Knowing the Unknown," Uppsala Peace Research Paper no. 7 (Uppsala University, Sweden, 2003), 46.

10. These, too, are contested terms.

11. See Barnett R. Rubin, *Blood on the Doorstep: The Politics of Preventive Action* (New York: Century Foundation Press, 2002), 131–32; Barnett R. Rubin and Bruce D. Jones, "Prevention of Violent Conflict: Tasks and Challenges for the United Nations," *Global Governance* 13 (2007): 393–94; and Michael S. Lund, "Conflict Prevention: Theory in Pursuit of Policy and Practice," in *Sage Handbook of Conflict Resolution*, ed. Jacob Bercovitch, Victor Kremenyuk, and I. William Zartman (Thousand Oaks, CA: Sage, 2009).

12. See, for example, the US Centers for Disease Control and Prevention definitions at http://www.cdc.gov/excite/skincancer/mod13.htm.

13. This section builds on and refines an earlier typology of preventive action contained in Paul B. Stares and Micah Zenko, *Enhancing US Preventive Action,* Council Special Report no. 48 (Council on Foreign Relations, Washington, DC, October 2009), 7–8.

14. See *Human Security Report 2009/2010,* 21–44.

15. See Wallensteen and Möller, "Conflict Prevention," 7–11.

16. See, for instance, the figure "Global Trends in Armed Conflict Onsets, 1946–2011," in Monty G. Marshall and Benjamin R. Cole, *Global Report 2011: Conflict, Governance, and State Fragility* (Vienna, VA: Center for Systemic Peace, 2011), http://www.systemicpeace.org/conflict.htm.

17. *Human Security Report 2009/2010,* 21–34.

18. Latin America is the other widely cited "zone of peace" where interstate conflict has been rare. Why is it the subject of considerable debate? To the extent that deliberate conflict prevention efforts have had any effect, the effect has derived from the development of region-wide norms of nonintervention and the use of international mediation in border disputes.

19. See the Schuman Declaration (May 9, 1950), http://europa.eu/about-eu/basic-information/symbols/europe-day/schuman-declaration/.

20. See Philip D. Zelikow and Condoleezza Rice, *Germany Unified and Europe Transformed: A Study in Statecraft* (Cambridge, MA: Harvard University Press, 1995).

21. See Polly Nayak and Michael Krepon, *US Crisis Management in South Asia's Twin Peaks Crisis* (Washington, DC: Stimson Center, 2006); Don Oberdorfer, *The Two Koreas: A Contemporary History* (Reading, MA: Addison-Wesley, 1997); Emery Brusset, "Evaluation of the Conflict Prevention Pools: Case Study: Sudan," Evaluation Report no. 647 (Department for International Development, London, March, 2004); and Bonnie Glaser, *Armed Clash in the South China Sea,* Contingency Planning Memorandum no. 14 (Council on Foreign Relations, Washington, DC, 2012).

22. Rubin and Jones, "Prevention of Violent Conflict," 395.

23. *Human Security Report 2009/2010,* 61–71.

24. For further discussion of various success stories, see Michael S. Lund, *Preventing Violent Conflicts: A Strategy for Preventive Diplomacy* (Washington, DC: United States Institute of Peace Press, 1996), 51–105; and Fen Osler Hampson and I. William Zartman, *The Global Power of Talk: Negotiating America's Interests* (Boulder, CO: Paradigm, 2012), 75–87.

25. See Reinhardt Rummel, "The EU's Involvement in Conflict Prevention Strategy and Practice," in *Conflict Prevention: Is the European Union Ready?* ed. Jan Wouters and Vincent Kronenberger (Brussels, 2004); and John Stremlau and Francisco Sagasti, *Preventing Deadly Conflict: Does The World Bank Have a Role?* (New York: Carnegie Corporation of New York, 1998).

26. See Paul B. Stares and Micah Zenko, *Partners in Preventive Action,* Council Special Report no. 62 (Council on Foreign Relations, Washington, DC, 2011), 13–21.

27. Rubin and Jones, "Prevention of Violent Conflict"; Report of the Secretary-General, *Preventive Diplomacy: Delivering Results* (New York: United Nations Department of Political Affairs, 2011); Richard Gowan, "Less Bound to the Desk: Ban Ki-moon, the UN, and Preventive Diplomacy," *Global Governance* 18 (2012): 387–404; and Chetan Kumar and Jos De la Haye, "Hybrid Peacemaking: Building National 'Infrastructures for Peace,'" *Global Governance* 18 (2001): 13–20.

28. See *Human Security Report 2009/2010,* 76–77.

29. For an excellent discussion of the early warning challenges, see Christoph Meyer, Chiara De Franco, John Brante, and Florian Otto, "Recasting the Warning-Response-Problem: Persuasion and Preventive Policy," *International Studies Review* 12, no. 4 (2010): 556–78.

30. See *Human Security Report 2009/2010,* 79.

31. See National Intelligence Council, *Global Trends 2030: Alternative Worlds* (National Intelligence Council, 2012), viii.

32. Ibid.

33. National Intelligence Council, *National Intelligence Assessment on the National Security Implications of Global Climate Change to 2030* (National Intelligence Council, 2008).

34. National Intelligence Council, *Global Trends 2030,* viii.

35. This section draws on Stares and Zenko, *Partners in Preventive Action*, 23.

36. Mark Mazower, *Governing the World: The History of an Idea* (New York: Penguin, 2012), 395.

37. See Lawrence Woocher, *Preventing Violent Conflict: Assessing Progress, Meeting Challenges*, Special Report no. 231 (United States Institute of Peace, Washington, DC, September 2009), 11.

28

REBUILDING WAR-TORN SOCIETIES
A CRITICAL REVIEW OF
INTERNATIONAL APPROACHES

Necla Tschirgi

Since the publication of UN Secretary-General Boutros Boutros-Ghali's much-cited report *An Agenda for Peace* in 1992, the knowledge base for postconflict peacebuilding has grown exponentially.[1] When Patricia Weiss Fagen put together a bibliography on rebuilding war-torn societies in 1995, she had a limited pool of resources to draw from.[2] Today, the academic as well as the practitioners' literature on postconflict peacebuilding is extensive and constantly growing—even if much of it remains inconclusive and highly contested.[3] Numerous academic programs, professional journals, research institutes, and policy and programming units are devoted to peacebuilding, including the United Nations' Peacebuilding Commission, Peacebuilding Fund, and Peacebuilding Support Office.[4] The World Bank, government agencies, nongovernmental organizations (NGOs), development donors, and international and regional organizations have produced extensive research, policy prescriptions, and practical guidelines on rebuilding war-torn societies. Peace-building has become a part of the international community's repertoire of conflict management tools, both to assist countries to overcome the legacies of violent conflict and to prevent their lapse or relapse into conflict. Although it is widely acknowledged that peacebuilding is an endogenous process, in the last two decades the international role in war-to-peace transitions has grown steadily.

Yet, the international record in assisting war-torn countries to get on the path to sustainable peace and development is meager and uneven. In addition to high levels of recidivism, countries emerging from conflict typically struggle with insecurity, instability, and poverty—problems that do not lend themselves to ready-made solutions or short-term fixes. The World Bank's *World Development Report 2011* notes that 90 percent of conflicts in the first decade of the twenty-first century occurred in countries that had previously experienced civil war.[5] Other research shows that since 2008, there has been a marked decline in the number of peace agreements, which suggests that the positive trend since the 1990s in favor of negotiated war termination might be coming to an end—with the increased likelihood of protracted transitions from war to peace.[6] Equally seriously, no low-income fragile or conflict-affected country has been able to achieve a single Millennium Development Goal.[7]

Paradoxically, as the knowledge base for rebuilding war-torn societies has expanded, the optimism and confidence that characterized the post–Cold War international commitment to peacebuilding have weakened. Instead, there are serious doubts, concerns, and questions about the viability and sustainability of the international peacebuilding project. Resting on this paradox, this chapter examines the evolution, achievements, limitations, and prospects of international efforts to assist countries emerging from war as part of the larger international conflict management strategy in the last twenty years. The chapter argues that international efforts to rebuild war-torn societies took shape incrementally and in response to concurrent changes in the international security context. The immediate post–Cold War phase, involving liberal peacebuilding approaches to the intrastate conflicts and humanitarian emergencies of the 1990s, was overtaken by larger security concerns after 9/11. With the global war on terror and the accompanying counterterrorism and counterinsurgency doctrines, peacebuilding was instrumentalized to serve multiple agendas. After the military interventions in Afghanistan and Iraq, peacebuilding efforts increasingly became conflated with stabilization, state building, and nation building in various countries that were seen to pose a threat to international peace and security. Since 2011, following popular uprisings and violent conflicts in the Arab region, some governments have advocated for regime change in Libya and Syria as an explicit goal of international assistance—further straining

the meaning of postconflict peacebuilding and its application in different contexts.

In light of the changing nature of international approaches to peacebuilding since 1992, this chapter is structured in four parts. The first part describes the evolution of the international peacebuilding enterprise in the immediate post–Cold War decade. The second part examines the transformation of the peacebuilding agenda in the aftermath of 9/11. The third part reviews key lessons that have been learned over the last twenty years and identifies some of the factors that contribute to effective peacebuilding. The final part explores where the international peacebuilding agenda might be headed as part of an evolving international peace and security agenda.

THE POST–COLD WAR INTERNATIONAL PEACEBUILDING PROJECT

The immediate post–Cold War peacebuilding agenda was shaped more by necessity than by deliberate design and reflected the multilateralist activism and optimism of the era. Throughout the 1990s, as protracted Cold War conflicts came to an end and intrastate conflicts and complex humanitarian emergencies were catapulted to center stage in international affairs, there was heightened demand for the United Nations and other international actors to assume a concerted role in assisting conflict-affected countries. Initially, it was not clear what form that assistance would take and how it would fit within existing policy and programming tools and frameworks. Nonetheless, the United Nations, other international and regional organizations, donor agencies, NGOs, and frontline development, human rights, and humanitarian practitioners became engaged in myriad activities, projects, and programs that went beyond the fragmented system of international assistance that had been in place since the end of World War II. International peacebuilding emerged in this highly fluid context and proved to be a particularly useful concept insofar as it pushed the boundaries of Cold War orthodoxies by emphasizing the interdependence between security and development in contemporary intrastate conflicts.[8]

Originally peacebuilding was presented in Boutros-Ghali's 1992 report *An Agenda for Peace* as part of a progression of discrete interventions from peacemaking and peacekeeping to post-conflict peacebuilding. Yet, in practice, international actors quickly realized that post–Cold War transitions from war to peace were not unilinear in nature; nor could they be addressed sequentially. Recognizing the limitations of fragmented mandates and institutional silos, early peacebuilders worked at the still-uncharted nexus between humanitarian assistance, peacemaking, peacekeeping, and development. Going beyond state-centric perspectives, a growing number of international actors began to address intrastate conflicts through novel approaches.

The new peacebuilding agenda offered an unusual opportunity for innovative multilateral action at a time when long-established Cold War policies and instruments were clearly inadequate to address intrastate conflicts and civil wars. Thus, in the first decade after the Cold War, peacebuilding heralded a new era in international cooperation and multilateral assistance with a distinctly humanitarian and developmental impulse. As diverse actors working on human rights, humanitarian affairs, conflict resolution, peacekeeping, and development became engaged in conflict-affected countries, there was a proliferation of activities, projects, programs, and policies that collectively came to be known as peacebuilding.

Initially defined as postconflict "action to identify and support structures which tend to strengthen and solidify peace to avoid a relapse into conflict," peacebuilding gradu-

ally acquired a broader definition as the link between peace, security, and development.[9] Throughout the 1990s, the main focus of international peacebuilding was on intrastate conflict or civil wars, with the international community providing a combination of humanitarian aid, political mediation, multidimensional peace operations, and development. Largely inspired by the liberal peace thesis and led by Western governments, the underlying model was to promote transition from conflict to peace through international support for political and economic liberalization. Although there were several successful interventions—especially ending proxy wars in countries such as Mozambique, Cambodia, and El Salvador—the decade also witnessed a series of new conflicts that erupted once the Cold War balance of power no longer held.

The United Nations played an important role in shaping the peacebuilding agenda. In the complex internal conflicts of the 1990s, where the boundaries between war and peace were often blurred, humanitarian relief, peacemaking, peacekeeping, and peacebuilding became interlinked. Building on *An Agenda for Peace*, a series of documents helped refine the United Nations' understanding of peacebuilding, while different parts of the UN system revised or expanded their work to respond to the changing nature of contemporary conflicts.[10] The tragic consequences of failed peace agreements in Angola, renewed conflicts in Haiti and Rwanda, and protracted wars in Afghanistan, Sudan, and the Democratic Republic of the Congo (DRC) highlighted the need for new instruments and approaches to support sustainable peace in complex emergencies and intrastate conflicts. The emergence of multidimensional peace operations, the creation of new conflict units such as the Bureau of Conflict Prevention and Reconstruction at the United Nations Development Programme, and the design of new service lines on security sector reform, disarmament, demobilization, and reintegration, and the rule of law heralded the growing convergence of mandates among humanitarian, development, political, security, and human rights actors in conflict contexts. Relapse into violence in Haiti and Timor-Leste following UN interventions in those countries reinforced the need for carefully planned exit strategies to prevent possible reversals and to lay the foundation for sustainable peace. Gradually, multidimensional peace operations with civilian and military components became the model for multilateral engagement in conflict contexts. UN peace operations were increasingly characterized by peacekeeping mandates based on internationally mediated peace agreements and included civilian components dealing with a wide range of issues, such as the reintegration of ex-combatants, the resettlement of refugees and internally displaced persons, demining, transitional justice mechanisms, election and human rights monitoring, and institutional reforms. Yet, from Somalia and Rwanda to the Balkans, multidimensional UN peace operations proved inadequate or ill prepared to deal with the resurgence of violence. In the Balkans, conventional military forces from the North Atlantic Treaty Organization (NATO) were brought in to support UN peace operations—becoming a precursor for post-9/11 peace operations in Afghanistan.

With some exceptions, such as in the Balkans, major countries did not consider the violent conflicts of the 1990s a direct threat to their vital security and national interests. Instead, violent conflicts were seen as products of local or national pathologies—largely exogenous to the international system despite their spillover effects. Largely motivated by humanitarian concerns and inspired by a liberal peace agenda, peacebuilding interventions of the 1990s were ad

hoc, piecemeal, and highly fragmented.[11] Despite the mantra of local ownership, they consisted of externally driven projects and programs that were often not well grounded in local realities. As documented in numerous evaluation studies, there was no coherent peacebuilding framework or strategy.[12] This strategy deficit was reflected in the disconnect between the various issue areas, such as public security, economic rehabilitation, social reconciliation, and justice, as well as in the diverse approaches pursued by different actors. Significantly, little attention was paid to the external dimensions of intrastate conflicts in an increasingly interdependent global world order. Donors designed innovative projects on transitional justice, social reconciliation, or gender equality, but did not deal with the external drivers of conflict—with some notable exceptions, such as illegal trade in natural resources.

Thus, despite policy statements on the indivisibility of peace in the post–Cold War era, peacebuilding was approached as a collective effort to address problems in zones of conflict at the periphery of the international system. It was after the terrorist attacks on the United States on September 11, 2001, that the direct links between peacebuilding in the periphery and international peace and security gained serious attention—albeit in ways that departed significantly from the Western-led multilateralist and humanitarian approaches of the 1990s.

DIVERGING APPROACHES TO WAR-TORN AND FRAGILE SOCIETIES AFTER 9/11

The events of September 11, 2001, radically changed the international security environment. The global war on terror and US-led wars in Afghanistan and Iraq represented dramatic departures from the multilateral approaches to peace and security that had been gaining ground since the end of the Cold War. The 1990s had witnessed concerted efforts to limit the use of force in international affairs with the decline of interstate wars and the growing focus on human security, conflict prevention, peacemaking, peacekeeping, and postconflict peacebuilding to address a range of intrastate wars and regional conflicts. After 9/11, state-centric national security doctrines reemerged alongside multilateral approaches that had increasingly focused on human security, conflict prevention, and peacebuilding. Insecurity in distant places was no longer seen as confined to zones of conflict. Instead, it became clear that conflict in the periphery could reach to the very core of the international system via non-state actors, terrorist and criminal networks, and failed and failing states. The US National Security Strategy of 2002 clearly stated that "America is now threatened less by conquering states than we are by failing ones."[13] Other governments adopted strategic doctrines to prevent or limit the impact of violent conflicts in distant countries on their own peace and security. State building, stabilization, postconflict recovery, and reconstruction became instruments of national security policies of major powers in responding to threats posed by civil wars, failed states, and unstable countries. In the process, post-9/11 approaches to peacebuilding also became securitized—especially in Afghanistan and Iraq.[14] The US-led wars in Afghanistan and Iraq were significantly different from the intrastate conflicts and complex political emergencies of the post–Cold War era. Nonetheless, these wars confronted the international community with the same challenge: how to assist these two countries in transitioning to self-sustaining peace.

The international experiences of the 1990s offered few lessons for building peace in the context of ongoing wars involving the vital interests of major powers. Thus, there was a new wave of interest in postconflict stabilization and reconstruction by major governments and policy planners as they prepared for the conclusion of military operations in Iraq and Afghanistan. Presciently, a 2004 publication by the Washington, D.C.–based Center for Strategic and International Studies distinguished among three generations of American approaches to postconflict reconstruction: post–World War II occupations; post–Cold War humanitarian interventions; and post-9/11 interventions in an era of global terrorism and weapons of mass destruction. This publication argued that "Iraq is the case that could define the newest generation of nation building. The situation on the ground and how the Bush administration responds to it will determine whether this effort becomes a real post-conflict reconstruction effort or else becomes a counter insurgency strategy that uses post-conflict reconstruction tools."[15] Indeed, the next decade witnessed the emergence of such a model.

The spirit of multilateral cooperation and collective action that had characterized the 1990s also changed dramatically after 9/11. The US-led war in Iraq without UN Security Council authorization led to sharp cleavages within the international community. Interest in conflict prevention and peacebuilding that had been gathering momentum throughout the 1990s was sidelined by the US-led global war on terror—deepening differences over the use of force as an instrument of national and international policy. The United Nations was unable to articulate a new agenda for collective security in the post-9/11 era. Secretary-General Kofi Annan warned that the United Nations could either rise to the challenge of meeting new threats to collective security or risk erosion in the face of growing discord among member states as well as unilateral action by them.[16]

He convened a high-level panel on Threats, Challenges, and Change to generate ideas about collective security and to propose policies and institutions for a more effective United Nations in the twenty-first century. The panel's report, *A More Secure World: Our Shared Responsibility*, drew attention to the "international obligation to assist States in developing their capacity to perform their sovereign functions effectively and responsibly." It also recommended the creation of a new intergovernmental peacebuilding commission:

> to identify countries which are under stress and risk sliding towards State collapse; to organize, in partnership with the national Government, proactive assistance in preventing that process from developing further; to assist in the planning for transitions between conflict and post-conflict peacebuilding; and in particular to marshal and sustain the efforts of the international community in post-conflict peacebuilding over whatever period may be necessary.[17]

State failure was, of course, not a new phenomenon—as reflected in the breakup of Yugoslavia, the collapse of Somalia, and protracted insurgencies in other African countries. However, as Cousens and Call note, "Historically, international peacebuilding efforts tended to neglect state building in favor of emphasis on social relations among conflicting groups or economic determinants of peace. . . . They tended to assume state capacity as a given and did not problematize contestation over state design, form, or function."[18] After 9/11, state building gained prominence as a peacebuilding as well as a security priority.

In his 2005 report, *In Larger Freedom*, Secretary-General Annan declared: "Sovereign States are the basic and indispensable building blocks of the international system. . . . If States are fragile, the peoples of

the world will not enjoy the security, development and justice that are their right. Therefore, one of the great challenges of the new millennium is to ensure that all States are strong enough to meet the many challenges they face."[19]

By the time leaders met at the World Summit in New York in 2005, assisting states to avoid state collapse and to transition from conflict had gained urgency as a challenge for the international community. However, there were different conceptions of the nature of the challenge and the appropriate responses. Major governments saw state failure as a vital threat to their security, as reflected in the 2008 UK National Security Strategy and the 2008 US National Defense Strategy.[20] Thus, one of the impacts of 9/11 on peacebuilding was the emergence of a security-oriented stabilization and state-building agenda in failed, fragile, or conflict-affected states alongside the development-oriented agenda that had prevailed in the 1990s.[21]

Yet, the policy and programming implications of linking state building and peacebuilding were far from clear because the two are not necessarily mutually reinforcing.[22] As demonstrated in the state-building efforts of the Cold War era, many new states that lacked local legitimacy were propped up by external powers for larger geo-strategic purposes and ruled without the support of their own populations. Not surprisingly, these were some of the same states that were now on the international agenda as weak, failing, or fragile states. Given its narrow security focus, the post-9/11 state-building agenda carried the similar risk of reinforcing the security capabilities of weak states at the expense of the imperative to strengthen their domestic legitimacy as the basis for sustainable peace and long-term development.

Inevitably, multiple approaches to state building emerged, and these have tended to pull in different directions in the design and implementation of key programs such as security sector reform, rule of law, and measures against organized crime. The tensions between developmentally oriented and security-driven strategies manifested themselves within key donor governments. Although some donor countries adopted whole-of-government strategies and the so-called 3D approach to ensure greater coherence among their diplomacy, defense, and development policies, the tensions between competing priorities have not been easy to resolve.[23] This was particularly true in the case of the United States, where the challenges of stabilizing Iraq and Afghanistan led to the development of a new counterinsurgency doctrine that incorporated "stability operations, also known as peace support operations, reconstruction and nation building." These had previously been "considered a separate category of military activity closely associated with multinationals or United Nations peacekeeping operations in which force is rarely used."[24]

The international peacebuilding agenda in the shadow of 9/11 and the wars in Afghanistan and Iraq was inevitably affected by the new security environment.[25] The rise of hard security concerns due to the transnational effects of state failure; the heightened military role in fighting terrorism, insurgency, and organized crime; and the vastly increased security budgets radically shifted international priorities. But the ramifications of the new security agenda were felt in other areas as well. One prominent example relates to the limitations placed on peacebuilding organizations in the United States. Following 9/11, the United States made it a crime to provide "material support" (including training, service, personnel, and expert advice, even about preparing for peace negotiations) to any foreign organization designated as terrorist by the US secretary of state. After the statute was challenged in

lower courts, the US Supreme Court's *Holder vs. Humanitarian Law Project* decision of June 21, 2010, upholding the statute, had a chilling effect on the US peacebuilding community.[26] The American example was not lost on other governments and international organizations as they reassessed their peacebuilding strategies in a highly securitized international context.

Reluctantly but inescapably, the United Nations became involved in both Iraq and Afghanistan, although these countries were hardly representative of the wide range of conflict-affected countries whose problems required international attention. Thus, beyond Iraq and Afghanistan, the United Nations pursued a distinctive and integrated approach to fragile and conflict-affected states in collaboration with key development actors including the World Bank, Organisation for Economic Cooperation and Development (OECD) Development Assistance Committee (DAC), and donor agencies. The newly established Peacebuilding Commission focused on countries such as Sierra Leone and Burundi, both of which were at a critical stage in their transitions and required concerted and integrated international support. A series of UN policy documents reiterated the linkages between development, democratization, and security in the context of supporting weak or fragile states, but the United Nations would not subscribe to a narrow security-driven stabilization or statebuilding agenda.[27] Instead, the UN system collectively expressed support for an expanded peacebuilding agenda based on state sovereignty that prioritized building national capacity for conflict management and development.

In May 2007, the secretary-general's Policy Committee restated the United Nations' understanding of peacebuilding as "a range of measures targeted to reduce the risk of lapsing or relapsing into conflict by strengthening national capacities at all levels for conflict management, and to lay the foundations for sustainable peace and development." The committee held that peacebuilding strategies must be "tailored to the specific needs of the country concerned, based on national ownership, and should comprise a carefully prioritized, sequenced, and therefore relatively narrow set of activities aimed at achieving the above objectives."[28]

The refocused spotlight on sovereignty and state capacity generated an extensive body of literature, policy, and programming exploring the linkages between peacebuilding and state building from a development perspective. In this context, several initiatives merit attention because they signaled the growing role of conflict-affected and fragile states in international policy discussions on sustainable peacebuilding that had hitherto been driven largely by donor countries and international organizations.

Launched in 2008, the International Dialogue on Statebuilding and Peacebuilding brought conflict-affected and fragile countries together with international partners and civil society to catalyze successful transitions from conflict and fragility by aligning these twin goals. Similarly, the International Network on Conflict and Fragility was established in 2009 to monitor international engagement with the world's forty-plus fragile and conflict-affected states and to help improve international engagement in these countries. Meanwhile, a group of fragile and conflict-affected countries came together to establish the g7+, with a secretariat based in Dili, Timor Leste, to formulate a common agenda for peacebuilding and state building. This led to a historic meeting between the g7+ and international donors in Busan, South Korea, in November 2011 to adopt the New Deal for Engagement in Fragile States. The New Deal has become an important platform to align international assistance behind local peacebuilding needs

and priorities. It also sets the terms of engagement to support country-owned and country-led transitions out of conflict and fragility and outlines a series of commitments to achieve better results. Efforts are underway to operationalize the goals embodied in the New Deal in several pilot countries and to develop new methodological and analytical tools to monitor progress in these countries.

Alongside these initiatives, research and publications reexamined the requirements for sustainable peace in conflict-affected and fragile states. Influential reports such as OECD DAC's *Supporting Statebuilding in Situations of Conflict and Fragility,* the World Bank's *World Development Report 2011: Conflict, Security, and Development,* and the UN Development Programme's *Governance for Peace: Securing the Social Contract* drew attention to the centrality of good governance, legitimate and responsive institutions, inclusive political processes, and resilient state-society relations for development as well as for peacebuilding. Similarly, in a speech on fragile states on January 8, 2009, World Bank President Robert B. Zoellick made a strong plea for the international community to focus on "bringing security and development together first to smooth the transition from conflict to peace and then to embed stability so that development can take hold over a decade and beyond." Zoellick argued that only "by securing development can we put down roots deep enough to *break* [his emphasis] the cycle of fragility and violence."[29] This approach was surprisingly similar to the early post–Cold War paradigm on peacebuilding as the link between security and development.

However, as already discussed, the security environment has changed dramatically in the last decade and this is reflected in the international community's approaches to peacebuilding in concrete contexts after

9/11. The critical question today is how to balance the long-term development needs of conflict-affected and fragile countries with the larger security interests of key international actors. From Afghanistan to Mali, there are many fragile countries where hard security concerns trump the requirements for sustainable peace and development. Moreover, following the Arab Spring and the violent conflicts in Libya and Syria, an emerging policy of regime change has further confounded the international community's role in conflict and postconflict contexts.

Thus, twenty years after its entry into the international conflict management tool kit, peacebuilding policies and programs reflect deep tensions and contradictions. On the one hand, there is a strong body of evidence that peacebuilding in conflict-affected countries rests on multifaceted, broad-based, and participatory processes of reconciliation and conflict transformation that depend on effective local agency and ownership. Yet, many conflicts today are no longer internal in nature but have significant regional and international dimensions with myriad stakeholders, interests, and agendas. Similarly, the centrality of security for peacebuilding is well recognized. But, top-down, state-centric strategies primarily designed to contain the transnational spillover of internal conflicts can seriously undermine long-term peace and security both domestically and internationally. The twin goals of security and development are clearly interdependent. Ultimately, however, they are influenced by the strategies that drive international interventions in fragile and conflict-affected countries. Although it is not realistic to ignore the larger security agendas that shape international approaches to war-torn societies, it is critical not to conflate the diverse agendas by generalizing about postconflict peacebuilding under very different circumstances. Accordingly, the next section fo-

cuses on lessons learned in contexts where international assistance was primarily and purposefully designed to support war-affected countries to make the transition from war to peace rather than contexts where peacebuilding was instrumentalized for other purposes.

A Sobering Assessment: What Have We Learned?

The international experience with peacebuilding in the last two decades has been far from uniform or consistent. It is difficult to speak of a coherent peacebuilding doctrine with clear goals, operational principles, and commonly accepted criteria for success in different contexts. Neither policymakers nor analysts have been able to agree whether postconflict peacebuilding should have minimalist goals to prevent renewed conflict (negative peace) or maximalist goals to address the root causes of conflict (positive peace). Although a middle ground has emerged to define success in terms of ending violence and instituting effective governance, what this would encompass in different contexts is hard to determine.[30] In the absence of a robust comparative methodology or framework, evaluating the effectiveness of peacebuilding interventions remains largely a subjective and highly contingent enterprise with widely differing interpretations of success.[31]

Nonetheless, twenty years of peacebuilding practice, experience, and knowledge in diverse contexts has generated a rich body of literature at the intersection of theory, policy, and practice. This literature has also demonstrated some of the difficult tensions, dilemmas, and contractions confronting peacebuilding. Before turning to an analysis of key lessons, it is important to note that the peacebuilding literature consists of two parallel streams that represent differing perspectives on the international peacebuilding enterprise: the mainstream problem-solving approach and the critical approach.[32] The mainstream approach basically accepts peacebuilding as an essential part of the liberal international agenda of the post–Cold War era, recognizes its mixed results, and focuses primarily on the deficiencies in its design and implementation. Although few systematic and cross-country evaluation studies offer comparative insights from different contexts, country or sector-based case studies have convincingly documented the many shortcomings of international peacebuilding.[33] These include the absence of a coherent strategy; the continuing disconnect in international support for peacemaking, peacekeeping, and peacebuilding; the lack of coordination among external actors; the short time frame of donor-supported development programs; and the dysfunctionalities of the international aid system, not least due to the lack of timely, adequate, and predictable financial resources.[34] This body of literature has come to be known as the problem-solving paradigm because it holds that the shortcomings of peacebuilding can be alleviated through more effective policies, practices, and institutions. The problem-solving literature has been highly influential as policymakers and practitioners have come to rely on its insights in designing and implementing peacebuilding interventions. As a result, there has been considerable cross-fertilization and mutual influence among policy, practice, and research, leading to a distinct epistemic community around mainstream peacebuilding.[35]

Meanwhile, a parallel body of literature has emerged that questions the main assumptions of international peacebuilding and its instrumentalization to serve larger agendas. Initially operating on the margins of mainstream discourse, the critical approach has steadily gained ground. The critical literature challenges the liberal peacebuilding agenda by raising questions about what type of peace is being built and whether the model promoted by the international community is sustainable. After 9/11, this debate was further affected by the conflation of peacebuilding with international security concerns. As peacebuilding became securitized, with increased reliance on the use of force, analysts began to question the motivations and objectives of the international peacebuilding agenda and interrogated the viability of the liberal peacebuilding model in conflict-affected non-Western societies.[36] They contend not only that mainstream peacebuilding strategies are inappropriate for addressing the multifaceted and structural problems facing countries emerging from conflict but also that they might in fact contribute to the perpetuation of those structural problems. Critical researchers turned their attention to the underlying normative and structural issues rather than the operational challenges that afflict international peacebuilding. Among other things, these issues include global as well as domestic power asymmetries, the economic drivers of conflict, and the impacts of the policies of key states and international organizations in fueling conflicts in peripheral regions. Unlike the mainstream approach that seeks practical solutions to improve peacebuilding's effectiveness, the critical approach argues that the strategies promoted by liberal peacebuilding are flawed because they are out of sync with local realities, needs, and aspirations and do not take into account the central issue of state formation and state legitimacy.[37]

Insights from both the mainstream and the critical approaches have inspired important debates and unresolved controversies on what constitutes sustainable peace and how it might be attained. In reality, both approaches are considerably more diverse and heterogeneous than is suggested in this quick review. Where they converge, however, is their shared understanding that although peacebuilding is a messy process with unpredictable outcomes, international approaches do make a difference. Thus, notwithstanding the divergent agendas and the heated debates that characterize current postconflict peacebuilding, several key lessons can be drawn about the international community's experiences with peacebuilding since the early 1990s.

Peacebuilding Is Political

Contemporary conflicts are predominantly intrastate in nature and therefore involve external intervention in what traditionally were considered a state's sovereign affairs. Accordingly, peacebuilding strategies need to be firmly grounded in an accurate understanding of the relations among multiple domestic and international actors with different motivations and agendas. How these relations are perceived, defined, and managed is an essential aspect of peacebuilding. Much of the mainstream literature defines engagement between locals and internationals in terms of promoting local ownership rather than the political role played by international actors in the difficult processes of contestation, negotiation, and political accommodation among diverse actors. The recent emphasis on inclusive and legitimate politics is a belated recognition of the importance of politics for peacebuilding.[38]

Peacebuilding Is a Context-Specific Enterprise Encompassing Interconnected Agendas for Security and Development

Although intrastate conflicts represent the breakdown of politics, they are often fueled by deep-rooted social, political, economic, and environmental problems, including horizontal inequalities, poverty, natural resource scarcities, and population pressures. These problems require multifaceted strategies. Although various institutions and analytical frameworks label them differently, rebuilding war-torn societies rests on several interrelated pillars, including security and public order; governance and political participation; justice, reconciliation, and rule of law; psycho-social recovery; economic reconstruction; and environmental rehabilitation.[39] The breadth of issues that require attention is vast. One of the main challenges is how to prioritize and sequence various peacebuilding initiatives for the most effective impact. For example, it is agreed that security is a prerequisite for sustainable peace, but which security measures require urgent attention depends on the context. Similarly, there is no single formula for reconciling the difficult trade-off between competing demands such as employment, poverty alleviation, and private-sector growth or stabilization and the promotion of democracy or justice and reconciliation.[40]

Peacebuilding Is an Endogenous Process that Requires a Long-Term National Strategy

Despite repeated lip service to local ownership, the international peacebuilding agenda remains largely an externally driven project that is dependent on strategies designed in donor capitals. Short-term, isolated, donor-driven projects do not add up to self-sustaining peace at the country level. Countries that are heavily dependent on external assistance over the long haul risk losing their legitimacy and ability to chart their own future. Thus, peacebuilding requires country-led and nationally owned strategies that reflect local needs and aspirations and provide a long-term vision for development.[41]

The Sustainability of Peacebuilding Depends on Its Institutionalization within Local Structures, Systems, and Processes

Because conflict results in the destruction or weakening of capacities at multiple levels, a central plank of peacebuilding is strengthening local capacities.[42] The limitations of international capacity development strategies, especially the misallocation of scarce resources, are well documented. One of the major criticisms of the state-building agenda is its focus on the formal institutions of the state at the expense of various local structures, informal mechanisms, and grassroots initiatives that can help anchor peacebuilding. Another shortcoming of international peacebuilding is its tendency to replace local capacities with external technical experts, consultants, and advisors.[43]

Strategies that Address Broader Regional and Transnational Factors Are Essential to Secure Peacebuilding at the Country Level

Although contemporary conflicts occur within states, they are not exclusively internal in nature. Factors such as cross-border flow of arms, refugees, and natural resources as well as transnational organized crime and terrorism fuel and exacerbate local-level conflicts. The international community needs more effective policies to deal with factors that are not country specific and that tend to mutate rapidly in a globalized world. In this context, the role of regional and subregional organizations in peacebuilding takes on added importance.[44]

Key Factors for Effective International Support for Peacebuilding

Peacebuilding research and evaluations have yet to generate robust findings that allow for cross-country comparisons. Moreover, there is little consensus about the definition or the end goals of peacebuilding, with the result that analysts differ in evaluating peacebuilding outcomes. Nonetheless, with various countries at different stages in their transition from war to peace, researchers have identified a range of factors that accompany successful peacebuilding interventions. Among these, concerted and timely action by international actors, integrated strategies aligned with national priorities, sustained political will, and the commitment of timely and adequate resources are particularly compelling. Although there are many context-specific factors for success, such as the nature of the war termination and the character of the ensuing political process, there is strong evidence that lack of adequate financial resources, wavering political will, and competing international agendas have contributed to the mixed record of international peacebuilding. Indeed, unlike the post–World War II era, which occasioned high levels of political commitment and financial resources for the reconstruction of Europe and Japan, international assistance for peacebuilding remains meager as reflected in the level of aid to fragile and conflict-affected countries.[45] With military and security budgets continuing to dwarf international peacebuilding assistance, donors' heightened focus on aid effectiveness has worked against conflict-affected countries—a fact that is increasingly recognized by the donor community.

From Afghanistan to the DRC and Guinea-Bissau, peacebuilding remains a fragile and reversible undertaking. As Roland Paris notes:

> The global experiment in post-conflict peacebuilding, underway since the end of the Cold War, has arrived at a crossroads and it is uncertain how it will proceed. While the United Nations (UN) and its member states continue to reaffirm their support for peacebuilding

and to mount new missions aimed at helping countries emerging from civil wars, observers have questioned the effectiveness and legitimacy of these missions. Many of these criticisms are warranted: the record of peacebuilding has indeed been disappointing. Efforts to promote liberal democratic governing systems and market-oriented economic growth—both core elements of the prevailing liberal peacebuilding model—have been more difficult and unpredictable than initially expected, in some cases producing destabilizing side effects.[46]

The Future of Peacebuilding in a Turbulent International Environment

This chapter argued that in the last twenty years, the international peacebuilding project has been transformed in response to complex challenges facing countries emerging from conflict as well as far-reaching changes in the international security environment. Initially, peacebuilding focused primarily on the multifaceted needs of conflict-affected countries. It was human centered and developmentally oriented and had a distinctly liberal agenda. After 9/11, rebuilding war-torn societies became part of a larger security agenda and was appropriated by military and security institutions. Currently, actors and institutions continue to use the terms "peacebuilding," "nation building," "stabilization," and "reconstruction" interchangeably, although there are significant differences of emphasis in terms of the basic principles, short-term and long-term strategies, and ultimate goals.

In many countries (including those on the agenda of the Peacebuilding Commission) that are of relatively minor geostrategic, political, or economic interest for powerful international actors, the United Nations, regional organizations, and various

humanitarian and development actors are engaged in multidimensional peacebuilding that encompasses peacemaking, peacekeeping, public order and citizen security, good governance, human rights, and socioeconomic development. In other countries—most prominently Afghanistan but also Somalia and Mali—peacebuilding has been securitized and conflated with other agendas, including counterterrorism and counterinsurgency. It is not clear which model will inform the next generation of peacebuilding interventions in countries such as Syria and Yemen that are caught in the throes of violent conflict or Libya, which has experienced forceful regime change. However, it is clear that the demand for international support for rebuilding war-torn countries is unlikely to diminish. One particularly disturbing trend is the marked decrease in peace agreements since 2008, which suggests that the international community will likely find itself engaged in situations where there is no clear transition from war to peace but a prolonged uneasy state of no-war and no-peace.

Based on the experiences of the last two decades, two seemingly contradictory conclusions coexist: peacebuilding is always a context-specific undertaking and dominant international approaches to rebuilding war-torn societies have long-lasting repercussions on local conflict dynamics and peacebuilding outcomes. The specificity of each conflict militates against a ready-made peacebuilding model, however well-conceived it might be. Thus, it would be folly to assume that what worked in Liberia and Guinea-Bissau would be suitable for Mali or Yemen. Given the heightened role of international actors in these countries, systematic and comparative evaluation studies to consolidate and deepen cross-country learning are essential if international assistance for peacebuilding is to yield more sustained and effective outcomes than has been the case so far. Luckily, it seems assured that peacebuilding will continue to be an area of growing interest for academics, policymakers, and practitioners alike.

NOTES

1. *An Agenda for Peace: Preventive Diplomacy, Peacemaking, and Peace-Keeping*, Report of the Secretary-General (New York: United Nations, 2002).

2. Patricia Weiss Fagen, *After the Conflict: A Review of Selected Sources on Rebuilding War-Torn Societies* (Geneva: UNRISD, 1995).

3. In this chapter, the terms "rebuilding war-torn societies" and "postconflict peacebuilding" are used interchangeably to refer primarily to international efforts to assist countries emerging from war. Peacebuilding is a fluid and elusive term that is used to encompass a range of preconflict, in-conflict, and postconflict interventions. For a review of the different uses of the term, see Michael Barnett et al., "Peacebuilding: What Is in a Name?" *Global Governance: A Review of Multilateralism and International Organizations* 13, no. 1 (2007): 35–58.

4. A quick search of the word "peacebuilding" under books on Amazon.com in January 2014 yielded 1,584 entries. There are now several academic journals with "peacebuilding" in their titles; in addition, there are a growing number of specialized journals on related fields such as state building, stabilization, transitional justice, and the rule of law.

5. World Bank, *World Development Report 2011: Conflict, Peace, and Security* (Washington, DC: World Bank, 2011), 2.

6. Stina Högbladh, "Peace Agreements, 1975–2011: Updating the UCDP Peace Agreement Dataset," Uppsala University: Department of Peace and Conflict Research Report 99 (2011), http://www.pcr.uu.se/digitalAssets/142/142371 _peace-agreements-1975-2011final.pdf.

7. World Bank, *World Development Report 2011*, 5

8. Necla Tschirgi, "Post-Conflict Peacebuilding Revisited: Achievements, Limitations, Challenges," IPA Policy Paper (International Peace

Academy, New York, 2004); Albert Cutillo, "International Assistance to Countries Emerging from Conflict: A Review of Fifteen Years of Interventions and the Future of Peacebuilding," IPA Policy Paper (International Peace Academy, New York, 2006); and Victor Chetail, "Post-Conflict Peacebuilding: Ambiguity and Identity," in *Post-Conflict Peacebuilding: A Lexicon*, ed. Vincent Chetail (London: Oxford University Press, 2009).

9. *Agenda for Peace*, 2002.

10. For a list of relevant UN documents of the era, see United Nations, *Peacebuilding: An Orientation* (New York: United Nations, 2010).

11. Tschirgi, "Post-Conflict Peacebuilding Revisited"; Cutillo, "International Assistance"; and Stephen Ryan, "The Evolution of Peacebuilding" in *Routledge Handbook of Peacebuilding*, ed. Roger Mac Ginty (London: Routledge, 2013).

12. See, for example, Dan Smith, "Getting Their Act Together: Toward a Strategic Framework for Peacebuilding," Report of the Joint Utstein Study of Peacebuilding (Oslo: The Royal Norwegian Ministry of Foreign Affairs, 1998).

13. United States, *The National Security Strategy of the United States of America* (Washington, DC: US Department of Defense, 2002), 1.

14. Edward E. Newman, "Peacebuilding as Security in 'Failing' and Conflict-Prone States," *Journal of Intervention and Statebuilding* 4 (2010): 305–22; and Necla Tschirgi, "Peacebuilding and Securitization" in *Handbook of Peacebuilding*, ed. Roger Mac Ginty (London: Routledge, 2013).

15. Robert C. Orr, ed., *Winning the Peace: An American Strategy for Post-Conflict Reconstruction* (Washington, DC: Center for Strategic and International Affairs, 2002), 7.

16. United Nations, "Address of the Secretary-General to the General Assembly" (September 23, 2003).

17. United Nations, *A More Secure World: Our Shared Responsibility*, Report of the High-Level Panel on Threats, Challenges and Change (New York: United Nations, 2004), 84.

18. Charles T. Call and Elizabeth Cousens, "Ending Wars and Building Peace in War-Torn Societies," *International Studies* 9, no. 1 (2008): 9.

19. *In Larger Freedom: Towards Security, Development, and Human Rights for All*, Report of the

Secretary-General (New York: United Nations, 2005), 6, para. 19.

20. United Kingdom, *National Security Strategy* (Norwich: Her Majesty's Stationary Office, 2008); United States, *National Defense Strategy* (Washington, DC: US Department of Defense, 2008).

21. The definition of failed, weak, and fragile states remains highly controversial, which is reflected in approaches to state building.

22. Call and Cousens, "Ending Wars and Building Peace"; Newman, "Peacebuilding as Security."

23. Stewart Patrick and Kaysie Brown, *Greater Than the Sum of Its Parts? Assessing "Whole of Government" Approaches to Fragile States* (New York: International Peace Academy, 2007); OECD DAC, *Whole of Government Approaches in Fragile States* (Paris: OECD, 2006).

24. United States Army-Marine Corps, *US Army-Marine Corps Counterinsurgency Field Manual* (Chicago: University of Chicago Press, 2007), xxiii.

25. Newman, "Peacebuilding as Security"; Tschirgi, "Peacebuilding and Securitization."

26. For more on the impact of this decision on the NGO community, see http://ccrjustice.org /holder-v-humanitarian-law-project.

27. For a list of relevant UN documents, see UN Peacebuilding Support Office, *Peacebuilding: An Orientation* (New York: United Nations, 2010).

28. Ibid., 5.

29. World Bank, "Securing Development" by President Robert B. Zoellick at http://siteresources .worldbank.org/NEWS/Resources/RBZUSIP Speech010809.pdf, 2.

30. For a useful discussion of this, see Call and Cousens.

31. There is a growing body of literature on peacebuilding evaluations. Nonetheless, the field is fraught with difficulties, not least because of the fluidity of the phenomenon to be evaluated. See, for example, Paul F. Diehl and Daniel Druckman, *Evaluating Peace Operations* (Boulder, CO: Lynne Rienner, 2010).

32. For a discussion of the two streams, see Michael Pugh, "The Problem-Solving and Critical Paradigm," in *Routledge Handbook of Peacebuilding*, ed. Roger Mac Ginty (London: Routledge, 2013).

33. One of the most systematic efforts to examine the record of international peacebuilding is by Michael W. Doyle and Nicholas Sambanis, *Making Wars and Building Peace: United Nations Peace Operations* (Princeton, NJ: Princeton University Press, 2006).

34. See, for example, Jock Covey, Michael J. Dziedzic, and Leonard R. Hawley, eds., *The Quest for Viable Peace: International Intervention and Strategies for Conflict Transformation* (Washington, DC: United States Institute of Peace Press, 2005); William J. Durch, *Twenty-First-Century Peace Operations* (Washington, DC: Stimson Center and United States Institute of Peace Press, 2006); James Dobbins et al., *The UN's Role in Nation-Building: From the Congo to Iraq* (Santa Monica, CA: Rand, 2005); and Roland Paris, *At War's End: Building Peace after Civil Conflict* (Cambridge: Cambridge University Press, 2004).

35. The *2011 World Development Report* is a good example of the cross-fertilization between the academic and policy communities.

36. See, for example, Stephen Baranyi, ed., *The Paradoxes of Peacebuilding Post–9/11* (Vancouver: UBC Press, 2008); Alejandro Bendaña, "Critical Assessments from the South," in *What Kind of Peace Is Being Built? Reflections on the State of Building Ten Years after the Agenda for Peace* (Ottawa: International Development Research Centre, 2003); Mark M. Duffield, *Global Governance and the New Wars: The Merging of Development and Security* (New York: Zed, 2001); Edward Newman, Roland Paris, and Oliver P. Richmond, eds., *New Perspectives on Liberal Peacebuilding* (Tokyo: UN University Press, 2009); and Shahrbanou Tadjbashsh, ed., *Rethinking the Liberal Peace: External Models and Local Alternatives* (London: Routledge, 2011).

37. Interestingly, the emergence of the state-building agenda has helped to stimulate some cross-fertilization between the mainstream and critical approaches and generated a new wave of literature at the intersection of peacebuilding and state building. See, for example, Charles T. Call, with Vanessa Wyeth, eds., *Building States to Build Peace* (Boulder, CO: Lynne Rienner, 2008); Simon Chesterman, Michael Ignatieff, and Ramesh Thakur, eds., *Making States Work: State Failure and the Crisis of Governance* (Tokyo: United Nations

University, 2005); and Roland Paris and Timothy D. Sisk, *The Dilemmas of Statebuilding: Confronting the Contradictions of Postwar Peace Operations* (London: Routledge, 2009).

38. For an early formulation of this point, see Elizabeth Cousens and Chetan Kumar, with Karin Wermester, eds., *Peacebuilding as Politics: Cultivating Peace in Fragile Societies* (Boulder, CO: Lynne Rienner, 2001). For further exploration of the relations between domestic and external actors, see Michael Barnett and Christoph Zürcher, "The Peace-builder's Contract: How External Statebuilding Reinforces Weak Statehood," in *The Dilemmas of Statebuilding,* ed. Paris and Sisk; and Christoph Zürcher et al., *Costly Democracy: Peacebuilding and Democratization after War* (Stanford, CA: Stanford University Press, 2013).

39. One of the earliest and most comprehensive frameworks is the Post-Conflict Reconstruction Task Force Framework, which was jointly produced by the Center for Strategic and International Studies (CSIS) and the Association of the United States Army (AUSA) in May 2002, available as appendix 1 in Orr, *Winning the Peace.* That framework has since been adapted by other international actors, including the United Nations and the African Union. For a useful discussion of the different pillars of peacebuilding, see the website Peacebuildinginitiative.org.

40. The literature on competing priorities in peacebuilding is rapidly growing. See, for example,

Chandra Lekha Sriram and Suren Pillay, eds., *Peace versus Justice? The Dilemma of Transitional Justice in Africa* (South Africa: University of Kwa-Zulu-Natal Press, 2009).

41. Local ownership has become a popular research topic. See, for example, Béatrice Pouligny, *Peace Operations from Below: UN Missions and Local People* (Bloomfield, CT: Kumarian Press, 2006). See also Tadjbashsh, *Rethinking the Liberal Peace.*

42. Volker Turk, "Capacity-Building" in Chetail, *Post-Conflict Peacebuilding.*

43. The United Nations continues to grapple with this problem despite many decades of capacity building on the ground. See, for example, the report of the secretary-general's Senior Advisory Group for the Review of International Civilian Capacities, submitted in January 2011, http://www.un.org/en/ga/search/view_doc.asp?symbol=A/65/747.

44. Necla Tschirgi, "Regional Approaches to Peacebuilding," *Journal of Peacebuilding and Development* 1, no. 1, (2002): 25–38.

45. For an interesting comparison of the experiences of the United States and the United Nations in rebuilding war-torn societies, see James Dobbins et al., *America's Role in Nation-Building: From Germany to Iraq* (Santa Monica, CA: Rand, 2008); and Dobbins et al., *The UN's Role in Nation-Building.*

46. Roland Paris, "Saving Liberal Peacebuilding," *Review of International Studies* 36 (2010): 337.

29

DEALING WITH TERRORISM

Martha Crenshaw

The problems of terrorism and counterterrorism are closely related to
other themes stressed in this volume:
sovereignty; state building, nation building,
and peacebuilding; norms; responsibility to
prevent and protect; legitimacy of the use of
force; failed, failing, and fragile states; and
democratic transitions. In the second decade
of the twenty-first century, the threat of terrorism emanated principally from proponents of radical Islamism, as it did during
the first decade. Finding an effective response
remained a challenge. Although terrorism
receded as a global threat, it contributed to
state failure and civil war and continued to
provoke military intervention from targeted
states.

This chapter proceeds as follows: The first
section begins with an overview of changing
patterns in the incidence and location of terrorism since the end of the Cold War. It then
analyzes what the future is likely to produce
in terms of specific dimensions of terrorism:
causes, actors, and methods. The second
section assesses the threat of terrorism to
global security. Terrorism threatens international stability in two major ways: first, in
creating disorder within states, particularly
those that are already weak, fragile, or un-

dergoing rapid social, economic, and political dislocations; and second, in increasing
the likelihood of violent interstate conflict.
The third section focuses on the complex
challenges of managing terrorism in an uncertain world.

A definition of terrorism is a necessary
preface to analysis, because the term is contentious and sometimes used to mean quite
different things. Terrorism is one form of
clandestine political violence, distinguished
by the fact that it is aimed at impressing a
watching audience and often involves indiscriminate attacks on civilians, including ordinary people in public places as well as
government officials.[1] Terrorism can be regarded as a form of violent communication
of a political message. Much discussion of
terrorism assumes that it is the practice of
nonstate actors, but any entity can be responsible because terrorism is a type of practice.
In the twenty-first century it is associated
principally with radical Islamism, but it is
not the province of one particular ideology
or religion.

The overlap between civil conflict and
terrorism that is evident in the cases cited in
this chapter can blur the distinction between
insurgency and terrorism. Insurgency is a

491

form of revolutionary warfare in which armed rebels attempt to overthrow a government by mobilizing the population in opposition. Terrorism is one of the tactics armed groups may choose to employ, whether or not they can mobilize large numbers. It may seem reasonable to refer to "insurgents" as distinct from "terrorists," but the activities are often performed by the same groups engaged in asymmetrical conflict with the state. Terrorism in this context is a form of coercion. US strategy in Afghanistan and Pakistan accepted the distinction between "counterinsurgency" and "counterterrorism" under the assumption that the former involved a struggle for the hearts and minds of the population, whereas the latter did not. In practice, it is difficult to separate the two policies because harsh counterterrorism measures can easily alienate the people whose hearts and minds the government aims to win over. Terrorism also plays a part in the sectarian violence that often accompanies civil war.

THE THREAT OF TERRORISM

John McLaughlin, former deputy director of Central Intelligence, warned about the perils of prediction in an uncertain time:

> First, a large dose of humility is called for in estimating the threat; it will simply be harder to have a confident understanding of the scope and nature of extremism in areas of high concern—or to confidently predict what might happen there. This is already true in the areas undergoing political revolutions, but it will soon be true also in Afghanistan and Iraq as our drawdowns inevitably reduce our visibility.
>
> A second related implication is that the potential for surprise is going up. For some years, terrorists have been showing a capacity to adapt in the face of our successes. When we made it harder to get weapons on air-

planes, they tried liquids in the 2006 airline plot detected in London. When we banned liquids, they devised weapons that were neither metal nor liquid—the failed 2009 underwear bomber in a plane over Detroit. When we tightened access to the passenger cabin, they tried (and failed) in 2010 to plant a package bomb in cargo originating in Yemen. And there are reports that in 2011, Al Qaeda's Yemen affiliate was toying with the idea of surgically implanting an explosive device in a suicide bomber.

It seems only reasonable to assume that the more fluid environment to which terrorists now have access will allow them to continue this kind of experimentation, with perhaps a greater chance that they will surprise us with something more effective—or simply get lucky.[2]

Trends in Terrorism

This analysis begins with a brief survey of trends in terrorism from 1991 to 2011, essentially the twenty years from the end of the Cold War to the conclusion of the bin Laden era, with his death in May of 2011.[3] The pivotal point of these two decades is September 11, 2001, marking the most destructive terrorist attack by a nonstate actor in history and the launching by the United States of the "Global War on Terror" that profoundly altered the international landscape. The struggle has not ended, but the international response has decisively weakened the central organizational core of Al Qaeda (AQ). On its own, AQ has not committed a fatal terrorist attack against civilians outside Afghanistan and Pakistan since 2008. The mantle of radical Islamism and jihadism has passed to its local and regional affiliates.

Two changes stand out in a general comparison of the pre- and post-9/11 decades. One is that the geography of terrorism overall has shifted. Iraq followed by Afghanistan and Pakistan became the principal locations for terrorism, which in the aggregate more than doubled in the regions of South Asia and the Middle East and North Africa. After 2007, terrorism in Afghanistan and Pakistan pulled ahead of Middle Eastern and North African terrorism. Terrorism in Southeast Asia also increased significantly in the post-9/11 decade, with significant attacks in Indonesia and the Philippines. To a lesser extent, terrorism also expanded in Russia and the newly independent states, due to the Chechen nationalist movement and its deepening links to Al Qaeda. Before 9/11, the regions of Central and South America and Europe and North America experienced the most terrorist activity. The conflict between Israel and militant Palestinian groups also figured prominently as a source of terrorism.

The second notable trend is in the method of terrorism: suicide attacks increased dramatically in the post-9/11 decade, and the locus of this activity also shifted.[4] In the 1991–2001 decade, there were 170 suicide attacks, which caused 2,077 deaths. In the post-9/11 decade, including the 9/11 attacks, there were 2,130 total attacks causing 26,866 deaths. In the early period, the most avid practitioners of suicide missions were, in order of prominence, the Liberation Tigers of Tamil Eelam (LTTE), largely in Sri Lanka; Palestinian groups in Israel and the occupied territories; the Kurdish PKK (the abbreviation is commonly used for the Kurdistan Workers' Party) in Turkey; and Chechen groups against Russia. Al Qaeda was last. In the post-9/11 decade, leadership in this tactic passed to the Taliban; although a recent adopter of the method, the Taliban was responsible for double the number of suicide attacks of Al Qaeda. Following the Taliban were Hamas, the Pakistani Taliban (TTP), and Al Qaeda in Iraq (AQI).[5] In terms of location of suicide attacks, Iraq, Afghanistan, and Pakistan dominated the field after

9/11, just as they did in overall terrorist incidents.

Some characteristics of terrorism remained relatively constant over the twenty-year period. Around half of all terrorist attacks caused no fatalities, and the aggregate number of incidents was not remarkably greater after 9/11 than before, according to the Global Terrorism Database. Thus from September 12, 2001, through December 31, 2011, 31,395 incidents were recorded, 47 percent of which caused no fatalities. From January 1, 1991, through September 10, 2001, 28,033 incidents were recorded, 55 percent with no fatalities.[6] Although attacks causing more than ten fatalities are a minority of all terrorist incidents, they became more common in the post-9/11 period.

The global trend toward reliance on suicide missions, which are typically more lethal than other forms of terrorism, may explain this shift toward larger numbers of victims killed.

The US National Counterterrorism Center (NCTC), established in 2004, collected statistical data on terrorist attacks against noncombatant targets through 2011 but discontinued the database in April 2012.[7] Reviewing the period 2007–11, NCTC calculated that incidents of terrorism worldwide dropped by nearly 29 percent. Attacks in Iraq decreased as military occupation

Table 1. Trends in terrorism, 1991–2011

Fatalities	Pre-9/11	Post-9/11
0	15,548	14,645
1–10	10,652	14,580
11–50	1,157	1,364
51–100	87	122
101+	41	34

Source: Global Terrorism Database (GTD), maintained by the National Consortium for the Study of Terrorism and Responses to Terrorism (START), located at the University of Maryland.

forces withdrew, while those in Afghanistan increased. NCTC also noted that the peak for suicide attacks during this period was 2007. NCTC estimated that during the five-year period, Muslims bore the brunt of terrorism, suffering between 82 and 97 percent of all fatalities. Sunni extremists, principally Al Qaeda affiliates and the Taliban in both Afghanistan and Pakistan, accounted for most terrorist attacks in 2009, 2010, and 2011. There was variation among Al Qaeda affiliates: from 2010 to 2011 Al Shabab, in Somalia, increased its attacks while AQI decreased sharply. Al Qaeda in the Arabian Peninsula (AQAP), in Yemen, and Al Qaeda in the Islamic Maghreb (AQIM), in Algeria and the surrounding region, declined less abruptly. Boko Haram, in Nigeria, also expanded its terrorist activities and in 2011 attacked a foreign target for the first time (a UN compound).

Causes

It is not easy to identify the causes of terrorism in general or the causes of suicide terrorism in particular.[8] Possible explanations include (1) underlying conditions, or "root causes"; (2) specific but unpredictable tipping events that serve as catalysts; (3) the strategies of actors who prefer terrorism to other means; and (4) psychological predispositions and beliefs of individuals and their process of radicalization into extreme ideologies that not only justify but also require violence. The problem with explanations in categories (1) and (2) is that many people experience adverse conditions that might lead them to feel aggrieved (e.g., government repression, poverty, social and economic discrimination, the pressures of globalization, foreign occupation), yet few of them resort to terrorism. The same qualifier applies to reactions to specific instigating events. Notwithstanding, a problem with individual-level analysis is that uncovering

deep psychological motivations is probably impossible, although tracing life histories can be informative in retrospect. Focusing on individuals can also lead to the neglect of the political and social dimensions of terrorism, which is a group activity highly dependent on context.

The approach taken here is that terrorism is a deliberate strategy of clandestine political violence chosen by organized nonstate groups sometimes facilitated by supportive states. Its advantages are regarded as superior to its disadvantages in particular historical settings. It is a means to an end. Extremist organizations often seize the opportunities afforded by the activation of popular grievances to pursue a political agenda. They use ideological and religious belief systems to legitimize and justify violence, including terrorism.

The aggregate-trend overview shows that terrorism frequently occurs in the context of violent and extensive civil conflict: examples include Iraq, Yemen, Afghanistan, Pakistan, Somalia, and, more recently, Syria and North and Northwest Africa, including Mali and Nigeria. Instability and violent and chaotic transitions create opportunities for extremist factions to pursue their agendas. For example, the Al Nusra Front, a jihadist group affiliated with Al Qaeda, assumed a dominant role in the opposition and introduced suicide bombings to the conflict in Syria. Subsequently its rival, the Islamic State of Iraq and Syria (ISIS), was denounced for its extremism by Al Qaeda itself. The killing of the US ambassador to Libya in 2012 was also at the hands of a jihadist faction taking advantage of widespread insecurity during the transition from the Gaddafi regime to the new government. Its ties to Al Qaeda are a matter of dispute.

Terrorism against targets outside of hot-conflict zones is typically explained by the perpetrators as punishment for intervention in external conflicts, not by internal conditions in the targeted country. In 2010, for example, Al Shabab bombed crowds in Kampala, Uganda, as revenge for Uganda's leadership of the African Union peacekeeping force in Somalia. Also in 2010, Faisal Shahzad claimed that he left a car filled with explosives in New York's Times Square to avenge American drone strikes against leaders of the Pakistani Taliban (TTP) and AQAP.

Actors

Looking to the future, what sorts of actors are likely to regard terrorism as a useful strategy, and under what circumstances? Will the world of terrorism shift to a post–Al Qaeda or post-jihadist era? Al Qaeda and its predecessors and successors in the jihadist universe have been threats for some twenty years, since at least 1993 and the first bombing of the World Trade Center in New York. This danger has shifted in form, declining as a threat to the West, but it has not disappeared.

It is unlikely that a strong core Al Qaeda organization will be resurrected, so in a strict sense a post–Al Qaeda era has already begun. The center was in decline well before Osama bin Laden was killed in Abbottabad in 2011, although his death at the hands of US special operations forces was clearly a blow to his followers. Headed by his much less charismatic successor Ayman al Zawahiri, Al Qaeda Central most likely remains headquartered in Pakistan, where it is under heavy pressure from US military and intelligence services, largely through drone strikes. Al Qaeda Central still maintains its communications capabilities, but terrorist attacks directed from the center have become infrequent. It is, however, operationally linked to other active groups in Afghanistan and Pakistan. In addition, the Al Qaeda advertising brand has retained its value.

Generally the Al Qaeda label is represented by affiliates, associates, and imitators in the jihadist universe, displaying varied degrees of linkage to the center. No single unified and monolithic transnational organization controls terrorism. There are or have been over thirty such allied but differentiated groups around the world.[9] They share Al Qaeda's general ideology and aim of replacing secular governments with religious regimes ruled by strict forms of sharia law. However, they are more likely to focus on defeating a local government than following the traditional Al Qaeda emphasis on the "far enemy." Leaders among them are AQI (transformed into the Islamic State of Iraq), AQAP) in Yemen, and AQIM. AQAP has been the most likely affiliate to act outside the local conflict arena, possibly because of the influence of the late Anwar al-Awlaki as much as US military assistance for the Yemeni government. Consequently, the United States has regarded AQAP as the most dangerous of the Al Qaeda–affiliated organizations.

Terrorism is typically thought of as the weapon of choice for weak nonstate actors, but state sponsors with other means at their disposal can also be powerful players. Iran's behavior has been troubling for over thirty years, since the regime helped establish Hezbollah in Lebanon in the early 1980s (taking advantage of the civil war to assert its regional influence). Hezbollah is a unique organization, representing much more than a client of Iran. It challenges Israel directly and militarily (e.g., in the 2006 war), and at the same time plays a major role in Lebanese politics. Hezbollah has attacked Israeli civilians traveling outside Israel (e.g., tourists in Bulgaria in the summer of 2012) and is designated as a terrorist organization by the US State Department. In the summer of 2013, the European Union also designated Hezbollah's military wing as a terrorist organization. In addition, Iran has threatened

Israel further by helping fund and arm Hamas and other Palestinian groups, even though they are Sunni. After the 2003 American invasion of Iraq, Iran supported Shia militias combatting coalition forces.

Concern about Hezbollah's intentions and capabilities as well as state sponsorship of terrorism increased with the descent of Syria into civil war in 2011. Iran became a committed supporter of the Assad regime, and Hezbollah's military power and geographical proximity enabled its forces to intervene directly in the fighting on behalf of the Syrian government. Adding to the risk that the Syrian civil war could metastasize into a regional conflict was the Assad regime's attempt to transfer advanced missiles to Hezbollah, leading Israel to launch preventive air strikes, and the possibility that Syria's chemical weapons could follow the same path until agreement was reached to destroy these weapons. The regime had already defied international norms about the treatment of civilians, so it was reasonable to fear that imminent collapse might lead a reckless Assad regime to ignore warnings about the use or transfer of weapons of mass destruction (WMD).

Another question relevant to the agency side of terrorism is the relationship between politically motivated violent organizations and transnational organized crime. Terrorist financing is of particular concern to the international community, resulting in a substantial degree of US-led cooperation in cutting off funding for terrorism. Hezbollah, for example, has mutually remunerative relationships with Lebanese diasporas in Latin America and West Africa. Jihadist groups in West Africa engage in kidnappings for ransom, especially since counterterrorism measures against terrorist financing and money laundering were strengthened. The Taliban in Afghanistan is reputed to profit from the opium trade. The line be-

tween criminal and political motivations is often blurred, and it is possible that more hybrid organizations will appear in the future.

As noted above, terrorism spills over well outside of active conflict zones as in the eyes of perpetrators the war is taken to the homelands of their enemies. These attacks and plots are relatively sporadic, as compared to the sustained campaigns of terrorism in prolonged civil conflicts such as Iraq, Afghanistan, Syria, Pakistan, Somalia, or Yemen. They are, however, of immense concern to Western states sensitive to homeland security and to the precedents of 9/11 and the London and Madrid bombings in 2005 and 2004, respectively. The diffusion of jihadist terrorism raises a number of questions about the future organization of violence. Contagion or diffusion effects in the jihadist universe range from strong (conspiracies with operational Al Qaeda or affiliate direction) to weak (no outside organizational connection, and ideological inspiration drawn largely from online sources). In the latter case, references are frequently made to "self-radicalization" and "homegrown terrorism." In a transnational structure characterized by weak diffusion processes, individual "lone wolves" may be more prevalent than tightly organized conspiracies engaging the services of multiple participants. However, such plots and attacks are not strictly domestic, and the perpetrators' extremist tendencies are not entirely self-generated. The links between operational jihadist organizations and their imitators abroad may be weak, but the inspiration for terrorism is distinctly transnational rather than local. The purpose of most terrorism in Western democracies post–9/11, for example, is not to overthrow the government but to avenge what is regarded by jihadist sympathizers as a Western assault on the Muslim world.

Methods

How can such relatively powerless actors threaten international order and security? What are the future forms and methods of terrorist activity?

Predicting innovation in terrorist strategy and tactics is difficult.[10] For example, just when hijackings were thought to be a relic of the past, Al Qaeda combined them with suicide missions to achieve the devastating 9/11 surprise. It is equally difficult to predict when an innovation will be widely imitated. The 9/11 method was not copied, possibly because of enhanced security measures and public awareness of the danger, but also because it was an extraordinarily complex plot requiring specialized resources (trained commercial pilots in particular) and thus difficult to imitate. Nor have the surprisingly successful (from the terrorists' point of view) 2008 Mumbai attacks led to imitation elsewhere. In the fall of 2010, Al Qaeda operatives in Pakistan were apparently planning a Mumbai–style attack in Western capitals, but American drone strikes interrupted them. However, such attacks might not have been feasible in Europe or the United States. The November 2008 Mumbai attacks, which killed 166 people, were conducted under unusual circumstances that would be hard to replicate. The terrorists bypassed Indian border controls with a secret amphibious landing in the Mumbai harbor and proceeded to use guns and grenades in a sequence of assaults against soft targets, including the famous Taj Mahal hotel. The perpetrators were members of Lashkar-e-Taiba (LeT), a group affiliated not only with jihadist goals but also with the Pakistani intelligence service ISI. Caught off-guard, Indian security forces were slow to react.[11]

Terrorist tactics are usually thought of as highly adaptable if not necessarily innovative. John McLaughlin's statement quoted at the beginning of this chapter refers to terrorist "experimentation," essentially a substitution or displacement effect. This proposition predicts that when one avenue for terrorist success is blocked, those thwarted cleverly substitute another tactic. Thus government defenses are always one step behind a versatile adversary.

Actually, terrorist tactics may not be so easily substitutable, and much terrorism is consistent over time. Groups may repeat the same tactic over and over, even if it does not work. For example, Al Qaeda and affiliates persistently targeted aircraft after 9/11 despite successive failures. According to a report issued in 2011 by the Combating Terrorism Center at the US Military Academy at West Point:

> A number of al-Qa'ida-affiliated plots sought to target commercial aviation since 9/11. A sampling of these include the "shoe bomber" plot in December 2001, an attempt to shoot down an Israeli airliner in Kenya in 2002, the liquid explosives plot against transatlantic flights in 2006, the Christmas Day plot in 2009, and the cargo bomb plots in 2010. Other prominent operations attempted or executed by Islamist extremists during this period include a 2002 plot to hijack an airliner and crash it into Changi International Airport in Singapore, the 2002 El Al ticket counter shootings at Los Angeles International Airport, the 2004 bombings of two Russian airliners, the 2007 Glasgow airport attack, a 2007 plot against Frankfurt Airport by the Sauerland cell, a 2007 attempt by extremists to target fuel lines at JFK International Airport in New York, the 2011 suicide bombing at Moscow's Domodedovo International Airport, and the 2011 shootings of U.S. military personnel at Frankfurt International Airport.[12]

Public transportation—trains, buses, subways, ferries, and aircraft—has been a favorite terrorist target since the nineteenth century. Symbolic targets such as iconic buildings and crowds of civilians will always be vulnerable to groups seeking to cause shock and horror and thereby gain attention. It also appears unlikely that suicide tactics will disappear, considering how rapidly and widely they spread after 1983. This innovative tactic, introduced in 1983, "stuck" although there is still no satisfactory explanation as to why. Bombings will always be a favored means, and kidnappings for ransom persist.

A key question for the future concerns the conditions under which significant escalation in terrorist destructiveness could occur. In particular, what is the prospect of nuclear, radiological, chemical, or biological terrorism? The threat of nuclear terrorism is a first-order US national security priority, although it would be the most challenging avenue for terrorist WMD use. This chapter has referred to fears that Syria would provide chemical weapons to Hezbollah. However, the only consequential incident of terrorist use of chemical weapons was Aum Shinrikyo's attacks on the Tokyo subway in Japan in 1995. In 2006–7 AQI used chlorine gas in bombs, but the initiative was short-lived. Again in 2013, there were reports of AQI attempts to construct chemical weapons, specifically using sarin gas. A critical question is why WMD have not been successfully exploited as a terrorist tactic. Are the acquisition and use of such weapons too difficult, especially compared to the relative ease and convenience of other "conventional" but enormously destructive means of killing large numbers of people? Are there normative inhibitions against the use of such weapons? Do terrorists have self-imposed limits? Are they sensitive to the risk they would incur? The answers are still elusive.

Another area of uncertainty in the second decade of the twenty-first century is the prospect of "cyberterrorism." Could violent cyber attacks be a central part of a terrorist campaign? So far, highly disruptive cyber attacks such as the Stuxnet virus used to destroy Iranian centrifuges have been the work of governments, and powerful governments at that. Underground conspiracies operating from remote locations and/or sympathetic jihadist hackers in the West lack the capacity for serious attacks on critical infrastructure or financial systems, despite frequent expressions of alarm at the prospect.[13] They primarily use the Internet as an information, communication, and propaganda tool—and in doing so open themselves to the cyber tools of counterterrorism agencies. It would not be prudent to ignore the risk of terrorist adoption of more sophisticated techniques, but the harm they could cause pales in comparison to that potentially resulting from the use of WMD.

THE IMPACT OF TERRORISM ON INTERNATIONAL SECURITY

Two dangers stand out. One stems from changes within states, the other from tensions among states. First, terrorism destabilizes regimes, contributing to state failure, power vacuums, and sometimes revolution. The second risk is that terrorist attacks will provoke external state intervention or interstate war, especially if the target implicates a state adversary. The terrorist assassination that sparked the First World War is a cautionary reminder of the potential repercussions stemming from seemingly minor actions by small conspiracies backed by powerful states with reputations at stake. Miscalculations and misperceptions can turn crisis into war.

Terrorism and Domestic Political Order

It is possible that a nonstate actor using terrorist tactics could overthrow the government of a country and replace it with an aggressively hostile regime. However, actually seizing power takes more than terrorism, and it is hard to measure the independent effectiveness of terrorism within a general campaign of insurgent violence that pits armed combatants and a mobilized population against a government's security forces. Still, Al Shabab in Somalia came close to victory until defeated by armed intervention on the part of the African Union. The Afghan Taliban is a formidable contender for power after the American withdrawal. The Al Nusra Front, officially designated by the United States as a terrorist organization in December 2012, or ISIS could emerge to dominate the fractured opposition in Syria.[14]

More likely is acute destabilization of already weak and vulnerable states. Terrorism can spread disorder and chaos, consequences that are especially dangerous in key geostrategic regions. Ungoverned spaces then furnish groups such as Al Qaeda or affiliates safe havens for launching attacks against their "far enemies" as well as the "near enemy." The case of Mali is instructive. AQIM along with local allies managed to drive the government's security forces out of northern Mali and seize control of a significant portion of the territory of the state. Only an armed French intervention drove them out. It is not clear whether the rebels intended or would have been able to overthrow the government in Bamako, but the risk of state collapse was genuine.

Terrorism also threatens democratic institutions and values even if it does not propel a country into complete breakdown. Indeed, terrorism is often a deliberate attempt to overturn democratic as well as secular rule. In the eyes of radical Islamists, the two principles are equally abhorrent. In Pakistan, for example, democratic institutions are the direct targets of terrorism—the victims are judges, prosecutors, officials, candidates for office, and voters. The assassination of Benazir Bhutto in 2007 is tragic

evidence of its impact, as was the 2013 assassination of the prosecutor in the case against her assailants. Terrorism did not determine the outcome of the 2013 elections in Pakistan, which represented the first transfer of power from one democratically elected government to another, but the high levels of violence reflected poorly on the ability of the government to maintain order and security.

As the example of Pakistan also reveals, one way in which terrorism intensifies domestic unrest is through its association with religious sectarianism within Islam or between Muslim and other religious communities. Sectarian violence inflames preexisting communal tensions and exposes government incapacity or partisanship in failing to protect religious communities, especially minorities. These effects are evident, for example, in contemporary Pakistan, Iraq, and Syria. In Pakistan, the most sectarian Sunni groups are also those most devoted to jihadist causes. Lashkar-e-Jhangvi, a group banned since 2001, is a case in point. As an analyst with the International Crisis Group concluded, "The primary source of terrorism in Pakistan is in fact not a Pashtun-led insurgency, but sectarian conflict; and the most dangerous and resourceful organizations are radical Sunni outfits headquartered not in FATA [the Federally Administered Tribal Areas bordering Afghanistan] but in the country's largest province, Punjab."[15]

In post-2003 Iraq, the Islamic State of Iraq took the lead in attacking Shia, including mosques, funeral processions, markets, and other purely civilian targets. The bombing of the Golden Mosque in Samarra in 2006 was the event that precipitated the turn toward civil war. Although there were no casualties (and it was not a suicide attack), the dome of the revered Shia shrine was destroyed, leading to reciprocal attacks by Shia militias against Sunni religious institutions that the Iraqi government was unable or unwilling to suppress. Terrorism might have surged originally as a reaction to foreign occupation, but the US withdrawal from Iraq did not end it. By 2013–14, Iraq was experiencing its highest levels of tit-for-tat violence between Sunni and Shia since the US withdrawal in December 2011, as the Shia-dominated government resisted Sunni demands for inclusion and the war in Syria became increasingly sectarian and emerged as the new magnet for foreign fighters.

TERRORISM AND INTERNATIONAL CONFLICT

A second way terrorism threatens international security is by (1) drawing outside powers (patrons) to support opposing parties (clients or proxies) in civil conflicts, or (2) provoking retaliatory strikes, or even direct military intervention, by the armed forces of powerful states. Either development can potentially escalate to interstate war.

What begins as internal conflict can draw in outside powers with a stake in supporting opposing local partners, thus transforming disputes into complex internationalized civil wars. The Lebanese civil war, for example, gave Syria an incentive to intervene in 1976, followed by Israel in 1978 and 1982, and subsequently the United States in conjunction with a multinational peacekeeping force in which France, Italy, and Great Britain joined. Israel's invasion of Lebanon in 1982 was an effort to destroy the Palestine Liberation Organization (PLO), which was regarded at the time as the major source of the terrorist threat to Israel. A result, however, was to set the stage for the formation of Hezbollah. Israel withdrew from southern Lebanon only in 2000, and Syria did not withdraw from Lebanon until 2005.

Some thirty years later, Iran and Russia, as well as Hezbollah, support the Assad regime while Western powers, major Arab countries, and Turkey support the resistance, sometimes reluctantly since AQ or radical Islamist influence is strong. Cooperation in finding a resolution to the conflict has been stymied by these divisions. The dilemma for the anti-Assad camp is that a rebel victory may mean an Al Qaeda or ISIS victory. Equally alarming is the prospect that violence will spread to surrounding states and that civil war will widen into regional conflict, especially after Hezbollah deployed its forces to assist Assad and violence spilled over into Lebanon. In turn, Israel has used precision air power to block Syrian moves to transfer advanced missiles to Hezbollah (probably supplied by Iran). Iran or Hezbollah could instigate terrorist attacks against Israeli or US targets outside the region, a capacity that has been demonstrated many times over (e.g., attacks on Israeli and Jewish targets in Argentina during the 1990s).

A puzzle is why terrorism would make it harder to cooperate to end civil war. One possible answer is that civilian deaths, caused by terrorism or excessive government reaction to what it calls terrorism, create pressures for humanitarian intervention that actually widen the scope of the conflict. Paradoxically, however, third-party intervention is often thought to be a positive factor in conflict resolution. Another possibility is that terrorism prolongs and embitters conflict, as atrocities on both sides destroy communal trust and impede reconciliation. Terrorism also makes it risky for moderates to seek compromise. It can destroy the middle ground.

Terrorism creates even greater disturbance when it provokes large-scale military intervention with ground forces, overthrow of the government that tolerates or supports terrorism, and lengthy occupation. Admittedly, the US response to 9/11 was exceptional, as was the act of terrorism that provoked it. Nevertheless, the long war in

Afghanistan (surpassing the Vietnam War in duration) was explicitly justified as counterterrorism, and the invasion of Iraq in 2003 would not have taken place had the 9/11 attacks not occurred. Both interventions had a profound impact on critical geopolitical regions, on the US military, and on US standing in the world. As noted earlier in this chapter, it is unlikely that the United States will be tempted to repeat these costly engagements, but it is not inconceivable should there be a provocation of the magnitude of the 9/11 attacks (for example, if nuclear or chemical weapons were used against US citizens).

The French operation in Mali in 2013 is another instance of military intervention in response to terrorism. The catalyst was not an attack on the homeland but a terrorist campaign that destabilized Mali. France, as well as its supporters in Africa and the West, feared that Mali would fall under the control of Islamist groups affiliated with AQIM, thus altering the strategic landscape in the Sahel and West Africa. The French action was at the request of the nominal government of Mali, thus not a violation of sovereignty, and France immediately communicated the intention to transfer the task to an international or regional organization. The United Nations later deployed soldiers and police.

The flow of arms from post-Gaddafi Libya also augmented the fortunes of terrorist groups in the region. Arms transfers represent another example of the spill-over effects of the insecurity that often accompanies regime transition. Even if the governments that replace authoritarian rule aim for democracy and tolerance, they are too weak to maintain internal security or guard borders.

Even limited military retaliation, typically the use of air power, against terrorists outside a state's borders is historically rare, with the exception of Israel. Israel has routinely retaliated outside its borders, but generally within the region, since the 1950s. Before 2001, at the international level military force was used at a distance sparingly and infrequently, to send a message as much as inflict consequential material damage on an enemy. It usually involved limited strikes by bombers or, later, cruise missiles, not defeat of the adversary. Thus the United States retaliated against Libya in 1986, Iraq in 1993, and Sudan and Afghanistan in 1998, but not against Hezbollah in 1983 or Al Qaeda in 2000 (when the USS *Cole* was bombed in Yemen). After 9/11, technological changes in air power made it much faster and easier to strike back with great power from a distance. Cruise missiles had the advantage of being unmanned and thus low-risk for military personnel, but they were also relatively slow. The US deployment of drones against Al Qaeda targets outside of active conflict zones where troops are committed—whether one considers this practice to be retaliatory punishment, preemption, prevention, or warfare—is a watershed development with as yet unknown ramifications. The future of drone warfare is a challenge for the management of the response to terrorism, which will be addressed in the last section of this chapter.

One problem is that there is no guarantee that limited retaliation will have limited effects. Even precision strikes could lead to escalation and major interstate conflict or war. Catalysts for crisis include major terrorist attacks in unstable but highly militarized regional conflict theaters such as India-Pakistan. In the post-9/11 time frame, at least two serious provocations, fortunately, did not elicit retaliation. This chapter has already referred to the 2008 Mumbai attacks by Lashkar-e-Taiba, the Pakistani militant organization with ties to the Pakistani intelligence services. Previously, in December 2001, terrorists linked to Pakistan attacked the Indian Parliament in New Delhi. Had India struck back either time, the crisis could have escalated to a nuclear exchange between India and Pakistan. Pakistan's strategic doctrine calls for the deployment of nuclear weapons in the face of a conventional Indian attack. India might not exercise similar restraint if there were a repetition of these assaults.

Looking to the future, the use of nuclear, biological, or chemical weapons would be highly provocative, crossing a thick red line, and possibly changing the international dynamic of terrorism and counterterrorism. The employment of such weapons would increase the likelihood of large-scale retaliation (official US policy since 2008 is to deter nuclear terrorism through the threat of overwhelming force). Carrying through on a policy of retaliatory deterrence is not simple, however. For example, in 2012 the United States announced that Syria's use of chemical weapons would be unacceptable, but when reports of such use surfaced, the United States showed considerable reluctance to act.

Outside powers provoked to the use of military force by terrorism risk blowback if a provocation-retaliation spiral sets in. Their homelands in turn may become the target of retaliatory terrorism, whether "homegrown" and inspirational or directed by terrorist organizations abroad.[16] Actually, retaliation by targeted states is rare, in part because of the attribution problem. It is not easy to identify perpetrators in a way that is both timely and convincing, as the United States found in trying to respond to the killing of the US ambassador to Libya in 2012.[17] In addition, over the decade since 9/11, the number of deadly terrorist attacks on the territory of states that involve themselves in conflicts abroad has declined. One reason is the efficiency of intelligence and security services in Western democracies. Enhanced internal security measures come with a price in civil liberties and individual

privacy, but most citizens seem to have accepted this trade-off.

CHALLENGES OF MANAGING TERRORISM

There is no clear international consensus about how to deal with terrorism or what the goals of a common strategy should be, even though international agreements and institutions devoted to counterterrorism—from the United Nations, through regional organizations, to informal bilateral arrangements—have expanded at a steady pace. Even allies may disagree, as the United States, for example, aimed at "defeating" Al Qaeda as a specific enemy, whereas Europeans tended to stress the containment of terrorism and enhanced resilience at home. The long history of formal and informal international cooperation in dealing with terrorism began in the 1960s. It is seen in numerous treaties, conventions, conferences, resolutions, high-level panels, committees, commissions, plenaries, working groups, action groups, strategies, initiatives, summits, and task forces, many at the level of the United Nations.[18] There are even nongovernmental organizations (NGOs) devoted to improving global cooperation.[19] Enforcing international regulations has been problematic, however; it is often difficult for the United Nations to monitor compliance, much less enforce it.

Despite sometime political disagreements among allies, much progress has been made in bilateral and multilateral cooperation to improve law enforcement, border controls, intelligence-sharing, and restrictions on financing for terrorism. The US-European relationship is a case in point. Here the challenge of management has been met well. These like-minded states face similar threats: attacks on their citizens, officials, and interests abroad, terrorist strikes at home directed by foreign jihadist organizations, and "homegrown" terrorism whether local (typically far right) or inspired by jihadist ideologies and publicists. "Radicalization" of citizens or residents who then turn to violence is a common concern.

Despite the often-cited contrast between the European "terrorism as crime" and American "terrorism as war" approaches, cooperation on the "civilian" or law enforcement side of counterterrorism has been extensive.[20] Much activity is at the working level of police and judicial bodies and intelligence agencies as opposed to the national level, and much of day-to-day cooperation is bilateral. However, as the European Union has increased its powers in the homeland security arena, it has become a partner as well. Concrete achievements were reached in areas of information-sharing, transportation security, and countering terrorist financing. Disagreement rose over data privacy and protection (especially with regard to airline passenger data) and terrorist designation lists. The United States consistently prodded the European Union to include Hezbollah, a move that was resisted until Hezbollah became involved in the Syrian civil war. European attitudes were also hardened by Hezbollah's attacks against Israeli tourists in Europe, including the conviction of a Hezbollah operative in a Cyprus court for a failed attempt, as well as Bulgaria's naming of Hezbollah as responsible for the lethal bombing of a tourist bus.

Europeans welcomed the election of President Obama in 2008, especially his promises to end many of the policies of the Bush administration that Europeans rejected— harsh interrogation practices, black prisons, extraordinary rendition, and the imprisonment of "unlawful combatants" at Guantanamo Bay. President Obama's failure to carry through on all these reforms, especially his inability or unwillingness to close the Guantanamo Bay facility, disappointed many Europeans, and many Americans for that matter. Nevertheless, these doubts did

not prevent the formation of a common front against terrorism. Actually, the pattern toward close cooperation began under President Bush, when political controversy was highest, and it is worth noting that during his second term, the US government placed a much greater emphasis on cooperating with allies than it had during the unilateralist first term.

The challenges for managing terrorism go beyond the control and prevention of terrorism itself, because, as noted throughout this chapter, terrorism is closely linked to other threats to international stability. The problems associated with responding effectively to terrorism are also interconnected. With so many complex challenges, it is hard to single out the most serious and pressing. To complicate matters, measures that reduce terrorism in the short term can increase its likelihood in the long term.

Managing Military Force

Studies of how terrorism ends conclude that military force is not generally the answer to terrorism over the long run.[21] However, in the 2001–13 period, the use of military force abroad was the centerpiece of US counterterrorism. Because the United States is the world's largest military power with the biggest footprint around the world, and the leader in global counterterrorism efforts, the US reliance on force to combat terrorism shapes international politics. President Obama recognized the need to go beyond the war on terrorism in a major policy speech in May 2013, but he continued to authorize drone strikes against Al Qaeda and its affiliates.[22] Should there be a redirection of US foreign policy, the global management of terrorism will shift correspondingly.

The resort to the use of force by threatened outside powers reflects an underlying structural problem in the international system, not just (or at all) a state's particular

propensity for one method over another: local governments in states where terrorists
operate are often ineffective at prevention.
Their sovereignty is weakened by their inability or unwillingness to prevent terrorist
groups affiliated with the loose Al Qaeda
network from establishing safe havens within
their borders, and their sovereignty is further eroded if an outside power intervenes.
The result is a downward spiral in their
ability to govern. Compounding the problem is the fact that the counterterrorism
strategies of many weak or poorly governed
states are based on the indiscriminate application of force. The result is popular dis-
affection, rising unrest, and further erosion
of legitimacy. In other instances, governments use force efficiently to suppress terrorism, but rather than solving the problem
deflect it beyond their borders (e.g., from
Saudi Arabia to Yemen). At the most extreme
level, local state breakdown results in full-
fledged civil wars, so that managing terrorism becomes part of civil war prevention or
mitigation.

The first decade of the global war on terror was defined by the two US-led wars in
Iraq and Afghanistan; in the second decade,
the United States withdrew its forces from
Iraq (completed in 2011) and began a drawdown in Afghanistan (scheduled for completion in 2014). However, the ending of
these two wars will not necessarily mean
less American reliance on fighting terrorists
with military means. The era of large-scale
military intervention to overthrow governments and occupy foreign countries is probably over, but the age of drones is not. Drones
are a highly efficient means of implementing
a policy of targeted killings of leaders of
militant groups.

The reliance on armed drones, or remotely
piloted aerial vehicles, as a key instrument of
offensive counterterrorism strategy at the interstate level was one of the most important
developments in the global war on terror

under the Obama administration.[23] The
policy began under the Bush administration,
and usage peaked in 2010. The United States
deployed armed drones in military campaigns to defeat adversaries in Afghanistan,
Libya, and Iraq. But their use has not been
restricted to combat zones. The battlefield is
potentially worldwide. Strikes have been
conducted against Al Qaeda and affiliates in
Pakistan, Yemen, and Somalia, and possibly
the Philippines. In 2013, the United States
established a drone base in Niger as disorder
spread to Mali. Future US counterterrorism
strategy will rely on the covert use of limited
force, utilizing drones and special operations
forces.

What are the implications of drone warfare for the management of global conflict?
The United States sought coalition partners
to legitimize ground interventions in Afghanistan and Iraq, but the use of drones
has been unilateral. There are no global
standards for their employment, whether for
surveillance or for offensive military operations. The American program has been
questioned in terms of international law as
well as lack of transparency and accountability in making decisions about who to
target. Drone warfare violates national sovereignty if the country where the target is
located objects or is not consulted. Even if
the government agrees, its citizens may not.
Despite their precision, drone strikes kill civilians. The numbers of civilian casualties
are disputed, but popular backlash against
the use of drones in targeted killings has intensified (in Pakistan, for example). The authority of the weak states that are the source
of the problem can be further undermined
by anti-drone protest.

Another unsettling effect is that proliferation is already under way. Few if any countries can reach the US level of drone
capability, which depends on much more
than technological prowess. However, even
states without global reach will probably be

able to use remotely piloted aircraft at or near home to attack their opponents.

The prospect of limited reach points to the next challenge: the conduct of counterterrorism operations in developing countries. For example, the Nigerian government's response to the militant group Boko Haram has involved significant human rights violations. In 2013, the government declared a state of emergency in the northern part of the country where Boko Haram operates. It is not that the threat from Boko Haram is not real—over three thousand people have been killed since the conflict started in 2009—but that the response to terrorism has involved abuses of human rights that are likely to precipitate more violence over the long run. The United States and the European Union provide counterterrorism assistance to Nigeria and call for respect for human rights and engagement with the communities likely to support Boko Haram, but their appeals have carried little weight.

Still, there have been relative success stories such as Indonesia and the Philippines. Indonesia employed a comprehensive counterterrorism campaign against Islamist militant groups, including Jemaah Islamiya and its offshoots, which combined improvements in law enforcement and intelligence, efficient prosecution of terrorists in the courts, and the organization of deradicalization programs in prisons. The Philippines, by contrast, benefited from the presence of US military advisers, who deployed on the ground after 2001. The threat of terrorism from the Abu Sayaf Group and Jemaah Islamiya has diminished considerably because of military campaigns in the south, and the Moro Islamic Liberation Front entered a peace process with the government. At the same time, the United Nations has been active in building up the civilian side of counterterrorism.

If analysis of the effectiveness of forceful responses to terrorism extends to the realm of ethnonationalist or separatist violence, it is clear that sometimes states can decisively crush such movements through the harsh application of military force. The military defeat of the LTTE at the hands of the Sri Lankan government in 2009, after twenty-six years of fighting interspersed with brief periods of negotiating, effectively ended the civil war between Tamils and Sinhalese, but at a high cost in terms of civilian casualties and international reputation. The same could be said for the Russian war in Chechnya, which left an embittered remnant of fighters that became the Caucasus Emirates organization.

Prevention and Building State Capacity

Clearly, the task of preventing terrorism goes well beyond designing and implementing specific counterterrorism measures. State capacity building must be developed long before countries face an urgent threat of terrorism. Lack of effective local governance permits extremist groups to flourish, and the absence of viable alternatives to coercion compels governments to use blunt force. Consider Pakistan, for example. The government is incapable of managing the multiple militant groups that increasingly threaten the state. Some of Pakistan's problems are due to the spillover of the war in Afghanistan, others due to lack of control over the border regions, yet others due to the rivalry with India, but the fact remains that the state functions poorly in all areas of governance. Rivalries among government agencies, particularly the civilian-military divide, create more inefficiencies.

The international community recognizes the need to improve local governance and counterterrorism effectiveness, and many bilateral as well as UN initiatives focus on capacity building. The United States is a leader in promoting international cooperation, although the effort has been less successful among non-likeminded states (seen in US relations with Russia, for example). In 2011, in an attempt to go beyond Western-centric frameworks and encourage greater diversity and inclusiveness, the US State Department announced the launch of the Global Counterterrorism Forum (GCTF), symbolically cochaired by the United States and Turkey. Members include the Western powers and Japan (along with the European Union), Russia and China, India and Pakistan (but not Afghanistan), and Nigeria. In the Middle East and North Africa, the partners are Algeria, Morocco, the United Arab Emirates, Saudi Arabia, Egypt, and Jordan. Neither Iraq nor Iran is a member, nor is Israel or Lebanon, or, needless to say, Syria. The GCTF is self-described as "an informal, multilateral counterterrorism (CT) platform that focuses on identifying critical civilian CT needs, mobilizing the necessary expertise and resources to address such needs and enhance global cooperation."[24] The goal of the GCTF is to prevent, combat, and prosecute terrorism and to counter incitement and recruitment. Its priority is civilian capacity building in the areas of law enforcement, border management, and countering violent extremism. Its aim is also to implement the Global Counter-Terrorism Strategy adopted by the UN General Assembly in 2006, thus to link up to a broader multilateral initiative.

The GCTF was not intended to resolve the possible "root causes" of terrorism such as poverty, demographic pressures, repression of dissent, lack of education, or intolerance. It does not aim to alter the structural economic and social conditions that could potentially permit or motivate terrorism. The limited scope of the GCTF may reflect the conclusion by its founders that promoting development and democracy on a global scale is not feasible. Such an ambitious task is formidably difficult, expensive, and slow,

and it is not certain that there is a payoff in ending terrorism. As noted earlier in this chapter, it cannot be shown that terrorism necessarily results from underlying conditions. The restricted GCTF mission may also be a result of its mixed composition: a successful outcome requires cooperation between democracies and nondemocracies. Citing authoritarian regimes as a "root cause" of terrorism could stop the project in its tracks. A third obstacle to ending terrorism through addressing "root causes" is that in the short run the process of democratization can create opportunities for terrorism, as the chapter in this volume by Jack Snyder, Dawn Brancati, and Edward D. Mansfield demonstrates.

CONCLUSIONS

It is not prudent to be complacent about the impact of terrorism on international security, although it is by no means an "existential threat" for developed democracies. Its destructive potential was neglected at great peril prior to 9/11, as few people thought that terrorism by nonstate actors posed any threat at all to international order. Exceedingly rare events, however unpredictable, can have momentous consequences, and the potential for surprise remains. Al Qaeda's capacity to mount major terrorist attacks on a global scale has diminished, but its local and regional effects and those of its affiliates can be disastrous. And terrorism-related crises can quickly rise to the global level.

Before the 9/11 attacks, it was unimaginable that terrorism would provoke a US-led global war against it, much less that the dynamic of terrorism and counterterrorism would shape the international politics of the first decade of the twenty-first century. A key problem for the future is moving beyond the reliance on military force in a "war on terrorism" to find more effective ways of dealing with the threat, as an internal or an external problem, or a mixture of the two.

An important question for the future concerns whether and when it is wise for governments to recognize or negotiate with entities that they have defined as "terrorist organizations." The United States faces this dilemma in planning a role for the Taliban in a future Afghanistan, and Israel confronts it in relations with Hamas. Similarly, the problem complicates international efforts to deal with Hezbollah. Pakistan also faces the problem in its relations with the many violent opposition movements it must manage. Can violent groups be transformed into political actors and co-opted into the political system through a process of negotiations and power-sharing arrangements? Is compromise possible? While the experiences of Sri Lanka and Colombia are ones of frustration and repeated failed negotiations, the example of Northern Ireland shows that politicization and incorporation of a violent adversary is possible—but that the process is long, requiring patience and sustained commitment on all sides. Instructive cases also include the transformation of Fatah and the PLO after a formal renunciation of terrorism in the 1980s and, in 2003, the rejection of terrorism by the Egyptian Islamist group Al-Gama'a al-Islamiyya.

The different outcomes in these various cases show that third-party initiatives to resolve local conflicts do not automatically produce positive results, however well-intentioned they may be. The mixed results also indicate that not all militant or terrorist organizations are alike. A solution that is persuasive and credible for one type of actor might not be for another.

Perhaps the most important lesson for the international community is that the process of ending terrorism is likely to be slow and arduous, requiring gradualism, endurance, and commitment despite setbacks. It is also likely to be incomplete. Peace processes often lead to the splintering of formerly cohesive adversaries, with extreme factions breaking away to continue terrorism because they are unwilling to accept a settlement that a moderate majority has agreed to. It has proved extremely difficult to delegitimize the deliberate killing of "enemy" civilians in order to promote a political cause. Some authors have argued that it is hard to end terrorism because terrorism is an effective method of bringing about political change.[25] However, it may be that the ideological justifications for terrorism are too compelling; that revenge is too strong a psychological force; that the practitioners have no other means of pursuing their goals, as they so often claim; that punishment is not swift or sure; or that the elites who issue moral injunctions condemning terrorism are dismissed as hypocritical.[26] Whatever the reason, terrorism and the response it provokes will continue to be a source of disorder within and among states. States may not be able to prevent or eradicate terrorism, but they can try to manage their own reactions to it.

NOTES

1. Donatella della Porta, *Clandestine Political Violence* (Cambridge: Cambridge University Press, 2013).

2. John McLaughlin, "The New Battlefield," *Foreign Policy*, www.foreignpolicy.com/articles/2012/11/13/the_new_battlefield?page-full, November 13, 2012.

3. These data are from the Global Terrorism Database (GTD), maintained by the National Consortium for the Study of Terrorism and Responses to Terrorism (START), www.start.umd.edu/gtd/. The GTD includes information on incidents from 1970 to the present.

4. Data from the Chicago Project on Security and Terrorism (CPOST), cpost.uchicago.edu/.

5. It is important to remember, however, that it is difficult to link attacks to specific groups; for example, well over half the post-9/11 attacks were attributed to an "unknown group" by CPOST.

6. This comparison excluded 9/11 itself. It can be counted as one incident or as three or four. Fatalities numbered 2,955. Also note the important caveat that the GTD lacks figures for the year 1993, so events of the pre-9/11 decade are undercounted.

7. The data were the basis for the "Annex of Statistical Information," in the *Country Reports on Terrorism 2011*, issued July 31, 2012, by the US Department of State, Office of the Coordinator for Counterterrorism. From 2012 on, statistical data are provided by START, using the GTD (see note 3).

8. On suicide terrorism, see Ariel Merari, *Driven to Death: Psychological and Social Aspects of Suicide Terrorism* (New York: Oxford University Press, 2010). See also Assaf Moghadam, *The Globalization of Martyrdom: Al Qaeda, Salafi Jihad, and the Diffusion of Suicide Attacks* (Baltimore, MD: Johns Hopkins University Press, 2008).

9. The website *Mapping Militant Organizations* displays a chart of global Al Qaeda affiliates, with profiles of each group. Available at http://www.mappingmilitants.stanford.edu.

10. Martha Crenshaw, "Innovation: Decision Points in the Trajectory of Terrorism," in *Terrorist Innovations in Weapons of Mass Effect: Preconditions, Causes and Predictive Indicators*, Maria Rasmussen and Mohammed Hafez, ed. (Washington, DC: Defense Threat Reduction Agency, 2010).

11. Angel Rabasa et al., *The Lessons of Mumbai* (occasional paper prepared for the Rand Corporation, Santa Monica, CA, 2009).

12. Ben Brandt, "Terrorist Threats to Commercial Aviation: A Contemporary Assessment," *CTC Sentinel*, US Military Academy, November 30, 2011.

13. See Peter W. Singer, "The Cyber Terror Bogeyman" (report, Brookings Institution, Washington, DC, November 2012). See also Christopher Heffelfinger, "The Risks Posed by Jihadist Hackers," *CTC Sentinel*, US Military Academy, July, 23, 2013.

14. In May 2013, the UN Security Council's Al Qaeda sanctions committee designated Al Nusra as well, since Al Nusra pledged allegiance to Al Qaeda in April of the same year.

15. Shehryar Fazli, "Sectarianism and Conflict: The View from Pakistan," Religion and Violence

Series Report (Danish Institute for International Studies, Copenhagen, June 2012).

16. Emanuel Adler, "Damned If You Do, Damned If You Don't: Performative Power and the Strategy of Conventional and Nuclear Defusing," *Security Studies* 19 (2010): 199–229. Adler argues that the provocation-retaliation dilemma is the defining structural feature of post–Cold War international politics.

17. For an argument to the contrary—that attribution is not a difficult problem—see Keir A. Lieber and Daryl G. Press, "Why States Won't Give Nuclear Weapons to Terrorists," *International Security* 38, no. 1 (Summer 2013): 80–104. I explain my perspective more fully in Martha Crenshaw, "Will Threats Deter Nuclear Terrorism?" in *Deterring Terrorism: Theory and Practice*, Andreas Wenger and Alex Wilner, ed. (Stanford, CA: Stanford University Press, 2012).

18. Two examples of work on this subject are Barak Mendelsohn, *Combating Jihadism: American Hegemony and Interstate Cooperation in the War on Terrorism* (Chicago: University of Chicago Press, 2009); and Peter Romaniuk, *Multilateral Counter-Terrorism: The Global Politics of Cooperation and Contestation* (London and New York: Routledge, 2010). A contemporary assessment can be found in "The Global Regime for Terrorism" (issue brief, Council on Foreign Relations, August 2011; updated May 2013), http://www.cfr.org/asia-and-pacific/global-regime-terrorism/p25729.

19. For example, in 2004 the Fourth Freedom Forum created a Center on Global Counterterrorism Cooperation with offices in Washington, DC, New York, and Brussels.

20. Kristin Archick, "U.S.-EU Cooperation against Terrorism," Report for Congress, (Congressional Research Service, Washington, DC, April 22, 2013).

21. See Seth G. Jones and Martin C. Libicki, *How Terrorist Groups End: Lessons for Countering al Qa'ida* (Santa Monica, CA: Rand Corporation, 2008); and Audrey Kurth Cronin, *How Terrorism Ends: Understanding the Decline and Demise of Terrorist Campaigns* (Princeton, NJ: Princeton University Press, 2009).

22. The text of the speech is available on the White House website, http://www.whitehouse.gov

/the-press-office/2013/05/23/remarks-president
-barack-obama.

23. The drone program is highly secretive, but press reports indicate that as of 2012 they were based in Niger, Ethiopia, the Seychelles, Djibouti, Saudi Arabia, Qatar, the United Arab Emirates, Yemen, Turkey, Italy, the Philippines, and Afghanistan. The US Navy also began experimenting with flying drones from aircraft carriers. See, for example, Micah Zenko and Emma Welch, "Where the Drones Are," *Foreign Policy*, May 29, 2012, http://www.foreignpolicy.com/articles/2012/05/29/where_the_drones_are.

24. From the GCTF website: http://www.the gctf.org/web/guest;jsessionid=8441CDA5D19A4 52811392C5FD06A4F19.w142.

25. An assessment of this debate can be found in Peter Krause, "The Political Effectiveness of Non-State Violence: A Two-Level Framework to Transform a Deceptive Debate," *Security Studies* 22 (2013): 259–94.

26. For a discussion of the psychological processes of radicalization, see Clark McCauley and Sophia Moskalenko, *Friction: How Radicalization Happens to Them and Us* (New York: Oxford University Press, 2011).

PART V

DILEMMAS AND DEBATES

30

WHAT IS THE "INTERNATIONAL COMMUNITY"?

Tod Lindberg

Discourse on global affairs often refers to the "international community." Political leaders and diplomats across the globe sometimes exhort it, as in "the international community must act"; they sometimes lament its passivity, as in "the international community has done nothing"; and sometimes they speak in its name, as in "the international community condemns this outrage."

When an earthquake devastated Haiti in 2010, the "international community" mobilized its resources for disaster relief and rebuilding efforts.[1] When a repressive government in Burma kept one of the world's leading human rights and democracy activists locked in prison, the "international community" condemned the persecution and mobilized to put pressure on the ruling junta.[2] When postelection ethnic clashes in Kenya in 2007–08 threatened to escalate into atrocities on a mass scale, the "international community" sent emissaries to help defuse the tension.[3] When Serbian strongman Slobodan Milosevic threatened ethnic cleans-

ing in the secessionist territory of Kosovo in 1999, the "international community" came to the rescue of the imperiled Kosovar Albanians.[4] When the SARS plague broke out in China in 2003 and threatened to turn into a global pandemic, the "international community" mustered its resources to identify a cause, develop treatments, and isolate those infected.[5] As forces loyal to Syrian dictator Bashar al-Assad shelled civilians in the rebel stronghold of Homs in 2012, the "international community" struggled to find a response.[6]

In no two of the specific cases just mentioned, from Burma to Kenya, does the term "international community" refer to precisely the same grouping of constituent parts. Yet, clearly there is a common meaning to its use in all of them. So what *do* we mean when we refer to the "international community" (and by "we" I simply mean those of us who practice or talk about international politics—though I will later be discussing a "we" in international politics whose content is richer in terms of normative agreement)? Where did our understanding of it come from? What exactly *is* the "international community"?

As we shall see in the course of this chapter, international politics is something more than the sum of the activities of state interaction in the pursuit of the national interest of each state. Nonstate organizations and institutions, as well as international organizations, and even individuals operating without state sanction, have played a significant role.

From time to time, they join states in pursuit of a commonly held sense of the good. Both the form of their interaction (unanimity of purpose) and the content (the good pursued) reflect the classically liberal desire for the application of universal moral principles. Although many invocations of "international community" fall short, at its best the international community is the embodiment of liberal normative aspiration exerting an influence on international politics.

FROM THEORY TO PRACTICE

A proper understanding of the international community begins with an examination of how such an entity might fit into the theories that attempt to explain international politics. These theories rightly begin with the observation that the distinguishing characteristic of international politics is the absence of a sovereign power over states. In fact, this absence of authority precedes the development of the modern state system. One could say that sovereign power is itself the solution to the absence of authority, and therefore security, in a particular territory.[7]

One modern school of international relations theory, neorealism, describes this condition of the absence of central authority internationally as "anarchy." A state has no one to rely on but itself. Its pursuit of its own security creates conflicts with other states pursuing their security. The result, in the title of John Mearsheimer's book, is *The Tragedy of Great Power Politics*.[8]

Another school of international relations theory, liberal internationalism, explores the ways in which states, specifically liberal or liberal-leaning states, can act together to shape an international order that is itself liberal.[9] States can agree on international law they accept as binding and on juridical mechanisms for resolving their disputes.

Typically, the means of doing so is through the establishment of international institutions that can help nudge the behavior of states in a liberal direction. Examples would be the United Nations Security Council, which UN member-states granted "primary responsibility for the maintenance of international peace and security," in the words of the UN Charter,[10] and the World Trade Organization, which member states have granted enforcement powers in the case of trade disputes. And the International Criminal Court, designed to hold perpetrators of atrocity crimes such as genocide and ethnic cleansing to account when national courts are unavailing.

A newer perspective on international relations theory is constructivism, whose central holding is that "anarchy is what states make of it."[11] Conflict can indeed ensue from the international system but need not automatically ensue as an inherent property of the system. States can be "friends." This is a quasi-sociological perspective that delves deeply into the role that shared ideas and identity have in shaping international politics, whether in accordance with liberal norms or not.[12]

None of these perspectives maps directly onto foreign policymaking by real-world governments and policymakers, nor are they really intended to; collectively, they constitute a more basic argument about how international politics works. Nevertheless, these perspectives are indeed associated with approaches to policymaking, at least in somewhat bastardized form. Neorealism becomes a "realist" approach to international politics, with an emphasis on the hard-headed pursuit of national interests. Liberal internationalism leads generally into a multilateral approach in pursuit of a common good. Constructivism generally tracks into liberal multilateralism, but its emphasis on the role of ideas in international politics is not in principle limited to liberal ideas, nor is the central tenet that "anarchy is what states make of it" necessarily a precursor to *collective* pursuit of liberal order. Constructivists everywhere may be horrified by the suggestion, but contemporary neoconservatism bears the characteristics of a constructivist perspective applied to the real world. At the core of neoconservatism is belief in the efficacy of the use of US power to promote US values, that is, "ideas," abroad; often doctrinally unilateralist in outlook, it accords the United States, as a powerful country, a primary role in shaping international politics. It is beyond the scope of this chapter to try to offer a full discussion of how neoconservative foreign policy preferences differ from traditionally conservative preferences. It may be observed, however, that neoconservatism's neoconstructivism is more ambitious internationally, whereas classical conservatism seeks primarily to protect the principle of sovereign prerogative against efforts to encroach upon it.

These different perspectives on actual policymaking in turn invite varying conceptions of the international community. The realist perspective effectively dismisses the idea of an international community as an oxymoron in a world of states pursuing their national interests.[13] The simple answer to the question of what the international community *is* would be, "nothing of consequence." There remains ample room in this perspective for states to act together, perhaps by "bandwagoning" with a bigger power to fend off a hostile power, perhaps by joining with others to balance a bigger power. The result is concerted international action—but hardly

an "international community" in the sense of the examples presented at the outset of this chapter.

The liberal perspectives, by contrast, whether institution- or values-oriented, do allow for the possibility of a consequential transnational grouping of states on the basis of liberal ideas and affinities shared across international borders. But the extent to which states sharing ideas constitute an international "community," let alone *the* international community, remains somewhat obscure.[14] Liberalism is, in principle, universal in its aspirations, but there remains a substantial gap between universal aspiration and its actualization. There is also the question of what those on the outside of liberal aspiration think of its universal claims.

From the neoconservative and conservative perspectives, the "international community" would seem to be an object of suspicion—not on grounds of its existence per se, as in the realist perspective, but in the sense of the legitimacy of its constitution, of those who claim to speak for it, and of its precepts for action.[15] It may, in short, be a type of fraud, an act of collusion by a group seeking to extend its influence and advance its agenda by representing itself as the view of all humanity. As such, the "international community" may seek to inhibit the ability of powerful states (such as the United States) to act on their own to shape international politics in accordance with its (liberal) values—or simply seek to restrict the ability of the United States to act as it pleases as a sovereign state.

In viewing the "international community," then, the policymaking perspectives discussed above have characteristic limitations. Realists cannot see it at all. Liberals tends to universalize a liberal normative agenda and call it the view of the international community, regardless of dissenting opinion. Neoconservatives and conservatives proffer a critique of the liberal view in which the "international community" is an invention of dubious value when it is not, indeed, a menace.

Each of these three perspectives throws some light on the problem of what we mean when we say "international community," but each is at best partial. A fully persuasive account of the international community would therefore have to persuade those of realist inclination that the international community has actuality that demands their attention at least from time to time; persuade liberals that the tendency to universalize liberalism creates avoidable problems with the evocation of the international community; and persuade neoconservatives and conservatives that the international community, properly understood, might be helpful in their ambition to shape international politics and to preserve US freedom of action.

This is what this chapter attempts. But because it is a tall order, it begins by offering a selective critical survey of views of the "international community" that at least clarifies some of the issues at stake, and concludes with some practical suggestions for policymakers that may enable them to speak more clearly about the "international community."

UNCERTAIN TERMS

This chapter is hardly the first attempt to speak coherently about the "international community," whatever it may be, nor the first attempt to recognize the difficulty of doing so. It began with the observation that the phrase is in common parlance, especially among officials (who presumably have some influence on the conduct and content of international politics) and advocates (those who wish to influence international politics).

The phrase has two elements, "international" and "community," each of which poses (or at least opens the door to) conceptual problems. Both elements also have synonyms that sometimes enter the discussions:

for example "world," "global," or "transnational" for "international"; "society" for "community." "International community" or one of its variants seems to have superseded a phrase common in the nineteenth and early twentieth centuries, the "family of nations." Countries were often said to be joining the "family of nations" by virtue of their increasing interaction with states presumably already members of this "family."[16]

Notwithstanding that the monarchs of European powers at the time were in many cases blood relatives, "family" is clearly a metaphor. The use of "community" and "society" seems to represent an effort to pin down the relationship among those concerned more exactly, or at least nonmetaphorically. Yet before we turn our noses up at the phrase "family of nations," it might be worthwhile to consider the possibility that those who used it a hundred or more years ago were trying to capture the same thing that people are reaching for today when they use the term "international community."

Each of the possible variants seems to have proponents as well as detractors who favor a different formulation. Hedley Bull, a leading member of the English School (considered by some to prefigure the emergence of constructivism in the United States), was closely identified with the term "international society," which he described as follows: "A *society of states* (or international society) exists when a group of states, conscious of certain common interests and common values, form a society in the sense that they conceive themselves to be bound by a common set of rules in their relations with one another, and share in the working of common institutions."[17] Here is a society whose members are states. Robert H. Jackson, meanwhile, distinguishes "'world society' (human beings with equal rights) versus 'international society' (among sovereign states, on a continuum from 'mere awareness . . . to extensive and continuous interaction through a highly developed institutional framework of international relations')."[18] Chris Brown prefers "world community," noting similarly the "essentially state-centric" character of "international community."[19]

Andreas Paulus sees an intrinsic normative element to the idea of community. He asks, "What distinguishes a 'community' from a 'society'? . . . [O]ne may say—with the necessary caution—that a community adds a normative element, a minimum of subjective cohesion to the social bond between its members. Whereas 'society' emphasizes factual interconnections and interrelations, 'community' looks to values, beliefs, and subjective feelings of commonality."[20] For Pemmaraju Sreenivasa Rao, the normative component of community is an element underlying international law. He proffers the observation that "the concept of international community has been a steady driving force behind the progressive development of international law and its codification."[21]

The terminological variety here points toward several important questions: Who is eligible for membership in the "international community"? Is it a group of states only, or does it also include nonstate actors? Does the glue that holds it together consist of shared normative views of some kind, and if so, what are they? And how sticky is the glue? Or is "international community" just a shorthand description for the interacting actors of the world in toto, regardless of how they interact? Is the "international community" already a coherent whole as is, or is it in the process of coming into being? Do we benefit most by thinking about the international community in terms of existing international institutions such as the United Nations? Is it better to think about international community in terms of international law (a legal perspective), or is it better to think of international law in terms of a nascent and evolving international community

(a sociological perspective)? This brief tour begins with an institutional perspective on international community, then looks at some legal perspectives and then at more sociological viewpoints.

INSTITUTIONS OF COMMUNITY

Writing in 1994, William D. Jackson noted the increase in the prevalence of the use of the term "international community" or something similar from the 1950s through the 1980s in speeches at the UN General Assembly.[22] Bruno Simma and Andreas Paulus note, "Resolutions of international conferences, of the UN General Assembly, and even the Security Council have used this term in an almost inflationary way."[23] And of course one of the leading promoters of the idea of "international community" was the former secretary-general of the United Nations, Kofi Annan. In a widely quoted 1999 speech, he asked and answered the question:

> What binds us into an international community? In the broadest sense there is a shared vision of a better world for all people, as set out, for example in the founding Charter of the United Nations. There is our sense of common vulnerability in the face of global warming and the threat posed by the spread of weapons of mass destruction. There is the framework of international law, treaties and human rights conventions. There is equally our sense of shared opportunity, which is why we build common markets and joint institutions such as the United Nations. Together, we are stronger.[24]

Here, institutions such as the United Nations are the locus where the international community manifests itself.

The United Nations has not been the only source of institutional articulation of a sense of international community. So, too, have some of the holdings of the Permanent

Court of International Justice, the body created by the Covenant of the League of Nations for the resolution of international legal disputes and the predecessor institution to the International Court of Justice, established at the same time as the United Nations. Antonios Tzanakopoulos notes:

> A number of pronouncements of the Permanent Court aim at dispelling any idea that the international community and its law is whatever is left after the scope of the various "sovereign" or "reserved" domains are determined—rather, the Permanent Court establishes that the purview of international law may expand without the sovereign domains "contracting" or "diminishing" in any way. This is because, as it states in *SS "Wimbledon,"* in the *Exchange of Greek and Turkish Populations*, and as Judge Anzilotti makes clear in his dissent in *Customs Union*, the assumption of international obligations is in and of itself an exercise of sovereignty.[25]

Tzanakopoulos seeks to "reverse-engineer" the Permanent Court's sense of "international community" by seeking in its holdings what he usefully designates as "'hallmarks' of an (international) community, or at least those commonly associated with the idea: the makeup of the community; the concept of obligations and action in the 'general' interest—as distinct from any individual interest of a member, even if that happens to coincide with the individual interests of other members (thereby constituting a 'common' or 'shared'—but not a general—interest); and the existence of institutions providing protection of the community interest."[26]

In addition to the United Nations, a number of functional international institutions play a role in regulating international interaction in fields ranging from aviation to trade, to development, to telecommunications. It would make little sense to discuss the regulation of global air travel solely in terms of state actors, without reference to the International Civil Aviation Organization (ICAO), an organ of the United Nations. It is true that states created the ICAO by treaty and are members of it (or not). But the body itself is certainly an actor that shapes international conduct in its sphere of competence. To the extent that civil aviation is ever a concern of the "international community," it makes sense to consider the ICAO a member of this community. And we can probably conclude that the will on the part of states to create the ICAO is clear indication that civil aviation is indeed a concern of *the* international community. There is no rival treaty organization to indicate a split among states so deep as to moot all consideration of a single international community with regard to regulation of civil aviation.

In *The Parliament of Man*, Paul Kennedy offers a history of the United Nations and its associated organs suggesting that they embody the best hope of the international community for a truly global government.[27] The United Nations is the universal body for states. Yet Kennedy himself notes the need for reform of the United Nations before it can make good on the broad promises of the preamble to its charter. Although there is arguably no higher standard for the legality and legitimacy of action on behalf of the "international community" than a unanimous Security Council resolution, decisions of the Security Council "are essentially reflective of the self-interest of its permanent members," as Rao notes.[28] Others have raised more wide-ranging questions about the utility of viewing the United Nations as the evolving global government of the international community.[29]

Nevertheless, the existence of international institutions created by states is an indication of a will to participate in *some* kind of international community. The ability of such institutions to influence international relations in their own right, and not merely as tools of states, is an indication that the international community in question includes nonstate actors as well as states. And the fact that certain international institutions exist without rival in international politics—the United Nations, the International Court of Justice, the ICAO, the World Bank, the World Trade Organization, to name but a few—is an indication that *the* international community is at work in their creation and perpetuation. But following Rao, this is not to say that *every* action on the part of such institutions is the work of the "international community," though some may be.

A COMMUNITY OF LAW

From time immemorial, states (or their precursors) have sought to establish rules for interaction that elevate international politics into something better than a permanent condition of the "war of every man against every man," in Thomas Hobbes's description of the notional "state of nature," out of which (and against which) sovereign authority arises.[30] Thus international law.

One especially influential legal perspective on international community comes from the twentieth-century legal theorist Hans Kelsen. He often refers to the "international community,"[31] but he uses the term narrowly and specifically, to refer to states that are bound to each other by treaty or by customary international law (law that is established by the routine practice of states): "All the states are members of the international community constituted by general international law, and hence are subject to that law; and a state may, without losing its character as a state, be a member of an international community constituted by particular international law, i.e., by a treaty to which the state is a contracting party."[32]

For many specialists in international law, the question of "international community" is fundamentally a question of the states to which international law applies (and to the individuals acting on the authority of a state). Kelsen's view of international law is hardly that of a minimalist: he believes that international law is superior to national law (whether one considers international law to embody a higher order of law per se or to obtain its purchase through the national law of states). But his system does not require much in the way of sociology to account for the ongoing working of international law. Once we know that there is such a thing as international law, the question of the society or community out of which it arose is of no pressing contemporary importance, whatever its historical interest. There is, for example, no general entry in the index to *Principles of International Law* for "international community."

For Kelsen, coercive authority does indeed operate in the international community of (general) international law.[33] But it is the *decentralized* authority characteristic of primitive law, rather than the centralized authority characteristic of the nation-state, with its courts and police forces. States can act on their own or with others in order to enforce international law. For example, "The state which, authorized by international law, i.e., under the conditions determined by international law, resorts to reprisals may be considered to be acting as an organ of the international community constituted by international law. The enforcement action may be interpreted as an action of this community, its reaction against a violation of international law."[34] The same principle may apply when a state goes to war against a violator of international law. Or it may be that the law may go unenforced in certain circumstances, as when a violator is too powerful to be stopped. The inability of the international community to stop any and all violators is, to Kelsen, no indication of the absence of law, which holds in all cases that violators *ought* to be punished.[35] That they sometimes go unpunished is only a product of the absence of centralization in the form of specialized organs possessing sufficient power to enforce the law.

Thomas M. Franck is especially interested in the question of states' compliance with the rules of international order. He begins his analysis of how the international system works with the observation, "In the international system, rules are not enforced and yet they are mostly obeyed."[36] In his view, the reason for this is that these rules and the institutions that support them "have a high degree of legitimacy," which "exerts a pull to compliance" that is not "powered by coercive authority."[37] The compliance is voluntary, and it is also variable based on the perception of the legitimacy of the rule. If a state (or those acting under its authority) believe that a rule is legitimate, they will adhere to it, perhaps even if certain other states do not adhere to it.

Franck believes states do this out of a sense of obligation "rooted in the notion of community." He writes: "The international system appears to be evolving a rather sophisticated normative structure without police enforcement. A sense of obligation pulls states in the direction of compliance. . . ."

Franck is not content to end the discussion on the question of voluntary compliance, however. He continues, "Though states' *compliance* with the rules may be voluntary, states' *obligation* to them is not. Nations, or those who govern them, recognize that the obligation to comply is owed by them to the community of states as the reciprocal of that community's validation of the nations' statehood."[38] Here, "community" is doing the heavy lifting of providing the "ought." What begins, in Franck, as apparently voluntary behavior based on a perception of the legitimacy of a rule becomes, in the end,

something done to preserve the "validation" of one's "statehood" by other states, though it is not entirely clear what the revocation of such "validation" would look like. Franck writes explicitly in opposition to Kelsen's invocation of decentralized coercive authority. But as a practical matter, this community-derived sense of obligation looks to be secured by a threat not readily distinguishable from that present in Kelsen's decentralized coercive authority—or perhaps is a similar work-around given the absence of such authority.

Both Kelsen and Franck seem to be seeking in international law a sovereign power above states. If they have established that such a power exists, however, it seems at most a shared normative vision about the law: that one should obey it (which most states do most of the time). Though this shared normative view may underlie the desire on the part of states and their agents to create international law, this collective will is something that the law as such does not provide.

Kelsen sees international law as binding on individuals through the mediation of the states that create it. Franck's position seems similar. Agents acting internationally on behalf of a state, including as head of state, are obliged (perhaps only in a very weak sense) to act in conformity with international law. The "international community" construed as states bound by law thus incorporates individuals as members as well, at least insofar as they are state agents.

It may be that agents of a state face domestic sanction for the failure to act in accordance with international law. Here, the coercive power of the state reasserts itself. However, there may be instances in which no domestic law compels an individual acting as agent of a state to comply with international law. President George H. W. Bush, for example, believed that he had sufficient authority under US law to undertake a military operation to eject Saddam Hussein's invading army from Kuwait in 1990–91. He nevertheless chose to seek and was able to attain Security Council authorization for military action. His decision to do so is not best understood as a case in which he was *bound* by international law, but as product of a will on his part to undertake the mission in maximal accordance with international law.

Another element of "international community," of particular importance among international lawyers, is agreement among states and their agents that certain types of political action, such as genocide and other atrocity crimes, are so offensive as to constitute crimes against humanity as a whole, and to which all governments are obliged to respond. These are known as *jus cogens* crimes, the "compelling law," out of which follow the *obligatio erga omnes*: "Above all, the characterization of certain crimes as *jus cogens* places upon states the *obligatio erga omnes* not to grant impunity to the violators of such crimes."[39] Rao argues that

> the concept of international community is at the base of the development of these two concepts which are being invoked frequently for the development and application of international law. It has also been a potent instrument in integrating the community of States and the peoples they represent into a composite legal community of mankind in as much as certain norms are set out as of higher and fundamental value to the community. The higher purposes and values represented by these superior norms, which are deemed non-derogable, constitute the basic elements of a world "constitution."[40]

The "compelling law" here has at its origin a shared normative conviction about how things should be. This conviction is something arrived at voluntarily.

Robert McCorquodale writes in opposition to what he calls "the legal doctrine that has dominated the understanding of the international legal system for centuries, . . . [giving] complete prominence to the actions of States and ignor[ing] the actions of others."[41] He describes the state as a "legal fiction" whose supposed "actions and statements are actually made by an elite of people who control decision-making inside a territorial boundary."[42] As with the state, so with the "international community." He shows how nongovernmental organizations, transnational corporations, and individuals have contributed to international politics in their own right and not solely as subunits of state actions. "Those participating in the international community will change depending on the nature of the issue involved (for example, landmines and climate change) and the requirements of international life (for example, regulating world trade). Similarly, as the international community changes and the areas governed by international law develop, then so will participation in the international legal system."[43] It is unnecessary to accept McCorquodale's description of the state as a "legal fiction"—in the modern state system, "legal fact" might be better, in contrast to natural facts concerning the physical world—in order to accept the value of his contention that the international community includes actors that are not states, nor to profit from his observation that the international community is not a fixed and permanent entity, but one whose properties and membership shift depending on the issue at hand.

The dominant state-centered legal doctrine to which McCorquodale refers and against which he argues is, in the view of Dino Kritsiotis, in the process of change: Kritsiotis notes "an incremental and increasing turn within the discipline of international law from accounts of the requirements for statehood to the idea of the formation of an *international community*." He calls this focus on the individual rather than the state "a radical alternative."[44] Bringing individuals and nonstate groupings of individuals into consideration in thinking about international politics has substantial repercussions, but it would be "radical" only if we tried to quit thinking about states altogether. Otherwise, it seems not radical but eminently reasonable.

THE SOCIOLOGY OF COMMUNITY

The prism of international law is not the only one through which the international community can refract, nor necessarily the best. As noted above, the will to comply with international law comes from somewhere other than the law itself, lacking as the international legal system does the coercive power of national law. It is born of normative preference. To speak of the "international community" is to gesture toward a widely shared vision of the good and the will to act in accordance with it.

Bruno Simma and Andreas L. Paulus argue that "the assumption that a society/community could be held together by means of legal norms alone overestimates the capacity of law and, conversely, underestimates the necessity of a societal consensus as a precondition for the formation of, and particularly respect for, legal rules."[45] The more fundamental inquiry is into the "societal consensus" or community. This applies not only within national borders but across them.

Which perhaps takes us to the sociology of community. Amitai Etzioni defines a community as "a shared moral culture and bonds of affection."[46] While the historical origins of "community" are local, there is no reason in principle why "a shared moral culture and bonds of affection" cannot exist across national borders. Indeed, in the case of major world religions, the existence of such communities is well understood. However, it is not solely *states* interacting to form an "international community" so much as

people (including statesmen). Their "shared moral culture" also gives rise to concerted action by states in setting an agenda for the international community. The voluntariness of the interchange, rather than the imposition of law in some fashion or other, would therefore seem to be at the heart of international community.

The voluntary and associational aspect of "international community" has also come to inform some contemporary legal perspectives. Harold Hongju Koh, in an article that begins as a review of Franck's book along with another, offers "transnational legal process" as the answer to the question posed in his title, "Why Do Nations Obey International Law?"[47]

> As transnational actors interact, they create patterns of behavior that ripen into institutions, regimes, and transnational networks. Their interactions generate both general norms of external conduct (such as treaties) and specific interpretation of those norms in particular circumstances . . . [such as treaty interpretations], which they in turn internalize into their domestic legal and political structures through executive action, legislation, and judicial decisions. . . . Domestic decision-making becomes "enmeshed" with international legal norms, as institutional arrangements for the making and maintenance of an international commitment become entrenched in domestic legal and political processes.[48]

Koh's approach is avowedly constructivist. A shared vision of the good becomes in many policy areas a key driver of international politics.

Anne-Marie Slaughter takes a similar approach in describing the emergence of transnational networks of policymakers, regulators, jurists, and others whose collective interaction in their areas of interest and expertise in turn shapes the behavior of their respective national governments and therefore international politics. "Even in their current form, government networks promote convergence, compliance with international agreements, and improved cooperation among nations on a wide range of regulatory and judicial issues. A world order self-consciously created out of horizontal and vertical government networks could go much further. It could create a genuine global rule of law without centralized global institutions and could engage, socialize, support and constrain government officials of every type in every nation."[49]

For both Koh and Slaughter, the associational activities of nonstate actors seem to be the glue holding the "international community" together: Their interactions end up driving the decisions and policies of national governments. It is striking that both envision the processes they depict as trending in the direction of the "entrench[ment]" (Koh) of international norms in national practice and "constrain[t]" (Slaughter) on government officials to act in accordance with them. Both seem to be reaching for something more binding than voluntary adherence.

Adeno Addis, also taking a constructivist perspective, proposes that the legal doctrine of "universal jurisdiction," according to which a government can hold a perpetrator of a *jus cogens* crime accountable regardless of whether the crime took place on its territory or involved any of its nationals, can have a constitutive effect for "international community."[50] Noting the connection of territoriality to both "community" and the idea of "jurisdiction," Addis argues that universal jurisdiction (in addition to what he sees as its instrumental utility in holding perpetrators of atrocities to account) "is partly a process through which the international community imagines its identity."[51]

These constructivist perspectives give rise to an interesting conceptual difficulty: the fluidity between descriptive and normative views of the "international community." If anarchy is what states make of it, then "international community" is what its members make of it: the interaction of states and agents of states, and other individuals and groupings of people, constitutes the international community. But Addis, in proffering this view of universal jurisdiction, is not so much describing an aspect of international community as it is. Rather, he is advocating for a more robust sense of international community, or identity, through the spread of the idea of universal jurisdiction. The constructivist perspective seeks to obtain an "is" from an "ought": If enough people (and the entities they create) act in accordance with their shared belief that certain principles should govern international conduct (or that transnational principles should govern all conduct), then, lo and behold, it is so.

The problem arises when people who seek a more robust identity for the international community realize the power of "ought" in shaping "is" and seek to hasten it along by saying that what they think *ought to be* actually *already is*. Here, it can become difficult to distinguish *advocacy* on behalf of a richer identity for the international community with a *description* of what the international community is. Here, one might run into *soi-disant* descriptions whose purpose is actually polemical—to get people to accept a particular point of view as true. If enough do so, then the polemical point of view *becomes* the truth, or so the hope runs.

Kelsen's references to "primitive law" are also telling. While in Kelsen's view we need hardly be ashamed of the condition of international law as it is now—which is to say, a law that is permanent and binding on all states and individuals acting as organs of a state—we can perhaps foresee a greater degree of centralization of the coercive enforcement power of the international community over time. Kelsen's insistence that international law is indeed backed up by coercive authority, albeit decentralized, is perhaps best understood as the judgment that international law *ought to be* backed up by coercive authority.

Etzioni, for his part, also foresees the expansion of "Global Authorities" to deal with transnational problems. He sees a de facto "Global Antiterrorism Authority" as having emerged in the aftermath of the 9/11 attack and its possible evolution into a broader "Global Safety Authority."[52] Note that international cooperation in opposition to groups that use terror tactics, though hardly lawless, is not primarily a manifestation of a legal state of affairs in which states are bound to join in fighting terrorists. Rather, it is interest-based and affinity-based: terrorists pose a common danger *and* what they do is wrong. It is therefore not only sensible but also right or just to try to stop them. This widely (but not universally) shared liberal normative aspiration is a valid expression of community whether or not coercive authority ever becomes a characteristic of international politics. Voluntariness is enough.

POWER AND "COMMUNITY"

Even the partial picture of approaches to "international community" presented here would be incomplete without taking note of some of the critical perspectives that have been offered on the subject of "international community." These views offer valuable perspective on the question of what the international community is by providing insight into potential misuses of the term.

Perhaps the most policy-relevant of these is the view that the idea of "international community," though it presents itself as the general interest of all its constituent parts, is in fact the preoccupation of a subset of international actors whose claim to speak for all is highly dubious. Rao refers to the

strong and justifiable view that the third world perspective and interests are often ignored and neglected in the development and application of international law. According to this view, many areas of international law are neither just nor equitable and hence cannot be regarded as legitimately reflecting the aspiration, needs and interests of the majority of the international community. . . . As long as self-help in international relations is made to seem inevitable and States are not obliged to stand as equals before the law, the emerging concept of international community will remain more a theory than a reality.[53]

If this is true to any degree, then it is also possible to call into question the motives of those who presume to speak in the name of the "international community." As William D. Jackson writes, "The importance of the quest for legitimacy in international politics should not be underestimated. In this general and continuing quest, states or international institutions find it useful to claim that their actions are expressions of or are done in the service of an international community. The nature of the international community in whose name so much is claimed is rarely indicated by those who invoke its authority. Indeed, the legitimizing function of the concept of the *international community* is served by its mystification."[54]

In particular, views of "international community" may be shaped by such considerations as who has power in the international political arena and how one stands in relation to the powerful.[55] As a very powerful country (if not indeed a hegemon, whether in fact or by aspiration), the United States might be prone to a view of "international community" that both reflects and justifies its position of preeminence. Andreas Paulus has identified what he considers

the specific incidence of the US approach to the characteristics of the international community: [1] the enthusiasm about the universalization of democratic and liberal values after the end of communism; [2] the significance, if any, of institutions as an intervening, not as an independent, variable; [3] the informality of legal processes, ultimately resulting in the lack of distinction between "is" and "ought"; and, not least [4] the distinction between "liberal" and "non-liberal" law [especially as articulated by John Rawls], resulting in an apparent disregard for the remaining pluralism in the multifaceted international community.[56]

These views are of a piece with

the distinctive features of American ideology at the beginning of the twenty-first century, [which] point in three directions: 1. a reluctance with regard to an all-encompassing institutionalization of the international realm, combined with an insistence on national prerogatives; 2. a reliance on the universality of democracy, human rights and the market economy as basic conditions for international welfare and as minimal conditions for the legitimacy of governments, protecting them from foreign intervention; and 3. the realist insistence on the relevance of (national) power and capabilities compared to the lack of resources at the international level, and the insistence on super-power prerogatives.[57]

Paulus essentially warns of the danger of an "Americanized" international community, in which Americans advance a view of "international community" and its aspirations that is not readily distinguishable from American habits and aspirations. This is indeed a serious problem with regard to diverging views of what the international community *ought to be*. Non-American perspectives might seek more powerful international institutions and less leeway for the exercise of national power. But as the international community *is*, as it actually mani-

fests itself, the liberal normative aspiration that it does indeed embody is not distinctly American but much broader.

THE INCLUSIVE "WE"

Most of those who write about "community," including the "international community," regard "community" in a positive light. A more radical critique argues that the "we-feeling" of community can exist only in relation to an excluded "Other," and therefore refuses to accord "difference" the respect it deserves. Simma and Paulus write that

> a "community" does not only possess an inside aspect but also presupposes an outside, an environment against which it defines and delineates its identity. In the case of an all-embracing community like the international one, it is unclear who or what constitutes this "outside": Does it only consist of those with whom nobody wants to deal, namely, terrorist "rogue states"? But even these outcasts are not fully excluded from international relations and institutions. Does the "international community" personify a particular civilization and value system, namely, a "Western" way of life, and therefore exclude groups opposing those values—religious fundamentalists or advocates of "Asian values," to name a few? But if this is the case, how can the international community engage people and peoples from different cultural backgrounds?[58]

Etzioni recognizes the problem for communitarianism associated with disregard for the Other and proposes to solve it as follows: "the new 'they' are weapons of mass destruction and pandemics; they fully qualify as enemies of humanity."[59] He seems to be reaching for a nonhuman "they" in order to avoid the charge of exclusion of a class of human beings. But the "they-ness" of weapons of mass destruction may depend at least to a degree on whether the case at hand involves a state with a nuclear deterrent capability or an individual with a quantity of sarin seeking to release it to kill others. It is possible that a perpetrator of *jus cogens* crimes is an Other rightly excluded.

But a better answer to the radical critique that "we" implies an excluded "they" might be to ask why this is necessarily so. Certainly, it is true that "we" *can* imply "they," and historically, the manifestation of this phenomenon has led to monstrous consequences. But "we" do not require the living presence of the human perpetrators of an ongoing Holocaust in order to oppose genocide and *genocidaires*. "We" harbor the aspiration that everyone voluntarily considers herself a part of this "we"—chooses to associate with "us." The content of the association may be very limited—say, that "we" agree that genocide is wrong. But it is also potentially richer: "We" may agree that even though "we" acknowledge the possibility that "we" will fight wars against each other, "we" will conduct these wars only within codes of conduct "we" have specified in detail. Or richer still: "we" agree "we" will never resort to force to settle our disputes. In none of these instances does "we-ness" imply an excluded Other. Rather, it contains an invitation to join.

And if the invitee rejects the invitation? That would seem to depend on the character of the rejection. If it is a total rejection— another group with a sense of "we" that is deliberately imagined with an excluded "they," which in this case is us—then "we" had better keep our distance and respond to threatening behavior as it arises. But at the state level, it is a long way to get to total rejection—one would be looking for something like the slaughter of all foreign visitors as an indication of it. In almost all cases, there is at least some level of stable interaction between states, such as the guarantee of safe passage for envoys of other states. "We" can consider this bare minimum a partially accepted invitation—and work to build on this de minimis sense of international community if "we" wish.

As McCorquodale writes: "While humans wish to form communities, there are . . . great varieties of ideas and values within a community and so there does not have to be an exact sharing of values for a community to exist. In fact a vast array of 'communities' exist, from epistemic to intentional, and include religious communities and other self-identifying communities."[60] Similarly, Georges Abi-Saab notes, "Sociologically speaking, . . . 'community' is a relative concept and its existence is a question of degree. It can exist in one group with regard to one point, but not necessarily with regard to others, and may similarly exist in different degrees of intensity."[61]

The point of this sense of community in relation to the international community is that what begins as the barest minimum of stable interaction beyond total rejection is something upon which those in that relation may build, overlaying other elements of "community" to the degree the parties themselves wish. "Identity" is not necessarily fixed, and for many it may be possible to layer on different identities without having them come into conflict with one another. Where such a conflict arises, the buildup of "community" may stop until the conflict is resolved, if indeed it can be. But the cessation of additional overlaying does not necessarily (or even routinely) undo the layers already in place. World War I brought early-twentieth-century globalization to a halt. But even so cataclysmic an event, and the even more destructive war that followed, did not undo the desire for richer international interaction, or international community. Few were the countries that pursued policies of isolation, autarky, and self-sufficiency, spurning all interaction with foreigners in the manner of Japan in the two-plus centuries before the arrival of Commodore Matthew Perry in

1854. Perhaps North Korean *juche* is the exception that proves the rule.

I have written elsewhere of what I then considered the most highly developed "transnational ethical community," namely the "Atlanticist community," joining the United States and Canada with Europe.[62] By now, the project of European integration probably deserves acknowledgment for pushing a transnational ethical community to a new level—though not necessarily at the expense of the Atlanticist community. The recent movement toward a trans-Atlantic trade agreement indicates a desire for further integration, likely resulting in a deepening sense of community. The desire may be based in mutual interest, but the likely effect will also include a deepening sense of community.

But though it is an element of the "international community," the Atlanticist community must be careful not to represent itself as *the* "international community" or everywhere a spokesman for the aspirations of the international community. When the Indian ambassador to the United Nations in 1999 rebuked the NATO secretary-general for saying that the alliance was taking military action against Slobodan Milosevic over Kosovo in the name of the "international community," pointing out that the governments of half of humankind opposed the action, he had a compelling point regardless of one's view about whether the military action was justified.[63] The Atlanticist community does not constitute some sort of authoritative layer of international community and should not represent itself as such.

To say as much is also to acknowledge that other transnational communities may gather and pursue common ends. The Non-Aligned Movement is one example, as is the Group of Seventy-Seven developing countries, whose membership now numbers 132. At the other end of global economic development is the Organisation for Economic Co-operation and Development (OECD). These organizations, likewise, have considerable reach and influence, but they too lack authority to speak for the international community as a whole, even though they may at times express the view of the international community. To look at it another way, if the international community is truly speaking, it will find itself doing so in harmony with the views of such transnational associations.

The International Community at Work

It is not hard to see some of the layers of international community in operation. At the most rudimentary level, states send and receive ambassadors, who enjoy diplomatic immunity. They gather at the United Nations, the universal body for states. They appear as parties at the International Court of Justice. They participate and deliberate in functional institutions, such as the International Civil Aviation Organization, whose decisions they accept voluntarily as those of the international community even though their preferred outcome might have differed. They agree to and abide by rules regulating international commerce. They band together in association with nongovernmental organizations (NGOs) to provide relief to countries struck by natural disasters. Often through the prodding of individuals and NGOs, they enshrine in treaties rules that govern the conduct of states, such as the prohibition of genocide and the use of chemical weapons. In all these instances, the international community is a liberal force regulating international politics.

The international community is not a world government, in the sense of a sovereign power. There is no such power, and it makes no sense to speak of the "international community" as if it were an actor asserting sovereign power, or aspiring to do so. In what sense is the secretary-general of the United Nations president of the world? In exactly no sense. Yet there are examples of states, acting in concert, that claim the mantle of the "international community" and do seem to represent something more than an aggregation of self-interested state action. Disaster relief operations often fall into this category—concerted executive action *by* governments in the name of the "international community." Turning to the realm of coercive force, the action with the best claim to have been undertaken on behalf of the international community was probably the ejection of Saddam Hussein from Kuwait in 1991. In addition to drawing a broad coalition of support, the military action took place with the authorization of the Security Council.[64]

This sort of executive action on behalf of the international community seems to require a strongly articulated and widely accepted moral justification beyond the national interests of the states involved. A humanitarian relief operation would enjoy no such legitimacy if, for example, it were merely a pretext for the introduction of military forces of the intervening state or states into the territory where the disaster struck. Although "No war for oil" was a slogan of the opposition to the 1991 Iraq war, supporters insisted that Iraq's aggression against Kuwait should not stand because aggression in pursuit of territorial aggrandizement is wrong.

Just as the international community is not synonymous with *world government*, neither is it synonymous with *global governance*, the latter understood here to mean the proceedings of the broad array of international and regional institutions, organizations, and other mechanisms that seek to structure and shape international politics, including through international law. Yet the proliferation over the past century of these institutions, as well as less formal associations, is noteworthy in

its own right, and especially for the extent to which states and their agents have actively sought the creation of new institutions. These institutions truly do facilitate coordinated state action.

But not just *any* kind of state action: There is, for example, no Organization of Pirate States. Nor is there a Geneva-based World Genocide Organization devoted to the collection and dissemination of information to improve the practice of atrocity. There is, however, an International Criminal Court designed to go after *genocidaires*. The direction of this quasi-governance seems unmistakable: The moral principles being advanced are those of classical liberalism.

Synonymous with neither *world government* nor *global governance*, the international community is likewise not simply the aggregation of the individuals who speak in its name, though people do. Humanity as a whole has never appointed a spokesperson. From time to time, many individuals and governments can and will oppose the judgments of such a self-styled "international community," and their dissent is proof in itself that the "international community" is not the speaker. A highly networked transnational group of like-minded individuals cannot constitute itself as the conscience of humanity if large segments of humanity are entirely deaf to its appeals.

Yet such a transnational network (or network of networks) actually does exist. When members speak in the name of humanity, they may be engaging in a bit of self-aggrandizement, and may even be seeking to further private interests (an elevation in the pecking order within the world of international NGOs, for example). The claims members make may overstate normative agreement even within the network. But this network is something more than merely an aggregation of self-interested individuals who have determined that they can better attain their common interests by ganging up on their opponents. As a counterexample of a purely self-interested network, think of an organized crime family, or, at the state level, perhaps the Axis powers during World War II.

On the contrary, there is *content* to the consort, a vision of the good that extends beyond simply what is good for members of the network. The content is not uncontested among members of the network. For example, the "international community" does not want Iran to acquire a nuclear weapons capability, but disagrees on whether a military strike on Iran should be an option. Yet not everything is up for grabs. One will find no members of the international community arguing in favor of the return of slavery, or for government based on the "divine right of kings."

So the international community is not the executive actor of some notional world government but does sometimes act; is not the agent of global governance but sometimes governs; and is not all those who claim to speak in its name, though sometimes those who speak in its name are right to do so. Rather, the "international community" is on the one hand the voice of classically liberal normative aspiration: what the world should be like. But on the other hand, this is an aspiration whose avatar can and does appear in the world, in various forms, and actually does influence politics among nations. Its appearance on the scene has something to do with the workings of traditional diplomacy and the interplay of the national interest of various states, but also encompasses an ongoing transnational dialogue about right and wrong.

So with the term "international community," we find ourselves at the always interesting intersection of morality and politics, but on a global scale. Classically liberal normative aspiration comes in many guises, from various forms of cosmopolitanism and

universalism on one side to various particular iterations such as "American exceptionalism" or "Western civilization" on the other. Those who feel an affinity for this normative aspiration already have a layer of membership in the international community atop their other layers of identity. There is an evident willingness to consider right and wrong on a global scale.

Currently, there seem to be some practical limits to the scope of this dialogue. Thomas Franck, following John Rawls, has proposed "fairness" as a standard for international law and the action of international institutions. The pursuit of Rawlsian fairness, or distributive justice, would seek to answer the basic question Franck identifies as that of Socrates and Jeremy Bentham: "'What shall we do about sharing and conserving in order to maximize human well-being?'"[65] It is easy to see how international efforts to address such subjects as global poverty and development, environmental regulation, and climate change might fall within such a "fairness" rubric.

It is also easy to see that these are subjects with which international politics and the international community have a hard time dealing effectively. Adoption of a global reform agenda aimed at "sharing and conserving in order to maximize human well-being" seems particularly difficult in light of the difficulties such endeavors encounter even at the national level. Of course, this is not to say that the difficulty of obtaining a comprehensive and permanent answer precludes the search for provisional and incremental improvement.

International politics may be somewhat more responsive when it comes to sudden negative departures from the status quo. Here, earthquakes and tsunamis enter the picture, as well as wars for territorial expansion. Genocide and other atrocities may be joining the list. If justice or morality (or even law) can be construed first as a matter of annulling an instance of injustice or mitigating the effects of the occurrence of something bad, with the aim of restoring a status quo ante that was better, we may be on firmer footing about what we can hope for from the international community.

Even here, however, we should be careful about loose talk of "international community." A hallmark of the true operation of the international community is unanimity of purpose, or something very close to it. When a tsunami strikes, what emerges nowadays is a single, coordinated effort to provide relief. Although NGOs working on such problems perceive competition among themselves and jockey for relative influence, we do not generally see a "Red Team/Blue Team" conflict over the provision of aid. While complete consensus on the propriety of ejecting Saddam Hussein from Kuwait by force if necessary was elusive, no coalition emerged in support of his contention that Kuwait was rightfully Iraq's nineteenth province. If there is an international coalition in favor of Iran obtaining a nuclear arsenal, it seems not to be one that speaks up to that effect.

But when there is significant opposition to a favored course, even if that course is favored by many, including all of one's friends and colleagues, it is surely disingenuous to invoke the "international community." Policymakers should take heed. One can and should offer one's reasons for the course one believes is right without suggesting that all of humankind agrees. It is a matter of reason and elemental respect for others, and it has the practical benefit of warding off self-delusion and the negative consequences that flow from it.

Our loose talk of "international community" comes at a price, in terms of sometimes inflated, sometimes diminished expectations about the ability of international politics to be brought into alignment with an evolving yet classically liberal moral order—

whose political authority consists in its voluntary acceptance by growing numbers of people, even including governments.

Those of realist inclination should be willing to make room in their view of the world for, at a minimum, an international community that comes and goes depending on the issue and the competing demands of international politics. When almost all the world lines up one way and not another—for trade, against piracy, for tsunami relief, against territorial expansion by conquest—a realist (or indeed anyone) might see the result as (merely) common interest. But when almost all the world talks about what may be merely common interest in terms of right and wrong, the notion of an international community constituted thereby is hardly far-fetched.

Perhaps those of liberal persuasion can avoid the temptation to substitute their normative desires regarding the "international community" for acknowledgment that the universal aspirations of classical liberalism are far from realized. In exchange, they can take comfort that the liberal vision is indeed the animating force behind international community.

Conservatives and neoconservatives could perhaps recognize that a key ingredient of US exceptionalism from the beginning was its classical liberalism, a sentiment non-Americans nowadays can and do share—forming an international community that perpetuates, defends, and seeks to spread a classically liberal perspective on right and wrong.

We policymakers and students of policymaking need to be careful what we are asking for and of whom we ask it when we ask something of the "international community." Otherwise, we are likely to end up disappointed in "its" inability to fulfill our expectations—a disappointment that is actually the product of our own failure to think about the international community clearly. The purpose of this chapter is to try to tighten up our discussion of the "international community" in order to improve our ability to conceive and execute policy in a moral framework. This liberal moral framework has found itself embraced and embodied from time to time, at least in part, in particular states, institutions, organizations, offices, and individuals—and in the interactions among them. This is the international community, and its significance in international politics is growing.

NOTES

Thanks to Ben Atlas for research assistance.

1. For example, "The damages caused in Haiti by the earthquake of January 12, 2010 are unimaginable. But the response from the international community—from Asia to Africa, from the United States, from Canada, from all of Latin America, from the Caribbean, from Europe, all the way to the Middle East—this response, thanks to its swiftness, thanks to its size, was commensurate with the disaster." President René Préval, "Joint Remarks in the White House with President Obama" (March 10, 2010), http://www.whitehouse.gov/the-press-office/remarks-president-obama-and-president-preval-republic-haiti.

2. See, for example, International Federation for Human Rights, Burma's "Critical Human Rights Situation: Time for the International Community to Act," *Refworld*, April 10, 2010, http://www.refworld.org/docid/4bfd1bcf28.html, accessed July 3, 2013.

3. For example, "While Kenya has experienced election-related violence since the early 1990s, the 2008 post-poll violence remains etched on the minds of the international community and we shall do all we can to stop a repeat of the same." UN Special Advisor of the Prevention of Genocide Adama Dieng, quoted in Fred Oluoch, "UN official warns against poll-related violence in Kenya," *The East African,* February 16, 2013, http://www.theeastafrican.co.ke/news/UN-official-warns-against-poll-related-violence-in-Kenya-/-/2558/1696148/-/3nn7noz/-/index.html.

4. For example, "This military action is intended to support the political aims of the international community." Press statement by NATO Secretary-General Javier Solana, March 23, 1999, http://www.nato.int/docu/pr/1999/p99-040e.htm.

5. For example, "SARS was a wake-up call for the international community, demonstrating just how quickly diseases can emerge and spread around the world." Public Health Agency of Canada, "Responding to an Infectious Disease Outbreak: Progress between SARS and Pandemic Influenza H1N1" (Public Health Agency of Canada, April 11, 2012), http://www.phac-aspc.gc.ca/ep-mu/rido-iemi/index-eng.php.

6. For example, "Humanitarian needs are escalating, in and beyond Syria. The international community should not look the other way as violence spirals out of control. Brutal human rights abuses continue to be committed, mainly by the Government, but also by opposition groups." United Nations Secretary-General Ban Ki-moon, "Address to the 67th General Assembly general debate," September 25, 2012, http://www.un.org/apps/news/infocus/sgspeeches/statments_full.asp?statID=1660#.UcJR-T771G4.

7. See Karl W. Deutsch, "From Aristotle to the Modern Nation-State," chap. 1 in *Political Community at the International Level,* reprint edition (Salt Lake City, UT: Aardvark Global Publishing, 1954), 3–43.

8. In addition to Mearsheimer's *Tragedy of Great Power Politics* (New York: W. W. Norton, 2001); see Kenneth N. Waltz, *Theory of International Politics* (New York: McGraw-Hill, 1979).

9. For a brief survey, see G. John Ikenberry, "Liberal Internationalism 3.0: America and the Dilemmas of Liberal Order," *Perspectives on Politics* 7, no. 1 (March 2009): 71–87.

10. Charter of the United Nations, Article 24.

11. Alexander Wendt, "Anarchy Is What States Make of It: The Social Construction of Power Politics," *International Organization* 46, no. 2 (Spring 1992): 391–425.

12. Postmodern critical theory also warrants a place in this discussion and would seem to map readily onto a constructivist perspective. See, for example, David Kennedy, "The Disciplines of International Law and Policy," *Leiden Journal of International Law* 12 (1999): 9–133; and Richard

Price and Christian Reus-Smit, "Dangerous Liaisons? Critical International Theory and Constructivism," *European Journal of International Relations* 4, no. 3 (1998): 259–94.

13. "Foreign policy in a Republican administration will . . . proceed from the firm ground of the national interest, not from the interests of an illusory international community." Condoleezza Rice, "Promoting the National Interest," *Foreign Affairs* 79, no. 1 (January–February 2000): 45–62. Subsequently, as secretary of state, Rice embraced the utility of the phrase, for example, "States where corruption and chaos and cruelty reign, invariably pose threats to their neighbors, threats to their regions and potential threats to the entire international community." Address at Sciences-politiques, Paris, February 8, 2005, http://www.washingtonpost.com/wp-dyn/articles/A7965-2005Feb8.html.

14. For example: "It is clear that NATO will not listen to the Security Council. It would appear that it believes itself to be above the law. . . . Those who continue to attack the Federal Republic of Yugoslavia profess to do so on behalf of the international community and on pressing humanitarian grounds. They say that they are acting in the name of humanity. Very few members of the international community have spoken in this debate, but even among those who have, NATO would have noted that China, Russia and India have all opposed the violence that it has unleashed. The international community can hardly be said to have endorsed their actions when already representatives of half of humanity have said that they do not agree with what they have done." Kamlesh Sharma, permanent representative of the Republic of India to the United Nations (March 26, 1999). United Nations S/PV 3989, http://www.un.org/ga/search/view_doc.asp?symbol=S/PV.3989.

15. For example: "By 2015, will Israel be even more isolated by a hostile international community?" Mitt Romney (speech at The Citadel, Charleston, South Carolina, October 7, 2011), http://blogs.wsj.com/washwire/2011/10/07/text-of-mitt-romneys-speech-on-foreign-policy-at-the-citadel//.

16. Yasuaki Onuma, "When Was the Law of International Society Born? An Inquiry of the History of International Law from an Intercivilizational Perspective," *Journal of the History of International Law* 2 (2000): 62–64.

17. Hedley Bull, *The Anarchical Society*, 3rd ed. (New York: Columbia University Press, 2002), 13.

18. Robert H. Jackson, "The Political Theory of International Society," in *International Relations Theory Today*, ed. Ken Booth and Steve Smith (University Park: Pennsylvania State University Press, 1995), 110.

19. Chris Brown, "International Political Theory and the Idea of World Community," in Ken Booth and Steve Smith, eds., *International Relations Theory Today*, 90.

20. Andreas Paulus, "The Influence of the United States on the Concept of the 'International Community,'" chap. 2 in *United States Hegemony and the Foundations of International Law*, ed. Michael Byers and Georg Nolte (Cambridge: Cambridge University Press, 2003).

21. Pemmaraju Sreenivasa Rao, "The Concept of International Community in International Law: Theory and Reality," in *International Law between Universalism and Fragmentation: Festschrift in Honour of Gerhard Hafner*, ed. Isabelle Busford et al. (Leiden: Martinus Nijhoff, 2008), 85.

22. William D. Jackson, "Thinking about *International Community* and Its Alternatives," in *Community, Diversity, and a New World Order: Essays in Honor of Inis L. Claude, Jr.*, Kenneth W. Thompson (Lanham, MD: University Press of America, 1994), 4.

23. Bruno Simma and Andreas L. Paulus, "The 'International Community': Facing the Challenge of Globalization," *European Journal of International Law* 9 (1998): 267.

24. Kofi A. Annan, "The Meaning of International Community," UNIS/SG/2478 (December 30, 1999).

25. Antonios Tzanakopoulos, "The Permanent Court of International Justice and the 'International Community,'" in *Legacies of the Permanent Court of International Justice*, ed. M. Fitzmaurice and C. J. Tams (Leiden: Martinus Nijhoff, 2013), 339–59, accessed through Social Science Research Network (SSRN), http://papers.ssrn.com/sol3/papers.cfm?abstract_id=2043914 (passage at SSRN: 9–10).

26. Tzanakopoulos, "Permanent Court," 3–4.

27. Paul Kennedy, *The Parliament of Man: The Past, Present and Future of the United Nations* (New York: Random House, 2006).

28. Rao, "Concept of International Community," 102.

29. See Kenneth Anderson, *Living with the UN: American Responsibilities and International Order* (Stanford, CA: Hoover Institution Press, 2012).

30. Thomas Hobbes, *Leviathan* (1651, Oxford University Press reprint, 2012), chap. XIII.

31. For examples, see Hans Kelsen, *Principles of International Law* (New York: Rinehart and Co., 1952; Lawbook Exchange ed., 2003, 2012), 19, 22, 25, 111.

32. Ibid., 110–11.

33. Ibid., 16, 36, 110–14.

34. Ibid., 25.

35. Ibid., 6–10.

36. Thomas M. Franck, *The Power of Legitimacy among Nations* (Oxford: Oxford University Press, 1990), 3. The observation echoes that of Louis Henkin: "It is probably the case that almost all nations observe almost all principles of international law and almost all of their obligations almost all the time." See Louis Henkin, *How Nations Behave: Law and Foreign Policy*, 2nd ed. (New York: Columbia University Press, 1979), 47.

37. Ibid., 24–25.

38. Ibid., 196.

39. M. Cherif Bassiouni, "International Crimes: *Jus Cogens* and *Obligatio Erga Omnes*," *Law and Contemporary Problems* 59, no. 4 (Autumn 1996): 66.

40. Rao, "Concept of International Community," 93–94.

41. Robert McCorquodale, "International Community and State Sovereignty: An Uneasy Symbiotic Relationship" in *Towards an "International Legal Community"? The Sovereignty of States and the Sovereignty of International Law,* ed. Colin Warbrick and Stephen Tierney (British Institute of International and Comparative Law, 2006), 241–65, http://ssrn.com/abstract=2088888 (passage at SSRN: 2).

42. Ibid., 4.

43. Ibid., 13.

44. Dino Kritsiotis, "Imagining the International Community," *European Journal of International Law* 13, no. 4 (2002): 963.

45. Simma and Paulus, "International Community," 267–68.

46. Amitai Etzioni, *From Empire to Community: A New Approach to International Relations* (New York: Palgrave Macmillan, 2004), 49.

47. Harold Hongju Koh, "Why Do Nations Obey International Law?" *Yale Law Journal,* 106 (1996–97): 2645–59.

48. Ibid., 2654.

49. Anne-Marie Slaughter, *A New World Order* (Princeton, NJ: Princeton University Press, 2005), 261.

50. Adeno Addis, "Imagining the International Community: The Constitutive Dimension of Universal Jurisdiction," *Human Rights Quarterly* 31 (2009): 129–62.

51. Ibid., 132.

52. Etzioni, *Empire to Community*, 124–25.

53. Rao, "Concept of International Community," 103–4.

54. Jackson, "Thinking about *International Community*," 6.

55. As it applies to the United States, this is David Kennedy's subject in "Disciplines of International Law and Policy."

56. Paulus, "Influence of the United States," 74–75.

57. Ibid., 87.

58. Simma and Paulus, "International Community, 268.

59. Etzioni, *Empire to Community*, 195.

60. McCorquodale, "International Community and State Sovereignty," 241–65.

61. Georges Abi-Saab, "Whither the International Community?" *European Journal of International Law* 9 (1998): 249.

62. Tod Lindberg, "The Atlanticist Community," in *Beyond Paradise and Power: Europe, America and the Future of a Troubled Partnership,* ed. Tod Lindberg (New York: Routledge, 2005), 215–36. Also published as "'We,'" *Policy Review* 128 (December 2008–January 2009), http://www.hoover.org/publications/policy-review/article/7054.

63. See note 14.

64. United Nations Security Council Resolution 678. Available at: http://daccess-dds-ny.un.org/doc/RESOLUTION/GEN/NR0/575/28/IMG/NR057528.pdf?OpenElement. Even here, however, the vote was not unanimous, with Cuba and Yemen opposing and China abstaining.

65. Thomas Franck, *Fairness in International Law and Institutions* (Oxford: Oxford University Press, 1995), 9.

31

POSTBELLUM PEACEBUILDING
LAW, JUSTICE, AND DEMOCRATIC PEACEBUILDING

Michael W. Doyle

One of the best ways to prevent future wars is to prevent repeat wars—to successfully build a peace where before there was armed conflict.[1] Unfortunately, we all know that defensive wars successfully fought to victory can sometimes produce only a short peace. And even well-motivated armed interventions can produce more harm than good if the intervention is incapable of transitioning to a self-determining, rights-respecting, welfare-enhancing, stable government. Most interventions, whether well intentioned or not, produce one of the three harmful consequences that John Stuart Mill hypothesized in his classic 1859 critical essay on intervention: another civil war, an oppressive regime, or a dependent colony.[2] Just and successful interventions leading to a postbellum peace are not impossible, but they are very difficult; about half of the consent-based peacekeeping operations fail.

The general record of repeat wars and harmful interventions suggests that victors,

even in just defensive wars, and interveners, even in just interventions, should have an obligation to take care that a justifiable postbellum transition is achieved. This, in turn, raises three questions: First, what are the applicable rules under international law for lawful occupations, and are they adequate? Second, what postbellum transformations are ethically permissible (or even required) in order to better realize widely recognized basic human rights? And third, are the permissible transformations effective in achieving a just and stable peace?

This chapter leads to three conclusions. Existing occupation law is inadequate to address these challenges. It should be reformed to permit ethically permissible and advantageous transformational peacebuilding. And legitimate peacebuilding strategies can work, provided they win the self-determining consent of the temporarily occupied, and are appropriately planned and resourced.

To explore these issues, this chapter describes existing international legal standards for occupation before turning to the external and internal policy measures that have been designed to make a peace just and lasting. The chapter comments on the "unconditional surrender" of Japan, the UN Security Council's mandate for the occupation of Iraq in 2003, and the peacebuilding strategy in Cambodia (1991–93) as examples of efforts to build peace while avoiding what has been called "liberal imperial peacebuilding." The chapter concludes with a discussion of what can make peacebuilding feasible and effective.

INTERNATIONAL LAW

In traditional international law, the use of armed force was not unlawful. States were permitted to, at their will, conquer territories, annex them, and assume sovereign rights over their populations.[3] Although the Peace of Westphalia of 1648 imposed limits against forcible religious conversion, there were few other limits on the use of force.[4] In the nineteenth century, a set of norms emerged to civilize war by constraining the rights of belligerent occupation. These norms emphasized an occupation's temporary character, one preliminary to the disposition of a peace treaty. An occupation could not legalize annexation, which was permitted only through a surrender agreement of an established sovereign.[5] In the meantime, the laws of occupation established rights for occupiers and rights for the occupied. When the Kellogg-Briand Pact of 1928 and the UN Charter of 1945 outlawed wars of aggression and established the principle of national self-determination, territory acquired by force was generally deemed illegitimate.

There thus emerged a tension between, on the one hand, the record of surrenders—which seemed to allow for complete discretion, even (as after World War II, "unconditional surrender") transferring complete sovereignty to the occupier—and, on the other hand, the law of occupation, which became the only operative, general law governing postbellum responsibilities.

Today, both sets of rules are governed by the UN Charter. Article 2(4) prohibits the use or threat of force among states other than in individual or collective self-defense, and Article 2(7) prohibits the United Nations' interference in domestic affairs, other than as required to preserve international peace and security when so determined by the Security Council. No occupation—and nothing but a defensive war—can be fully legal without multilateral authorization.

The Hague Regulations of 1907 and the Fourth Geneva Convention of 1949 define the accepted laws of occupation. Their essence is conservation: occupiers have a duty to protect the occupied, maintain law and order, protect private property, and ensure the delivery of social services, such as public health care (Geneva IV, Article 56), within the limits of what is reasonable. In turn, the occupied population has duties not to resist the occupiers (if they wish to enjoy protected civilian status), follow lawful regulations, and even pay taxes to cover the expenses of the occupation. Conservation thus supplanted transformation—occupiers are not permitted to reform the laws, promote human rights not already recognized in local law, change the constitution, democratize, or promote social equity. They must instead preserve the status quo antebellum. Article 43 of the Hague Convention summarizes the requirements as follows:

> The authority of the legitimate power having in fact passed into the hands of the occupant, the latter shall take all the measures in his power to restore, and ensure, as far as possible, public order and safety, while respecting, unless absolutely prevented, the laws in force in the country.[6]

The Geneva Convention shifts the focus of responsibilities directly to the rights of "protected persons" in the occupied territory and substantially enhances those rights. But, while more flexible, the Geneva Convention also stresses conservation of laws and the constitution, unless changes are necessary to respect the rights of the protected set forth in the convention, as in Articles 47 and 64:

> Article 47. Protected persons who are in occupied territory shall not be deprived, in any case or in any manner whatsoever, of the benefits of the present Convention by any change introduced, as the result of the occupation of a territory, into the institutions or government of the said territory, nor by any agreement concluded between the authorities of the occupied territories and the Occupying Power, nor by any annexation by the latter of the whole or part of the occupied territory.[7]

> Article 64. The penal laws of the occupied territory shall remain in force, with the exception that they may be repealed or suspended by the Occupying Power in cases where they constitute a threat to its security or an obstacle to the application of the present Convention. Subject to the latter consideration and to the necessity for ensuring the effective administration of justice, the tribunals of the occupied territory shall continue to function in respect of all offences covered by the said laws. The Occupying Power may, however, subject the population of the occupied territory to provisions which are essential to enable the Occupying Power to fulfill its obligations under the present Convention, to maintain the orderly government of the territory, and to ensure the security of the Occupying Power, of the members and property of the occupying forces or administration, and likewise of the establishments and lines of communication used by them.[8]

Article 43 of the Hague Convention, concluded seven years before the outbreak of World War I, is understandable as a rule to limit constitutional changes among European states sharing a common sense of civilized comity. Barring a "standing menace" or the collapse of civil order, occupations of other legitimate sovereigns should be temporary and conservative. But the Geneva Conventions of 1949 are harder to explain. In the aftermath of World War II and the Holocaust, and in the middle of radical attempts to de-Nazify Germany and create new legal orders across Western and Eastern Europe, the conventions may reflect attempts by each bloc, capitalist and communist, to limit the transformations imposed by the other. But they do not reflect what each did in its own sphere based on the unconditional surrender agreements they imposed. Nor do they reflect what one might want to, or should, do in the aftermath of anything but a limited war among states recognizing each other's legitimacy.

JUS POST BELLUM

Turning to the ethics of just war, what should occupiers be allowed to do and what should they be held responsible for doing? Complementing traditional *jus ad bellum* (justification for war) and *jus in bello* (just conduct in war), scholars are arguing that we must also assess *jus post bellum*, or "justice after war." This raises the question of whether, like the traditional *justices*, justice after war should be judged semi-independently. Can interventions be in accordance with the requirements of *jus ad bellum* and *jus in bello*, but fail the principles of *jus post bellum*, and vice versa? Whatever one thinks of the justice of going to war with Iraq, can the United States leave without helping Iraqis build a legitimate state? Former US secretary of state Colin Powell has reportedly called this (in regard to occupying Iraq in 2003) the "Pottery Barn Doctrine: You break it, you own it."[9] But is it possible?

In our time, the classic reference is "de-Nazification" in Germany following World

War II and the breaking up of the imperial principle, the militarist faction, and the *zaibatsu*, in Japan. The Allies clearly had a right to end German and Japanese aggression and drive their armies back to their borders. But were they entitled to also reform Germany and Japan? If so, what cost, Michael Walzer asks, should the victors and vanquished pay to guarantee reliable security?[10] Alternatively, when instead should the victors relinquish the goals of unconditional surrender and peacebuilding in order to spare the lives that a campaign for total conquest will cost?

Walzer poses, and also sharpens, this modern moral conundrum, but without fully resolving it. Should a negotiated arrangement have been struck with Nazi Germany, had it been willing to surrender to the Western Allies? The special nature of the evil of Nazism makes it apparent that this was not a deal many, including Walzer, would have wanted to be made, even to save the lives of many Allied soldiers and noncombatant Germans. But Walzer does not address the preventive arguments for postwar pacific reconstruction. He, like many liberals, would have preferred a German revolution that toppled Nazism and with which the Allies could then have made peace. But he also argues that Nazi leaders should have been punished and, lacking a German revolution, that occupying Germany was necessary. The Nazis' trial would have been an act of "collective abhorrence" for their crimes, rather than an act to prevent future aggression.[11]

Walzer further argues that Japan's government should have been accommodated. Thus, the atomic bombs dropped on Hiroshima and Nagasaki, along with the firebombing of Tokyo and other Japanese cities, were unjustified as violating *jus in bello* restrictions on killing noncombatants. Indeed, the United States dropped the two atomic bombs on military targets, but with radically disproportionate effects on noncombatants. The evident purpose behind the destruction of those cities was to coerce the Japanese war cabinet into surrender. Unfortunately, the two bombs were barely adequate for the purpose of persuading the war cabinet to surrender on terms likely to make the peace last. The victors conceded the continuation of an imperial figurehead, but demanded the authority to reconstruct Japan. It is not at all clear that the war cabinet would have accepted this demand without the shock of the two bombs or the entry of the Soviet Union into the war against Japan. Both together seemed to have tipped the decision toward surrender.[12]

Leaving Japan in the hands of those who launched the conquest of Asia would have been unwise. For some skeptics, talking about noncombatant protection in the era of the bombings of Shanghai, Nanjing, Coventry, London, Hamburg, and Dresden is akin to handing out speeding tickets at the Indianapolis 500. Nonetheless, it is reasonable to ask whether there were other, more just means of coercing the Japanese war cabinet into a sufficiently complete surrender that would have permitted political reconstruction. For example, would the detonation of a demonstration bomb have worked? What about a protracted naval blockade that prohibited Japan's access to any goods other than food and medicine necessary for survival? Neither of these seemed promising at the time. The looming competition with the Soviet Union also colored US estimations of how to end the war.[13] But, in retrospect, humane alternatives may have been worth further exploration.

Ethical Peacebuilding

In a seminal article on the ethics of postwar peacebuilding, Gary Bass addresses the ethics of political reconstruction. He sensibly suggests that justice after war should be tailored to addressing the causes that brought about the war.[14] If, on the one hand, genocide provoked a humanitarian response, then the criminal regime that committed genocide should be reconstructed, the perpetrators prosecuted, and the victims compensated. The obvious model here is de-Nazification following World War II, along with the Nuremberg Tribunals and Germany's financial compensation for Holocaust victims. If, on the other hand, a traditional aggression takes place, such as an attempt to seize a province or valuable oil field, other rules should apply. Under these circumstances, the right response is a return to the status quo while perhaps imposing additional external measures to ensure the aggressor is unlikely to repeat the aggression.

External Measures

The just defender thus has a right to improve the prospects that aggression will not be repeated. Historically, beyond the return of conquered territory, defenders have demanded the cession of strategic provinces or outposts to reduce the capacity for renewed aggression. Following World War I, Germany lost its overseas colonies and substantial contiguous territories, including most of Alsace-Lorraine to France and West Prussia to a reconstituted Poland. So, too, the United States demanded the cession of strategic islands from Japan following World War II. Some of these territories were held in residual sovereignty for Japan, as Okinawa was until 1972, while others were held as UN trust territories under a special strategic mandate of the Security Council.[15] Their purpose was to put the United States in a dominant position in the western Pacific, in part to deter a remilitarization of Japan. But each ran up against the competing demand of self-determination, and, in the end, ceded to it.

Reflecting the challenges of holding strategic territory permanently, reparations and other restrictions on future capacities have been levied on past aggressors. The most famous (or infamous) of these was the reparations against Germany following World War I, mandated by the "war guilt clause" (Article 231) of the Treaty of Versailles. Reparations were set at 132 billion marks (about $442 billion in 2012 US dollars).[16] This imposition raises questions of who should pay: were all parties equally responsible? And whether the effects are counterproductive: would they produce resentment or impoverish the world economy? Restrictions have also been placed on armaments. After World War I, the German army was limited to one hundred thousand troops (and no tanks) and to fifteen thousand sailors and six battleships. This may well be a better strategy for peace, but, again, one needs to consider whether it produces incentives to evade, how it will be enforced, and whether the limitations are credible.

External measures might well indeed be sufficient to reduce the capacity for future aggression, but they sometimes come at high costs to innocent civilians. The most prominent modern example of capacity-limiting *jus post bellum* is the peace imposed on Iraq following Saddam Hussein's aggression against Kuwait in 1990. The UN Security Council imposed the peace with Resolution 687, the so-called "Mother of All Resolutions" (named in mockery of Saddam's empty threat of inflicting the "Mother of All Battles" in defense of his occupation of Kuwait). The cease-fire resolution dictated the demarcation of Iraqi-Kuwaiti contested borders and imposed compensation obligations on Iraq for damage done in Kuwait and to Iraq's foreign financial creditors. It also mandated a disarmament regime enforced by international economic sanctions that unfortunately imposed its most severe burdens on innocent Iraqis.[17]

While external measures, such as those mentioned above, have the virtue of preserving the internal self-determination of even aggressor states, they can easily fall short of what seems necessary both as a matter of national security and humanitarian sympathy. As Bass notes, wars sometimes leave defeated aggressors on "the verge of anarchy," with broken governments incapable of providing security or minimal social protections.[18] An occupation thus becomes morally necessary. It then produces legal obligations of occupation, but also a conundrum of how to leave justly. To whom is sovereignty to be restored if the state is itself collapsed or "failed"?

Sometimes, the root causes of aggression are deep within a regime's structure. This militarism, the "perpetual menace" that Mill identified in Napoleon's rule of France, is an ideology and set of institutions fostered by the rulers.[19] It is itself the problem and must be changed.

And lastly, interventions, unlike ordinary wars of self-defense, presuppose a focus on the domestic regime of the state intervened against. Just interventions are necessarily grounded in overriding or disregarding a state's sovereignty in order to rescue a population from its government or free an oppressed nation seeking to secede. External measures do not address these problems.[20]

Internal Measures

The principles of UN trusteeship that applied to colonial trust territories after World War II are one guide to just peacebuilding for foreigners exercising authority over another people. Article 76 of the UN Charter requires state trust holders "to promote the political, economic, social and educational advancement of the inhabitants of the trust territories and their progressive development towards self-government or independence." This only applied to designated trust territories and specifically not to UN member-states (according to Article 78).

Legally, states are either independent, or, if conquered, protected by the laws of occupation of the Geneva Conventions, which prohibit transformation. Transformation thus can only be guided by broad ethical principles, specific surrender agreements, and Security Council authorizations.

Assuming that sovereignty is temporarily in the hands of another state or international organization, what is permissible and what is required in the way of transformation? In these circumstances, the occupying state is something like a "trustee," or "conservator," for the interests of the people.[21] Three guiding principles seem appropriate.

First are the terms of the surrender, the enabling Security Council resolution, or the peace treaty between competing factions in a civil war that the foreign force is mediating or implementing. These are decisive legal and ethical constraints on postbellum reconstruction, the legally binding standards for authoritative action. Their authorizing and limiting role is discussed below in regard to the peace process in Cambodia. These constraining principles are essential, but they are not a sufficient guide by themselves because there may be no formal surrender (as in Iraq in 2003). Moreover, the Security Council will itself need guidance in the design of the mandate it authorizes. And when the peace post–civil war is less than voluntary, the issue becomes what terms the foreign mediator should pressure the parties to accept. This will require standards.

Thus, second are the basic norms of human rights, such as those embodied in the Universal Declaration of Human Rights (1948), claimable by all persons. Those basic norms of individual, civic, political and economic rights should limit what the peacebuilder or occupier can do and indicate what it should strive to foster. They cannot, however, be a fixed rule, or recipe, for action. No state today fully meets these exacting standards of human rights or those of the subsequent human rights treaties inspired by them. But peacebuilders in temporary sovereign authority should regard them as normative: to be fostered where feasible and not to be violated without cause.

And third, the principle of self-determination should guide. Peace treaties are ambiguous, and human rights are abstract, open-ended, and inevitably need to be balanced and given local specificity by culture and methods of actual consent.[22] The challenge of legitimate and effective peacebuilding is balancing these three, often contradictory principles and adjusting to the particular circumstances of each case.

Transforming Iraq, 2003

The UN Security Council faced these questions as it considered what mandate to give the coalition that invaded Iraq. Importantly, it asserted in Resolution 1483 that the occupation was indeed an "occupation" and that therefore the Geneva Conventions applied.[23] This entailed responsibilities for maintaining public order, such as preventing looting and protecting the inhabitants from abuses, including torture or other inhumane treatment.[24] It then went on to specify that the Oil for Food program (the provision of humanitarian assistance funded through Iraqi oil sales and monitored by the Security Council) should be concluded, but that the remaining financial balances of the program and ongoing oil sales should be handled according to best international market practices, with the proceeds to be used for the benefit of the Iraqi population.[25]

The most striking provision of Resolution 1483, given the limitations of occupation law, was the requirement that the "Authority" (later termed Coalition Provisional Authority, or CPA) facilitate the "establishment of an internationally recognized, representative government of Iraq."[26] This purpose was further elaborated in the preambular paragraphs as "Encouraging the efforts of the people of Iraq to form a representative government based on the rule of law that affords equal rights and justice to all Iraqi citizens without regard to ethnicity, religion, or gender. . . ." The resolution probably reflected long-standing norms in favor of democratic governance as integral parts of peacebuilding, and UN standards more generally.[27] It may also have reflected concerns that some members of the US Defense Department had been contemplating handing over sovereignty to an unrepresentative (and shady) group of former exiles led by Ahmed Chalabi, though the US State Department sought to assure them that this was not the case.[28]

In any case, Resolution 1483 filled the gaps in occupation law. Authorized under Chapter VII of the UN Charter, the resolution was legally binding on all states as part of the United Nations' authority to address breaches of international peace and security. It could not rewrite occupation law (only a treaty can), but it provided definitive authority for this particular case, for transforming Iraq.

Self-determination, human rights, and occupation authority are often in tension. In a thoughtful study of what should have been occupation policy in Iraq, Noah Feldman set out principles drawing on the idea of trusteeship as a duty to facilitate self-determination.[29] He described four steps that occupiers should take. The first is establishing order, providing the security that the population has a right to expect when a government has been overturned and that is necessary for the population to begin to express itself. Second is guaranteeing freedom of speech and assembly, allowing the population to define itself and its goals. Third is serving as an impartial mediator between factions, giving each a chance to present its case to the people. Finally, the fourth step is holding democratic elections for a constituent assembly that will itself shape a constitution and government. These elections should neither be too early—before a viable state has been restored (police and courts are functioning), parties have formed, and a responsible press can inform the public—nor too late, when the occupation appears colonial and the population is rebelling against its paternalism. Then, when all the above have been met, the occupier must leave, having returned self-determination to the people and their own government.

"Liberal Peacebuilding" as Multilateral Imperialism?

A concern has arisen in the literature on peacebuilding that both state reconstruction and holding elections as exit strategies are new forms of imperialism, imposed by the United Nations or regional organizations such as NATO on vulnerable postconflict societies.[30] This view gains some persuasive force when one adds that neither states nor democracy are absolute requirements of justice. Both state reconstruction and elections respond to a need for secure protection and human rights, but as John Rawls has argued in his last work, *The Law of Peoples*, neither peace nor basic rights logically require either a liberal order or an electoral democracy.[31]

Rawls argues that a concern for the basic human rights—including subsistence, the absence of extreme abuses such as torture, and guarantees of freedom of speech and religion—that are essential for human dignity and for international security are compatible with what he calls "decent hierarchical societies." These do not meet the egalitarian standards of "justice as fairness" that would be chosen by free and independent individuals (including the equality of opportunity and democracy standards of his *Theory of Justice*, for example).[32] They are instead hierarchical societies without elected govern-

ment. But they do not abuse basic rights and, having pledged nonaggression, can be assumed by liberal democratic peoples to be sufficiently safe that they warrant respect for their sovereignty and a mutual regime of nonintervention and peace. These societies do not guarantee equal protection of the laws. They tolerate, for example, systematic discrimination against racial or other minorities, women, or other religions, and they limit voting rights or legislative and bureaucratic posts to males or members of the established religion. But they do have consultation mechanisms, such that even those without equal rights have their interests listened to and taken into account by the established hierarchy. Together, Rawls argues, these guarantees are sufficient for liberal peoples to extend the democratic peace they institute among themselves to decent hierarchical societies, which he significantly calls "Kazanistans" (implying that certain traditional Muslim hierarchical societies might qualify).[33]

Some liberal philosophers disagree with Rawls, holding that, even in ideal theory, Rawls's rights are insufficiently egalitarian to guarantee mutual respect for human dignity. Political scientists have speculated that the regime Rawls described is such an abstract construct that few actual states will meet its criteria for rights and peace without also being electoral democracies.[34] But Rawls's argument is hypothetical, advocating the possibility of complete toleration of nondemocratic, nonliberal societies by liberal societies. He makes a powerful case for a duty of toleration, including, most importantly, nonintervention with regard to these decent hierarchical societies.[35] And these arguments build on a long tradition of liberal thought, exemplified by Mill and others, in favor of indigenously determined self-determination.

But these arguments for nonintervention, though legitimate, are not equally relevant for peacebuilding. Peacebuilding involves what foreigners should and should not do when they are in a position of legal or legitimate authority—not what locals can do and what foreigners, as part of an established international order of sovereign independence, should tolerate.

In a post–civil war conflict situation, the peace treaty will govern the norms of foreign interference. But in the age of human rights and where UN peacebuilders have discretion, it would be hard to understand how foreigners on their own authority could deny equal participation in constitution-making to women or minority claimants. Partly, of course, this is a product of UN norms in favor of equal human rights. In addition to free speech and assembly, the Universal Declaration of Human Rights specifies in Article 21 that:

1. Everyone has the right to take part in the government of his country, directly or through freely chosen representatives.
2. Everyone has the right of equal access to public service in his country.
3. The will of the people shall be the basis of the authority of government; this will shall be expressed in periodic and genuine elections which shall be by universal and equal suffrage and shall be held by secret vote or by equivalent free voting procedures.[36]

But the preference for democratic decisions is also a product of the fact that in the postconflict situation, it is not clear *ex ante* who should have leading authority to determine the content of self-determination, again unless that has been settled by a peace treaty. If temporary peacebuilding authority has been delegated to the United Nations, peacekeepers cannot say to one minority or religion, class, race, gender, or ethnicity that they do not have legitimate standing in an

effort to write a constitution specifically delegated to the supervision of international authorities. It is not sufficient that such groups merely be consulted. The question of what constitutes equitable participation may indeed have been the root of the preceding armed conflict.

The deputy head of the United Nations' peacekeeping department, Edmond Mulet, recently recounted how the electoral logic works. When he was special representative overseeing the peacebuilding process in Haiti, he consulted local politically influential actors about what should be done about upcoming elections, looming in the wake of the devastating earthquake the country had just experienced. All agreed that the country was not ready to go through an electoral contest. The governing party offered to simply retain political power—backed up with international support. The opposition was equally happy to carve up the ministries among themselves and began suggesting friends and relatives for the various posts. But neither agreed that the other had a legitimate right to govern. In these circumstances, with both the opposition and governing parties nominating themselves to take power illegitimately, an election seemed the least corrupt and most legitimate alternative.[37]

Moreover, peacebuilding authority only arises in distinct circumstances. States that possess effective sovereignty—a monopoly on domestic violence—are not candidates for peacebuilding, no matter what their domestic regime. As long as they do not engage in aggressive war or genocide and suffer defeat, these states are members in good standing of the international legal order. The current world order tolerates military and civilian oligarchies (China, for example, is a permanent member of the Security Council), and numerous monarchies and personalist dictatorships (as in Saudi Arabia, Myanmar, or, until recently, Libya, Syria and North Korea), with and without elections.

Nor are most civil wars settled by international peacebuilding. When a civil war is resolved by conquest, the winner imposes its constitutional regime. When it is resolved by a negotiated elite pact, the reconstituted oligarchy rules. It is only when there is no victor, and the elites, warlords, or others are incapable of arriving at their own peace agreement, that international mediators and peacebuilders become relevant.

Cambodia, 1992–93: A "System of Liberal Democracy, on the Basis of Pluralism"[38]

This was the story of the Cambodian peace process: Following the toppling of Prince Sihanouk's regime by a US-inspired coup led by Lon Nol in 1970 and the devastation inflicted by the Khmer Rouge autogenocide of the late 1970s, Vietnam invaded in December 1978. But Hun Sen, the Vietnamese-installed strongman, could not root out the Khmer Rouge and its Sihanoukist allies in the 1980s. And Hun Sen's forces could not come to a power-sharing agreement with the Khmer Rouge and the Sihanoukist faction in negotiations held between 1987 and 1990, mediated by Indonesia and Australia.[39] It was only then that UN Security Council mediators stepped in.

The Paris Peace Agreements of 1991 incorporated substantial compromises with justice that governed the activities of international peacebuilders. The autogenocide inflicted by the Khmer Rouge was brushed aside (at least temporarily) in the peace treaty as the "unfortunate practices of the recent past." But an essential element of the bargain struck was that the factions agreed to designate the United Nations as an interim administrator, which would conduct a "free and fair" election to determine the future sovereignty of Cambodia. One could not count on the commitment of any one of the four factions—ex-Leninist, ex-Maoist,

ex-military, or ex-royalist—to "liberal democratic pluralism" the peace accords envisaged. But democracy was the only constitution available after autocracy and oligarchy had failed. One value of elections as a coordinating solution was their very uncertainty *ex ante*—each faction thought it could win.[40] A second value was important but much more difficult to achieve in practice. This was a commitment that the next set of elections would also be free and fair. Tolerating a loss in one election was a precondition of being able to compete again and perhaps win.

The usual norm in peacebuilding is that forming a government should be left to the process itself in which all relevant groups have prima facie equal standing. This produces a bias in favor of democratic procedures that allow, but make unlikely, that the wide range of participants will hand authority to one ruler, such as a small oligarchy, a military junta, one ethnicity, or one religion. In short, it does not preclude tyranny, but it structurally limits tyrannies to tyrannies of the majority. And it biases procedures for drafting new constitutions in favor of power-sharing pacts and constitutional limitations that protect minorities in order to represent the widest possible consent.

Thus, the UN secretary-general's 2001 report "No Exit Without Strategy" (also known as "News") explores criteria of success and failure in peacekeeping operations and outlines when to close an operation, either because it has succeeded or failed. It offers a menu of peacebuilding activities that includes building state institutions such as a bureaucracy, army, and police force; economic development; and democratic elections. These are ideals toward which most operations should strive.[41] Elections are seen as part of a typical exit strategy because they permit a transfer of state authority, temporarily in the hands of international peacekeepers, to a government chosen by the majority of the voters.

As do many strategy documents, "News" sets forth ideals. It indicates, but does not develop, all the actual hard and incompatible choices that vary from conflict to conflict. In an ideal world, special representatives heading peacebuilding operations can choose security first, or establish the rule of law, or implement a rational budgetary and fiscal process in which the government relies on nationally derived revenues, or foster local self-governance, or launch self-sustaining economic development.[42] All these would serve as better, even ideal, exit strategies compared to democratic elections or the mere expiration of a mandate. If elections are held before there is stable order, both nationally and locally, or reliable information from a free press, or responsible political parties, they can simply ratify hatreds and extremism.[43] Calendar-driven exit dates neglect rational assessments of whether the purposes of the intervention or peacebuilding were actually fulfilled.[44]

Unfortunately, special representatives do not operate in those ideal worlds. Instead, they need to take into account what the factions will tolerate, and measure that against what sustainable peace seems to require. Ideally, again, this balance will be incorporated in the peace treaty that the parties will have negotiated. But this will be far from a perfect consensus. Factions will be tempted to defect (become "spoilers" in Stephen Stedman's phrasing)[45] and resort to force unless they can be assuaged, sidelined, or overawed. For example, in Cambodia, the Khmer Rouge defected quickly and UN Special Representative Akashi, in charge of the UN peacekeeping operation, had to rely on, and balance, the rivalry between Hun Sen's "State of Cambodia," which had military and bureaucratic capacity, and Prince Ranariddh's FUNCINPEC Party, which enjoyed the traditional legitimacy of his father, Prince Sihanouk.

If that is not enough compromise, they will also have to take into account what the troop contributors will bear in terms of cost, time, and casualties, and what their own missions will accept as achievable mandates. Elections became the Cambodian exit strategy in 1993 not only because the factions could not agree on who would rule but also because the troop contributors insisted on leaving in the summer of 1993 rather than bearing the additional costs of staying until order, the rule of law, and fiscal sustainability were in place.[46]

The alternative to an electoral exit strategy in the vast majority of cases is thus not an organic, ground-up, or locally derived communal consensus. Nor is it a stable, economically viable state experiencing the rule of law. The alternative in most cases, as it was in Cambodia, is a return to civil war. In these circumstances, democratic election as an exit strategy is what is tried when everything else has been tried and failed. It is the last, not the first, choice. And elections are—unfortunately, but frequently—conducted before state institutions are secure, before a reliable rule of law is in place, before a responsible press and well-organized political parties have been established, and before the electorate is well informed. Elections in Cambodia in 1993 were held in the midst of escalating civil violence inflicted by the Khmer Rouge insurgency and by Hun Sen's violent provocations—conditions far short of the ideal circumstances favoring "free and fair" polls of the popular will. But they were held *then* because the peacekeepers were unwilling to take additional casualties, and ordinary Cambodians were fed up with the inflation that the spending by the UN operation had helped engender. The alternative to elections was a return to full-scale civil war. The elections created a government that could be internationally recognized, and thus legally assisted, to combat the Khmer Rouge insurgency, as well as a constituent assembly authorized to write a constitution.[47]

THE POLITICAL LOGISTICS OF PEACEBUILDING

Can international peacebuilding actually work? There have been many failures to impose a legitimate and stable domestic regime through foreign occupation. We need only think of the US intervention in Cuba in 1898 and again in 1907; in the Philippines from 1898; in Nicaragua in 1912; and Haiti in 1915. Rule of law, private property, democracy promotion, and strategic dominance were joint aims in those cases. But in all those cases, there was a failure to establish a democratic government. From 1920 to 1932, the United Kingdom failed in Iraq and Palestine—and from 1882 to 1954 in Egypt—to leave behind friendly, rule-of-law–abiding, and semidemocratic governments. In the postwar period, the Soviet Union failed in Eastern Europe to leave behind stable, self-sustainable communist governments.

On the other hand, the postwar occupations by the United States, United Kingdom, and France in Germany and western Austria, as well as the US occupation in Japan, were all instances of successful democratic transplants. How was this done, and how can these successes be repeated?

First of all, they were preceded by a complete defeat. In no case was there just a liberation of one group that was then freed to rule in its own interests. A complete defeat offered a fresh slate for transformation. Second, the occupiers were able to draw upon indigenous traditions of liberal capitalism and representative rule, including the liberal constitutional regimes that governed both Germany and Japan in the 1920s. The occupation thus had a restorative aspect to it. Third, the occupation could identify a common foreign enemy against which the new regime could mobilize alongside occupiers. Soviet communism served this purpose for the Allies in postwar Germany. Or, relatedly, a domestic "enemy" was exploited

through a strategy that often included offering new opportunities for hitherto subordinated classes now advantaged by expropriating former landlord or ruling classes. In Korea and Japan, land reform and labor rights operated in this fashion. Fourth, there was an assured departure. That is, the occupiers drew a public distinction between occupation and imperial rule. The occupiers were known to be temporary.

And fifth, the occupiers were well prepared. As David Edelstein has noted, as early as 1943, the United States set up schools at the University of Virginia and at Yale to train future administrators of Germany and Japan. In 1943, it was not clear the Allies were going to win the war. Nonetheless, that year the United States began to develop adequate language and other civil administration skills, and undertook long-term planning.[48] Compare this with the US occupation of Iraq in 2003. A story in *The New York Times* quotes a senior US staff officer of the Third Infantry Division saying that, after successfully taking Baghdad, his division had "*no further orders whatsoever.*"[49] That is, expecting that the war would be an easy victory (it was) and that peace would almost automatically follow (it rarely does), the Defense Department had provided no instructions on how to occupy or govern, or on what was to happen next. The United States had prepared for humanitarian assistance; it left out the politics. This was a striking, and, as we now know, consequential difference. Add this lack of preparedness to the weakness of democratic traditions in Iraq, the incomplete defeat of the insurgents (to put it mildly), and the very slow pace of reconstruction, and the challenges of a successful occupation in Iraq become clear.

Much can be learned from these unilateral measures, but they need to be supplemented by the lessons of multilateral peacebuilding. Multilateralism introduces severe coordination costs, but it also mobilizes new capacities, curbs the more extreme forms of national self-dealing, and adds impartial implementation through multilateral management, which can elicit widespread cooperation.[50] The question, of course, is how to do this.

There have been many successes in establishing self-sustaining self-government. They include Namibia, El Salvador, Cambodia, Mozambique, and East Timor. "Success" here means an end to large-scale civil war (fewer than one thousand battle deaths) and something very modest on the scale of democratic rule—that is, some degree of participation, a national election, but not necessarily a resolution of all the other problems associated with early democracy. There have also been equally striking failures to establish a democratic rule of law, including Rwanda in 1994, Bosnia throughout the 1990s, Liberia and Angola for a decade, and Somalia from the 1990s up until the present.

Though slow learners, the international community is beginning to learn the key factors to success. Nicholas Sambanis and I have identified what we think to be two key factors: consent and international capacity.

First, it helps if you have consent through a comprehensive and negotiated peace settlement. In short, a good exit depends on a good entrance. This requires a genuine, comprehensive, negotiated agreement (not just a truce) that brings all the relevant players together to negotiate a future preliminary constitution under which they are all prepared to compete peacefully. This kind of agreement seems to make a difference. When the United Nations enters under Chapter VII enforcement authority, without consent, as in Bosnia or Somalia, or with heavily coerced consent, as NATO did in Bosnia after Dayton, achieving a successful participatory peace is much more difficult.[51] It is not impossible. The peace in East Timor and between East Timor and Indonesia is still holding, but it is very important that the peace enforcement operation transforms itself into a consent-based operation. It can do this by organizing a national convention to outline a peacebuilding strategy, as Lakhdar Brahimi attempted to do for Afghanistan in the Bonn meetings in 2002. There, he helped identify plans to call a *loya jirga* (grand council) to ratify a peacebuilding strategy.

Second, a major international investment of peacebuilding resources helps transform agreements into self-determining successes. Multidimensional peacebuilding on the cheap is a prescription for failure. One needs to have as much "international capacity" as is needed to counterbalance both "local incapacity" and "local hostility." The more local hostility (measured by deaths, refugee displacements, and the relative strength and numbers of the factions) and the less local capacity (measured by the incapacity of the government and poverty of the economy), then the larger the "international capacity" (measured by troops, money, and authority) needs to be. International capacity offsets local incapacity and can launch a process of peacebuilding that restores order, builds new institutions, and launches economic development. The three can be seen as constituting three dimensions of a triangle (Figure 1), whose "area" represents the peacebuilding probability and prospect for peace and whose shape differs for each country.

If the international community engages in a conflict area, such as Rwanda in 1993–94, with a cheap operation designed merely to monitor and facilitate, when the extremists are determined and all factions are hostile and distrustful, disaster is likely inevitable. But democratic peacebuilding can be done effectively, and successes in Namibia, El Salvador, Cambodia, Mozambique, and East Timor are the result of significant international efforts to help transfer democratic

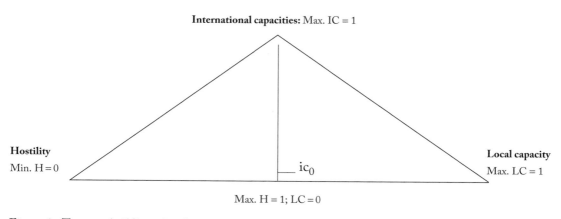

International capacities: Max. IC = 1

Hostility
Min. H = 0

ic_0

Local capacity
Max. LC = 1

Max. H = 1; LC = 0

Figure 1. The peacebuilding triangle

Source: Michael W. Doyle and Nicholas Sambanis, *Making War and Building Peace: United Nations Peace Operations* (Princeton, NJ: Princeton University Press, 2006).

institutions to societies that are otherwise extremely problematic prospects for democratic rule. The keys were matching the right degree of international authority (from monitoring to quasi-sovereign trusteeship); military and civilian governance assistance; and economic redevelopment to fit the nature of the dispute in question. By balancing the international capacity with the amount of destruction sustained and deaths and displacements suffered, these transformations were well positioned for success.

The key to an effective strategy is a combined portfolio. Good peacemaking, composed of mediation and negotiation, generates consent and authorizes the legitimate capacities that allow peacekeeping civilians and battalions to manage a peace process. Similarly, effective peacekeeping organizes the reconstructive peacebuilding that creates new institutions and new actors through which genuine transformation toward peace can take place. Discrete peace enforcement and bribes are the inducements that stop the gaps in peacemaking, peacekeeping, and peacebuilding, and that prevent a peace operation from becoming hostage to total spoilers who are determined to prevent peace under any terms. The force works in

these circumstances because it rests on a process that incorporates the consent of the vast majority of the relevant actors and draws upon resources that the peacebuilding process has mobilized.[52] Peacemaking, peacekeeping, peacebuilding, and discrete peace enforcement work together, each reinforcing the other in a successful combination. The absence of any is an invitation to failure.

A recent study by the UN Department of Peacekeeping Operations has identified key features in the operational success of these missions. They include:

- Genuine commitment to a political process by the parties to work toward peace
- Clear, credible, and achievable mandates, with matching resources
- Unity of purpose in the Security Council, with active diplomacy in support
- Supportive engagement by neighboring countries and regional actors
- Host-country commitment to unhindered operations and freedom of movement
- Integrated UN approach, effective coordination with other actors, and

good communication with host-country authorities and population
- Missions need to demonstrate their credibility, strengthen their legitimacy, and promote national and local ownership[53]

All these can clearly make a positive difference, but no one should argue that the ethical problems of *jus post bellum* have been solved by multilateral authorization and new strategies of mutilaterally managed peacebuilding.[54] Manifestly, they haven't been. On too many occasions, the international community, as represented in the Security Council, has chosen to authorize less-than-adequate missions, perhaps most notably in Rwanda and Srebrenica. Under pressure from a Security Council unwilling to expend resources and assign troops, General Roméo Dallaire, the force commander of the UN operation in Rwanda, was told to "situate the estimate": to design the mission to fit available resources rather than to fit the challenges on the ground.[55] Elsewhere, the Security Council has refused to act, or has taken measures clearly inadequate toward ending humanitarian emergencies with which it has been confronted, such as in Bosnia before 1995, Darfur from 2003, and Syria today.

Nonetheless, with the revival of the Security Council after the Cold War, multilateral authorization constrained many of the dangers of unilateral exploitation. With the slow buildup of lessons—what worked and what did not—multilateral intervention has acquired the tools to avoid both political collapse and dependency. It learned, moreover, how to help build self-sustaining, self-determining peace. We should not, therefore, be judging these new forms of interventionism by the same tropes we have used to judge unilateral interventions. They can be different and, sometimes, justifiable.

NOTES

This chapter draws on points I developed in the Castle Lectures delivered at Yale University and that will appear in *The Question of Intervention: John Stuart Mill and the Responsibility to Protect* (forthcoming, 2014). It has also benefited from suggestions made by Chester Crocker, Fen Hampson, and Pamela Aall, and the participants of a seminar organized by them at the Centre for International Governance Innovation, University of Waterloo, Canada. Stefano Recchia added valuable critical comments; Jan Messerschmidt provided research assistance; and Olena Jennings and Maggie Powers assisted with proofreading.

1. For examples, see Virginia Page Fortna, *Does Peacekeeping Work? Shaping Belligerents' Choices after Civil War* (Princeton, NJ: Princeton University Press, 2008); and Michael Doyle and Nicholas Sambanis, *Making War and Building Peace: United Nations Peace Operations* (Princeton, NJ: Princeton University Press, 2006).

2. J. S. Mill, "A Few Words on Nonintervention," from *The Collected Works of John Stuart Mill, Volume XXI—Essays on Equality, Law, and Education,* ed. John M. Robson, introduction by Stefan Collini (Toronto: University of Toronto Press, London: Routledge and Kegan Paul, 1984). I discuss interventions and their outcomes in *The Question of Intervention: John Stuart Mill and the Responsibility to Protect* (New Haven, CT: Yale University Press, forthcoming 2014).

3. L. Oppenheim, *International Law*, vol. 1: *Peace*, ed. Ronald Roxburgh, 3rd ed. (London: Longmans, 1920–21), 372–406.

4. Leo Gross, "The Peace of Westphalia, 1648–1948," *American Journal of International Law* 42, no. 1 (1948): 20–41.

5. Needless to say, that does not imply that the surrender agreement was voluntary in any larger sense, or that these same norms applied outside the developed world of Europe, North America, and Japan. For influential treatments of the law of occupation, see Eyal Benvenisti, *The International Law of Occupation* (Princeton, NJ: Princeton University Press, 1993); and Morris Greenspan, *The Modern Law of Land Warfare* (Berkeley: University of California Press, 1959).

6. Hague Convention no. IV, Respecting the Laws and Customs of War on Land, Annex, art. 43, October 18, 1907, 36 stat. 2277; T.S. no. 539 (hereinafter Hague Convention).

7. Geneva Convention Relative to the Protection of Civilian Persons in Time of War, art. 47, Aug. 12, 1949, 75 U.N.T.S. 287, 6 U.S.T. 3516 (hereinafter Geneva Convention).

8. Geneva Convention, art. 64. For a thorough discussion of the Geneva Convention and a critique of US and UK occupation policy in Iraq, see Adam Roberts, "Transformative Military Occupation: Applying the Laws of War and Human Rights," *American Journal of International Law* 100 (2006): 580–622. And for an insightful discussion of the lack of connections between occupation law and UN peacebuilding, see Kristen Boon, "Obligations of the New Occupier: The Contours of a Jus Post Bellum," *Loyola of Los Angeles International and Comparative Law Review* 31, no. 1 (2009): 57–84; Gregory H. Fox, *Humanitarian Occupation* (Cambridge: Cambridge University Press, 2008); and Ralph Wilde, *International Territorial Administration* (Oxford: Oxford University Press, 2008).

9. Bob Woodward, *Plan of Attack* (New York: Simon and Schuster, 2004), 150.

10. Michael Walzer, *Just and Unjust Wars* (New York: Basic Books, 1977), 111–24. In a recent essay, he revises his arguments, noting the importance of reforming regimes subject to humanitarian interventions, for who would want to leave *génocidaires* in power? See the chapter "The Triumph of Just War Theory," in Michael Walzer, *Arguing about War* (New Haven, CT: Yale University Press, 2004), 3–22.

11. Walzer, *Just and Unjust Wars*, 117. See also Gary Bass, "Jus Post Bellum: Postwar Justice and Reconstruction," *Philosophy and Public Affairs* 32, no. 4 (2004): 384–412 (exploring the justice of these kinds of settlements, particularly the case of post-genocide); and for a valuable overview, see Stefano Recchia, "Just and Unjust Postwar Reconstruction," *Ethics and International Affairs* 23, no. 2 (Summer 2009): 165–88.

12. Ian Buruma surveys the debate on the issue in "The War over the Bomb," *New York Review of Books*, September 21, 1995, 26–34. Tsuyoshi Hasegawa, in *Racing the Enemy: Stalin, Truman, and the Surrender of Japan* (Cambridge, MA: Harvard University Press, 2005), discusses the difficulty of persuading the Japanese cabinet to limit negotiations to the preservation of the emperor, after the atomic bombs on Hiroshima and Nagasaki had been dropped, 205–51.

13. For insights on the debate within the United States, see Leon Sigal, *Fighting to a Finish: The Politics of War Termination in the United States and Japan, 1945* (Ithaca, NY: Cornell University Press, 1988); and McGeorge Bundy, *Danger and Survival: Choices about the Bomb in the First Fifty Years* (New York: Vintage, 1988). For a balanced assessment of Truman's moral leadership, see Joseph Nye, *Presidential Leadership and the Creation of the American Era* (Princeton, NJ: Princeton University Press, 2013), esp. 81–83.

14. See Bass, "Jus Post Bellum." For a wide-ranging analytic survey of the elements of transitional justice, see Jon Elster's *Closing the Books: Transitional Justice in Historical Perspective* (New York: Cambridge University Press, 2004). The discussion of "restoration" France in 1814 and 1815 is especially apposite.

15. Palau, independent in 1994, was the last of these.

16. See Margaret MacMillan, *Peacemakers: The Paris Conference of 1919 and Its Attempt to End War* (London: Murray, 2001). Adding to the penalty of the reparations (and thus eroding the prospects for long-term peace), the Treaty of Versailles required Germany to acknowledge "war guilt" and try the kaiser and other senior officials (the last, observed only in the breach).

17. For a thorough analysis, see Ian Johnstone, *Aftermath of the Gulf War: An Assessment of UN Action* (Boulder, CO: Lynne Rienner, 1994). The disarmament regime and its sanctions were later lightened by Oil for Food, a UN program designed to protect vulnerable civilians and their nutritional and medical needs from the effects of the sanctions imposed to coerce Iraqi compliance. The effects, nonetheless, were devastating on Iraqi civilians, and the regime engendered massive corruption, some of which spilled over onto UN officials, as described in Kofi Annan, *Interventions: A Life in War and Peace* (New York: Penguin, 2012), 319–34.

18. Bass, "Jus Post Bellum," 403.

19. For a discussion of John Stuart Mill's views on intervention, see his famous 1859 essay "A Few Words on Non-Intervention"; and my *Question of Intervention*, which comments on it.

20. See Brian Orend, "Justice After War," *Ethics and International Affairs* 16, no. 1 (2002): 43–57, on the democratic norms for reconstructing domestic regimes.

21. Gerald Helman and Steven Ratner, "Saving Failed States," *Foreign Policy*, no. 89 (Winter 1992–93): 3–21.

22. My views on this question owe much to conversations with legal advisers and peacekeepers in Cambodia (1993), El Salvador (1994), Vukovar (1998 and 1999), and Brcko (1999 and 2000). For an eminently pragmatic rendering of these issues and how to make them effective, see Ambassador R. William Farrand's *Reconstruction and Peace Building in the Balkans: The Brcko Experience* (Lanham, MD: Rowman and Littlefield, 2011). This book is remarkable for, among other reasons, being one of the very few studies of peacebuilding written by someone intimately informed of (not to mention responsible for) the complexities of transitional governance as they emerge at the leadership level.

23. Paragraph 5 of the resolution specifically cites The Hague and Geneva Conventions. See UN Security Council Resolution 1483 (UN document S/RES/1483), May 22, 2003.

24. Neither occupation law nor SCR 1483 ensures adequate implementation. The looting of the National Museum and National Library of Iraq had already occurred when UNSC Resolution 1483 passed. Paragraph 6 requires the occupying authorities to assist in the return of stolen goods. The abuses at Abu Ghraib prison were revealed subsequently. The United States and the United Kingdom, apparently key drafters of the resolution, were under pressure to recognize their "occupancy."

25. The agreement also specified that 5 percent be used for the Kuwait compensation fund established following the first Iraq War.

26. UNSC Resolution 1483, para. 22.

27. See Thomas Franck's influential survey of the issue, "The Emerging Right to Democratic Governance," *American Journal of International Law* 86, no. 1 (1992): 46–91.

28. See David Phillips, *Losing Iraq: Inside the Postwar Reconstruction Fiasco* (New York: Basic Books, 2005); and Thomas Ricks, *Fiasco: The American Military Adventure in Iraq* (New York: Penguin, 2006), 56–57.

29. Noah Feldman, *What We Owe Iraq: War and the Ethics of Nation Building* (Princeton, NJ: Princeton University Press, 2004), 59–62.

30. For a good recent survey, see Philip Cunliffe, "Still the Spectre at the Feast: Comparisons between Peacekeeping and Imperialism in Peacekeeping Studies Today," *International Peacekeeping* 19, no. 4 (August 2012): 426–42. For the seminal but still relevant critique, see Roland Paris, "Peacebuilding and the Limits of Liberal Internationalism," *International Security* 22, no. 2 (Fall 1997): 54–89; and his updated reassessment, "Saving Liberal Peacebuilding," *Review of International Studies* 36, no. 2 (April 2010): 337–65.

31. John Rawls, *The Law of Peoples* (Princeton, NJ: Princeton University Press, 1999).

32. John Rawls, *A Theory of Justice* (Cambridge, MA: Belknap, 1971).

33. Rawls, *Law of Peoples*, 69.

34. As exemplified in critiques such as that by Charles Beitz, "Rawls's Law of Peoples," *Ethics* 110, no. 4 (2000): 669–96. The issue is discussed in Michael Doyle, "One World, Many Peoples: International Justice in John Rawls's *The Law of Peoples*," *Perspectives on Politics* 4, no. 1 (March 2006): 111–23.

35. He parallels, with differing grounds, the arguments made for nonintervention by Kant for all societies but the aggressive, and by Mill for all but the cases for which nonintervention should be overridden or disregarded.

36. Universal Declaration of Human Rights, General Assembly Resolution 217A(III) (UN document A/810), December 10, 1948.

37. See his remarks at the International Day of Democracy, September 16, 2013, hosted by the International Peace Institute and available on the IPI website at http://www.ipinst.org/news/general announcement/397-video-democratization-at-the -sharp-end.html.

38. The phrase is from the Agreements on a Comprehensive Political Settlement of the Cambodia Conflict, also known as the Paris Peace Agreements of 1991.

39. See Steven Ratner, "The Cambodian Settlement Agreements," *American Journal of International Law* 87, no. 1 (1993): 1–41; Richard Solomon, *Exiting Indochina* (Washington, DC: United States Institute of Peace Press, 2000); the chapters by Jin Song and Nishkala Suntharalingam in *Keeping the Peace: Multidimensional Operations in Cambodia and El Salvador*, ed. Michael Doyle, Ian Johnstone, and Robert Orr (New York: Cambridge University Press, 1997); and Doyle and Sambanis, *Making War and Building Peace*, chap. 5.

40. Michael Doyle, *UN Peacekeeping in Cambodia: UNTAC's Civil Mandate* (Boulder, CO: Lynne Rienner, 1995). Disclosure: I served as an international monitor during the Cambodian elections that were organized and certified by the United Nations, April–June 1993.

41. Report of the Secretary-General, "No Exit Without Strategy: Security Council Decision-Making and the Closure or Transition of United Nations Peacekeeping Operations" (UN document S/2001/394), April 20, 2001. Disclosure: In March 2001, I chaired the UN Secretariat working group that drafted this report and presented it to the Security Council in April for its approval.

42. Numerous scholars in the field are recommending priorities along these various lines, including Kimberly Zisk Marten's *Enforcing the Peace: Learning from the Imperial Past* (New York: Columbia University Press, 2004); Séverine Autesserre's *The Trouble with the Congo: Local Violence and the Failure of International Peacebuilding* (New York: Cambridge University Press, 2010); Ashraf Ghani and Clare Lockhart's *Fixing Failed States: A Framework for Rebuilding a Fractured World* (Oxford: Oxford University Press, 2008); and Nicholas Sambanis and my own list (including our "seven-step plan," with security first) in *Making War and Building Peace*, 337–42.

43. Edward D. Mansfield and Jack Snyder, "Democratic Transitions, Institutional Strength, and War," *International Organization* 56, no. 2 (2002): 297–337.

44. Fen Hampson and Tod Lindberg, "'No Exit' Strategy," *Policy Review*, no. 176 (2012): 15–33.

45. Stephen Stedman, "Spoiler Problems in Peace Processes," *International Security* 22, no. 2 (1997): 5–53.

46. In spring 1993, both the Japanese and Australian battalions had announced their decisions to leave. The Japanese had been driven out by the traumatic loss of a Japanese national murdered by disgruntled electoral division employees (not by the Khmer Rouge, as originally thought). The Australian Parliament resolved on the rapid exit as security deteriorated throughout Cambodia in March and April 1993.

47. The constitutional assembly was required to operate on the basis of a two-thirds supermajority for ratification, thus ensuring the agreement of the two major factions, FUNCINPEC (the princely party of Sihanouk's son) and SOC (Hun Sen's State of Cambodia) to the ratification. This had the fortunate and not accidental effect that a coalition government was the likely outcome. No other government would have been functional and legitimate, because FUNCINPEC had the most votes, and the SOC controlled the military and civil capacities of the state.

48. For a thorough analysis of establishing strategically friendly regimes, see David Edelstein, "Occupational Hazards," *International Security* 29, no. 1 (Summer 2004): 49–91. Edelstein is defining success differently, not in terms of democracy or self-determination, but in terms of US security interests. For a discussion of democracy promotion, see Carnegie Council on Ethics and International Affairs, *Multilateral Strategies to Promote Democracy* (New York: Carnegie Council, 2004).

49. Michael Gordon, "Catastrophic Success: The Strategy to Secure Iraq Did Not Foresee a Second War," *New York Times*, October 19, 2004; and Thomas Ricks, *Fiasco*.

50. Nicholas Sambanis and I address the costs and value of multilateral peacebuilding at some length in *Making War and Building Peace*; Page Fortna, in *Does Peacekeeping Work?* offers a cogent argument for its successes; and Charles Call, in *Why Peace Fails: The Causes and Prevention of Civil War Recurrence* (Washington, DC: Georgetown University Press, 2012), addresses its record of many failures.

51. As Stefano Recchia commented on a draft of this argument, this unfortunately means that peacebuilding is most likely to succeed in the easier cases, when comprehensive peace agreements can be achieved. Because the United Nations often tackles the harder cases, when the parties cannot settle the conflicts on their own, the challenges of successful peacebuilding become evident.

52. For example, preventing the Khmer Rouge from disrupting the election after their defection from the peace process was tolerated by their former ally (Prince Ranariddh's FUNCINPEC), supported by Hun Sen's military forces, and conducted with the support of the UN operation. Attacks on the KR by Hun Sen prior to the peacebuilding process met the political opposition of FUNCINPEC, China, and Thailand. I have explored the combined portfolio strategy in "Building Peace: The John W. Holmes Lecture," *Global Governance* 13, no. 1 (2007): 1–15.

53. UN Department of Peacekeeping Operations and Department of Field Support, "A New Partnership Agenda: Charting the New Horizon for UN Peacekeeping" (New York: July 2009), 2.

54. For thoughtful criticisms, see Chandra Lekha Sriram, *Confronting Past Human Rights Violations: Justice vs. Peace in Times of Transition* (London: Frank Cass, 2004). For the challenges of restoring the rule of law, see Agnes Hurwitz, ed., *Civil War and the Rule of Law* (Boulder, CO: Lynne Rienner, 2008); and Jane Stromseth, David Wippman, and Rosa Brooks, *Can Might Make Rights? Building the Rule of Law after Military Interventions* (New York: Cambridge University Press, 2008).

55. Roméo Dallaire, *Shake Hands with the Devil: The Failure of Humanity in Rwanda* (New York: Carroll and Graf, 2003), 56.

32

THE LONG DECADE OF STATE BUILDING

Astri Suhrke

Just as the nineteenth century was a "long century" of state formation in Europe,[1] the post–Cold War years formed a "long decade" of externally assisted state building. From 1989 to 2007, the United Nations or its members mounted twenty-two international interventions with partial or full state-building agendas. The US invasion of Iraq in 2003 and the long engagement in Afghanistan starting in 2001 were the most ambitious interventions of this kind. The interventions were situated in a fast-developing international regime designed to assist state building in the aftermath of civil wars, internal strife, the implosion of weak regimes, or the persistence of states unwilling or incapable of meeting international standards of justice and security. In an inversion of previous security doctrines, weak rather than strong states were seen as the problem, a source of anarchy that spelled violence at home and threats to international peace. The state building prescription was premised on ideal notions of a legitimate and responsible state. Constructing such states, it was believed, required building formal state structures

that, with international assistance, could provide basic security, justice, and good governance, enabling them to take their place as responsible members of the international community.

Toward the end of the "long decade," the can-do convictions were more muted, and received orthodoxies about internationally assisted state building were modified. Many factors account for these changes. On the intervening side, there was growing recognition that prevailing strategies of state building carried high costs and had limited results, as shown by the interventions in Iraq and Afghanistan. In the target states, local elites often pursued their own agendas, which undercut international state building strategies. Ambitious national reform movements wanting to fill the political room reduced the space for international actors, as demonstrated during the Arab Spring in 2011. In response, the transnational community concerned with state- and peace-building elevated the notion of "national ownership" to central doctrine. The policy discourse increasingly questioned conventional thinking that emphasized the role of foreign assistance and state-centric approaches. Some state functions, it seemed, could be provided without having to reform or (re)build the state.

This chapter examines the orthodoxies in the state building discourse during the "long decade," as well as their critics. It then outlines emerging thinking in the policy discussion about alternative approaches to state building as a road to peace.

STATE BUILDING AND PEACEBUILDING: INSTITUTIONAL ORTHODOXIES

The end of the Cold War triggered a series of developments that placed questions of the nature and role of the state—until then, a subject of political ideologies and academic inquiry—squarely on the table of the major international organizations and Western foreign policy establishments. New conflicts had developed on the rim of the old superpower rivalries. Some governments that had depended on foreign patrons during the Cold War now "failed," at times spectacularly, and some countries imploded in violence along ethnic lines. But the end of the Cold War also opened the way for numerous peace settlements. A revitalized United Nations, assisted by other international agencies, often mediated the terms of the settlement and the framework for postwar development. In the process, strategies for reform and reconstruction were developed that came to be called "state building." Three principal producers of knowledge in this respect were the World Bank, the Organisation for Economic Co-operation and Development (OECD), and the United Nations.

The World Bank's first contribution was in the form of the 1997 *World Development Report* (WDR), which assessed the optimal role of the state for development, and—by implication—for stability and peace.[2] The report set an implicit threshold for "failed

states" by outlining minimum functions that all states must fulfill, and it offered strategies for reform to achieve this goal. Beyond these basic functions, the size and role of the state should be tailored to its capabilities, leaving the rest to the market, according to the report.

The WDR 1997 became the framework for the many missions later undertaken by the World Bank alongside other international financial institutions (IFIs), UN agencies, bilateral donors, and nongovernmental organizations (NGOs) to reconstruct or reform states in postwar situations. In Afghanistan after the 2001 US-led intervention, for instance, the World Bank promoted institutional reform of the public administration (including downsizing the civil service and privatizing several functions); initiated public financial management, currency reform, and policies for macroeconomic stability (including calls to increase revenue collection and limit military spending); supported anticorruption measures; and assumed fiduciary responsibilities for managing donor aid flows to the Afghan government. The lending portfolio was relatively small, focusing on supporting institutions that would make money productive and facilitate private-sector development. Overall, the World Bank's activities were designed to establish what were considered "basic functions" in the schema laid out in 1997, now called "state building."[3]

The OECD became engaged in state- and peacebuilding because of the organization's concern with aid effectiveness and the problems that so-called failed or fragile states posed for economic development. The OECD's Development Assistance Committee (DAC) made "focus on state building" the third principle in its guidelines to donor governments providing aid in conflict and postconflict situations.[4] Like the World Bank's WDR 1997, the DAC's guidelines identified some parameters considered basic state functions necessary to reduce poverty and generate development. Because respect for human rights and a measure of state legitimacy were included, state building that followed these markers was assumed to contribute to domestic peace and international order.

The guidelines, adopted by the OECD in 2007, became a foundational text for donor development assistance policies and evaluations. A comprehensive survey of thirteen recipient countries in 2011 found that donors were "increasingly committed to statebuilding," mostly by programs to strengthen formal institutions at the executive level, including public-sector management and service delivery, as well as election support. Also included, but on a smaller scale, were programs to strengthen institutional structures of the judiciary, legislatures, and local administration.[5]

The World Bank and the OECD/DAC backed into peacebuilding via state building from a development agenda; the United Nations did the reverse, backing into state building from its mandate to promote and safeguard international peace. The first comprehensive peace mission in the 1990s, in Cambodia, illustrates the dynamic. The UN Transitional Authority in Cambodia (UNTAC) gave the United Nations authority to administer Cambodia in a transition period after the 1991 peace agreement. A mission with multiple functions, UNTAC focused on free and fair elections designed to enable the bitterly rival Khmer factions to settle their conflict peacefully, a goal contingent on the Cambodian state apparatus acting in a neutral fashion. At the time of the peace agreement, however, the state was controlled by one faction (led by Hun Sen), and neutrality could not be expected. The United Nations therefore effectively took over the state. The mandate was written into the peace agreement:

In order to ensure a neutral political environment conducive to free and fair general elections, administrative agencies, bodies and offices which could directly influence the outcome of elections will be placed under direct United Nations supervision or control. In that context, special attention will be given to foreign affairs, national defence, finance, public security and information. To reflect the importance of these subjects UNTAC needs to exercise such control as is necessary to ensure the strict neutrality of the bodies responsible for them.[6]

Strictly speaking, it was state management rather than transformative state building. The United Nations established a parallel structure to monitor and make the necessary corrections in the administrative offices of the state, as well as the political organizations of the competing Khmer factions. UNTAC had the formal power to examine books and practices and to fire and hire Cambodian civil servants and political staff. The results were mixed. Elections were held, leading to a coalition government, but the Hun Sen faction expertly circumvented UN controls to keep a firm grip on the state administration and the police, laying the foundation for what became a long autocratic rule.

Several years elapsed before the United Nations again undertook a similar trusteeship-like mission (in Kosovo and East Timor in 1999). But the importance of an effective and impartial state echoed in the subsequent UN discourse on peacebuilding and state building.[7] By the mid-2000s, the growing international attention to "failed states" had reinforced the concern. As spelled out in a high-level report to the UN secretary-general in 2004, serious threats to international peace and security were now seen to emanate from weak, poor, and violence-ridden countries who could spread disease, illegal migrants, terrorism, organized crime, and warfare to their neighbors and, in a globalized world, the rest of the international community. Underlying these perceived threats was a "crisis of State capacity and legitimacy."[8]

The United Nations responded by sharpening its state-building capabilities as part of the organization's peacebuilding agenda. The next year, the UN Peacebuilding Commission was established with a mandate to coordinate international peacebuilding, including activities by donors and the international financial institutions involved in state building as defined above. Its very first country report, on Burundi, emphasized the need to reform the state.

> The consolidation of peace . . . requires that the State has the technical, human and financial means to manage public affairs in a transparent and efficient manner. However, years of conflict in Burundi have significantly weakened the national institutions and lowered the confidence of Burundians in the capacity of their State to defend and protect their interests. . . . Corruption and the poor quality of public services are a manifestation of this counter-performance, while the expectations of the population from the Government are enormous. . . . [T]he comprehensive reform of the public administration . . . constitutes an essential condition for the re-establishment of trust between individual citizens and the State.[9]

FIRST-ORDER QUESTIONS
Understanding the State

What kind of state was the unspoken model for these recommendations? The Burundi report brings out the curious combination of Hobbesian and Lockean thinking that marked the development of the international discourse on state building. The ultimate "failed state" was commonly

understood as a Hobbesian state of nature—a war of all against all. But the apparatus needed to tame these forces was not an oppressive Hobbesian Leviathan; it was a liberal state founded on reason, tolerance, and trust that would "manage public affairs in a transparent and efficient manner," as the Burundi report put it. This state corresponded to Max Weber's model of "the modern state," characterized by a monopoly of legitimate force, an effective administration, and a legal-rational framework for public transactions. But the model state in the orthodox state building discourse was also more: it was a social contract kind of state, constituted from below and playing by democratic rules. This state did not act on behalf of particular social segments, nor was it an actor with interests of its own. Rather, the state was simply a neutral *arena* where competing groups pursued their interests through a fair and free political process.

To what extent any existing state is—or can be—an arena, neutral and separate from society, has long occupied philosophers and social scientists.[10] Class theorists claim that a state's structure and functions reflect the mode of production of society and therefore can have only relative autonomy from society. In this view, the principal function of the state in a capitalist society is to serve the accumulation of capital and regulate class relations, hence necessitating certain basic functions as identified, for instance, in the 1997 World Bank report. By contrast, the view of the state as an arena, separate from but responding to parties and pressure groups in society, is central to the pluralist paradigm that has been developed in conventional North American political science as an explanation for how Western democracies work. In this perspective, the basic function of the state is to maintain a free and fair arena for diverse political forces to operate.

The contemporary internationally assisted state-building project has taken Western democracies as its model, with an emphasis on periodic elections, development of legislatures, political parties, and principles of good governance. Less obvious, and certainly less recognized, is the further borrowing of a particular set of underlying assumptions of the state as a neutral arena, autonomous from but responding to society. These assumptions may not hold even in Western political democracies. Given the problems of realizing such a model, particularly in societies with very different histories, radical critics suspected that the model masked more self-serving interests of the rich and powerful states and the organizations they led—that is, to preserve their hegemony in the international system.[11] Such views fed into a larger body of criticism of "the liberal peace," as we shall see below.

Can States Be Built?

Another fundamental question is whether states can be *built*—one floor at a time, as it were. The language of state building has emphasized agency and political will, which contrasts with the well-known historical record of most states being *formed* by broader historical forces over a long period. The proponents of state building acknowledged the need for time and long-term commitments, but claimed that the process in the contemporary world could be shortened because critical ingredients—knowledge, capital, and coercion—were largely available from the outside in the form of international assistance. The challenge for international aid was rather to identify the right sequence, timing, and dosage of reforms; to be sensitive to local context and respect the need for local ownership; and to mobilize the political will to maintain aid commitments for the long

haul. This view was elaborated in a fast-growing how-to literature on building the model state, produced in universities, aid organizations, and think tanks where analysts worked in close proximity to the donor community to produce knowledge that could influence policy and be readily integrated in practice.[12]

Is State Building Linked to War Making?

Another fundamental question is whether the process of building a state is so inherently conflictual that it undermines peace, making state building and peacebuilding contradictory processes.

The now-classic formulation of the relationship between violence and state building is Charles Tilly's analysis of state formation in Europe.[13] Tilly argued that the modern European state is essentially a product of war. A later "bellicist literature" likewise found that state formation in parts of Africa and Asia was stimulated by wars.[14] The main argument is that waging war requires extraction of resources that necessitates control—bureaucracies capable of mobilizing and managing men, money, and material, in other words, the raw material of a state. War making and state building are thus joined at the hip, and, as the process of resource extraction predictably meets with resistance, infused with conflict also on the state-building side.

Critics argued, as noted above, that external assistance can mitigate the elements of violence. In the contemporary world, foreign capital reduces the potential for local conflict over resource extraction, and international peacekeepers are in place to deter or control collective violence.[15] The claim is supported by some quantitative and comparative studies, which find that multifunctional international peace operations tend to prevent a recurrence of civil war.[16] The case study literature, however, is ambiguous.

Take the case of Liberia, a country that has suffered enormous physical and institutional destruction during fourteen years of civil war. Some fifteen thousand international peacekeepers and civilian police were deployed to secure the 2003 peace agreement. International assistance financed an ambitious reconstruction and state-building program, accounting for about two-thirds of all official income in the postwar years.[17] Numerous international experts arrived for hands-on control to improve public financial management and reduce corruption. For a small country (3 million people), it was a formidable international presence and undoubtedly helped sustain Liberia's postwar peace. Even collective violence on a lesser scale (related to, for example, organized crime, riots, strikes, and the abuse of state power against citizens) was quite limited when compared to some other postwar situations.[18]

On the other hand, state building entails the setting of constitutive rules for access to power and authoritative allocation of public goods. This is an inherently conflictual process that produces winners and losers, with a corresponding potential for violence. A large influx of foreign aid might simply increase the stakes and whet the appetite. A joint World Bank and UN Development Programme (UNDP) mission to Liberia in 2009 found that: "state building processes which themselves significantly shape the distribution of power are lightning rods for conflict."[19] Liberia's peace agreement nevertheless proved durable, with tensions unfolding below the level of collective violence.

Somalia was not so fortunate. After prolonged civil war, the establishment of a transitional federal government in 2004 marked efforts to restore the writ of the central state. At the time, a close observer found that many Somalis viewed state building as a deeply contested, zero-sum endgame, fearing the restoration of a central state which they associated with repression, corruption, and patronage-based politics, and warned against conflating state building with peacebuilding.[20] The period that followed was indeed violent. Competing groups fought for territory and power. A local Islamist movement (the Islamic Courts Union) challenged the federal authority but was defeated when Ethiopian troops entered the fray, supported by the US government which considered the Islamic Courts potential international terrorists. Only in 2012 did the fighting die down, and a road map for peace was drawn up, a provisional constitution approved, and a large-scale reconstruction program started.

In general, the most obvious aspect of the relationship between state building and peacebuilding resembles that between democracy and peace: fully liberal democratic states tend to have domestic peace, but the process of getting there is, statistically speaking, likely to be conflictual and often violent.[21]

THE "LIBERAL PEACE" AND ITS CRITICS

The increasingly standardized international reform package introduced after wars or regime change was built around institutions of liberal political democracy and a market economy, based on the tacit, and sometimes explicit, assumption that this would promote peace (hence the term "the liberal peace"). The assumption has a strong intellectual tradition, going back to Immanuel Kant. One component had, by the mid-1990s, been certified by quantitative social science research, which found that democratic states rarely experience civil wars or wage war against each other.[22] The findings reinforced the natural inclinations of Western liberal states, encouraged by the ideological hegemony of Western liberal democracy after the collapse of Soviet-style socialism, to reproduce their own institutions elsewhere. As a third wave of democratization occurred in former communist states and elsewhere,[23] it seemed self-evident that democratic elections was the first step toward peace in postwar states. This, in turn, assumed at least a minimally functioning state. Pioneered in Cambodia, state building, peacebuilding and democratization thus merged in the increasingly standardized international regime for transitioning countries from war to peace.

Economic liberalization was introduced as another standard component with strong support from the International Monetary Fund and the World Bank. Privatization was in line with the principle of the World Bank's 1997 state-building formula, that state functions should match state capabilities and be suitable for failed or fragile states that by definition were weak. The further link between economic reform and conflict was developed in another major World Bank study, which showed that rapid growth with poverty reduction reduced the probability that countries that once had experienced civil war would experience renewed, major conflict.[24]

The "liberal peace" was soon attacked from several directions. The most radical critique viewed internationally supported state-cum-peacebuilding as a form of neocolonialism that was morally indefensible and, by denying autonomous development, was genuinely illiberal.[25] A more narrow instrumentalist perspective focused on the technical limitations of strategies to achieve peace, democracy, and development. Bridging the two positions, other critics argued that the strategies were failing in large part precisely because they were externally promoted and directed.

Institutionalize First

The assumption that economic and political liberalization would promote peace was attacked in a pioneering 2004 study by Roland Paris.[26] Echoing the much earlier work of Samuel Huntington on modernization and violence in developing countries,[27] Paris called for institutionalization before liberalization in order to blunt the potential for renewed violence in societies emerging from civil war where common institutions were still weak and consensus frail. Liberalizing reforms that embedded principles of competition in both economic and political life would, under these conditions, produce more conflict than peace, he argued. Similar findings emerged from studies of early postwar elections, although there were significant variations.[28] As for rapid economic liberalization, the negative consequences of rapid privatization driven by donors and the IFIs were documented in postwar situations as diverse as Cambodia, Mozambique, Angola, and Bosnia. The reforms enabled well-positioned individuals and factions to capture the process and its dividends, fueling massive corruption, inequality, organized crime, and human rights violations.[29]

The limitations of prevailing strategies of early liberalization masked deeper problems that defied easy solutions. International agencies tried to build institutions to counter the misuse and conflict associated with economic liberalization and elections, but creating effective institutions in the sense of consensual, binding rules is perhaps the most difficult of all building tasks. Donors seeking to speed up the postwar transition typically created empty institutions that outwardly fit the template of reform, while real power resided elsewhere. Not surprisingly, the expected results were not forthcoming.[30]

Empty institutions in turn reflect underlying problems of legitimacy. Even in areas where international interventions were welcomed as a liberation—as in East Timor and Kosovo—local resentment over limited participation and perceived excessive foreign control soon developed.[31] In East Timor, it took exactly three months after the UN transitional regime (UNTAET) was established until angry demonstrators converged on the plaza before the office of the UN Special Representative, located in the palatial building of the earlier Portuguese colonial rulers. Problems of legitimacy were most obvious in "the new protectorates,"[32] that is, where the UN administered an area directly. Yet they were evident in all state- and peacebuilding operations where aid came with a reform agenda fine-tuned by international organizations, donor agencies, and external consultants.

Local Ownership

In theory, the principle of "local ownership" of aid strategies would address problems of legitimacy and effectiveness, as much of the policy-oriented literature in support of state building emphasized.[33] But the problem remained. International actors understandably wished to control events in order to secure outcomes in accordance with their own interests. This clashed in principle and often in practice with the concept of local ownership, made more difficult by the presence of many and often rival local groups, all claiming ownership. The consequent contradiction between local ownership and external control seemed embedded in the state building venture. It was striking in cases of deep international involvement, as in Afghanistan,[34] where local postwar elites had vested interests in the war or postwar aid economy,[35] or where politics were shaped by the power of patronage networks or patrimonial rule, thinly disguised by what Abrams famously called "the mask of the state."[36] Such elites had little interests in Weberian-

inspired reforms designed to establish the state as a neutral arena for all players and prevent state resources from being tapped for private gain.

The difficulties of translating the principle of local ownership into practice helps explain why building a legitimate, effective, and neutral state is a slow and uncertain process. One recent ranking of countries based on their democratic properties is indicative. Of the 167 countries on the list, twenty-one had experienced civil war and received considerable postconflict assistance. Of these, none made it into the top category ("democracies"), five were in the second highest category ("flawed democracies"), ten ranked lower ("hybrid regimes"), and six were on the bottom ("authoritarian regimes").[37]

Building a Rentier State

Externally assisted state building contains another contradiction that makes it an uncertain tool of democratization and, to that extent, of building a legitimate state. A large influx of aid relative to local revenue generation will foster so-called rentier states. Heavy dependence on foreign assistance gives elites in such states stronger incentives to please their foreign patrons than to develop long-term political bargains with their own people for local revenue extraction in ways that entail democratic accountability. As a result, rentier-state elites are typically corrupt and narrowly self-serving. Elites more dependent on local taxation, by contrast, have stronger incentives to improve local governance, administration, and democratic accountability.[38]

The state-building project in Afghanistan illustrates the point.[39] For the entire decade after the 2001 US-led intervention, foreign funds accounted for around 85 percent of all official expenditures. By 2012, local revenue collection had increased but remained comparatively unimportant. The inflow of external funds crowded out Afghan strategies for capital accumulation in the service of long-term development and institutions of good governance and democratization. Responding to the easy availability of foreign money, Afghan elites looked to donor assistance and the war economy for funds to run the state and, for many, to enrich their families through corruption on a truly grand scale. The international actors, for their part, appeared powerless to promote good governance and democratization, in part because of their reciprocal dependence on Afghan authorities to pursue the war against the Taliban and Al Qaeda, but also because of the inherent difficulties of imposing democratic processes on an unwilling but generously funded partner.

REAPPRAISALS

The growing awareness of dilemmas, problems, and contradictions of state building led to a reappraisal that was gathering momentum in the second half of the 2000s. The reappraisal took place against the sobering realization that the most ambitious and costly international interventions at the time—in Iraq and Afghanistan—showed very modest results. "Fixing failed states" was obviously not as easy as some analysts had confidently proclaimed.[40] Even state-building projects unfolding under more peaceful conditions seemed to stall. The 2009 World Bank-UNDP mission to Liberia cited above was deeply pessimistic. Despite the huge international investment and a national leader recognized for her integrity, cooperation, and will to reform, the Liberian state remained fragile. In the words of their joint report, "It is even possible that the unspoken overall goal of the aid community, i.e. reconstituting Liberia as a functioning Weberian state, is not attainable."[41] The Economist Intelligence Unit in 2012

gave Liberia a score of 0.79 on a scale of 0 to 10 for "functioning of the government"—the same score earned by Afghanistan.[42]

New Key Words

A comprehensive survey of internationally assisted state-building operations in Africa published in a major American academic journal found the results "paltry" and recommended a radical rethinking.[43] In the policy-oriented world of academia and think tanks, the rethinking had already begun. Analysts were scanning recent state-cum-peacebuilding experiences in order to uncover underlying problems and contradictions. While such tensions might not be resolved, hopefully they could be managed better.[44] In this spirit, new key words appeared: "tailor-made reforms," "local context," "local knowledge," and "external long-term commitment and patience." Strategies on how to exit from transformative interventions were studied with new interest.[45]

As part of this reappraisal, analysts started to investigate alternative approaches to state building and the state-centric paradigm that had dominated the "long decade." Given the difficulty of (re)building or reforming states, it seemed better to work from structures other than the state that did—or could—provide equivalent core functions in areas of security, justice, and social services. Researchers documented various forms of governance without a state[46] and the possibility of governing "ungoverned spaces."[47] The new trend built on earlier awareness of the problems of empty institutions and the argument that effective reform must build on existing local practices to create hybrid institutions.[48] It was an implicit recognition of the pioneering work by Menkhaus on Somalia, which demonstrated that even in the rubble of a totally collapsed state, forms of governance did exist to provide a modicum of security and justice.[49]

Security, for instance, could in some situations be provided by armed groups with ties to the local community,[50] or by communities mobilizing against rival hostile groups.[51] On the other hand, analysts using economic models acknowledged that "security markets" might not function optimally by providing security to all (a collective good) rather than only to those who were included in the scheme (a "club good"), and competition among armed groups would create insecurity all around.[52] Some analysts placed faith in the capacity of non-state actors to provide justice by building on institutions of so-called traditional justice in the form of customary law, often administered by local village institutions of elders, or Islamic law interpreted by local religious authorities.[53] Similarly, public-private partnerships (PPPs) and civil society organizations were important providers of social services under conditions of "limited statehood,"[54] often with external support and informed by international norms and standards. A measure of governance was thus possible despite low state capacity.

Alternatives to the conventional state-centric approach were gaining some traction in aid organizations. The 2011 *World Development Report* focused on policies and functions rather than structures and institutions; the priority now was to build transnational coalitions in support of right policies and appropriate reforms.[55] Among the major donor agencies, the UK Department for International Development (DFID), which maintained a large research program, launched a new multiyear project to identify local voices and structures and to explore hybrid institutions in "states in fragile situations," as was now the preferred term.[56] It was an admission of the limits of orthodox state building of the top-down, outside-in variety, more obviously so because the previous DFID research program of this kind had been state-centric.

Yet interest in new approaches did not signal a lessened concern to guide developments in turbulent parts of the world. Strong transnational constituencies for poverty reduction, human rights, and peace were joined by powerful actors such as the US Department of Defense, which articulated security doctrines that held "ungoverned spaces" to be sources of international terrorism and narco-trafficking. In Afghanistan, the main international driver for support to traditional justice was the US military, which saw it as part of a counterinsurgency strategy.[57] Moreover, the World Bank significantly contributed to the sense of an anarchic and violent world with its 2011 *World Development Report*, which skewed interpretation of figures on conflict toward the highest possible estimates and conflated quite diverse types of violence. To the general reader, it appeared as a strong rationale for external intervention in so-called fragile states.[58] In this respect, it echoed the 2004 UN report on international security threats discussed above.[59] Methods and strategies, however, were changing in response to critics, failures on the ground, and accumulated lessons learned.[60]

Voices from the South: The g7+

Within the fragile states themselves, lessons had been learned as well. To counter the growing criticism of prevailing state building approaches, as well as to prevent possible aid cuts prompted by the 2008 financial crisis, governments in fragile states became proactive. Calling itself g7+ (with a small g) after the initial seven members, the group soon grew to eighteen states which formulated revised principles for assistance to state building and peacebuilding and for joint monitoring of implementation.[61] Their efforts were recognized at OECD's high-level meeting in Busan, South Korea, in November 2011, which endorsed a "New Deal for

Engagement in Fragile States."[62] The New Deal differed from the "old deal" formulated by the donors in the earlier OECD Principles in two main respects. First, national leadership and ownership were now emphasized as the only way out of fragility. Second, the criteria for evaluating external assistance should include progress in peacebuilding and state building as defined by the g7+ and cover several areas: legitimate politics, security, justice, economic foundations, and revenues and services.

It was an initiative from below to seize the agenda, although worked out in close cooperation with donors. As such, the New Deal reflected a compromise. The governments of so-called fragile states committed to the key strategies of state building that donors long had promoted (increasing local revenues, improving public financial management and transparency,) and to the use of state building as an instrument of peace (through inclusive political settlements and conflict resolution, strengthening "people's security," and addressing injustices). In return, they hoped to secure long-term assistance, and also to exert greater control over the aid process and the regular evaluations. The New Deal was a response to the growing criticism that local elites lacked the will or the capacity to support reforms, and to the equally pointed criticism that external actors imposed standardized packages that created empty institutions. As such, it embodied the evolving consensus on guidelines for development cooperation that all parties, without much difficulty, could agree to in principle. The test was how the guidelines would be interpreted and followed in practice.

The View from the North

In the United States and Europe, where the ambitious state- and peacebuilding agenda had been formulated and financed, there was a parallel reassessment. NATO's intervention in Libya in 2011 is indicative: it was a limited military action, followed by a limited international civilian presence to aid state building. The contrast with the comprehensive and deep international engagement in Afghanistan is striking. Admittedly, the two cases were different. Unlike Afghanistan, Libya had a relatively functioning, if nondemocratic, state at the time of regime change. The country's oil resources made it independent of foreign financial assistance and the related demands for reform. Instead, foreign consultants and companies lined up for contracts with the Libyan government, as the UN Support Mission in Libya (UNSMIL) noted.[63]

But the contrasting response also expressed the erosion of confidence in Europe and the United States in ambitious programs of internationally assisted state building. The costly and controversial interventions in Iraq and Afghanistan had left little taste for a repeat, and the demonstrations of Arab nationalism during the nationally driven regime changes elsewhere in the Middle East had given "local ownership" a new meaning. The general change in mood was noted by the UN Peacebuilding Commission as well. In a remarkably frank report in early 2013, the commission highlighted "the lack of strong political support" from member countries for its work and chided the Security Council for not engaging with the peacebuilding agenda.[64]

Economic considerations worked in the same direction. Economic crisis in several European states, and economic austerity in most of the European Union and United States, caused marked reductions in official development aid. Aid from OECD members fell in real terms by 2 percent in 2011 and another 4 percent in 2012. There was also a noticeable shift in aid allocations away from the poorest countries and toward the middle-income countries.[65] As typically low-income countries, so-called fragile states with state- and peacebuilding programs were certain to feel the cuts. Outside the OECD, the new emerging major powers—Brazil, China, and India—showed little interest in multilateral programs of this kind.

CONCLUSIONS

The "long decade" of state building that started after the Cold War was premised on what soon proved to be optimistic and unwarranted assumptions about the facility of state building and the positive relationship between building states and building peace. As criticism based on experience on the ground mounted, readjustments and reappraisals took place. One main challenge to the orthodoxies of the 1990s—which lasted well into the 2000s—aimed at the donor-directed process. Articulated in the literature, the criticism was placed on the policy agenda by a group of self-styled "fragile states"—the g7+ (with a small g)—with ambitions to turn the policy rhetoric of local ownership and local-led processes into reality. Another main challenge was to the state-centric approach itself, although this was received with some caution in the world of states.

Both criticisms reflected the difficulties of externally assisted state building. External actors and local elites often did not have congruent interests in building states and peace. The process of state building—while carrying the promise of peace in the long run—was itself conflictual. To produce quick and desired results, assistance missions tended to be intrusive, crowd out local initiatives, and create institutions with weak legitimacy. Weak internal legitimacy in turn eroded the foundation of the state being built. The counterproductive dynamic was most obvious where international involvement was heavy, as in Afghanistan, and in-

cluded fighting a major war. Here building peace while waging war generated so many internal tensions that the principal tasks of creating an effective state and a sustainable peace were not accomplished, although progress was made in service sectors heavily funded by donors, such as health and education. But even in Liberia—a country formally at peace and led by a capable president dedicated to reforms—huge inflows of aid money and international consultants had, after almost a decade of efforts, failed to establish an even minimally effective state.

The main reasons seem to lie in the very nature of the state-building process. As noted above, historically most states have been *formed* over long periods of time, not built over a few years. The exceptional cases of state *building* in modern history have occurred under truly exceptional circumstances, characterized by existential national security threats, exceptional national leadership with a vision for the future, and the presence of national resources to finance reform. This was the case of Turkey under Kemal Ataturk, the Meiji Restoration in Japan, and the Chakri dynasty in late nineteenth-century Thailand. If there are any lessons from these events for the present, it is that *building* states indeed requires exceptional national efforts and national leadership.

The presence of external threats is particularly important in relation to the question of legitimacy. In the above three cases, acute national awareness of external threats seemed to legitimize the costs, sacrifices, and losses incurred by building a stronger state. A similar dynamic has been observed in the contemporary emergence of the "Asian Tigers." Perceived existential national security threats gave the governments of South Korea, Taiwan, and Singapore the capacity and legitimacy necessary to harness resources and reshape the state into a more effective apparatus for economic growth and development.[66] By contrast, in the long decade of state building examined above, international actors have been visibly on the inside of the process, making nationalism a marginally relevant source of legitimacy for the new state. Promises of good governance and an implicit social contract were invoked instead, but these sources of legitimacy are tied to future service deliveries, which mostly are slow or modest in coming. Good governance, in short, lacks the ideational force of nationalism or religion.

The policy implication of this analysis is twofold. First, state *formation* rather than state *building* must be the operative word in most of the so-called fragile countries. State formation connotes a long-term and often conflictual process. Second, international assistance does have a role, but the declaratory emphasis on local ownership must be taken seriously to give room for autonomous local development, and a sustainable process. This means that international actors need to take a backseat role in the aid relationship, pay more attention to local absorptive capacity than quick results, develop rather than import capacity, hold a long-term view, recognize the kind of limitations and systemic restraint that became evident during the "long decade," and scale down expectations accordingly.

A New Deal along these lines can have several consequences, most obviously less aid and fewer external consultants. Moreover, developments on the ground may well conflict with the interests of external actors concerned and with their criteria for an effective state and a sustainable peace. Yet the alternative strategy of intrusive and directive external assistance did not deliver the expected results and in important respects was clearly counter-productive. Viewed in this light, a genuine New Deal appears to reflect a fortuitous harmony between what is desirable and what is realistic in the present international environment.

NOTES

1. Michael Mann, *The Sources of Social Power*, vol. 2. *The Rise of Classes and Nation-States, 1760–1914* (Cambridge: Cambridge University Press, 1993).

2. World Bank, *World Development Report 1997: The State in a Changing World* (Washington, DC: World Bank, 1997).

3. World Bank, *Afghanistan: State Building, Sustaining Growth, and Reducing Poverty* (Washington, DC: World Bank, 2005).

4. Organisation for Economic Co-operation and Development (OECD), "Principles for Good International Engagement in Fragile States and Situations," April 2007.

5. OECD, *International Engagement in Fragile States: Can't We Do Better?* (Paris: OECD, 2011).

6. United Nations, "Agreement on a Comprehensive Political Settlement of the Cambodia Conflict, Article 6" (UN Document A/8/608-S23177), October 30, 1991, United States Institute of Peace, Peace Agreements Digital Collection, http://www.usip.org/sites/default/files/file/resources/collections/peace_agreements/agree_comppol_10231991.pdf.

7. The point was made in the 2000 report of the high-level panel chaired by Lakhdar Brahimi. The "Report of the Panel on United Nations Peace Operations" (UN document A/55/305-S/2000/809), or Brahimi Report, recommended a stronger UN role to support tasks such as improving the civilian police, rule of law, and human rights; demobilizing belligerent armies; and holding elections. All this presumed a minimally effective state.

8. United Nations, *A More Secure World: Our Shared Responsibility. Report of the High-Level Panel on Threats, Challenges and Change* (New York: UN, 2004).

9. UN Peacebuilding Commission, "Strategic Framework for Peacebuilding in Burundi" (UN document PBC/1/BDI/4), July 2007, *ReliefWeb*, http://reliefweb.int/report/burundi/strategic -framework-peacebuilding-burundi.

10. Mann, *Sources of Social Power*, vol. 2.

11. Mark R. Duffield, *Development, Security and Unending War: Governing the World of Peoples* (Cambridge: Polity, 2007); and David Chandler, *Empire in Denial: The Politics of State-Building* (London: Pluto, 2006).

12. The literature is huge, but the following titles are suggestive. An early main volume is Elizabeth Cousens, Chetan Kumar, and Karin Wermester, eds., *Peacebuilding as Politics: Cultivating Peace in Fragile Societies* (Boulder, CO: Lynne Rienner, 2000). Most confidently can-do is Ashraf Ghani and Clare Lockhart, *Fixing Failed States: A Framework for Rebuilding a Fractured World* (Oxford: Oxford University Press, 2008). The anthology edited by Charles Call and Vanessa Wyeth, *Building States to Build Peace* (Boulder, CO: Lynne Rienner, 2008), has some skeptics, while Timothy Sisk's recent book, *Statebuilding* (Cambridge: Polity, 2013), reviews the literature in detail, concluding that externally assisted state building for peace can succeed if properly designed.

13. Charles Tilly, *Coercion, Capital, and European States, AD 990–1990* (Cambridge, MA: Blackwell, 1990).

14. Brian D. Taylor and Roxana Botea, "Tilly Tally: War-Making and State-Making in the Contemporary Third World," *International Studies Review* 10 (2008): 27–56.

15. George Sørensen, "War and State-Making: Why Doesn't It Work in the Third World?" *Security Dialogue* 32, no. 3 (2001): 341–54; and Barnett R. Rubin, "Constructing Sovereignty for Security," *Survival* 47, no. 4 (2005): 93–106.

16. Michael W. Doyle and Nicholas Sambanis, "International Peacebuilding: A Theoretical and Quantitative Analysis," *American Political Science Review* 94, no. 4 (2000): 779–801; and Michael W. Doyle and Nicholas Sambanis, *Making War and Building Peace: United Nations Peace Operations* (Princeton, NJ: Princeton University Press, 2006).

17. World Bank and United Nations Development Programme, "Report of the Technical Mission to Liberia on State Building in Fragile and Post-Conflict Contexts" (Washington, DC: World Bank, 2009).

18. Torunn Wimpelmann Chaudhary, "The Political Economies of Violence in Post-War Liberia," in *The Peace in Between: Post-War Violence and Peacebuilding*, ed. Astri Suhrke and Mats Berdal (London: Routledge, 2012), 248–66.

19. World Bank and United Nations Development Programme, "Report of the Technical Mission to Liberia."

20. Ken Menkhaus, "Governance without Government in Somalia: Spoilers, Statebuilding, and the Politics of Coping," *International Security* 31, no. 3 (2006): 74–106.

21. Håvard Hegre, Tanja Ellingsen, Scott Gates, and Nils Petter Gleditsch, "Toward a Democratic Civil Peace? Democracy, Political Change, and Civil War, 1816–1992," *American Political Science Review* 95, no. 1 (2001): 33–48.

22. Bruce Russett, *Grasping the Democratic Peace: Principles for a Post–Cold War World* (Princeton, NJ: Princeton University Press, 1993).

23. Samuel P. Huntington, *The Third Wave: Democratization in the Late Twentieth Century* (Norman: University of Oklahoma Press, 1991).

24. World Bank, *Breaking the Conflict Trap: Civil War and Development Policy* (New York: Oxford University Press, 2003).

25. David Chandler, *International Statebuilding: The Rise of Post-Liberal Governance* (London: Routledge, 2010).

26. Roland Paris, *At War's End: Building Peace after Civil Conflict* (New York: Cambridge University Press, 2004).

27. Samuel P. Huntington, *Political Order in Changing Societies* (New Haven, CT: Yale University Press, 1968).

28. Anna K. Jarstad and Timothy D. Sisk, eds., *From War to Democracy: Dilemmas of Peacebuilding* (New York: Cambridge University Press, 2008).

29. Michael Pugh, Neil Cooper, and Jonathan Goodhand, *War Economies in a Regional Context: Challenges of Transformation* (Boulder, CO: Lynne Rienner, 2004); and Christopher Cramer, "Trajectories of Accumulation through War and Peace," in *The Dilemmas of Statebuilding: Confronting Contradictions of Postwar Operations*, ed. Roland Paris and Timothy D. Sisk (London: Routledge, 2009).

30. Roger Mac Ginty and Oliver Richmond, "Myth or Reality: Opposing Views on the Liberal Peace and Post-War Reconstruction," in *The Liberal Peace and Post-War Reconstruction*, ed. Roger Mac Ginty and Oliver Richmond (London: Routledge, 2009). For additional critical analysis of "the liberal peace" and state building, see Oliver Richmond, *A Post Liberal Peace* (London: Routledge, 2011), and Oliver Richmond, *Liberal Peace Transitions: Between Statebuilding and Peacebuilding* (Edinburgh: Edinburg University Press, 2009).

31. Richard Caplan, *A New Trusteeship? The International Administration of War-Torn Territories* (Oxford: Oxford University Press, 2002); Mats Berdal, *Building Peace after War* (London: International Institute of Strategic Studies, 2009); and Dominik Zaum, "The New Protectorates: Statebuilding and Legitimacy," in *The New Protectorates: International Tutelage and the Making of Liberal States*, ed. James Mayall and Ricardo Soares de Oliveira (New York: Columbia University Press, 2011), 281–342.

32. Mayall and Soares de Oliveira, *The New Protectorates*.

33. See note 12 above.

34. Astri Suhrke, *When More Is Less: The International Project in Afghanistan* (New York: Columbia University Press, 2011).

35. Michael Barnett and Christopher Zürcher, "The Peacebuilder's Contract: How External Statebuilding Reinforces Weak Statehood," in Paris and Sisk, *Dilemmas of Statebuilding*, 23–52.

36. Philip Abrams, "Notes on the Difficulty of Studying the State" [1977], *Journal of Historical Sociology* 1, no. 1 (1988): 58–89.

37. Economist Intelligence Unit, "Democracy Index 2012: Democracy at a Standstill," https://www.eiu.com/public/topical_report.aspx?campaignid=DemocracyIndex12. The index is based on five indicators (electoral processes/pluralism, functioning of government, political participation, political culture, and civil liberties), with a score range of 0 to 10. In 2012, the actual range was from 1.08 (North Korea) to 9.9 (Norway). As noted, twenty-one of the countries listed have been major recipients of postconflict assistance. Of these, Serbia, Slovenia, Croatia, El Salvador, and East Timor were "flawed democracies" (category score range 6 to 7.9); Guatemala, Nicaragua, Haiti, Uganda, Libya, Mozambique, Iraq, Nepal, Cambodia, and Bosnia and Herzegovina were "hybrid regimes" (category score range 4 to 5.9); and Liberia, Sierra Leone, Rwanda, Angola, Democratic Republic of the Congo, and Afghanistan were "authoritarian" (category score range 0 to 3.9).

38. Michael Ross, "Does Oil Hinder Democracy?" *World Politics* 53, no. 3 (2001): 325–61; and Deborah Bräutigam, Odd-Helge Fjeldstad, and Mick Moore, eds., *Taxation and Statebuilding in Developing Countries* (Cambridge: Cambridge University Press, 2008). For a broader discussion of the rentier state concept in relation to resource dependence and de facto international protectorates such as Bosnia, see Michael Danderstädt and Arne Schildberg, eds., *Dead Ends of Transition: Rentier Economies and Protectorates* (Frankfurt: Campus Verlag, 2006).

39. See Suhrke, *When More Is Less*.

40. See Ghani and Lockhart, *Fixing Failed States*.

41. World Bank and United Nations Development Programme, "Report of the Technical Mission to Liberia."

42. Economist Intelligence Unit, "Democracy Index 2012."

43. Pierre Englebert and Denis M. Tull, "Postconflict Reconstruction in Africa," *International Security* 32, no. 4 (2008): 106–39.

44. Paris and Sisk, *The Dilemmas of Statebuilding*, 304.

45. Richard Caplan, ed., *Exit Strategies and Statebuilding* (Oxford: Oxford University Press, 2012).

46. Thomas Risse, ed., *Governance without a State?* (New York: Columbia University Press, 2011).

47. Anne L. Clunan and Harold A. Trinkunas, eds., *Ungoverned Spaces: Alternatives to State Authority in an Era of Softened Sovereignty* (Stanford, CA: Stanford University Press, 2010).

48. Volker Boege, Anne Brown, Kevin Clements, and Anna Nolan, "On Hybrid Political Orders and Emerging States: What Is Failing—States in the Global South or Research and Politics in the West?" in *Building Peace in the Absence of States:*

Challenging the Discourse on State Failure, ed. Martina Fischer and Beatrix Schmelzle (Berlin: Berghof Foundation, 2009), 15–35.

49. Menkhaus, "Governance without Government in Somalia."

50. William Reno, "Persistent Insurgencies and Warlords: Who Is Nasty, Who Is Nice, and Why?" in Clunan and Trinkunas, *Ungoverned Spaces*, 57–76.

51. Mohammed Osman Tariq, "Tribal Security System (Arbakai) in Southeast Afghanistan," Crisis States Occasional Paper no. 7 (Crisis States Research Centre, UK Department for International Development, London, 2008), http://www.dfid.gov.uk/r4d/Output/179041/Default.aspx.

52. Sven Chojnacki and Zeljko Branovic, "New Modes of Security: The Violent Making and Unmaking of Governance in War-Torn Areas of Limited Statehood," in Risse, *Governance Without a State*, 89–114; and Stergios Skaperdas, "Warlord Competition," *Journal of Peace Research* 39, no. 4 (2002): 435–66.

53. Noah Coburn and John Dempsey, "Informal Dispute Resolution in Afghanistan," Special Report 247 (United States Institute of Peace, Washington, DC, 2010); and Danish Institute for International Studies (DIIS), *Non-State Actors in Justice and Security Reform* (Copenhagen: DIIS, 2011), http://www.diis.dk/sw111521.asp.

54. Risse, *Governance without a State*, 2.

55. World Bank, *World Development Report 2011: Conflict, Security and Development* (Washington, DC: World Bank, 2011).

56. "Governance, Security and Justice in Fragile and Conflict-Affected Situations" (Justice and Security Research Programme, UK Department for International Development, 2011), http://www.dfid.gov.uk/r4d/Project/60873/Default.aspx.

57. Suhrke, *When More Is Less*, 211–17.

58. Astri Suhrke and Ingrid Samset, "Cycles of Violence? WDR 2011: Three Issues and a Question" (forum, Nordic Africa Institute, July 1, 2011), http://www.naiforum.org/tag/astri-suhrke.

59. United Nations, *A More Secure World.*

60. Susan Woodward, "The IFIs and Post-Conflict Political Economy," in *Political Economy of Statebuilding: Power after Peace*, ed. Mats Berdal and Dominik Zaum (London: Routledge, 2013), 140–57.

61. Members listed on the g7+ website (http://www.g7plus.org/) at the time of writing were Afghanistan, Burundi, Central African Republic, Chad, Comoros, Côte d'Ivoire, Democratic Republic of the Congo, Guinea, Guinea-Bissau, Haiti, Liberia, Papua New Guinea, Sierra Leone, Solomon Islands, Somalia, South Sudan, Timor-Leste, and Togo. A principal founding member was Emilia Pires, Finance Minister of Timor-Leste.

62. Organization for Economic Cooperation and Development, "A New Deal for Engagement in Fragile States" (2011), http://www.newdeal4peace.org/.

63. United Nations, "Report of the Secretary-General on the United Nations Support Mission in Libya" (UN document S/2012/129), March 1, 2012.

64. UN Peacebuilding Commission, "Report of the Peacebuilding Commission on Its Sixth Session" (UN document A/67/715-S/2013/63), January 29, 2013, 3.

65. Organization for Economic Cooperation and Development, "Aid to Poor Countries Slips Further as Governments Tighten Budgets," March 4, 2013, http://www.oecd.org/newsroom/aidtopoorcountriesslipsfurtherasgovernmentstightenbudgets.htm.

66. Richard F. Doner, Bryant K. Ritchie, and Dan Slater, "Systemic Vulnerability and the Origins of Developmental States: Northeast and Southeast Asia in Comparative Perspective," *International Organization* 59, no. 2 (2005): 327–61.

33

PEACEBUILDING AND TRANSITIONAL JUSTICE
THE ROAD AHEAD

Jane E. Stromseth

The pursuit of justice is central to peacebuilding after conflict. The architecture of "transitional justice" has developed dramatically since the early 1990s: international criminal tribunals for the former Yugoslavia and Rwanda were followed by hybrid national-international courts—as in Timor-Leste, Sierra Leone, Bosnia and Herzegovina, and Cambodia—and by the permanent International Criminal Court in The Hague. Truth and reconciliation commissions in many different countries reached out directly to victims of atrocities, often supplemented by reparations, both material and symbolic, and by institutional reforms in security and justice systems. Governments and international organizations, nongovernmental organizations (NGOs), universities, and civic organizations developed programs and expertise in postconflict justice, truth seeking, redress, reconciliation, and atrocity prevention.

Yet what do we really know about the impact of these dramatic developments? Impressive as the architecture is, a deeper understanding of how well these efforts are working is called for. As destructive conflicts continue in many parts of the world—and as men, women, and children suffer from crimes against humanity and unspeakable pain on a daily basis—what can the mechanisms of justice realistically expect to accomplish? As communities struggle to build peace after years of violent conflict and repression, what can be learned from the experiences of countries as diverse as Sierra Leone, Timor-Leste, Cambodia, Bosnia and Herzegovina, Peru, and Afghanistan? Beyond the unique experiences and lessons of particular countries, do efforts to seek justice in transitioning societies encounter recurring challenges that require systematic attention?

This chapter grapples with these questions. The pursuit of justice after conflict is an essential component of peacebuilding. Like a large boulder in the middle of a river, expectations about justice influence the flow and dynamic of peacebuilding waters.

Anyone navigating these turbulent currents needs to be aware of the developments, lessons, and dilemmas of transitional justice during the past several decades. Tensions between some forms of justice and peace processes may exist in particular contexts, as may tensions between international goals and local aspirations, but so too do ways to mitigate tensions and build constructive synergies.

This chapter begins by examining the "what, why, and how" of transitional justice. After discussing different understandings of transitional justice, it examines diverse goals of this complicated enterprise, the evolution of mechanisms to achieve these goals, and trends in the field since the early 1990s. Three enduring challenges are explored in detail, together with emerging opportunities growing out of these challenges. The chapter then examines what empirical studies suggest about the impact of transitional justice efforts; it looks ahead to where this field is going as a component of conflict management and global security; and it concludes with observations for the future.

EVOLUTION OF TRANSITIONAL JUSTICE SINCE THE 1990S

Fundamentally, transitional justice involves measures that countries transitioning out of conflict take to address a legacy of atrocities and massive human rights abuses committed during armed conflict or under repressive regimes. The concept emerged prominently in the late 1980s and early 1990s as countries in Latin America transitioned from periods of conflict and repression to more democratic societies, although the term has earlier roots.[1] As the phrase implies, transitional justice is always a work in progress—dynamic, evolving, and never fully complete. As Mahatma Gandhi responded when asked what he thought of Western civilization: "It would be a good idea."[2] So too is transitional justice.

Whether transitional justice should be conceived broadly or more precisely is a source of some debate. A core understanding of transitional justice focuses on seeking accountability for egregious crimes that violate international law, such as genocide, war crimes, and crimes against humanity, and for other severe human rights abuses committed during conflicts. Other observers advocate for a broader conception that also addresses larger issues of domestic societal transformation: for instance, looking at systemic causes of abuse and seeking to work for fundamental changes in governmental and social institutions—changes that will reduce human rights abuses and consolidate democracy moving forward.[3] Some observers contend that economic crimes, corruption, and development imperatives should be given greater attention as part of transitional justice.[4] But common to most conceptions is a central focus on seeking some measure of justice for victims, some accountability for perpetrators, and some meaningful reforms to deter a recurrence of atrocities and severe human rights violations.

Goals of Transitional Justice

Why seek transitional justice? Every country emerging from a period of conflict, trauma, or repression will face unique circumstances, constraints, and possibilities in confronting its past. Moreover, within societies, groups often differ over which goals should take priority as the country transitions to stability. Increasingly, though, many civil society leaders have emphasized that peace will not endure without some sustained effort to confront past abuses and build public confidence in the rule of law moving forward. As these issues are contested and resolved, if uneasily and imperfectly, proponents of transitional justice have sought to advance a number of important goals that—taken together—can help address and fairly adjudicate the grievances that afflict societies torn apart by violence.

An overarching goal is *accountability*. Holding perpetrators of egregious international crimes personally liable, whether they are government actors or militia leaders, helps dismantle a legacy of impunity for such crimes. Demonstrating that their conduct was wrong and in violation of agreed norms of international law, and showing that impunity for such crimes is ending and that even the high and mighty are now bound by the law, is a central aspect of providing meaningful substantive *justice*.[5] Justice in the sense of *fair process* is also a crucial goal: providing due process to alleged perpetrators and ensuring impartial and even-handed adjudication are particularly important to building expectations of fair legal process in deeply skeptical populations navigating toward postconflict stability.[6]

Redress for victims (or reparative justice) is another crucial goal of transitional justice processes.[7] Acknowledgement and recognition of the harm and pain that victims have endured is, for many, a critical form of redress. Victims may seek apology from perpetrators as well as other forms of reparation, both material and symbolic, as recognition of the wrong they have suffered.

Truth seeking is fundamental to reckoning with the past.[8] How did the human rights abuses and atrocities happen, who was responsible (including governmental as well as nonstate militia groups), what are the root causes, and what needs to change to prevent such abuses from happening again? Developing a public understanding—a historical truth that is widely acknowledged—can help ensure that abuses are not forgotten or swept under the table. *Truth telling* and *truth hearing* can be vital elements of a deeper and less contested understanding of a common past.

Prevention of the recurrence of atrocities and abuses is a central aspiration of transitional justice. Effective prevention is a web that must operate at many mutually reinforcing levels. One central but challenging element of prevention is *deterrence*: holding individual perpetrators accountable and removing them from positions in which they can intimidate and abuse others can begin the process of demonstrating that certain conduct is out of bounds, identifying redlines and putting others on notice that they too may face justice if they cross those lines.[9] Also crucial are structural and systemic reforms that focus on the underlying causes of human rights abuses.

Reconciliation, in the sense of working to overcome deep divisions and antagonisms among long-contending groups that ultimately must face a common future, is often highlighted as a goal of transitional justice processes. Reconciliation can be enormously challenging at many different levels. At a national level, a country and its political and civic leaders may aim to move forward constructively, including and welcoming previously contending groups in the political process. Civil society organizations can take steps to advance intergroup understanding and the ability to see the "other" in more empathetic terms. But moving beyond long-standing, deeply felt divisions and grievances can take years. Prospects for reconciliation at the community and the personal level will depend on many unique factors, including individual willingness to take responsibility for misdeeds and individual willingness to forgive.[10]

Additional ambitious goals of transitional justice include consolidating democracy and improving governance as well as strengthening human rights compliance more generally. These and other aims are only imperfectly realizable, as the discussion below elaborates. Moreover, the means to seek such ambitious goals are themselves works in progress.

Mechanisms of Transitional Justice

How can justice be sought after conflict? No single mechanism can possibly achieve all the goals of transitional justice. Different mechanisms are better at advancing some goals than others, and some combination of measures over a considerable period of time will usually be part of a country's transitional justice strategy.

Criminal prosecutions, for example, are a way to try individuals and to hold personally accountable those convicted of genocide, war crimes, and crimes against humanity. Ideally, prosecutions can help remove specific offenders from positions of power in which they abuse and intimidate others; they can document individual responsibility for horrific atrocities; they can provide concrete examples of fair judicial process; and they can provide some measure of justice to victims who have suffered at the hands of perpetrators. Criminal prosecutions, as discussed below, have been held before international tribunals, before hybrid courts consisting of both national and international judges and lawyers, and before domestic courts. But because trials inevitably focus on a small number of individuals and gather facts for the specific purpose of proving particular crimes, they are only a partial, albeit critical, response to the widespread harm that so often accompanies periods of intense conflict and repressive rule.

Truth commissions play a central role in many transitional justice processes.[11] Structured in different ways, truth commissions are often able to reach out to large numbers of victims and survivors of atrocities, to gain a fuller understanding of the harms experienced, to assess the underlying causes, and to bring communities together to confront a hurtful past. Truth commissions can some-

times uncover patterns of abuse that might otherwise go unaddressed and hear voices that might otherwise go unheard. They can offer a confidential venue in which victims of crimes such as sexual violence may feel more comfortable coming forward than in a public adversarial process. In Peru and in Timor-Leste, for example, women who had experienced sexual violence spoke out before truth commissions after initial reluctance to share their experiences.[12] Also, because truth commissions can take an overarching view of conflict and the causes of atrocities and abuses, they generally offer recommendations for structural reforms to prevent recurrence. Truth commissions may also include reconciliation measures, as in the community-based reconciliation processes in Timor-Leste, where perpetrators confessed to misdeeds and offered apologies and, in some instances, specific forms of redress to their victims.[13]

Reparations, both as part of truth commissions and independently of them, are also a valued part of transitional justice. Material reparations can take many forms, such as payments, free health care, and education benefits. Symbolic reparations, such as public apologies, public memorials, and listing the names of victims, may be just as important. In Timor-Leste, for instance, Balide Prison, the site of torture and abuse during the Indonesian occupation, is now a public memorial and museum.[14]

Transitional justice is also about looking forward: to ending and transforming abusive circumstances and preventing their recurrence. *Institutional reforms* are vital to this process. Security sector reforms may include vetting of military and police forces and removing from authority individuals who consistently violate fundamental human rights, in a process of "lustration."[15] Better training and professionalization of security forces, including training in international humanitarian law and human rights, and transparent mechanisms of monitoring and accountability for these forces, are often a critical part of the mix. Systematic justice sector reforms are also crucial, complex, and long-term elements of transitional justice strategies.[16] "Supply-side" reforms that aim to strengthen a country's ability to provide fairer mechanisms of dispute resolution must also be joined by "demand side" reforms that focus on bottom-up efforts to build public confidence through better access to justice and more responsive, accountable officials.[17]

If this all sounds logical and coherent in principle, it is enormously difficult in practice. There is no self-evident template of mechanisms or easy agreement on priorities and goals across the diverse societies struggling with legacies of violent conflict and brutal atrocities. Moreover, for many residents of countries racked by violence, halting the violence—achieving a basic peace—is the overriding near-term priority and precondition to living a normal life. Economic and development needs cry out for attention alongside struggles for justice and accountability.

TRENDS IN TRANSITIONAL JUSTICE

Across the diverse global terrain of countries emerging from conflict, repression, and massive human rights abuses, three overarching trends since 1990 are clear.

The Development of International and Hybrid Criminal Courts and Law

The most striking development since the early 1990s has been the creation of international and so-called hybrid, or mixed, criminal tribunals to hold perpetrators of atrocities individually accountable. The corresponding development and refinement of international criminal law is equally notable. When I embarked on my career as a law professor in 1991, the field of international criminal

law had hardly developed since Nuremberg; today, it is an active focus of scholarship, practice, and advocacy, attracting the commitment and passion of huge numbers of students and practitioners from around the globe.

To be sure, the International Criminal Tribunal for the former Yugoslavia (ICTY) and the International Criminal Tribunal for Rwanda (ICTR) were established belatedly, in the face of failure to prevent egregious crimes against humanity and genocide. Yet, despite their limitations, both tribunals sought to hold accountable perpetrators of atrocities in fair trials, and both courts can point to significant accomplishments. Since the UN Security Council established the ICTY in 1993, the tribunal has indicted 161 individuals, convicted and sentenced 69 defendants, and acquitted 18, with 12 cases involving 25 defendants ongoing as of November 2013.[18] In addition to bringing many individuals to account, establishing facts and creating a historical record, bringing some measure of justice to victims, and developing international criminal law, the ICTY has worked with judiciaries in the former Yugoslavia to support domestic prosecutions. The ICTR, created by the UN Security Council in 1994 to address atrocities in Rwanda, became the first tribunal to try and convict a head of government for genocide.[19] Each tribunal's record of outreach to victims is more mixed, however, as are views of the ICTY and ICTR among directly affected populations.[20]

In part because of the physical and psychological distance of these tribunals from the countries directly affected, a model of hybrid, or mixed, courts took root. In Timor-Leste, Sierra Leone, Bosnia and Herzegovina, and Cambodia, international and domestic leaders created new courts made up both of international *and* national judges, prosecutors, defense counsel, and administrators, located not in some far-off place but directly in the country that endured atrocities. The specifics differed—the hybrid concept is shaped in different ways: Timor-Leste's special panels were part of the domestic justice system, as is Bosnia's War Crimes Chamber, which phased out international actors over time; the Special Court for Sierra Leone, created by an agreement between the United Nations and the government, included a majority of internationally appointed judges; the hybrid court in Cambodia (the Extraordinary Chambers in the Courts of Cambodia, or the ECCC), following more contentious negotiations, provided for a majority of domestic judges alongside international ones.[21] Other examples of "internationalized criminal courts"—or domestic courts with substantial international involvement—exist, for example, in Kosovo and in Uganda.[22] The varied experiences of mixed tribunals notwithstanding, creators hoped that the hybrid nature and in-country location would enhance their domestic legitimacy, inject international support, and enable more domestic legal capacity building than the more distant purely international tribunals.

The creation of the International Criminal Court (ICC), whose jurisdiction took effect in 2002, did not halt the interest in strengthening domestic ability to prosecute atrocity cases. On the contrary, the ICC is designed to be complementary to domestic proceedings. Created by a treaty called the Rome Statute, the ICC has jurisdiction over crimes against humanity, genocide, and war crimes—if the country on whose territory a crime occurred, or the country whose nation is accused of such a crime, is a party to the statute or otherwise consents to the court's jurisdiction.[23] These directly affected states have the first opportunity to take action. Under the complementarity principle, the ICC itself has jurisdiction to prosecute atrocity crimes only if countries that other-

wise have jurisdiction are "unwilling or unable genuinely" to investigate or prosecute.[24] Sitting at The Hague in the Netherlands, with ambitious goals that include advancing justice and "end[ing] impunity" for international crimes,[25] the ICC hopes that its very existence will prod affected countries to take action themselves. Yet complementarity, as discussed below, is anything but simple in practice.

Whose Justice? Engaging Local Populations More Effectively

Another trend since the 1990s is the recognized need to engage local populations more effectively in conceiving and implementing transitional justice. All too often, transitional justice has been a top-down exercise, with insufficient understanding of the aspirations and goals of domestic communities. The ICTY and ICTR—physically distant from the people who suffered atrocities—engaged in outreach only belatedly. Learning from this, the Special Court for Sierra Leone made community engagement central: teams of young outreach officers traveled throughout the country discussing the court's focus on "those most responsible" for serious crimes and responding to public questions and criticisms of the court's work, including that its concentration on a few "big fish" let direct perpetrators go unpunished.[26] Truth commissions by their nature engage with a broad range of local populations, but even they realize that some voices and communities need more of a chance to participate and be heard. Women in Peru who had suffered sexual violence were initially reluctant to discuss their experiences but, with time, provided a fuller picture of the harms of the conflict.[27] In Timor-Leste, the Commission on Reception and Reconciliation made sure to include women and young people among those leading community-based reconciliation proceedings.[28]

Engaging local populations more thoughtfully and systematically inevitably reveals how complicated and divergent perceptions of fair justice can be. In particular, whether justice is evenhanded, treating like cases alike, or instead looks like winners simply prevailing over losers, is a difficult and recurring issue that profoundly shapes public understandings of justice going forward. Unfortunately, justice processes sometimes look like a continuation of politics by other means, to borrow from Clausewitz.[29] Moreover, in postconflict societies recovering from wrenching violence and horrific atrocities, where citizens have little confidence in the legal system or in government officials, reaching out directly to affected communities and better appreciating their concerns can be essential to providing any sense of meaningful justice. Learning from earlier experiences, the ICC has engaged in more systematic outreach in the countries involved in its cases, facing challenging questions and critiques from local audiences, as in Uganda.[30] NGOs often play an essential supplementary role in community outreach and education. In the Democratic Republic of the Congo, for example, the NGO Interactive Radio for Justice provides not only information about the ICC but also regular broadcasts focused on domestic laws and justice issues.[31] In Afghanistan, the Afghan Independent Human Rights Commission surveyed the local population to gain a better sense of people's goals and hopes for transitional justice, though progress in achieving those aspirations has been limited.[32] Although local settings can vary enormously—including the mix of perpetrators, victims, and their links to government or insurgent groups—public education and participation are critical ingredients for catalyzing local support for fair-minded judicial remedies.

Combined, Multifaceted Approaches to Transitional Justice

The very complexity of the goals sought in transitional justice—accountability, justice, truth, reparation, prevention, among others—has influenced a third prominent trend. This is the growing pattern of combining multiple, different mechanisms of transitional justice as countries emerge from conflict and reckon with their past. Some countries, such as South Africa, with its Truth and Reconciliation Commission (TRC), choose to make one approach central.[33] Other countries have prosecuted high-level offenders while giving a truth commission jurisdiction over lesser crimes. Although some combination of trials, truth commissions, reparations, and reforms is increasingly common, there is no one-size-fits-all template, and the uniqueness and diversity of countries' circumstances must be taken into account—such as the condition of the domestic legal system; public attitudes and expectations about postconflict justice; the degree of tension among different groups or factions; the commitment (or lack thereof) of domestic leaders to accountability for atrocities and human rights abuses; and whether or not fair trials can be held domestically. Furthermore, combined, multifaceted approaches require working out a constructive relationship and division of labor among different initiatives, which often is not easy.

Tensions can arise between different mechanisms, and publics can be confused about their roles. But they can work together with careful planning and some goodwill. In Timor-Leste, for example, individuals who committed lesser offenses were eligible for the community reconciliation process before the Commission on Reception and Reconciliation, but only after their cases were reviewed and screened by the special panels for serious crimes.[34] Although this yielded some level of accountability, victims understandably were frustrated by the fact that many serious offenders ultimately were never tried before the court. In Sierra Leone, the relationship between the truth commission and the special court was complicated and at times uneasy.[35] Even as combined approaches become more common, and offer possibilities for different forms of justice and redress, acute challenges in moving ahead to pursue meaningful accountability and to prevent the recurrence of atrocities are all too apparent.

Enduring Challenges in Transitional Justice

Across the unique circumstances, constraints, and choices of different countries emerging from conflict, a number of recurring challenges stand out. This section focuses on three in particular: the sometimes uneasy relationship between peace and justice; tensions over local versus international ownership and roles; and the need for clearer linkages between accounting for the past and rule of law capacity building going forward. A fourth and overarching challenge, which cuts across all the others, is the more effective prevention of atrocities and massive human rights abuses, a challenge that calls for renewed commitment and a wide range of responses.[36]

Justice and Peace: Tensions or Synergies?

Few issues in transitional justice have generated more controversy than the so-called justice versus peace debate. Are justice and peacebuilding in tension or mutually reinforcing? Specifically, does pursuing criminal accountability impede negotiations to end conflicts? Does it hamper peacebuilding after conflict? Or is seeking justice in some

form vital to establishing an enduring peace? These are issues on which experts disagree, be they negotiators, political leaders, former combatants, human rights advocates, victims, or civil society leaders. At the two poles of the peace versus justice debate are two contending positions.

At one end of the spectrum are "realists," who argue that the quest for justice and accountability undercuts peace negotiations. This, the realists claim, is because contending forces—or tyrannical leaders—may be unwilling to lay down their arms if they face prosecution, a reluctance that "in turn prolongs the conflict, enables the continuation of atrocities, and increases human suffering."[37] Even after a conflict ends and peace is being consolidated, realists argue that criminal prosecutions of major perpetrators can be destabilizing and that conditional amnesties may be needed to remove "spoilers" and thus improve prospects for a stable peace and rule of law development. Pursuing accountability without establishing "political and institutional preconditions," they contend, "risks weakening norms of justice by revealing their ineffectiveness and hindering necessary political bargaining."[38] Once political bargains are struck among contending groups, they argue, "institutions based on the rule of law become more feasible."[39] Realists, in short, place priority on peace understood as stability and the absence of armed conflict, and they urge that measures of justice and accountability accommodate to this priority.

At the other end of the spectrum are those who take a "justice is essential" view. Proponents of this position argue that peace ultimately is not sustainable without justice, and that major perpetrators of atrocities must be held legally accountable if a country is to make an effective transition to a society marked by the rule of law. Justice advocates regard legal impunity as the biggest barrier to sustainable peace and argue that vigorous prosecution of at least major offenders is the only way to remove the stain of impunity from traumatized societies. Fair trials affirm that atrocities are wrong and unacceptable—drawing a clear line for all to see—and incarceration prevents the guilty from repeat offenses, potentially serves as a deterrent to others, and provides some reassurance to the public.[40] Trials also give victims a sense of justice that helps them move forward without the need to seek personal vengeance. Truth commissions can supplement trials and acknowledge more fully the truth of what occurred, in turn acknowledging and empowering victims and survivors, and potentially, many argue, contributing to reforms and reconciliation over time.[41] Justice advocates also stress the legal obligations of states to prosecute perpetrators of egregious international crimes and the rights of victims to redress.[42]

Trends on the ground are, to some degree, overtaking and moving beyond the broad, at times theological, debate over peace versus justice. There is no one answer to the question of the optimal relationship among these vital goals. Practical realities and constraints differ dramatically across counties. Context matters enormously: the unique circumstances of each conflict shape the prospects for consolidating peace, and the nature and severity of atrocities influence the urgency and complexity of accountability. Sierra Leone is not Uganda is not Afghanistan is not Sudan is not Guatemala is not the Central African Republic. The particular struggles in securing peace, the particular legacy of abuses, and the unique domestic culture and politics all shape the concrete possibilities for combining peace and justice.

Some examples give a sense of the diverse challenges. In countries where a conflict has ended and a new domestic regime is squarely in place, having replaced a discredited, evicted prior regime, as in Timor-Leste, there may be greater chances for pursuing

criminal justice than in a multiparty conflict that continues to fester. Even in Timor-Leste, though, domestic leaders placed priority on building a strong relationship with Indonesia as part of securing the peace.[43] In Uganda, some argue that the ICC's indictment of Lord's Resistance Army leader Joseph Kony delayed and complicated peace negotiations; others contend that it brought the LRA to the negotiating table and has helped to undercut Kony's legitimacy and constrain his movements.[44] In the case of Sudan, the African Union has called on its members not to cooperate in the arrest and surrender of President Omar al Bashir for trial at the ICC, contending that the ICC indictment has had "unfortunate consequences" on "delicate peace processes underway."[45] In Afghanistan, the government has resisted calls to remove and hold accountable perpetrators of human rights abuses, and international actors concerned about stabilizing the country have not pressed as hard as justice advocates would like.[46]

Yet, despite sometimes difficult tensions and tradeoffs, historical trends have elevated the role and importance of justice. Gone are the days when peace negotiators could presume upon blanket amnesties as part of a peace settlement. Amnesty patterns of the past, even as recently as the 1991 Paris Peace Accords concerning Cambodia, are no longer supported by the United Nations.[47] As Secretary-General Kofi Annan made clear during Sierra Leone's 1999 Lomé Peace Accord negotiations, the United Nations will not support amnesties for international crimes including genocide, war crimes, and crimes against humanity.[48] Furthermore, international and regional courts have held that international law places limits on amnesties;[49] and countries have treaty obligations to extradite or prosecute perpetrators of genocide, torture, and war crimes.[50] The development and refinement of international criminal law, and the elevation of the "responsibility to protect" as a normative concept since 2005, have also influenced the terrain on which conflicts are ended and peace processes commenced.[51] Expectations of accountability have increased among populations that have endured atrocities and among advocates of justice. Perpetrators can no longer presume impunity or amnesty.

It's also not at all clear how well amnesties actually have worked to promote or consolidate peace across a variety of historical examples. Historical accounts indicate that Hitler took note of the failure to hold leaders of the Ottoman Empire accountable for the Armenian genocide, commenting to his military officers, "Who after all is today speaking about the destruction of the Armenians?"[52] In addition to undercutting deterrence, amnesties may be overstated as vehicles to end conflicts. In Sierra Leone, for instance, domestic amnesties granted to rebel leader Foday Sankoh and others in an effort to stop the fighting did not bring an end to a conflict rooted in greed and self-interest; a British military intervention was necessary to halt the violence.[53] Varying experiences in Latin America with amnesties warrant continued close study.[54] Many more cases need to be examined to assess the impact—in both the near term and the longer term—of *conditional* amnesties as part of ending a conflict.[55]

Whether criminal *indictments* ultimately impede peacebuilding—beyond posing initial complications—is also a contested and context-specific question. Initial fears often prove to be exaggerated. Balkan peace negotiators, for example, worried that the indictments of Radovan Karadzic and Ratko Mladic would hamper the Dayton peace negotiations; but subsequent accounts suggest that their absence was crucial to attendance by Bosnia's Muslim leadership at Dayton and likely helped rather than undermined the process.[56] Likewise, Charles Taylor's indictment during negotiations to end the Li-

berian conflict raised fears of complicating the delicate deliberations. Yet, taking a longer view, the conviction of Taylor for crimes against humanity and war crimes, and his removal from a position of power and of intimidation, was crucial to bringing peace to West Africa.[57]

As noted earlier, the pursuit of criminal justice and accountability as a form of transitional justice is like a boulder in the river—and it will be a component of any future peace process, requiring skillful navigation while accommodating it as part of the terrain. Practical realities and normative constraints are converging to give justice a more central role.

The growing emphasis on justice as a necessary part of peacebuilding processes creates challenges but also opportunities for the future. There's no question that ending violent conflict is a crucial priority: there can be no justice without a basic peace. As a result, stopping violent conflict and the harms and atrocities that too often accompany it, and consolidating a workable peace, may influence the *timing* and forms of justice sought, and may entail *sequencing*. In some cases, it has taken years to grapple systematically with the legacy of past abuses and to hold perpetrators accountable. In Guatemala, for example, former head of state Efrain Rios Montt was convicted of genocide and other crimes in a national court years after the conflict came to an end.[58]

Yet, even in situations where political leaders resist accountability, civil society organizations (often supported by international actors) can gather and preserve evidence for use when the time is ripe. In Afghanistan, the Afghan Independent Human Rights Commission has assisted such efforts.[59] In Syria, international support is helping Syrians document abuses and preserve evidence for future accountability proceedings.[60] Years earlier, determined efforts to preserve evidence of Khmer Rouge atrocities assisted subsequent prosecutions of Khmer Rouge leaders before the ECCC.[61] Although justice delayed may sometimes be justice denied—particularly when perpetrators, witnesses, and survivors are no longer alive to complete the process—reckoning with the past can also take place in phases and layers over time, and the transformation it invites is always a work in progress.

Whose Justice? Local versus International Ownership and Roles

A second recurring dilemma in struggles over transitional justice is the question of ownership. Whose justice is being pursued? Whose goals and priorities are at the heart of the process, and whose initiative is driving the endeavor? Is justice being pursued in an even-handed way, or are some groups being singled out unfairly? What are the respective roles and division of labor among global, regional, and local actors? Both internationally and domestically, how much of the process is top down or bottom up? Struggles over these issues mark most experiences with transitional justice across different countries and continents. Are there any guidelines for how to think about all this?

An initial point to make here is that everybody has a stake, or interest, in how transitional justice unfolds. No one is completely neutral. The so-called international community has a stake in making sure that internationally supported legal processes comport with international standards of due process, whether they be international courts, hybrid tribunals, or domestic courts supplemented by international assistance. At the same time, individual states have their own interests that play out in how hard they push for accountability and in which form, how they want to frame the temporal and subject matter jurisdiction of courts, and what sort of assistance they are prepared to provide. Thus, it's no surprise that the jurisdiction of

the Cambodia tribunal excludes the time period during which major states actively supported the Khmer Rouge, for example.[62] The ICC's broader temporal jurisdiction, which essentially applies from the point that a country becomes a party, is designed, in part, to address such concerns by providing a forum that is generally available when states are unwilling or unable themselves to investigate or prosecute offenses within the subject matter jurisdiction of the court.[63]

Domestically, too, everyone has a stake. At the national level, political and civic leaders often contest the goals that should take precedence in moving ahead after conflict. Not surprisingly, their priorities and conceptions of justice may not always align with those who emphasize criminal justice. In Timor-Leste, for example, the former foreign minister and later prime minister and president Jose Ramos-Horta stressed that "independence is a form of justice."[64] This is an important point from someone who, along with former president Xanana Gusmao and many others, devoted his career to Timor-Leste's long and historic struggle for independence. Moreover, Gusmao stressed the importance of social justice as he worked to consolidate the country's long-sought independence, build its economy, and develop constructive relationships with its neighbors.[65] Yet, lack of accountability has been a bitter pill to swallow for human rights advocates, church leaders, and civil society organizations advocating meaningful justice and redress for victims and survivors of atrocities before, during, and after Timor-Leste's historic referendum for independence.

Are there guidelines for addressing the complicated questions of local versus international ownership and roles? Let me suggest several. First, local ownership and a basic degree of public support for the aims and means of transitional justice are crucially important. Public engagement and debate over justice and what it ought to look like is part of the point of transitional justice. The intensive public dialogues and critiques in villages across Sierra Leone over the work of the special court helped build local understanding of fundamental rules of international law and human rights, as well as of fair judicial process, even as citizens expressed frustration with some aspects of the court's work. In Peru, hearing from previously excluded, neglected, and victimized populations in truth and reconciliation processes opened up better public awareness of long-hidden grievances and inequalities. This is not to romanticize local justice. Governments can also use local mechanisms to consolidate power and restrain public debate.[66] Moreover, certain groups (such as recipients of disarmament, demobilization, and reintegration assistance, often former combatants) may be privileged over others. But as a starting point, engaging local audiences and hearing many voices, including those of women and young people, in addition to the usual power holders, should be a central part of transitional justice processes.

When it comes to preventing atrocities and holding perpetrators accountable, a second key precept is the primacy of domestic responsibility. In committing themselves to the "responsibility to protect" in 2005, heads of state from around the world affirmed the responsibility of all countries to protect their populations from genocide, war crimes, crimes against humanity, and ethnic cleansing.[67] If a state fails to fulfill this responsibility, even with international assistance, states agreed that "the international community, through the United Nations" has a responsibility to protect populations from these crimes through diplomatic and humanitarian means and, if necessary, through collective action under Chapter VII of the UN Charter should peaceful means be insufficient.[68] This emphasis on the primacy of domestic responsibility, but with international action as a fallback in the event a state

fails to protect against atrocities, echoes the complementarity principle of the ICC, which allocates responsibility to investigate and prosecute international crimes.

Complementarity gives states with jurisdiction the first opportunity to investigate and prosecute atrocity crimes, with the ICC stepping in if those governments are unwilling or unable "genuinely" to do so. This precept is another touchstone in the relationship between domestic and international actors navigating transitional justice. The hope is that the impulses of sovereignty and the prospect of ICC action will lead states to take action to prevent and to prosecute atrocity crimes themselves. Or, at the very least, these factors will prod states to commence serious domestic transitional justice dialogues and processes of some kind, with the possibility of some major cases potentially going to the ICC. Prodding by the ICC has had an impact, for instance, in Colombia, where the prospect of possible ICC action has likely encouraged greater domestic attention to accountability issues.[69]

Compelling and straightforward in principle, complementarity nevertheless can be complicated and contentious in practice, exposing tensions between domestic and international decision makers. For example, what if a state decides to prosecute only members of certain groups in a conflict, avoiding prosecution of its own leaders? What if a state opts for a truth commission over prosecution? What if a state is genuinely willing to prosecute but is unable to do so fairly and effectively without substantial external support? What if a state "self-refers" a situation to the ICC even though it could potentially prosecute? Issues such as these have prompted the ICC prosecutor as well as scholars and practitioners to offer guidelines for complementarity.[70]

One way to navigate, although not avoid, challenges inherent in charting constructive national-international relationships is to put more energy into "positive" or "proactive" complementarity.[71] The idea here is that international actors, including the ICC, should be proactive in *assisting* countries willing to credibly investigate and prosecute international crimes. Some of this work has already begun: in the Democratic Republic of the Congo, international actors, including the United Nations and NGOs, have assisted war crimes prosecutions before domestic military courts, including mobile courts;[72] in Uganda, internationals are assisting in the work of the domestic war crimes division of the Ugandan High Court.[73]

Positive complementarity presents its own issues. International concerns about fair and impartial process in resource-challenged or politically influenced domestic systems are often well founded and not easily allayed, nor are domestic sensitivities to international pressure and guidance. But, in the right circumstances, proactive complementarity can assist willing countries to undertake fair trials and, depending on how international assistance is structured, can help build longer-term improvements in domestic justice systems. Moreover, a workable division of labor may be possible in which the ICC tries some suspects and domestic authorities try others. And because international and hybrid tribunals tend to focus on "those most responsible," there will generally be a need for other, more inclusive domestic transitional justice measures as well. Reaching out to affected populations and *linking* accountability mechanisms and forward-looking reforms more effectively remains a central challenge.

Rule of Law Reform: Building Justice on the Ground?

A third recurring struggle in the transitional justice experiences of many countries is the challenge of building "justice on the ground" at the national and subnational level.[74] This includes the challenge of combining meaningful accountability for the past with much-needed capacity-building contributions to domestic justice systems and rule of law more generally. After all, transitional justice includes the goal of transitioning to a situation where domestic institutions are able to resolve disputes more fairly and peacefully; avoiding future atrocities and massive human rights abuses depends on this. So the imperative to move forward while looking backward—of giving greater attention to the potential linkages and synergies between accountability proceedings and domestic capacity building—warrants more attention and effort.

This is much easier said than done, for many reasons. One is the enormous difficulty and complexity of efforts to strengthen the rule of law in societies that have been torn apart by violence and conflict. So many needs cry out for attention in the face of devastated, resource-poor, and often dysfunctional court systems; mixed experiences with customary justice; police or military forces marred by patterns of human rights abuses; unfettered patronage networks; poverty and lack of fair access to resources or power; and discrimination based on gender and other grounds. It is understandable that international and domestic actors responsible for managing the prosecution of atrocity crimes, or postconflict truth and reconciliation processes, would prefer to focus intensively on their particular missions, already fraught with Herculean challenges.

Unfortunately, what's understandable is not always beneficial. All too often, those who work on forward-looking justice system and security sector reform are a completely separate community from those who work on transitional justice processes such as criminal trials and truth commissions. Furthermore, practitioners and officials involved in rule of law initiatives often are "stovepiped" in their areas of specialty (e.g., judicial training, code writing, and police reform), with little direct linkage to those involved in related fields or with criminal tribunals or other accountability proceedings.[75] As a consequence, possibilities for capacity-building synergies are underexplored.

Resource tensions are a perennial challenge, to be sure. International and hybrid war crimes tribunals—with their air-conditioned offices, computers, experienced and relatively well-paid staff, administrative support, and access to legal materials—stand in stark contrast to often dilapidated, sweltering, resource-poor, struggling domestic justice systems. In Sierra Leone, I saw firsthand the disparities between the special court and the domestic system, and experienced directly the resulting frustration of national Supreme Court judges, then engaged in a tug-of-war with the special court over a talented administrator that both courts wanted.[76] But these realities argue all the more for thoughtful efforts at developing capacity-building synergies between war crimes courts and domestic justice systems, which will require focused international financial assistance that aims to link support for accountability mechanisms with related, longer-term justice system reforms.[77]

Opportunities for such capacity-building synergies often are greater when tribunals are located in conflict-affected societies, as in Sierra Leone and Timor-Leste, or when international assistance is provided directly to domestic courts, as in Bosnia and Herzegovina, Uganda, and the Democratic Republic of the Congo. Even so, capacity building that will endure after prosecutions cease takes considerable effort and forethought. In Sierra Leone, for example, the special court worked closely with domestic investigators to provide training in evidence gathering and witness protection, and these investigators continue to work in the domestic system.[78] Timorese judges who worked on war crimes cases at the special panels continue to serve in the domestic justice system.[79]

Even so, justice system capacity building often has a mixed track record,[80] and these efforts require systematic attention and resources.

Rule of law reform and capacity building after conflict cannot focus solely on the supply side of building fairer and more effective state institutions. Also crucial are demand-side reforms that address public demand for, access to, and expectations of fair justice. All too often, international and hybrid tribunals seem to domestic audiences like alien spaceships that land for a time, do their business, and take off, leaving befuddled local populations scratching their heads wondering what this had to do with their ongoing struggle for justice.[81] One welcome response has been the development of more thoughtful, extensive engagement programs with local audiences on issues of justice, accountability, and fair process—programs in which tribunal staff, NGOs, and local citizens are brought together to wrestle with justice issues of common concern. Sierra Leone's special court is probably the best example—it held forthright community-based discussions across the country, established "Accountability Now" clubs at local universities, and regularly met with NGOs in an interactive forum to discuss the court's work and accountability more generally.[82]

Truth commissions have the potential for even wider engagement with the public, for probing deeper causes of systemic abuses, and for putting far-reaching reforms on the public agenda. Putting long-suppressed or untold injustices on the agenda and providing a basis for public education and dialogue can be empowering and generate pressure for change.[83]

Building justice on the ground, like all aspects of transitional justice, is always a work in progress requiring determination, creativity, and multiple reinforcing reforms. Guatemala's Attorney General Claudia Paz y Paz provides an inspiring example: building "one-stop" 24-hour courts where domestic violence victims can come for medical support, counseling, and initiation of prosecutions against perpetrators.[84] Such examples of innovation and empowerment can help build people's confidence that justice really is available to them "on the ground."

LOOKING AHEAD:
CONCLUDING OBSERVATIONS

Looking ahead, it is worth pondering the lessons learned about transitional justice over the past several decades and what is left to learn. These efforts are complex, challenging, and important, and increasingly there is better empirical information about the impacts of different mechanisms and approaches in varying conflict situations. Qualitative and quantitative studies, including detailed case studies, provide insight into the impact and effectiveness of tribunals, truth commissions, reparations, and other mechanisms in meeting key goals. Not only political scientists but also anthropologists, historians, sociologists, regional experts, practitioners, law professors, and others offer thoughtful accounts of the complicated experiences and impacts of transitional justice efforts across different societies.[85]

One major recent study, *Transitional Justice in Balance*, offers a nuanced portrait of the "efficacy" of different measures singly and in combination.[86] It examines transitional justice processes and mechanisms (including trials, truth commissions, amnesties, reparations, and lustration/vetting) in 161 countries over time from 1970 to 2007, using data sets to explore the impact of these processes on two broad goals of transitional justice, "strengthening democracy and reducing human rights violations."[87] Among the study's empirical findings are that new democratic governments are "more likely to prosecute perpetrators if the old regime collapsed" than in situations of negotiated transitions; that "when new democracies use trials with amnesties" or trials "with amnesties and truth commissions, whether in a regime collapse or in a negotiated transition, they contribute to the success of democracy and human rights"; and that although "trials alone do not bring the desired results of stronger democracy and improved human rights," neither do trials "jeopardize democratic transitions."[88] The study recommends a "balanced" approach to transitional justice that navigates political and economic constraints through a combination of mechanisms and careful sequencing.

More empirical work on transitional justice such as this, including studies of the perceptions of victims and survivors who have participated in different justice processes, is needed.[89] Have these processes empowered victims and given them greater confidence in fair justice, or not? In addition, further analysis of the impact of "proactive complementarity" initiatives—in which international actors assist domestic accountability processes—could shape the design of more effective and sustainable capacity-building synergies.

Transitional justice has become an indispensable part of peacebuilding's architecture. States have normative responsibilities to protect their populations from genocide, war crimes, crimes against humanity, and other serious human rights abuses, and the 2005 commitment to the responsibility to protect, though imperfect in execution, reflects a shift in the normative landscape in which states, international organizations, and NGOs operate. State's parties to the Genocide Convention, the Torture Convention, and the Geneva Conventions have undertaken legal obligations to refrain from genocide, torture, and war crimes and to punish such offenses.[90] More than 120 states have joined the ICC,[91] and even powerful countries that have not, like the United States, have supported the work of the court in particular cases.

In short, the normative terrain on which conflict resolution takes place has changed, and expectations of accountability for those most responsible for atrocity crimes are increasingly widespread. Social media that crosses the globe with the speed of a text message or a mouse click can expose once-hidden atrocities to the world at large. Greater transparency about misconduct has generated a global constituency for justice rooted in public outrage and in a widely shared desire for basic human rights.

Transitional justice is fraught with both moral urgency and complexity: achieving meaningful accountability, or any degree of fair justice, or a fuller and more truthful account of past abuses, or institutional reforms that promise lasting impact is incredibly difficult. It takes extraordinary patience and commitment, based on realistic expectations of what justice processes can deliver. However, it also takes boldness and a degree of impatience: a determination to press ahead, often against overwhelming odds, to seek justice and to develop institutions that can rectify grievances that unaddressed will metastasize into violence. Failure to prevent egregious atrocities and massive human rights abuses occur every single day. These failures come at an excruciating human cost, and they demand the best efforts of everyone to learn more—and to do more—about effective prevention.

NOTES

1. Ruti Teitel, *Transitional Justice* (New York: Oxford University Press, 2000). The literature on transitional justice is vast and expanding. See, for example, Tricia C. Olsen, Leigh A. Payne, and Andrew G. Reiter, *Transitional Justice in Balance: Comparing Processes, Weighing Efficacy* (Washington, DC: United States Institute of Peace Press, 2010), especially chapter 1 (discussing the origins of the term "transitional justice"); Neil J. Kritz, ed., *Transitional Justice: How Emerging Democracies Reckon with Former Regimes*, vols. 1–3 (Washington, DC:

United States Institute of Peace Press, 1995); and M. Cherif Bassiouni, *Post-Conflict Justice* (Ardsley, NY: Transnational, 2002). The International Center for Transitional Justice (ICTJ) defines transitional justice as "the set of judicial and non-judicial measures that have been implemented by different countries in order to redress the legacies of massive human rights abuses," including "criminal prosecutions, truth commissions, reparations programs, and various kinds of institutional reforms." ICTJ, "What is Transitional Justice?" 2014, available at www.ictj.org/about/transitional-justice.

2. Cited in Fred R. Shapiro, *The Yale Book of Quotations* (New Haven, CT: Yale University Press, 2006), 299; see discussion at www.quoteinvestiga tor.com/2013/04/23/good-idea/.

3. Olsen, Payne, and Reiter, *Transitional Justice in Balance*, 12–13.

4. Roger Duthie, "Toward a Development-Sensitive Approach to Transitional Justice," *International Journal of Transitional Justice* 2 (2008): 292–309.

5. Jane Stromseth, David Wippman, and Rosa Brooks, *Can Might Make Rights? Building the Rule of Law after Military Interventions* (New York: Cambridge University Press, 2006), 259–60.

6. Ibid.

7. Rama Mani, *Beyond Retribution: Seeking Justice in the Shadows of War* (Oxford: Blackwell, 2002), 173–78 (discussing reparative justice).

8. Priscilla B. Hayner, *Unspeakable Truths: Transitional Justice and the Challenge of Truth Commissions* (New York: Routledge, 2011); *Rule-of-Law Tools for Post-Conflict States: Truth Commissions* (New York and Geneva: Office of the UN High Commissioner for Human Rights, 2006), available at www.ohchr.org/Documents/Publications/Ruleoflaw TruthCommissions.pdf.

9. Payam Akhavan, "Beyond Impunity: Can International Criminal Justice Prevent Future Atrocities?" *American Journal of International Law* 95 (2001): 7–31.

10. For a courageous speech that rejects hate and revenge and advocates education, see Malala Yousafzai, speech at the United Nations (New York, July 12, 2013), available at www.aworl datschool.org/pages/the-text-of-malala-yousafzais -speech-at-the-united-nations.

11. See Hayner, *Unspeakable Truths*.

12. Julissa Mantilla Falcon, "The Peruvian Truth and Reconciliation Commission's Treatment of Sexual Violence Against Women," *Human Rights Brief* 12, no. 2 (2005): 1–4, available at www.wcl.american.edu/hrbrief/12/2falcon.pdf; and *Chega!: Final Report of the Commission for Reception, Truth and Reconciliation in East Timor* (2005), chap. 7.7: Sexual Violence, available at www.cavr-timorleste.org/en/chegaReport.htm.

13. Stromseth, Wippman, and Brooks, *Can Might Make Rights?* 285–88; and *Chega!* part 9: Community Reconciliation.

14. See www.etan.org/et2009/09september/12/13comarc.htm.

15. *Rule-of-Law Tools for Post-Conflict States: Vetting: An Operational Framework* (New York and Geneva: Office of the UN High Commissioner for Human Rights, 2006), available at www.ohchr.org/Documents/Publications/RuleoflawVettingen.pdf.

16. Stromseth, Wippman, and Brooks, *Can Might Make Rights?* chap. 6.

17. Jane Stromseth, "Strengthening Demand for the Rule of Law in Post-Conflict Societies," *Minnesota Journal of International Law* 18, no. 2 (2009): 415–24.

18. Assessment and report of Judge Theodor Meron, president of the International Tribunal for the former Yugoslavia, UN Doc. S/2013/678 (November 18, 2013), Annex I, 3. The UN Security Council established the ICTY in 1993 by adopting Resolution 827, S/Res/827 (May 25, 1993). For an empirical survey of nine international criminal tribunals, see Alette Smeulers, Barbora Hola, and Tom van den Berg, "Sixty-Five Years of International Criminal Justice: The Facts and Figures," *International Criminal Law Review* 13 (2013): 7–41.

19. See *Prosecutor v. Jean Kambanda*, ICTR-97-23-S, Judgment and Sentence, September 4, 1998. The UN Security Council created the ICTR in 1994 by adopting Resolution 955, S/Res/955 (November 8, 1994).

20. Stromseth, Wippman, and Brooks, *Can Might Make Rights?* 263–74; and Diane F. Orentlicher, *That Someone Guilty Be Punished: The Impact of the ICTY in Bosnia* (New York: Open Society Justice Initiative, 2010), available at www.opensoci

etyfoundations.org/publications/someone-guilty-be-punished-impact-icty-bosnia.

21. Stromseth, Wippman, and Brooks, *Can Might Make Rights?* 265–68, 274–99; Cesare Romano, Andre Nollkaemper, and Jann Kleffner, eds., *Internationalized Criminal Courts: Sierra Leone, East Timor, Kosovo, and Cambodia* (Oxford: Oxford University Press, 2004).

22. Romano, Nollkaemper, and Kleffner, *Internationalized Criminal Courts*, chap. 4 (Kosovo); and Jane E. Stromseth, "The International Criminal Court and Justice on the Ground," *Arizona State Law Journal* 43, no. 2 (2011), 438–42 (Uganda).

23. Rome Statute of the International Criminal Court, Article 12, available at www.un.org/law/icc/. The Statute entered into force on July 1, 2002.

24. Rome Statute, Article 17.

25. Rome Statute, preamble. The states parties to the Rome Statute affirm in the preamble their determination "to put an end to impunity for the perpetrators of these crimes and thus to contribute to the prevention of such crimes" and their resolve "to guarantee lasting respect for and the enforcement of international justice." Ibid.

26. Stromseth, Wippman, and Brooks, *Can Might Make Rights?* 295–97.

27. Falcon, "The Peruvian Truth and Reconciliation Commission's Treatment of Sexual Violence against Women"; and Jelke Boesten and Melissa Fisher, "Sexual Violence and Justice in Postconflict Peru," Special Report no. 310 (United States Institute of Peace, Washington, DC, June 2012).

28. Stromseth, Wippman, and Brooks, *Can Might Make Rights?* 286. The CAVR followed the requirement of its mandate "that a minimum 30% of all Regional Commissioners be women" and that community reconciliation panels have "appropriate gender representation." *Chega!: Final Report*, part 9, 43 (para. 154).

29. Carl von Clausewitz, *On War* (Princeton, NJ: Princeton University Press, 1976), chap. 1, section 24.

30. Stromseth, "The International Criminal Court and Justice on the Ground," 440.

31. Interactive Radio for Justice, www.irfj.org; Sarah Katz-Lavigne, *Interactive Radio for Justice:*

Mid-Project Impact Assessment Analysis (2010), available at www.comminit.com/global/node/324478.

32. See Afghan Independent Human Rights Commission, *A Call for Justice: A National Consultation on Past Human Rights Violations in Afghanistan*, available at www.aihrc.org/af/rep_Eng_29 _01_05.htm, reporting on the surveys and focus groups conducted by the Afghan Independent Human Rights Commission.

33. See Martha Minow, *Between Vengeance and Forgiveness: Facing History after Genocide and Mass Violence* (Boston: Beacon, 1998).

34. Stromseth, Wippman, and Brooks, *Can Might Make Rights?* 286.

35. William A. Schabas, "Internationalized Courts and their Relationship with Alternative Accountability Mechanisms: The Case of Sierra Leone," in Romano, Nollkaemper, and Kleffner, *Internationalized Criminal Courts*, 165–80.

36. On recurring failures to prevent genocide and other atrocities, see Samantha Power, *"A Problem from Hell": America and the Age of Genocide* (New York: Basic Books, 2002). As special assistant to President Obama and senior director for multilateral affairs and human rights at the National Security Council, Samantha Power led the administration's efforts under Presidential Study Directive 10 (PSD 10) to improve US capacity to prevent atrocities, including through the creation of the interagency Atrocity Prevention Board.

37. Anonymous, "Human Rights in Peace Negotiations," *Human Rights Quarterly* 18 (1996): 256.

38. Jack Snyder and Leslie Vinjamuri, "Trials and Errors: Principle and Pragmatism in Strategies of International Justice," *International Security* 28 (Winter 2003/04): 6–7.

39. Ibid.

40. This paragraph draws directly from Stromseth, Wippman, and Brooks, *Can Might Make Rights?* 250.

41. See Hayner, *Unspeakable Truths.*

42. Diane F. Orentlicher, "Settling Accounts: The Duty to Prosecute Human Rights Violations of a Prior Regime," *Yale Law Journal* 100, no. 8 (1991): 2537–2615; Steven R. Ratner and Jason S. Abrams, *Accountability for Human Rights Atrocities in International Law: Beyond the Nuremberg Legacy*, 2nd ed. (Oxford: Oxford University Press, 2001),

163–66, 335; and Naomi Roht-Arriaza, "State Responsibility to Investigate and Prosecute Grave Human Rights Violations in International Law," *California Law Review* 78, no. 2 (1990): 451–513. The UN General Assembly has adopted "Basic Principles and Guidelines on the Right to a Remedy and Reparation for Victims of Gross Violations of International Human Rights Law and Serious Violations of International Humanitarian Law," UN Doc. A/RES/60/147 (December 16, 2005), available at www.ohchr.org/english/law/remedy.htm.

43. Stromseth, Wippman, and Brooks, *Can Might Make Rights?* 281–82.

44. Scott Worden, "The Justice Dilemma in Uganda," *USIPeace Briefing* (Washington, DC: United States Institute of Peace, February 2008), 4–5, available at www.usip.org/sites/default/files /resources/1_3.pdf; and Stromseth, "The International Criminal Court and Justice on the Ground," 439. Others question whether Kony was fully aware of the indictment's consequences or the ICC.

45. Assembly of the African Union, *Decision on the Meeting of African States Parties to the Rome Statute of the International Criminal Court (ICC)*, Doc. Assembly/AU/13 (XIII) 1–3 July 2009, 2, available at www.au.int/en/sites/default/files /ASSEMBLY_EN_1_3_JULY_2009_AUC _THIRTEENTH_ORDINARY_SESSION _DECISIONS_DECLARATIONS_%20MES SAGE_CONGRATULATIONS_MOTION_0.

46. "Afghanistan Universal Periodic Review 2013," *Human Rights Watch*, January 7, 2014, available at www.hrw.org/print/news/2014/01/07/af ghanistan-universal-periodic-review-2013; Nick Grono, "Peace, Justice and Reconciliation in Afghanistan," *International Crisis Group* (speech, conference on Afghanistan before the European Parliament in Brussels, Belgium, March 16, 2011), available at www.crisisgroup.org/en/publication -type/speeches/2011/peace-justice-and-reconcili ation-in-afghanistan.aspx.

47. United Nations, Department of Public Information, Agreements on a Comprehensive Political Settlement of the Cambodia Conflict: Paris, 23 October 1991, January 1992. The 2004 *Report of the Secretary-General on the Rule of Law and Transitional Justice in Conflict and Post-Conflict Societies*, U.N. Doc. S/2004/66 (August 3, 2004), para. 10, made clear that "United Nations-endorsed peace agreements can never promise amnesties for genocide, war crimes, crimes against humanity or gross violations of human rights."

48. *Seventh Report of the Secretary-General on the United Nations Observer Mission in Sierra Leone*, U.N. Doc. S/1999/836 (July 30, 1999), para. 54 ("Hence the instruction to my Special Representative to enter a reservation when he signed the peace agreement, explicitly stating that, for the United Nations, the amnesty cannot cover international crimes of genocide, crimes against humanity, war crimes and other serious violations of international humanitarian law").

49. *Prosecutor v. Morris Kallon and Brima Bazzy Kamara* (Decision on Challenge to Jurisdiction: Lomé Accord Amnesty) (Decision of the Appeals Chamber), 2004 Case no. SCSL-2004-15-AR72(E) & SCSL-2004-16-AR72(E), paras. 66–71; *Prosecutor v. Allieu Kondewa* (Decision on Lack of Jurisdiction/Abuse of Process, Amnesty Provided by the Lomé Accord) (Decision of the Appeals Chamber), 2004 Case no. SCSL-2004-14-AR72 (E), paras. 48–51; Case of *Gelman v. Uruguay* (Judgment on Merits and Reparations), 2011, IACHR, paras. 195–214; Case of *Gomez Lund et al. ("Guerrilha Do Araguaia") v. Brazil* (Judgment on Preliminary Objections, Merits, Reparations, and Costs), 2010, IACHR, paras. 147–48; Case of *Barrios Altos v. Peru* (Judgment on Merits), 2001, IACHR, paras. 41–44.

50. Ratner and Abrams, *Accountability for Human Rights Atrocities in International Law*, 163–66.

51. On the responsibility to protect, see 2005 World Summit Outcome Document, High-Level Plenary Meeting, Sept. 14–16, 2005, at paras. 138–39. See also Gareth Evans, *The Responsibility to Protect: Ending Mass Atrocity Crimes Once and for All* (Washington, DC: Brookings Institution Press, 2008).

52. Michael P. Scharf and Nigel Rodley, "International Law Principles on Accountability," in *Post-Conflict Justice*, ed. M. Cherif Bassiouni (New York: Transnational Publishers, 2002), 91 (quoting Adolph Hitler).

53. Stromseth, Wippman, and Brooks, *Can Might Make Rights?* 251–52.

54. Francesca Lessa, Tricia Olsen, Leigh Payne, Gabriel Pereira, and Andrew Reiter, "Overcoming Impunity: Pathways to Accountability in Latin America," *The International Journal of Transitional Justice* 8, no. 1 (2014): 95–97.

55. Olsen, Payne, and Reiter, *Transitional Justice in Balance*, 35–37.

56. Richard Holbrooke, *To End a War* (New York: Random House, 1998), 107–8, 226, 315–16; and Richard Goldstone, "Peace Versus Justice," *Nevada Law Journal* 6, no. 2 (2005–2006): 421–22. ("There can be no doubt that had Karadzic been a participant at Dayton, the Bosniak leaders, a mere two months after the [Srebrenica] massacre, would not have been prepared to attend the meeting. That was indeed confirmed in my presence some months later by the then-Bosnian foreign minister, Mohamed Sacirby").

57. Stromseth, Wippman, and Brooks, *Can Might Make Rights?* 292–95; "Appeals Chamber Upholds Charles Taylor's Conviction, 50 Year Sentence," Special Court for Sierra Leone press release, September 26, 2013, available at www.sc-sl.org/LinkClick.aspx?fileticket=gEJ2L%2B5/rBo%3D&tabid=53.

58. Naomi Roht-Arriaza, "Genocide and War Crimes in National Courts: The Conviction of Rios Montt in Guatemala and its Aftermath," *ASIL Insights* 17, no. 14 (May 23, 2013): available at www.asil.org/insights/volume/17/issue/14/genocide-and-war-crimes-national-courts-conviction-rios-montt-guatemala. A subsequent ruling by Guatemala's Constitutional Court led to the cancellation of the guilty verdict. Open Society Justice Initiative, *Judging a Dictator: The Trial of Guatemala's Rios Montt* (November 2013), 17–19. There are tentative plans for the trial to be restarted in 2015.

59. *Citizens Access to Justice (Report on Monitoring of Decree no. 45 of the President of the Islamic Republic of Afghanistan)* (Kabul, Afghanistan Independent Human Rights Commission, 2012), 5–6, available at www.aihrc.org.af/media/files/AIHRC%20Report%20on%20Decree%2045%20(English)-final.pdf.

60. "Syria Justice and Accountability Center," 2014, www.syriaaccountability.org/.

61. Craig Etcheson, "The Politics of Genocide Justice in Cambodia," in Romano, Nollkaemper, and Kleffner, *Internationalized Criminal Courts*, 196 (discussing Documentation Center of Cambodia).

62. Wendy Lambourne, "The Khmer Rouge Tribunal: Justice for Genocide in Cambodia?" (paper presented at the Law and Society Association Australia and New Zealand Conference, "W(h)ither Human Rights," Sydney, Australia, December 10–12, 2008), 7; and David Scheffer, *All the Missing Souls: A Personal History of the War Crimes Tribunals* (Princeton, NJ: Princeton University Press, 2012), 349, 378, 387.

63. Rome Statute, art. 11 (temporal jurisdiction).

64. Stromseth, Wippman, and Brooks, *Can Might Make Rights?* 281.

65. Ibid.

66. Susan Thomson, "The Darker Side of Transitional Justice: The Power Dynamics Behind Rwanda's *Gacaca* Courts," *Africa* 81, no. 3 (2011): 373–90.

67. 2005 World Summit Outcome Document, High-Level Plenary Meeting (September 14–16, 2005), at paras. 138–39.

68. Ibid.

69. Tiller, Justine, "The ICC Prosecutor and Positive Complementarity: Strengthening the Rule of Law?" *International Criminal Law Review* 13, no. 2 (2013): 530–31.

70. International Criminal Court-Assembly of States Parties, *Report of the Court on Complementarity, delivered to the Tenth Session of the Assembly of States Parties*, ICC-ASP/10/23 (November 11, 2011), paras. 28–55; ICC-OTP, Policy Paper on Preliminary Examinations (2013), paras. 46–58, 100–103; ICC-OTP, Informal Expert Paper: The Principle of Complementarity in Practice (2003), paras. 71–74; William W. Burke-White, "Proactive Complementarity: The International Criminal Court and National Courts in the Rome System of International Justice," *Harvard International Law Journal* 49, no. 1 (2008): 85–105.

71. Burke-White, "Proactive Complementarity," 53–107.

72. Elena Baylis, "Reassessing the Role of International Criminal Law: Rebuilding National Courts through Transnational Networks," *Boston College Law Review*, no. 50 (2009): 1–86; Tessa Khan and Jim Wormington, *Mobile Courts in the DRC: Lessons from Development for International Criminal Justice*, Oxford Transitional Justice Research Working Paper Series (Oxford University, Oxford, March 2014), http://otjr.crim.ox.ac.uk/materials/papers/178/mobile%20courts%20DRC.pdf and Randi Aho, et al., *Barriers to Justice: Implementing Reparations for Sexual Violence in the DRC* (New York: Columbia University School of International and Public Affairs, 2013), www.new.sipa.columbia.edu/academics/capstone-workshops/awarding-and-enforcing-reparations-in-mobile-courts-judgments-in-the-democratic-republic-of-the.

73. *Justice for Serious Crimes Before National Courts: Uganda's International Crimes Division*, Human Rights Watch, January 2012, available at www.hrw.org/sites/default/files/reports/uganda0112ForUpload_0.pdf; and Eric Witte, *Putting Complementarity into Practice: Domestic Justice for International Crimes in the Democratic Republic of Congo, Uganda, and Kenya*, Open Society Justice Initiative Report, January 2011, available at www.opensocietyfoundations.org/reports/putting-complementarity-practice.

74. Jane Stromseth, "Justice on the Ground: Can International Criminal Courts Strengthen Domestic Rule of Law in Post-Conflict Societies?" *Hague Journal on the Rule of Law* 1 (2009): 87–97.

75. Jane Stromseth, "Post-Conflict Rule of Law Building: The Need for a Multi-layered, Synergistic Approach," *William and Mary Law Review*, 49 no. 4 (2008): 1453–54.

76. Stromseth, "The International Criminal Court and Justice on the Ground," 436.

77. Stromseth, "Justice on the Ground," 94–97. See also Stromseth, Wippman, and Brooks, *Can Might Make Rights?* chap. 9, which discusses funding challenges more generally for rule of law building after conflict.

78. Stromseth, Wippman, and Brooks, *Can Might Make Rights?* 298.

79. Ibid, 283.

80. For a discussion of some of the challenges in Cambodia, for example, see Jane Stromseth, "Justice on the Ground?: International Criminal Courts and Domestic Rule of Law Building in Conflict-Affected Societies," in James Fleming ed., *Getting to the Rule of Law* (New York: New York University Press, 2011), 193–200.

81. I am grateful to my Georgetown colleague Professor David Luban for this spaceship metaphor.

82. Stromseth, Wippman, and Brooks, *Can Might Make Rights?* 295–98.

83. For an insightful and related analysis of how countries signing up to human rights treaties may open up possibilities for improved human rights protection through agenda-setting, litigation, and popular mobilization, see Beth Simmons, *Mobilizing for Human Rights: International Law in Domestic Politics* (New York: Cambridge University Press, 2009).

84. Guatemala's 24-Hour Courts: Changing the Way Women Access Justice, www.blog.usaid.gov/2013/03/guatemalas-24-hour-courts-changing-the-way-women-access-justice/.

85. For a sense of the wide range of publications on transitional justice, see "Transitional Justice Bibliography," Andrew G. Reiter, compiler, available at http://sites.google.com/site/transitionaljusticedatabase/transitional-justice-bibliography (accessed March 13, 2014).

86. Olsen, Payne, and Reiter, *Transitional Justice in Balance.*

87. Ibid, 16.

88. Ibid, 155–56.

89. For example, several studies examine views of the participants, including victims, in Timor-Leste's Commission for Reception, Truth and Reconciliation. See Spencer Zifcak, *Restorative Justice in East Timor: An Evaluation of the Community Reconciliation Process of the CAVR* (New York: Asia Foundation, 2004), 20–22, 25–26; Piers Pigou, *The Community Reconciliation Process of the Commission for Reception, Truth and Reconciliation* (New York: United Nations Development Programme, 2004), 81–83. See also Memunatu Baby Pratt, *Nation-Wide Survey on Public Perceptions of the Special Court for Sierra Leone* (2007).

90. Ratner and Abrams, *Accountability for Human Rights Atrocities in International Law*, 163–66.

91. For ICC membership, see www.icc-cpi.int/en_menus/asp/states%20parties/Pages/the%20states%20parties%20to%20the%20rome%20statute.aspx.

PART VI

CONCLUSION

34

LEARNING FROM THE OCTOPUS
WHAT NATURE CAN TELL US
ABOUT ADAPTING TO A
CHANGING WORLD

Rafe Sagarin

Editors' note: As editors, we recognize that the study of conflict management is inherently a multidisciplinary enterprise, but we are also aware that with few exceptions, scholars and practitioners of conflict management rarely venture out of the social sciences. With this in mind, we end this volume on a note that may challenge and inspire our readers, turning to marine ecologist Rafe D. Sagarin to give his perspective on dynamic systems. Extrapolating from the natural world, Sagarin's work (more fully developed in his book Learning from the Octopus: How Secrets from Nature Can Help Us Fight Terrorist Attacks, Natural Disasters, and Disease*)[1] sheds interesting light on how the "international ecosystem" may need to evolve in an era when there is no longer a "dominant community" to direct global affairs. Key concepts include the role of symbiotic relationships between a variety of actors; the development of mitigation strategies; the importance of remaining flexible and adaptable; and the usefulness of redundant capabilities. These may be useful pointers for managing conflict in a world adrift.*

◆ ◆ ◆

The basic ground rules under which nature evolved are simple but somewhat counterintuitive. Namely, nature doesn't waste energy trying to *plan* or make *predictions* in a complex world, and doesn't try to *perfect* itself. Rather, nature *adapts* to live with whatever challenges the complex world produces. Because adaptation is essentially carrying the weight of all that planning, predicting, and striving for perfection (that we tend to pour abundant resources into), it is a powerful concept that needs to be understood mechanistically. Here, I try to identify some key aspects of adaptability within the context of challenges that will be familiar to scholars and practitioners who try to understand and mitigate international change and conflict.

1. Seeing Trouble. How we see trouble is essential to how we avert trouble from flaring up into catastrophe. The most adaptable systems in nature use a highly decentralized network to sense change in the environment. An octopus, for example, doesn't use its highly developed brain to tell all its arms what color to turn when it needs to be camouflaged. Rather, millions of individual skin cells change to match their own immediate environment, giving the octopus a collective camouflage. An example on the human scale is Google's "Flu Trends" product, which uses all of us as the decentralized agents that are recording flu outbreaks when we individually search Google for flu-related terms like, "what are flu symptoms?" Google can have all our searches instantly compiled and provide accurate flu data up to two weeks before government agency reports.

Nature also has a lesson here, simply because it doesn't have the luxury of observing trouble through a theoretical lens. My recent work on the history of science (*Observation and Ecology*)[2] argues that we are entering a period in the life sciences where, because of large-scale human impacts to the Earth, we can no longer study life solely in well-controlled experimental or theoretical systems but have to greatly increase our reliance on observations of the changing world to understand it. My sense is that many academic fields that began with observational and comparative methods have later gone through periods where theoretical approaches and experimental simulations came to dominate, and are now reversing course back to the observational approaches because of the inadequacy of theory and controlled simulations to deal with real-world complexity.

2. Responding to the Unexpected. We can never be sharp enough in our observations to catch every situation before it flares up. How well we deal with the unexpected is related to how redundant our systems are for dealing with change. We tend to think of redundancy as wasteful and inefficient, but nature continually uses redundant systems to mitigate the effects of the unknown. From DNA to individual species to whole ecosystems, redundancy confers the resiliency that allows natural adaptive systems to respond to a wide range of unpredictable perturbations. In this model, efficiency is much less important than getting the job done.

Smoke detectors, tsunami detectors, and most chemical alarms efficiently look for a particular signal and then react (usually with a piercing sound) when they find it. This doesn't work too well when there are harmless signals that appear similar to the harmful signal, leading to false alarms. Nor does it work when the harmful signal doesn't fit a predetermined pattern. Because of false alarms, millions of homes in North America have dismantled their smoke alarms, and even communities in Southeast Asia hardest hit by the Boxing Day tsunami have dismantled the tsunami alarms provided to them by the international community after that catastrophe. Animals, which showed strange behaviors hours before the Boxing Day tsunami, remain the best alarm systems because they continually and redundantly resample their environment for signs of change. The lesson is that looking for patterns of change from a predetermined "watch list" and responding with a predetermined action will always run into limitations in a complex and changing world.

3. Dealing with Entrenched Conflict. We can't prevent trouble everywhere. There are already many areas in the world where conflict is deeply entrenched, and even recently emerging conflicts seem to quickly appear intractable. How we deal with entrenched conflict is in many ways dependent upon our methods of communication. In the Cold War, it was easy to rely on what I call "fiddler crab diplomacy." Fiddler crab males grow one enormous claw that they wave menacingly at other males to vie for females and territory. They never actually fight with this claw, because of the likelihood of "mutually assured destruction," but the crabs have a very keen sense of whose claw is just a tiny bit bigger than the other's. This kind of communication only works between adversaries with similar resources, similar goals, and similar motivations, but in the current international arena, as in most of nature, conflict is asymmetrical with respect to all of these factors—a virus doesn't care about the size of a fiddler crab's claw.

One way organisms deal with asymmetric conflict is not just to communicate with their adversaries but to communicate in a way that their adversaries are sure to understand clearly. For example, ground squirrels make shrill calls to their mammalian and avian predators. This essentially tells the coyote or hawk, "don't waste your energy trying to grab me, I already know you are there." But they don't do this when they see a snake, because snakes don't hear. Rather, they puff up their tails in an aggressive display that usually deters the snake. And if the snake happens to be a rattlesnake, the squirrel also *heats up* its tail, because rattlesnakes see in infrared. The West would have done well to pay attention to this kind of empathetic communication following the killing of Osama bin Laden. Western newspaper headlines crowed over videos released by the US government supposedly showing how pathetic bin Laden was in his final days, with his unkempt appearance and strange bobbing up and down on the floor of a decrepit house. In fact, all of these signals were powerful affirmations to radical Muslims that bin Laden was living to his last days in accordance with the way of the Prophet—he kept his beard despite needing to hide, he prayed, and he lived humbly despite his wealth.

4. Transcending Conflict. All organisms on Earth reach the limits of their ability to adapt at some point, and when they do, they engage in *symbiotic* partnerships with other organisms. Symbiosis can arise between completely unlikely partners—like large predatory fish allowing small fish to clean parasites from their mouths—and symbioses throughout the history of life have generally emerged out of relationships that used to be agonistic. Such symbioses are possible even within the most entrenched human conflicts. The biggest drop in the IED threat to American soldiers in Iraq didn't come through better armor or better detection methods but through symbiotic partnerships between low-ranking American officers and their former enemies: local leaders and combatants who found it beneficial to provide intel on bombs and bomb makers to American soldiers. Israeli, Palestinian, and Jordanian doctors now work together to detect and mitigate the threat of infectious diseases, no matter which side of which disputed territories they arise. These symbioses work, as in nature, because they aren't aiming for perfect solutions, but because they are intently focused on solving the problem at hand. The Middle Eastern doctors are not trying to create a road map to peace, they are just trying to solve real problems.

Often, the tradeoffs required to create symbioses among human groups in conflict are not material and obvious, but *symbolic tradeoffs* (see the work of Scott Atran)[3] that speak to a particular group's cultural identifiers. A good example of a symbolic tradeoff is Nelson Mandela's protection of the name and colors of South Africa's national Springbok rugby team, which most black South Africans wanted to see destroyed as a vestige of Apartheid. Rather than take an opportunity for petty revenge, Mandela saw an opportunity to make a symbolic gesture to white South Africans that he was serious about forming a multicultural society. Keeping the Springboks was not extremely costly to black South Africans (who didn't much care about rugby, anyway), but was enormously valuable to white South Africans, and the tradeoff required neither side to abandon their cultural identifiers.

5. Remaining Adaptable. Too often, we think we are adaptable because we changed what we did one time to solve a particularly thorny problem, but adaptability in nature is a *recursive* process that continually builds off of its own successes. When we are insulated from the continual force of natural selection, it is easy to forget to keep adaptable practices alive, and this can leave us vulnerable. One way to remain adaptable is to focus intently on past successes. While it is important to "learn from history's mistakes, lest we repeat them," this is actually a defensive posture that, at best, ensures that things don't get any worse. If we want to move forward, grow, get better at what we do, the only basis we have is building off practices that were successful. Indeed, every living thing on Earth is an example of learning from its ancestors' successes. In nature, failure is literally a dead-end: you don't reproduce and you don't pass on your genes. The one turtle out of a hundred nest mates that survives from its infancy to adulthood is the only important turtle to turtle evolution. Likewise, identifying even small successes out of a larger operational failure can be the most important way to improve performance in the future. Too many "after action" reports in organizations are overwhelmingly focused on failure, and many don't mention successes at all.

BECOMING ADAPTABLE

The way we jumpstart the natural process of adaptability in any organization, no matter how large or small, is simply to shift from giving orders to issuing challenges. Challenge-based problem solving—when leaders don't tell people what to do, but rather frame a challenge that anyone is invited to solve—produces faster, cheaper, and far more effective

solutions than a centralized command-and-control model. Challenges activate every practice of adaptable systems described above because they engage decentralized and redundant problem solvers, and these problem solvers often find they need to form symbiotic partnerships with differently skilled people to fully address the challenges. The role of leadership then becomes that of a selective agent that identifies successful results and directs new challenges to build off previous successes.

I can cite dozens of examples of remarkable challenge-based solutions that have emerged just in the last few years in a dazzling array of fields including mathematics, weapons development, space exploration, education, environmental protection, corporate stewardship, marketing, medicine, proteomics, and even individuals finding lost stuff, but examples from international relationships and conflict management are less well known.

What may help here is moving beyond the view that there is an "international community" and toward a view of an "international ecosystem." In ecology, a "community" is a relatively well-constrained unit defined by largely predictable dominant players, such as a "white fir/Douglas fir woodland community." By contrast, an "ecosystem" is a more broadly encompassing term that includes not just the species involved, but the stocks and flows of energy and materials across a complex landscape. Ecologists have come to acknowledge that our traditional notions of "community" are being torn apart by climate change, never to be replicated, whereas the ecosystem concept is more congruous with continual shifting and change in the roles and relationships of its parts. In an ecosystem, historical events can make even very small players enormously important. For example, a sudden pulse of waste nitrogen to a bay can cause a massive bloom and subsequent die-off of microscopic algae that depletes all the oxygen and creates an enormous "dead zone" throughout the system. Taking an ecosystem view of international relations disabuses us of the notion that there is a dominant community that can direct the systems' evolution, and opens us to the likelihood that the most important players in the system may be ones we have not even identified yet. Broadly challenging the international ecosystem to address its threats may be an effective way to understand and mitigate conflict in an awakening world.

NOTES

1. Rafe Sagarin, *Learning from the Octopus: How Secrets from Nature Can Help Us Fight Terrorist Attacks, Natural Disasters, and Disease* (New York: Basic Books, 2012).

2. Rafe Sagarin and Anibal Pauchard, *Observation and Ecology: Broadening the Scope of Science to Understand a Complex World* (Washington, DC: Island Press, 2012).

3. Scott Atran, Robert Axelrod, and Richard Davis, "Sacred Barriers to Conflict Resolution," *Science* 317 (August 24, 2007): 1039–40.

Index

United States Institute of Peace Press

Since its inception in 1991, the United States Institute of Peace Press has published more than 175 books on the prevention, management, and peaceful resolution of international conflicts—among them such venerable titles as Raymond Cohen's *Negotiating Across Cultures*; John Paul Lederach's *Building Peace*; *Leashing the Dogs of War* by Chester A. Crocker, Fen Osler Hampson, and Pamela Aall; and *The Iran Primer*, edited by Robin Wright. All our books arise from research and fieldwork sponsored by the Institute's many programs, and the Press is committed to extending the reach of the Institute's work by continuing to publish significant and sustainable works for practitioners, scholars, diplomats, and students. In keeping with the best traditions of scholarly publishing, each volume undergoes thorough internal review and blind peer review by external subject experts to ensure that the research and conclusions are balanced, relevant, and sound.

About the United States Institute of Peace

The United States Institute of Peace is an independent, nonpartisan institution established and funded by Congress. The Institute provides analysis, training, and tools to help prevent, manage, and end violent international conflicts, promote stability, and professionalize the field of peacebuilding.

Chairman of the Board: Stephen J. Hadley
Vice Chairman: George E. Moose
Chief Financial Officer: Michael Graham

About the Centre for International Governance Innovation

About CIGI

The Centre for International Governance Innovation is an independent, non-partisan think tank focused on international governance. Led by experienced practitioners and distinguished academics, CIGI supports research, forms networks, advances policy debate, and generates ideas for multilateral governance improvements. Conducting an active agenda of research, events and publications, CIGI's interdisciplinary work includes collaboration with policy, business and academic communities around the world.

CIGI's current research programs focus on three themes: the global economy, global security & politics and international law.

CIGI was founded in 2001 by Jim Balsillie, then co-CEO of Research In Motion (BlackBerry), and collaborates with and gratefully acknowledges support from a number of strategic partners, in particular the Government of Canada and the Government of Ontario.

Le CIGI a été fondé en 2001 par Jim Balsillie, qui était alors co-chef de la direction de Research In Motion (BlackBerry). Il collabore avec de nombreux partenaires stratégiques et exprime sa reconnaissance du soutien reçu de ceux-ci, notamment de l'appui reçu du gouvernement du Canada et de celui du gouvernement de l'Ontario.

For more information, please visit www.cigionline.org.

CIGI Masthead

Managing Editor, Publications	Carol Bonnett
Publications Editor	Jennifer Goyder
Publications Editor	Patricia Holmes
Publications Editor	Vivian Moser
Media Designer	Melodie Wakefield

Executive

President	Rohinton Medhora
Vice President of Programs	David Dewitt
Vice President of Public Affairs	Fred Kuntz
Vice President of Finance	Mark Menard

Communications

Communications Specialist	Kevin Dias	kdias@cigionline.org (1 519 885 2444 x 7238)
Public Affairs Coordinator	Erin Baxter	ebaxter@cigionline.org (1 519 885 2444 x 7265)